Operation Crossroads

OPERATION

Naval Institute Press / Annapolis, Maryland

CROSSROADS

The Atomic Tests at Bikini Atoll

Jonathan M. Weisgall

Library of Congress Cataloging-in-Publication Data
Weisgall, Jonathan M., 1949–
    Operation crossroads : the atomic tests at Bikini Atoll / Jonathan
M. Weisgall.
            p.   cm.
    Includes bibliographical references and index.
    ISBN 1-55750-919-0
    1. Operation Crossroads, 1946. 2. Nuclear weapons—Marshall
Islands—Bikini Atoll—Testing. 3. Nuclear weapons—United States.
I. Title.
U264.3.W43   1994
363.17'99—dc20   93-42134
                                                                 CIP

Printed in the United States of America on acid-free paper ∞

9 8 7 6 5 4 3 2

First printing

To *the People of Bikini*

Everything is in God's hands.

> —Words of Bikini leader "King" Juda when asked by the U.S. Navy in March 1946 if his people would be willing to leave their homeland.

CHAPLAIN: We're in God's hands now.
MOTHER COURAGE: Oh, I hope we're not as desperate as *that!*

> —Bertolt Brecht, *Mother Courage*, scene 3

And the second angel sounded, and as it were a great mountain burning with fire was cast into the sea: and the third part of the sea became blood;

And the third part of the creatures which were in the sea, and had life, died; and the third part of the ships were destroyed.

And I stood upon the sand of the sea, and saw a beast rise out of the sea. . . . Who is like unto the beast? Who is able to make war with him?

> Revelation 8:8–9, 13–14

Contents

Foreword   *ix*

Preface   *xv*

Prologue: "The World Disappears"   *1*

1. "I Don't See How a Ship Can Resist the Atomic Bomb"   *11*

2. "Battleships Can't Be Sunk by Bomber Aircraft"   *18*

3. "Bikini Won Out"   *24*

4. "They Are a Fine Race of People If Those in the Canoe Were a Fair Specimen"   *34*

5. "The Buck Rogers of the Navy"   *45*

6. "I'm Tired of Babying the Soviets"   *53*

7. "I Am Not an Atomic Playboy"   *63*

8. "The Greatest Event in the History of Mankind Except Only the Birth of Christ Himself"   *73*

9. "Operation Crossroads, Known . . . Unofficially as 'The Great Boondoggle'"   *82*

10. "It Would Be Very Helpful If the Test Could Be Postponed or Never Held at All"   *89*

11. "If an Atomic Bomb Comes Close Enough to a Ship . . . It Will Sink It"   *95*

12. "One Hell of a Good Sales Job"   *104*

13. "We Want Radiation-Sick Animals, But Not Radiation-Dead Animals"   *116*

14. "It Will Merely Be a Waste of Money and Effort to Take These Ships to the Test"   *124*

15. "In Fact, They Say It Is a Very Pleasant Way to Die"   *132*

16. "The Girl We Would Most Like to Split Atoms With"   *141*

17. "The Whole Project Sounds Like Bad Boys Playing with Matches in the Hay Mow"   *153*

18. "Thank God That Someone Had the Sentiment Not to Anchor Her at Bikini!" *163*

19. "So We Strive to Save Civilization, and We Learn How to Wreck It, All on the Same Weekend" *173*

20. "Listen World, This Is Crossroads!" *182*

21. "The Fleet Looked as Though It Had Returned from a Quick Trip to Hell" *193*

22. "The Water Near a Recent Surface Explosion Will Be a Witch's Brew" *206*

23. "Why Doesn't the Captain Take This Ship Out of Here?" *218*

24. "I Never Want to Go Through the Experience of the Last Three Weeks of August Again" *227*

25. "These Ships Must Not Be Considered as Casualties in the Sunken Ship Sense of the Word" *235*

26. "The Atomic Bomb Did Explode Something More Important than a Couple of Out-of-Date Warships" *246*

27. "I Would Call Down the Wrath of God upon Such an Obscenity" *256*

28. "General Groves Is Very Much Afraid of Claims Being Instituted by Men Who Participated in the Bikini Tests" *266*

29. "The Best Defense against the Atomic Bomb Is Not to Be There When It Goes Off" *279*

30. "It Scared the Hell Out of Me" *288*

31. "Leave 'Thermonuclear' Out of Press Releases and Speeches" *299*

32. "Bikini and Rongerik Look as Alike as Two Idaho Potatoes" *308*

Appendix: Disposition of Target Vessels at Operation Crossroads *317*

Notes *323*

Bibliography *375*

Index *397*

Foreword

JONATHAN WEISGALL HAS WRITTEN a comprehensive, significant, and readable account of an event of considerable historic impact—the two nuclear tests that were conducted by the U.S. government in 1946 at Bikini Atoll in the Marshall Islands.

As the first historical account of the atomic tests written by a non-government source, *Operation Crossroads* brings to light many newsworthy revelations, the most important of which is that the second shot in Operation Crossroads—the underwater Baker test—was the world's first nuclear disaster, and one that had been predicted by our own scientists.

A Los Alamos report had warned that "the water near a recent surface explosion will be a witch's brew" and that there would be enough plutonium near the water's surface "to poison the combined armed forces of the United States at their highest wartime strength." Los Alamos therefore cautioned the Navy against conducting an underwater test because of the hazards involved.

The radiological safety monitors for the test, headed by Col. Stafford Warren, faced a nightmare of hazards after Baker, as many of their warnings were ignored and men routinely boarded target ships, swept them, scraped them, and even ate their meals and slept aboard them, constantly being exposed to the danger of inhaling plutonium and fission products. The government was concerned that the radiological hazards would lead to lawsuits, and they finally materialized—nearly four decades after the tests.

Stafford Warren's concern about the toxicity of plutonium reminds me of my first realization of the magnitude of this problem. This occurred at the wartime Metallurgical Laboratory of the Plutonium Project at the University of Chicago early in 1944, when we first began to receive visible amounts of plutonium from the pilot plant in Oak Ridge, Tennessee. I was struck by the fact that despite the great care in planning by the project medical people (in providing protection against gamma-ray activity), no one had anticipated and made special provisions for the wide-scale handling of alpha-particle-active material, which presented special hazards of ingestion.

It became clear to me that our ordinary laboratory hoods were inadequate for this task and that rather extensive rebuilding of our laboratory facilities to emphasize adequate air flow and extraordinarily clean operations would be necessary. I immediately, on January 5, 1944, wrote Robert S. Stone (director of the health division) as follows:

> It has occurred to me that the physiological hazards of working with plutonium and its compounds may be very great. Due to its alpha radiation and long life, it may be that the permanent location in the body of even very small amounts, say one milligram or less, may be very harmful. The ingestion of such extraordinarily small amounts as some few tens of micrograms might be unpleasant, if it locates itself in a permanent position. In the handling of the relatively large amounts soon to begin here and at Site Y [at Los Alamos], there are many conceivable methods by which amounts of this order might be taken in unless the greatest care is exercised.

As a result our laboratory facilities were immediately rebuilt and no adverse effects were experienced by the scientists in my research group.

Even before the first three atomic bombs were detonated in July and August 1945, a number of scientists at the Metallurgical Laboratory became concerned about the impending use of the bomb. In June 1945, six committees were established at the Met Lab to make recommendations to the government regarding postwar policy. One was a Committee on Social and Political Implications headed by German-born James Franck, a venerated Nobel laureate (1925) in physics. I was a member of this group. Other members, all chosen by Franck, were Donald Hughes, James Nickson, Eugene Rabinowitch, Joyce Stearns, and Leo Szilard.

The committee's report, shaped mainly by Szilard, with some drafting help from Rabinowitch, was completed on June 11, 1945, and signed by every member of the group. It made basically three points. The first was that the United States could not avoid a nuclear arms race through a policy of secrecy. The second was that the best hope for national and world safety from the consequences of the bomb lay in international control of atomic energy. The third was that the military use of the bomb against Japan was "inadvisable" because it would "sacrifice public support throughout the world, precipitate the race for armaments, and prejudice the possibility of reaching an international agreement on the future control of weapons." We suggested, instead, that the power of the bomb first be demonstrated in an uninhabited "desert or barren island."

For various reasons our recommendation was not accepted. I have mixed feelings about this because the use of the atomic bomb did bring an abrupt end to World War II, sparing many American and Japanese lives. On the other hand, a world in which the atomic bomb had never been used in warfare might have offered a more fertile field for the successful international control of this fearsome power.

U.S. policy in the early postwar years was based on the "Baruch Plan," as presented to the UN Atomic Energy Commission in 1946. Under this proposal the manufacture of nuclear weapons was to cease, existing weapons were to be destroyed, and their nuclear materials were to be transferred to an international authority for use in peaceful applications. Rigid controls were contemplated, with punishments for violators not subject to a Security Council veto.

While it seemed that the United States was being unprecedentedly generous in offering to surrender a great military advantage, its atomic monopoly, the Baruch Plan was unacceptable to the Soviet Union for a number of reasons: (1) it involved intrusive inspection procedures that conflicted with the Soviet penchant for military and industrial secrecy; (2) any time the plan failed, the United States would have been left with its monopoly of atomic know-how, if not actual weapons; (3) Soviet development of its own atomic capability, which was being pursued vigorously, would have been nipped in the bud; and (4) the United States would have reaped an enormous propaganda harvest.

The Soviet Union responded to the Baruch Plan with a proposal of its own. As presented to the UN by the young Andrei Gromyko, this would have outlawed at once the production and use of atomic weapons. Three months later all existing atomic weapons were to be destroyed. Only after another three months was a control system to be considered, and any penalties for violators were to be meted out by the Security Council, where the great powers had the veto.

Among the many differences between the U.S. and Soviet approaches, clearly one of the most fundamental had to do with the timing of the various steps. We wanted controls to be established first, then disarmament would follow. The Russians said it had to be the other way around. The United States, finding its exclusive possession of atomic weapons a heavy moral burden, was willing to give up this advantage but needed strong guarantees before doing so. The U.S.S.R. wanted to exploit what it hoped to be worldwide moral outrage against nuclear weapons in order to blunt the advantage of the United States but was unwilling to accept any physical intrusion on its domain in return.

Disarmament discussions for the next several years focused on efforts to bridge the wide gap between the U.S. and Soviet approaches. There was little chance of agreement, however, especially after the first Soviet nuclear test in 1949 and the onset of the Korean War in 1950. While both East and West offered several new proposals during these years, they seemed designed primarily to influence world opinion, not as bases for serious negotiation.

The international climate improved somewhat beginning in 1953 as the Korean War ended and both superpowers acquired new leadership. The collective leadership that succeeded Joseph Stalin and the new administration of Dwight Eisenhower both seemed more flexible in their approaches to disarmament questions.

Nuclear weapons tests first became an object of widespread public concern in 1954. On March 1 of that year, the Atomic Energy Commission detonated a hydrogen bomb, code named Bravo, as part of a test series at Bikini Atoll in the Pacific. Because of a yield more than twice that anticipated—equivalent to 15 million tons of TNT, to this day the most powerful explosion ever detonated by the United States—and because of unexpected wind conditions, Bravo showered a Japanese tuna trawler with radioactive debris. The crew of twenty-three suffered from severe radiation sickness and one crew member subsequently died, allegedly from effects of the radiation. Some inhabitants of the Marshall Islands were also affected, although less severely.

The shock of these events was compounded by the news that contaminated fish were reaching the Japanese market from the test area and by further fallout on Japan from a Soviet test soon afterward. A wave of protests followed. Highly respected world leaders, including Prime Minister Nehru of India, Albert Schweitzer, Albert Einstein, and Pope Pius XII, joined in the call for an end to nuclear tests.

Continuing negotiations between the United States and the Soviet Union for a nuclear test ban were not successful; however, a mutual moratorium on testing went into effect in 1958. This continued into the administration of John F. Kennedy until the Soviets unexpectedly conducted a nuclear weapons test (150 kilotons) in the atmosphere on September 1, 1961, to initiate a series of tests. Following an atmospheric test series by the United States and another one by the Soviet Union in 1962, and the searing influence of the Cuban missile crisis in October 1962, serious test ban negotiations took place in Moscow during July 1963. During a historic twelve days President Kennedy's representative, W. Averell Harriman, and Premier Nikita Khrushchev's delegate, Andrei Gromyko, negotiated a Limited Test Ban Treaty (outlawing all but underground testing of nuclear weapons).

I was privileged, in my role as chairman of the U.S. Atomic Energy Commission (and an ardent test ban advocate), to serve as a member of Secretary of State Dean Rusk's delegation attending the signing of the treaty in Moscow on August 5, 1963. Following our delegation's meeting with an ebullient (and impressive) Khrushchev in his Kremlin office during the morning, the historic ceremony took place in Catherine's Hall. Although this treaty undoubtedly represented the greatest advance in arms control in decades, I was disappointed that we failed to achieve the much sought-after, desperately needed agreement on a treaty banning all nuclear tests (a comprehensive test ban). I am one of those who believe that if John F. Kennedy had lived and served out a second term, and if Nikita Khrushchev had survived in office, significant further steps in arms control, including a comprehensive test ban, would have ensued.

A small step toward further limitation on testing took place in 1974 when President Richard M. Nixon and Soviet Chairman Leonid Brezhnev signed the Threshold Test Ban Treaty limiting the yield of underground tests by the superpowers to 150 kilotons. This treaty was not ratified by the U.S. Senate until 1989, after repeatedly being decried as a sham by those favoring a comprehensive test ban. However, both sides have observed its terms since its specified effective date of March 31, 1976.

The chances for a comprehensive treaty have taken an upward swing with the election of Bill Clinton as president. Under pressure from Congress, the United States had already declared a moratorium on nuclear weapons testing in fall 1992, following the declarations by Russia and France of such temporary moratoria. The other two countries known to possess nuclear weapons are Great Britain and the People's Republic of China. Great Britain is following the lead of the United States. Unfortunately, China conducted an underground nuclear weapons test in October 1993. This has put a strain on the moratorium but has not yet broken it.

A possible mechanism for achieving a comprehensive test ban is through a provision in the Limited Test Ban Treaty that states that a conference to consider amendments to the treaty must be convened if requested by one-third or more of the parties. A proposed amendment would then enter into force if ratified by a majority of the parties, including all three of the "original parties" (the United States, the United Kingdom, and Russia as a successor to the Soviet Union). The Parliamentarians for Global Action, an international organization of national legislators, has taken the lead in advocating this approach, which has many advantages.

All in all, there is much cause for optimism for outlawing all testing of nuclear weapons within the next few years. We have reached a point where this goal may be within our grasp, and Jonathan Weisgall's book is bound to aid in the ongoing debate.

Glenn T. Seaborg
University of California at Berkeley

Preface

"**J**onathan, could you take a call on my line? It's got something to do with atom bombs." That is how I became involved with Bikini Atoll.

It was 1975, and I had just begun practicing law with the Washington, D.C., law firm of Covington & Burling. My office was next to that of John Douglas, a senior partner who headed the civil rights division of the Justice Department under President Kennedy and had become involved in many pro bono activities since returning to Covington & Burling.

John was late for lunch that day, so he asked me to step into his office and take the call. It was from the Legal Aid Society of Hawaii, which had been asked by a sister organization, the Micronesian Legal Services Corporation, to help the people of Bikini Atoll in the Marshall Islands. The islanders were in the process of returning to their atoll, but U.S. scientists were telling them that they should limit their consumption of coconuts—the staple of their diet—to only one or two a day. Otherwise, there might be a problem with radiation, or "poison," as the Bikinians called it, because there is no word in Marshallese for "radiation." The Bikinians were worried. They thought their homeland might not be safe, and they did not know what to do.

After reviewing the available scientific data on Bikini with several experts, I filed a lawsuit on the Bikinians' behalf in U.S. District Court in Honolulu, asking the court to order the government to file an environmental impact statement and conduct a thorough radiological survey of Bikini. I flew to Honolulu in October 1975 to argue some preliminary motions in the case, less worried about my legal abilities before Judge Samuel P. King than how I was going to justify a trip to Hawaii to my law firm's pro bono committee.

Twelve of the fourteen years from 1975 through 1988 were spent litigating three separate lawsuits against the federal government on behalf of the islanders. Much of the work required historical research to buttress the legal arguments. For instance, an essential element to one of the lawsuits was proving that the United States had entered into a contract with the Bikinians, that the Bikinians had offered to leave their atoll in 1946 in return for America's promise to care for them. It was also important to show that the United States intended to remove the Bikinians only temporarily. The work combined my love of law with my love of history; as a European history major at Columbia, I had had the privilege of studying under the likes of Fritz Stern, Jacques Barzun, and Peter Gay.

Appeals to the U.S. and international agencies meant telling the story of Bikini, of the tests and the people. Congressional testimony and lobbying meant not just moral proclamations and appeals, but facts and figures showing the value of the tests to U.S. nuclear security and how the tests led directly to huge savings in the defense budget. The documents began to build up, from the National Archives, the Department of Energy, the Navy, the Department of Interior, the Department of Justice, and elsewhere, and they told a fascinating story, one that I hope I have told without regard to my advocate's role as the Bikinians' lawyer.

As it has taken ten years to research and write this book, it is difficult to list all those who have provided encouragement, reviewed parts of the manuscript, and offered criticism and assistance. I interviewed many people for this book, and several of them later read relevant chapters and corrected many errors. My thanks go to them, to Covington & Burling, and to David R. Addis, David R. Anderson, James D. Berg, Barton J. Bernstein, Therese D. Boyd, Charles W. Brodhead, Bernard F. Cavalcante, Abram Chayes, Benjamin S. Cooper, Bill Curtsinger, Gordon P. Erspamer, Alissa Friedman, Jordana Friedman, Lloyd Graybar, Barton C. Hacker, James Hamilton, Glenn E. Helm, Chuck Hansen, Pamela Henson, Eric Hiner, Kent Hiner, Laura Hudson, Ellen Hume, Giff Johnson, Kathy Johnson, Robert C. Kiste, Joel Klein, Louisa Lancetti, Ralph E. Lapp, Jane Freundel Levey, Barry W. Levine, Sanford V. Levinson, Martin Lobel, Margaret M. Macdonald, Rudy Maxa, Priscilla McMillan, Roger Meade, Consuella C. Miles, Andrew Nelson,

John M. Niedenthal, Ed Reese, Alisa Rivkin, David Alan Rosenberg, Virginia Rowthorn, Thomas Scoville, Glenn T. Seaborg, Martin Sherwin, John T. Smith II, Robert Stone, James W. Symington, Kirk Talbott, Evan Thomas, Alison von Klemperer, Ralph Waltz, Paul C. Warnke, Dean Warren, Gary E. Weir, John Noble Wilford, and John H. Zentay. At the same time they are absolved of any errors, which are all mine to bear. Special thanks as well to my wife, Ruth, for her judgment, suggestions, and willingness to tolerate a perpetually cluttered dining room, and to my children, Alison, Andrew, and Benjamin, who were patient, curious, and forgiving beyond their years.

Operation Crossroads

Prologue

"The World Disappears"

Thousands of radio stations around the world broadcast the test. It was nine o'clock on the morning of July 1, 1946. More than 42,000 military and scientific personnel were assembled at Bikini Atoll, a tiny ring of islands in the Pacific some 2,500 miles southwest of Hawaii, for the world's fourth explosion of an atomic bomb. The first three—at Alamogordo in the New Mexico desert, then over Hiroshima and Nagasaki—were shrouded in wartime secrecy, but this one, code-named Operation Crossroads, was different. At Bikini the world watched and listened as a B-29 Superfortress prepared to drop an atomic bomb on a guinea-pig fleet of ninety-five ships. More than 175 reporters from around the world were there, as well as congressmen, senators, a cabinet member, and United Nations observers.

About an hour before the explosion, an electronically operated metronome began ticking away the last minutes aboard the abandoned battleship *Pennsylvania,* anchored several hundred yards from the expected site of the blast. The metronome was hooked up to a radio transmitter, and its steady beat was heard in millions of homes around the world. "It came to sound like a voice of doom tolling the world's last minutes," wrote the *New York Times*'s William L. Laurence, who had witnessed the Alamogordo and Nagasaki explosions.

Suddenly a staccato voice came across the radio amid the ticking. "Thirty minutes to go, thirty minutes to go." Then the ticking. The

1

voice spoke again after twenty minutes. "Ten minutes to go, ten minutes to go." The countdown began, with the voice repeating itself like an echo. "Two minutes to go, two minutes to go."

Zero hour. "Bomb away," said the voice on the radio, and another voice blared, "Listen world, this is Crossroads!" Then it happened. The chain reaction lasted only one ten-millionth of a second, but in that time it released the explosive energy of 23,000 tons of TNT. The temperature at the center of the blast was 10,000 times greater than the sun's surface. Later generations have become inured to film clips of the bomb, but in 1946 it was new and terrifying. "It was like watching the birth and the death of a star, born and disintegrated in the instant of its birth," wrote Laurence.[1]

The explosion briefly obliterated the morning sun as a ball of fire shot upward into the sky, first red, then turning purple. From the swirling clouds of fire emerged a column of white smoke, rising five miles. The mushroom cloud rose another two miles from the top of the column, covering the stratosphere with all the colors of the spectrum. Bikini captured the imagination of the world, which witnessed for the first time the sounds and sights of an atomic bomb explosion.

The second test, three weeks later, was at once magnificent and terrifying. In one second, an underwater bomb pushed a one-mile-wide dome of water into the sky. Ten seconds later, as if in slow motion, the millions of tons of water and debris collapsed back into the lagoon, creating a gigantic curtain of mist and spray that moved outward at more than 60 miles an hour and soon engulfed almost all of the target ships. The blast, which sank the 26,000-ton battleship *Arkansas* in a matter of seconds, unleashed the greatest waves ever known to humanity, one of which lifted the huge aircraft carrier *Saratoga* 43 feet. It also unleashed the greatest amount of radioactivity ever known up to that time.

The apocalyptic sight of an atomic explosion and mushroom cloud was indelibly seared into the public's conscience. The images from Bikini have been used countless times since 1946 to evoke fear and terror mixed with curiosity and awe. Footage of the blast appears at the end of the movie *Dr. Strangelove: Or, How I Learned to Stop Worrying and Love the Bomb*, a nuclear comedy about what might happen if a madman actually pressed *the* button, as well as in the Japanese film *Godzilla*, in which a 400-foot dinosaur-like sea beast ravages Tokyo after being aroused from the depths of the Pacific by the bomb bursts at Bikini. Just the name of Bikini Atoll has become synonymous with Doomsday. In his screenplay of the 1956 movie version of *Moby Dick*, science fiction writer Ray Bradbury updated the allegory of humanity's struggle against natural forces by linking the tremendous elemental power of the Great White Whale to the destructive force of the bomb, foreboding disaster for Captain Ahab and the ill-fated crew of the *Pequod*. In one scene, Ahab tells his first mate that he has studied all the logbooks of New Bedford whalers to determine the hidden journey of Moby Dick. "He now swims the waters off Good Hope," says Ahab, "and all the Indian Ocean lies before him. Next month he cruises the Bengal Bay. In March the Sulu Sea." As the camera cuts to a map of the Pacific, Ahab's finger points to Bikini Atoll. "Running eastward to the gateway of the Pacific, I shall be waiting for him here, at new moon in April."[2]

The symbolism of Bikini provided an ironic contrast to Operation Crossroads. Bikini was the Pacific paradise, a dream-like Pacific Ocean setting where humans and nature had for centuries coexisted so peacefully, largely undisturbed by Western influences. Islanders sailed their outrigger canoes, lived in thatched huts, and fished for their dinner. To the eye, Bikini was only land, sea, and sky. To the ear, it was gently lapping waves and endless trade winds.

Into this setting came a new group of men. The islanders were moved away and Westerners began to tinker dangerously with nature. After Operation Crossroads, ships wiped out by the bomb rested on the floor of Bikini's lagoon. Multicolored coral reefs were gradually bleached white as radiation destroyed the algae. Thousands of dead fish floated in the lagoon and radioactive isotopes in others created x-ray pictures when placed on photographic plates. The story of Bikini is the story of the fear and destruction, the arrogance and ignorance of the atomic age. Bikini was the world in miniature, where humans, once so close to nature, now built a proving ground to alter and destroy it.

Bikini has a rich and romantic history. Its discovery is linked to such people as Otto von Kotzebue, a Russian explorer and son of a well-known German novelist and playwright; Nikolai Rimsky-Korsakov, a Russian naval officer and uncle of the great Russian composer of the same name; Adelbert von Chamisso, a brilliant German writer, poet and, later, botanist, whose ballads were set to music by Robert Schumann; and Charles Darwin, who studied Chamisso's notes on the coral beneath Bikini's reef.

As a weapons test site, Bikini was rocked by twenty-three atomic and hydrogen bombs between 1946 and 1958. Today, its lagoon is a graveyard for some of the dozens of World War II ships that served as guinea pigs to test the effects of an atomic bomb on naval vessels. These ships told stories of their own: *Saratoga*, at one time the largest aircraft carrier in the world, which survived two torpedo attacks and five kamikazes from Wake to Guadalcanal, Rabaul, Tarawa, and Iwo Jima; *Arkansas*, the oldest capital ship in the U.S. Navy during World War II; *Nevada*, run aground at Pearl Harbor but raised in time to see service from Omaha Beach to Okinawa; the German cruiser *Prinz Eugen,* which joined the *Bismarck* in sinking the HMS *Hood,* the pride of the British navy; and the Japanese battleship *Nagato,* the flagship of Admiral Yamamoto.

In its first eight years of notoriety, Bikini was responsible for introducing to the world two rather extraordinarily diverse words: *bikini* and *fallout.* The exotic—and, presumably, atomic—allure of Bikini was responsible for the adoption of its name in 1946 to describe the revealing new two-piece bathing suit. According to Webster's, *bikini* was derived "from the comparison of the effects wrought by a scantily clad woman to the effects of an atomic bomb." Then, in 1954, radioactive fallout from a thermonuclear shot, code-named Bravo, contaminated several hundred inhabitants of the Marshall Islands as well as the crew of a Japanese fishing vessel. The Bravo test at Bikini dramatically raised the stakes in the nuclear arms race and touched off a debate in the scientific community on fallout and low-level radiation that still rages today.

Operation Crossroads had all the trappings of a three-ring circus. It was to be the contest between the atom bomb and the battleship, two heavyweights slugging it out in the Pacific. Behind all the hoopla, though, was a horrifying, sinister lesson in warfare: Radioactive fallout was a new weapon of terror. As with chemical and biological warfare, it can wipe out entire cities and, to magnify the terror, its victims cannot smell it, touch it, feel it, see it, or hear it. It casts its net over a huge area, catching anything in its way, but its time of impact, unlike a bullet or a missile, is not specific or limited. Like a bomb that never stops exploding, its effects can be felt days, weeks, or years later. It is a weapon of biological extinction, truly designed more for genocide than for the destruction of buildings or military targets. Hiroshima and Nagasaki showed that the instant blast and heat of an atomic bomb can kill tens of thousands of people in a matter of seconds. The story of Operation Crossroads, and the Bravo shot eight years later, is that the killing power of lingering radioactive fallout far surpasses the instant sledgehammer effect of the bomb's blast.

The story of nuclear testing at Bikini is also the story of the Bikini people, and theirs is a case history of bureaucratic incompetence and neglect. In 1946 the U.S. Navy executed a well-planned and swift logistical operation in uprooting the 167 islanders from their homeland. Unfortunately, that was the only time the U.S. government acted toward them with such urgency and commitment. The islanders became nuclear nomads, as the United States moved them to three different atolls and islands in two years. They nearly starved to death on one and were eventually resettled on Kili, a tiny, solitary island with little reef and no lagoon.

This is a story of a fatal combination of ignorance and arrogance. There is no conspiracy and no genuine villain—only victims. The story could have been different, but no one knew the true danger of radioactivity. Men were playing with atomic fire, and they simply did not know all the facts. A French physicist, Henri Becquerel, had discovered radioactivity half a century earlier, yet much remained unknown.

The world's first atomic bomb test, code-named Trinity, had occurred a year earlier at Alamogordo in the New Mexico desert. At the request of J. Robert Oppenheimer, the director of the Los Alamos National Laboratory that built the atomic bomb, arrangements were made with the governor of New Mexico to declare martial law and evacuate the state in case of a catastrophe. Robert Krohn, one of the physicists who worked on the test, reported that "prior to the shot, back at the lab, there had been some speculation that it might be possible to explode the atmosphere—in which case the world disappears."[3] Brig. Gen. Leslie R. Groves, the head of the Manhattan Project, became annoyed the night before the test when Nobel Prize–winning physicist Enrico Fermi offered to take bets from the other scientists as to whether or not the bomb would ignite the atmosphere, and if so, whether it would destroy only New Mexico or the entire world. Contingency plans were put in place to evacuate the inhabitants from the surrounding farms, and numerous doctors were flown to Los Alamos the week before the test to free Los Alamos physicians to race to Trinity in case of a disaster.[4]

No one really knew how big a bang the bomb would make. Some worried that it would not work at all. President Truman's chief of staff, Adm. William D. Leahy, warned the president: "The damn thing will never go off, and I say that as an expert in explosives."[5] These doubts were expressed in a gloomy ditty that became known as the "Los Alamos Blues":

> From this crude lab that spawned a dud,
>   Their necks to Truman's axe uncurled,
> Lo, the embattled savants stood
>   And fired the flop heard round the world.[6]

A drizzle started the day before the test, and the scientists were concerned about what is now called fallout. The wind blowing from the south might carry radioactive debris right over Albuquerque or Amarillo, 300 miles away, and rain would bring down excessive fallout over a small area. The long-range weather forecasters had been accurate for many days, but they had not predicted the blustery rain and mist the evening before the test. The base camp became disorganized as many of Oppenheimer's advisors besieged him, urging a 24-hour postponement.

Someone had to make a decision. Leslie Groves took Oppenheimer aside into a small office to discuss matters quietly. They called in the weather forecasters. "Since it was obvious that they were completely upset by the failure of the long-range predictions, I soon excused them," explained Groves, but his subsequent actions did not augur well for the coming of the nuclear age. "After that, it was necessary for me to make my own weather predictions—a field in which I had nothing more than very general knowledge."[7]

At the control bunker, five miles south of the 100-foot-high tower on which the bomb was perched, some of the scientists were discussing the betting pool, which cost a dollar. Edward Teller had bet on a yield of the equivalent of 45,000 tons of TNT. Oppenheimer had bet low, at just 300 tons, and Norman Ramsey bet zero. No one knew. As it turned out, the yield was about 20,000 tons, and I. I. Rabi won the $103 pool. He had bet 18,000 tons because that was the only number left to choose.[8]

William Laurence, the science editor of the *New York Times,* had been selected by Groves to document the development of the atomic bomb. Groves instructed him to prepare four separate press releases on the July 16 test to cover four different scenarios. The first two were easy: a loud explosion in the desert accompanied by a burst of light, with no deaths or property damage, or a louder explosion, heard over a wider area, with some property damage. The third possibility was more troublesome, as Laurence had to write about an even larger explosion, accompanied by several deaths and major property damage. But the fourth press release was the most difficult to prepare, because it covered the deaths of some of the most prominent scientists of the age. Moreover, Laurence would have to answer the obvious question: "What, in heaven's name, were they doing in the desert at that hour of the morning?" He wrote that they had accidentally set off an Army munitions dump while vacationing at Oppenheimer's ranch in New Mexico. Laurence would be among the eyewitnesses, so the fourth press release carried his own obituary. No one knew what would happen.[9]

Moments before the blast, it was still cloudy, with light rain and high humidity. A Nobel Prize winner was heard to murmur, "I'm scared witless, absolutely witless." Then came the blast. "Just at that instant there rose from the bowels of the earth a light not of this world, the light of many suns in one," wrote Laurence. George B. Kistiakowsky of Harvard described the spectacle as "the nearest thing to Doomsday that one could possibly imagine."[10] As the dazzling light of the predawn blast covered the base camp, Gen. Thomas Farrell, Leslie Groves's deputy, shouted in horror, "The long-hairs have let it get away from them!"[11]

The 100-foot-high steel tower holding the bomb was vaporized. A quarter mile from the tower a 16-foot-high, 4-inch-thick iron pipe set in concrete had disappeared. One-half mile from the Zeropoint, or point of explosion, was a 220-ton massive steel cylinder surrounded by a strong steel tower 70 feet high, the height of a six-story building. Forty tons of steel had been used to fabricate the tower, and the cross bracing was much stronger than that normally used in ordinary steel construction. The blast tore the tower from its foundations, ripped it apart, and flattened it. "None of us had expected it to be damaged," wrote Groves.[12]

Ignorance turned to arrogance three days after Hiroshima. Tokyo Rose, Japan's English-speaking propagandist, went on the radio to report numerous radiation injuries among the survivors. The Los Alamos scientists were incredulous. The bomb was designed to kill people from the force of its explosion, not from radiation injuries. "Any person with radiation damage would have been killed with a brick first," said Norman Ramsey, one of the laboratory's chief scientists. Oppenheimer agreed. The bomb added nothing new to warfare except a bigger explosion; it would simply produce a "very big bang," he said, and would kill only about 20,000 people.[13] The *New York Times* said the Japanese might be attempting to capitalize on the horrors of an atomic bombing "in an effort to win sympathy." According to American propaganda experts, it reported, the Japanese "jumped at the chance of converting an abstract horror theory into allegations that they count upon to arouse humanitarian reactions in this country."[14] In fact, the bomb killed 80,000 people instantly and another 50,000 to 60,000 in the next several months.

But the reports continued, even after Japan surrendered. In early September, Hiroshima survivors were continuing to die at the rate of about 100 daily from burns and infections that Japanese doctors were unable to treat. A reliable Japanese news agency reported "uncanny effects" resulting from the bomb. General Groves asked Los Alamos to investigate, but he said that the charges of radiation sickness were "hoax or propaganda." The laboratory leaders agreed. The reports were "definitely a hoax," Los Alamos's ranking radiation expert said, "because the data which the Japanese gave did not correspond to any experience known here."[15] At the very same time, Los Alamos scientists discovered severe radiation burns on cattle 40 miles north of the Trinity site, as seventy-five cattle lost hair along their backs and sides and had severe skin blistering.[16]

The Manhattan Project's senior physician, Stafford Warren, told Congress shortly after Hiroshima that only 5 to 7 percent of the deaths at Hiroshima and Nagasaki were caused by radiation, and Groves testified that "there were no after-effects from radiation," adding that "there was no radioactivity damage done to any human being excepting at the

time that the bomb actually went off."[17] Groves's understanding of the
medical consequences of radiation exposure was based on misinforma-
tion sprinkled with wishful thinking. Contrary to the medical estimates
at the time, at least 20,000 deaths at Hiroshima were the result of radiation exposure, and another 20,000 people suffered radiation injuries.[18]

In some ways, the seeds of the arrogance of the U.S. nuclear testing
program were sown at the outset of the Manhattan Project, on October
9, 1941, when President Franklin D. Roosevelt, on his own, directed
Vannevar Bush of the National Defense Research Committee to move
ahead with the development of the atomic bomb. It was imperative, of
course, that the program be carried out in complete secrecy, but Roosevelt kept the program so isolated that he did not even establish a mechanism to consider the broader issues that might be raised by this new
weapon of mass destruction.

This secrecy, and the implications of national security that accompanied the bomb, continued after the war as military leaders decided to
hold Operation Crossroads to test the effects of an atomic bomb on
ships. There was no civilian agency within the government to question
whether the tests made any sense. In fact, only two high-ranking officials in the U.S. government even knew how many atomic bombs were
in America's stockpile—and the new president of the United States,
Harry S. Truman, was not one of the them. Only Leslie Groves and
General of the Army Dwight D. Eisenhower had this information. Truman did not know, nor did his secretary of state, James F. Byrnes, nor
his secretary of the navy, James V. Forrestal. In fact, Truman even told
one cabinet meeting that he really did not want to know the number.
"Mr. President, you *should* know," replied Commerce Secretary Henry
Wallace incredulously. "Also the Secretary of War should know, and
the Secretary of the Navy."[19]

The fact of the matter is that Operation Crossroads arose out of a
bitter rivalry between the Navy and the Army Air Forces over the
impact of the atomic bomb on their future budgets, missions, and prestige. The military took over complete control, from conception through
planning, the tests themselves, and even the post-test reports. Having
relinquished control to the bureaucracy, the Truman White House,
barely into its first year, played no significant role in many crucial
aspects of Operation Crossroads, such as public relations issues, disputes over the significance of the tests, preparations for dealing with
radioactive fallout from the second test and resulting radiation overexposures, the debate over the release of a secret report on the tests by
the Joint Chiefs of Staff, mistreatment of the Bikini islanders, and the
first hints of public fear and anxiety over the atomic bomb. Although
the tests were cited as the most important news event of 1946, Presi-

dent Truman paid no attention to them, except for one White House meeting to discuss a civilian committee to observe them and one cabinet meeting to discuss their postponement. The bomb had won the war, but now the war was over, and Truman turned his attention to domestic affairs. The president's self-imposed ignorance did not catch up with him until months later, when he realized that in approving Operation Crossroads he had authorized the detonation of one-third of America's nuclear stockpile.[20]

When they were moved in 1946, the Bikinians were told that they could return when the atoll was no longer needed for nuclear testing. But no one knew what the effects of atomic testing at Bikini would be. "Our scientific friends went from one extreme to the other," recalled Rear Adm. Draper L. Kauffman, one of Operation Crossroads's planners. "One extreme even thought that the island would disappear and that it would be weeks before we could go back into the lagoon. Another extreme said that we could go back in right away, that there would be very little residual radiation."[21]

There was concern that the second bomb test at Bikini, an underwater shot code-named Baker, would tear ships from their anchorages and toss them up onto Bikini's coral reef. Planning for the third test, a deep underwater shot code-named Charlie, was actually held up at one point for fear that it might cause a giant tidal wave to sweep thousands of miles across the Pacific. A high Navy source revealed that "some of the experts feel that [the test] might set up a great tidal wave which nothing could check." The experts knew what would happen with an atomic explosion in the air, he added, but "when it is exploded under water . . . anything may happen."[22] No one knew.

Some scientists warned the military about the danger of fallout. If the radioactive cloud from the underwater shot did not rise at least 10,000 feet, they wrote, the deadly fission products would collapse back into the lagoon and onto the target ships. Other scientists had already predicted that the cloud would rise only 8,000 or 10,000 feet. It was thus highly likely that the ships would be contaminated by radioactive materials falling from the cloud, but no emergency decontamination procedures were planned. No one even knew how to decontaminate. The scientists' predictions came true, and the Baker test became the world's first nuclear accident. Despite the scientists' warnings, the Navy ordered men to board contaminated ships. Many even ate and slept aboard them, and some received radiation doses well above the daily tolerance standard. Ignorance had met arrogance.

Eight years later, in 1954, the Bravo shot was detonated at Bikini. It was more than twice the estimated yield. The Atomic Energy Commission (AEC) said that no one knew the wind direction was going to shift, carrying the 20-mile-high cloud of lethal radioactive particles right over Bikini Island and eastward over several inhabited Marshallese atolls.

When President Johnson declared Bikini safe in 1968, he was backed up by an AEC study and an independent review of that study by a blue-ribbon panel of scientists. But no one caught a mathematical error in the AEC study, which threw off the figures by a factor of as much as 100. The AEC study was wrong; Bikini wasn't safe, but no one knew.

1

"I Don't See How a Ship Can Resist the Atomic Bomb"

On August 6, 1945, a B-29 bomber named the *Enola Gay* dropped the world's second atomic bomb, a uranium device code-named Little Boy, over Hiroshima.[1] Within seconds, thousands of people in the center of town were scorched by a wave of searing heat. Every person and object within 500 yards of ground zero became incandescent in the million-degree heat. Many others within a half-mile radius lay writhing on the ground screaming in agony from the intolerable pain of their burned bodies. Trains and streetcars were tossed off their rails as though they were toys. Over 80,000 people were killed within minutes, including twelve U.S. Navy men imprisoned in the city jail.[2]

When President Truman received the news, sailing back from the Potsdam Conference, he declared, "This is the greatest thing in history!"[3] He boasted a broad, proud smile as he walked about the ship spreading the news. "We are now prepared to obliterate more rapidly and completely every productive enterprise the Japanese have above ground in any city," he stated in an announcement released by the White House. "We shall destroy their docks, their factories and their communications. Let there be no mistake; we shall completely destroy Japan's power to make war."[4] Pearl Harbor, atrocities, kamikaze attacks, and suicide charges had hardened Americans toward Japan. "When you deal with a beast you have to treat him as a beast," Truman wrote a few days later.[5]

Truman's hope that only one bomb would be dropped on Japan was not realized. "There was no debate ever on the matter of dropping a second bomb," Leslie Groves later recalled. "The debate had all been on whether to use the atomic bomb as a weapon at all." The first bomb was to demonstrate to Japan the power of atomic weapons, and the second was to prove that America did not have a limited supply. Indeed, military plans called for the assembly and use of a third bomb in late August and others in September if necessary.[6]

The decision on the timing of the second bomb was left entirely to the military. The second raid had been scheduled for August 11, which would have allowed Japan five days to respond to the first bomb, but, due partly to weather forecast, the date was moved up to August 9. That day, 40,000 people in Nagasaki died in the explosion of the world's third atomic bomb, a plutonium device code-named Fat Man, the same type of "gadget" (as the bombs were called) as had been tested at Trinity.[7]

The atomic bomb, built to win the war, did the job, as Japan announced its surrender on August 14. Publicly, Truman had no qualms about his decision. "I regarded the bomb as a military weapon and never had any doubt that it should be used," he wrote in his memoirs. In fact, just three hours before reports of Japan's surrender reached the White House on August 14, Truman, frustrated at Japan's silence, told British officials that he had no choice but to drop an atomic bomb on Tokyo.[8] Privately, though, he was troubled. "It was a terrible decision," he told his sister after the war, and in his private journal he wrote that "even if the Japs are savages, ruthless, merciless and fanatic, we as the leader of the world for the common welfare cannot drop this terrible bomb on the old capital [Kyoto] or [Tokyo]."[9]

The atomic bomb represented a quantum leap in the technology of warfare. It made geographical boundaries meaningless and wiped out all previous rules of warfare. At the same time, though, some saw it as too destructive to be used again as an offensive weapon. In a conversation about postwar politics, Budget Director Harold D. Smith said to Truman, "Mr. President, you have an atomic bomb up your sleeve," to which Truman replied, "Yes, but I am not sure it can ever be used."[10] As Vannevar Bush, Truman's science advisor, observed, "There was no powder in the gun, for it could not be drawn."[11]

The United States had a new weapon on its hands, but did not know what to do with it. Literally within days of the war's end, the press, politicians, scientists, and academic leaders began a public debate over three basic questions: Should America share the secret of the bomb with other countries? Should there be military or civilian control over the bomb? How would the bomb change the face of war?

In late June, nearly two months before the end of the war, the Navy approved testing high explosives on captured enemy ships and Navy vessels about to be stricken from the active list, but Hiroshima changed these plans, as the Navy's chief of the Bureau of Ships called for atomic bomb experiments "to clear up its major influence on naval warfare" before proceeding with the TNT tests. Meanwhile, just three days after Japan's surrender, Army Chief of Staff Gen. George C. Marshall directed the Joint Chiefs of Staff to determine the effect of the bomb on warfare and military organization.[12]

In the public's mind, the advent of the atomic bomb was a blow to the Navy. After all, the Army and its air branch, the Army Air Forces (AAF), had the bomb; the Navy did not. The Army, under the direction of General Groves, was given the job of building the atomic bomb, and its air force dropped the bombs over Japan. This fact was compounded by the nearly universal belief that the atomic bomb had rendered navies obsolete. "I don't want to pose as an expert or a crystal ball gazer," Senator Edwin C. Johnson told Vice Adm. William H. P. Blandy, the Navy's new deputy chief of naval operations, at a hearing in December 1945 before the Senate's new Special Committee on Atomic Energy. "However, it does seem to me . . . that atomic energy has driven ships off the surface of the sea. I don't see how a ship can resist the atomic bomb."[13]

In reality, the situation was exactly the opposite of public perception. The AAF had played no role in developing the bomb; it was nothing more than an atomic bomb delivery agency, whose only contribution to the Manhattan Project was modifying the B-29 aircraft to accommodate the large weapon for loading and delivery. In fact, the two men who armed the Hiroshima and Nagasaki bombs in flight were Navy officers who had major responsibilities at Los Alamos during the war. Moreover, Navy facilities had manufactured nonnuclear ordnance material for the Hiroshima Little Boy bomb and the armored shell for the Nagasaki Fat Man bomb.[14]

The AAF, at first, also felt threatened by the advent of the atomic bomb. After all, the AAF's key goal in the war had been to prove that strategic bombing—long-range aerial bombardment—was the decisive factor in modern warfare.[15] If one atomic bomb, delivered by one airplane, could sink a navy or level a city, why did the United States need a large fleet of strategic bombers? The answer lay less in logic than in the unspoken tenet of popular U.S. strategic policy in the two world wars: Capitalizing on American technological superiority and using few ground troops, the U.S. military must quickly defeat the enemy at a point far from the United States itself. Before World War II, the Navy seemed to satisfy this concept; now the AAF did. The atomic bomb had made the Navy obsolete not only because ships were vulnerable to atomic attack, but also because no navy could deliver the bomb.

However, despite the fact that the atomic bomb may have made strategic bombing as obsolete as a navy, the undeniable fact remained that only the AAF could carry this devastating weapon to the enemy. "The influence of atomic energy on Air Power can be stated very simply," wrote AAF Commanding General Henry H. "Hap" Arnold in his final report on World War II, parts of which were published in *Life*. "It has made Air Power all-important. . . . Bombers can now range the world." The message was clear: The atomic bomb was the AAF's weapon. "The only known effective means of delivering atomic bombs . . . is the very heavy bomber," Arnold concluded. "Development of the air arm, especially with the concurrent development of the atomic explosive, guided missiles, and other modern devices, will reduce the requirement for or employment of mass armies and navies."[16] Congress bought Arnold's argument in its entirety. "The atomic bomb . . . we recognize as absolutely connected to the Air Force," declared Senator Warren R. Austin at a congressional hearing in 1945, "there being no other means or method of handling the atomic bomb."[17]

Faced with these widespread public views, the Navy responded quickly. On August 16, Lewis L. Strauss, who would later become chairman of the AEC, wrote a memorandum urging his boss, Navy Secretary James Forrestal, to test ships' ability to withstand the atomic bomb. Concerned that the Navy's "penurious policy" for research and development prior to the war had led to inadequate testing of torpedo warheads, Strauss clearly grasped the Navy's political dilemma, and he recommended that the atomic tests be held as soon as possible. "If such a test is not made," he warned Forrestal, "there will be loose talk to the effect that the fleet is obsolete in the face of this new weapon and this will militate against appropriations to preserve a postwar Navy of the size now planned." Strauss suggested both air and underwater tests of the bomb on surplus ships, and he urged Forrestal to act quickly. "If this suggestion has merit, it would have to be inaugurated before the ships in question are laid up or scrapped—that is to say, promptly."[18]

Forrestal acted immediately. A World War I Navy flier and later president of the investment firm of Dillon, Read, he was one of the few Wall Street financiers who supported the New Deal. An ambitious, hard-driving workaholic, Forrestal had served briefly as an administrative assistant to President Roosevelt in 1940 and then in the Navy Department for nearly six years, first as undersecretary and then, since 1944, as secretary. He favored Strauss's suggestion, and he immediately created a new Office of Special Weapons with responsibility for nuclear research and the development of guided missiles. The head of the new organization, Vice Adm. William H. P. Blandy, was given the title of Deputy Chief of Naval Operations for Special Weapons (OP-06), thus placing him on a par with the Navy's five other deputy chiefs and just below Adm. Ernest J. King, commander-in-chief of the U.S. fleet and chief of naval operations (CNO). The OP-06 office was small, but its four officers were all top Navy men, and, with the exception of Blandy, all had worked on the Manhattan Project.[19]

While the public and the press pointed to the vulnerability of the Navy, AAF strategists were actually envious of Forrestal's quick adjustment to the strategic importance of nuclear weapons. "The Army Air Forces is, in a scientific sense, on trial for its life," wrote Maj. Gen. St. Clair Streett to General Arnold just weeks after Hiroshima. "The whole concept of air warfare is undergoing a rapid change and unless we grasp the impact of these changes and adapt ourselves to them quickly, they will be lost to us." If the AAF did not keep up with scientific advances, warned Streett, "they will be snatched at random by all other branches and the confusion and loss of effectiveness will be tremendous." Calling Arnold's attention to Forrestal's "very active reorganization" of the Navy, Streett recommended a similar program of research and development within the AAF, contacts with private university laboratories, and the fostering among scientists of "a spirit of intense interest in the Air Forces and its problems."[20]

Meanwhile, Senator Brien McMahon of Connecticut, a freshman who would later become chairman of the Senate Special Committee on Atomic Energy, proposed in a speech on August 25 that an atomic bomb be dropped on captured Japanese ships. "The resulting explosion should prove to us just how effective the atomic bomb is when used against the giant naval ships," he said. "I can think of no better use for these Jap ships."[21] However, in late August, Admiral King, unaware of Strauss's memorandum and Forrestal's thinking, passed on to Secretary of State James Byrnes a recommendation from Adm. Chester W. Nimitz that the thirty-eight surviving ships in the Japanese fleet be routinely destroyed. Byrnes left for London a few days later and was out of Washington until October 4, so he took no action on Nimitz's proposal.[22]

Army and AAF officials, though, immediately picked up on McMahon's suggestion. On September 14, Lt. Gen. Barney Giles, commanding general of the Army's Strategic Air Forces, cabled a message from his Guam headquarters to Hap Arnold in Washington. "We now have full information on the atomic bomb on land targets," wrote Giles. "Strongly recommend that we use at least two more atomic bombs in the destruction of remnants of the Japanese fleet." Giles added that Gen. Douglas MacArthur, the supreme allied commander, was "in full agreement" with his proposal. Four days later, General Arnold proposed to the Joint Chiefs that Admiral King's recommendation be countermanded and that ten Japanese ships be made available instead to the AAF for testing atomic bombs "and other possible new weapons."[23]

These were not the first suggestions that atomic bombs be used on ships. In fact, at Potsdam, Hap Arnold had suggested testing an atomic bomb buried in hundreds of feet of mud beneath a Japanese harbor, and the Army had considered dropping the bomb on Japanese fleet concentrations during the war. Indeed, had the bomb been developed in time, it would probably have been used against the Japanese fleet in Truk lagoon, just 800 miles southwest of Bikini.[24]

Admiral King was on the spot. The chiefs of two Navy bureaus were calling for full-scale tests to determine the effect of the atomic bomb on ships. General Arnold's proposal, though, meant the Navy might have no role to play in the tests. King clearly understood the potential impact of the bomb on the armed services, telling the Joint Chiefs in mid-October that the "threat of atomic explosives is producing radical thinking about future warfare, which will influence the size and nature of the Army and Navy." He countered Arnold with a new twist, suggesting that both the Army *and* Navy participate in the tests, with the entire operation under the direction of neither service, but rather under the Joint Chiefs of Staff. As if to demarcate each service's responsibility, he proposed two tests, one an air drop and the other an underwater shot, and he also suggested including U.S. vessels among the targets. King recognized that the number of tests was limited by the virtually nonexistent U.S. nuclear arsenal. "The supply of atomic bombs is so small and their cost so great," he wrote, "that the numbers expended for all purposes must certainly be held to the essential minimum."[25] In fact, by June 1946 the U.S. nuclear weapon stockpile consisted of exactly nine bombs, two of which were not operational.[26]

Admiral King disclosed plans for the tests at a press conference in Kansas City on October 27, without mentioning the role of the AAF. He said that between 80 and 100 ships would be used in the experiment. "We're going to have plenty of ships to work with," he declared. "We're going to discard at least one-third of the ships we wound up the war with. The Japs have a number, not much good for anything else. We also may look at the German fleet for some." In fact, four days later Navy Secretary Forrestal earmarked 158 surplus U.S. vessels for atomic bomb tests.[27]

The Joint Chiefs, which then consisted of generals Arnold and Marshall and admirals King and Leahy, accepted King's recommendations, and its planning staff appointed an Army-Navy subcommittee to make a detailed proposal on the atomic tests. The LeMay Subcommittee, as it became known, was headed by World War II hero Maj. Gen. Curtis E. LeMay, who led the firebombing against Japanese cities. The committee met frequently during the next weeks to select target vessels, plan logistics, determine the array of ships, and set fuel and ammunition loads for the target ships.

Many military men quickly viewed the tests as a public relations challenge as much as a military test. "To the public, the test looms as one in which the future of the Navy is at stake, the question being whether the Navy can withstand the atomic bomb onslaught," wrote Assistant Secretary of War Howard C. Petersen to the Army's public affairs director. "If the Navy withstands [the tests] better than the public imagines it will, in the public mind the Navy will have 'won.' This the Navy will play to the limit."[28]

2

"Battleships Can't Be Sunk by Bomber Aircraft"

Operation Crossroads was billed as a cooperative Army-Navy venture, but in fact it represented one more chapter in the decades-old rivalry and mistrust between the Army and the Navy and the culmination of the 25-year debate over the role of airplanes and ships. The tests also came at a time that, as Samuel P. Huntington has written, "stand[s] out in American military history as a high-water mark of interservice competition."[1]

Some of the differences between the services were bitter and tragic. For example, while German submarines sank 7 million tons of Allied shipping in the Atlantic Ocean between December 1941 and March 1943, the Army and Navy fought over which service would deploy the aircraft and airborne radar to fight the antisubmarine war. Other disagreements were simply petty, such as the Navy's unwillingness to share the new Pentagon building with the Army in 1942, despite President Roosevelt's directive. Similarly, the Cabinet debated for nearly 90 minutes whether to hold the 1943 Army-Navy game, and President Roosevelt personally ordered the site of the 1944 game to be switched from either of the two academies to New York.[2]

In the view of Secretary of War Henry L. Stimson, the Army-Navy rivalry "grew mainly from the peculiar psychology of the Navy Department, which frequently seemed to retire from the realm of logic into a dim religious world in which Neptune was God, Mahan his prophet,

18

and the United States Navy the only true Church." The "high priests of this Church" were the career Navy bureaucrats, a group of men to whom he always referred collectively as "the Admirals." Stimson described them as "both anonymous and continuous," and not subject to anyone's control—not even the president's.[3]

The most serious disputes between the two services concerned the role of the airplane, the organization of the air forces, and the challenge by the AAF to come into its own as a separate service. The AAF remained part of the Army until 1947, when it finally became the U.S. Air Force, a separate branch of the military. Although the Navy had an air branch, most aviators served in the Army, first under the Army Signal Corps, then the Army Air Service in World War I, the Army Air Corps in the 1920s, and finally the Army Air Forces in World War II. The appropriate role of an air force, under the Army or Navy or as a separate branch, caused constant tension between the two armed services. The creation of the Joint Chiefs of Staff early in the war did little to relieve this rivalry, because the Joint Chiefs frequently split differences between the services, as in its decision to divide the conquest of the Pacific between Gen. Douglas MacArthur and Adm. Chester Nimitz.

Until World War I, there was no dispute as to the appropriate roles of the Army and the Navy. The Army's mission was to fight on land, while the Navy's was to control the seas. The emergence of military aviation, however, complicated this division of functions and revolutionized the traditional view of the U.S. coastline as the dividing point between the services. The aviators' first leader was the flamboyant Brig. Gen. William "Billy" Mitchell, who commanded a joint French-U.S. air force in World War I. Upon returning from France after the war, Mitchell sounded the first call for an independent air force. The argument lasted well into World War II, and it became a major part of the debate over the atomic tests at Bikini in 1946.

Great Britain had created an independent Royal Air Force in 1918, but U.S. aviators remained the stepchildren of the two older services. Mitchell, frustrated by air power's subordinate role, mounted a propaganda campaign to convince the American public that an air force was as important as a navy and an army and should therefore be autonomous. "The air service should be organized as of co-ordinate importance to the army itself," he proclaimed in 1919, "and not only of equal but of greater importance than the naval organization."[4] He also leveled a charge that would be repeated verbatim in 1945: "Air power alone won this war."[5]

Both the Army and the Navy opposed Mitchell, but for different reasons. For the Army, the issue was simple; the Air Service was part of the Army, and the Army wanted to keep it. For the Navy, the issue took on the trappings of a holy war because Mitchell directly attacked the Navy's basic functions. He challenged the Navy's strategic vision of itself as the country's "first line of defense," the service that would first meet an approaching enemy. Historically, the Army's jurisdiction was the land and the Navy's the water. The advent of the airplane, which functioned over both land and water, created overlapping jurisdiction. Naval air power did not impinge on the traditional role of the Army, but if the Army's air force could sink a fleet of approaching enemy ships, what would happen to the Navy's role as the first line of defense?

Mitchell's argument was simple: The Navy was obsolete, because all surface vessels were subject to aerial bombardment. Air power could defend America's coastline better than the Navy by mounting a long-range preemptive bombardment to knock out an approaching enemy fleet—and at great savings to the taxpayer. Battleships could not support air attacks on an enemy and were defenseless against bombers. They could not defend the coastline as efficiently as airplanes, and they were much too costly. An autonomous air force was the answer, and it could do the job for the cost of two or three battleships a year, Mitchell asserted, telling a congressional committee that the Army could build 1,000 airplanes for the cost of each new $45-million battleship.[6]

Newspapers doted on Mitchell and his quotable attacks on the military establishment, but they never questioned his faulty logic of applying European models of air strategy to the United States. World War I taught that independent air forces—capable of both defensive measures and offensive air strikes—were important to European nations, which are in close proximity to one another. But short-range bombers were of no use to a nation as geographically insular as the United States, and there was no technology on the drawing boards that would permit heavy bombers to cross the Atlantic or Pacific oceans. The aircraft carrier would soon change these assumptions, but Mitchell's ideas on strategic bombing were years ahead of their time. Undaunted, he took dead aim at the Navy, proclaiming that the new aircraft carrier was really an "airplane transport," not part of a fleet, and should thus be under the control of the air services.[7] "The air will prevail over the water in a very short space of time," he predicted in 1919, and the next year he told a congressional committee that his airplanes could "destroy, put out of commission and sink any ship in existence."[8]

"Battleships can't be sunk by bomber aircraft," replied Navy Secretary Josephus Daniels to Congress, boasting that he would "stand bareheaded on the deck of a battleship and let . . . Mitchell take a crack at me."[9] Adm. Charles B. McVay, the chief of the Navy's Bureau of Ordnance, agreed, telling the Navy's General Board that it was impossible "to sink a ship—a modern ship—by a bomb."[10] With the press in the early 1920s fostering rivalries between baseball heroes Babe Ruth and Rogers Hornsby and tennis stars Helen Wills and Suzanne Lenglen, these Army-Navy challenges and boasts took on all the trappings of a sports contest, as Secretary Daniels agreed to permit Mitchell's aviators to bomb the captured German battleship *Ostfriesland* off the Virginia coast in late July of 1921.

The *Ostfriesland* tests would be invoked repeatedly 25 years later in the debate over Operation Crossroads. Planning for the 1921 bombing revealed fundamental differences between the services regarding the purpose of the tests. At a joint Army-Navy conference in May, Mitchell argued that his planes should be allowed to attack with bombs of any size and in any number, but the Navy emphasized that the purpose of the tests was to assess the damage to the *Ostfriesland,* not prove the Air Corps's ability to sink it.

"We want to follow up our attacks and push it," Mitchell told the planners.

"That's all right if you want to destroy it," replied a Navy representative, "but we want to determine the effect."[11]

There was no doubt that the *Ostfriesland* would eventually sink, but the Navy's intent in conducting the exercise was to learn how to build ships in the future that would be less vulnerable to air attacks. Mitchell's goals, on the other hand, were to create the impression that the experiments were a battleship-versus-aircraft duel, win the propaganda war, and capture the most publicity.

The tests commanded worldwide attention. With the war and navy secretaries, senators, congressmen, and hundreds of other government officials, foreign military attachés, and reporters lining the decks of the battleships, cruisers, and destroyers of the Atlantic Fleet, the long-awaited tests began on the morning of July 20, 1921. Army and Navy fliers dropped fifty-seven bombs on the *Ostfriesland,* scoring eight direct hits, but they failed to sink the ship. The next morning, though, Mitchell hoodwinked the Navy. He had agreed to halt bombing after each hit by a 2,000-pound bomb, but he now instructed his men to try for near-misses, believing that these would be more damaging than direct hits. Four bombs in rapid succession hit as close as 20 feet from the ship, and she sank in 21 minutes. The spectators on the observer ships stared incredulously as the huge dreadnought rolled to port, her bow rising high in the air, and then sank.[12]

Mitchell's stunt turned him into a national folk hero overnight. The Navy never did obtain the technical data it sought on bomb damage and control, and it faced a tremendous problem in dealing with the public's reaction to the tests, just as it would with the advent of the atomic bomb. Senator William E. Borah declared on the Senate floor that the tests demonstrated that "the battleship is practically obsolete," and he urged the Navy to stop work on six battleships then under construction.[13] The *New York Times* editorialized that "Mitchell's dictum that 'the air force will constitute the first line of defense of the country' no longer seems fanciful."[14] Mitchell categorically declared victory for the airplane. "Aircraft now in existence . . . can find and destroy all classes of seacraft under war conditions with a negligible loss," he declared after the tests.[15]

The Navy took a completely different view of the exercise. "I cannot conceive of any use the fleet will ever have for aircraft," declared the chief of naval operations before the tests.[16] Afterwards, Capt. William Leahy, the director of naval gunnery (who would later rise to the rank of fleet admiral and chief of staff to President Roosevelt), told the secretary of the navy that Mitchell's "experiment . . . pointed to the improbability of a modern battleship being either destroyed or put out of action by aerial bombs."[17] Another report conceded that aviation's influence on naval warfare would undoubtedly increase in the future, "but the prediction that it will assume paramount importance in sea warfare will not be realized."[18]

The Navy insisted that the tests were purely experimental and that Mitchell had invalidated them by violating the ground rules. As one historian has noted, though, "there was an element of truth in subsequent charges that [the Navy] did not want to see a battleship sunk by bombing and did what it could to prevent it."[19] The Navy also claimed that the tests were artificial and rigged. Mitchell's planes were able to locate the *Ostfriesland* only because the Army Air Service laid out a Hansel and Gretel trail of destroyers acting as markers leading up to the ship, which was at anchor, unmanned and undefended. In a sense, therefore, the Navy was right, but the public viewed the stunt as a victory for air power.

The charismatic and brashly self-confident Billy Mitchell kept up his proselytizing, arguing that air power could destroy an enemy's vital industrial and military centers at a cost of fewer men and dollars than either the Army or Navy. The son of a U.S. senator from Wisconsin and friend of Rep. Fiorello LaGuardia of New York, Mitchell had strong and vocal allies on Capitol Hill. As early as 1919, his supporters in Congress introduced bills to establish a Department of Aeronautics, separate from the Army, but the War Department's opposition killed every measure. Mitchell characterized his opponents as "lineal prototypes of the champions of the long-bow,"[20] and he promised a public crusade to "jar the bureaucrats out of their swivel chairs,"[21] but he went too far in September 1925 when the crash of a Navy dirigible in a storm led him to accuse both the Navy and War departments of "incompetency, criminal negligence, and almost treasonable administration of the national defense." In a highly publicized court-martial, he was convicted of insubordination and was suspended from the Army.[22]

Ironically, Mitchell's relentless demand that Army and Navy aviation be consolidated into an autonomous air force caused the armed services to place greater emphasis on air power and, in some cases, coopt the aviators. The Navy upgraded the role of naval aviators with the creation of its own Bureau of Aeronautics in 1921, and it began to place more emphasis on the design of airplanes and aircraft carriers. The creation of BuAer, as it was called, also appeased the naval aviators; it tied them more closely to the Navy and ensured that they would not join Mitchell's campaign for an autonomous air force.

Meanwhile, the Army Air Corps, newly created out of the old Army Air Service in 1926, achieved extraordinary autonomy even while under the Army. By June 1941, the renamed Army Air Forces was virtually recognized as an independent service, and Hap Arnold, the Air Force chief, was appointed to the Joint Chiefs of Staff in 1942, where he sat as an equal to his nominal superior, General Marshall. Nevertheless, Mitchell's forces kept up their campaign into World War II. "The blood of all the men who have died in this war for lack of air support . . . is on the heads of those who obstructed the development of our air strength," wrote one AAF publicist.[23] In fact, Wendell Willkie even made a campaign issue of Army Air Corps independence, promising it autonomy in the 1940 presidential campaign.[24] As military historian Ronald Spector has noted wryly, "No foreign power seemed as menacing to the army in the interwar period as did rivalry from the navy and the Army Air Corps."[25]

The summer of 1946 would see a repetition of the armed services' identical arguments from the summer of 1921. The AAF's goal at Bikini would be to sink as many ships as possible, while the Navy would seek to preserve as many as possible for scientific study. Where naval pride ended and science began would remain a murky dividing point.

3

"Bikini Won Out"

On Sunday morning, December 7, 1941, eight of the nine battleships in America's Pacific fleet were at anchor in Pearl Harbor. By sheer luck, the aircraft carriers *Lexington* and *Enterprise* were at sea with their escorting cruisers and destroyers, and the *Saratoga* was just entering San Diego harbor after an overhaul at the Puget Sound Navy Yard. The trauma of Pearl Harbor proved Billy Mitchell's point. Without a single shot being fired from a battleship, more than 350 Japanese planes launched from six aircraft carriers destroyed or damaged eight U.S. battleships, three destroyers, three cruisers, and over 300 airplanes, all neatly lined up in rows on airfields. All but twenty-nine of the Japanese planes returned safely to their carriers and the fleet got away safely. With ninety-six ships anchored inside crowded Pearl Harbor like sitting ducks, a surprise air attack from aircraft carriers easily destroyed many of them.

At Griffith Stadium in Washington, D.C., 27,000 fans, including a young ensign named John F. Kennedy, watched the Washington Redskins play the Philadelphia Eagles in the last game of the football season. The news had reached the press box and spread down the seats, row by row. Then came a series of loudspeaker announcements. "Admiral W. H. P. Blandy is asked to report to his office at once," said the public address announcer, and he followed with a list of other generals and admirals. Most of the fans, though, kept their attention on the field, where Sammy Baugh led the Redskins to a 20–14 victory.[1]

24

Two days later, when Japanese bombers appeared over the fortified naval base of Singapore—the "Gibraltar of the East"—the British dispatched the battle cruiser *Repulse* and the new battleship *Prince of Wales* to search for a Japanese convoy. Japanese reconnaissance planes sighted the two ships on the evening of December 9, and eighty-five torpedo planes and bombers attacked in successive waves the next morning.

This was neither Pearl Harbor nor a staged Billy Mitchell attack on a defenseless target. Both the *Repulse* and the *Prince of Wales* were fully armed. They maneuvered and fought as skillfully as possible, but the 20-year debate over battleships versus airplanes ended on December 10, 1941, as heavy bombers attacked and sank capital ships underway in combat for the first time in history. The *Repulse* sank 15 minutes after the first Japanese torpedo hit, and the *Prince of Wales* some three hours later, as nearly 850 British sailors went down with their ship in a naval victory for Japan nearly as great as Pearl Harbor.[2]

Fifty years of naval strategy changed overnight, and with it the role of aviators and ships. The battleship faded as an offensive weapon. The prewar naval strategy of using the airplane for scouting and patrol for battleships ended with Pearl Harbor and the sinking of the *Prince of Wales* and *Repulse*. The main weapon of the naval fleet soon became the aircraft carrier, and the carrier-borne airplane became the most potent weapon of war. It displayed more flexibility, power, and speed against a greater variety of enemy forces on land or at sea than any other naval weapon.

Ironically, the sinking of eight battleships at Pearl Harbor proved to be the loss of obsolescent equipment and ideas, as fleets of aircraft carrier task forces, rather than Mahan's fleets of battleships, proved decisive. As the war progressed, the battleship's role evolved into one of protecting aircraft carriers and assisting in preinvasion bombardments. Newer battleships teamed up with fast carrier task forces, while older ones, such as the *Arkansas, New York,* and *Nevada,* supported landings at Normandy and throughout the Pacific. At one point in the spring of 1943, the United States had one active aircraft carrier—the *Saratoga.* By the summer of 1944, nearly 100 were operating. On the other hand, from Pearl Harbor until the end of the war, the Navy launched only five new battleships.[3]

With victory inevitable, smoldering service disagreements on unification and autonomy for the AAF resurfaced. The combined Army-Navy opposition to an independent air force broke down toward the end of the war, as the Army unequivocally supported air force independence, unification of all the armed services, and even the elimination of naval aviation. The Army also supported unification because it feared it would lose ground after the war to the more glamorous and popular Navy and AAF. The AAF, seeking independence from the War Department, supported consolidation because unification, rather than the creation of a separate and rival department, was the best way to attain autonomy.

When General Marshall, Army Chief of Staff, endorsed unification of the services in November 1943, the Navy suddenly stood alone. It feared the loss of its aviation branch to the AAF and its Marine Corps to the Army.[4] These deep and seemingly irreconcilable differences became public in congressional hearings in the spring of 1944. For three days, witness after witness from the War Department, starting with Secretary of War Stimson, urged the creation of a single defense department embracing all the armed services, with the Air Force becoming a separate, independent service.

Stimson knew that most of the Navy brass were opposed to unification, but he also knew that Navy Secretary Frank Knox had come around and now strongly supported unification. Knox, though, died suddenly on the fifth day of the hearings, just after the Army had completed its testimony. His successor, James Forrestal, a reclusive, humorless, brooding man of cold intensity, adamantly opposed unification and elimination of the Navy's air units. He argued that competition between the armed services was healthy and that independence would leave each service free to develop as it best saw fit.[5]

Representative Carl Vinson, the Navy's stalking horse and chairman of the House Naval Affairs Committee, immediately went after the contradictions in the War Department's testimony. How could it urge unifying the Army and Navy under one department while at the same time recommend autonomy for the air force and thus create three services in place of two? Through his questioning, Vinson successfully revealed that the Army Air Forces wanted unification—but only if unification included a separate and autonomous air force. Stimson was now worried that the hearings "might become a free-for-all in which nothing but bitterness would be produced."[6] With D-day a month away, front-page articles on the Army-Navy dispute could have a serious impact on morale. Stimson quickly convened a meeting of key representatives and military brass, and the hearings abruptly ended a week later. The Navy had won for the short-term. It had raised doubts about unification, and the hearings ended without congressional support for the War Department.[7]

The end of World War II rekindled the interservice debate on unification and air force autonomy. The postwar years would mean fewer dollars, and unification would mean even more competition for funds and positioning within the new organization. On August 25, 1945, the *New York Times* reported that Army and AAF proponents of unification "regard the cessation of hostilities as the green light to resume their campaign, and Navy leaders are preparing for the coming fight."[8] This was no exaggeration. A statement by Air Force General LeMay that the B-29 had rendered the aircraft carrier obsolete was "the first overt act in the coming battle for funds," wrote Adm. John S. McCain to Forrestal. "It is beginning to look to me that the war after the war will be more bitter than the actual war."[9]

It was difficult to keep these disagreements from the public eye, and they turned ugly on occasion. Asked at a Senate hearing to comment on statements by admirals Nimitz and Marc A. Mitscher that sea power and carrier-based planes had forced Japan to surrender, AAF General James H. "Jimmy" Doolittle shot back, "Our B-29 boys are resting uneasily in their graves as a result of those two comments." Doolittle, who led the first air raid on Tokyo, said "it was not sea power that compelled Japan to sue for peace, [and] it was not carrier strength that won the air war." In his view, the aircraft carrier was "going into obsolescence, having reached the peak of its usefulness." The carrier had two attributes: "First, it can move about, and second, it can be sunk. When we get aircraft with sufficient range, we will not need carriers." The real lesson of the war, he maintained, "is that you can't lose a war if you have command of the air, and you can't win a war if you haven't." Forrestal protested within hours to the secretary of war, Robert P. Patterson, stating that Doolittle's comments could cause "irreparable harm" to "the comradeship of all branches of the armed services."[10] Meanwhile, at another hearing, AAF head Hap Arnold asked, "Why should we have a Navy at all?" and then answered his own question: "There are no enemies for it to fight except apparently the Army Air Force."[11]

As chairman of the Senate Special Committee to Investigate the National Defense Program, Harry Truman saw the Army-Navy rivalry and waste firsthand, and he was determined to reorganize the armed services when the war ended. "We are turning out a very large number of planes and could turn out more if the navy and army boys could make up their minds just what they want," he wrote his wife from an inspection trip in San Diego.[12] The United States, he liked to say, was lucky to have won World War II. "I have the feeling that if the Army and the Navy had fought our enemies as hard as they fought each other, the war would have ended much earlier."[13]

The dropping of the atomic bomb on Hiroshima and Nagasaki and the sudden surrender of Japan led to public perceptions that served only to intensify the interservice debate. The atomic bomb, of course, revolutionized strategic planning, and the Navy seemed to be the most vulnerable to this new weapon. The advent of the bomb, though, was not the only threat the Navy faced at the end of the war. Many congressmen were openly critical of Navy policies during the war, beginning with

Pearl Harbor. In addition, with the Soviet Union rapidly emerging as America's new enemy, the Navy could neither defend the European landmass in case of a Russian invasion nor strike at targets in the Soviet Union. Moreover, Russia's small navy only strengthened the arguments of those who wanted to cut the size of the U.S. Navy, and the extraordinary public pressure to speed demobilization was quickly translated into calls for drastic cuts in the size of the postwar Navy. The United States was demobilizing 1.5 million men each month in the fall of 1945. The number of servicemen declined from a wartime high of 12 million to 1.5 million by 1947, the annual budget for military spending dropped from over $90 billion to less than $11 billion, and the number of combatant vessels dropped from nearly 1,500 to fewer than 300.[14]

President Truman, who supported unification, did not sympathize with the Navy. He complained privately that the Navy's budget demands for 1946 were "profligate and unrealistic," told Forrestal that he was "seriously offended" by the Navy's behavior in the unification debate, and confided to his budget director that "Navy people had a complex."[15] The fact that Truman was an Army man and Roosevelt a former Navy assistant secretary did not ease the Navy's concerns. In 1939 Roosevelt had boasted to his former boss, Navy Secretary Josephus Daniels, "You know I am my own Secretary of the Navy," and he constantly referred to the Navy as "us" and to the Army as "them."[16] "During the Roosevelt administration, the White House was a Navy wardroom," one of Truman's military aides remarked in an informal talk. "We're going to fix all that."[17]

Less than three weeks after Japan's surrender, Carl Vinson's House Naval Affairs Committee held hearings on the future of the Navy. The view of most congressmen was expressed by Rep. Clarence Cannon, who declared that "one bomb, such as destroyed the city of Nagasaki, would prove equally effective in decimating any naval force that could be assembled."[18] The war had seen the triumph of the aircraft carrier and naval aviation, but now, suddenly, the entire future of the Navy seemed to be at stake. Navy Secretary Forrestal was clearly on the defensive as he opened his testimony by addressing the issue directly. "Why should we maintain any Navy after this war?" he asked. "Does the atomic bomb immediately destroy the usefulness of all navies now in existence?" For Forrestal, though, the question was not whether the Navy should continue to exist. "It is patently obvious," he said, "that all we are dealing with is the question of degree of size of that Navy."[19]

Forrestal was not yet convinced of the bomb's effectiveness. "In the first place," he told the committee, "the atomic bomb, although immensely destructive, is still a bomb, requiring land- or carrier-based planes to deliver it." He then cautioned the lawmakers about the bomb's "limitations and uncertainties," and he reminded them of Germany's glide bomb, which could penetrate three decks of armor and was viewed as a threat to American operations in the Mediterranean. Within a short time, though, the weapon was effectively neutralized. "I only cite that to show the speed with which countermeasures can be devised to meet a situation," he added, suggesting that there might be a way of defending against an atomic bomb. In fact, at a cabinet meeting that same month he decried the dependence on "gadgets, as these instruments do not win wars."[20]

The advent of the atomic bomb did not change Forrestal's perception of the Navy's mission. "In each of the past two wars," he testified, "our enemies failed to control the seas—and they were defeated. In the future, as in the past, attacks upon us or attacks by us must cross on, over, or under the sea." His conclusion was simple and forceful: "The control of the sea and of the air above it is the mission of the United States Navy—and the Navy will continue to discharge that mission with whatever weapons are most effective." To Forrestal, that weapon was still the aircraft carrier task force, although at the same time he dramatically announced the Navy's intention to develop an atomic bombing capability for aircraft carrier task forces, so that the Navy, as well as the AAF, could deliver the bomb.[21]

Nevertheless, Forrestal could not shake the view of many budget-conscious congressmen that the bomb had rendered navies obsolete. Prior to the advent of the atomic bomb, Forrestal's question as to whether there should even be a Navy "would have been ridiculous," the committee reported after the hearing. "However, some opinion has been expressed that the Navy is the principal casualty of the atomic bomb—that the atomic bomb . . . [has] eliminated the necessity of a Navy." Congress was determined to cut his proposed budget for fiscal year 1947 from $5.1 to $4.1 billion, and many saw naval aviation as an expensive luxury, especially in light of the AAF's proven ability to deliver the atomic bomb. Faced with this widespread interpretation of the significance of the bomb, a return to a peacetime economy, rapid demobilization, and a renewed call for unification of the services, the Navy had no choice but to move ahead with demonstration tests to show that ships could withstand atomic attacks.[22]

As planning for the atomic tests began, both services used leaks to the press to jockey for position and power.[23] The *New York Herald Tribune* wrote that the tests would "settle the controversy over the atomic bomb versus the battleship," while the *New York Times* reported that "some leaders of the Army Air Force . . . in private conversation will tell you flatly that they consider the Navy 'finished.'" In fact, the *Times* noted,

> it would not be at all surprising if . . . a proposal should emanate from AAF circles to test the effect of the new atomic bomb on Navy warships. There has been speculation concerning whether the atomic bomb, if dropped in the midst of a fleet at anchor, might cause the bottoms of steel ships to disintegrate and thus sink the entire fleet.

How the Navy brass would react to this Billy Mitchell–like demonstration was not known, the *Times* said. "But even if the results were bad for the Navy, they would no more consent to scrapping the battleships and carriers than the admirals did after Colonel Mitchell's bomber sank the *Ostfriesland.*"[24]

Headlines in the fall reflected the internal Navy-AAF debate within the Joint Chiefs of Staff over control of the tests. "Navy to Test Atom Bomb," *New York Times* columnist Arthur Krock reported in October.[25] The balance had shifted by November, as the *Times* reported that the AAF "expects not only to fly the bombs but to propose conditions under which the test should be conducted." No AAF official would speak publicly, it noted, "in the hope that the tests can be arranged in a spirit of complete cooperation and harmony," but the AAF said it was struggling to make sure the tests "would not be an all-Navy affair." AAF officers, the *Times* wrote, thought the tests would "prove the danger of operating surface ships anywhere near the scene of possible [atomic] explosions."[26]

Within the LeMay Subcommittee, the AAF-Navy rivalry went unchecked. The Navy wanted full control over the tests, but the AAF resisted. At one point, LeMay even met with President Truman to voice the AAF's concerns that the tests were not fair to its needs. Then, on December 14 LeMay proposed that Leslie Groves, head of the wartime Manhattan Project, be placed in charge of the tests. The Joint Chiefs, though, reasoning that the vast majority of personnel, ships, and material would be drawn from the Navy, decided that the commander of Joint Task Force One, as the organization was called, should be a Navy officer. The next day, Commodore William S. "Deak" Parsons, the senior Navy member of the LeMay Subcommittee, nominated Vice Adm. William H. P. Blandy.[27]

Two days later, on December 17, the Joint Chiefs' Joint Planning Staff reported that the Navy and the AAF were still stalemated on many aspects of the tests. The AAF, maintaining that "the atomic bomb is an air weapon" and that its value "will depend largely upon the ability of the airplane to deliver it to the target," insisted upon assembly and preparation of the bomb in the airplane, air delivery under simulated battle conditions, and studies designed to show the effects of the bomb on AAF equipment and installations.[28]

On December 22, three days after President Truman's message to Congress recommending unification of the armed services, the Joint Planning Staff submitted an outline of the tests to the Joint Chiefs. The planners recommended three tests, one an air burst, one at ground level or a shallow underwater depth, and a third several thousand feet underwater. The planners also urged the Joint Chiefs to appoint a military evaluation board, with representatives from the Army, Navy, Manhattan Project, and civilian scientists. The Joint Chiefs approved the plans a week later and directed the secretaries of war and navy to seek President Truman's approval.[29]

With many of the details still to be worked out, Forrestal and Acting Secretary of War Kenneth C. Royall sent a joint memorandum to President Truman on January 8, 1946. "These tests are necessary," they wrote, "to evaluate the strategic implications of the advent of the atomic bomb," including "the consequences of this powerful aerial weapon with respect to the size, composition and employment of the armed forces and . . . particularly . . . an analysis of future naval design and tactics." President Truman wrote the single word "Approved" on the memorandum on January 10, and planning moved forward quickly. The president had just approved the detonation of one-third of America's atomic bomb stockpile.[30]

The Joint Chiefs, acting on Deak Parsons's recommendation, appointed Vice Admiral Blandy as commander of Joint Task Force One. On January 11, by direction of President Truman, they formally ordered him to conduct the tests and to select a "suitable site which will permit accomplishment of the tests with acceptable risk and minimum hazard."[31] The site had to meet numerous conditions: It had to be in an area controlled by the United States, in a climatic zone with predictable winds and free from storms and cold temperatures, and with a large, sheltered area for anchoring target vessels and measuring radiation effects. It had to be located within 1,000 miles of a B-29 air base, as the first test was to be an air drop. The site had to be uninhabited or have a small population that could be easily relocated. As Blandy later wrote, "It was important that the local population be small and co-operative so that they could be moved to a new location with a minimum of trouble."[32] But most important, given the risk of radioactive contamination, the site had to be far away from population centers in the United States. As the AEC later stated to Congress, it felt that "tests should be held overseas until it could be established more definitely that continental detonations would not endanger the public health and safety."[33]

Military planners began working to select a test site as early as October 1945. Frederick L. Ashworth and Horacio Rivero, two of the four officers in the Navy's new OP-06 Office of Special Weapons, were in charge of the search. "We just took out dozens of maps and started looking for remote sites," recalled Rivero. "After checking the Atlantic, we moved to the West Coast and just kept looking." By mid-December they had not reached a decision. "We are in the throes of trying to figure out something about locations for this test business," Ashworth told a colleague on December 19. "We haven't come to any particular conclusion. It looks like pretty far away is going to be the answer."[34]

On January 13, 1946, Fleet Admiral Nimitz, the new chief of naval operations, called a press conference in Washington to announce the selection of Admiral Blandy. Blandy said that the tests, planned for the upcoming summer, would be a "thoroughly joint operation," not a "contest," between the Army and the Navy.[35] He did not reveal the location of the tests but, in retrospect, it was perhaps not surprising that two days later, on January 15, President Truman announced that the United States would insist that it be sole trustee under the United Nations of the Pacific islands captured from Japan during the war.[36]

On January 24, 1946, Admiral Blandy appeared before the Senate Special Committee on Atomic Energy to announce the tests. The project was code-named "Operation Crossroads," Blandy told the senators, a term he coined himself. Blandy took great pride in his choice of the code name, but the words were already in use in certain code work. Blandy cut through the red tape, though, and obtained the name for the tests.[37] In solemn tones, he explained that the name was deliberately chosen because "seapower, airpower, and perhaps humanity itself—are at the crossroads."[38] The choice of names was brilliant, implying to some that the military was unsure of its direction and was truly in awe of the atomic bomb. The ominous code name, remarked one observer, "has been greatly admired in literary and non-violent circles."[39]

Admiral Blandy also revealed the test site. More than a dozen locations throughout the Pacific, Atlantic, and the Caribbean were studied. Most were ruled out because the waters were too shallow, the population too large, or the weather undependable. Early deliberations favored one of the Caroline Islands, west of the Marshalls, partly because target ships were readily available in the area and could be retained there and, as a Navy memorandum noted, "partly because evacuation of natives would not be a major problem."[40] Serious consideration was also given to Ecuador's Galapagos Islands, 600 miles off the coast of South America in the eastern Pacific, Ulithi in the western Carolines in Micronesia, and two other sites in the Marshall Islands, Bikar and Taongi.[41]

In the end, however, Rivero and Ashworth picked Bikini. Indeed, Manhattan Project scientists had suggested a demonstration of the bomb on a barren island instead of dropping it on Japan.[42] "Bikini just popped up as the one atoll that made all sorts of sense," recalled Ashworth. "It had a good-sized lagoon, a few large islands for observing stations, good access through wide channels and a reasonably shallow area a few miles off the main island to anchor the target ships."[43]

Bikini also formed the apex of an obtuse-angle triangle with Kwajalein and Enewetak atolls, which could accommodate B-29 and B-17 aircraft for the tests. Kwajalein to Enewetak was a bit far—400 miles—but Bikini was perfect, just 200 miles from Enewetak and 250 from Kwajalein.[44] As the official U.S. history of Operation Crossroads phrased it, "Bikini won out."[45] In less grave tones, the comedian Bob Hope explained the selection process. "As soon as the war ended, we located the one spot on earth that hadn't been touched by war and blew it to hell."[46]

4

"They Are a Fine Race of People If Those in the Canoe Were a Fair Specimen"

The Pacific Ocean, more than twice the size of the Atlantic, covers one-third of the globe and is equal in size to the entire land surface of the world. At its widest part it extends 12,000 miles—halfway around the globe—from Panama to the western tip of the China Sea. Bikini Atoll, located 2,500 miles southwest of Honolulu at 11 degrees north of the equator, is a tiny pinpoint in the massive Pacific. It is one of twenty-nine atolls and five islands comprising the Marshall Islands, which are scattered over 357,000 square miles just north of the equator in the central Pacific Ocean, an area more than twice the size of California. By contrast, the total land area of all the Marshallese atolls and islands is only 70 square miles, about the size of Washington, D.C. The Marshalls, together with the Caroline and Mariana islands, constitute Micronesia, which consists of more than 2,000 islands and atolls dispersed throughout an ocean area of the Pacific nearly equal to the size of the continental United States.[1]

To the atoll-dweller of the Marshall Islands, the world is a necklace-like chain of low, flat islands surrounding a lagoon. Here, millions of years ago, a coral shelf began to build upward from a submerged volcano that rose about 15,000 feet from the ocean floor. As the coral polyps grew, they formed islands and a circular reef of live coral surrounding a shallow lagoon. Seeds blown by the wind were deposited over time, and trees and vegetation grew up.[2] Only a handful of the

1,152 islets in the Marshalls are more than one mile long. The highest elevation is only about 15 feet above sea level, and no single spot is more than a few hundred yards from the lagoon or ocean. "An atoll island is nothing but a sandspit," a U.S. official in the Marshalls once observed. "Living on an atoll is like living on a ship, except that the ship will get to a port, but the atoll will never go anyplace."³ An atoll's lagoon is completely surrounded by islands and the reefs that connect them, although this chain is usually broken by several channels deep enough for ships to pass through. Depending on the tide, two neighboring islands in the same atoll may be only a short, easy walk apart or they may be miles apart, so separated by reef or channel as to prevent the populations from traveling back and forth except by boat.

Bikini's reef and islands protect the lagoon from rough ocean currents. The lagoon sides of many islands have sandy beaches that provide easy access to the water for fishing, sailing, and bathing. Water on the ocean side, though, can be approached at low tide only by a slick and frequently painful walk across an unforgiving coral reef, an area larger than Bikini's land surface. At high tide, these reefs are covered with two to four feet of water, but at low tide the water recedes, leaving vast expanses of limestone reef cut by crevices and dotted by small pools that contain crabs, snails, eels, and other fish.

A tropical marine climate prevails throughout the Marshalls, with high temperatures and humidity. The temperature is remarkably uniform, deviating little from the annual mean of 81 degrees Fahrenheit, and the humidity averages 85 percent. The rainfall distribution in the islands differs greatly from north to south. Bikini and the other northern atolls are located in the middle of the northeast belt of trade winds, which bring strong winds but little rain during the fall and winter. As a result, the northern atolls receive only an average of 60 inches of rain per year, while the annual rainfall in the southern atolls is nearly three times greater. The southern islands therefore have richer soils, superior vegetation cover, and a greater variety of crops than the northern islands, whose poor soil cover can sustain only three basic subsistence crops—coconut, pandanus, and breadfruit. This difference in resources was historically reflected in the islands' population. Bikini, typical of the other northern atolls, had only 167 residents in 1946, while some of the southern atolls sustained populations in excess of 1,000.

Bikini Atoll's twenty-three islands have a combined land area of 1,780 acres, or less than three square miles, and only four islands are large enough to support more than a few families. Indeed, prior to the evacuation of the islanders in 1946, the entire population lived on Bikini Island, the largest in the atoll, which covers 600 acres, an area less than three-quarters the size of New York's Central Park.

Bikini's islands enclose a 243-square mile oval lagoon, which extends 26 miles east to west and 15 miles north to south, with an average depth of 180 feet. A reef connects most of the islands in the east, north, and west, but there are several channels on the southern side of the atoll, the largest being the nine-mile wide Eneu (pronounced "Enyu") channel. The atoll's only fresh water is rainwater, caught and stored in cisterns and tanks.

As the northernmost atoll in the Marshall Islands' western chain, Bikini is relatively distant and isolated from other atolls. Its closest neighbor, Rongelap Atoll, is more than 80 miles to the east. Before 1946, the Bikinians maintained no regular contacts with outside communities, and they were among the last Marshallese people subject to foreign influences. Indeed, while some of the Marshalls were sighted in 1787, Bikini was not located until nearly 40 years later. There are no written records of Marshallese history before 1825, but carbon dating of human remains and other archaeological discoveries at Bikini indicate that people may have lived on the atoll as early as 2000 B.C.[4]

The Pacific was one of the last areas to be explored by European navigators and traders. In 1519, six years after Balboa's sighting of the Pacific Ocean, Charles I of Spain dispatched Ferdinand Magellan to the Pacific with five ships and 265 men to find cloves, peppers, curry, nutmeg, mace, and cinnamon. These fragrant spices, which the Crusaders had first brought back to Europe from the East, were used for perfumes, medicinal drugs, and cosmetics, and they were in great demand throughout Europe. Cloves, the most sought-after spice, were used to season and preserve meats.[5] The Spice Islands (Moluccas), located off the coast of Indonesia, were the main source of these spices and the only source of cloves, but Portuguese ships controlled access via the coast of Africa and India, so Magellan proposed a westerly route around the Americas.

By almost any standard, Magellan's voyage was catastrophic. Two ships were lost in the strait that bears his name, one by shipwreck and the other by desertion. After leaving the west coast of South America, the remaining ships sailed for nearly four months without sighting land, and the sailors were reduced to chewing worm-ridden biscuits and gnawing on leather. Then, on March 6, 1521, Magellan spotted land and natives paddled out in canoes to meet his ship. Magellan had reached Guam.

It was perhaps prophetic that this first meeting between Western man and the Micronesians was disastrous. The Guamanians, fascinated by so many new tools and devices, snatched away everything that was not nailed down, and Magellan's men were forced to drive the islanders back with pointed crossbars. The islanders retaliated the next day, as forty spear-wielding men attacked a landing team searching for provisions, but the Spaniards held their own, killing seven warriors. Magellan contemptuously dubbed Guam and two small nearby islands Islas de Ladrones (Islands of Thieves) and sailed on to the Philippines, where he and forty of his men were killed. Only one of his five ships, with just eighteen men aboard, returned to Spain in 1522. Despite these losses, the voyage was a great financial success because the ship had reached the Moluccas and returned to Spain with 25 tons of valuable cloves.[6]

The "pursuit of the clove" had begun, and the Spaniards steadily charted Micronesia in a search for new routes to the Spice Islands not controlled by Portugal. Alvaro de Saavedra Ceron sailed to the Marshall Islands in 1528, stopping at what was probably Enewetak. His encounter with the Marshallese was more friendly than Magellan's in Guam. His crew was welcomed at the beach by islanders who sang and danced to the beat of drums and accompanied the sailors to the house of their chief. At dinner, the chief pointed to Saavedra's musket, curious as to its purpose. Saavedra fired it, and in the ensuing pandemonium most of the Marshallese ran out of the house and fled in their canoes. Others fell to the ground in a dead faint, but the chief stood his ground, trembling uncontrollably.[7]

The visit ended peacefully, although Saavedra died shortly after leaving the Marshall Islands. Other Spanish explorers in the late sixteenth and early seventeenth centuries discovered the Solomon Islands, New Hebrides, and New Guinea. The Dutch came from Indonesia early in the seventeenth century, and the eighteenth century brought the British and the French. In 1765 the English admiral John Byron (grandfather of the poet) discovered some of the southern Gilbert Islands, while Tahiti was discovered and claimed by explorers from France, England, and Spain between 1768 and 1774. The greatest Pacific explorer of the century, James Cook, made three voyages between 1769 and 1779, and discovered the Hawaiian islands, Christmas Island, the Marquesas, Fiji, New Caledonia, and the Cook Islands.

The Marshall Islands were sighted during these years. In 1767, Samuel Wallis spotted what is believed to be Rongelap and Rongerik atolls, east of Bikini, and named them the Pescadores. Twenty years later, in 1787, two British captains working for the East India Company, William Marshall and Thomas Gilbert, sailed through the islands and atolls that later bore their names. And in 1794, Thomas Butler sighted Enewetak, more than 200 miles west of Bikini. He named it Browne's Range in honor of an East India Company agent at Canton. Mr. Browne's name, slightly altered, stayed with Enewetak into the atomic age, as World War II charts of the atoll referred to it as Eniwetok (Brown) Atoll.[8]

But no Westerner discovered Bikini until well after the major Pacific discoveries. The first sighting of the atoll was not by a Dutchman, Spaniard, Frenchman, or Englishman, but by a captain in the Russian Imperial Navy, Otto von Kotzebue. His father, August von Kotzebue, a successful German playwright, left Weimar following a disagreement with Goethe and entered the service of the Russian czars, eventually obtaining a political appointment in Estonia. Otto, born in Reval in 1787, sailed at the age of 16 on the first Russian expedition to circle the world.

In 1815, Count Romanzov, grand chancellor of the Russian empire, placed the 28-year-old Kotzebue in command of the *Rurik,* a small 180-ton brig, to lead a Russian expedition to the Arctic. One of the most remarkable men to join Kotzebue for this voyage was Adelbert von Chamisso, a brilliant young German writer and poet-turned botanist. Chamisso, six years older than Kotzebue, had fled with his family to Berlin at the outbreak of the French Revolution and later fought with the Prussians against Napoleon in 1806. From 1803 to 1806 he edited a literary journal in Berlin that published his first poems, although several years later he turned his attention to botany. Chamisso achieved his first literary success in 1814 with the publication of the narrative *Peter Schlemihls wundersame Geschichte,* a story of a man who sells his shadow to the devil. The narrative became a classic and was translated into many languages; the artist George Cruikshank illustrated the English version. Chamisso's later poems were much admired by Heine, and Robert Schumann set some of them to music.[9]

This poet, dramatist, literary editor, linguist, soldier, and botanist was just beginning to be recognized as a major literary figure when he joined Kotzebue on the *Rurik*'s voyage. Another member of the expedition was a 22-year-old Estonian surgeon and entomologist, Ivan Ivanovich Eschscholtz, who joined the *Rurik* as the ship's surgeon and zoologist and later returned to teach at the university in Dorpat. Chamisso and Eschscholtz became close friends during the three-year voyage of the *Rurik;* indeed, during the expedition's stay in San Francisco Chamisso named what is commonly known as the California poppy as *Eschscholtzia californica.*[10]

The voyage of the *Rurik* took Kotzebue, Chamisso, and Eschscholtz throughout the Pacific from the Bering Sea to Cape Horn and the west coast of North America. Kotzebue's major goal, long a dream of European explorers, was to discover an Arctic passage from the Pacific to the Atlantic Ocean. The expedition succeeded in mapping large portions of the Alaskan coastline, and then headed into the Arctic Ocean but, unable to penetrate the ice, it turned south into the warmer waters of the Pacific, visiting some of the Marshall Islands before returning to Russia in 1818.

In 1823, Czar Alexander I placed Kotzebue in charge of another scientific expedition to the Pacific on a larger ship, the *Predpriatie* (Enterprise), built especially for the expedition. Chamisso did not join Kotzebue on this expedition, but Eschscholtz did, as did 2d Lt. Nikolai Petrovich Rimsky-Korsakov and Lt. Ivan Chramtschenko, who would return to Bikini in 1858. The crew of 145 men embarked with great fanfare, as the czar himself traveled to Kronstadt to see them off.[11] The explorers reached the northern Marshalls in October 1825, as Kotzebue searched for the Pescadores (Rongelap and Rongerik), discovered by Samuel Wallis 58 years earlier. On October 6 he sighted Rongerik, but he did not alter Wallis's nomenclature on his charts. The next day he sailed more than 50 miles along the ocean side of what he thought was a single atoll, but which were in fact the neighboring atolls of Rongelap and Ailinginae. He named them in his chart the Rimsky-Korsakov Islands in honor of his second lieutenant, who was to become an admiral, the director of Russia's Marine Corps in the 1840s, a favorite of Emperor Nicholas I, and the uncle of the great Russian composer of the same name.[12]

On the morning of October 9, Kotzebue wrote in his journal, "We had scarcely spread our sails before the man at the mast-head discovered some low islands to the north." Kotzebue was 11 miles windward of Bikini Atoll. He tried to tack, but a strong easterly current prevented him from approaching any closer. A second attempt failed, so he continued westward, contenting himself with determining the position of the western islands. "These, like other coral islands," wrote Kotzebue, "probably lie round a basin; of population we could see no trace, though there was every appearance of their being habitable."[13]

Kotzebue named the island "after our worthy Doctor and Professor, Eschscholtz." This name, like Rimsky-Korsakov (Rongelap and Ailinginae) and Pescadores (Rongelap and Rongerik), remained on navigational charts. Indeed, when Bikini was first selected as an atomic test site, the *New York Times* referred to it as "the Bikini (or Eschholtz [sic]) Atoll."[14] While Eschscholtz's name no longer graces Bikini, it is still found on the map of Alaska, thanks to Kotzebue, who had named three sites after himself and his two friends in 1816, when the *Rurik* anchored on the lee side of a small island in a bay near the Arctic Circle. This is today Chamisso Island in Eschscholtz Bay, and both are located on the east end of Kotzebue Sound.[15]

Chamisso's observations on the coral atolls of the Marshalls were published in 1821, and Charles Darwin relied on them 21 years later in his study on coral reefs.[16] Kotzebue's own accounts of the 1815–18 expedition had an equally interesting history. They were studied by many naturalists and writers, including Herman Melville, whose views on Tahiti in his novel *Typee* were shaped largely by Kotzebue's observations of the island.[17] Ironically, the Alaskan town of Kotzebue, named after the discoverer of Bikini, served as the supply and transport site for Project Chariot, a study by the AEC in the late 1950s and early '60s on the use of nuclear explosions to excavate a harbor on the Chukchi Sea, which separates Alaska from the Soviet Union. The enterprise was never attempted, but the AEC's environmental survey of the flora and fauna of the Arctic relied on Kotzebue's accounts of his voyage to the area nearly 150 years earlier.

The first recorded meeting of the Bikinians with non-Marshallese occurred in 1858, when Kotzebue's lieutenant, Chramtschenko, revisited Eschscholtz Atoll. This time the crew located a three-mile-wide channel and entered Bikini lagoon. Crossing the lagoon, Chramtschenko reported, his crew came upon a canoe "with a chief aboard, who informed us that the name of the group was Bigini." "They are a fine race of people," wrote Chramtschenko, "if those in the canoe were a fair specimen."[18]

The Bikinians tell their own story of their origins. As related by one of the elders, an iroij (paramount chief) named Larkelon returned to his home at Wotje Atoll one day to discover that his wife had left him to live with his cousin. Marshallese tradition forbade him from going to war with his own clan, so he and a group of his clan members sailed away, never to return home. When they came upon Bikini they sailed across the lagoon to Nam Island, where Larkelon challenged the iroij of Bikini and demanded that the Bikinians bring him food and other goods. At this, said the elder, the iroij of Bikini and his people fled in their canoes across the lagoon and out to sea, "where they have not been heard of since."[19] Larkelon's matrilineal descendants succeeded him as iroij, and the leader of the Bikini community in 1946, dubbed "King" Juda by the Western press, was a fifth-generation descendant from Larkelon. Using a figure of 25 years to a generation, it is possible that Chramtschenko may actually have met Larkelon in Bikini's lagoon in 1858.

As more and more contacts developed between the Marshall Islands and the outside world during the nineteenth and twentieth centuries, Bikini remained virtually isolated. As a result, the islanders developed their own dialect, distinct from other Marshallese. Those few Bikinians who ventured beyond the reef to travel in the Marshalls were looked down upon by other Marshallese, who found their speech variations humorous and viewed them as culturally inferior. Indeed, the Bikinians seemed to accept this unflattering description. They thought of themselves distinctly as "Bikinians," not as Marshallese, and most preferred to remain within the confines of Bikini Atoll.[20]

In the meantime, other parts of the Marshall Islands began to come under foreign influences, although the islands had a notorious reputation for hostility toward outsiders. The mutineers of the Nantucket whaler *Globe* were murdered on Mili Atoll in 1824, as were twelve men from the British whaling ship *Elizabeth* who went ashore at Ebon in 1833. There was murder at Bikini as well, as the captain and two crew members of a trading schooner that called at the atoll in 1834 were killed by the islanders. Three ships subsequently returned to Bikini in the belief that the captain was being held hostage, and the crew of one reportedly killed thirty Bikinians, which would have represented about one-third of the atoll's entire population at that time.[21]

In 1857, the year before Chramtschenko visited Bikini, Protestant missionaries from New England established their first mission on Ebon Atoll in the southern Marshalls. Christianity spread quickly, together with modesty, as the missionaries persuaded Marshallese women to cover their bodies with ungainly, ankle-length Mother Hubbards. Missionaries did not travel to the northern atolls until late in the century, however, and the first mission at Bikini was not established until 1908, when a Marshallese pastor arrived from a southern atoll.

In the 1860s a German trader named Adolf Capelle settled in the Marshalls and developed a copra business. Copra, or dried coconut meat, remains the cash crop of the Marshalls; when processed, it yields coconut oil. The copra industry, strong in the southern Marshalls, never flourished in the north, where the coconut was more of a subsistence crop. Capelle and other German traders taught the Marshallese how to process copra, exchanging it for metal tools, cloth, and tobacco. Germany, eager for colonial expansion in the Pacific, saw an opportunity in the Marshall Islands, an area to which no other Western power had asserted a substantial claim. In 1878 it signed a treaty with a paramount chief named Kabua to receive the right to establish a coaling station at Jaluit Atoll and access to other ports in the archipelago. With Britain's approval, Germany declared the Marshall Islands a protectorate in 1885, and by the end of the century it had purchased Spain's entire Pacific holdings for $4.5 million.[22]

Meanwhile, life at Bikini had changed little since Kotzebue and Eschscholtz had sailed by the islands in 1825. Although Marshallese in the southern atolls, influenced by German traders and missionaries, had begun to adopt western dressing styles by 1900, the Bikinians wore fiber skirts and mats well into the twentieth century. A tribal system of rule, led by paramount chiefs, had developed within the Marshall Islands, but the Bikinians maintained a large degree of political independence until the late nineteenth century.

Germany established its colonial headquarters on Jaluit Atoll, in the southern Marshalls, through a government-sponsored trading company that carried out commercial activities and collected a tax on the copra trade by working through the paramount chiefs. Earlier tributes to the iroij had consisted of food products, coconut sennit, and personal services, but with the arrival of the copra industry the paramount chiefs collected copra, sold it to the Germans, and took a substantial share of the income. The chiefs dispatched several boats for the purpose of gathering copra, but these operated almost exclusively in the southern atolls.

Japan seized most of Germany's Micronesian possessions at the outbreak of World War I, and at the Versailles Peace Conference in 1919 it was awarded Micronesia as a class "C" mandate of the League of Nations. The League of Nations Covenant recognized that the peoples of mandated territories were "not yet able to stand by themselves under the strenuous conditions of the modern world," and it therefore "entrusted . . . the tutelage of such peoples . . . to advanced nations who by reason of their resources, their experience, or their geographical location can best undertake this responsibility."[23] Japan immediately initiated a program of intensive economic development throughout the Marshall Islands and the rest of Micronesia, dramatically increasing production in agriculture, copra, and fishing. The entire area soon became completely integrated into Japan's economy; the Marianas were converted into sugarcane plantations, the Carolines became large fishing centers, and phosphate and bauxite were mined on Palau.

Although the Mandate Agreement forbade the establishment of fortifications or military bases, Japan closed off Micronesia to all foreigners in the 1930s and began to fortify strategic islands and atolls in anticipation of its military invasion of the Pacific.[24] Japan launched its attack on Pearl Harbor from Micronesia, and America would later end the war from Micronesia, as the B-29s for Hiroshima and Nagasaki took off from Tinian Island in the Marianas. In between, Micronesia was the site of many of the bloodiest battles of the war, with the exotic names of its previously unheard-of islands—Tarawa, Saipan, Kwajalein, Enewetak, Peleliu, and Truk—becoming household words in America.

As the war in the Pacific slowly turned in America's favor, Navy brass saw the Marshall Islands as one of their first targets. Kwajalein, the world's largest atoll, was at the geographic center, surrounded by Japanese air bases at Enewetak, Mili, Maloelap, Wotje, and Jaluit. Nimitz did not want to give the Japanese time to improve their defensive positions in the Marshall Islands, so he boldly called for a strike right at Kwajalein. This was to be the first strike at the Japanese empire, against land it had controlled for 25 years and had fortified for a decade.

Forty-thousand U.S. Marines and Army assault troops landed on Kwajalein on January 31 and February 1, 1944, and by February 7 the atoll had fallen. American forces suffered 2,000 casualties, including 372 dead, while nearly 8,000 Japanese were killed. Meanwhile, 260 miles to the southeast, Adm. Raymond A. Spruance's forces took Majuro on January 31 without a single casualty. Majuro was the first territory of the prewar Japanese empire taken by the United States. A garrison force of 7,000 men landed within days and converted the atoll to an advanced air and naval base. In less than three months a new 5,800-foot airstrip was completed and 150 ships were anchored from one end of the lagoon to the other.[25]

With casualties at Kwajalein much lower than expected, Nimitz ordered an immediate attack on Enewetak. The invasion went forward successfully on February 17, at a cost of 710 American casualties and 2,700 Japanese losses. Four atolls—Jaluit, Mili, Wotje, and Maloelap—remained fortified by thousands of Japanese soldiers, but their capture was no longer critical, so they were bypassed and left to wither until Japan surrendered. Meanwhile, Kwajalein and Enewetak were turned into U.S. military bases. By early March, Kwajalein became the Army's main air base in Micronesia, and its two new runways supported U.S. bombers. By April 1, 22,000 men were based at Kwajalein and 11,200 at Enewetak, whose lagoon was filled with more than 100 ships.[26]

The Marshalls campaign was a spectacular success. The huge losses at Tarawa in November 1943 had shocked the American people, but the liberation of the Marshalls raised morale and restored public confidence in the Navy. It gave the Japanese no time to fortify their defensives in the Marianas, and it advanced by four months Nimitz's march across the Pacific.[27]

While Bikini was spared serious fighting during World War II, the impact of the war had a profound effect on the islanders. Three Bikini men who had attended a Japanese school at Jaluit were drafted as laborers and sent to Enewetak Atoll, where they were killed during the American invasion. Meanwhile, six Japanese soldiers established a weather station at Bikini Island during the war, making them the first foreigners to reside at Bikini. They told the Bikinians of Japan's conquest of Asia, said that Bikini belonged to the emperor of Japan, and left the people with the impression that Japan was the most powerful nation on earth. The soldiers imposed a strict regimen on the islanders; they suspended Christian services, set curfews, and conscripted labor.

An American plane strafed the weather station at Bikini on March 27, 1944, killing one Japanese soldier and injuring two others. The next day, recalled a Bikini elder, a second plane appeared. "We were all very afraid and so we ran to hide in the bushes at the other end of the island." When an American ship entered the lagoon on the afternoon of March 28, several Bikinians sailed out to it on an outrigger canoe and reported the location of the Japanese soldiers. The islanders were sent back with a surrender demand to give to the Japanese and instructions to advise the Bikinians to move to the northern end of the island the next morning in order to avoid the Marines, who would be landing at the southern end.

American forces came ashore on March 29 and unfurled an American flag. The Bikinians, like the other Marshallese, feared and hated the Japanese and gave the Americans every assistance they could. The troops could not find the Japanese, but the next morning two Bikinians located them and led the Americans to their foxhole. When the five Japanese heard the Americans' voices, they opened their hand grenades and killed themselves.[28]

The damage to Bikini was slight, but as American troops moved closer and closer to Japan, the most awesome weapon—the atomic bomb—was being prepared to enter the scene, and it was destined to change the face of Bikini forever.

"The Buck Rogers of the Navy"

The appointment of William Henry Purnell Blandy as the commander of Operation Crossroads's Joint Task Force One marked the culmination of the 33-year career of one of the Navy's most innovative leaders. "Spike" Blandy, as he was nicknamed, was known as the "Navy's Gun Man" during the years he headed the Navy's Bureau of Ordnance. Now back in the public eye, he was dubbed the "Atomic Admiral."

Blandy, a native of New York City, was born in 1890. His grandfather, Dr. William Henry Purnell, after whom he was named, was president of the University of Delaware, and his great-grandfather was a naval officer in the Mexican War. Blandy studied at Delaware College until 1909, when he was appointed to the Naval Academy by Senator Henry A. du Pont of Delaware. There he was a wizard at mathematics, won two prizes in gunnery and ordnance, and excelled in high jumping and fencing. He graduated first in his class of 1913, and the yearbook called him "the best Cadet Commander the Academy has known during the life of this class."

Blandy saw action in Europe during World War I, and he was present when the German fleet surrendered at the end of the war. He returned to the United States to do postgraduate work in ordnance engineering at the Naval Gun Factory in Washington, D.C., and in 1924 was appointed chief of the gun section of the Navy's Bureau of Ordnance. Over the next

15 years he became the top ordnance expert in the Navy, combining his mastery of the practical aspects of gunnery with his vast knowledge of gun design and manufacturing. He overhauled gunnery training procedures and developed improved manufacturing techniques for several guns that remained in use at the end of World War II. He wrote and lectured extensively on gunnery during these years, and a 1925 talk he gave at the Naval Academy on gunnery safety precautions remained as part of a World War II guide for naval officers.[1]

Blandy returned to sea in 1938 as captain of the pre–World War I battleship *Utah*, which served as a target for 10,000 water-filled bombs and torpedoes, as well as experimental drone planes, which the ship's crew would try to shoot down. The bombs put holes in the ship's deck, while the drones, precursors of the Japanese kamikazes, occasionally crashed onto the deck. "Even if those bombs didn't carry explosives," he recalled, "it was no nerve-soothing experience to watch them coming at you at 700 feet a second, to hit near your conning tower." The ship was hit by more than 1,000 bombs, and Blandy later compared its deck to a piece of Swiss cheese. After one exercise left sixty holes in the deck, he permitted his officers to shift their staterooms whenever a bomb exposed their bunks to the sky.[2]

In February 1941, at the age of 50, Blandy became the youngest line admiral in the Navy, as he was selected from over 100 officers senior to him to head the Navy's Bureau of Ordnance, which oversaw the design, development, and production of ammunition, guns, and fire control systems.[3] The Navy's munitions output soared under Admiral Blandy. Production in 1942 was fifteen times higher than in 1941; the entire U.S. automotive industry in its most successful prewar year was smaller than the naval ordnance industry in 1942. The bureau's officer complement grew from 80 to over 2,000 under Blandy, and at its peak it handled more than $1 billion in war production contracts per month.

Blandy quickly developed a reputation for getting the job done, frequently by going around the bureau's entrenched bureaucracy. He ruthlessly slashed red tape and changed a long-standing bureau policy of manufacturing weapons exclusively in government-owned and -operated plants. "If . . . this Bureau had not taken the bull by the horns in the beginning," he said in response to criticism that he favored private companies, "[we] would be eating nothing but fish and rice today, with damn little saki to go with it. We would also be wearing socks with the big toe separate." He developed the idea of awarding the Navy "E," a merit flag symbolizing excellence and efficiency, to outstanding ordnance plants. The gimmick was a huge success, as thousands of workers attended ceremonies dedicating "E" pennants. Other Navy bureaus soon took up the practice, as did the Army, and by 1942 the award became an Army-Navy "E."[4]

When Blandy took over the bureau, its seventeen sections were virtually independent fiefdoms, each responsible for every phase of a particular type of ordnance, such as armor or torpedoes, from development through production and eventual scrapping. Blandy completely reorganized this vertical system with a horizontal structure organized along five functional lines, such as production and administration. Instead of seventeen coequal heads reporting directly to him, he now had five. Determined to reverse the Navy's longstanding failure to provide necessary funds for research, he created a separate division of research and development, an action that later led to his selection as commander of Joint Task Force One. He was also instrumental in establishing the Naval Ordnance Test Station at Inyokern, California, to develop rockets and other new weapons.[5]

Blandy was an excellent administrator and worked well with Navy Secretary Forrestal, who recalled after the war that Blandy's appointment as chief of the bureau "was hailed with gratitude by the people in the service who knew his capabilities."[6] He had an intimate knowledge of metallurgy, chemistry, armor, projectiles, and forgings—all the subjects involved in the manufacturing of guns, shells, and torpedoes. He also attracted talented men, including Bernard Brodie, the future nuclear strategist, who became Blandy's speechwriter and assistant in 1943. His office was surrounded by gunnery pictures and ordnance flags, and his desk was decorated with model guns and gadgets made from shell casings. His conferences were short and to the point; he asked concise questions and expected quick, direct answers from others.[7]

Blandy's experience in charge of the *Utah* tests convinced him that high-altitude bombing of ships was nowhere near as serious a threat as low-level dive-bombing attacks or aerial torpedoes, so he ordered the installation of antiaircraft guns at every possible station on all ships. The Navy, though, had not developed adequate short-range antiaircraft guns, a predicament Blandy blamed on the Billy Mitchell–inspired rush to develop air power and what he called a "defeatist" attitude regarding the ability of ships to defend themselves against hostile aircraft.[8]

Undaunted, Blandy moved quickly to obtain licenses to build two foreign models, the Swedish 40mm Bofors machine gun and the Swiss 20mm Oerlikon, two guns that had gained an excellent reputation for efficiency during the Spanish Civil War. Blandy's directive was implemented immediately, and it saved countless hundreds of lives. The battleship *Nevada,* which had 20 antiaircraft gun mounts in place during the attack on Pearl Harbor, had 56 one year later, while the number of antiaircraft guns on the battleship *South Dakota* more than quadrupled between 1941 and 1943, from 23 to 102.[9]

In contrast to his success with antiaircraft guns, Blandy was confronted with extraordinary problems facing the Navy's submarine fleet, whose main weapon, the Mark XIV torpedo, ran 11 feet deeper than it was set for. Part of the problem was due to inadequate testing. "Prior to the war," recalled Lewis Strauss, one of Blandy's aides, "we never tested a torpedo with a live warhead because it would destroy the torpedo and the bureau couldn't afford the $12,000. The Navy was starved that way and the Bureau of Ordnance was more or less a stepchild of the Navy."[10]

Rear Adm. Charles A. Lockwood discovered the trouble with the Mark XIV's depth-control mechanism, but Bureau of Ordnance technicians blamed the crews for the problem and said that no reliable conclusions could be drawn from Lockwood's tests. In desperation, Lockwood sent off a dispatch to Blandy, his old friend who was one year his junior at the Naval Academy. "Please lend us a hand to clear the air and give us the dope we need," he wrote. Blandy ran new tests, and eight months after Pearl Harbor the bureau conceded that Lockwood was right and ordered commanders to adjust their settings.[11]

Blandy explained his decisions in an interview after the war:

My policy was to be radical in experimentation, and somewhat more conservative in adoption. If I found something good, I would take a chance. I would have the thing produced in a hurry and sent out for combat testing, rather than wait until the designers achieved perfection. Of course, we busted once or twice on ideas that did not work out, but on the whole, it was a correct policy. It saved many months and an unestimated number of lives and ships.[12]

Blandy left the Bureau of Ordnance in late 1943 to become commander of Amphibious Task Group I in the Pacific. He saw action at Kwajalein in the Marshall Islands in 1944, just a few hundred miles from Bikini, led amphibious forces at Saipan and Palau, and commanded all preinvasion activities at Iwo Jima and Okinawa, including bombardment, minesweeping, and underwater demolition. Blandy's record, though, was somewhat tarnished at Iwo Jima, where he was caught in the rivalry between the Navy and the AAF. His experience there fully prepared him for the interservice rivalry that was to hamper Operation Crossroads.

The decision to take Iwo Jima was dictated by the AAF's new bomber, the B-29 Superfortress. B-29 groups began operating out of Saipan, Tinian, and Guam in the Marianas in late 1944, but the results were disappointing. The planes were plagued by ineffective high-altitude bombing techniques, mechanical defects, navigational hazards, inadequate maintenance facilities, and long overwater flights that used up most of the plane's fuel and left little margin for unforeseen headwinds. Nevertheless, the Navy was concerned about the advent of the B-29s. Some naval planners dismissed them "as a sideshow of the stunt category," but others saw the Superfortress raids as an attempt by the AAF to wrest control of the Pacific War from the Navy. "The interests of the AAF and the Navy clash seriously in the Central Pacific campaign," wrote one of Admiral King's assistants. "The danger is obvious of our amphibious campaign being turned into one that is auxiliary support to permit the AAF to get into position to win the war."[13]

"This outfit has been getting a hell of a lot of publicity without having really accomplished a hell of a lot in bombing results," barked Gen. Curtis LeMay when he took over command of the B-29 raids in early 1945.[14] Iwo Jima was the problem. Japanese planes from the island disrupted B-29 missions and warned Tokyo of approaching raids. Moreover, avoiding the island required the B-29s to fly a long dogleg course that consumed more fuel, reduced bomb loads, and complicated navigation. Taking the island would wipe out these problems as well as provide an air base midway between Japan and the Marianas that the B-29s could use for refueling and emergency landings.[15]

By mid-February 1945, 250,000 U.S. servicemen were poised to invade Iwo Jima. The Marines, suspecting the island was highly fortified, asked for ten days of continuous naval bombardment before the landing, but their request competed with several political issues. The assault on Iwo Jima had already been delayed a month by General MacArthur's return to the Philippines, accompanied by six battleships. Furthermore, Adm. Raymond A. Spruance planned to use other ships to mount a carrier-based raid on Tokyo to coincide with the preinvasion bombardment of Iwo Jima. The ostensible reason for Spruance's raid was to neutralize Japanese planes that might attack during the invasion, but he was also determined to show that the Navy could attack Tokyo's aircraft factories that the Army's B-29s could barely touch. He did not hide his disdain for the B-29. "We cannot afford to await the outcome of bombing 'with precision instruments' from 30,000 feet, often through solid overcast," he wrote to a friend.[16]

Anxious to launch his attack on Tokyo with Navy planes, Spruance reduced the Marines' request for naval bombardment from ten days to three, with an option for a fourth day, if commanders on the scene believed it necessary. "In retrospect," wrote military historian Ronald Spector, "it is hard to see how bombing aircraft plants in Japan could have had an immediate effect on the situation at Iwo Jima, and it is hard to escape the conclusion that the Navy was eager to have a go at upstaging the Army Air Forces."[17]

The task of bombarding Iwo Jima fell to Admiral Blandy. He had only six battleships, all of which were built before the United States entered World War I. Four were the oldest in commission in the Navy; in fact, the *New York* would soon lose her propeller blades because of metal fatigue. Three had started their careers as coal burners, and three others were up from the mud of Pearl Harbor. To make matters worse, bad weather and poor visibility at Iwo Jima severely hampered bombardment for two of the three days. At midnight on the third day, Blandy sent an ominous wire to Adm. Kelly Turner: "Though weather has not permitted complete expenditure of entire ammunition allowance, and more installations can be found and destroyed with one more day of bombardment," Blandy reported, "I believe landing can be accomplished tomorrow as scheduled, if necessary."[18]

Blandy's decision to decline Spruance's offer of an extra day of bombardment was harshly criticized. "Blandy and his fellow gunfire officers weren't going to cross the beaches in the morning as were the Marines, with khaki shirts their only armor," wrote one chronicler of the invasion. Marine Maj. Gen. Holland M. Smith "would never forget or forgive the fact that Blandy's battleships had retired for the night with hundreds of shells still in ammunition lockers."[19] But Blandy felt the bombardment had done all that was needed.

In retrospect, one or two additional days of bombardment would probably have shortened the battle, as the estimated four-day capture of Iwo Jima took a month. All but a handful of the 21,000 Japanese defenders died, but the Marines' losses were also staggering. Their 6,821 dead and 19,217 wounded marked the only time in the Pacific that American casualties exceeded Japanese, as reporters called the campaign the worst since Gettysburg. Ironically, the island never became the B-29 base envisioned by Spruance and LeMay. Japanese air strength was decreasing rapidly, eliminating the need for fighter escorts. The B-29s continued to operate out of the Marianas, although the bombers would make more than 2,400 emergency landings on Iwo Jima, saving many lives.[20]

Blandy was a model of stern command and authority, and he inspired men in combat. "He had that rare quality of leadership which elicited respect and absolute confidence from those who served under him," wrote Lewis Strauss. "I have heard many junior officers who were with him in the Pacific say that they had rather go into battle with Blandy on the bridge than any other commander."[21] Blandy's courage, efficiency, and competence were complemented by his intellectual curiosity. He was fluent in French, and even translated into English a lengthy technical paper by a French naval engineer on transverse resistance of guns, and he lectured and wrote extensively on naval history.[22]

Well before Operation Crossroads, Blandy found himself defending battleships and destroyers against the AAF. "With the romance of air power there has been a tendency to forget the old surface ship," he told an interviewer during the war. "Nelson always said he never had enough frigates and I always think we never have enough destroyers." He added that the surface ship would remain a major weapon until such time as an enemy could be brought to total defeat by air power. "Then the death knell will sound for the surface ship, but I don't expect to live to see that day," he smiled.[23] Lewis Strauss later described Blandy as a battleship admiral, adding that Blandy was "proud of that tag although it was already beginning to be used as a term to indicate obsolescent naval thinking." Like other Annapolis graduates, wrote Strauss, Blandy "sincerely believed in the doctrine that the Navy was the one indispensable service which could defend and preserve the nation against all aggression."[24]

In November 1945 Forrestal appointed Blandy deputy chief of naval operations for special weapons to oversee the development of atomic bombs and guided missiles. The man who had been called the "Navy's Gun Man" now became the "Buck Rogers of the Navy."[25] Blandy was realistic, even provocative, about the future of the Navy. The "battleship admiral," he told an interviewer, "is a generic term for all admirals who are too slow to recognize new developments." He even suggested that conservative naval strategists of the future might be labeled carrier admirals rather than battleship admirals. "In this new age," he explained, "the old battleship may get its face lifted and emerge as a giant rocket ship—perhaps with atomic rockets. . . . We may see submarines operating submerged at a greater radius by atomic energy, and capable of striking with robot atomic rockets." Indeed, when asked by Admiral King to comment on a proposed plan for the makeup of the postwar Navy, Blandy recommended against demobilizing additional battleships instead of aircraft carriers, leading one naval historian to label him a representative of "the old 'Gun Club.'"[26]

Blandy's wartime experience as head of the Bureau of Ordnance strongly influenced his postwar views on the proposed atomic bomb tests on ships. Ironically, he had proposed in 1943 that enemy ships and surplus U.S. vessels be used as targets after the war to test the effects of newly developed weapons.[27] In an off-the-record meeting with reporters after his appointment as commander of Joint Task Force One, he recalled that the Navy's ability to test any sort of weapon, particularly torpedoes, was severely hampered by a lack of test targets. "I'd had the idea" at the bureau, he said, "that after the war obsolete ships of our own and captured enemy ships should be reserved . . . for the purpose of trying out new weapons, because I had seen in the previous peace period that we were always short of full-sized hulls to experiment with."[28]

Even before leaving the Bureau of Ordnance in 1943, Blandy had given serious thought to the question of postwar planning and research. Determined to avoid what he saw as the Navy's shortsightedness after World War I, he was instrumental in ensuring that the new ordnance testing facility in California would serve not only the Navy's wartime needs, but also remain after the war as a permanent center for weapons research and development. "In the postwar period, which, of course, will also be the next prewar period," he wrote to Navy Secretary Knox in his final report as ordnance chief, "determined efforts must be made to maintain the contact now existing between the Bureau of Ordnance and the best scientific brains and research facilities in the country." His efforts bore fruit, leading the historians of the Naval Weapons Center in China Lake, California, to describe Blandy as "the most visionary prophet of a permanent, postwar Navy ordnance research center."[29]

Blandy's good relationship with the press would also help him in Operation Crossroads. The *New York Times* called Blandy a "resourceful, quick-thinking man" with "complete composure and steel-trap efficiency," adding that he is "widely recognized as one of the Navy's ablest young admirals and, incidentally, one of its most articulate spokesmen." The consensus in naval circles, it reported, was that Blandy "is the best possible choice for the atomic bomb test, which calls for a combination of technical background and command experience, plus qualities of forward-thinking and . . . diplomacy." The *Honolulu Star-Bulletin* wrote that "he is considered by many to be the greatest ordnance man the navy ever had," and *Newsweek* concluded that the choice of Blandy to head Joint Task Force One "was excellent."[30]

Although Admiral Blandy was certainly a card-carrying member of the "Gun Club," he transcended the traditional narrow mold of naval officers. He recognized the importance of naval aviation in the late 1930s, consistently championed innovations and improvements at the Bureau of Ordnance, and was always concerned about the Navy's future. "Blandy was a high-minded man," recalled Townsend Hoopes, an aide to Forrestal and one-time undersecretary of the Air Force, who used to watch Blandy mingle with other admirals at the Rhode Island home of Congressman Walter Gresham. On one summer afternoon, as politicians and naval officers sipped drinks, the young Hoopes stared in amazement as Blandy swam nearly a mile straight out into the Atlantic Ocean. Mrs. Blandy assured him that Blandy was fine; this was his normal exercise. Blandy, thought Hoopes, took a different approach to life. "He was not a narrowly indoctrinated black shoe naval officer; he was curious and adventurous, broader than most of the Navy brass."[31]

6

"I'm Tired of Babying the Soviets"

The announcement of Operation Crossroads came at the birth of the Cold War, as the Truman administration began to view the Soviet Union not as its estranged wartime ally but as America's next enemy. The postwar relationship between the two countries had already turned rocky as Eastern Europe, liberated by Russia from the Nazis, quickly turned into a Soviet sphere of influence. A secret report by the Office of Strategic Services in early April 1945 warned President Roosevelt that a postwar Russia might pose even more of a threat to the United States than the combined Axis powers. "Russia will emerge from the present conflict as by far the strongest nation in Europe and Asia—strong enough, if the United States should stand aside, to dominate Europe and at the same time to establish her hegemony over Asia," the report predicted.[1] Just three days later, Averell W. Harriman, the American ambassador to Moscow, urged Roosevelt to "make it plain to the Soviet Government that they cannot expect our cooperation on terms laid down by them."[2]

Roosevelt did not believe that the Russians were determined to dominate Europe. "They have got a large enough 'hunk of bread' right in Russia to keep them busy for a great many years to come without taking on any more headaches," he said in 1944.[3] The Yalta Conference, though, in February 1945 changed his mind. "Averell is right," he said three weeks before he died. "We can't do business with Stalin. He has broken every one of the promises he made at Yalta."[4] In just a few months Roosevelt had undergone a profound change in his attitude, telling a reporter before leaving for Warm Springs, Georgia, that Stalin was not a man of his word.[5]

Two weeks later, America had a new president, Harry S. Truman, who had no experience or background in foreign affairs. He had not met Stalin and did not even know his own secretary of state, Edward R. Stettinius, Jr. "If we see that Germany is winning we ought to help Russia," he had said as a senator shortly after Germany's invasion of Russia in 1941, "and if Russia is winning we ought to help Germany and that way kill as many as possible. Neither of them think anything of their pledged word."[6]

Truman tempered his public views after succeeding Roosevelt and did not break abruptly with any of Roosevelt's policies. But styles speak loudly, and the shift from Roosevelt's indirect, manipulative approach to Truman's bluntness resulted in clearer signals being sent, frequently with harder edges. His first public meeting as president with Soviet Foreign Minister Vyacheslav Molotov was a stormy one. When Truman abruptly cut him off and terminated the meeting, Molotov turned ashen and left quickly. To Commerce Secretary Henry A. Wallace, Truman compared the Russians to "people from across the tracks whose manners were very bad." Five months later, though, he told his Cabinet that "we were not going to let the public know the extent to which the Russians had tried our patience but that we were going to find some way to get along with the Russians."[7]

In fact, Harry Truman's vacillating views toward the Kremlin mirrored the ambivalence and uncertainty within his new administration. As the war in Europe came to a close, some of his advisors who distrusted the Soviet Union, such as Harriman, Leahy, and Forrestal, recommended a hard line against the Russians, while others, such as generals Marshall, Dwight D. Eisenhower, and Lucius Clay, who had worked closely with Russian military leaders during the war, thought the Soviets would be more concerned with postwar domestic reconstruction than expansion.

The advent of the atomic bomb only reinforced these divergent views. Harriman, for example, thought the bomb would rekindle Russia's siege mentality and revive its feelings of insecurity. Henry Stimson wrote in his diary at Potsdam that "we might have to have it out with the Russians" after the war.[8] The successful test of the atomic bomb during the conference only hardened his thinking on postwar international cooperation. The problem, he wrote to Truman, "arises out of the fundamental differences between . . . a really free people [and] a nation . . . which is systematically controlled from above by secret police and in which free speech is not permitted." Every proposal on postwar cooperation in a "world composed of two such radically different systems is subject to frustration by misunderstandings arising out of natural suspicion."[9]

Returning to the United States, Stimson began to rethink the logic of his Potsdam paper. A long talk with Harriman convinced him that there was no hope for a change in Soviet society or its distrust of the West. Perhaps, then, he wrote on September 11, "might it not be better to reverse the process, to meet Russian suspicion with American candor, to discuss the bomb directly with them and try to reach agreement on control?" Starting with the proposition that the problem of the atomic bomb would dominate future U.S.-Soviet relations, Stimson suggested a direct approach by the United States to control the use of the atomic bomb, with the United States, Britain, and Russia agreeing to stop work on bomb development and production. "If we fail to approach them now and merely continue to negotiate with them, having this weapon rather ostentatiously on our hip," he wrote, "their suspicions and their distrust of our purposes and motives will increase."[10] A dedicated internationalist who had served in the same post 35 years earlier under President Taft and as secretary of state under President Hoover, Stimson believed deeply in mutual trust and honor among nations. In 1929 he opposed the establishment of an intelligence service in the State Department, declaring, "Gentlemen do not read other people's mail."[11]

Stimson went to the White House and reviewed his four-page memorandum with Truman paragraph by paragraph. "We must take Russia into our confidence," he told the president.[12] This was the first time any of Truman's advisors had formally approached him to discuss atomic policy. He told Stimson that he was "in full accord" with his views and asked him to present them to the Cabinet on September 21, Stimson's seventy-eighth birthday and last day in government service.[13]

The Cabinet was split on Stimson's proposal, and to many at the meeting his basic point—direct discussions with the Russians—was changed into the idea of sharing the atomic "secret" with the Soviets. At one extreme was Commerce Secretary Wallace, who stated that failure to share information about the bomb with the Russians would make them an "embittered and sour people." Robert P. Patterson, who was to succeed Stimson, and Dean Acheson, acting secretary of state, agreed with Stimson that direct talks were necessary. At the other extreme was Navy Secretary Forrestal, an early convert to Russophobia, who led the opposition to Stimson. The Russians, whom he described as "essentially Oriental in their thinking," deserved neither America's understanding nor its sympathy. "We tried that once with Hitler," he said. "There are no returns on appeasement." The bomb, he asserted, belonged to the American people, and "we should exercise a trusteeship over [it] on behalf of the United Nations."[14]

The key question, of course, was how long America's atomic monopoly would last. The scientists and engineers who developed the bomb predicted that Russia would have a bomb by 1950. The secret—that a bomb would work—was known, so the Russians' task was largely an engineering, design, organizational, and manufacturing problem. As Vannevar Bush explained to Truman's Cabinet, the Russians could have the bomb in five years, "provided they devote a very large part of their scientific and industrial effort to it." Those who favored a direct approach to the Russians, such as Stimson, Wallace, and Acheson, accepted this evaluation and assumed that the Soviets' acquisition of atomic energy was inevitable in any case. However, military leaders, led by Leslie Groves, predicted that America's atomic monopoly would last at least 20 years. Those who opposed Stimson's proposal—Byrnes, Forrestal, and Leahy—accepted this view, which, as Bush wrote, naively and incorrectly assumed the existence of an "atomic 'secret,' written perhaps on a single sheet of paper, some sort of magic formula."[15]

Where Truman fit into this debate is hard to say, because at this time he was not of one mind regarding the Soviet Union. Direct and unpretentious, he deeply believed in America's moral righteousness, but he was also convinced that the United States could rely on this strength only with the military might to back it up. As he told Congress just two months after Hiroshima, "The surest guaranty that no nation will dare again to attack us is to remain strong in the only kind of strength an aggressor understands—military power."[16]

Truman's actions, though, did not square with his words, largely because the rapid pace of demobilization was eroding America's military strength. It was not demobilization, he told his cabinet members; it was really "disintegration." However, as his biographer David McCullough has noted, Truman faced such tremendous pressure from the American public to demobilize that he might well have been impeached if he had tried to stem the tide. Moreover, with the war over, he was determined to cut expenditures in order to reduce the deficit, balance the budget, and stifle inflation, and demobilization would help achieve these goals, albeit at the cost of achieving national security objectives.[17]

In the first few months of his presidency, Truman relied heavily on his new secretary of state, James F. Byrnes, a familiar and friendly figure from his early Senate days, for leadership on foreign policy issues. A former senator from South Carolina and Supreme Court justice, Byrnes had twice just missed the vice-presidential nomination, losing to Henry Wallace in 1940 and to Truman in 1944. He had served in all three branches of the federal government—the only American ever to serve as governor, secretary of state, Supreme Court justice, congressman, and senator—and he believed himself much more qualified to serve as president than Truman.[18]

Eager to assert his new power, Byrnes was convinced that America's atomic monopoly would help him win concessions from the Soviet Union at the upcoming London Conference of Foreign Ministers. He was determined not to brandish the bomb, he told Stimson, but to rely instead simply on its existence as an "implied threat" to strengthen his negotiating position.[19] The Russians, though, made light of the bomb. At a reception in the House of Lords shortly after the start of the conference in September 1945, Byrnes approached Russia's Foreign Minister Molotov and asked him when the sightseeing would end so the conferees could "get down to business." Molotov, sounding like Stimson in Washington, asked Byrnes in turn if he had an "atomic bomb in his side pocket."

"You don't know Southerners," Byrnes replied. "We carry our artillery in our hip pocket. If you don't cut out all this stalling and let us get down to work, I am going to pull an atomic bomb out of my hip pocket and let you have it."[20]

If Byrnes really believed that the atomic bomb would make the Soviet Union more manageable, he was mistaken. If anything, Molotov proved to be more stubborn than ever, and atomic diplomacy failed to achieve American objectives. The three-week conference was a failure and ended without even a final communiqué. Determined to try a new approach after London, Byrnes abruptly decided to adopt Stimson's proposal for U.S.-Soviet cooperation on the bomb. In November, he proposed a second meeting of the Council of Foreign Ministers in Moscow in late December, hoping to use the conference to reach an agreement on the control of atomic weapons as a means of resolving other East-West issues. This time he would use the atomic bomb as a carrot, not as a stick, and he would go right to Stalin. George F. Kennan, the State Department's top Soviet expert and future ambassador to Russia, questioned Byrnes's motives. His weakness in dealing with the Russians, thought Kennan, was that his purpose was "to achieve some sort of an agreement, he doesn't much care what."[21]

Truman remained of two minds. Publicly he took a tough stance. At a Navy Day speech in New York on October 27, 1945, with forty-seven U.S. warships displayed along the Hudson River and 1,200 Navy planes flying overhead, Truman spoke of America's military strength. Clearly directing his remarks toward Moscow, he declared that the United States would not "recognize any government imposed upon any nation by the force of any foreign power," and he emphasized that America would hold the atomic bomb as a "sacred trust" for humanity.[22] Privately, though, he told aides it was "inevitable that we should have real difficulties but we should not take them too seriously." These differences could be resolved "amicably if we gave ourselves time." Truman thought the Russians were having "very real problems at home," and he viewed Stalin as a "moderating influence" on more conservative Kremlin leaders, such as Molotov. "It would be a real catastrophe if Stalin should die at the present time," he said.[23] Given this assessment, the strategy of approaching Stalin directly made sense. Byrnes and Truman thought that a generous American offer on the control of atomic weapons would create a give-and-take atmosphere in which Stalin would make concessions as well.

Byrnes held two meetings with Stalin during the Moscow conference and achieved some small agreements, all the while keeping Washington largely uninformed. Much to Byrnes's surprise, Stalin even agreed to the American plan for the creation of a United Nations Atomic Energy Commission under the jurisdiction of the Security Council. Byrnes, acting pleased with the results of the conference, spoke to the country on the major radio networks upon his return to the United States on December 30. "The meeting in Moscow did serve to bring about better understanding," he said. Peace required both justice and wisdom, he declared, and there was "ample scope for the achievement of these essential results" at Moscow.[24]

Leahy and other hardliners saw Byrnes as too eager to accommodate the Russians. Truman, buffeted about by his advisors and more concerned with domestic issues such as mounting labor strife and inflation, seemed to agree with all sides. He certainly wanted to get along with the Russians, and he felt that he could negotiate with Stalin. "I like Stalin. He is straightforward," he wrote his wife from Potsdam after their first meeting. He noted in his diary that the Russian leader was frank, honest, and willing to compromise, and he told Henry Wallace that Stalin was a "fine man" who simply wanted to do the right thing.[25] His trust in the Russians, though, had waned considerably by the end of 1945. "There is no evidence as yet that the Russians intend to change their habits as far as honoring contracts is concerned," he told Forrestal in early December.[26]

Shortly after Byrnes's radio talk, Truman summoned him to the White House and told him the Moscow agreements were just a general promise from the Russians. The president, reading from the text of a handwritten letter, told Byrnes that the "Russians have been a headache to us" since Potsdam, and he proceeded to tick off his grievances. Truman no longer doubted Soviet intentions. "Unless Russia is faced with an iron fist and strong language another war is in the making." The continued presence of Soviet troops in Iran was an "outrage if I ever saw one," and he was convinced that Russia intended to invade Turkey and seize the Black Sea Straits. "I'm tired of babying the Soviets," he exclaimed, and on January 8 he announced that he did not consider himself bound by the Moscow agreement.[27]

Truman undoubtedly hoped for international control of atomic weapons, but he also recognized that America was not ready for international control of a new technology monopolized by the United States. "Maybe we could get world government in a thousand years or something like that," he told a friend in October 1945, but it was nothing more than a theory.[28] He was not alone. His proposal to Congress in October to consider a program of international cooperation on atomic energy met with a chilly response. "We have the jump on the rest of the world in [the bomb's] development and use," declared Senator Edwin C. Johnson of Colorado. "We should not . . . fritter away that significant and tremendous advantage by surrendering its know-how and its formulas to anyone." Ninety percent of those Congressmen polled opposed sharing information on the bomb with any country at all, and a nationwide poll showed that nearly the same percentage of Americans shared these views.[29]

The new year brought on the formal end of the World War II Grand Alliance and the emergence of the Cold War. As the historian Melvyn Leffler has noted, "It is hard to overstate how portentous the international situation appeared to U.S. officials in early 1946."[30] Truman and his top advisors had spent the previous eight months vacillating in their views toward the Russians and trying to develop a cohesive policy. The Cabinet was split between confrontation and cooperation, but neither approach seemed to make a difference. Truman, however, was unable to focus much of his attention on foreign affairs because of the increasingly serious domestic problems of wages, prices, and strikes. On January 19, 800,000 steel workers walked off their jobs in the biggest strike in U.S. history. At one point in the first part of the year, more than 1 million workers were on strike. John L. Lewis called a nationwide coal strike, General Motors workers struck, and a nationwide rail strike virtually brought the country to a standstill.

Every day in the new year seemed to bring more ominous news. On February 3, Drew Pearson stunned listeners to his evening radio program with the disclosure that a Russian spy ring was operating in Canada. When Canadian authorities arrested twenty-two government scientists and technicians on February 15, Moscow did not even deny the allegations. Stalin left no doubts about Soviet intentions in a February 9 speech at the Bolshoi Theater. His blunt tone marked the return of ideological rhetoric. World War II was a victory for the "Soviet system," and gone were the usual references to Russia's wartime allies. The "hostile" international environment facing Russia and the "capitalist encirclement" of his country, he said, could lead to another war. He declared that international peace was "impossible under the present capitalist development of world economy," and he announced a five-year plan to more than double Russia's output of iron, steel, coal, and oil "to guarantee our country against any eventuality." Harriman was now convinced that Stalin was intent on exporting communism to the rest of the world, and even Supreme Court Justice William O. Douglas, a leading liberal, called it "the declaration of World War III."[31]

Three days later, on February 12, the Soviets announced that a new Communist government had been formed in North Korea, and there were reports of large Soviet troop movements in the area. A February 21 report from the Joint Chiefs of Staff to President Truman reflected the military's hardening position toward the Soviets. "The consolidation and development of the power of Russia is the greatest threat to the United States in the foreseeable future," it stated, adding that the proliferation of the atomic bomb would wipe out the military advantage America enjoyed during the war. Atomic warfare would mean that "our long term potential . . . owing to the length of time required for mobilization . . . might not be sufficient to avert disaster."[32]

The very next day, George F. Kennan, the chief of mission at the U.S. embassy in Moscow, sent his famous "Long Telegram" to Washington. Taking his cue from Stalin's February 9 speech, Kennan asserted that Russian leaders were motivated by a "political force committed fanatically to the belief that . . . there can be no permanent *modus vivendi*" with America. Marxism, he reasoned, was merely a "fig leaf" for the "neurotic" Kremlin leaders, who couched themselves in a new ideology, but, like the czars before them, were obsessed with the "instinctive Russian sense of insecurity." As a response, he recommended military preparedness. "Soviet power," he wrote, is "impervious to the logic of reason, and it is highly sensitive to the logic of force." This policy, later dubbed containment, was dependent upon the West drawing a line against further Soviet expansion.

As Kennan later wrote, the effect of his Long Telegram was "nothing less than sensational." It was "one of those moments when official Washington . . . was ready to receive a given message," and it galvanized American thinking. Truman read it, Forrestal circulated it throughout the government, and it was soon released to the press. Hardliners such as Harriman and Forrestal shared Kennan's frustrations in dealing with Russian intransigence, but Kennan proposed a solution no one else had offered: concede Eastern Europe to the Soviets but draw the line there and forge an alliance with other Western nations to counter this Russian sphere of influence.[33]

The crucial event of those months was the crisis in Iran. Moscow refused to honor a March 2 deadline to remove troops from parts of Iran it had occupied during the war, and it supported a Communist-led separatist movement in a northern province bordering on the Soviet Union. This was not Eastern Europe, where the Soviet Union could make out a claim for legitimate security concerns and a sphere of influence, but an area of vital strategic and economic importance to the West. It was appearing more and more clear that Russia's search for security had ended and its quest for expansion had begun. In response to new cables from Kennan warning that the Soviets' goal was the "virtual subjugation, penetration and domination of the entire country" and Bahrain, Kuwait, and Turkey as well, Truman sent the battleship *Missouri* to the eastern Mediterranean and began to supply aid to the Tehran government.[34]

If there was a single moment during these first postwar years that was seen as the breaking point between East and West, it was Winston Churchill's speech in Fulton, Missouri, on March 5. With Truman's presence on the podium seen as a U.S. endorsement, Churchill declared that an "iron curtain" had descended from "Stettin in the Baltic to Trieste in the Adriatic," and he called for a revival of the Anglo-American wartime alliance against a new enemy—the Soviet Union. The key to this association was the atomic bomb, asserted Churchill. It would be "wrong and imprudent to entrust the secret knowledge or experience of the atomic bomb" to the new United Nations, and it would constitute "criminal madness to cast it adrift in this still agitated and un-united world."[35]

Operation Crossroads's critics would charge that the 1946 tests were designed to send a clear signal to Moscow that the United States, with its atomic monopoly, was prepared to perfect the bomb and use it on the Soviet Union. Their views were similar to those of others who argued that the atomic bombs were dropped on Japan with a real eye toward the Soviet Union. The atomic bomb was superfluous, these critics argued, because Japan was already on the verge of collapse and ready to surrender. Rather, this show of force was intended to impress the Soviets and warn them not to overrun Eastern Europe.[36] As P.M.S. Blackett, the Nobel Prize–winning British physicist, suggested, "The dropping of the atomic bombs was not so much the last military act of the second world war, as the first major operation of the cold diplomatic war with Russia."[37] Truman's comment at Potsdam about the bomb's effect—"I'll have a hammer on these boys"—lent credence to this theory, but few historians have accepted it.[38]

The timing of Operation Crossroads led many critics to view the tests as yet another saber-rattling gesture toward the Soviet Union, and President Truman took no measures to change that view. The tests were first conceived in August 1945, however, well before U.S.-Soviet relations deteriorated, and they grew directly out of the decades-old Army-Navy rivalry that resurfaced with the advent of the atomic bomb and the end of World War II. The AAF emerged from the war challenging the Navy's traditional role as the nation's first line of defense, and both services sought to stake out their roles in a postwar nuclear age that would see new strategic doctrines, unification of the services and, inevitably, fewer defense dollars.[39]

In just one year, though, Truman had radically changed his perception of U.S.-Soviet relations. By the spring of 1946, he no longer trusted Russia and no longer viewed disputes with the Soviets as the inevitable results of competing national interests that could be resolved through quiet diplomacy. Like Kennan, he viewed the Russians as trying to extend their power and their sphere of influence. He still believed in coexistence, but it could only be achieved from a position of U.S. military strength, and the atomic bomb epitomized that strength. Harvard University president James B. Conant, Roosevelt's science advisor and administrator of the Manhattan Project, shared Truman's views and thought the Bikini tests would intimidate the Russians. Asked at an off-the-record talk sponsored by the Council on Foreign Relations in April whether Operation Crossroads would help or hurt the goal of international control of atomic weapons, he replied that "the Russians are more rather than less likely to come to an effective agreement for the control of atomic energy if we keep our strength and continue to produce bombs."[40] As the Joint Chiefs of Staff remarked just before Operation Crossroads, the fact remained that the atomic bomb was the "one military weapon which may for the period until Russia obtains it exert a deterrent effect upon her will to expand."[41] Operation Crossroads, like Hiroshima and Nagasaki, was not designed to intimidate the Kremlin, but Washington certainly saw the bomb as a strong diplomatic tool and was anxious to reap its anticipated benefits.

"I Am Not an Atomic Playboy"

Operation Crossroads was opposed and even ridiculed from the moment of Admiral Blandy's announcement of the tests on January 24. The first shot, Test Able, was less than four months away and required a tremendous amount of planning, but Blandy and his staff spent much of their time responding to critics and Cassandras in the press, Congress, and the scientific community.

Some of the press reaction was pure sensationalism, caused in large part by the novelty of the atomic bomb. Even such a respected columnist as Arthur Krock of the *New York Times* suggested that Operation Crossroads "may be proof that a great fleet, including the most powerful modern vessels of war, can . . . be dissolved" and that "the energy thus released can change the contours of the ocean bed and of distant coast lines."[1] The *Times* reported that the second test, scheduled as a surface shot, "will tear ships from their anchorage [and] hurl them onto the coral reefs." An artist's drawing accompanying the article showed a destroyer tossed into the air, completely upside-down.[2] In fact, the Navy was the source of some of the sensationalism. For example, according to a Navy spokesman, plans for the underwater shot were being held up for fear that it "might set up a great tidal wave which nothing could check."[3]

A Yale University physics professor announced that the "mathematical probability that a crack or crevasse or hole may be blasted in the ocean floor assuredly is not zero." According to the professor, water rushing into the crevasse might come into contact with molten rock and set off explosions that would create mile-high waves moving at high speeds. The permanent shift of such a large mass of material, he warned, would affect the rotational inertia of the world, thus decreasing the length of the day, and if material was no longer uniformly distributed, a new axis of rotation would be sought, causing "unthinkable earthquakes, gyroscopic shudderings and readjustments."[4]

"Tidal Disaster, World Climate Change Seen After Bikini Tests," blared a headline in the Boston Herald, and a Johns Hopkins University seismologist predicted that an underwater shot could set off a major earthquake and tidal wave that would swamp all the ships.[5] Senator Brien McMahon of Connecticut, chairman of the Senate's new Special Committee on Atomic Energy, expressed concern that a subsurface atomic blast might set off an underwater chain reaction, blow up the entire ocean and with it the world. Even a spokesman for a group of physicists en route to Bikini told reporters that an underwater explosion might cause a chain reaction "impossible to control" and that the damage to marine life would be "almost incalculable."[6] Other critics predicted cracking in the earth's crust and water pressure so great that fish would be killed throughout the Pacific Ocean.[7]

Admiral Blandy replied to these charges in a February 21 speech he repeated over the next three months:

> The bomb will not kill half the fish in the sea, and poison the other half so they will kill all the people who eat fish hereafter. The bomb will not cause an earthquake or push up new mountain ranges. . . . The bomb will not start a chain reaction in the water, converting it all to gas and letting all the ships on all the oceans drop down to the bottom. It will not blow out the bottom of the sea and let all the water run down the hole. It will not destroy gravity. I am not an atomic playboy, as one of my critics labeled me, exploding these bombs to satisfy my personal whim.[8]

Other Operation Crossroads officials also tried to downplay these dire warnings. "We do not know how many of the target ships in the Bikini lagoon will be destroyed," Crossroads's technical director Ralph A. Sawyer, a University of Michigan physicist, told a Washington news conference. "A great many will not be damaged at all." Comdr. Roger Revelle, who headed oceanography and wave measurement studies, scoffed at the notion of a tidal wave or even mild aftereffects from the blast. The bomb, he explained, was less than one one-thousandth as powerful as a moderate earthquake, and most of its energy would head into the atmosphere anyway, with only a small fraction spent on the atoll and its lagoon. "It is doubtful if the Bikini explosion will be picked up on seismographs more than a few hundred miles away," he told reporters.[9] Edward Teller and Hans Bethe, two prominent members of the Manhattan Project, assured the public that Operation Crossroads would cause only local disturbances, adding that it was impossible that the tests would result in the "explosion of the globe."[10] Testifying at a congressional hearing in April, Sawyer branded as "irresponsible" the predictions of catastrophe. "We positively will not burn up the atmosphere or the ocean," he declared. "After all, I'm going out as a volunteer, not as a guinea pig."[11]

A much greater problem for Blandy than tidal waves and holes in the ocean floor was the fact that the military nature of the tests seemed to work at cross-purposes both with Congress's effort to place domestic control of atomic energy in civilian hands and with the Truman administration's attempt to formulate a UN plan for the international control of atomic weapons. The debate on these new questions of domestic and international control of nuclear weapons and atomic energy was affected by deteriorating East-West relations, and the upcoming Crossroads tests began to be seen as a litmus test on the administration's views on both issues.

On October 3, 1945, President Truman sent a message to Congress calling for legislation to establish the Atomic Energy Commission (AEC) to set policy for the domestic control of atomic energy. Two different Senate bills reflected the public debate on this issue. The May-Johnson bill, introduced the day after Truman's message by Rep. Andrew J. May of Kentucky and Senator Edwin Johnson of Colorado, would have granted vast powers to the four military and five civilian members of the commission, essentially leaving control of America's nuclear program in the hands of General Groves. Three notable physicists—J. Robert Oppenheimer, Enrico Fermi, and Ernest O. Lawrence—endorsed the bill a week after it was introduced, stating that "the broad powers granted the Commission by the legislation are justified by the importance and perils of the subject."[12]

Most atomic scientists, however, denounced the bill as a peacetime extension of the Manhattan Project, with continued compartmentalization of research, secrecy, and other military restrictions on their research. "I must confess," wrote physicist Herbert Anderson to the chairman of the Association of Los Alamos Scientists, "my confidence in our leaders Oppenheimer, Lawrence, Compton, and Fermi, . . . who enjoined us to have faith in them and not influence this legislation, is shaken."[13] Sixty leading citizens, including Albert Einstein and twenty-seven atomic scientists, sent a telegram to Capitol Hill claiming that the bill would establish "totalitarian authority" in the field of atomic physics and might "promote a competitive armament race, while at the same time tying American scientific hands and brains."[14]

Sensing the growing opposition to the May-Johnson bill, Senator McMahon, a Democrat, introduced a rival bill later in the fall to create an atomic energy commission composed entirely of civilians and subject to presidential authority. A short, husky, well-dressed lawyer, McMahon had served in the Justice Department for six years during the Depression, specializing in tax and criminal matters. He had argued several cases before the Supreme Court and represented the government in highly publicized cases against John Dillinger and the Harlan County Coal Operators Association. McMahon was both able and ambitious. Just weeks after Hiroshima, he introduced a bill to create a Senate Special Committee on Atomic Energy, and when it passed on October 23 he became its chairman, establishing his claim to leadership in this new field. Although he had just been elected to the Senate in 1944, he now presided over a committee that included such veteran Democrats as Richard B. Russell of Georgia, Tom Connally of Texas, Millard E. Tydings of Maryland, and Harry F. Byrd of Virginia, as well as Republicans Arthur H. Vandenberg of Michigan, Thomas C. Hart of Connecticut, and Warren R. Austin of Vermont.[15]

Truman publicly vacillated on the two bills. At first he threw his support behind the May-Johnson proposal, but he abruptly switched sides in February 1946, publicly endorsing civilian control. Support for the McMahon bill, though, nearly evaporated overnight when Washington newspaper columnist Frank McNaughton, relying on a tip from a "confidential source," revealed that Soviet agents were operating in the United States and Canada. McMahon, under pressure from his colleagues, reconvened hearings on domestic control and called on Leslie Groves to testify before his committee for the third time on February 27.[16]

In an atmosphere charged with spy scares and distrust of Russia, Groves urged a strong role for the military on the commission. He viewed atomic energy as a weapon and therefore believed it should stay under military control. He told the committee that an atomic energy commissioner should be "a man who is not going to forget for a minute that as long as this is the prime military weapon of the country, defense must come first and other things afterwards."[17] His arguments suddenly gained new respect. There was little love lost between Groves and McMahon. Both men lived in Darien, Connecticut, and Groves, a life-long conservative Republican, briefly considered running for the Senate against McMahon.[18] Groves would later write about "political opportunists" in the Senate and "a few politically ambitious people [who] decided that they could advance their careers by displaying an interest in atomic energy matters," an obvious reference to McMahon.[19] The senator had asked Groves the previous November to supply his committee with detailed information on the bomb, but Groves flatly refused, lending more credence to supporters of the McMahon bill.[20]

At the February hearing, McMahon mockingly suggested that Groves's call for military representation on the AEC formed a perfect job description for the general. "You have always exercised becoming modesty," McMahon noted sarcastically, "but it seems to me you have drawn a bill of particulars here which you could pretty well fit."[21] Groves did not fall for the bait. He had already made his point, and the timing of his testimony during the spy scare was not coincidental; it was revealed years later that he was Frank McNaughton's "confidential source" as to the existence of the alleged Soviet spy ring.[22] Two weeks later, the committee voted, over McMahon's sole dissent, to adopt Senator Vandenberg's amendment to establish an AEC military liaison board with the power to appeal commission decisions to the president.[23]

While public debate on the McMahon bill dominated the headlines, the identical issue of civilian versus military control of the bomb was being debated in connection with the upcoming atomic bomb tests. In announcing Operation Crossroads on January 24, Admiral Blandy said that a military review board would be established to evaluate the tests. He wanted to appoint an all-Navy board, but the AAF balked. Ostensibly concerned about objectivity, the AAF insisted on representation and suggested its own commission to report directly to the president.

However, an all-military panel, whether all-Navy or more broadly based, was out of the question for Senator McMahon, who called for a civilian board of scientists and engineers to evaluate the tests. "It is very important that the people of the United States be entirely and completely convinced that these tests are being planned and will be executed . . . fairly," he wrote to Truman in February. "I believe it is placing too great a burden on any Department of Government to require it to be solely responsible for conducting operations which might well indeed determine its very existence."[24]

In a February 7 speech, McMahon made his point publicly, pointing out that the Navy would "preside over what possibly will be its own funeral" under Blandy's plan. "I am not insinuating for one moment that the Navy is out to prove anything in these tests," he said, adding, "I simply believe that such independent commission findings would avoid protracted controversy over the results."[25]

The press also criticized the idea of a military review board. Hanson W. Baldwin, the military affairs correspondent of the *New York Times,* reported that many scientists believed that the "Navy has more or less constituted itself both judge and jury and is sitting in judgment on its own future."[26] Henry Wallace told President Truman in early February that because Operation Crossroads was being run "entirely by the Navy," critics were suggesting that the tests would be conducted "in a prejudiced way to further Navy interests." The aerial shot, said Wallace, "will teach very little that is not already known, and the Navy knows this." The underwater shot, "the only significant test, . . . is being unduly delayed," he added, and "it is being insinuated that the real reason is that the Navy would not like to have the results . . . known at this time." These criticisms, Wallace told Truman, reinforced the need for an independent review board to take the evaluation of the tests out of "the hands of men who are prejudicially interested in the results."[27]

On February 8, Truman asked the War and Navy departments to comment on the idea of a civilian board. Secretary of War Patterson responded that the Joint Chiefs' decision to appoint two civilian members, together with the presence at Bikini of numerous congressmen, reporters, and civilian scientists, would avoid the possibility of bias, and Forrestal agreed.[28] Privately, though, Forrestal was more critical of the Navy. On February 4, Bradley Dewey, president of the American Chemical Society, telephoned Forrestal to discuss his invitation to serve as one of the two members. Dewey was inclined to accept, but he had misgivings.

"I'm going to tell Patterson—I can't bother with Blandy—I think the public relations end of the test has been handled rottenly," said Dewey.

"I quite agree with you," responded Forrestal, who mentioned that Supreme Court Justice William Douglas was a leading candidate as the other civilian on the board. "I said this morning to Blandy that I believe that the people who are handling this on a military level did not appreciate the breadth of what they were dealing with, particularly the unusual public interest."[29]

Truman, under fire from McMahon and Wallace, realized that his recent tacit endorsement of the McMahon bill was at odds with placing the upcoming Crossroads tests entirely in military hands. Admiral Blandy had scheduled a 4 P.M. press conference on February 13 to announce his all-military evaluation board, but a call came from the White House at 10 A.M. to delay the announcement. At a White House meeting that afternoon with Byrnes, Forrestal, Nimitz, Patterson, Leahy, and Eisenhower, Truman said that he did not want the tests to be conducted in a manner that would permit the military to prove whatever it wanted to prove. "The president said . . . that reports were getting around that these tests were not going to be entirely on the level, and he wanted to squelch them," wrote Eben A. Ayers, assistant White House press secretary in his diary.[30]

Truman, an astute student of American history, also recalled the Billy

Mitchell incident. He said Mitchell had rigged the tests, creating the exact conditions that permitted him to sink the *Ostfriesland* with his airplanes and thus prove what he wanted to prove.[31] According to Forrestal, Truman told the group that he had "to be sure that this test met all of the crackpot criticisms and that not only would it need to be objective but we had to convince the public it was objective."[32] Two days later, on February 15, Truman raised these issues again in a cabinet meeting devoted exclusively to Operation Crossroads, at which Forrestal announced that Blandy had selected as two of his civilian advisors Bradley Dewey and Karl T. Compton, president of the Massachusetts Institute of Technology, both of whom had worked on the Manhattan Project. As Blandy was already planning to invite a civilian group to observe the tests, it was agreed that this group, together with some senators and congressmen, would constitute a civilian review board to report directly to the president. Truman's action was not lost on observers of the debate on domestic control of atomic energy. The establishment of a civilian review board for Operation Crossroads "has sharpened the issue raised by . . . the [McMahon] bill [as] to . . . whether a civilian commission shall be the custodian of all atomic production and the ultimate authority over its use," wrote Arthur Krock in the *New York Times*. "To the Army and Navy the President's latest decision is a step farther in that direction."[33]

During the early months of 1946, the Truman administration was also trying to formulate a policy on the international control of the atomic bomb. Byrnes had created a committee in January 1946, headed by his undersecretary, Dean Acheson, to develop a plan and present it the following June to the newly formed UN Atomic Energy Commission. Acheson, in turn, persuaded the committee to establish a five-man board of technical consultants, headed by David E. Lilienthal, whom Truman would later select as the first chairman of the AEC. By March the group issued what became known as the Acheson-Lilienthal Report, which marked the high-water mark in the postwar effort to obtain international cooperation in the control of atomic energy. The key to the plan was the creation of an international atomic development authority to own, mine, and oversee all uranium and thorium deposits, the raw materials for an atomic bomb. The authority would "denature" fissionable material, rendering it useless for atomic bombs but usable for peaceful purposes, such as nuclear power plants, which it would license, construct, and monitor. With its broad inspection powers and monopoly on the raw materials, the authority could easily detect a wayward country's attempt to divert atomic resources to develop a bomb.

The report, publicly released in late March, received widespread praise, and deservedly so. It was designed to create a cooperative international venture to share America's atomic monopoly while at the same time prevent the spread of the atomic bomb. "In plain words," said Acheson and Bush in a radio address, "the Report sets up a plan under which no nation would make atomic bombs or the materials for them." A bipartisan resolution was promptly introduced in the Senate to adopt the report as the American proposal at the upcoming meeting of the UN AEC.[34]

Oppenheimer was proud of his work on the Acheson-Lilienthal Report, but FBI wiretaps of his telephone conversations, transcripts of which J. Edgar Hoover regularly sent to his friend Byrnes, revealed that he was not optimistic about its chances of success in the hands of Secretary of State Byrnes. In a May 27, 1946, conversation with a friend, Oppenheimer remarked that the Acheson-Lilienthal Report "was pretty good," but he warned that "the British and Russians will be very difficult." In response to his friend's statement that Byrnes's public release of the report "was extremely cagey," Oppenheimer said, "All this attributes to Mr. Byrnes considerably more thought than he gave the subject. I think you shouldn't look for such highfalutin' arguments on the part of a man who is punch drunk."[35]

On the day after Acheson submitted his report, President Truman, at the strong urging of Byrnes, appointed Bernard M. Baruch, the 75-year-old Wall Street financier, as the U.S. delegate to the UN AEC. "That was the day I gave up hope," Oppenheimer later recalled.[36] Lilienthal and Acheson were also appalled by the choice of Baruch. They regarded him as a vain and shallow self-promoter who lacked the expertise, vision, and skill for the job and whose innate Wall Street conservatism and distrust of Russia would bring a jingoistic tone to the negotiations. Baruch's staff of publicists successfully cultivated his reputation as a confidant of presidents who dispensed advice from a bench in Lafayette Park across the street from the White House. Acheson told Byrnes that Baruch's reputation was "without foundation in fact and entirely self-propagated," and Lilienthal wrote that he was "quite sick" upon learning of Baruch's appointment. "We need a man who is young, vigorous, not vain, and whom the Russians would feel isn't out simply to put them in a hole, not really caring about international cooperation. Mr. Baruch has none of these qualifications."[37]

Truman did not disagree with their personal assessment of this legendary park-bench sage. "Asked old man Baruch to act as U.S. representative," he jotted on a note in March. "He wants to run the world, the moon and maybe Jupiter—but we'll see." Several months later he wrote to his wife about this "stuffed shirt," who now "will have something more to do than sit on a park bench and give out impossible advice. There never was a greater egotist unless it was Franklin D."[38]

Politically, though, the choice was an excellent one. Baruch, a tall, silver-haired, elder statesman from South Carolina, was the darling of conservatives in the Senate, where Truman was seeking support for the McMahon bill. Press reaction was uniformly positive. "No private citizen in this country enjoys the prestige both here and abroad that is Mr. Baruch's," wrote the *New York Herald Tribune,* and another newspaper editorialized, "We will sleep more comfortably in our beds because clear-eyed Barney Baruch is on guard."[39]

Baruch wanted Oppenheimer as his scientific advisor, and he did his best to charm the physicist, but Oppenheimer was troubled by what he heard from Baruch. "They talk about preparing the American people for a refusal by Russia," he told Lilienthal.[40] In fact, Baruch probably wanted Oppenheimer only for cosmetic purposes, to show he had the endorsement of the Acheson-Lilienthal group. Baruch had already told Lilienthal that "he wasn't much on technical scientific stuff, but he could smell his way through it," and his comments to others showed that he did not intend to rely on advice from scientists about the bomb. "I knew all I wanted to know," he told Vannevar Bush. "It went boom and it killed millions of people and I thought it was an ethical and political problem and I would proceed on that theory."[41]

Oppenheimer turned down Baruch's offer, but Truman and Acheson told him that "it might not look right if I got out right now, so I said I would be present at meetings," he later recalled.[42] Baruch probably knew Oppenheimer's intentions anyway, thanks to the FBI tap on Oppenheimer's telephone. "I think that if the price of it is that I have to live with the old man, it may be too high," Oppenheimer told a friend in one of the tapped telephone conversations. "If I can work on his conscience, that is the best angle I have." He also considered contacting colleagues in Europe to lobby for effective international controls.[43] Oppenheimer had already been severely criticized by his colleagues for siding with conservative leaders in supporting the May-Johnson bill, and he may simply have been reluctant to align himself again with Baruch's conservative crowd. Baruch, meanwhile, began to rely more and more on Leslie Groves for technical and policy advice.[44]

These issues of atomic policy, coinciding with the birth of the Cold War, quickly took on ominous political overtones. Questions of civilian or military control, secrecy versus openness, building bombs or abolishing them, became litmus tests for the label of liberal or conservative—and sometimes patriot or Communist. Admiral Blandy was straightforward in reconciling the upcoming atomic tests with the goals of abolishing the bomb and using atomic energy for peaceful purposes. "Of course we all do wish for these results," he told an audience in February. "But it is a far cry from wanting to abolish the bomb, and succeeding in doing it." Until then, he said, "it is the Army's and the Navy's business to learn more about the destructive power of this new weapon, both in order to be ready to use it, and to defend against it, in case we should be forced to do either."[45]

FBI director J. Edgar Hoover saw matters in a different light. Just one month before the first test at Bikini, he warned his close friend George E. Allen, director of the Reconstruction Finance Corporation, of an alleged Soviet espionage network in Washington, D.C., "operating with the view of obtaining all information possible with reference to atomic energy." The list of government officials with "pro-Soviet leanings" was staggering. It included Dean Acheson, Henry Wallace, Assistant Secretary of War Howard Petersen, State Department officials Herbert Marks and John J. McCloy, Alger Hiss, and two advisors to Senator McMahon's committee. He also singled out two officials in the Bureau of the Budget who were advising President Truman on Operation Crossroads and the impact of the atomic bomb on the size of U.S. armed forces. Their advice, wrote Hoover, was "pro-Soviet propaganda, which, when reduced to its simplest form, advances the argument that 'why keep a large Army and Navy when the use of atomic energy eliminates the necessity for such a large force.'" There was no evidence yet, Hoover concluded, that the group had committed any wrongdoing, but in light of the "pro-Russian political views" of Acheson, Petersen, and Wallace, "it is not beyond the realm of conjecture that they would fit into a scheme as set out above."[46]

8

"The Greatest Event in the History of Mankind Except Only the Birth of Christ Himself"

With Congress considering civilian control of the AEC and ready to embrace the Acheson-Lilienthal Report, some members began to question the purpose of Operation Crossroads. One of the first congressmen to raise the issue was Senator Scott Lucas of Illinois, a member of McMahon's committee and a friend of the atomic scientists at the University of Chicago. Lucas had been considered a dark-horse candidate for vice-president in 1944 and would later serve briefly as Senate Democratic majority leader until he lost his Senate seat in 1950 to Republican Everett McKinley Dirksen.[1]

"I may be treading on thin ice," Lucas conceded when he spoke on the Senate floor on January 31, but he asked the obvious question: "If we are to outlaw the use of the atomic bomb for military purposes, why should we be making plans to display atomic power as an instrument of destruction?" He questioned the deliberate destruction of U.S. ships, invoking the miracle of Dunkirk, when "every conceivable ship which could be found, even rowboats and skiffs," were used to transport British soldiers across the English Channel, and the Lend-Lease program, when the United States sent England fifty old destroyers that "could hardly move across the Atlantic, but they performed good service during the last war."

Lucas also argued that the target vessels were not obsolete, and he suggested that they could be better used as floating dormitories to

73

relieve the severe housing shortage caused by so many returning veterans. The country was facing the most severe housing shortage in history. Fifty thousand people were living in Army Quonset huts, and in Chicago, which had more than 100,000 homeless veterans, 250 used trolley cars were sold for use as houses.[2] Lucas proposed no formal action to stop the tests. "I am merely thinking more or less out loud," he explained to his colleagues. "But the more I think about it, the more I am convinced we should stop, look, listen, hesitate, and pause before going through with this particular project."[3]

Admiral Blandy's problems with Congress were just beginning. In an odd twist on military secrecy, he wanted the tests to be as open to the public as possible, but the House Naval Affairs Committee disagreed. "I am against . . . the idea of giving to the world the results of these experiments carried on at our own expense," said one committee member. "They don't give us anything; why should we give them what we have got?" Another agreed. "We've got to trust somebody, I suppose. But I just hope we don't wake up some morning and find out there was another meeting like Yalta and the whole atom story has been told." The committee eventually approved an amendment directing the secretaries of war and the navy to ban the release of information about the tests to foreign governments "except as they may determine to be not prejudicial to the best interests of the United States." Others on the committee took an even harder line. Rep. Sterling Cole of New York thought the amendment "allow[ed] too much leeway," and he argued that the tests should be closed to the public and other nations and treated "as any other military secret."[4]

Blandy had already sparred with the Senate over the upcoming tests even before his appointment as the commander of Joint Task Force One. In testimony before the Senate's Special Committee on Atomic Energy in December 1945, Chairman Brien McMahon had asked him to predict the "life expectancy of surface ships" in view of the atomic bomb. Blandy jumped on McMahon's question to blast what he called the "fallacy" of the impression that the utility of a ship or airplane is determined by what can destroy it. What makes a weapon obsolete, he argued, was not what could destroy it, but rather what could replace its function. The aircraft carrier, he said, was more vulnerable than a battleship because of the large amount of gasoline, bombs, and ammunition it carried, but nothing could replace it, so when they were sunk they were replaced with more carriers.

"But if the destruction is so effective that a ship cannot perform a useful function," countered Senator Edwin Johnson of Colorado, "then of course it becomes obsolete just as the bow and arrow did."

Senator Thomas C. Hart of Connecticut, a former admiral, came to

Blandy's rescue, asking him whether ships would continue to be used in the future to transport men and goods across oceans.

"Yes, sir," replied Blandy.

"And in the event of war, with transportation absolutely a necessary part, men will be fighting from, and on, and in, ships no matter what weapons are in existence to destroy them. Is that the case?"

"That is my belief, Senator," said Blandy.

Senator Johnson, however, thought that the Navy's only effective response to the atomic bomb was the submarine. "If [navies] will go below the surface, they will still be in the picture," he asserted. "If they don't, it will be just too bad."

"There are a lot of people who will agree with you, Senator," bristled Blandy. "I think I will wait for the tests."

"Yes, I will wait for the tests," retorted Johnson, "but the physicists and experts have convinced me that ships on the surface of the sea are going to be ducks on the pond, and I want to see them go down below where they cannot be seen and reached by the atomic bomb."[5]

In announcing that Operation Crossroads would be conducted on nearly 100 target ships, ranging from aircraft carriers and battleships to submarines, barges, and landing craft, Blandy had not consulted with the "Swamp Fox," Rep. Carl Vinson of Georgia, chairman of the House Naval Affairs Committee and the Navy's strongest supporter in Congress. Tall and a bit stooped, Vinson wore navy blue suits, brown and white striped shirts with overlarge collars, and ankle-high shoes. He frequently affected Navy terminology, telling the driver of his big black Hudson to "swing to starboard" or to "blow up the steam." Ironically, Vinson never went near a warship before arriving in Washington, and he represented a rural district of inland Georgia with no naval installations. Described by the press as the "owner" of the Navy, he was dubbed "The Admiral" by his colleagues. He would frequently refer to "his" Navy and to the secretary of the navy as "my Secretary"—and with good reason. By 1946, Vinson had already spent more than half of his 62 years in the House and was beginning his fifteenth year as chairman of the Naval Affairs Committee; he would eventually serve in the House for 51 years, breaking Sam Rayburn's record.[6]

Vinson was the Navy's most important ally in the House. He was also jealous of his prerogatives, though, and he felt that the Navy's plans to use ships as targets for the tests required congressional approval. Vinson's views on this small issue reflected broader changes taking place on Capitol Hill. Congress had spent the better part of the previous five years deferring to Franklin Roosevelt and the executive branch on national security and foreign policy issues. The end of the war marked the return of congressional authority in those areas and a corresponding diminution of authority within the executive branch. To Senator Arthur Vandenberg, Harry Truman's visit to Capitol Hill the day after Roosevelt's death marked an end to years of "executive contempt for Congress" under Roosevelt.[7] The Senate's establishment of a Special Committee on Atomic Energy in October 1945 clearly showed its intent to influence policy in that field, and Senator Vandenberg's stinging criticisms of Byrnes led the secretary of state to include both him and Senator Tom Connally, chairman of the Senate Foreign Relations Committee, in the American delegation to the 1946 Paris Peace Conference in a year when both senators faced reelection.

With the press reporting in early January 1946 that such venerable American ships as the aircraft carriers *Saratoga* and *Enterprise* would be used as targets for the atomic bomb, Vinson said that he thought there were enough German and Japanese ships available for the tests, and on January 18 he announced plans to introduce a bill in the House to make both the *Saratoga* and *Enterprise* national museums instead of target ships for atomic bombs. The Navy had obviously not kept him informed of its plans, though, because when Admiral Blandy announced the tests a week later, he listed dozens of U.S. ships as target vessels, but only two Japanese ships and one German cruiser. Vinson, in turn, promptly reminded the Navy that, under a 1882 law still on the books, it could only use as targets those vessels found unfit for further service by a special Navy board of inspection or as specifically authorized by Congress.[8]

The target vessels slated as guinea pigs in Operation Crossroads were hardly unfit for service. Virtually all had seen service in World War II, and eighteen of them were less than two years old, so legislation was needed to use them as bomb targets. Accordingly, on January 28 Vinson introduced House Joint Resolution 307, which he regarded as a routine measure to authorize use of the ships as bomb targets at Bikini. "In order that the atomic test may be realistic and valuable, some ships of fairly modern construction must be used," he explained on March 11, when the House took up the legislation. The battleships "are old and of no further naval value," he said, and the *Saratoga* "is a stout ship but advances in carrier design have outmoded her." Many of the ships, he added, "would be disposed of by other methods if not used for this test."

No board had declared the ships to be unfit, Vinson admitted, but he declared them so himself. "These are obsolete and surplus ships. We have no need for them." In fact, in the months after Japan's surrender the Navy had canceled construction orders on more than 9,800 combat vessels and declared 7,000 ships to be surplus to the needs of the postwar Navy.[9] Vinson was defensive about the cost of the tests and yet adamant about the need to destroy modern ships. He conceded that the book value of the target vessels was about $450 million, but he argued that their cost was not as great as it seemed, because if sold for scrap they would bring only a small part of their book value, a figure he pegged at $1 million.

Vinson's remarks set off a raucous two-hour debate on the House floor, reflecting congressional anxiety and skepticism over Operation Crossroads. "Why all this great party to the Pacific for this sensational bombing and holocaust at this time?" asked Rep. Robert Thomason of Texas, the senior member of the House Military Affairs Committee and one of the most influential members of Congress on issues of national defense. "Why is the Navy so anxious for this experiment? . . . Why the necessity of that grand destruction of property at this time? In one of the most critical periods of the world's history, with everything chaotic," he asked, "why all the haste in this matter? We ought to talk a little about peace."[10]

"We have this surplus property," Vinson responded. "It is going to be expended in one way or the other. The best way would be for the Government to find out something about the atomic bomb so that it will be helpful and guide us in the future as to the building of ships." He mentioned an upcoming appropriations bill for the Navy. "We are coming in here in a day or two to ask for three and a half billion dollars to support the Navy. You would be in a far better position knowing what effect the most modern destructive weapon ever devised would have on ships of that Navy." He agreed with Thomason that the atomic bomb could destroy a city and kill tens of thousands of people. "But cities will continue to be built and human beings will continue to be born. We are going to try to find out if it can destroy navies."

Thomason surprised many of his colleagues by denouncing Vinson's proposal. "We all know that at Nagasaki and Hiroshima it was proved that the bomb could do such tremendous damage that it really does not make so much difference whether the bomb sinks a ship or not. We know that it will . . . wreck anything in its path. Our airplane bombs sank ships." He was unconvinced by Vinson's argument on appropriations, pointing out that at least nine of the target ships were less than a year old. "Yet the gentleman from Georgia says he is going to soon ask for a large appropriation for new ships. Sink or damage them one day— build new ones the next day."[11]

Thomason's arguments went beyond money, though. His committee was just then grappling with the McMahon bill and control of the atomic bomb, issues he thought clearly at odds with another demonstration of the bomb's power. "I think the timing . . . is bad and that this glorified experiment is not wise or necessary at this time," he argued.

"Our boys back from Japan know what the atomic bomb can do. . . . The question for the immediate future is to determine what we are going to do with the weapon and who is to be its custodian." Thomason saw the tests solely as a military display. "In less than ten months after V-E Day, with all the war talk that is going on, you are sending these ships out to the Far Pacific for a vast display, when the world is on fire and everybody thinks we are going to have another war with a great power." He also questioned the scientific value of the tests. "To go out and sink or damage 90 ships . . . just as an experiment for men who are not scientists is ridiculous." The top scientists who worked on the Manhattan Project were not being sent, said Thomason. "Why do you not also send those men over there along with the brass hats?" he asked, adding that the military men who were headed for Bikini "do not know any more about the atomic bomb than the man in the moon."[12]

Vinson called Thomason's bluff on the timing of the tests. "Will the gentleman advise the House when he thinks it would be the proper time?"

"I do not know," Thomason responded, although he suggested that it should be after the establishment of the AEC. In his view it made more sense to "keep our secret instead of going out there for a great display that will prove nothing at this time except perhaps to arouse suspicion in other countries."

Vinson defended the military nature of the tests. Operation Crossroads "is to be strictly under the guidance of the Joint Chiefs of Staff and not of any scientists," he explained. Scientists would aid in the tests and be invited to attend, but "this is a military test as to the effect something the scientists have created, the atomic bomb, will have on ships."

Representative Justin Johnson of California rose to support Thomason. "What are we trying to do here," he asked, "except to put on a glorious show, impress Russia and other countries, and sink a whole fleet of ships?" He, too, was "amazed" by the absence of the leading scientists, calling Operation Crossroads "strictly a military show." Johnson, like several other congressmen, was also troubled by the prospect of sinking so many new and serviceable ships. "To give our blessing to the sinking of a whole fleet is so absurd that it is ridiculous."[13]

Admiral Blandy sought to blunt the congressional criticism and to minimize the cost of the tests. He admitted that the total cost of the tests was originally calculated at over $500 million, but because many of the ships were obsolete it was more accurate to appraise their cost only in terms of their scrap value. "Many of them are obsolete and they were already scheduled for disposal, which meant only one thing, the junk heap," he told reporters in April. With scrap prices then at about $13 a ton, their value came out to less than 1 percent of the original cost of the ships. "So instead of being over $400,000,000, we would be lucky to get $4,000,000," he said. The $100 million cost of running the tests, he added, "has no foundation at all." He could not estimate the actual cost, saying that "we will have a closer approximation when we get closer to accomplishment," but under his analysis the entire cost of the tests would "not exceed the total cost of one large new ship."[14]

When asked directly at a congressional hearing what the tests would cost, Blandy evaded the question. "I could not give an exact figure," he replied, "because in the first place it would be difficult to place the exact value on the ships, but my own feeling is that the net result will be a profit." The Navy continued to assert that the only real cost of the tests would be the scrap value of the 370,000 tons of target ships, estimated to be $10 per ton, or $3,700,000.[15] Blandy later put the cost at $70 million, exclusive of the cost of the atomic bomb itself. "Practically all of this," he added, "is being absorbed in current appropriations and in the general cost of finishing off the war."[16]

Blandy disingenuously sought to characterize Operation Crossroads as defensive in nature:

> Some people fear that these tests may be construed by other nations as a "martial gesture." But the principal targets are naval ships. Great Britain, the only other country possessing a strong navy, certainly does not believe that we are planning to use the bomb against her fleet. Therefore the tests stand out clearly as a defensive measure. These are measures of caution and economy, not aggression.

Blandy frequently reached for metaphors to defend the upcoming tests. "The city Fire Chief cannot predict where or when the next fire will occur, but the City Council does not reduce his force or equipment to a dangerous fraction of his needs because of that," he told one audience. He assured them that he was not making a plea to keep the atomic bomb in the world's arsenal. "But whatever our weapons are to be, we still need weapons, whether we join an international police force or not," he concluded. "A large unarmed nation is not a power for peace; it is a prey for aggressors."[17] He also sought to portray Operation Crossroads's critics as somehow unpatriotic. "If, because of a desire to avoid offending other nations, we failed to carry out these experiments," he asserted, ship designers "would be groping their way along a dark road which might well lead to perilous national weakness." This road, he continued, "may lead to another and worse Pearl Harbor."[18]

For some congressional supporters of the tests, the advent of the bomb was a religious event. "When the scientists released atomic energy," declared Democratic representative Jerry Voorhis of California, "the greatest event in the history of mankind except only the birth of Christ Himself took place; there is no question about that." Over in the Senate, Edwin Johnson of Colorado conjured up an updated version of Theodore Roosevelt's warning to speak softly but carry a big stick. "God Almighty in His infinite wisdom [has] dropped the atomic bomb in our lap," he told the Senate. Now the United States, "with vision and guts and plenty of atomic bombs, . . . can outlaw wars of aggression . . . and . . . compel mankind to adopt the policy of lasting peace . . . or be burned to a crisp."[19]

As the House wound up its debate on Vinson's resolution to authorize the use of Navy ships as targets at Bikini, Rep. John Rankin of Mississippi, a member of the House Un-American Activities Committee, delivered a homily on the upcoming tests. "Almighty God has placed this great weapon in our hands at a time when atheistic barbarism is threatening to wipe Christianity from the face of the earth," he declared, adding that Operation Crossroads "would probably insure the peace of the world for generations to come" and thus further the cause of Christianity. "As the leading Christian nation in the world," he said on the House floor, "we are charged with . . . furthering the cause of our Christian civilization, and helping to maintain peace among the nations of the earth." Rankin, a fiery debater who was known for his uninhibited language and fits of temper, having once physically attacked a fellow congressman, now raised his voice in support of Vinson's proposal and shouted to the House, "We are going to stop this appeasement stuff! If we find some outfit is getting ready to attack us with an atom bomb we are going to be first on the draw! I'm tired of appeasement. I'm tired of foreign powers sending agents here to undermine and destroy what we have."[20]

In the end, Vinson's resolution carried the day. The only issue that raised enough questions in the House to modify the legislation was the military's control of the tests. Echoing Truman's concerns at the White House cabinet meeting several weeks earlier, several congressmen recalled the Billy Mitchell incident and suggested that the Navy should not both conduct the tests and report on them. "It is natural to expect the military people will view these tests through rose colored glasses," noted Rep. Sterling Cole of New York. He therefore offered an amendment to the resolution on March 11 that would direct the president to appoint an eleven-member independent advisory board, with five civilian and six military members, to evaluate the tests and make recommendations to the military. After more posturing, including questions concerning whether the Communist *Daily Worker* would be permitted to witness the tests and the number of congressmen to be invited, Vinson's resolution, together with Cole's amendment establishing an independent board, passed the House the next day by a vote of 314 to 25.[21]

Blandy opposed the mixed civilian-military board when he testified a week later before the Senate Naval Affairs Committee, but the committee did not kill Cole's proposal. Instead, it voted unanimously to leave the makeup of the committee to the president's discretion.[22] Reflecting his vacillation on both the McMahon bill and the May-Johnson proposal (the *New York Times* pointed out that he had endorsed both bills), Truman decided to appoint a civilian board of his own and, at the same time, permit the Joint Chiefs to name its own evaluation committee. By late March, though, it appeared that the tests might not be held at all.

9

"Operation Crossroads, Known . . . Unofficially as 'The Great Boondoggle'"

The 1946 debate on Operation Crossroads saw the breakdown of the wartime alliance between scientists and the military. Leslie Groves's characterization of the Manhattan Project scientists as the "greatest bunch of prima donnas ever assembled in one place" typified the attitude of many military leaders. Groves questioned whether the atomic scientists' loyalty ran to the United States or to a different calling of truth and knowledge, and leading atomic scientists sometimes did little to discourage this perception. They were a "kind of international brotherhood, comparable in many ways to a religious order," wrote the Nobel Prize–winning physicist James Franck, and their public activities were "dictated solely by [their] social conscience."[1]

The scientific-military alliance in the Manhattan Project, fragile at best, barely survived the war. In May 1945, Leo Szilard, who had prepared Albert Einstein's famous 1939 letter to President Roosevelt urging the United States to develop the atomic bomb, appealed to Secretary of State Byrnes for a delay in the use of the bomb against Japan. He argued that an arms race might be avoided by keeping the bomb a secret and letting the Russians think that it had not succeeded. Byrnes responded that $2 billion had been spent on the tests and Congress was entitled to know the results.[2] In July, Szilard drew up a petition signed by nearly seventy Manhattan Project scientists urging Truman not to drop the bomb without first publicly announcing the terms the Allies intended to impose on Japan after the war. Groves, who later described Szilard as "continually a disruptive force," withheld the petition from Truman until after Hiroshima.[3]

Nuclear scientists began to organize on a large scale immediately after the war, and they quickly joined the debate on Operation Crossroads, international control of atomic weapons, and civilian control of atomic energy within the United States. On December 10, 1945, scientists at the University of Chicago's Metallurgical Laboratory published the first issue of the *Bulletin of the Atomic Scientists,* whose circulation grew to 10,000 in less than one year. The group called for the establishment of international control of atomic weapons, and it described the hearings before Senator McMahon's committee as the "most important event happening in the world today." Another new group, the Federation of Atomic (later "American") Scientists, which represented another 1,500 Manhattan Project scientists, endorsed the McMahon bill in late January. It, too, published a newsletter and opened a Washington office to conduct what *Newsweek* described as the atomic scientists' "reluctant lobby."[4]

The public venerated the new atomic scientists. Max Lerner wrote of their "almost miraculous clarity" in analyzing issues concerning the bomb. "As witnesses before the Senate and House committees, and in their newspaper conferences, they were quiet, modest, lucid and compellingly convincing," said the broadcaster Gram Swing on the ABC radio network. "They have proved to be as impressive a group of men as ever came to modern Washington."[5] *Harper's* noted wryly that "no dinner party is a success without at least one physicist to explain . . . the nature of the new age in which we live."[6]

J. Robert Oppenheimer burst into the limelight three days after Hiroshima, telling reporters that Manhattan Project scientists believed in the "desperate necessity" of world cooperation and understanding. Within three months, friends were urging him to run for Congress from California.[7] The atomic scientists were instant celebrities with a keen sense of good public relations. They wrote articles for leading newspapers and magazines. *Time* reported that sixty congressmen listened "in absolute stillness" to an "A-B-C course" in nuclear physics taught by "atomic scientists half their age," and Oppenheimer's lectures on quantum theory at the California Institute of Technology attracted such large crowds that loudspeakers had to be set up for people outside the lecture hall.[8] Oppenheimer, Hans Bethe, and Harold C. Urey regularly spoke on intermission programs of New York Philharmonic broadcasts. Nuclear physicists, wrote Joseph and Stewart Alsop, "acquired something of the position in our society of the Mathematician-Astronomer-Priests of the ancient Mayas, who were at once feared and revered as the knowers of the mystery of the seasons and the helpers of the sun and the stars in their life-giving courses."[9]

The atomic scientists' chief target was Leslie Groves, their brusque and aloof boss during the war and already the kingpin of postwar nuclear policy. Groves was physically imposing, nearly six feet tall and weighing over 250 pounds. The son of an Army chaplain, he grew up on Army posts, studied engineering at the University of Washington and MIT, and then went on to West Point, where he graduated fourth in his class in 1918 and joined the Army Corps of Engineers. He supervised construction of Army barracks after Pearl Harbor, then built the Pentagon, and by 1942 was in charge of all military construction in the United States, which totaled an extraordinary $600 million per month. He wanted to command troops in combat, but Stimson and Roosevelt picked him to head the Manhattan Project instead.[10]

Groves's deputy, Kenneth D. Nichols, described his boss as "abrasive and often very critical, . . . the biggest sonovabitch I've ever met in my life, but also one of the most capable individuals." Groves "had an ego second to none," said Nichols. "He had absolute confidence in his decisions and he was absolutely ruthless in how he approached a problem to get it done."[11] General Eisenhower had little respect for his colleague. "He was a czar during the war, and everything is a comedown for a man of his type," Eisenhower told David Lilienthal in 1947. "There are ways of getting things done that don't require humiliating people and making enemies of them. . . . Groves will never understand about these things."[12]

Groves was obsessed with security concerns. He created a category of "ultra-secret" for some of his documents, higher than the government's top-secret category, and he proudly defended his policy of compartmentalization during the Manhattan Project. "Compartmentalization of knowledge," he wrote, "was the very heart of security. My rule was simple—each man should know everything he needed to know to do his job and nothing else." Adherence to this rule, he asserted, improved efficiency and "made quite clear to all concerned that the project existed to produce a specific end product—not to enable individuals to satisfy their curiosity and to increase their scientific knowledge."[13]

After the war, atomic scientists clashed with Groves on virtually every issue concerning the bomb. In a speech in Chicago just three weeks after Hiroshima, physicist Samuel Allison described Los Alamos as a "luxurious concentration camp" and ridiculed Groves's emphasis on security, warning that if security restrictions on atomic research were not lifted, scientists would leave the field and "devote themselves to the study of the color of butterfly wings."[14] Leo Szilard lashed out at Groves in testimony before Senator McMahon's committee, saying that Groves's insistence on compartmentalization had caused an 18-month delay in the development of the bomb by preventing scientists from "putting 2 and 2 together."[15] Joseph and Stewart Alsop wrote that Groves was "heartily detested" by most of the scientific consultants working on the Acheson-Lilienthal Report, and the *New York Times* reported on the "hostility" toward Groves in the scientific community.[16]

Virtually every leading atomic scientist went on record to say that Russia would have the bomb within five years, but Groves, noting sarcastically that "the more they talk the shorter the time seems to get," said repeatedly that it would take a generation.[17] Speaking in Los Angeles after inspecting ships being prepared for Operation Crossroads, Groves assured reporters that the secrets of the atomic bomb were safe. "The bomb project is a little like a giant jigsaw puzzle with 100,000 pieces," he said. "A chance betrayal by one of our scientists might reveal five or 10 pieces out of 100,000, but that would mean almost nothing."[18] At his last press conference before he retired in 1948, Groves continued to insist that Russia's atomic bomb was a generation away. As it turned out, the scientists were right and Groves was wrong, as Russia exploded its first atomic bomb in 1949.

Despite the public's adulation of the atomic scientists, most policymakers in Washington during the immediate postwar years relied more on Groves, the "Atom General," than on the scientists. Ironically, those who were wary of the Russians simply did not want to hear that a Russian bomb was only three or four years away. Instead, they found more comfort in Groves's emphasis on atomic secrecy and his assurance of an American monopoly of 15 or 20 years. When Robert Oppenheimer urged Secretary of State Byrnes to speed up negotiations with the Russians over international control of atomic energy, Byrnes replied that while he greatly admired Oppenheimer's scientific achievements, he and the president had the responsibility for handling international affairs.[19] Forrestal viewed Groves as more responsible than the scientists, whom he considered naive, untrustworthy, and unstable, and Truman shared these views.[20] When Dean Acheson brought Oppenheimer into the Oval Office, the physicist blurted out that he had blood on his hands from his work on the bomb. Truman mockingly offered him a handkerchief and responded, "Would you like to wipe them?" The president was livid. "Don't you bring that son of a bitch around here again," he told Acheson after the meeting. "After all, all he did was make the bomb. I'm the guy who fired it off."[21]

The debate over secrecy versus openness and the duration of America's atomic monopoly reflected what McGeorge Bundy has described as the tension between fear of the atomic bomb and reliance on its protection, a tension that would also be reflected in the debate on Operation

Crossroads. Robert Oppenheimer and most other atomic scientists saw the bomb as the "destroyer of worlds," while Bernard Baruch and most military leaders saw it as the "winning weapon."[22]

Operation Crossroads only deepened this scientist-military rift, especially when the House Naval Affairs Committee on January 30 proposed legislation that would keep many of the test results secret. That same day, William A. Higinbotham, chairman of the new Association of Los Alamos Scientists, told reporters that he saw little value in the upcoming tests. The damage to the ships "is not going to be impressive," he said, and the results "will sound like a considerable disappointment."[23] Atomic scientists hoped that science had the power to force diplomats' hands. *Life* wrote that the scientists "take a poor view" of Operation Crossroads. They believed that Hiroshima and Nagasaki showed "that the atomic bomb is too powerful a weapon to leave outside the confines of international control and that Operation Crossroads will simply underline this truth without contributing much to atomic knowledge."[24]

"The value of the proposed tests for their avowed purpose, setting Navy policy, is dubious in the extreme," wrote Louis N. Ridenour, professor of physics at the University of Pennsylvania and spokesman for the new Federation of American Scientists. "No one should be surprised if only one ship is sunk by the first Bikini bomb," he stated in a magazine article entitled "Bikini: What Can It Prove?" The article contained a photograph of Admiral Blandy surrounded by eleven Army and Navy officers, with a caption that read: "High command of 'Operation Crossroads,' known officially as Joint Task Force 1, unofficially as 'The Great Boondoggle.'"[25]

Albert S. Cahn, a University of Chicago physicist, charged that the tests were "silly" and "meaningless" and would only give the American people a false sense of atomic power. "The danger is that as a result of this test the people will think we are safe from an atomic attack," asserted Cahn. "Actually, that isn't so. In case of war, no power is going to be foolish enough to waste its bombs on a few boats. They are going to bomb the cities and harbors."[26]

Lee A. DuBridge, the newly appointed president of the California Institute of Technology, argued that the tests would not answer basic military questions. "Suppose only two or three ships are sunk—do we then conclude that the Navy is still supreme as our first line of defense and we need not fear atomic warfare?" he asked in the *Bulletin of the Atomic Scientists*. He claimed that Operation Crossroads ignored the basic strategic question of whether an enemy would find it worthwhile to use its atomic bombs to destroy ships. If it did, "no one doubts that a properly placed atomic bomb can put a battleship or carrier out of action." But, DuBridge asked, "does this mean we abandon the navy?"

Hundreds of pages of secret reports would be written about the effects of the atomic bomb on gun turrets, ordnance, and radar, said DuBridge, but "regardless of the volumes of empirical data collected, these tests still leave unanswered the basic strategic question of whether navies or armies are obsolete and how future warfare might be conducted." Cahn saw a more sinister motive. "This isn't a test of atomic power," he declared. "This is a demonstration of power by the Navy. They are staging it for Congress so that the Navy will look pretty good and they can get bigger appropriations and a bigger Navy."

Despite Admiral Blandy's description of the atomic tests as a scientific experiment, the scientific community remained skeptical. The results of the tests will not "make a ripple on the surface of basic nuclear science," DuBridge asserted. "The study of nuclear fission will not be advanced one iota by all these figures. The value to pure science will be nil."[27] *Time* reported that some scientists were flatly calling Operation Crossroads a "put-up job," and it quoted one who called it a "ridiculous test. The Navy men will either prove that our Navy is safe from attack or that we need a new Navy."[28] The *Bulletin of the Atomic Scientists* editorialized that Operation Crossroads's greatest flaw was the failure to study the effects of the bomb's radiation on ships' crews. In real combat, a ship one mile from the blast would probably not sink, but the crew would be killed by radiation, and "only a ghost ship would remain, floating unattended on the vast waters of the ocean."[29] The Navy, for its part, either did not understand the effects of radiation or else assumed that ships and their crews could somehow withstand a direct hit from an atomic bomb. "We want ships which are tough, even when threatened by atomic bombs," wrote the official historian of Operation Crossroads. "We want to keep the ships afloat, propellers turning, guns firing; we want to protect the crews so that, if fighting is necessary, they can fight well today and return home unharmed tomorrow."[30]

Many atomic scientists were also concerned about the political implications of the tests. With the exception of a few skeptics, who received most of the media's attention, nearly all atomic scientists believed that the devastation inflicted at Hiroshima and Nagasaki would not be repeated at Bikini, for the simple reason that ships are stronger than buildings and are designed to withstand the tremendous pressure of an explosion. Destruction of only a few target ships was going to disappoint the public, reasoned the *Bulletin of the Atomic Scientists,* which was concerned that public opinion might thus be lulled into a feeling of false security, "along the lines of 'Oh, the atomic bomb is not so terrible—it's just another big bomb.'" Lee DuBridge was also concerned about the message Operation Crossroads would send to other countries.

"Are international relations to be improved by these tests?" he wondered. "Not even the greatest enthusiasts for them has claimed this. . . . I will say only that at this critical hour they are in poor taste."

Last, the atomic scientists were concerned about the risks and costs of the experiment. The *Bulletin of the Atomic Scientists* speculated that the aerial shot would reveal nothing about mechanical damage, which could not be estimated from the previous three atomic explosions. DuBridge shared these views. "Wouldn't science and engineering be far better off if the 100 million dollars or so which tests will cost could be devoted to laboratory research under controlled conditions?" he asked. He also worried about an unknown danger, fallout. "Who can say that a sudden rain storm could not precipitate dangerous quantities of this material onto one or more of the ships packed with observers?" he asked. "The surface burst will raise a great cloud of water spray and where will it be carried?" Ten weeks later, these fears would be realized at Bikini. "Or," he continued, "might not a cloud of this lethal dust be carried hundreds of miles and deposited on unsuspecting inhabitants?"[31] Eight years later, this exact prediction also came true, but at the time of Operation Crossroads DuBridge's concerns were dismissed. "He has been wrong before," commented Rep. Walter G. Andrews of New York, a member of President Truman's evaluation board.[32] Nevertheless, it was these atomic scientists who accurately predicted the results of Operation Crossroads and asked the tough questions military analysts would grapple with in top-secret reports after the tests.

One month after the tests were announced, no high-ranking member of the Los Alamos team of scientists that built the atomic bomb was planning to participate in Operation Crossroads. The Navy's technical director for the tests, Dr. Ralph Sawyer, was not a nuclear physicist, but rather an expert in the field of spectroscopy. Prior to his appointment, his knowledge of the atomic bomb came solely from what he had read about it. He was not a member of the Manhattan Project and had played no role in the development of the bomb. Robert Oppenheimer had been asked to participate only as an observer, and most of the other top Manhattan Project scientists had returned to teaching and research. "Many of the men who have been invited to take part declined because of the nature of the test," suggested the *New York Herald Tribune*. "They fear a test in which ninety-four of the ninety-seven target ships will come out unscathed. The public reaction, they believe, will be to discount the atom bomb and support a large navy."[33]

10

"It Would Be Very Helpful If the Test Could Be Postponed or Never Held at All"

The newly famous Manhattan Project scientists shunned Operation Crossroads, but congressmen did not. Congressional pressure to travel to Bikini was so great that Admiral Nimitz made arrangement in early March to increase the congressional allocation from thirty to sixty spaces. Speaker of the House of Representatives Sam Rayburn, though, was not informed of this increase, and he assumed that only the four congressional members of the president's evaluation board were planning to go to Bikini. Rayburn strongly opposed junkets that interrupted congressional sessions, and he was particularly opposed to this trip because of important pending legislation and upcoming primaries.

With public pressure against Operation Crossroads continuing to mount, President Truman considered postponing the tests or canceling them altogether. According to Henry Wallace, the president told several cabinet members at a White House luncheon meeting on March 19 that Rayburn "had been putting him on the spot with regard to sending a lot of congressmen to witness the test. The President didn't want a lot of Democratic congressmen out witnessing the test when their votes were needed here in Washington."[1] Blandy's office drafted a letter to Rayburn and Senator Kenneth McKellar of Tennessee, president pro tem of the Senate, to be signed by the War and Navy departments, asking the two leaders to submit a list of congressmen who would attend the tests. Navy Secretary Forrestal signed the letter, but the War Department did not after learning of Rayburn's opposition.[2]

Truman was in a bind. He told Wallace at the March 19 meeting that he would postpone the tests until 1947, but first he called a cabinet meeting for March 22 to hear from his advisors.[3] The president opened the meeting by proposing that Operation Crossroads be postponed. Forrestal, who brought along Admiral Blandy to defend the tests, read a written memorandum that he prepared for the meeting. "The postponement of Operation Crossroads," argued Forrestal to the Cabinet, "would entail very substantial waste, not merely in money, but of time and effort," and much of that investment "would be completely lost if a decision were made to abandon the operation." Moreover, the Los Alamos scientists recruited for the tests would be leaving the government to return to university work in September. "There have been upwards of 20,000 men actively engaged on it for the last two months," he said, and the "whole organization is one which probably would be most difficult to assemble again."[4]

After Forrestal spoke, Blandy explained that the aerial shot was scheduled for May 15, a surface test for July 1, and a deep underwater shot for early 1947. He suggested that senators and congressmen be invited to attend only the second test on July 1, at a time more suitable to Congress than the first test. Truman responded that he needed congressional support for the McMahon bill and that he thought most congressmen traveling to Bikini wanted to see both shots. Wallace then proposed holding the tests during Congress's two-week Christmas recess, but Blandy explained that the absolute deadline for the second test was September 1.

Wallace asked whether the third test, which he said would be the most destructive, should be held first. "It might make the others unnecessary," he said. Blandy responded that he did not want to hold the third test first "for fear that he might lose all his ships and not have them for the first and second tests." Wallace replied that "it might not be necessary to hold any tests at all if we could arrange for a really effective inspection service in every nation in the world."

While Wallace argued that the tests made no sense, Secretary of State Byrnes was concerned with the upcoming Paris Council of Foreign Ministers, scheduled to meet in late April and May to lay the groundwork for the Paris Peace Conference to be held over the summer. Although Byrnes had by now joined the hardliners on the question of dealing with Russia, he told the cabinet meeting that the May 15 date for the first test "would be extremely unwise," adding that "from the standpoint of international relations it would be very helpful if the test could be postponed or never held at all." In his opinion, "this Crossroads Operation has developed into a big show on the strength of the atomic dictator," and the results of the test "would be negligible." He preferred "that the tests were not held at all, but certainly the later the better."

Forrestal fought back. "Scientists have strong views on both sides in connection with the value of the tests and the procedures to be followed," he conceded, but he and Blandy called the tests "invaluable" and warned that Senator McMahon had "threatened to forbid any further appropriations for the Navy under the assumption that the present Navy is obsolete." The War Department added that cancellation would give Russia "the impression that we are becoming secretive," and Byrnes admitted that "Russia wants the tests to go ahead and they want to be present at the location of the tests."

Truman said that a decision had to be made "here and now." According to Forrestal, Truman "said it was essential for Congress to be in Washington at the date set for the first test, and he neither desired to have them away at the bomb tests then, or hold the tests without inviting them." The president was also concerned about the cost, an argument reminiscent of Byrnes's justification to Leo Szilard for dropping the bomb on Japan. "This test," Truman said, "will cost 100 million dollars and if the tests are canceled this amount of money will be wasted." With one group of advisors calling for outright cancellation and another group urging no change, Truman played the role of judge and came to a compromise decision, ordering Operation Crossroads postponed for six weeks, until July 1.[5]

The news was immediately leaked to the press by a Navy source. Just hours after the cabinet meeting, Eben Ayers, assistant White House press secretary, received a telephone call from a reporter asking for confirmation of a United Press report that the tests had been postponed. President Truman intended to announce the delay over the weekend, but now Ayers and Charlie Ross, the president's press secretary, had to confer with Truman and prepare a statement.[6]

It was after 9:00 P.M. on March 22, a Friday night, when Charlie Ross read a short announcement to reporters. "The postponement," he said, "is prompted by the fact that a large number of congressmen have expressed a desire to witness both these tests, but, owing to their heavy legislative schedule, would be prevented from doing so if the tests were held on the dates originally fixed."

"Is there no other reason?" a reporter asked.

"This statement covers the ground," Ross answered.

"Does the present international situation have any bearing on the decision?"

"I can't go beyond the statement," Ross replied.[7]

The press reacted skeptically because the announcement came on the heels of two separate messages from the Soviet Union. Two days earlier, Moscow radio, in a direct reference to the tests, had accused the United States of "brandishing the atomic weapon for purposes which have little in common with the peace and security of the nations." Then, just 10 hours before the White House announcement of the postponement of the tests, Stalin strongly endorsed the role of the United Nations, stating that the United Nations' strength "is based on the principle of equality of states and not on the domination of one state over others."[8] The view that a postponement would have a reassuring effect on the upcoming UN Security Council meeting, which was scheduled for the following Monday, March 25, was reinforced by the fact that both Senate Foreign Relations Committee chairman Tom Connally and Soviet UN Security Council Representative Andrei Gromyko met with Truman just hours before the announcement of the postponement.

Two high-ranking administration sources who were involved in Operation Crossroads confirmed that the postponement was related to international events. They pointed to a "hopeful trend in the disturbed United Nations picture" and suggested that the tests might be postponed indefinitely, "until the nations are pulling together better." Another high administration official said it was "obvious" that the desire of congressmen to witness the tests was not the only reason for the postponement, but he added that it would be "rather dangerous" to discuss the "real reason."[9]

Assistant Secretary of War Howard C. Petersen, who attended the cabinet meeting for Secretary of War Patterson, confirmed that the uncertain international situation weighed heavily in Truman's decision. In a top-secret memorandum prepared just after the Friday cabinet meeting, Petersen wrote that Truman postponed the tests both to allay concerns about congressional observers and "to meet Secretary Byrnes' point that holding the test on May 15 . . . may appear as a threatening demonstration of force." Patterson later told an aide that Truman ordered the delay because of "the very increased expenditures that were required, the large number of personnel to be committed to it . . . [and] the unsettled conditions of the time."[10]

Admiral Blandy, informed of the postponement less than five hours before Ross's announcement, was taken completely by surprise, as he had announced on Friday afternoon that 600 observers would be leaving for Bikini the following Monday. Joint Task Force One issued a short press release on Saturday stating that the postponement would have no effect on the tests, but speculation continued over the weekend that Operation Crossroads would be canceled altogether. Part of the blame was due to Blandy himself. Just three days before the postponement, he had testified before Congress that Bikini's easterly winds were favorable for a test in May or June, but that the weather would become worse in the summer. The admission by Blandy's intelligence chief on Saturday that the delay made the tests "a little nervy" only served to

fuel rumors that the tests would be called off, as the press speculated
that uncertain weather might create radioactive clouds that would
endanger safety at the test site.[11]

At a news conference on Saturday morning, March 23, Charlie Ross
said the decision to postpone Operation Crossroads was not a "sudden
one." He stated that many congressmen had asked President Truman for
the postponement so they might see the tests, and he denied that the president's decision was a conciliatory move made in response to Stalin's
expression of confidence in the United Nations. Told that speculation
was rampant that the postponement was inspired by the upcoming meeting of the UN Security Council, Ross replied tersely, "I know that."[12]

That same day, Ross noted in his diary that newspapers were suggesting "international reasons" for the postponement, but this was not the
case. "Reason officially stated was valid," noted Ross. "Many congressmen wanted to attend test (under encouragement by Navy). An exodus
around May 15, date for the first bomb detonation, would interfere with
legislative program." Ironically, with all the press speculation about Stalin
and the United Nations, Truman told Ross on Friday night that he was
"less worried over the situation vis-a-vis Russia than most people."[13]

President Truman told the Friday cabinet meeting that sixty congressmen would observe the tests, but the White House, anxious to
show that the tests were on track, doubled this number on Saturday,
announcing that 120 senators and representatives would attend the
tests. On Monday, March 25, still scrambling to squelch rumors that
the tests would be canceled, the White House announced the appointees
to the president's civilian evaluation board, now called the President's
Evaluation Commission for the Atomic Bomb Tests. This action had the
desired effect. The *New York Times* noted that it "was taken as full
assurance that the Crossroads Operation at Bikini Atoll would neither
be postponed indefinitely nor called off," adding that Blandy's task
force was in session all through the day, "trying to come out of the 'tail-
spin,' as one official put it, into which test plans were hurled by the six-
week postponement."[14]

Three days later, in a continued effort to squelch rumors that Operation Crossroads was on the verge of cancellation, Blandy announced the
members of the Joint Chiefs mixed civilian-military evaluation board. In
fact, two members of Truman's evaluation commission—Karl T. Compton and Bradley Dewey—were also named to the Joint Chiefs' committee, which Blandy viewed as neither unusual nor undesirable. "I don't
see anything particularly unique about that," he told a press conference.
"I think it possible it will afford a good tie-in between them."[15]

President Truman emphasized again at his March 28 news conference
that the only reason for the postponement was that a May 15 test

would take too many congressmen out of Washington. This justification, dubious when announced, seemed even more transparent now, because Speaker Rayburn had announced the day before that Congress was making such good progress on passing emergency legislation that he anticipated a spring recess. "How do these two things fit together?" asked a reporter. Truman responded that he had not discussed a recess with Rayburn, and he held firm to his explanation.[16] At Pearl Harbor, though, where most of the men preparing for the tests were assembled, morale was low. "Some men are frankly skeptical that the tests will be held, even though we have every assurance they will be," said one Navy captain on March 27. "Nobody here believes the reason behind the postponement is to permit more congressmen to sit in on the show."[17]

Meanwhile, the four congressional members of Truman's new evaluation commission warned Blandy's officers at a March 30 meeting that Congress believed that the Joint Chiefs of Staff were not entirely backing the tests and that some members favored outright cancellation. Military leaders were divided on how to respond. Admiral Nimitz wanted to reaffirm the military's backing for the tests, as did Leslie Groves, who urged the Joint Chiefs to make their support clear. Admiral Leahy, on the other hand, did not think any useful purpose would be served by the Joint Chiefs' "gratuitous repetition" of their previous recommendation. The Joint Chiefs' planning staff recommended against a statement, arguing that a reaffirmation "would give the impression that there is a difference of opinion between the President and the military authorities and that the latter are attempting to carry their case to the public."

The Joint Chiefs, however, concluded that only the president could stem the tide of criticism. Accordingly, Patterson and Forrestal wrote a joint letter to Truman on April 6 stating that the postponement had "raised some question concerning the solidarity of the military opinion as to the importance of these tests," and they urged him to make a public statement.[18] Truman agreed. "Preparations for the atomic bomb tests in the Pacific are being pressed forward," he told the nation on April 12, "and I have been assured that the present target dates for the explosions will be met." Calling the tests a "laboratory experiment," he added that they "are of vital importance in obtaining information for the national defense" and "should give us the information which is essential to intelligent planning in the future and an evaluation of the effect of atomic energy on our defense establishment."[19] The New York Times, which had speculated for weeks that the tests would be canceled, reported that Truman's announcement "settled rumors that, because of the delicate international situation, he might call off the tests entirely."[20] Operation Crossroads was on again.

11

"If an Atomic Bomb Comes Close Enough to a Ship . . . It Will Sink It"

President Truman's postponement of Operation Crossroads revived congressional efforts to abandon the tests altogether. In a March 23 letter to the president, Rep. Herman P. Kopplemann of Connecticut applauded the postponement and assured him that the American public approved of his decision. "I am glad you have wisely seen fit to cancel an expedition which at best might have aggravated tension and suspicion," Kopplemann wrote.[1]

James W. Huffman, Ohio's freshman Democratic senator, introduced a resolution on March 29 to cancel Operation Crossroads. The president's postponement, he declared, was a step in the right direction, but it did not go far enough, and he called for the outright cancellation until the cause of international cooperation and peace was given an opportunity to succeed. "This is no time for martial gestures," Huffman declared in his first speech before the Senate. "Are we preparing for peace or are we preparing for war?" he asked. If the country was preparing for war, he argued, why destroy ninety-five ships and show the world America's improved atomic strength? However, if the country was preparing for peace, why indulge in "this wanton destruction of property and display of atomic power?" With the United Nations in its infancy, he concluded, "it is unthinkable that the United States should even remotely indicate that she is preparing for an atomic war."

Senator Scott Lucas, who had raised these issues two months earlier, rose to support the resolution and cautioned against "a grandiose display of atomic power." On the one hand, argued Lucas, the president had nominated Bernard Baruch "to devise some plan to destroy the most deadly weapon that mankind has ever seen. On the other, we are considering this great experiment in the Pacific Ocean which tends to promote the very opposite."[2] Senator J. William Fulbright of Arkansas, then in his second of 29 years in the Senate, also supported the resolution. He criticized the cost of Operation Crossroads and argued that the tests would contribute more to other countries' suspicions than to world peace. "I felt we should be doing all we could to get along with the Russians," recalled Fulbright nearly five decades later, "and these tests were taking us in the other direction."[3] The three senators also noted that leading atomic scientists opposed the tests. Lucas said he had talked with four of the most prominent scientists in the country, none of whom favored Operation Crossroads, and Fulbright added that Oppenheimer, Harold Urey, and others opposed the tests.

Senator David I. Walsh of Massachusetts, a former admiral and chairman of the Committee on Naval Affairs, shocked his colleagues by endorsing Huffman's resolution. Two days earlier, on March 27, Walsh's committee had approved House Joint Resolution 307, which authorized the use of $425 million of Navy ships for the tests, and sent it to the full Senate for a vote. With the legislation pending, Walsh was thrown off by Truman's postponement. "I see no objection to having the Senate consider the resolution," he said. "In fact, I think it desirable that the Senate and the President should reflect further upon whether it is wise to proceed with the experiment."[4]

Walsh was most concerned with the open-ended nature of the joint resolution, which would have permitted the Navy to use three enemy combat ships and up to ninety-seven American combat ships as targets at Bikini. On April 1, he wrote to Forrestal stating that favorable action by the Senate on the joint resolution would be forthcoming if the Navy restudied its needs and reduced the number of combat vessels. He also indicated that President Truman's postponement of the tests and the subsequent uncertainty among some senators as to whether the president was wholeheartedly in favor of Operation Crossroads were interfering with prompt favorable action by the Senate. Forrestal later reduced the number of combat ships to thirty-three.[5]

Huffman was hoping to use the Senate's vote on the use of Navy ships for targets as another forum to debate the tests. If Operation Crossroads went forward, he warned, "Russia can say we are perfecting a terrible war weapon and she must look out for her own interests. I don't think we ought to provide that excuse at this time." But Senator Carl A. Hatch of New Mexico, newly appointed chairman of President

Truman's Evaluation Commission for the Atomic Bomb Tests, served notice that the tests would move ahead on the new July 1 schedule. Hatch, a close friend of the president's who had first been elected to the Senate with Truman, told reporters that "it would be criminal negligence to call the tests off now."[6] In the end, Huffman's resolution to cancel the tests went nowhere. He was unable to persuade Senate leaders to refer it to a committee for a hearing, and it was never voted on.

In the House, Rep. Louis Ludlow of Indiana made one last attempt to stop the tests. On April 18, he introduced a resolution calling for the United States to cancel the tests and cease manufacturing atomic bombs. Operation Crossroads "cuts across all the claims and pretensions we have made that we would take the leadership in creating a world of peace and security," he declared on the House floor. "If we go ahead with the Bikini Atoll demonstration, we will be saying, in effect, to every other nation: 'We are going to show you how many of you we can kill if you get ugly. So don't start anything.' What an approach to world peace. What a travesty!" Holding the tests, he insisted, "will be poking a pistol in their faces and asking how they like it. How is that for a start for world peace?"[7]

The atomic scientists' organizations praised Truman's postponement. "The tests are purely military, not scientific," declared the Federation of American Scientists. "Scientists expect nothing of scientific value and little of technical value to peacetime uses of atomic energy. Scientists are cooperating in these tests at the request of their country's armed forces, although they do so with heavy hearts, and without enthusiasm."[8] These efforts to stop the tests, though, received little support in the media. Most newspapers supported the tests, and *Newsweek* wrote that advocates of cancellation "seem to be walking along the trail which nearly led us to disaster after the First World War."[9]

Several prominent Manhattan Project scientists steered clear of Operation Crossroads altogether. Harvard University president James B. Conant, a member of the State Department committee that formulated the Acheson-Lilienthal Report, said he found a "certain degree of incompatibility" between the tests and his work on the international control of the atomic bomb. "There might be a tendency on the part of some people to confuse evaluation of a weapon with enthusiasm for its use," he wrote to Forrestal and Patterson in early February. "This would be quite erroneous, of course, but the present atmosphere which surrounds the debate on the atomic bomb is not one which produces the utmost clarity of thinking." He therefore declined their invitation to serve on the military board to evaluate the tests.[10]

Robert Oppenheimer, already suspicious of Baruch and U.S. efforts to achieve domestic control of atomic energy, was growing increasingly concerned about Operation Crossroads as well. Having already been criticized by many fellow scientists for supporting the May-Johnson bill, Oppenheimer was reluctant to support Operation Crossroads, but when Truman asked him in February to serve on his civilian evaluation commission, he reluctantly accepted, after first declining.[11]

Truman and his advisors knew the value of Oppenheimer's imprimatur. His name carried magic, and his involvement would lend greater credibility to the tests and help offset criticism that the tests were of no scientific value. Groves, though, anticipating Oppenheimer's hostility toward Operation Crossroads, decided that he should be permitted to attend the tests but not evaluate them. He carefully drafted Truman's telegram to Oppenheimer, which invited him to serve on the president's commission "to observe the atomic bomb tests to be conducted by the Navy in May." As an aide pointed out in a memorandum, "General Groves wished to point out the fact that the phrase 'and evaluate' is not included in this telegram."[12]

Oppenheimer was feeling increasingly dejected—and guilty—over the course of U.S. atomic policy. "If atomic bombs are to be added as new weapons to the arsenals of a warring world," he said on October 16, 1945, his last day as director of Los Alamos, "then the time will come when mankind will curse the names of Los Alamos and Hiroshima."[13] Six months later and now a private citizen, he desperately wanted to help the U.S. government develop international controls, but he could not abide Bernard Baruch. He prepared some memoranda "merely [in] an attempt to be helpful to him," as he wrote, but he remained "still very heavy of heart."[14] Moreover, his growing doubts about Operation Crossroads left him uneasy with his assignment to serve on the president's evaluation commission, so on May 3, 1946, he wrote a remarkable letter to Truman asking to be excused from serving. "I am concerned," he wrote, "lest the nature of my misgivings make my participation . . . not a help to you but an embarrassment."

Oppenheimer summarized his objections to the tests in one sentence. "I do not think that naval applications are the important ones to test, nor that the test as it will be carried out will in fact be a good measure of naval applications, nor that the measurements which are to be made are the right measurements to make." He went on to explain each point in detail. The tests were designed to determine the effect of atomic weapons on ships, he began, but the answer was no secret: "If an atomic bomb comes close enough to a ship, even a capital one, it will sink it." The only real question, he said, was how close to the ship the bomb must be. Attempts to simulate combat conditions in the field would be crude at best. More reliable data could be obtained by model tests and calculations, and at far less expense than the estimated $100 million cost of the tests. "For less than one per cent of this, one could obtain useful information." Similarly, he said, scientific data concerning the effects of radiation on animals, equipment, and rations could better be obtained by simple laboratory testing methods.

Oppenheimer also told Truman that he saw no reason to devote such large resources to studying the effects of the atomic bomb on ships. In the event of atomic warfare, he reasoned, atomic weapons would be used primarily to bomb cities and industrial centers. "In comparison with these issues, the detailed determination of the destructiveness of atomic weapons against naval craft would appear trivial." Oppenheimer also felt that the juxtaposition of the Bikini tests and the upcoming UN meeting would undermine the peace process, and he questioned "the appropriateness of a purely military test of atomic weapons at a time when our plans for effectively eliminating them from national armaments are in their earliest beginnings."

Oppenheimer's political message to Truman was clear: He was opposed to Operation Crossroads, and he was prepared to write a report critical of the tests. Even if the tests were successful, he said, "many of my misgivings will still apply," and he acknowledged that "it could well be most undesirable" for him to produce a critical report. Under these circumstances, he hoped the president would agree that "I can better serve you if I am not a member of your committee than if I am."[15] Oppenheimer resigned a few days later, but not, as one of his biographers has noted, "without the feeling from some people that perhaps, like Lady Macbeth, he was washing his hands too often for past sins."[16]

The White House, perhaps concerned about adverse publicity and pressure to cancel the tests, sat on Oppenheimer's letter for seven weeks and did not announce his resignation from the president's evaluation commission for nearly two months.[17] By late May, Oppenheimer still did not know whether his resignation would be accepted. "I am supposed to go to Crossroads, which I don't want to do, but I haven't been excused from it," he told a friend in a taped telephone conversation. "I expect I will have to turn up at the United Nations meetings, but it's not clear."[18] In a June letter to Senator Hatch, Oppenheimer showed little enthusiasm for his task. "For the immediate future," he wrote, "I have consented to try to be of assistance to Mr. Baruch and to his staff. For this reason it hardly seems possible for me to participate in the observation of the tests at Bikini, nor to serve effectively on the President's Committee."[19]

On the weekend of May 17–19, Baruch and his advisors met with Oppenheimer, Lilienthal, Acheson, and Bush over changing the Acheson-Lilienthal Report into what was becoming the Baruch Plan. The essence of the Acheson-Lilienthal Report remained, but its new emphasis on sanctions, enforcement, and inspection changed the tone of the report. Baruch even proposed atomic attack on any country that violated the plan, with no veto available in the UN Security Council. "It was unrealistic, silly, . . . mischievous in the extreme," wrote Lilienthal, and Acheson agreed that it would wreck the possibility of Russian acceptance.[20] Even America's military leaders, whose advice Baruch did not seek until the eleventh hour, questioned his ideas. "I do not believe that the people of this country are prepared now to enter into an agreement for automatic punishment of other nations for acts which do not directly concern the United States," wrote Admiral Nimitz to Baruch. "We face the incongruity that the atomic bomb is necessary to enforce an agreement to outlaw its use."[21] But Baruch, mindful of his experiences working on the Treaty of Versailles after World War I, was determined to prevent an agreement on the control of atomic energy from becoming, in his words, "another in the long line of history's empty declarations and gestures. . . . If I had learned anything out of my experience in international affairs, it was that world peace is impossible without the force to sustain it."[22]

The Acheson-Lilienthal group grew increasingly despondent about reaching an agreement with Baruch and his advisors. Oppenheimer told Lilienthal that he was not optimistic about the talks, "because the negotiations require insight, judgment, knowledge, and luck of a high order," qualities he found lacking in Baruch's team. Dean Acheson tried to work with Baruch in late May, but to no avail. "He was pretty badly mixed up still," Acheson told Lilienthal. "He starts by saying that he accepts the Report in its entirety, and then begins these vague excursions." Acheson was certain that Baruch deeply distrusted him, and in fact later that summer Baruch accused him of secretly taping their telephone conversations. Lilienthal even declined Baruch's invitation to attend the opening session of the UN Atomic Energy Commission; "I don't want to be roped into that," he wrote in his journal. Byrnes, too, who had recommended Baruch to Truman, had lost hope. "This is the worst mistake I have ever made," he told Acheson on the eve of the UN meeting. "But we can't fire him now, not with all the other trouble."[23]

Despite the turf battles and personality clashes, though, Baruch implemented the basic goal of the Acheson-Lilienthal Report—a system of controls leading up to disarmament—and he strengthened the enforcement provisions. "Mr. Baruch's principal contribution to the atomic energy program," President Truman later wrote, "was that he transformed the Acheson-Lilienthal Report from a working paper into a formal, systematic proposal and that he added a section that called for sanctions against any nation violating the rules."[24]

At eleven o'clock on the morning of June 14, Baruch, dressed in pinstripe trousers and a dark double-breasted jacket, sat to address the delegates to the UN Atomic Energy Commission gathered at the Hunter College gymnasium in the Bronx, which had been transformed into a stately international meeting hall. Sound-absorbent tiles covered the ceiling's iron girders, and mahogany plywood had been placed over the gym's brick wall. Baruch and the other delegates sat in green upholstered chairs around a large horseshoe table. Some of the leading Manhattan Project scientists—Arthur Compton, Harold Urey, Charles A. Thomas—sat with the American delegation in the hall; Oppenheimer, haggard and anxious, sat with them. Test Able, the first shot in Operation Crossroads, was only two weeks away, and the link between Bikini and the Bronx was obvious. "The decisive 'Operation Crossroads' will not take place at Bikini," wrote Anne O'Hare McCormick of the *New York Times*. "It will take place here, in the Bronx."[25]

Baruch began his speech with an apocalyptic prophesy. "My fellow citizens of the world, we are here to make a choice between the quick and the dead." He spoke directly, in a clear and resounding tone. "Behind the black portent of the new atomic age lies a hope which, seized upon with faith, can work our salvation. If we fail, then we have damned every man to be the slave of fear. Let us not deceive ourselves: We must elect world peace or world destruction."

Baruch called for an "international law with teeth in it," and he did not back down from sanctions. "Before a country is ready to relinquish any winning weapons," as he called the bomb, "it must have more than words to reassure it." He spoke of outlawing war and total disarmament, but only in the context of abolishing the atomic bomb. "The light at the end of the tunnel is dim," he told the delegates. "The way is long and thorny but supremely worth traveling. All of us want to stand erect with our faces to the sun, instead of being forced to burrow into the earth like rats."[26] Baruch ended his speech around noon, and the story hit page 1 of early editions of afternoon papers. The praise was instantaneous and overwhelming. "There is not type in any newspaper office anywhere big enough to emphasize the importance of the American proposal today," exclaimed a typical editorial.[27]

Just a few hours later, the Senate began its final debate on Operation Crossroads. Up for a vote that afternoon was House Joint Resolution 307, regarding the Navy's use of target ships. Senator Lucas held up a newspaper and read out an account of Baruch's speech earlier that day. He predicted that the United States would be accused of "double talk" in light of Baruch's speech. "If the United States wishes to strengthen Mr. Baruch's hand," he exclaimed, "if the United States wishes to show the world that we mean business in the renunciation of the atom bomb as an instrument of warfare, we should now call off this test, or at least it should be delayed until we can see what constructive results can come from the noble and wonderful proposal which has been made by this great man, Bernard Baruch."

Senator Huffman joined in, stating that it was impossible to square the tests with Baruch's statement at the United Nations that America desired to use atomic energy only for peaceful purposes. He denounced Operation Crossroads as a dangerous "Roman holiday in the Pacific" and said that the "only important impression these tests are going to give the world is that the United States is not done with war."

Senator McMahon snapped back. "We are using the bomb on our property, in waters which are controlled by this Government," he said. "We do not threaten to hurl the bomb at the property of any other nation."

"We are not attacking any other nation, but we are attacking peace itself," retorted Huffman. Lucas agreed, arguing that the tests would antagonize the Soviet Union and undermine U.S. security. "If the situation were reversed," he said, "and at this very moment Russia were in the Aleutians, conducting such a test as we are about to conduct in the Pacific, I am sure the Senator from Connecticut would be doing a little talking about Russia holding such an experiment in our backyard, and wondering why Russia was doing it."

"What would the Senator feel as to the old philosophy of 'Speak softly and carry a big stick'?" interjected Senator Ralph O. Brewster of Maine.

"We have done that right along," replied Lucas.

"No; we have not; we have not had the big stick. That has been the trouble."

Senator Warren Magnuson suggested that the tests, by showing the devastating power of the bomb, would lend support to Baruch's call for international controls. "We might show the rest of the world . . . what a terrifying thing the atomic bomb is," said Magnuson. "Then I think we will reach the point where we accomplish the very thing the Senator from Illinois wants to accomplish."

"I do not know why our Army and Navy men want any more demonstrations of what an atomic bomb will do, after what was done to Nagasaki and Hiroshima," answered Lucas. Huffman tried another approach, asserting that the tests would furnish America's enemies with information about the bomb. "Other nations of the world are going to glean almost all the information developed, and some of them have been invited to witness the event. . . . By these tests we are simply educating would-be aggressors in atomic warfare, just as surely as the sun will rise tomorrow."

Despite the objections of Lucas and Huffman, House Joint Resolution 307 was passed by the Senate and signed by President Truman that afternoon, just hours after Bernard Baruch called for total disarmament. "This is not a demonstration to scare anybody," said McMahon. "The test should not affect the New York United Nations conference in any way." Huffman, calling the resolution a prelude to an atomic arms race, did not see it that way. "Our actions are simply not squaring up with our professed intentions."[28]

12

"One Hell of a Good Sales Job"

Bikini Atoll was in newspaper headlines around the world, but at Bikini the islanders had no idea that their lives were about to change forever. Ironically, the Bikinians' geographical isolation—the very factor that had limited their contact with the outside world—was about to end their isolation and thrust them onto the center stage of world events.

Conditions at Bikini had improved dramatically in the two years since America had liberated the Marshalls and imposed military government rule over the occupied islands. During the war the islanders had survived on their own resources as best they could. Cut off from other Marshallese, they made no copra for export and received no trade goods. Their physical condition in 1944 was poor. Their clothing was ragged, and the food shortage on Bikini was worse than on other atolls. American troops at Bikini immediately turned over to the islanders all the Japanese food supplies, which included canned meat, fish, and over a ton of rice. Regular visits every few months from military officials quickly brought the Bikinians into closer contact with the United States than they had ever been with the German or Japanese administrations. American ships brought food and supplies, as well as doctors who provided free medical care. By the end of 1945 the Americans had built a school and a medical dispensary at Bikini. Each was staffed by a Bikinian trained at Kwajalein by the Navy, with salaries paid by the Navy as

104

well. The U.S. military administration also provided textbooks, blackboards, and school supplies, while an education officer designed the curriculum and made frequent inspection trips to Bikini to evaluate the program. The United States provided for many of the Bikinians' needs, and the islanders thought highly of their American friends.

The Americans brought other innovations as well. An economic affairs officer encouraged the people to make handicrafts, which were eagerly purchased by Americans at Kwajalein, now being developed as a military base. The Navy also introduced a new form of community government, modeled after the local governments the British had successfully established in the Gilbert Islands. A council was created, consisting of the community's eleven family heads, or alabs. They in turn named Juda, their hereditary chief and descendant of the legendary Larkelon, as their chief, or magistrate under the American model.

The Bikinians quickly returned to their prewar traditions. They began to process coconuts into copra, which they sold in order to buy rice, flour, sugar, tea, coffee, kerosene lamps, utensils, fishhooks, clothes, and canoe sails. Men fished, gathered crops, and maintained their homes and canoes, while women tended to the household and wove baskets from coconut fronds and mats from pandanus leaves. The Bikinians, who were among the best sailors in the Marshall Islands, patched up their outrigger canoes after years of wartime disrepair. Eight 30-foot canoes were rigged with sails on 20-foot masts. Built mostly from the wood of breadfruit trees, each canoe was connected by a strong frame with the outrigger, which sat in the water nearly 10 feet away from the canoe. These boats, which required a three-person crew, could easily transport as many as seven or eight passengers the entire 26-mile length of the atoll. The islanders also built seven one-person paddle canoes for use in the immediate area of Bikini Island. They used their boats for fishing and for recreational sailing to islands across the atoll, thus breaking the monotony of life on the main island.

The entire community attended church every Sunday, when all work and most recreation were strictly prohibited. The services, led by a Bikini pastor trained by Protestant missionaries, combined Christian and Marshallese beliefs. The pastor conducted morning and afternoon services on Sundays as well as two afternoon services during the week, and church elders met on the first evening of each month to plan services and conduct church business.[1]

American ships had visited Bikini regularly since 1944, so the islanders were not surprised when the *Sumner* arrived at the atoll on February 6, 1946. The crew's first task was to blast three channels in the reef off Bikini Island so that a Navy LST, used during the war to put ashore tanks and equipment, could reach the beach in order to move the

167 islanders. Most of the Bikinians watched the ship curiously from the shoreline, while others raced out into the lagoon in their outrigger canoes to gather fish killed by the dynamite charges used by the *Sumner*'s crew.[2]

Back in Washington, the Navy viewed the removal of the Bikinians as only one small step in an otherwise massive logistical operation. In congressional testimony five days after Operation Crossroads was announced, Admiral Blandy made only one brief reference to the Bikinians, telling the House Naval Affairs Committee that the islanders would be "removed to another atoll, in accordance with proper procedure, and their interests safeguarded."

"Has our Government or the Navy Department yet undertaken any means to compensate those people?" asked Rep. Michael Bradley of Pennsylvania, concerned that the Bikinians would lose their livelihood from the destruction of the atoll's fish life. "There are not a great number of people, but they ought to be provided for."

"Yes," replied Blandy. "Their interests will be safeguarded in that respect."[3]

The Navy did not care which atoll the Bikinians selected, as long as they were out of the danger zone. A confidential Navy cable from the Marshall Islands recommended resettlement on "any of atolls to east or south [of] Bikini," and reported that the only relevant criterion was "drift of air and sea currents," while another cable asked for more information on "safe distance criteria."[4]

The task of telling the Bikinians they would have to leave their homeland fell to 52-year-old Navy Commodore Ben H. Wyatt, the military governor of the Marshall Islands. A native of Williamsburg, Kentucky, the soft-spoken Wyatt had been a 135-pound pint-sized end for Navy's football team, but his determination and speed earned him the nickname "Battling Ben," and he graduated in 1917 as one of the Naval Academy's top athletes. He became one of the Navy's first pilots and barnstormed around the United States in the 1920s. In 1936, Wyatt, lost in low-hanging clouds, almost caused an international incident by landing his plane on the Nuremberg airfield during a Nazi party rally. Hermann Goering demanded to see the brash pilot who had just landed in a restricted area, but Wyatt talked his way out of the problem and was released.[5]

Ten years later, Wyatt found himself in another hot spot that would require some persuasive talking. On Sunday morning, February 10, 1946, he flew to Bikini by seaplane from Kwajalein. The ostensible purpose of Wyatt's visit was to ask the Bikinians if the United States could use their atoll as an atomic test site, but he knew the islanders had no choice in the matter. President Truman had approved Bikini as the site for Operation Crossroads exactly one month earlier, and the *Sumner* was already blasting in the lagoon.

Church services had just ended when Wyatt arrived to meet with the people, who sat cross-legged on the ground under Bikini's coconut palms near their thatched-roof village. "Fortunately, the Commodore had the ability to translate the stark language of a Navy message into gentle words," the Navy reported. "It was an historic occasion, this impact of the accumulated scientific knowledge of centuries upon a primitive people, and it was staged with sincerity and poise."

Wyatt knew how to appeal to the Bikinians. He drew upon the Bible, the common denominator between the Bikinians and the Americans, and delivered a short homily. According to Wyatt's own account, he "compared the Bikinians to the children of Israel whom the Lord saved from their enemy and led into the Promised Land." He described the power of the atomic bomb and "the destruction it had wrought upon the enemy," and he told the people that the Americans "are trying to learn how to use it for the good of mankind and to end all world wars." The Navy had searched the entire world for the best place to test these powerful weapons, and Bikini was it. Wyatt then asked, "Would Juda and his people be willing to sacrifice their island for the welfare of all men?"

Wyatt provided two versions of the Bikinians' response. In 1952, six years after the events, he recalled that he left the Bikinians to discuss the issue among themselves. That afternoon, as he was walking along the beach, Juda approached him "and said that if the United States needed their island for a scientific experiment, the Bikinians were willing to surrender it."[6] However, in a message he sent to his superior officer just eight days after the meeting, Wyatt indicated that the Bikinians' decision was instantaneous. "After all plans had been explained to them and all personal questions answered their local chieftain, referred to as King Juda, arose and stated that the natives of Bikini were very proud to be a part of this wonderful undertaking," cabled Wyatt, "and if it was the desire of the United States Government for them to live elsewhere they would be very happy to do so."[7] Newspaper accounts, based on interviews with Wyatt, reported that Juda stood up and said, "If the United States government and the scientists of the world want to use our island and atoll for furthering development, which with God's blessing will result in kindness and benefit to all mankind, my people will be pleased to go elsewhere."[8]

In a matter of a few hours at most, the Bikinians had readily acquiesced in Wyatt's request, without even knowing where they would go. Why? Official Navy accounts notwithstanding, the Bikinians' decision was not based solely on a naive desire to see humanity benefit from testing the atomic bomb, as they had no real idea of the weapon's power. The people, though, were awed by America's defeat of Japan and the death of the six Japanese soldiers at Bikini, who had told them that Japan was the most powerful nation on earth. The islanders were also grateful to the Americans, who had brought them food and doctors and had constructed several community buildings on Bikini.

The persuasive power of the Americans, though, went beyond material largess. The Bikinians were devout Christians, and Wyatt's arrival right after church services on a Sunday was no coincidence, nor was his comparison of the Bikinians to the Children of Israel. His analogy undoubtedly had considerable emotional impact, despite the fact that it was inept; the Bikinians, after all, were about to be led *out* of their promised land, not into it. His description of the awesome power of the atomic bomb also led the people to believe that they were powerless to resist the wishes of the United States.

"This was a very difficult question," recalled Lore Kessibuki, a handsome, quiet alab, barely five feet tall, "but we didn't feel we had any other choice but to obey the Americans."[9] Some people did not want to leave, remembered Lore, but "that group didn't win because we were quite afraid. . . . We were so afraid of the words that that man said because he said you need to leave this atoll, because we're going to use it." The people wanted to please their American friends, but that friendship was tinged with fear, perhaps with memories of American planes strafing Bikini and killing Japanese who opposed them. "We just wanted to follow the words of the American man," said Lore. "It had just been the end of the war. We were still afraid and we wanted to heed his words."[10]

The option of staying on Bikini and telling the United States to look elsewhere was simply not realistic. Even a *New Yorker* cartoon depicted that alternative as a joke. With battleships in the background and a Navy LST on the shore, a Bikinian with a pot belly and wearing shorts and a Panama hat is shown talking to two Navy officials. "The residents have voted two to one against your conducting your experiments in this vicinity," he tells them.[11] The Bikinians, though, knew they had to go. Wyatt knew it, too, but he still went through the motions. And back in Washington, there was laughter at Admiral Blandy's press conference when he was asked whether the Bikinians had been told the atomic bomb was going to be dropped there. "You couldn't comment on their reaction?" asked one reporter. Laughing, Blandy said he didn't know.[12]

Several different factors—America's power, the destructive force of the bomb, the islanders' fear, Wyatt's invocation of the Bible—may have contributed to the Bikinians' decision. Another possibility remains, though, and that is that the Bikinians were willing to move because

Wyatt told them it would only be for a short time, a few years perhaps, in order for the Navy to conduct two tests in 1946 and a third in early 1947.

There is no contemporaneous record of what transpired on that Sunday afternoon at Bikini. The press reports and Navy history were based exclusively on Wyatt's recollections. The evidence, though, strongly suggests that he only asked the Bikinians to leave temporarily. There were no plans to use Bikini beyond the 1947 underwater bomb test. Moreover, little was known in early 1946 about the lingering effects of radiation in the environment, so there would have been no reason to suspect that Bikini would remain off-limits for much beyond the testing period.

Other evidence comes from statements of Admiral Blandy. For example, at Blandy's press conference the day the tests were announced, a reporter asked whether the Bikinians would be moved permanently, to which Blandy responded, "I don't think that it should necessarily be permanently."[13] At a later press conference he said that Bikini would be a restricted security area "for some time after the tests," and in several speeches, lectures, and interviews after the tests, Blandy said that the Bikinians' return to their atoll was being measured in terms of months. The import of Blandy's statements was clear: The Navy's intent was to return the Bikinians home sometime after Operation Crossroads.[14]

Blandy's statement was not an isolated incident. "All I can tell them," Commodore Wyatt told newsmen in November 1946, "is that they can't go home now."[15] And *Infantry Journal* reported in its April 1946 issue that "unless the resulting radioactivity is permanent, and experts are confident that it will not be, the inhabitants will be permitted to return to their homes when the operation is completed."[16]

The Bikinians clearly believed that they would be able to return home shortly. "The Navy told us we could live anywhere, even on a sand island," they told a Navy anthropologist in 1950. "The Navy would take care of us, we were told, until we went back to Bikini."[17] Another anthropologist who interviewed numerous Bikinians less than two years after they moved concluded that "these people understood that their enforced absence from the atoll was to be only short-lived."[18]

Navy records do not disclose whether Wyatt told the Bikinians when—or even if—they could move back to their atoll. Perhaps he never confronted the issue directly, promising the people instead that they could return home at some vague time in the future. "That was a tough job," he told reporters several weeks after he returned from Bikini. "If one man in that crowd said, 'I will not leave,' then it meant trouble and bad feelings. I told the story as simply as I could, and made no commitments."[19] Wyatt, though, was aware of potential legal problems that might result from the islanders' displacement and relocation. When he asked the Navy before flying to Bikini what commitments he could make to the people concerning reparations, he was told to tell them they could submit claims for damages.[20]

Wyatt told the Bikinians that they were free to move to any Marshallese atoll that they selected outside the danger area—the two atolls closest to Bikini—but their choice of a relocation site was made more difficult because Wyatt arrived at Bikini with Jeimata Kabua, an iroij lablab, or paramount chief, who asserted control over Bikini. Kabua suggested that the people move to Lae or Ujae, two inhabited atolls under his control. Ujae, though, posed serious navigational and beaching problems, and Lae, with a land area of just half a square mile and a small lagoon, was too small and limited in its resources to support an additional 167 people.

A third possibility was Rongerik, an atoll some 125 miles east of Bikini. The Bikinians were somewhat familiar with Rongerik, because it is close to Rongelap, where several Bikinians had previously traveled. Unlike Lae and Ujae, it was uninhabited, so resettlement there would permit the Bikinians to live their lives without interacting with other Marshallese. Kabua, though, strongly opposed resettlement there because it was not under his authority; it belonged to Lajore, another paramount chief. Moreover, its land area and lagoon were only a quarter the size of Bikini's, and it had few coconut trees.

The Navy, meanwhile, mounted a campaign to assure the public that the Bikinians were actually going to be much better off by leaving Bikini. "The atoll itself is unhealthy and produces little food besides coconuts and fish," wrote a retired Navy admiral in a *Newsweek* column, while Wyatt's chief of staff told reporters that Rongerik was better than Bikini. "It has more coconut, pandanus and breadfruit trees and is richer, from the natives' point of view," he said.[21]

The Bikini leaders deliberated for several days, and many began to rethink their decision to leave altogether. "The decision was okay with some," remembered Lore, "but most of us said 'no' because of the great sorrow we felt when thinking about leaving our homeland."[22] Finally, four days after Wyatt's visit, the council voted, and nine of the eleven alabs named Rongerik as their first choice. Four days later the other two alabs selected Rongerik so all the families could remain together.[23] Lore, one of the eleven alabs, explained that the other alabs selected Rongerik because it was uninhabited. "Another thing that was in their minds as they considered," he added, "was that we would not be staying there long. 'We'll go and stay there until we can return back to Bikini.'"[24]

The Bikinians, whose lives had been suddenly changed forever by the Americans, had just as suddenly changed Marshallese society by openly defying their own paramount chief. Part of this decision was due to the fact that they had seen Kabua only rarely, and not at all during the war when they were forced to garrison and feed the Japanese soldiers. These soldiers, moreover, told the people that Bikini belonged to Emperor Hirohito and that Marshallese paramount chiefs no longer had power. The postwar council system imposed by the U.S. Navy also undermined the iroij lablab, because he had no function in this new local government. The tax levied by the Americans was paid by the Bikinians themselves with money earned from the sale of handicrafts, and they gave no copra to the chief because they had made none since the war.

Kabua had no role in the Bikinians' world. They did not formally recognize him as the owner of Bikini, and he had not assisted them. In defying his wish to move to an atoll in his realm, they had, in effect, thrown in their lots with the Americans, who were providing for their every need and seemed to them to be more of an iroij lablab than Kabua. Lajore, the paramount chief of Rongerik, readily consented to the Bikinians' move, but the Navy did not compensate him or clarify Kabua's relationship with the Bikinians. If the relocation was to be only temporary, though, no such arrangements would be necessary.[25]

Preparations for the move proceeded rapidly. As a precaution against future lawsuits, Navy surveyors photographed each dwelling on Bikini and counted each family's coconut and pandanus trees. The Bikinians, meanwhile, dismantled their church and meeting hall for transport to Rongerik. Their homes and all the other buildings on Bikini, though, were to be destroyed, and the Navy transplanted 2,500 palm trees from Bikini and Rongerik "for the purpose of improving the appearance" of Kwajalein, as Wyatt wrote in a confidential April 13 memorandum.[26]

An LST landing craft arrived at Bikini from Kwajalein on February 25 with equipment and supplies for Rongerik, including tents, cement, roofing, shovels, buckets, saws, axes, masonry tools, 30,000 gallons of fresh water, one month's supply of food for 160 people, and a U.S. flag.[27] An advance party of twenty-two Bikinians loaded the dismantled buildings and left for Rongerik the next day with fifteen Seabees. The work crews built a complete village there under the supervision of Comdr. Harold W. Grieve of Los Angeles, described by Wyatt as "one of America's best-known architects and decorators."[28]

Back at Bikini, the islanders prepared to abandon the atoll. They packed up their few belongings—bedding, fishing equipment, kerosene lamps, pandanus leaves to thatch their new houses, and Bibles and Congregational hymnals left decades earlier by missionaries. The Bikinians, who had never seen movies before, were entertained on the deck of the *Sumner* with Mickey Mouse cartoons, a Roy Rogers western, and a Hollywood bedroom farce. The tempo of activity increased as Navy photographers and commercial newsreel teams arrived during the last week of February. Much to the displeasure of Kabua, Juda became known in the American press as "King Juda."[29]

Both Bikini and Rongerik were declared "native areas" and thus off-limits for Navy personnel. "There will be no unnecessary communication with the natives and no attempt to molest them in any way whatsoever," ordered the officer in charge of the resettlement.[30] "The operation may be said to have political implications of a supra-national character," read another order, "and it is desired that it be accomplished without any unfortunate incidents of any kind." Nevertheless, a 1948 census of the Bikinians on Rongerik contained several light-skinned youngsters whose unwed mothers listed "Navy" and "Seabee" as the father.[31]

The removal of the Bikinians became a major media event. The islanders had never received so much attention, and they seemed to enjoy it. "The young girls were particularly susceptible and giggled and posed as soon as a lens was turned their way," wrote a *National Geographic* reporter.[32] On Sunday, March 3, photographers and newsreel teams filmed the islanders' last church service on Bikini. The congregation, dressed in starched white shirts and dresses, sat on palm leaf matting out in the open where their church had once stood, as their pastor sat on a bench leading the service. Some cameramen were not satisfied with their angles, so the people obliged by repeating the service twice. Publicity was so intense that the demands of news agencies and Navy photographers forced a one-day postponement of the Bikinians' departure. "We were very confused," recollected Kilon Bauno, a Bikini elder. "I couldn't understand why they had to do everything so many times."[33]

On the morning of Wednesday, March 6, the Bikinians decorated the graves in the community cemetery with flowers and green coconut fronds. In a brief prayer, they bade farewell to their ancestors, entrusting their souls to the care of God. The mood of the simple and moving ceremony was unfortunately jarred by the needs of cameramen, though, who again had the Bikinians repeat their prayers. As movie cameras whirred, Wyatt and the Bikinians then reenacted their February 10 meeting.[34] "Now then James," said Wyatt to his Gilbertese translator, "tell them please that the United States Government now wants to turn this great destructive power into something good for the benefit of mankind, and that these experiments here at Bikini are the first step in that direction. They have heard of our plans for their evacuation, James. Will you ask King Juda to get up and tell us what his people think and if they are willing to go."

This time, though, Juda's ominous response reflected the fear and uncertainty about the move that Wyatt had not detected in February. "We are willing to go," answered Juda, adding, "Everything is in God's hands."

"Well," Wyatt retorted, "you tell them and King Juda that everything being in God's hands, it cannot be other than good."

Juda had served up Wyatt's biblical references back to him. The Bikinians knew they were powerless, and Juda invoked the only help he could; it was all up to God. Wyatt, though, wanted Juda to repeat his words from February—that his people would be pleased to go else-where—so the cameras kept rolling for at least seven more takes of the reenactment. Wyatt even added a new twist to his pitch. "Now, tell them over there at Rongerik we haven't got any flies and we hope they don't have any trouble with them," he said several times. Juda, how-ever, kept repeating that everything was in God's hands, so Wyatt finally gave up. Obviously bored by the repeated reenactments and botching his lines, he turned to the Navy cameraman at one point. "All right, is that all?" he asked into the camera, and then walked away from the meeting, leaving the Bikinians seated on the ground.[35]

The LST had returned from Rongerik and was now perched at the tip of the beach, its loading ramp lowered into the sand. A steady stream of men, women, and children began to pass back and forth from their houses to the loading ramp, carrying boxes, bundles, chickens, and nearly a ton of pandanus thatch panels from deserted dwellings. By now, though, the departure had been delayed a day. "The publicity requirements received priority," noted a Navy report.[36]

By Thursday morning, March 7, the last of the cargo was stowed. The Bikinians filed aboard, the loading ramp retracted, and the LST backed down the beach into the lagoon. The Bikinians crowded the rails. Until now, none of the islanders had shown much emotion over leaving. But now, the frenzied activity was over. Watching their islands fade in the distance, the enormity of the situation began to sink in. Some people sang songs of farewell; others wept. Most were silent. Some told a *Life* magazine photographer that they would return to Bikini one day.[37]

Lore Kessibuki stood on deck for hours until the LST had cleared the Eneu channel and he could no longer see any of Bikini's islands. He then composed a song, both sad and hopeful, which remains the Bikinians' anthem today:

> No longer can I stay; it's true.
> No longer can I live in peace and harmony
> And rest on my sleeping mat and pillow.
> No longer can I stay on my island;
> I must leave all the things there.

The thought overwhelms me and leaves me helpless.
My spirit has to travel, far away, lost
   Until it is caught in a great current.
Only then can I find peace.

The LST reached Rongerik the next day. Juda and some of the alabs went ashore in small landing crafts to assign each family a tent dwelling. Late in the afternoon the LST moved up to the beach and the loading ramp was lowered. The Bikinians streamed down, carrying all they could, and sought out their new homes. Soon the beach was littered with all their belongings. Floodlights lit the area until midnight, when all the possessions were finally secured in the Bikinians' new home. "The initial reaction of the people to their new home was one of satisfaction without enthusiasm," said an internal Navy report. "In some quarters there was a feeling of dispiritedness, and this was not easily dissipated."[38] A jocular reference to the islanders by Adm. DeWitt C. Ramsey, vice chief of naval operations, may have unwittingly revealed the Navy's strategy in the move. In a speech after the move, he praised the Bikinians' "contribution to the advancement of science and humanity," adding that "perhaps they were somewhat influenced by the homes our Seabees built for them on Rongerik."[39]

At precisely 8:00 A.M. on Sunday, March 10, in a solemn ceremony attended by all the Bikinians, the American flag was raised for the first time over Rongerik, flown from a gaff lashed to a coconut tree. "It was raised and lowered with military punctiliousness daily thereafter by the islanders," the Navy reported.[40] Less than a month had passed since the Bikinians had been told they would have to abandon their home. One military official called the removal "one hell of a good sales job." A *New York Times* article on the Bikinians, entitled "The Strange People from Bikini," stated, "Primitive they are, but they love one another and the American visitors who took their home."[41]

Back in Washington, the Navy announced that the move was successful, calling it the Bikinians' "contribution to the advancement of science," and Admiral Blandy said that "their chief states they are very proud to be a part of this great undertaking."[42] The Navy assured the public that the "natives are delighted, enthusiastic about the atom bomb, which has already brought them prosperity and a new and promising future," and Commodore Wyatt said he was pleased that "everything seems to be going so well." One Associated Press story, quoting a Navy spokesman, indicated that the move was actually a blessing in disguise. "Rongerik is about three times larger than Bikini. . . . Coconuts here are three or four times as large as those on Bikini and food is plentiful."[43]

Commodore Wyatt flew to Rongerik to visit the Bikinians several weeks after the move. At a formal ceremony in the islanders' transplanted thatched-roof church, he presented three illustrated books on America to Juda and Josia, the schoolteacher, who then led the community in songs to their American guests. The first was "My Faith Looks Up to Thee," which they sang from a missionary hymnal. Then, although none of them spoke English, they sang from memory "God Bless America" and "Good Night Ladies." In appreciation, Commodore Wyatt turned to the group and said, "Such lovely voices deserve a finer church," and he promised to send some beams from Kwajalein to support one side of the community church, which was sagging.[44]

In New York, meanwhile, the United Nations was looking for a permanent site in Connecticut or north of New York City. New York Rep. Sol Bloom urged the residents of the two areas to follow the Bikinians' example and leave their homes, explaining that the islanders agreed to leave Bikini to "help preserve world peace." A letter to the editor of the *New York Times* contrasted the actions of the Bikinians with the "selfish attitude" of the wealthy suburbanites who did not want the UN headquarters located on their land, adding, "This shows how much we have to learn from these Bikinians who practice what they preach." A State Department spokesman, however, warned that there would be no transfer of sovereignty over suburban land. The United Nations would get the land by paying a fair price for it, he said, and the legal rights of the residents would be protected.[45]

13

"We Want Radiation-Sick Animals, But Not Radiation-Dead Animals"

Admiral Blandy was under tremendous pressure to hold Operation Crossroads quickly. Nearly all the civilian scientists and consultants who agreed to participate had to return to university teaching jobs or graduate school by September. Moreover, military personnel and scientific resources from Los Alamos Laboratory were rapidly declining from their wartime peaks. Army and Navy budgets were about to be slashed, and the target vessels, especially the obsolete ships, could not be made available indefinitely. The Navy had 1,500 combatant ships at the war's end, but only 270 would be in the active fleet two years later. Meanwhile, the armed forces had been reduced from 12 million men and women in June 1945 to 3 million a year later.[1]

On the other hand, Operation Crossroads was a massive undertaking that required an extraordinary amount of planning, training, and coordination. New scientific instruments and special cameras had to be designed and tested. More than 10,000 instruments were to be placed on target ships, nontarget ships, aircraft, and the islands around the atoll. Some devices were relatively simple, while others were developed specifically for use at Bikini, covering a wide range of scientific fields, including radiation, electronics, radiometry, technical photography, wave motion, oceanography, and electromagnetic propagation. Tens of thousands of men had to be assembled, inoculated, fed, trained, assigned space, and transported two-thirds of the way across the Pacific.

116

Scientists had to develop a radiological safety program to protect the participants as well as Marshallese inhabitants of nearby atolls. More than 200 support ships were needed, and nearly 100 target vessels had to be prepared. Salvage facilities were needed to repair ships, make other target vessels seaworthy for the trip back across the Pacific, and destroy those that could not be salvaged. The task of simply assembling and supplying the ships and men equaled the size and complexity of a major wartime operation; indeed, Joint Task Force One would prove to be four times larger than the forces that invaded Guadalcanal.[2]

Faced with these conflicting pressures, Blandy announced on January 24 that the first test would be an air drop code-named Able, and the second test, Baker, would be exploded at or just below the surface of the water and would be held about six weeks later. "It is expected to produce waves a hundred feet high, winds reaching a thousand miles an hour, and heat measured in hundreds of millions of degrees," wrote Blandy. The third shot, Charlie, would be detonated several thousand feet below the open ocean. The engineering problems in constructing a bathysphere capable of holding the bomb and withstanding the tremendous water pressure precluded scheduling this test before the spring of 1947. "Here," said Blandy, "we are really exploring the unknown, and no one can be sure what the results will be. . . . Among the things that have to be considered here are whether this bomb might set up an endless chain reaction in the ocean, or radioactivize the water over large areas."[3]

The Navy's inclusion of modern ships in the target array lent support to its assertion that the tests were not merely intended to demonstrate the power of the atomic bomb, but were actually weapons-effects tests whose results would influence ship design and naval tactics.[4] "This operation is a joint scientific-military venture," Blandy said repeatedly. "It is not a military operation with scientific advisers."[5] He told the press in January that the bombs would be tested on ninety-three target ships and that Joint Task Force One would use about fifty support vessels. A total of about 20,000 military and civilian personnel would be involved, he said. Within three months, this number would double, as 41,963 men, 37 women nurses, 150 aircraft, and more than 200 ships traveled to the Marshall Islands to participate in what the *New York Times* described as the largest and "most stupendous single set of experiments in history."[6] Operation Crossroads was, above all else, an extravaganza. It was the grandest scientific experiment ever, more exhaustively photographed, reported, and measured than any previous event in history.

The logistical problems facing Blandy were immense. His staff prepared an operation plan several thousand pages long with twenty-nine annexes, many with appendices running hundreds of pages in length. When Oppenheimer and Groves saw the operation plan, they wrote that "it would be difficult to get it more complicated."[7] Described in overblown terms by the Navy as "so vast and detailed as to suggest the Book of Fate itself," the plan subdivided Joint Task Force One into eight task groups and detailed all aspects of Crossroads, covering communications and electronics, photography, instrumentation, safety and security, evacuation of Bikini, reentry, and inspection of the target ships. The detail was staggering, including, for example, exposure times for the 10,000 most important photographs. Virtually all contingencies were anticipated, including a typhoon plan, air-sea rescue, and even evacuation of the Bikinians from Rongerik. An air transport unit, dubbed "Crossroads Airline" and consisting of twenty C-46 aircraft and giant C-54s, was also established to provide regular airlift service for personnel, equipment, and supplies between Roswell Army Air Field in New Mexico and Kwajalein, as was an air shuttle serving Kwajalein, Bikini, and Enewetak.[8]

In both statistics and fanfare, Operation Crossroads was enormous. Just feeding the 42,000 men posed a major logistical challenge, as daily requirements included 4,000 pounds of coffee, 11,000 pounds of sugar, 22,000 pounds of flour, 38,000 pounds of fruit, 40,000 pounds of meat, 89,000 pounds of vegetables, and 70,000 candy bars. Plans were even made for a special cancellation stamp for 200,000 pieces of mail to be sent from Bikini on July 1, bearing the postmark "Atom Bomb Test, Bikini Atoll."[9]

Work at Bikini began with the arrival of the *Sumner* and *Bowditch* in early February to sound the lagoon, chart the shoal areas, establish navigational aids, and secure a nine-square-mile area to house the flotilla of target ships. The only available hydrographic charts of Bikini were Japanese, and they were inaccurate, so new charts were prepared. The names of many of the atoll's twenty-six islands were difficult to spell and would have caused havoc in military dispatches, so a new set of code names was adopted. The main islands of Bikini, Eneu, and Nam remained the same, but Ionchebi became Ion, and Bokoaetokutoku was shortened to Boku. Aomoen was changed to Amen and Eniman to Eman, but Amen and Eman started to cause confusion, so Eman's code name was soon changed to Prayer.[10]

Bikini's lagoon was dotted with coral heads that posed a serious obstruction to navigation. Composed of coral and algae, they rose up nearly 180 feet from the lagoon floor, and many extended up to the surface. Using over 100 tons of dynamite, Navy divers blasted off the tops of dozens of coral heads and huge explosions periodically rocked the peaceful lagoon, followed by clouds of spray rising hundreds of feet into the air.[11] Japanese mines, which had to be removed before the arrival of the target fleet and support ships, posed a more serious hazard. After the war, the Navy had located and removed thirty-five contact mines inside the approach to the Eneu channel. Some of the swept mines had exploded when hit by rifle fire, but nearly half were sunk without exploding and lay on the lagoon's floor near the channel. The Navy quickly searched out these mines and traced Japanese military sources familiar with the mining of the atoll. All mines in the Eneu channel were eventually destroyed, together with five others that were found washed up on other islands in the atoll.[12]

Scientists on the *Bowditch,* a 400-foot, one-time Grace Lines cargo and passenger ship, conducted detailed biological, geological, and hydrographic surveys of Bikini's lagoon. The ship's diverse group of scientists included zoologists, geologists, botanists, ichthyologists, meteorologists, and entomologists, with "about the only ology absent being astrology," as *Life* noted.[13] The scientists were drawn from numerous universities as well as the U.S. Geological Survey, the Interior Department's Fish and Wildlife Service, the Smithsonian Institution, and Wood's Hole Oceanographic Institution. Botanists surveyed the atoll's plant life, while other scientists and commercial fishermen conducted a census of the atoll's fish, animal, and coral life before and after the tests to determine the biological effects of the bomb on fisheries and animal life. Even a control group of fish and wildlife was taken from the neighboring atolls of Enewetak, Rongelap, and Rongerik. Over 20,000 fish were caught, including many formerly unknown species, and all were shipped back to Washington for study. Unfortunately, 98 percent of the fish were lost when the ship carrying them ran aground near San Francisco on September 13, 1946.[14]

Wave-motion experts surveyed Bikini lagoon's currents to predict the dispersion of radioactive material, while geologists studied the reef and beaches and the water exchange between the lagoon and the open ocean. A network of weather stations was established at Enewetak, Kwajalein, Tarawa, Marcus, and Wake to predict Bikini's weather, and their reports were augmented by numerous ship stations in the Marshall Islands, which sent weather information to Bikini every three hours. A complete photographic survey of the atoll was conducted, and the main islands of Bikini and Eneu were periodically sprayed with DDT. Pressure recorders and seismographs were placed on the lagoon's floor and on various islands to measure shock waves, spectrographs were to record the spectrum of the flash, and bolometers would indicate the radiant heat. It was no exaggeration for one of the scientists to write several years later that Bikini "has become perhaps the most thoroughly known atoll on earth."[15]

The Army's biological warfare division brought living bacteria to Bikini, sealed in eighty aluminum cases, to analyze mutations during radiation exposure. The Department of Agriculture, hoping to learn the effects of an atomic bomb on soil fertility, brought out soil samples from Maine, Georgia, and Texas, from which seeds would be grown after the tests.[16] Joint Task Force One also sponsored numerous experiments to detect and measure Bikini's explosions at sites around the world, including Hawaii, Wake, Guam, Midway, the Philippines, Australia, Peru, Puerto Rico, and Germany.[17]

In its first few public announcements, Joint Task Force One made no mention of using test animals at Bikini, and Blandy, concerned about pressure from animal protection societies, hinted in congressional testimony that no animals would be used. "The question is now under debate," he told a Senate committee the day the tests were announced. "Some of the scientific personnel hope that they can get all the information required from instruments placed on board the ships which would indicate what would happen to the crews of the ships." He made the same point at another hearing, but one month later he reversed his decision, although his public announcement stated only that a "minimum number" of animals would be used.[18]

In fact, an entire ship, the Navy attack transport *Burleson*, was deployed in late June to bring out to Bikini 200 pigs, 200 mice, 60 guinea pigs, 204 goats, and 5,000 rats. Each animal was tattooed with an identification number, because tags might be chewed off. The *Burleson* was outfitted with pens, feeding troughs, and 80 tons of hay and grain for the goats and pigs. Its steel decks were covered with a layer of concrete to provide sure footing for the animals, and special drainage and disposal chutes were constructed for sanitary purposes. "We regret that some of these animals may be sacrificed," Blandy wrote, "but we are more concerned about the men and women of the next generations than we are about the animals of this one. The Army and Navy simply can't be starry-eyed about this phase of the experiment."[19]

The 5,664 animals were to be placed on twenty-two target ships in the same positions as a human crew in battle, from decks and bridges to turrets, gun-tubs, and engine rooms. Some goats were covered with sunblock creams, while others had their hair clipped to human length for complete exposure.[20] Some of the pigs, whose skin is like a human's, were dressed in standard Navy antiflash suits and smeared with antiflash lotion. An Operation Crossroads press release stated that the animals would be treated well: "It is not the intention to kill a large portion of the animals since dead animals are of less value for study." As the head of the Navy's medical section put it, "We want radiation-sick animals, but not radiation-dead animals." Joint Task Force One, blithely assuming that the radiation diseases would soon pass, said that the animals would be returned to Washington, "where studies will be made until they die a natural death."[21]

With more than 700 cameras planned for use in the tests, the demand for photographers far exceeded the supply. About 500 photographers were eventually recruited, including Louis Hagemayer, one of the photographers who had filmed Billy Mitchell's battleship bomb test in 1921.[22] A total of 328 still and aerial-motion cameras were installed in every available location in the dozens of B-29 and C-54 airplanes that would fly over the blasts; some planes carried as many as twenty-eight still and motion-picture cameras. Other cameras were installed to photograph the readings on instruments at the moment of the blast, all timed automatically at one ten-thousandth of a second for the exact moment of detonation. Photographic planes had to be at their precise positions at the exact moment of the blast in order to ensure accuracy of timing, and constant rehearsals were held in Albuquerque and later at Bikini. Even then, photography would be a gamble; cameras on target ships faced certain destruction, and film spoilage from gamma radiation was a threat to surviving film. Indeed, photographic gelatin in a movie camera six miles from the Trinity site had been scorched so badly that it bubbled.[23]

The explosions were to be the most thoroughly photographed moment in history. Nearly half the world's supply of film was at Bikini for the tests, and photographers prepared specialized equipment that would take 1 million pictures in the first few seconds after the Able explosion. The AAF alone expected to take 9 million pictures; its motion-picture cameramen would use enough film during the first four seconds of the Able shot to make four full-length Hollywood feature pictures.[24] Among the cameras at Bikini was the world's largest still camera, with a giant 48-inch focal length telephoto lens capable of photographing legibly the dial of a wristwatch from a quarter of a mile away, a remarkable feat for 1946. Sixty high-speed movie cameras were designed to take 8,000 pictures a second and slower ones, shooting 3,500 pictures per second, would stretch each second of the explosion into three and one-half minutes of film. Cameras at Eneu Island were installed inside lead-walled vaults, whose doors were designed to close automatically after filming, thus protecting the film from exposure to the harmful effects of gamma radiation. Plans were also made to use television cameras to record the explosion for remote observers.[25]

Nearly as dramatic as the B-29 delivering the bomb would be unpiloted drone planes that would be radio-guided directly into Test Able's atomic cloud, many miles closer than manned planes could go. On the other side of the cloud, manned "mother" planes would "catch" them and lead them back to Kwajalein. These drones, then known as remote-controlled planes, were equipped with automatic cameras, telemeters, radiation-measuring devices, electronic recording instruments, and air filters and air collector bags to gather samples of the radioactive cloud. Four of the drones, huge B-17 Flying Fortresses, nicknamed Babe I, II, III and IV, would be launched from Enewetak Atoll, 200 miles west of Bikini. Navy drones from the aircraft carriers *Shangri-La* and *Saidor* just outside Bikini's lagoon would fly close to the blast and then back to Roi Island at Kwajalein. A few B-17s had been launched without crews in World War II, but they were deliberately crashed on targets with their cargoes of explosives. Operation Crossroads would mark the first successful pilotless takeoff, flight, and landing of a B-17.[26]

A reliable communications network was essential for both press broadcasts and teletype, as well as for Joint Task Force One's needs, such as radio signals for remote-controlled scientific instruments and control of drone boats and aircraft. The Navy's complex plan, developed in reliance on joint Army-Navy operations during the war, called for 203 channels and 348 frequencies, many of which were then utilized unofficially to exchange idle chatter throughout the lagoon. One officer denounced what he called the "adolescent brains of the Task Force personnel," and he urged others to "catch the juvenile sailors while actually engaged in sending their unmentionable stories over the air."[27]

The 3,000 Army personnel at Bikini were assigned to assess the damage to Army equipment exposed at varying distances from below Zero-point, the point of explosion. Joint Task Force One drew up detailed plans to place Army Corps of Engineers materiel, such as construction tractors and firefighting equipment, aboard attack transports and LSTs stationed between one-half mile and two miles from the bull's-eye. Similarly, Signal Corps equipment, such as switchboards, generators, batteries, and wires, were exposed on the decks of the target ships, as were ammunition, chemical warfare gas cylinders, jeeps, tanks, machine guns, rocket launchers, fuel, clothing, medical supplies, animal furs, rubber, paints, canned meats and fruits, Vienna sausages, and even seven-jeweled wrist watches.[28]

Both the target ships and the support vessels required considerable remodeling. Television, radio teletype facilities, and broadcast studios were installed both on the *Mount McKinley,* Admiral Blandy's flagship, and the *Appalachian,* the press ship. Special laboratories and instrumentation facilities were built on the *Haven, Wharton, Avery Island,* and *Kenneth Whiting,* while the *Burleson,* now dubbed "Noah's Ark," was, in the Navy's words, turned into "a great dirtless farm, a palatial hotel for animals." The *Cumberland Sound* and *Albemarle,* large seaplane tenders, were modified to accommodate the two atomic bombs, making them the only mobile storage and assembly sites for nuclear weapons, four years before aircraft carriers were modified for this purpose. All target ships, meanwhile, were carefully inspected and photographed both before and after the tests to document the damage. Some of the more war-weary ships required extensive repairs, and one of the most difficult tasks was making the vessels watertight so that pumping would not be required to keep them afloat.[29] In addition, seventy-one Navy airplanes were to be placed on the decks of twenty-two different target ships, and two seaplanes were to be moored between one and one-half and two miles from Zeropoint.[30]

The list of federal agencies, private companies, contractors, universities, and other organizations affiliated with Operation Crossroads seemed endless. More than fifteen universities were involved, as were dozens of private companies and organizations, including Western Electric, Westinghouse, Raytheon, Bell Telephone, Monsanto, Kodak, Polaroid, RCA, General Electric, Fairchild Camera, Lenox Hill Hospital in New York, the Mount Wilson Observatory, and even the American Red Cross.[31] "Planning this test has not been easy," Admiral Blandy wrote in the June 1946 issue of *Collier's*. "We who have worked on it during the past few months often thought the name 'Operation Crossroads' might well be changed to 'Operation Headache.'"[32]

14

"It Will Merely Be a Waste of Money and Effort to Take These Ships to the Test"

Planning for the technical aspects of Operation Crossroads was hampered both by ongoing Army-Navy rivalries and by the diverging views of scientists and the military. For example, the Navy's first proposed target array, submitted to the LeMay Subcommittee in December 1945, would have placed one aircraft carrier 1,000 yards from the Zeropoint, two battleships and one submarine at 1,500 yards, and the remainder at greater distances. The AAF, however, conceding that there could be a bombing error of up to 300 yards, proposed adding more ships to the array within this 300-yard area to compensate for a possible error. This factor, together with the revelation in January 1946 that pressures at Hiroshima and Nagasaki fell off more rapidly with distance than had been previously guessed, led Joint Task Force One planners to favor greater concentration of the ships in the center of the target array.[1]

The diverse views of the Navy and the AAF as to the purposes of the tests and their respective roles in them bore an eerie resemblance to the Navy–Air Corps dispute in 1921, when the Navy wanted to study the effects of air-dropped bombs on ships but Billy Mitchell wanted simply to sink the ships. Twenty-five years later at Bikini, the Navy still wanted to preserve as many ships as possible, while the AAF wanted to sink as many as possible. The Navy's rationale was that the ships served essentially as complex pressure instruments to record the blast effects of the new weapon. Accordingly, the lethal limits of the blast could be determined only by saving the ships. The AAF, on the other hand, faced with the task of delivering the bomb, took the position that a large number of target ships should be within the 1,000-yard circle of the bull's-eye. Otherwise, a miss of more than 300 yards—certainly a possibility from 30,000 feet—would do little damage and thus defeat the entire purpose of the tests.

The impasse was referred to the Joint Chiefs' Military Advisory Board. When it first considered the issue in December 1945, the board sided with the AAF, directing that the battleship *Nevada* be located 500 feet from the Zeropoint, eight times closer than the Navy proposed, with the other target ships close by. Within two months, though, it changed its position, deciding on February 4 that the target ships should be more scattered. The very next day the AAF formed a committee to protest the decision, pointing out that there were ballistic weaknesses in the bomb that might cause a serious error in the drop.[2]

Leslie Groves's top advisors, including Oppenheimer, Los Alamos director Norris E. Bradbury, James Conant, and British physicists William G. Penney and Sir Geoffrey Taylor, all believed that the proposed arrangement of ships was unsatisfactory and recommended a maximum concentration of ships at the center of the target. In addition to the *Nevada*, Groves told Blandy, four other capital ships should be placed at distances no greater than 300 yards from the Zeropoint, and all the other capital ships should be placed as close to that circle as possible. He did not mince his words to Blandy. "The proposed positions of [some ships] would give information of no value unless the bomb was very inaccurately placed. In their proposed locations it will merely be a waste of money and effort to take these ships to the test."[3]

Nineteen separate target arrays were eventually considered. In the end, twenty-four ships would be jampacked into the immediate bull's-eye area, a space normally used by only two or three capital ships at anchor and only one at sea, and all ninety-five target ships would be moored in an area where the Navy would normally place only fourteen vessels, or five in a cruising formation at sea.[4]

The AAF, led by General LeMay, also insisted that every ship in the target array carry a full load of fuel and ammunition. "LeMay wanted a big spectacle there, I suspect, . . . of all these ships burning," recalled Vice Adm. Frederick L. Ashworth.[5] All the scientists, though, were opposed. "We could imagine a situation where we might burst the oil tanks on some ship and get the lagoon covered with oil and have a fire start and lose all the scientific results right there," said Ralph Sawyer, technical director of Crossroads. He proposed instead that fuel loads and ammunitions on ships near the center of the target array range from one-tenth to one-third of capacity and the ammunition loadings not exceed two-thirds of the normal load.[6]

Nevertheless, LeMay held his ground. "He used to have a cigar that he switched around from one side of his mouth to the other," said Sawyer. "So Blandy asked everybody what they thought about oil and fuel. LeMay said, 'Every ship must have full loading of oil, ammunition and fuel.'" Sawyer and Deak Parsons made their points, and after an hour of discussion Blandy went around the room again. "LeMay shifted his cigar to the other side of his mouth and said, 'Every ship must have full loading of oil, of fuel and of ammunition.' So Blandy said, 'Well, very good, gentlemen, I think I have all the information I need.'" Blandy sided with the scientists.[7]

Similar arguments plagued the question of how the Able blast was to be delivered. Early discussions favored a tower shot of between 100 and 300 feet, as at the Trinity test in New Mexico. The obvious advantages of accuracy and convenience, though, were outweighed by an expected reduction in the effectiveness of the bomb explosion. In addition, a tower shot would have been similar to the second test, which was still being planned as a surface shot, and there were difficulties in constructing a high enough tower at Bikini.[8]

Preliminary discussions among Los Alamos, the AAF, and the Navy assumed the Able bomb would be suspended from a blimp anchored to one of the target ships or from a balloon. However, Norris Bradbury rejected the idea of using a tower or blimp for a blast of more than 100 feet, and Blandy agreed. The AAF was in a bind, because a higher altitude would cause less damage but a lower altitude would remove the need for an air drop. In rejecting the use of a blimp, the operation plan paid as much attention to the politics of Operation Crossroads as to the technological difficulties. It cited the "uncertainties and hazards" of using a blimp, including the possibility of the "loss of the bomb in water," and it noted that Able was "the only test of the three which can offer attack training to the Army Air Forces."[9]

Planners then debated the best height at which to detonate the bomb. A detonation at the 2,000-feet height of the Hiroshima and Nagasaki bombs would produce damage over a larger area than a detonation at 500 feet, but the higher shot might not sink any ships. As Ralph Sawyer explained, "No building can stand a thirty-degree roll very well, whereas a ship is built to stand a thirty-degree roll."[10] The group finally agreed on a detonation height of 515 feet, which required dropping the bomb from an altitude of 30,000 feet. This decision, in turn, brought other risks into the operation. At a minimum, target vessels and instruments could not be utilized with maximum efficiency because of a possible bombing error. In fact, a miss of more than 300 yards in any direction would destroy or invalidate a large amount of valuable data. In addition, weather restrictions might cause delays, and difficult timing signal problems would have to be overcome. Most of these problems would come back to haunt Operation Crossroads.[11]

Some scientists remained concerned about the trajectory of the bomb. "We have a bomb that doesn't fall uniformly," the chief Los Alamos engineer for the tests, Roger S. Warner, told the AAF in January.[12] Indeed, the Nagasaki bomb would have killed tens of thousands of more Japanese but for the fact that the bomb drop was off target by two miles.[13] At Roswell Field in New Mexico, twenty-five top B-29 crews competed for the honor of dropping the fourth atomic bomb. The men were now all part of the AAF's Strategic Air Command (SAC), which had just been established on March 21 to carry out long-range heavy bomber operations, and Operation Crossroads was to be the SAC's first operation with atomic weapons. Most teams came from the 509th Composite Group, which had been training for atomic missions when the war ended, and one of the leading contestants was Col. Paul W. Tibbets and his crew of the *Enola Gay,* which had dropped the atomic bomb on Hiroshima.[14]

An essential part of the bombing competition was acquiring information on the ballistics of the Fat Man bomb. The AAF also saw Operation Crossroads as a way to obtain expertise in arming and monitoring the bomb and thus to be independent of the Manhattan Project and the Navy once an atomic bomb was placed aboard a B-29. Extracting this top-secret information from the Manhattan Project, though, proved to be difficult. As a secret Air Force history put it, "AAF B-29 crews were cooperating with Manhattan personnel at the same time that Manhattan District was anything but willing to cooperate with AAF personnel." The AAF officer assigned to obtain the bombing tables "set out to get the information as part of the day's work," noted the Air Force. "He was baffled by the stone wall attitude of Manhattan representatives."[15] Still obsessed with wartime secrecy, Leslie Groves was unwilling to relinquish his exclusive control of bomb technology to another branch of the armed services, thus singlehandedly thwarting the AAF's attempt to integrate this new weapon into its military planning.

On April 23, Admiral Blandy directed Groves to supply the ballistics tables by May 15 at the latest. There was no reply, however, and repeated requests went unanswered. Indeed, when Blandy's flagship sailed from the West Coast on May 8, no one knew whether the bomb tables would be delivered to Bikini. Eventually, though, Groves relented and agreed to have the Manhattan Project train six AAF officers as bomb commanders and five junior officers as weaponeers.[16]

While the stonewalling was being resolved, the AAF moved ahead with bomb tests and training. Following a series of bomb drops in New Mexico, the top four teams moved to Kwajalein in mid-May to resume the competition at Bikini itself. To simulate the bombing conditions for Test Able, a 550- by 75-foot coral strip was cleared on Erik Island in the southwestern part of the atoll to approximate the dimensions of the *Nevada*, the bull's-eye target ship. Spotting towers and radar beacons were built on nearby islands, allowing the AAF to carry out practice runs by dropping high explosives on the coral target. As soon as practices began at Bikini, though, serious bombing errors started to occur, due mostly to the unique wind structure and severe wind sheers at the atoll, and the four crews had to work out unusually complex ballistics formulas.[17]

At a mid-April press conference, Maj. Gen. William E. Kepner, director of air operations at Bikini, explained the competition. In order to ensure the most accurate drop, he said, the AAF's method of selecting the crew would be "traditionally American—the boys who will do the job will win the position by straight competition."[18] Not everyone, however, agreed the competition was fair. The *Enola Gay* crew was one of the four finalists, and Paul Tibbets thought they had won the job based on their practice drops. However, as Tibbets later wrote, "Some sharp pencils reversed the outcome of the competition." Operations analysts reviewed the test results, "and they figured—making allowance for an intangible and completely irrelevant factor called 'ballistic winds'—that if the bombs had been dropped over the Pacific, the third crew would have come closest."[19]

Kepner did not tell the press that the first few months of training for the B-29 teams were disastrous, primarily because the AAF had given such a low priority to materiel and personnel for the 509th. Leslie Groves complained to Curtis LeMay that the AAF had not made enough aircraft available to provide sufficient training and practice for the crews. Six B-29 aircraft were assigned to the 509th, but only two were operable at any one time. Numerous engine problems occurred, and in one instance, four of five attempts to make practice drops were aborted due to mechanical failures. These troubles culminated in the crash of a B-29 during a practice run, killing the bombardier instructor, two radar observers, and other personnel. Neither the pilot nor copilot had been able to fly a B-29 for 30 days prior to the crash.[20] Improvements were made, but the Able test would still be flawed by a critical AAF mistake.

Operation Crossroads signaled the end of Leslie Groves's monopoly over atomic weapons. Passed over by the Joint Chiefs of Staff in favor of Blandy as the commander of Operation Crossroads, Groves responded by stalling, criticizing Joint Task Force One, refusing to release information, and personally attacking Admiral Blandy. As early as September

1945, he imperiously informed the Joint Chiefs of Staff that Los Alamos scientists had begun studies on the possible effects of an underwater shot and the resulting radioactivity, but the studies "would have to be carefully reviewed by me personally and I do not have sufficient time to do this just now."[21] In February 1946 he denied an AAF request that the 509th Composite Group be permitted to view six-month-old film footage on the Hiroshima and Nagasaki bombs, and he permitted the 509th to make a photographic record of Operation Crossroads only on the condition that no photographs would be taken of the bomb, related equipment, or handling techniques.[22]

Groves's obsession with security never subsided, and the Atom General resented the Atomic Admiral as the usurper of his ironclad control of atomic weapons. In March 1946, Groves drafted a memorandum warning Blandy that his public statements provided

> enough information to indicate that security . . . is far below the standard which was maintained prior to the initiation of Operation Crossroads. In view of my responsibilities for the security of the entire bomb project, from which responsibility I have not yet been relieved, it is requested that I be informed as to the steps which you propose to take in this respect.

After drafting the memorandum, though, Groves decided not to send it, telling his aide in a handwritten note, "Hold this—if security works out right we won't want it."[23]

He did not hold back two months later. On May 13, Blandy announced that the press would be permitted to view the target array before and after the tests to instill public confidence in the integrity of Operation Crossroads. The news release contained a map showing the approximate relative locations of the target ships for the first test, and it stated that photographs showing damage would be released immediately after each test, subject to security interests. Groves was livid. "It seems obvious that if an intent observer were to combine the map released of the array with pictures of ship damage and personal observations, he would be able to learn much more about the effect of an atomic bomb against ships than would ordinarily be released to a foreign government," he cabled Blandy. He was convinced that Blandy was going to release information that foreign governments could not obtain "without recourse to espionage," but Blandy disregarded his recommendation against the release of photographs.[24]

Blandy and Groves had radically different views about the openness of Operation Crossroads. Appearing at a press conference on March 1 for the first time with Groves, Blandy told reporters he hoped there would be no censorship of their stories. "My policy is to let you know everything we can about the test," said Blandy.

"There has already been too much discussion," interjected Groves, adding that he wanted the reporters "locked up on the press ship, taken out to a certain point, write what they can see of the explosion, and then send them back home."

"If you do that, you're going to have another explosion, too!" exclaimed one reporter.[25]

The next day, atomic scientists assailed Groves at a press conference called by Nobel Prize–winner Harold Urey and other members of the Federation of Atomic Scientists. Urey denied that a quarrel existed between atomic scientists and the Army. Rather, he said, "there is a quarrel between the atomic scientists and the Manhattan District Engineer Corps of the Army."[26] Six days later, Joint Task Force One announced that reporters would be permitted to write without censorship and would be permitted to cover all phases of the tests "which proper security will permit."[27] The Navy said it wanted the tests to be treated like "the story of the year, maybe of the decade, and possibly of a lifetime."[28]

The Navy won out, but Groves did not change his views. He never let up on Blandy or the Crossroads team. Asked to comment on several technical reports after the tests, he wrote to the Joint Crossroads Committee that he was "dumbfounded by the lack of appreciation for military security of the atomic bomb displayed in these reports," and he complained that top-secret information was being circulated to people not authorized to receive it. "I must admit that this performance is strictly in line with previous handling of security by JTF One, but I was hoping to see an improvement as the organization grew older."[29]

Groves did not reserve his contempt solely for Blandy. When a telegram arrived at his headquarters stating that Stafford Warren, Operation Crossroads's director of radiological safety, was taking a "badly needed vacation" in September 1946, Groves wrote in the margin, "This is laughable."[30] His Army bias may also have affected his views. Groves did not attend the tests, but he sent a group of Manhattan Project participants as observers. His aide, Col. H. C. Gee, reported that the members of the group returned home "with a feeling of definite friendship towards the Army for the excellent treatment accorded them wherever they were in Army hands. This was in strong contrast with their feeling concerning the treatment accorded by the Navy."[31]

The public announcement of Operation Crossroads thrust Blandy back into the public eye. In the three months between the announcement of the Crossroads tests and his departure for Bikini, he constantly gave speeches and press interviews and testified before congressional committees. He was also one of a few Navy officials to play a prominent role in the early development of U.S. policy on atomic energy. Just before his departure for the Marshall Islands, he met with Baruch, Eisenhower, LeMay, Groves, and other admirals to review the Acheson-Lilienthal Report. Blandy predicted that the Russians would insist that the United States cease producing the bomb as a prior condition to discussing UN control, an action that all agreed was contrary to the best interests of U.S. security. Just two days earlier, Blandy had publicly praised the Acheson-Lilienthal Report, although he warned that it "takes a seven-league stride across international boundaries."[32] Privately, he was much more skeptical, and he called for continued U.S. production and development of atomic weapons. "This course," he told Forrestal, "would probably be considered unethical by some of our more internationally minded citizens, who might succeed in tying our hands in such activities, on the basis that [this] would constitute a display of bad faith."[33]

Forrestal, who would later serve as the first secretary of defense, always had the highest regard for Blandy, even as his opinion of the Navy as a whole declined. In a conversation with Eisenhower in 1949, Forrestal listed the names of six Army leaders he trusted. As for the Navy, he named only Blandy and one other.[34] Indeed, eight months earlier, Forrestal, drafting a memorandum in his diary to establish a three-man committee to work out differences in the new Defense Department budget, proposed Blandy as one of the three, describing him as "free from the normal subjectivity and prejudices" of the Navy.[35]

Blandy also enjoyed the respect and enthusiastic support of his subordinates at Bikini. "Admiral Blandy was not just a capable man and naval officer and also a scientist," recalled Curtis Youngblood, a Crossroads participant, but "also a damn good politician."[36] Most of the scientists agreed with this assessment, because Blandy saw the tests, in large measure, as serving their needs. "When the scientific people would come up and explain things that we in the military thought were either pointless or impossible or something like that," said Draper Kauffman, a demolition expert, "Blandy would say, 'Now, look, this is important to the scientists. They know what they need. Our job is to furnish it.'"[37] Ralph Sawyer, Crossroads's technical director, agreed. "Most of these naval officers had never seen this kind of an operation, certainly, and didn't know what we were trying to do, and there were problems, but Blandy was a first rate man." Blandy, said the *New Yorker,* measured up "to even a reserve officer's dream of what a naval officer should be."[38]

15

"In Fact, They Say It Is a Very Pleasant Way to Die"

"Crossroads told us nothing new about atomic bombs," recalled Norris Bradbury, the Berkeley-trained physicist who succeeded Robert Oppenheimer as director of the Los Alamos National Laboratory. "We learned damned little at Crossroads. My major impression being out there was that this was a monumental waste of time and money. However, it gave the Navy something to do."[1]

It also gave Los Alamos something to do. Following the bombing of Hiroshima, Oppenheimer entered a packed auditorium to address a crowd of yelling, foot-stomping scientists. As he mounted the podium he clasped his hands together above his head like a prize fighter. "The place went up like we'd won the Army-Navy game," recalled his secretary. Within days, though, almost all technical activity at the laboratory ground to a halt. The goal had been achieved, and Washington was suddenly faced with developing a policy for a laboratory whose sole purpose had been achieved.[2]

"In the months immediately following the war, the Laboratory struggled for existence," Bradbury recalled. One group felt that Los Alamos should be turned into a monument or museum and that all work on the military uses of atomic energy should cease. A second group favored research on the peaceful uses of atomic energy, while a third argued that the laboratory should become a factory for the production of atomic weapons. There was talk in Congress of closing Los Alamos altogether, while Oppenheimer wanted to move the entire facility to California.[3]

Most of the atomic scientists wanted to return to academia. "Three-fourths of the lab people were trying to get out as rapidly as possible," recalled Bradbury.[4] Many of the laboratory's top scientists left to rejoin universities in time for the start of the 1945 fall semester. "It became common knowledge at Los Alamos that the first team was leaving and, by implication, those who remained were second team players," wrote one observer.[5]

The future of Los Alamos became even more doubtful in October 1945, when Oppenheimer resigned as director to teach at Cal Tech. On October 17, Leslie Groves named Bradbury as the new director for six months or until Congress passed legislation on the future of atomic energy, whichever came first. (Bradbury would serve for 25 years, until 1970.) In fact, the postwar problem at Los Alamos was not lack of support for ongoing weapons production but lack of political direction and funding. The secrecy of the Manhattan Project and its funding had come to an end. Congressional legislation was needed to fund the laboratory and to provide a transition from the Army to the new AEC, but that authority would not come until after Operation Crossroads. In the meantime, atomic bomb production virtually ground to a halt.[6]

Even before the public announcement of Operation Crossroads, Bradbury recognized the laboratory's political dilemma, and he asked for Admiral Blandy's assistance. "The absence of legislation on the subject of atomic energy," he wrote to Blandy in the first week of 1946, "will have a profound effect upon the adequacy and effective conduct of the proposed tests" and was making it impossible for Los Alamos scientists to predict even the general nature of future government-sponsored research on atomic energy. As a result of this uncertainty, he warned, so many top employees had left or were planning to leave that it would be barely possible to conduct Operation Crossroads in the early summer of 1946 and impossible after September 1. He asked Blandy to bring this matter "to the attention of those who may be in a position to indicate the urgency of this matter to Congress." Bradbury was not exaggerating. "As 1946 opened," wrote the official AEC historians, "the laboratory was in a crisis."[7]

Bradbury, a Navy reservist on leave from the Stanford faculty, forged a good working relationship with the Navy, whose tradition of postgraduate education and interest in science had produced such trained officers as Frederick Ashworth, the Nagasaki weaponeer, and Deak Parsons, the laboratory's ordnance division leader and weaponeer of the Little Boy bomb. As early as November 1943, Parsons had envisioned the atomic bomb delivered by torpedo as a naval weapon. Ironically, Oppenheimer recommended postponing work on the project, telling

Parsons that he had "no theoretical encouragement to believe that [an underwater atomic bomb] will be an effective weapon, and we have what I regard as a reliable answer to the effect that it will produce inadequate water blast."[8] Operation Crossroads would prove Oppenheimer wrong.

In late October 1945, the Navy's Office of Special Weapons, which consisted of Blandy, Parsons, Ashworth, and Horacio Rivero, met with other Navy officials to begin planning what would become Operation Crossroads. The Navy may have entertained the thought of building its own bombs, but Parsons quickly put those notions to rest. "The plain fact," he told the other Navy officials, "is that the 1945 Atomic Bomb is a one-laboratory instrument and that laboratory is at Los Alamos." The Navy considered using Wood's Hole Oceanographic Institution to do the instrumentation work, but Parsons insisted that Los Alamos take the lead role in the technical aspects of the tests, telling Bradbury that "it would be unsafe, unworkable and infinitely confusing to have any other organization attempt to dominate." Parsons ended on a prescient note. "It almost goes without saying," he wrote, "that all parties concerned should . . . prevent . . . ruining the test by allowing it to become the football in any publicity or . . . airplane vs. battleship argument."[9]

There was considerable debate at Los Alamos over which type of bomb should be used at Operation Crossroads. Bradbury recommended in October 1945 that the laboratory reengineer the Mark III Fat Man Nagasaki bomb in hopes of improving existing models and designing a radically improved weapon. The 10,000-pound Mark III bomb was crude and unwieldy. A specially trained thirty-nine-man team required two days to assemble it. Once assembled and loaded, the weapon could remain ready for firing for only 48 hours before having to be partially disassembled to recharge the short-lived batteries that powered its fusing and monitoring systems.

The bomb had other problems as well. Its ballistics had been problematic from the beginning. A huge 500-pound, five-foot-square aluminum fin assembly was welded onto the bomb in the hopes of improving its flight characteristics, but the enormous aerodynamic stresses on this unit made bombing accuracy even more unpredictable. In fact, early ballistics tests of the bomb at Dahlgren Naval Proving Ground in Virginia showed such poor flight characteristics that the testing ended after only a few days. Los Alamos scientists, though, believed the Mark III's ballistics to be better than they actually were, because they attributed practice misses to AAF pilot errors.

In addition, the bomb could only be delivered by a special B-29 Superfortress. Under the code name Project Silverplate, forty-six of these planes were modified during the war to accommodate the huge bomb, using new equipment and wiring. "Silverplating," as it was known, required more than 6,000 man-hours and created huge security problems for the Manhattan Project. Moreover, only about half of these planes remained operational by the summer of 1946.[10]

Work on a new, smaller bomb, code-named Mark IV, began at Los Alamos in early 1945, and the initial practice drops of the prototype units were held in December. The Mark IV had a new implosion core design and had been reengineered to provide a new tail assembly, better reliability, a more streamlined and aerodynamic casing, and simpler production and assembly. Although Los Alamos's ordnance division was anxious to test the new bomb, the laboratory eventually recommended that two older Nagasaki-type Mark III weapons be used at Bikini. After all, the purpose of the tests was military. The fact that the effects of an atomic weapon were to be studied rather than the weapon itself militated in favor of an already tested weapon and against a newly designed bomb that might give poor efficiency or whose behavior might be difficult to ascertain. Moreover, Leslie Groves, aware that Russian observers might be invited to Bikini, opposed testing newly designed weapons in their presence.[11]

Many Los Alamos scientists were disappointed with this decision. After all, they knew from Trinity and Nagasaki that the Fat Man plutonium device and the bomb design worked. Oppenheimer, though, was concerned because the Fat Man bomb had a one-in-fifteen chance of being a dud. "Bombs have been designed which do not have this weakness," he wrote to Truman in his letter of resignation from the president's evaluation commission, "but it is not planned to use them." In fact, Los Alamos scientists and Army officials had already dubbed these Nagasaki-type bombs primitive "Model T's," and *Time* reported that the scientists were "suspiciously" asking why the Navy was planning to use the outmoded Nagasaki model instead of an improved bomb.[12]

Admiral Blandy denied that any new bomb existed. The "standard type Nagasaki bomb is the best type which we have available and that is the reason it is being used," he told a May 13 press conference. "There is no desire . . . to hold back a more powerful bomb. If a more powerful bomb were now available, it would be employed." Ironically, Crossroads would have a short-term adverse impact on America's atomic weapons program. The tests burdened an already depleted staff at Los Alamos, and the ordnance engineering division's research and development efforts on the improved Mark IV bomb were severely curtailed by its preoccupation with preparing for Crossroads.[13]

Los Alamos agreed to provide all technical support for Operation Crossroads. "No new scientific knowledge emerged from this work," recalled Raemer E. Schreiber, who helped assemble the plutonium core for the two bombs, "but it was a real shot in the arm for people who weren't quite sure what the lab was going to do next." Los Alamos would produce, assemble, and test the weapon components, make recommendations on the height and depth of the shots and array of ships, estimate the weapons' equivalent high-explosive yield, control the timing of the Able shot, detonate the Baker bomb, and design a barge and caisson for the underwater Baker shot. Measuring the underwater shot posed serious problems, because no one knew for certain whether an atomic weapon would transfer energy to a denser medium such as water in the same manner as it transferred energy to air.[14]

Austrian emigré Victor F. Weisskopf, a key Los Alamos theoretician who was in charge of predicting the effects of the Trinity shot, was concerned about the lack of scientific planning for the tests. "We are now confronted with a completed program which I consider, in many respects, unsound from the scientific point of view," he wrote the Navy. "The people who prepared it had no first-hand knowledge of the phenomena occurring at the explosion." Weisskopf also felt the tests would convey the wrong impression to the public. "It is clear, from the available data, that only one or two ships, if any, will be sunk," he said. "Thus the planned exposure of ninety-seven ships will give the impression that the atomic bomb is an ineffective weapon. I see great dangers in the influence of this on public opinion for the future of international collaboration on atomic energy."[15] Weisskopf did not hide his opposition to Operation Crossroads. He resigned from the Navy's military review board just one month after the tests were announced.

The official history of Los Alamos candidly states that Operation Crossroads "was not generally popular with the scientists." Only a few were interested in the ordnance aspects of the tests, and most did not believe that scientific knowledge "would be advanced proportionately to the effort expended." In fact, in order to recruit personnel for the tests, the laboratory had to offer a hefty bonus for overseas duty to the 124 personnel who traveled to the Marshall Islands to work on the program.[16] One nuclear physicist called the tests "twenty per cent science and eighty per cent drama," and Los Alamos commonly referred to them in a matter-of-fact way as the "Navy tests."[17] The Navy was fully aware of this attitude, and even knowledgeable Navy officers privately questioned the scientific value of the tests. One was Capt. Ralph Larkin, who had taken over the Los Alamos liaison work from Deak Parsons and Frederick Ashworth. "The general attitude here is that this is a Navy test," Larkin told Ashworth in a telephone conversation in December 1945, one month before the tests were even announced. "The Manhattan District will pick up a little information, but not much."[18]

The Navy made two ships available to Los Alamos for use as a laboratory and for bomb assembly, the *Cumberland Sound* and the *Albe-marle*. Nearly 150 laboratory personnel, approximately one-eighth of the entire staff, were assigned to work on Crossroads for nine months. The relationship with the Navy was a good one, recalled Norris Bradbury, but there was some rivalry as well. "Please send us back photographs (non-classified) if this is possible, and human interest stories," he wrote to his assistants at Bikini in early May. "We are concerned that the Navy will get all the publicity and we are anxious to see that the Los Alamos party gets its break in the public press."[19] Forty-five years later Bradbury, still living in Los Alamos, recalled the laboratory's role in Crossroads. "The Navy was a hell of a lot better at public relations than we were," he reminisced. "I found this a big annoyance. We did all the work and the Navy got all credit and all the interviews."[20]

An advance party of Los Alamos scientists and technicians traveled to Bikini in late April. "I think we are only half effective, because of the novelty and unfamiliar working conditions," wrote 34-year-old Cornell physicist Marshall Holloway to Norris Bradbury on the voyage out. "Then, too, the trip so far has some aspects of a pleasure cruise."[21] Just coordinating matters within Bikini lagoon proved difficult. On one occasion, Los Alamos technicians were measuring the results of an AAF test drop of an inert bomb, called a pumpkin, when a second one came plummeting down perilously close to them. "Matters of this sort make me lose my lunch," lamented Roger Warner.[22] On another occasion, Holloway's team practiced loading dynamite aboard a barge and then hoisted a special flag signaling the presence of explosives on board the ship. Within minutes a tugboat arrived mistakenly with orders to tow the barge to the middle of the lagoon for bombing practice. Holloway pleaded with the captain and warned him of the explosives, but to no avail. Luckily the barge was not moved until the pumpkin drop, but Holloway was nearly hysterical. "After three weeks here at Bikini we are all finding tempers short," he wrote. "As an attempt to ease the tension I am calling a holiday. . . . All labs will be locked. People are going to relax by Executive Order."[23]

Back at Los Alamos, scientists continued to test and assemble the two bombs for delivery to Bikini. The most dangerous experimental work was conducted by the Critical Assemblies Group, headed by expatriate German physicist Otto R. Frisch, who in late 1944 proposed a daring experiment to determine exactly how much enriched uranium was needed to detonate the Hiroshima bomb. He arranged a series of uranium slugs into a cube shape, leaving a small hole in the center to prevent a chain reaction. Kept apart, these masses were lifeless. A slug of uranium hydride, guided carefully by four rails, was then dropped through the core. For a fraction of a second, the assembly would become "critical," and a chain reaction would start, creating the conditions for an explosion. "It was as near as we could possibly go towards starting an atomic explosion without actually being blown up," recalled Frisch.[24]

Richard Feynman, a young physicist at the lab, chuckled at the notion of Frisch's experiment, likening it to "tickling the tail of a sleeping dragon."[25] The "dragon experiment," as it became known, was conducted in a remote building in Los Alamos, known as Omega site. There Frisch's group built a 10-foot iron frame, known simply as the "Guillotine," that would guide the uranium slug through the center of the two hemispheres to create the chain reaction.

Working under Frisch was Louis Slotin, a skinny, 33-year-old physicist whose Russian parents had fled to Canada to escape the pogroms. Slotin was both fearless and brilliant. He enlisted in the Abraham Lincoln Brigade as an antiaircraft gunner in the Spanish Civil War and then joined the Royal Air Force at the outbreak of World War II. At Los Alamos, where he quickly became one of Oppenheimer's favorites, he read constantly, even on fishing trips with colleagues. After the war, he told friends, he hoped to pursue studies in microbiology. He began critical assemblies with uranium in January 1945, but in June he began to work with plutonium, the core of the Trinity bomb.

In an oblong, white-walled room at the Omega site, Slotin used only two screwdrivers to manipulate two plutonium hemispheres. As he prodded the two lumps, he would listen to the sounds of a Geiger counter and glance quickly to another instrument, which recorded on a roll of paper the radiation levels emitted by the two spheres. As he nudged the hemispheres closer together, the line jumped across the paper and the Geiger counter clicked faster and faster. If he passed the point of criticality and was unable to break contact, he knew he might produce a nuclear explosion in the laboratory. So did other nervous physicists at the laboratory. Indeed, Frisch himself had almost lost his life during one such experiment.[26]

Slotin continued his criticality experiments after the war, performing more than two dozen "crit tests," as they were called. "Those of us who were old hands felt impervious to the invisible danger," one member of the Critical Assemblies Group recollected. "I am afraid that familiarity indeed breeds contempt of danger."[27] Slotin's nonchalance amazed Enrico Fermi. "Keep doing that experiment that way and you'll be dead within a year," he once warned the young physicist.[28]

After Japan's surrender, Slotin went on vacation for a few weeks, and his assistant, Harry Daghlian, a 22-year-old graduate student, took over. On the evening of August 21, Daghlian was working on a criticality experiment with 13-pound tungsten carbide bricks. Just as the assembly was nearing critical mass, his fingers slipped, and a tungsten carbide brick fell uncontrolled into the assembly. As a sudden bluish glow filled the room, Daghlian hit the assembly and knocked out the brick, but it was too late; he had been exposed to a lethal dose of radiation. Within days, his right hand, which had received most of the radiation, swelled up tremendously, and skin fell off his body in whole clumps. Photographers from the laboratory's health group made a complete photographic record as Daghlian deteriorated over the next weeks, with Slotin constantly at his bedside. He developed a fever five days after the accident, and it rose to above 106 degrees. Delirium soon set in, and Daghlian complained of severe internal pains as radiation sickness spread. He died an agonizing death 24 days after the accident.[29]

Exactly nine months after Daghlian's accident, at 3:20 P.M. on May 21, 1946, the cheerful, brash Slotin was performing another crit test, this time on one of the bombs being assembled for Operation Crossroads. Slotin had just received his travel orders and was looking forward to traveling to Bikini to see the tests. Seven other scientists were with him in the room, including Alvin Graves, who was scheduled to go to Bikini as the top assistant to Ralph Sawyer, the technical director.[30]

Suddenly Slotin's screwdriver slipped and the hemispheres came too close together, starting a chain reaction. In less than a millisecond, deadly gamma radiation burst from the assembly. The same bluish glare filled the room as the assembly went critical and the air became momentarily ionized. Slotin, instead of ducking and possibly saving his own life, immediately hurled himself onto the hemispheres and tore them apart with his bare hands, stopping the chain reaction. By placing his body between his colleagues and the radiating mass, Slotin saved the lives of the other seven men, but he realized in an instant that he was doomed. Amazingly, he calmly told his colleagues to stand exactly where they had been at the moment of criticality. Then, in order to help doctors determine each man's level of radiation exposure, he sketched a diagram on the blackboard showing everyone's location in the room. Then he went out into the hallway and telephoned for help. "I'm sorry I got you into this," Slotin told his colleague Alvin Graves, who had stood closest to him, as the two waited for a car to take them to the hospital. "I am afraid that I have less than a fifty-fifty chance of living. I hope you do better than that."[31]

Slotin's treatment was limited to penicillin, 11 pints of blood, and ice packs to help relieve his high fever. But the doctors could do nothing. The radiation dose he received was as if he had been less than a mile from the Hiroshima bomb. Within 12 hours, he began to suffer bouts of nausea. His white cells virtually disappeared after three days, and his arms swelled up to nine inches in diameter. Slotin tried to maintain consciousness as much as possible to explain his symptoms to the doctors, but the pain was excruciating. Faced with a unique and invaluable opportunity to study the effects of ionizing radiation on human beings without any other complicating factors from a bomb explosion, experts flew in from around the country and closely studied Slotin and the other seven scientists. Doctors took radiation readings from their blood and bones, gold fillings in their teeth, silver belt buckles, and even a gold Sheaffer pen Slotin had been carrying in his pocket. The health group made what the laboratory's official history described as a "spectacular" photographic record of Slotin's deterioration.[32]

Eight days after the accident, with Slotin on his deathbed, many of his colleagues had to attend a cocktail party at the laboratory for some visiting dignitaries. No word of the accident was permitted; the laboratory wanted the whole affair hushed up. Slotin died in terrible agony the next day. The other seven men were all overexposed and became temporarily sterile. They recovered, though, and later had normal children. The laboratory turned to another physicist, Klaus Fuchs, to prepare a report on the accident.[33]

In the months between the deaths of Daghlian and Slotin, Leslie Groves testified in Washington before the Senate Special Committee on Atomic Energy. "The radioactive casualty can be of several classes," he told the committee. "He can have enough so that he will be killed instantly. He can have a smaller amount which will cause him to die rather soon, and as I understand it from the doctors, without undue suffering. In fact, they say it is a very pleasant way to die."[34]

16

"The Girl We Would Most Like to Split Atoms With"

The intense public interest created by Operation Crossroads led to thousands of requests from reporters, foreign observers, and congressmen to attend the tests. Within one week of the announcement of the tests, the Navy had received nearly 6,000 press requests to go to Bikini, but space was limited to 168 newsmen. Among those chosen were some of the best print and radio reporters of the day, including William Laurence and Hanson W. Baldwin (*New York Times*), Bob Considine and James L. Kilgallen (International News Service), William Randolph Hearst, Jr., Norman Cousins (*Saturday Review*), Bill Downs (CBS), Clete Roberts and Gram Swing (ABC), and Mutual correspondents Quentin Reynolds, Bill Chaplin, and Austin Pringle.

The Navy, hoping to obtain a representative cross-section of reporters, made some strange choices. Accredited correspondents included the fiction editor of *Charm*, a slick women's fashion magazine, a reporter for *Air Aces*, a bimonthly pulp comic book, and reporters for newspapers in Passaic, New Jersey, and Anderson, Georgia. Chicago, Boston, and Philadelphia newspapers had three reporters each, the same as for all of Great Britain. The Soviet Union and nine other countries were each allowed one. Several women correspondents applied to cover the tests, but Joint Task Force One issued a blanket rule excluding all female reporters. When the Women's National Press Club protested, the Army agreed to fly out a group, but the Navy held its ground and no women reporters were included.[1]

Most of the reporters were housed aboard the *Appalachian,* nick-named the "Big Apple" and described by Bob Considine as "a commu-nications ship noted for its abominable communications."[2] Built during the war as an amphibious force flagship to carry an admiral and his staff, the ship housed 117 correspondents. "We slept late, dressed like beachcombers, and threw cigarette butts on the deck, which we called the floor," recalled one.[3]

Joint Task Force One's public affairs officer was Capt. Fitzhugh Lee, an affable naval officer whose grandfather, a Confederate cavalry gen-eral, was Robert E. Lee's nephew. Captain Lee had successfully handled press coverage of the Japanese surrender aboard the *Missouri,* but the challenge of Operation Crossroads was much greater. "I had to get these . . . people out there," he recalled, "and keep them happy while we were there for some six weeks in the South Pacific in a non-alcoholic non-air conditioned ship in very overcrowded conditions, and hopefully bring them all back safely without radiation damage, and with their sto-ries well told."[4]

As the "Big Apple" plowed westward from San Francisco at a top speed of eight knots, some reporters turned to drink. "Sensing the prob-able need for such relief," wrote Bob Considine, "the Navy had been unusually clement. Our papers read that alcoholic beverages were strictly forbidden aboard all U.S. Navy ships, but for Operation Cross-roads there would be no baggage inspection." As a result, he said, many reporters brought two bags aboard the ship, "one for clothing, one for comfort."[5] Conditions on the "Big Apple" did not help matters. The ship was hot and crowded, and frequent communications breakdowns delayed dispatches as much as 12 hours. The reporters "were a restless, unhappy group," recalled Lee. "I couldn't blame them in many ways."[6]

The real problem, though, was there was no genuine news to report. The frustrations, as one participant noted, were due to "the absurdity of locking 117 newshawks up on a ship with nothing to do for days and days but write their heads off about something most of which was already known, and the rest Top Secret." No scientists or military observers were on the ship, and at Bikini the reporters met with Opera-tion Crossroads officials only at mob press conferences. A petition by thirty correspondents asking for permission to speak to scientists in small groups or one-on-one was turned down. The Navy had opened up the tests to reporters, but strictly on its terms. "We had freedom of action—on the end of a shrinkable leash," wrote one reporter after the tests.[7]

The question of foreign observers was not resolved when the tests were announced on January 24, although the Joint Chiefs had decided in December that nine British scientists could participate in the tests.

Senator McMahon led the call to open up the tests to all nations, but Secretary of State Byrnes sounded a more cautious note, telling a January 29 press conference that the issue was under study. Blandy recommended limiting observers to British and Canadian officers and scientists, but Acheson and Byrnes thought that failure to invite at least members of the UN Security Council would be seen abroad as a signal that the United States was unwilling to cooperate with the United Nations' effort to control atomic weapons.[8]

The real question concerned Russian observers. Just eight months earlier, General Marshall had proposed inviting two Soviet scientists to observe the Trinity test. At that time, Byrnes had put his foot down, but now the existence of the bomb was no longer a secret.[9] "Making the test an open one," editorialized the *New York Times*, "would show that we consider this new weapon a matter of world responsibility, not just our own," while the *Washington Post* reasoned that failure to include foreign observers would "fortify the world's fear that we think of the atom as our peculiar property and mean to brandish it as a weapon for our peculiar interests."[10]

At a meeting in early February, Byrnes, Forrestal, Patterson, and Blandy agreed to recommend that each member of the UN Atomic Energy Commission be permitted to send two observers. This plan, later approved by the Joint Chiefs and President Truman, permitted officials from eleven countries—the Soviet Union, France, Great Britain, China, Poland, the Netherlands, Brazil, Egypt, Mexico, Australia, and Canada—to attend the tests. Within hours of the meeting, Byrnes, who had been anxious to invite the Russians, sent off a cable to Kennan in Moscow to deliver to Molotov, telling him of this recommendation but cautioning that Congress had not yet authorized the tests and that no invitation could yet be extended. Meanwhile, Leslie Groves recommended that the United States extend an invitation to Trygve Lie, secretary-general of the United Nations. "I have been informed by Mr. Baruch that Mr. Lie desires such an invitation, although he probably will not accept it," Groves wrote to the Joint Chiefs, adding that "issuance of such an invitation will be helpful to the negotiations which Mr. Baruch is about to enter upon in the Atomic Energy Commission." Lie declined the invitation.[11]

The foreign observers faced a difficult trip. "In no sense of the word should this voyage be construed as a cruise or a pleasure jaunt," warned the Joint Chiefs, adding that a Navy ship, with limited berthing facilities on a two-month voyage in a tropical climate, did not "provide the comforts of a luxury liner." On top of this, all foreign observers were required to sign a waiver stating that they would not bring a claim against the United States for any injuries they might receive in connection with the tests, whether due to the hazards of Operation Crossroads or any other cause.[12]

The twenty-two foreign observers sailed to Bikini on the communications ship *Panamint,* which one of them described as a "strange Noah's Ark to which each country had sent pairs of different species, but always of the same sex: military men, naval, ordnance, and intelligence experts; parliamentarians; academics; and scientists."[13] The two British representatives were members of Parliament, one Labor and one Conservative, while the Soviets sent two scientists, one a nuclear physicist and the other an expert in mineral processing who was actually a KGB agent.[14] Other foreigners included Chung-Yao Chao, a young physicist at China's National Central University who would later play a major role in that country's nuclear weapons development program, and physicist Stefan Pienkowski, president of the University of Warsaw and one of the leaders of the Polish student resistance during World War II.[15]

The foreign observers were kept completely in the dark and did not even receive press releases. United by their resentment over the lack of information, the group's only distraction was the open-air movies shown on the *Panamint*'s afterdeck every evening. "We never missed this spectacle, even during tropical squalls," wrote French nuclear chemist Bertrand Goldschmidt, who watched movies fifty-seven evenings in a row and described his trip to Bikini as "the only exotic cruise on which I was bored."[16]

Competition for an invitation to the tests was intense on Capitol Hill. On March 19, Rep. Jack Z. Anderson of California, a member of the House Naval Affairs Committee, telephoned Navy Secretary Forrestal to lobby for an invitation. "I passed up two trips for the express purpose of seeing this test," he told Forrestal, adding that another congressman was determined to go to Bikini, even if "he has to go on a battleship." Anderson pressed Forrestal to invite all the members of the Naval Affairs Committee. "We authorized the legislation and held extensive hearings on it," he said, "so I think we're just going to have to call on you for a little assistance."[17]

At one point it seemed that most of the top Truman administration officials, including the president himself, were going to Bikini. Newspapers reported in late January that Truman, Byrnes, Forrestal, and Patterson would fly on the presidential airplane *Sacred Cow* to inspect the damage from the tests, but would not be present for the actual detonations because of concern for their safety. Others announcing their intentions to witness the tests included generals Groves and Eisenhower, Admiral Nimitz, Senator McMahon, and Representative Vinson.[18]

In the end, though, Truman did not go to Bikini. Neither did Byrnes, Patterson, Nimitz, Eisenhower, Groves, McMahon, Vinson, nor the vast majority of the 120 senators and representatives whose supposed attendance at the tests had caused Truman to postpone them. Admiral Blandy told an April 10 press conference that Congress had "considerable interest" in the tests, but a radio commentator said that same week that he had been unable to locate a single congressman who planned to go. The commentator was nearly correct. When the three ships carrying observers to Bikini sailed on June 12 from Oakland, just one congressman was aboard. A few others flew to Hawaii to meet the ships later, but eventually only fifteen congressmen and senators traveled to Bikini, of whom four were members of Truman's evaluation commission. Thirteen saw the Able test, and only three in addition to the evaluation commission members witnessed the Baker test.[19]

Navy Secretary Forrestal announced in mid-June that he would attend the tests, ending intense speculation that he would resign over the issue of armed services unification. Ironically, the two most prominent military officials who attended Operation Crossroads, Forrestal and his old golfing companion and social friend from New York, W. Stuart Symington, newly appointed assistant secretary of war for air, were now bitter adversaries in the armed services unification battle. The two friends and rivals aspired to many of the same goals, one under the influence of Carl Vinson and the admirals, the other indoctrinated by the AAF.[20] Less than a month before leaving for Bikini, Forrestal and Secretary of War Robert Patterson had written a joint letter to President Truman outlining their areas of continuing disagreement on unification, and in a private meeting with Truman before leaving for Bikini, Forrestal accused the Army of "steam roller tactics" and threatened to resign rather than support unification. Two years later, as secretary of defense, Forrestal would accuse Symington of "official disobedience and personal disloyalty."[21]

In early June, Leslie Groves, who continued to feel upstaged by Blandy, ordered his deputy, Kenneth D. Nichols, to represent him at Bikini on Blandy's flagship. "If the bomb does not go off," Groves told him, "you take over." Nichols pondered the order. "I didn't ask him how a brigadier general takes over from a vice admiral on his own flagship. However, the bomb probably would go off, so why worry about it?" Groves never did travel to Bikini. "He did not want to be in a position where he had no authority," recalled Nichols.[22]

The vast majority of Crossroads participants—the 38,200 Navy men, most of the 550 civilian scientists and technicians, the reporters and observers—lived aboard the more than 150 support ships in Bikini lagoon that were not to be used as targets. For an Army man like Kenneth Nichols, the Navy system was an eye-opener. Every afternoon he went to Bikini Island's beach for a swim and a drink at the officers' club. "I think I've been in the wrong service," Nichols wrote to his wife. "The Navy really has a very enjoyable caste system." Even when walking along the beach to pick shells, there was a pecking order, and Blandy came first. "He gets first choice of the shells," Nichols told his wife.[23]

Blandy delegated the technical work to his top two scientific assistants, Deak Parsons and Ralph Sawyer. Sawyer, dean of graduate studies at the University of Michigan, had previously served as laboratory director of the Dahlgren Naval Proving Ground in Virginia. Parsons, an outstanding scientist and naval officer, had worked on the three most important research and development programs that won World War II—radar, the proximity fuse, and the atomic bomb. A quiet, handsome man with a balding head and intelligent eyes, the 42-year-old Parsons had armed the Hiroshima bomb in the bomb bay of the *Enola Gay,* inserting the projectile and detonator, and he was the foremost nuclear authority in the Navy at the end of the war.[24] Well experienced in gunnery, high explosives, fusing, and ordnance, he had been recruited by Leslie Groves to head the ordnance division at Los Alamos, where he was in charge of ballistic testing and arming and detonating the weapons. "Within a few minutes I was sure he was the man for the job," wrote Groves. Parsons quickly gained the respect and friendship of the scientists, especially Oppenheimer, and became their key liaison to the military—a role he would repeat at Bikini.[25]

Both Parsons and Sawyer had radio call signals to receive messages around the lagoon. Sawyer's was "Between," he recalled, because he was between the scientists and the military. Parsons's was "Wet Nurse"—"when the scientists would cry he'd come."[26] Curtis Youngblood, a security administration officer at Operation Crossroads, recalled that Parsons and Sawyer "worked 24 hours a day. They carried the load." Admiral Blandy, by contrast, found plenty of time to relax once he arrived at Bikini. He went fishing two or three times a week and entertained visiting dignitaries. "At noon," reminisced Youngblood, "he'd come up on top of the ship, where the rest of us young squirts were taking sun baths and horsing around, and Blandy's boy would bring a cot up there and old Spike would lay there and read a Whiz Bang magazine with his colored glasses on, and maybe take a nap, . . . and then at night Blandy would have a bridge game."[27]

Security was a major concern at Bikini because of the public nature of the tests and the many scientists, technicians, and other civilians hired for Operation Crossroads. Blandy's staff utilized the security personnel of the Manhattan Project's intelligence division to check all civilian personnel and servicemen who would be exposed to highly sensitive information. No one, though, detected the true intentions of Klaus Fuchs, a

German-born British physicist and Russian spy who had come to Los Alamos during the war as a member of the British atomic energy mission, where he worked under Hans Bethe studying the development of a nuclear-weapon blast wave over time and distance.[28]

Fuchs, who described the plutonium bomb and Trinity test to Russian agents in Boston and Santa Fe, stayed on at Los Alamos after the war. He worked on a comprehensive report on the atomic bomb project, attended seminars on the future of nuclear power, heard Edward Teller lecture on the possibility of developing a thermonuclear bomb, calculated the blast effects at Hiroshima and Nagasaki, viewed films of the bomb drops over Hiroshima and Nagasaki, and analyzed the radiation effects from the Trinity test. "We poured drinks down him at Los Alamos, and he was part of the family," recalled Norris Bradbury. "He was also in great demand as a babysitter, being a single man."[29]

Ironically, Fuchs would have returned to England six months before Operation Crossroads but for the direct intervention of lab director Bradbury. "In Dr. Fuchs's case," wrote Bradbury to his British counterpart in early February, "we are anxious to retain his services at least until the completion of the Naval Tests." Bradbury needed Fuchs to provide advice on new models of the current bomb, weapons theory, and other Operation Crossroads matters on which Los Alamos's theoretical division was seriously short of personnel. Fuchs eventually left Los Alamos for England on June 14, where he provided the Soviet Union with a wealth of information, including the so-called Fuchs formula for radiation intensity as a function of distance, which was based on his work in planning for Operation Crossroads.[30]

As the real target of espionage would probably be the bomb itself, fifty Marines were assigned to guard classified installations at Kwajalein. They kept a close watch on *Dave's Dream,* the B-29 Superfortress that would carry the bomb to Bikini. It sat at the far end of the Kwajalein runway, nearly half a mile from the regular installations, alongside the *Enola Gay,* which was available as a backup. A special pit had been built there to load the bomb, and close by were a group of Quonset huts and a cement vault that housed the device. Another Marine detachment guarded instrumentation at Bikini, Eneu, and Amen islands at Bikini, while security officers were assigned to Admiral Blandy's flagship and ships carrying radiological monitors, Los Alamos scientists, congressmen, reporters, and foreign observers. The quality of the monitoring was typified by one incident in which a security officer reported "suspicious" and "vaguely communistic utterances" by two Los Alamos employees, one of whom, he said, "seems to be a first class dope regardless of his political tenets."[31]

At Bikini lagoon, shrill pipes woke the men early each morning. After breakfast, hundreds of boats criss-crossed the lagoon, depositing scientists and technicians at the target vessels to prepare for the tests. Men hoisted trucks, tanks, artillery pieces, airplane wing tanks, stabilizers, altimeters, fire extinguishers, and even a P-47 fuselage aboard ships of the ghost fleet and secured them to the decks. Canned goods, uniforms, medical supplies, field stoves, soap, insecticides, and even K-rations were made fast and labeled. More than 150 items of food, clothing, and supplies were scattered over eleven target vessels, while lubricants and fuels were exposed on four tank-landing craft and a concrete drydock. Ships' engineers worked out plans to shut down machinery and close all watertight compartments. Throughout the lagoon photographers recorded all the activities and inspectors took voluminous notes on prepared forms. So many people attended meetings on the *Mount McKinley,* Blandy's flagship, that there were frequently more than fifty small boats lying off her gangways.

Water taxis, Bikini's chief status symbol, were in great demand for ferrying scientists, technicians, and visitors around the lagoon, and there never seemed to be enough of them. Smithsonian scientists in particular complained about the lack of boats, which they needed to collect fish, birds, mammals, and plants from the atoll. Some gave up relying on Navy transportation and went camping on Bikini's outer islands. Others were forced to camp once when the Navy dropped them on a western island and forgot to pick them up for two days. In fact, the Smithsonian's curator of ichthyology became so disgusted with working conditions that he arranged for a replacement in early July. Unlike the ichthyologists and zoologists, though, whose work was of little interest to the Navy, the oceanographers and geologists at Bikini fared much better. The *Bowditch,* which housed many of the scientists, was equipped for ocean mapping, and the U.S. Geological Survey scientists had adequate equipment and transportation.[32]

Within four days of the Bikinians' removal from the atoll, the 53rd Naval Construction Battalion arrived from Guam to begin construction. Popularly known during the war as Seabees, these veterans of Guadalcanal, Bougainville, and Guam took down nearly all the structures on Bikini and Eneu and quickly transformed the face of the islands. Within weeks, the 1,000 Seabees, working around the clock, built twelve 75-foot steel towers for mounting cameras and other technical equipment, seven pontoon causeways, seaplane landing ramps, a water distillation and distribution system, a dispensary, power-generating units, shallow moorings for small boats, and countless huts to house seismographic, photographic, and other technical equipment.

By June, parts of Bikini looked like a huge playground. The island was equipped with five concrete basketball courts, ten volleyball courts, four baseball fields, a 100-foot-square concrete athletic court, swim floats, life-guard platforms, swimming beaches, a beer garden, an archery range, courts for horseshoe pitching, paddle tennis courts, twenty-six dressing huts, and a trap-shooting range. The island even had its own local radio station, "Radio Bikini," which interviewed Crossroads participants and broadcast the comings and goings of various dignitaries.[33]

The Seabees also built two thatched-roof clubs, the "Up and Atom" and "Studs Saloon," which sported a sign offering "No Wine, No Women, No Nothing." These simple frame structures, open on three sides with palm thatches to hold off the sun and rain, had a serving counter along the closed side and a few crude tables and benches to round out the decor. The clubs immediately buzzed with reporters looking for news and cheap drinks. "A curious tingling sensation in the limbs of hooch samplers can be traced, in all probability, to the shock they encountered on learning that the Navy's price for a priceless bottle of ice cold beer in this forlorn spot in the central Pacific is ten cents," wrote Bob Considine. "This case is a stunning experience to younger reporters raised in the brocaded clip joints of their homeland."[34] Reporters were not alone in taking advantage of the low-cost alcohol. "The hazards from having drunks push one off the landing docks or fall onto you in the shore boat is a far greater hazard to life & limb than the atomic bomb—and I'm not fooling," wrote a physicist to a friend.[35]

In the late afternoons, as many as 10,000 men headed to Bikini Island in small boats for beer, soda, and recreation. "We thought it was wonderful the way they were treating us there," recalled John Smither-man, who was just shy of his eighteenth birthday at the time. "We had all the ice cream we could eat and we had some of this what you call 3.2 beer, trying to cool off with that." The men played baseball, ping-pong, volleyball, and basketball, and the warm waters of the lagoon were always available for quick relief from Bikini's heat and humidity. "Our whole crew thought we had died and gone to heaven," said Anthony Guarisco, who served on a ship that supplied Bikini with cigarettes, liquor, soda, and athletic equipment. As Los Alamos told its civilian employees preparing to leave for Bikini, "There will be [an] unlimited supply of candy, Coke and ice cream."[36]

As sunset approached, everyone headed back to the ships for dinner, followed by movies on deck. Occasionally, some creative talents offered home-bred entertainment. A group of observers aboard the *Panamint* entertained the ship's officers and crew one night with a comic opera replete with mad scientists, cannibals, and sex-starved shipwrecked sailors. Even the press got into the act, staging a musical comedy in which they tried to defend King Juda as the Navy moved the Bikinians. The "Big Apple" reporters' theme song, dedicated to Blandy's press officer, was sung to the tune of "When I Was a Lad" from Gilbert and Sullivan's *HMS Pinafore*:

> *We are the boys of Fitzhugh Lee*
> > *We hate the Navy and we hate the sea.*
> *We hate the Army and we hate this ship.*
> > *But we're all signed up for the atomic trip.*
> *(We're all signed up for the atomic trip.)*
> > *We're all signed up and ready to go.*
> *To offer up our testicles for UNO.*

"It was a poor verse," admitted Bob Considine, "but there was little else to do at eight knots."[37]

The 42,000 men stationed at Bikini received several locally produced newspapers, including the *Daily Blast, Crossroads,* the *Atomic Bombshell* (published from "Guinea Pig Bay"), and the *Crossroads Pacific Breeze. Crossroads,* published aboard the *Bowditch,* kept its readers apprised of preparations for the tests, activities at Bikini, and the prolonged absence of women at the atoll. Each issue featured a "Miss Crossroads of the Week," or "The Girl We Would Most Like to Split Atoms With." The paper's headline in late April promised "Real Live Women to Appear Soon in Bikini Area," reporting that the *Haven,* a hospital ship, would be arriving shortly with female nurses. *Crossroads* apologized to its readers in the next issue, though, as the *Haven* brought only male scientists and radiological safety personnel. The newspaper reported that the Seabees were planning to build a four-lane highway from San Francisco to Bikini to accommodate the many VIPs coming to Bikini, and it also speculated that the purpose of goats at Bikini was either to "relieve responsible authorities of blame in case of the atom bomb's failure to amply mutilate the test ships" or "to eliminate the lagoon's sewage problems."[38]

Crossroads's humor reflected the uncertainties about the upcoming tests. As Bob Considine recalled, "There was mirthless jesting about the possible effect of the Bikini bombs on visiting genitals." Joint Task Force One issued wallet-sized cards to all personnel, signed by Admiral Blandy, stating that the participant had participated in Operation Crossroads. A similar-sized card, printed against a background drawing of a mermaid, was issued by the Royal Order of the Radiated Studs. Signed by the Omnipotentiary of the Bikini Chapter, the card recited that its holder, "having been subjected to non-propagating radiation during Operation Crossroads and having been sterilized but not devitalized, is hereby declared entitled to all the privileges of this order."[39]

The humor extended to the upper ranks of Joint Task Force One. Deak Parsons was granted a commendation from Sty No. 1 of the Grand Council, Exclusive Order of Guinea Pigs. Having "subjected his body to the rigors attendant to atom bombs, hundred-foot tidal waves, mermaids, vampires, sandfleas, typhoons, mal-de-mer, cannibals, canned beer, etc.," he was accorded full status as a "Brother Pig." The plaque was signed by the Keeper of the Trough, the Grand Guinea Swine (Brig. Gen. Roger M. Ramey) and the Little Guinea Swine (Col. William J. Blanchard), both of whom would later fly on *Dave's Dream* on Able Day. The faculty of the Radiological Safety College of the University of Bikini (Universitas Bikiniana) also conferred upon Parsons a doctor of phenomenology degree "in the year of our Lord, 1946, and of the University, 1."[40]

"Atomic Bill" Laurence was the undisputed dean of correspondents covering Crossroads. His eyewitness reports on Trinity and the bombing of Nagasaki had just won him a second Pulitzer Prize, and his views carried enormous weight among the U.S. and foreign correspondents at Bikini. He was harshly critical of scientists who criticized Crossroads. "When scientists say such a test will be useless before it has been conducted they are speaking as political propagandists," he said of Lee DuBridge, and he dismissed another scientist's prediction of an underwater earthquake as a "cheap shot at scare journalism, unworthy of a scientist." Other reporters, too, grew tired of the predictions of catastrophe. "The increasingly violent opposition of atomic scientists to the Bikini tests is rapidly draining the reservoir of goodwill which was there six months ago," wrote one.[41]

As radio reports of Bernard Baruch's speech before the United Nations reached the *Appalachian*, Laurence praised the American plan. "If you don't like this plan, what else is there you can propose?" he asked. "Either this or a war with atomic bombs!" Dissenters either agreed with Laurence or dropped out of the inner circle of reporters. Some correspondents, though, saw a sharp contrast between the Baruch Plan and Operation Crossroads. "We have two contrasting acts in the atomic drama," wrote Norman Cousins for the *Saturday Review*. "One act is in New York, where the nations are considering proposals made by Mr. Baruch to cut deeply into national sovereignties by setting up a rule of law against the manufacture of atomic weapons anywhere. The other act is out here in the Pacific, where Bikini is an expression of atomic power in a world of competitive national sovereignties." Cousins saw a clear choice for the United States. "If we go one way—the way of the Baruch proposals—we can make a pretty fair beginning in the hard struggle for world law. . . . But if we go the other way, it means that sooner or later other nations are going to have their own Bikinis."[42]

For some, Bikini was a symbol of American determination and military might. For others, it represented the end of a simple world of coconut palms and gentle breezes. "Bikini Lagoon, although we have never seen it, begins to seem like the one place in all the world we cannot spare," wrote E. B. White in the *New Yorker*. "It grows increasingly valuable in our eyes—the lagoon, the low-lying atoll, the steady wind from the east, the palms in the wind, the quiet natives who live without violence. It all seems unspeakably precious, like a lovely child stricken with a fatal disease."[43]

17

"The Whole Project Sounds Like Bad Boys Playing with Matches in the Hay Mow"

The Navy organized a sophisticated public relations campaign to explain Operation Crossroads. Admiral Blandy gave speeches and held news conferences in cities around the country, and Joint Task Force One issued a steady stream of press releases. Nevertheless, from the very beginning Operation Crossroads was a public relations nightmare.

Blandy emphasized that Operation Crossroads was a "joint effort in every sense of the word," but the press saw it as more of a battle than a test. "Are navies obsolete?" asked *Time.* "Chronically optimistic airmen . . . think so. Brassbound Navymen hold that atomic explosives are just another weapon." At a press conference, an Air Force major general was asked how many airplanes would participate in the tests. "The air will be about as full of planes as the Admiral wishes," he answered dryly. "Don't use my name," commented an AAF captain in Honolulu, "but you can say the Navy is cooperating very nicely in blasting itself out of existence."[1] Other AAF officials charged that the tests were rigged and that the Navy intended to use them as propaganda. The *New York Times* reported that the AAF "wants to make certain in advance that, if and when 90 percent of the 100 target ships survive the first test, Navy spokesmen abstain from pointing with pride to the fact that 'the fleet has survived.'"[2]

The syndicated columnists Joseph and Stewart Alsop charged in a February column that the "ancient demon of interservice rivalry has reared its head." Instead of being a serious attempt to determine the strategic implications of the atomic bomb, they said, Operation Crossroads showed signs of deteriorating into "another grim struggle between Navy and Air Forces." They, too, harked back to Billy Mitchell and warned that the evaluation of the tests would be heated and biased; the "danger is that each faction will seek, not to find out the truth, but to defend its own theories at all costs."[3]

Charges flew back and forth between the AAF and the Navy. "Again the Navy has 'bravely' accepted an unoffered challenge to prove that their powerful ships can withstand anything—even the atomic bomb," observed *Flying* magazine. "And again they are going to do it their way. The game (if you can call it that) is to be played with the Navy's own deck of cards and according to the Navy's own set of rules."[4] The Navy, AAF sources told the *Baltimore News Post,* "wants to protect its beloved battleships. No matter what happens, the admirals will draw the conclusions from Bikini that the Navy can survive atomic warfare."[5] Admiral Blandy tried to convince the public that the purpose of Operation Crossroads was to determine the effect of atomic weapons on ships, not whether navies were obsolete, but no one bought his argument. "Will not the Bikini tests, if successful, expose the Navy to an involuntary suicide?" the columnist Walter Lippmann asked his friend James Forrestal in June. "If all the ships in the proposed concentration should be destroyed or receive serious damage, will it not prove that navies are truly obsolete?"[6]

Admiral Nimitz, meanwhile, continued to defend the Navy. Five days after the announcement of Operation Crossroads, he reminded a National Press Club audience that the atomic bomb was carried to the Pacific in ships, that the airplanes that dropped the bombs were fueled by gasoline carried in ships, and that the bases from which these airplanes operated were seized by ships. "No matter what the outcome of the bomb experiments, we will need a fleet . . . until the commerce takes to the air," he said. "That day will not come in our lifetime."[7] He later charged that the argument that the atomic bomb was going to render navies obsolete was "a fantastic theory offered without practical proof," and he sought to downplay the notion that the bomb could sink a fleet of ships. "Let the 'false prophets' prepare the headlines in advance, such as 'atomic bombs sink ships in test' or 'navy is doomed.' But don't take them too seriously," he warned. "While the prophets of naval doom are shouting themselves hoarse, the Navy will be at work to make the changes needed to accommodate American sea power to the new weapon." This approach, though, backfired and led to the charge, as the *New York Herald Tribune* put it, that the Navy was going to hold the tests for the "satisfaction of proving how, if a ship is placed far enough away from an atomic bomb, it will ride out the blast unharmed."[8]

onically, both sides agreed with the atomic scientists that industrial sites were better targets for atomic bombs than ships. An AAF spokesman told reporters that ships were not a "worthy target for such expensive and devastating missiles," and Nimitz agreed.[9] "Ships are difficult and unprofitable targets for atomic bombing, because of the degree to which they are dispersed in naval tactical positions," he insisted. "Much more logical targets," he said, "would be the bases, naval and aviation, upon which the fleets of sea and sky depend."[10]

The AAF-Navy rivalry permeated the entire project. The assistant secretary of war bluntly told a colleague that the consequences of the Navy "winning" the tests "will be to strengthen the Navy's position as to the size of its establishment and the participation by it in the total funds appropriated for the military forces."[11] The Army Air Forces history of Operation Crossroads noted that the AAF's only ways of learning about Joint Task Force One's plans and decisions were visits and telephone calls to task force headquarters. "On these occasions, however, very little information was given voluntarily and much of it had to be extracted tactfully. Most of the information verbally received in this manner was seldom confirmed in writing." This was "a difficult situation at best," the AAF history charged.[12]

The combination of AAF-Navy bickering and mounting congressional concerns led part of the public to see an inconsistency between Operation Crossroads and the post-Hiroshima call for world government and international control or even abandonment of the atomic bomb. Protesters marched in Washington with signs reading "Wrong Road to Peace" and "Bikini: Rehearsal for World War 3."[13] Several veterans' organizations, irate that the New York was to be used as a target ship at Bikini, demanded that the battleship remain in New York as a war memorial and naval reserve center. Another veterans' group placed a full-page advertisement in the New York Times in late February protesting the tests. President Truman, declared the Military Order of the Purple Heart, had promised after Hiroshima and Nagasaki that the United States would harness atomic energy for peaceful uses, but at Bikini "we are serving notice on the world that we are pursuing the ways of war." The veterans also played on the public's fear of the bomb, warning that the underwater explosion might start a huge tidal wave. "These atomic explosions must not take place! They must be stopped!"[14] claimed the veterans, who called on the public to send penny postcards to the White House urging the president to cancel the tests and save the ships.

More than penny postcards arrived at the White House. In fact, protest letters by the thousands began pouring into Washington as soon as the tests were announced. Veterans and active servicemen protested the impending destruction of the target vessels, "ships which served admirably to bring us victory over Germany and Japan and which in the few months since the war ended have suddenly become 'obsolete,'" as one serviceman wrote. A Marine Corps veteran wrote that the proposed tests were "wasteful, unnecessary, and dangerous, dangerous not only for the uncertain results of this release of atomic energy, but also dangerous in the warlike attitude they display."

Hundreds of local organizations passed resolutions and sent in petitions opposing Operation Crossroads. A typical proclamation declared that the tests were "entirely out of step in a plan to bring about world harmony," a threat to world peace, a waste of material and money, and a "dangerous attempt to play with cosmic fire." Protest letters were sent by such diverse groups as the Massachusetts branch of the Women's International League for Peace and Freedom, the Public Forum of Spokane, the Society of Friends of Wilmington, Ohio, the YMCA of St. Petersburg, Florida, and Local 122 of the American Federation of Musicians.

Some protesters were indignant. One New Yorker called the tests an "appalling outrage," an "unspeakable madness and idiocy," and he called on Truman to stop "this Buck Rogers foolishness." Other letters were plaintive in tone and reflected deeply held religious views. "I simply feel the end results cannot possibly justify either the means employed nor make up for the attendant misfortunes which cannot possibly be foreseen by anyone but God," wrote a man from Wilmette, Illinois. Ten women from Oakland, California, were concerned about U.S.-Soviet relations. "We accuse Russia of being suspicious of us. Were this experiment hers would we not be suspicious of her?" they asked. "To claim that [Operation Crossroads] is in the interests of pure knowledge is a smoke-screen which will deceive no one."[15] Another protester said that the Navy's explanation for the tests was not clear. "If it destroys many ships, the Navy will want to build new ones. If it destroys no ships, the Navy will want to build more of the old kind. The whole thing is ridiculous."[16]

"The whole project sounds like bad boys playing with matches in the hay mow," wrote the dean of women at a New York college. "The expense, the danger, the possibility of its being construed as a show-off gesture by other nations—all these features I deplore." The most unpleasant letter Blandy received, he later recalled, was from someone who said he was worse than the German and Japanese generals then on trial. "I would not only be responsible for killing thousands of other men," said Blandy, "but would be killed myself, and thus would not be available for trial."[17]

Some eighty-five people wrote not to protest the tests but to volunteer as human guinea pigs on the target vessels. One offer came from a man who insisted that his name not be used lest the public think him crazy, while another volunteer offered his life in return for the support and education of his children. "Have been a Jack of all trades in my life," he wrote, "and this will make certain my kids won't have to follow the same groove I drifted into." Another volunteer pointed out that the Navy had no plans to determine the effect of the bomb on alcoholics. "Fifty per cent of our population are alcoholics and as an alcoholic I offer myself as a guinea pig. Do not think this will be murder because I am willing to sacrifice my life to science. I am worthless anyhow." Nevertheless, the urge to live still flickered, as the postscript added, "I'll bet you $1,000 I live."[18]

Some of the volunteers, though, were thoughtful, sincere, and articulate, and few asked for money. A serviceman in the Philippines wrote a pitiful letter to Truman. "This is not a bid for publicity, Sir," he said, "but an honest offer directed to the one who can grant me my one desire left in life. . . . I have no one to care for, as my mother and father are estranged, and my sweetheart, as so often happens now to servicemen, has decided to leave me for someone else, so I have no one to love me." Recognizing that "it means certain death," a 19-year-old ex-Marine who served at Iwo Jima volunteered for the tests, as did a Navy veteran with diabetes who said he had less than a year to live. A prisoner in the Washington State Penitentiary also volunteered, hoping to pay "my 'debt to society.' I feel that inasmuch as I was not in a position to contribute as much to my country's effort in the recently ended war as I would have liked to, I can make up for that by having my offer accepted."[19]

After Admiral Blandy announced that experimental animals would be used at Bikini, thousands more protest letters—from antivivisection societies, church organizations, and individual animal lovers—swamped the White House, Capitol Hill, and the War and Navy departments. "The Humane Societies all over the country will fine any ignorant stupid people for beating their pets or starving them," wrote a woman from Venice, California, "and yet people in high positions are allowed to plan such fiendish things. As a moral standard it speaks very poorly for America." Similar letters came from groups such as the Massachusetts Council of the Milk Goat Breeders Association, the Rochester (New York) Anti-Vivisection Society, and the Canadian Vegetarian Association. Members of the Southern Dairy Goat Owners and Breeders Association came to Washington to protest the tests. "Good goats are scarcer than good Congressmen," the association said, and it suggested using congressmen as substitutes for the animals.[20]

Protests also came from animal lovers abroad. In just one week, the

U.S. Embassy in London received irate letters from more than 500 British animal lovers and organizations, including the British Union for Abolition of Vivisection and the Cats' Protection League. "The whole idea is diabolical," wrote one group, "and shows to what depth of degradation some people have fallen."[21] In London, a Conservative member of Parliament was loudly cheered in the House of Commons when he asked, "Why choose innocent animals when there are so many guilty men available?" The Society for the Prevention of Cruelty to Animals of Vancouver, British Columbia, telegraphed President Truman to condemn the use of animals as "ghastly, cruel, barbarous and a serious reflection on your national character," and the president of the International League of Anti-Vivisectionists begged Truman to reconsider. Over half the protest letters from the public condemned the use of animals for experiments on the target vessels, and protests from dog lovers were so great that Blandy excluded them from the tests.[22]

"Public relations was a major problem throughout the entire operation," conceded Blandy after the tests, adding that all letters were answered "in the most courteous and reassuring manner."[23] The burden of replying to the 7,000 protest letters fell to Blandy's staff intelligence officer, Brig. Gen. Thomas J. Betts. "I hope you may realize that we were extremely reluctant to come to the decision to use even a single animal in the tests," was his standard response to animal lovers. "May I further say that all the animals used will be treated in the most humane manner possible and will not be exposed to any unnecessary suffering?" To writers protesting the destruction of ships, he explained that the badly damaged ones would be towed back to the United States and sold as scrap, while "others may be placed back into service."[24] He also wrote back to all volunteers who offered to be human guinea pigs. "Some people are obviously cranks," he told a press conference. "Some people are daredevils. Some of them want a little publicity. We try to be courteous to them."[25]

Even children wrote. "My little friends and I want to protest the using of all those ships in the Atomic Bomb Test," wrote an 11-year-old boy from East Chicago, Indiana. "Why don't you give some of them to the children of the country? My friends and I would like to have a real PT boat which we could run on Lake Michigan. . . . Please if you do leave the machine gun on the boat. We would take care of the high octane gas and oil ourselves and I know a little bit about running one."[26]

Some of the protests came from the Crossroads participants themselves. "Mom, I don't want to worry you," wrote an enlisted man aboard a gunboat at Bikini, "but this is the way it is: The Captain has already told us that there is not much of a chance for us. . . . If my time has come, I will go, but I never expected to go like this. I don't see why they send us out here when they know we will all get killed, but they said they expected to lose six or seven hundred men."

Within days, the sailor's letter was in the hands of his family's congressman, Admiral Blandy, General Betts, and White House naval aide Clark Clifford. Clifford met with Blandy on March 29 to discuss this obvious misunderstanding from a troubled and perhaps homesick serviceman, and Blandy sent back a memorandum explaining that the gunboat would be stationed 21 miles from the bomb site and would not reenter Bikini's lagoon until it was safe to do so.[27]

Many writers supported atomic testing, but urged that the experiments be held on a smaller scale. "Airplane engineers do not need to destroy full size planes to see just what the planes will do under certain conditions," wrote a man from Gardena, California. "They use small models. Scientists do not need to kill elephants to determine the reaction of chemicals and drugs. They use small mice." One writer was distressed that the Able test was scheduled for a Sunday, intended to be a day of quiet and prayer. He expressed great relief when he was informed that Bikini was across the international date line, so that Sunday in the United States was actually Monday in Bikini.[28]

Only a few newspapers and magazines joined the protests. The *Los Angeles Daily News* left no doubt about its views in an editorial entitled "Lunatics at Bikini." The *Seattle Post-Intelligencer* opposed the use of experimental animals, and the *Oregon Daily Journal,* in an editorial entitled "Mad Test," asked, "Is there no official mind for anything but destruction? Are we so eager to prove war vessels obsolete in order that the whole world may be launched into an armament race?" The Portland newspaper sympathized with the plight of the Bikinians and opposed the "slaughter of war veteran ships and living creatures."[29]

E. B. White, writing in the *New Yorker,* pondered what would happen if the tables were turned. "We like to sit and think about the editorials that would be appearing in the American press this spring if Japan were the nation conducting the A-bomb experiments in the Marshalls," he wrote. "That is one set of editorials we would hate to miss." He volunteered to join the experimental animals, "as it seems only right that the human race be represented on so vivid an occasion. As yet it has not been definitely established that an atomic bomb can kill a man if he is standing on the deck of a ship. And until we know that, how can anybody rest easy?"[30]

Barely a month after the announcement of Operation Crossroads, Capt. Fitzhugh Lee realized that the Navy had a public relations crisis on its hands. With Blandy's approval, Lee sent a confidential memorandum to top Joint Task Force One officials in early March reviewing aspects of the tests "which, to some, appear dangerous or ill-advised." He stressed that opposition was "sporadic, relatively unorganized, and ineffective," and that most of it "appears to come from the 'dissatisfied scientists.'" As a means to counter these criticisms, he provided a checklist of points for officers to emphasize or avoid in their public statements. Lee's suggestions, though, were contradictory and only served to create more public confusion and opposition. He urged officials to refer to the tests as "scientific experiments," while also telling them to emphasize that the tests were proper military measures necessary in order for the armed forces to discharge their responsibilities. To neutralize the "dissatisfied scientists," Lee told officials to "emphasize the fact that over 500 civilian scientists are actively cooperating in the operation," but he also told them to say that the "tests are not intended to 'prove' or 'disprove' anything."[31]

Lee's suggestions did little to change public perception of Operation Crossroads. Bradley Dewey, one of the two civilian members of the Joint Chiefs of Staff's evaluation board, raised some of these concerns in a June 10 telephone conversation with Navy Secretary Forrestal. "This is very much off the record and not for circulation," began Dewey, "but some of the press fellows have been chewing around and asking questions." Dewey said he was being asked by reporters whether he and Karl Compton, the other civilian member of the board, were "going to be free to speak [our] mind[s] after you have filed your official opinion." Dewey told Forrestal that it would be best if they could say yes, subject to military secrecy, adding that this was also the suggestion of the "best thinkers that I can get at in the press."

Dewey also wanted to be able to "get across the fact that the apparent results may not be the final conclusion." He felt it best to caution "against just accepting a box score as the entire story, so that the record would be written beforehand, that the whole test wasn't to be judged by how many ships were sunk."

Forrestal readily agreed. "That's right," he replied, "and as a matter of fact we are already beginning to get some of that, not directed against you but against the Navy. As you know, Oppenheimer is raising the broad general question of whether you should have these experiments at all."[32]

With Blandy becoming increasingly concerned about the impact of the tests on the public's perception of the Navy, Fitzhugh Lee sent him and two other admirals a secret memorandum in early June with some suggestions from a Hollywood publicist on Operation Crossroads. Lee pointed out that Joint Task Force One was required by the Joint Chiefs to be impartial, but he thought the suggestions might be interesting. Understandably, he did not send the publicist's ideas to any AAF officials.

"The actual technical results of the bomb tests are not nearly so important to Navy Public Relations as is the Public's interpretation of these results," wrote the Hollywood publicist, adding that public opinion, more than scientific findings, could determine the entire future of the Navy. Depending on the public's expectations, "the same identical results could be interpreted either as the Navy's funeral, or the beginning of a new and greater Navy." The problem was that the public viewed the tests as "The Navy vs. The Atomic Bomb," and the Navy was going to lose. "Even though the damage is less than anticipated, it is going to be difficult to explain to the mass public that this is good—there still will be damage, and that can always be made to look bad."

Why fight a losing battle? asked the publicist. "Rather than try to square off and lick the bomb—join it. The ships aren't being tested—the ocean is." Army ground forces could not withstand the bomb, nor could land-based airplanes, so the publicist's strategy was to make the public realize that the ocean and the Navy were America's last hope. "Just as the aircraft carrier was developed to answer Billy Mitchell's air bombing . . . this is an attempt to find a better defensive answer to the atomic bomb."[33]

In a way, the publicist was right, but the media seized on the bomb-versus-ship analogy from the outset and the Navy never could shake the image of a contest. As one newspaper put it the day after the tests were announced: "In one corner: A guinea pig fleet of vessels, ranging from carriers and battleships to submarines and transports. In the other corner: The Atom Bomb! . . . Remember the Monitor vs. the Merrimac? You ain't seen nothing yet!"[34]

The Navy was also concerned about the public's perception of its treatment of the Bikinians. Captain Lee and one of his assistants discussed this issue with a film studio in California, and in late April the studio telegraphed Lee's office with its suggestions. "We open the picture with an animated map of the Pacific," said the filmmakers, "and then pan down to the island of Bikini." The narrator would explain the purpose of Crossroads, followed by Commodore Wyatt "persuading the natives to leave." The next scene would show the evacuation of the Bikinians, "the narration treatment to explain how the Joint Task Force showed such great care and humane treatment in the evacuation."[35]

Newsreels that summer showed that exact scene, with a cartoon pencil zeroing in on an animated map of the Pacific Ocean. "The basic requirements call for a protected anchorage six miles in diameter in an unpopulated region of the world," says the narrator as the camera heads southwest across the Hawaiian islands, passing cartoon drawings of oceanliners and fish. "The site should be remote from fishing grounds, steamer lines and inhabited shores and must be controlled by the United States." The camera pans across the Marshall Islands and stops at Bikini. "Bikini Atoll, a dot on the map of the mid-Pacific, was destined to become a focal point for the eyes of the world!" Then faces of Bikinians appear on camera: a pretty young girl, a toothless man, King Juda next to Commodore Wyatt. "American officials discuss plans with the Bikini natives for the evacuation of the atoll," the narrator continues. "The islanders are a nomadic group, and are well pleased that the Yanks are going to add a little variety to their lives."[36]

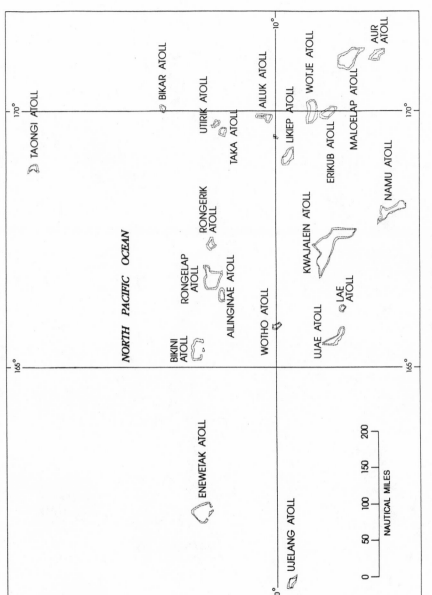

The northern Marshall Islands.

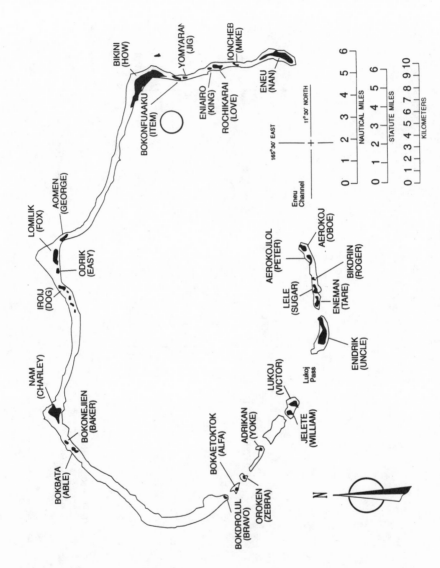

Bikini Atoll. Code names are in parentheses. The target area is circled.

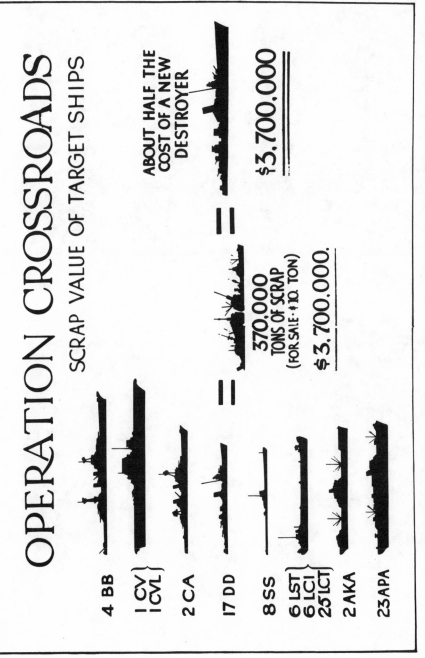

JTF-1 press release showing the scrap value of the target ships for Operation Crossroads. Admiral Blandy told Congress in March that the construction costs of the target ships totaled $450 million. In response to criticism of the cost, Blandy later argued that the ships' scrap value would not exceed the cost of one new destroyer. (U.S. Naval Institute Research Library)

"The residents have voted two to one against your conducting your experiments in this vicinity."

"The United States Government now wants to turn this great destructive power into something good for the benefit of mankind," Navy Commodore Ben H. Wyatt tells the Bikinians on March 6, 1946, the day before they are moved. With newsreel cameras rolling, Wyatt reenacted at least eight times his earlier meeting with the islanders. (Carl Markwith, © National Geographic Society)

Top left: Village life on placid, palm-covered Bikini Atoll one month before the removal of the islanders. (U.S. Naval Institute Research Library)

Bottom left: New Yorker cartoon from June 1946. The Bikinians' ability to tell the United States to test its atomic bombs elsewhere was depicted as a joke. (Drawing by Robt. Day; © 1946, 1974 *The New Yorker* Magazine, Inc.)

"King" Juda, leader of the Bikini people. "We are willing to go," he told Wyatt through an interpreter, adding ominously, "Everything is in God's hands." (National Archives)

Top right: An advance team of Bikini men leave Bikini to assist Seabees in building new homes for the islanders on Rongerik. (National Archives)

Bottom right: Three Bikini girls carrying their possessions from the village on Bikini Island to the waiting Navy LST. (Carl Markwith, © National Geographic Society)

In a quiet moment before leaving, Bikinians pay final respects to loved ones at the Bikini graveyard. (Carl Markwith, © National Geographic Society)

Bikini families huddled together aboard *LST-1108* with their household effects and belongings for the overnight trip to Rongerik. (National Archives)

Leslie R. Groves at his desk during World War II. (National Archives)

Adm. William H. P. "Spike" Blandy, commander of JTF-1. The "Atomic Admiral," as he was dubbed, defended Operation Crossroads against its critics. (National Archives)

J. Robert Oppenheimer and Leslie R. Groves (in protective footwear) at the site of the Trinity test in late 1945. (Los Alamos National Laboratory)

Navy Commodore William S. "Deak" Parsons, weaponeer aboard the *Enola Gay* and later Operation Crossroads's Deputy Task Force Commander for Technical Direction. (National Archives)

Admiral Blandy and members of the Joint Chiefs of Staff Evaluation Board view a model of Bikini lagoon showing the location of the target ships. *Left to right:* Bradley Dewey, Adm. William H. P. Blandy, Lt. Gen. Lewis H. Brereton, Dr. Karl T. Compton (chairman of the board), Rear Adm. Ralph A. Ofstie, Vice Adm. John H. Hoover, Maj. Gen. Thomas F. Farrell, and Gen. Joseph W. Stilwell. (U.S. Naval Institute Research Library)

Dr. Stafford L. Warren, head of the Radiological Safety Section, photographed at Bikini. (Courtesy of Dean Warren)

Navy Secretary James V. Forrestal and Admiral Blandy at Bikini. (AP/Wide World Photos)

The crew of *Dave's Dream,* the B-29 Superfortress that dropped the Able bomb. Maj. Woodrow P. "Woody" Swancutt, the pilot, is fourth from left, in the passenger's seat. Maj. Harold H. Wood, the bombardier, is next to Swancutt, in the driver's seat. (USAF photo)

"Stud's Saloon," operated by the Seabees. JTF-1's caption to this picture was "The boys manage to split a few atoms of some kind of liquid between them to wash the nuclear dust from their tonsils." (National Archives)

Three 75-foot steel towers on Eneu Island built to accommodate still and motion-picture cameras. (The Bettmann Archive)

Sailors aboard the target ship *New York* batten down the ship's hatches prior to evacuation for the Able shot. Some men remained on the ships up to two hours before the blast in order to start the operation of various recording instruments. To the right, with "Crossroads" painted on it, is one of the many types of gasoline tanks exposed to the atomic bomb tests. (U.S. Naval Institute Research Library)

As part of the "Queen Day" rehearsal on June 24, enlisted men remove their personal tags from a board hanging near the quarterdeck of the target ship *Pennsylvania*. The deck officer checked the tags against the ship's roster to ensure that every man had left the ship. (U.S. Naval Institute Research Library)

As if in prayer, sailors on the flight deck of the *Saidor* practice shielding their eyes from the expected intense light of the Able bomb. The protective goggles issued to other observers were ten times too dark and cut out over 99 percent of the light from the explosion, so most observers saw practically nothing. (U.S. Naval Institute Research Library)

Goats tethered to the deck of the target ship *Niagara* munch hay peacefully as they await the Able shot. Thousands of letters were sent to Washington protesting the use of more than 5,000 animals in the tests. (National Archives)

The resplendent *Prinz Eugen,* the most advanced ship of World War II, at anchor in Bikini lagoon. She was the most popular ship at Bikini, and many on her crew said that they would rather have served on her than any other U.S. ship. (National Archives)

The Baker bomb is suspended 90 degrees below the steel land ship *LSM-60 (middle),* whose tall mast is designed to pick up the detonation signal from the control ship *Cumberland Sound.* The *Saratoga (above)* and the *Arkansas* are nearly in final positions a few hundred yards from the *LSM-60.* (National Archives)

The *Saratoga,* home to nearly 100,000 sailors, nears San Francisco harbor on Magic Carpet service after World War II. She held the record for the number of aircraft landed on a carrier, and she transported nearly 30,000 veterans home from the Pacific after the war. (San Francisco Maritime National Historical Park, National Park Service)

Photographed from the air about two minutes after detonation, the atomic plume from the Able shot, looking like a giant cauliflower head suspended on an ever-stretching neck, rises over the lagoon, with Bikini and other islands and reefs in the atoll visible below. (USAF photo)

Baker shot: At the instant of explosion, as the steam and fission products reach the lagoon's surface, a white condensation cloud forms, which looks like a dome or bubble lit from within. This photograph was taken from a drone plane almost directly overhead at the instant of detonation. (U.S. Naval Institute Research Library)

This classic photograph of Baker was printed in newspapers around the world and remains the symbol of the atomic bomb today. Most observers thought the dark spot on the right showed the *Arkansas* upward on one end like a toy boat, but Admiral Blandy explained that this was created by a cloud of soot

and debris from the ship's stacks and boilers. In the left foreground is the cruiser *Salt Lake City;* in the right foreground is the Japanese battleship *Nagato.* (U.S. Naval Institute Research Library)

Baker shot: The cloud formation at its peak, as the water column erupts to a height of over one mile in one second. It looked like Niagara Falls in reverse. (USAF photo)

Baker shot: The dome of water that had surged into the atmosphere starts to settle down into a doughnut-like circle. (National Archives)

Ten seconds after the explosion the stern of the *Saratoga* rises 43 feet on the first wave crest. The Baker shot unleashed the greatest waves ever known; the first wave rose to a height of 94 feet. (National Archives)

As the cauliflower cloud looms darkly overhead, two million tons of water begin to fall back into the lagoon after the Baker shot, dwarfing the *Nagato* at the right. (National Archives)

The water column collapsing back into the lagoon creates the base surge, as the circle of radioactive water, spray, mist, and debris billows out in an ever-widening ring over the target ships. (National Archives)

The superstructure of the submarine *Skate* is crushed by the force of the Able blast, and a makeshift sign keeps visitors away. As reporters motored by her, Capt. Fitzhugh Lee, Blandy's public affairs officer, boomed, "Good as ever!" (National Archives)

Despite high radiation levels, the *Skate* is under way on July 2, with her crew standing on the deck as she passes Admiral Blandy's flagship, the *Mount McKinley*. (U.S. Naval Institute Research Library)

Able test damage to the *Sakawa*, which was anchored about 500 yards from the Zeropoint. She sank the day after the Able shot. (National Archives)

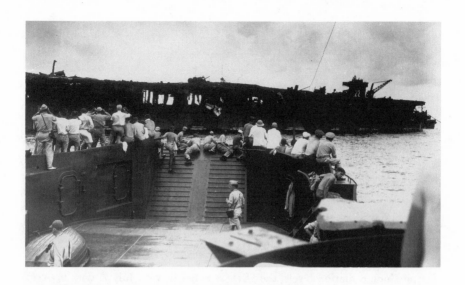

Observers inspecting burned test materials on the foredeck of the *Pensacola*. (National Archives)

Two radsafe monitors take Geiger-counter readings from the bow of a gunboat on the way into Bikini lagoon after the Baker test. Blandy tried to tour the ghost fleet the day after the shot, but he was forced to turn back in less than 30 minutes. (U.S. Naval Institute Research Library)

Top left: Reporters and observers on the *LCT-52* inspect damage to the *Independence* after the Able blast. Part of the flight deck was blown off, while the rest was buckled, and all twenty-five fighter planes were tossed overboard. (National Archives)

Surrounded by other target ships, the *Saratoga* slides beneath the waters of Bikini lagoon seven and one-half hours after the Baker detonation. All hands of the fleet were called on deck for the final moments, and many men wept openly while she sank. (U.S. Naval Institute Research Library)

Navy fireboats wash down the decks of the *New York* with seawater following the Baker shot in an attempt to decontaminate the ship. The Navy also tried blasting the target ships with corn cobs, rice, barley, ground coffee, sand, and coconut shells. (USAF photo)

The tried and true Navy method: scrubbing the deck of the *Prinz Eugen* to reduce radiation levels. Radsafe monitors on the target ships were fully clothed at all times, including rubber gloves and boots, but enlisted men were not. "I had on a pair of shorts and my tennis shoes and my . . . little t-shirt with a sailor hat," recalled one sailor. "And that's all the clothing that I had on me." (U.S. Naval Institute Research Library)

Underwater shot of *Saratoga* today. (Courtesy of Bill Curtsinger)

Admiral and Mrs. Blandy, together with Adm. Frank J. Lowry, celebrate the dissolution of JTF-1 in Washington, D.C., on November 7, 1946. The resemblance between Mrs. Blandy's hat and the mushroom cloud seems to have been coincidental. (Stock Montage)

The battered hulk of the *Independence* at San Francisco in January 1951, ready for sinking off the Farallon Islands after three years of radiological testing and use as a training ship for radsafe monitors. (San Francisco Maritime National Historical Park, National Park Service)

18

"Thank God That Someone Had the Sentiment Not to Anchor Her at Bikini!"

As Able Day approached, the main attraction at Bikini Atoll was the ghost fleet of ninety-five target ships, which ranged from 36-foot landing craft and concrete barges to submarines, destroyers, cruisers, five battleships, and two aircraft carriers, including the 888-foot *Saratoga*.[1] Together, the target fleet of ninety-two American and three foreign ships constituted the world's fifth largest navy, and included surviving ships of nearly every major naval battle of World War II—Pearl Harbor, Coral Sea, Midway, Leyte Gulf, the Solomons, the Aleutians, and the *Bismarck* breakout. The American ships had rich and proud histories of war service and held fond memories for thousands of American sailors, including many at Bikini.[2]

The ships selected as targets were, for the most part, overage vessels or those of obsolete design that would otherwise have been decommissioned and sold for scrap. The U.S. battleships—the *New York, Arkansas, Pennsylvania,* and *Nevada*—were commissioned between 1912 and 1916 and had escorted President Woodrow Wilson to the Versailles Peace Conference following World War I. These four were selected because they had shown great resistance to battle damage. All had heavy side and deck armor, elaborate torpedo protection systems, and nearly 600 watertight compartments, while the aircraft carrier *Saratoga* was selected to test the strength of her 1,000 watertight compartments. The concrete drydock and two concrete barges, on the other

163

hand, were selected as a result of bomb damage surveys at Hiroshima and Nagasaki, which showed that reinforced concrete structures were highly resistant to the atomic bomb.[3]

The twelve destroyers at Bikini included the *Ralph Talbot,* which was one of the first ships on the scene to rescue some of the 316 survivors in the worst sea disaster in American naval history—the sinking of the cruiser *Indianapolis* and her crew of 1,196 men off Guam three days after delivering vital parts of the atomic bomb that would destroy Hiroshima.[4] Closer to the Zeropoint was the destroyer *Anderson,* which had rescued 377 men from the aircraft carrier *Lexington* in the Battle of the Coral Sea and 204 men from the sinking carrier *Yorktown* at Midway. The eight submarines in the lagoon, which together had sunk over 130,000 tons of enemy shipping, had hull thicknesses ranging from 5/8 inch in the older *Tuna* and *Sea Raven* to as much as one inch in the newer *Dentuda, Apogon,* and *Pilotfish,* which were barely three years old.[5] Nineteen fairly new attack transports (AKAs) were targets, including the *Gilliam* and *Carlisle,* which were less than two years old, and the *Gasconade,* so new that it had not even seen action in the war. The lagoon was also spotted with numerous smaller vessels, including tank, infantry, and mechanized landing craft, personnel landing craft vehicles, and several concrete drydocks and barges.

The day after the tests were announced, the archaic battleship *New York* left her home port for Bikini. The squat, odd-looking battleship was the third oldest active ship in the Navy and had fought nearly a score of battles in two world wars. She was present for the surrender of the German High Seas Fleet at the end of World War I and later hosted as guests King George V, the Prince of Wales, and the young crown prince of Japan, Hirohito. After convoy patrol duty at the outbreak of World War II, the *New York* went into action in 1942 in the North African landings, where she saved two destroyers from severe damage by silencing a German battery. For a year she served as a gunnery training ship, as nearly 12,000 officers and enlisted men trained on her. She participated in the preinvasion bombardment of Iwo Jima and was the only major ship to stay on assignment for the entire Okinawa campaign. During her 78 days there she covered landings and furnished close support for the Army and Marines, firing off more shells than the combined total for all ships in the invasion of Tarawa.[6]

A week before the public announcement of Operation Crossroads, New York's Governor Thomas E. Dewey sent a telegram to the Navy asking that the sailing date of the *New York* be delayed until the state legislature had an opportunity to vote on a bill to appropriate funds to make her a state shrine. The Navy rejected this request, although Admiral Blandy told a congressional committee in late January that New

York might get her back if she survived the tests.[7] Other obsolete ships were spared from service at Bikini, such as the aircraft carrier *Enterprise*, which fought in nearly all the major Pacific campaigns. "Thank God that someone had the sentiment not to anchor her at Bikini!" wrote Fleet Adm. William F. "Bull" Halsey.[8]

Just as the *New York* left port, the largest surviving German ship from the war, the *Prinz Eugen*, slid into a dock in south Boston. The Tripartite Naval Commission awarded her to the United States after the war, and she was brought across the Atlantic from Bremen as the USS *IX-300* for use at Bikini. The arrival of the *Prinz Eugen* in Boston Harbor was an extraordinary sight. Eight Navy Hellcats buzzed her repeatedly, and a lone bomber swung over again and again. The Stars and Stripes flew at her stern, but the skeleton crew of American sailors was outnumbered by the ship's crew of 574 Germans, dressed in their full wartime brass-buttoned uniforms, with the exception of their swastikas, which had been removed.[9]

An American crew would not be available until late February, so the Germans moved the immaculate ship to the Philadelphia Navy Yard, where they were feted daily by as many as 2,000 German-American visitors. At Bikini, the *Prinz Eugen* was the most popular ship in the lagoon. Her American captain marveled at the ship's modern electrical system and many compartments, and crewmen aboard her said they would rather have served on her than on any other U.S. ship.[10]

The resplendent and graceful *Prinz Eugen* was perhaps the most advanced ship of World War II. More than three inches of steel armor protected the ship, and up to six inches protected the turrets. High-pressure steam turbines, generating 80,000 horsepower, produced speeds up to 33 knots. The handsome cruiser so closely resembled her running mate, the famous battleship *Bismarck*, that even trained German officers had difficulty distinguishing between the two ships at a distance.[11]

Constructed primarily for raiding Allied commerce on the high seas, the *Prinz Eugen* actually spent a large part of the war blockaded in port. Nevertheless, she did participate in two of the most famous episodes in the Atlantic war. Hounded by British planes, she was able to join the *Bismarck* in Norway in May 1941, and the two ships then made their famous breakout into the North Atlantic to raid Allied shipping. Passing between Iceland and Greenland, they were intercepted on the morning of May 24 by the battle cruiser *Hood*, the largest ship in either navy, and the ill-fated battleship *Prince of Wales*, the pride of the British fleet.[12] At 5:52 A.M., all four ships opened fire, at a distance of about 14 miles. Both the *Prinz Eugen* and the *Bismarck* placed direct shots on the *Hood*, and at 6:00 A.M., eight minutes into the battle, the *Hood* blew up and sank immediately. Only three of her crew of over 1,400 survived in one of Britain's greatest naval losses of the entire war, and the *Prince of Wales* broke off the battle after 20 minutes.[13]

For the next three days, the *Bismarck* maneuvered 1,750 miles in a running sea battle against seventeen British battleships, carriers, cruisers, and destroyers. She was finally sunk on May 29, just 77 hours after her great victory over the *Hood*. The *Prinz Eugen,* meanwhile, had broken off from the *Bismarck* to continue shipping raids. Churchill, hoping to precipitate America's entry into the war, wanted the United States involved in her capture. "It would be far better that she should be located by a United States ship," he wrote in a top-secret memorandum to Britain's First Sea Lord, "as this might tempt her to fire upon that ship, thus providing an incident for which the United States government would be so thankful."[14]

The *Prinz Eugen* did not oblige. She cruised 7,000 miles and twice managed to refuel from German tankers, but engine troubles forced the luckless cruiser to slip into Brest for repairs without firing on a single merchant ship. The British then blockaded Brest and harassed the *Prinz Eugen* with frequent air raids, including a direct hit on July 2, 1941, which destroyed the main gunnery control room, killing sixty men. Six months later, on February 11, 1942, the *Prinz Eugen* dramatically broke the British blockade in the famous "Channel dash," miraculously escaping to Germany by steaming directly up the English Channel in broad daylight, much to the chagrin of embarrassed British admirals. The *Prinz Eugen* sped to Norway, but within a week a torpedo from a British submarine blew off her stern, forcing her back to port again, and she saw little action for the rest of the war.[15]

By contrast, the most detested ships moored in Bikini's lagoon were the Japanese cruiser *Sakawa* and the hulking black battleship *Nagato*. The *Sakawa,* completed on November 30, 1944, was the only Japanese cruiser of her class to survive the war; she surrendered undamaged and intact. Both ships were filthy and foul-smelling and lacked adequate sanitary facilities. A Navy spokesman admitted that the trip from Japan to Bikini was uncomfortable; the sailors described it as a "nightmare." In fact, the *Sakawa* became the subject of some notoriety when a group of angry American sailors attempted to sabotage her while en route to Bikini. The five saboteurs let the ship drift at sea for several days alongside the *Nagato,* endangering the lives of crewmen. Two of the sailors were later court-martialed and sentenced to 18 months in prison.[16]

The *Nagato,* a huge, strange-looking, pagoda-like battleship, was nearly as long as the *Saratoga*. At the time of her completion in 1920 she was the world's largest warship and the first to be armed with 16-inch guns.[17] In 1941, she served as the flagship for Adm. Isoroku Yamamoto, commander-in-chief of the Imperial Japanese Fleet, who expected to die in battle aboard her. Staff meetings were held on the *Nagato* as Yamamoto and his staff prepared final plans for the attack on the ninety-six ships of the U.S. Pacific Fleet inside the crowded anchorage of Pearl Harbor, deployed, as at Bikini, like sitting ducks. Each high-level Japanese bomber carried only one bomb—a nearly one-ton projectile constructed from the 16-inch shells of the *Nagato* and her sister ship, the *Mutsu,* and designed to penetrate the thick deck armor of U.S. battleships. One of these 16-inch shells sank the battleship *Arizona,* together with more than 1,200 of the 1,400 men on board, thereby accounting for nearly half the deaths at Pearl Harbor.[18]

Yamamoto replaced the *Nagato* as his flagship two months after Pearl Harbor, but its name would always be associated with him and the attack on Pearl Harbor. The battleship was part of the force that attempted to take Midway and the Aleutians in May 1942 and later saw action in the Marianas and the Battle of Leyte Gulf in 1944, where she was hit by two torpedoes and four bombs from carrier planes. Shortly afterwards she reached port at Yokosuka, Japan, to await repairs that never came. In July 1945, carrier bombers from Bull Halsey's Third Fleet blasted off her mainmast and badly damaged the deck and superstructure, but they could not sink her. The *Nagato* ended the war out of action, the only Japanese battleship or carrier not sunk in the fighting, and on August 30, 1945, a special ceremonial detail from Halsey's staff took over the ship and hauled down her flag to symbolize the unconditional surrender of the Japanese navy.[19]

When the crippled *Nagato* arrived at Bikini, an LST alongside supplied all the water and electricity, and the ship quickly became a tourist attraction of sorts, although one observer described her as the "stinkingest, filthiest place you could imagine." Visitors became so frequent that the Navy issued an order limiting sightseeing parties to groups of twenty. The Navy stored a considerable amount of ammunition on the despised ship, and several mines were strapped onto either side of the deck, "apparently with the idea of helping the A-bomb do its stuff," as one visitor noted.[20]

The oldest ship in Bikini's lagoon—and the oldest active battleship in the Navy—was the *Arkansas.* Three months after being commissioned in September 1912, she carried President William Taft to Panama to inspect work on the canal. She supported Marine landings at Veracruz, Mexico, in 1914 and sailed to Europe in July 1918 to fight against Germany. During World War II, the *Arkansas* provided fire support for U.S. troops at Omaha Beach on D-day and then moved to the Pacific in time to bombard Iwo Jima and Okinawa. She sailed more than 130,000 miles during the war and made three additional voyages in Operation Magic Carpet, returning servicemen to the States after the war.[21]

Moored off the port beam of the *Arkansas* was the 30-year-old battleship *Nevada,* which was selected as the bull's-eye for the Able test because, according to the Navy, she was the "most rugged ship available."[22] When the Japanese attacked Pearl Harbor, most of her officers were ashore for the weekend. Despite bomb and torpedo attacks, the *Nevada*'s machine guns opened fire on approaching torpedo planes. With fuel oil from the nearby *Arizona* burning on the water's surface, the *Nevada* had to move. Out of Pearl Harbor's acrid, billowing clouds of smoke came a sight so extraordinary, wrote the historian Gordon W. Prange, that those who saw it "could not have been more dumbfounded had it been the legendary Flying Dutchman—*Nevada,* heading into the channel, a hole the size of a house in her bow, her torn flag rippling defiance." The *Nevada* was the only capital ship to get under way. Bombers swarmed over her like bees, as the Japanese saw a golden opportunity to bottle up all of Pearl Harbor. Luckily, the Navy reservist commanding the *Nevada* also realized this, and he successfully grounded her into the mud short of the harbor's entrance. The fore part of the ship was nearly gone and the superstructure badly damaged; 50 men were dead and 109 wounded.

Refloated and modernized, the *Nevada,* now known as the "ghost of Pearl Harbor," served in the Aleutian Islands and then moved to the North Atlantic. She saw constant action during the Normandy invasion and bombardment of Cherbourg, firing her guns at the rate of 300 rounds an hour while German shore batteries straddled her twenty-seven times. She served with the *Arkansas* at Iwo Jima and Okinawa, where she took five hits from a Japanese shore battery and was struck by a kamikaze plane, losing thirteen men.[23]

A return visitor to the Marshall Islands was the venerable battleship *Pennsylvania,* commissioned three months after the *Arkansas* and for many years the flagship of the American fleet. Ironically, she had served as the Navy's flagship during the 1921 Billy Mitchell tests. "Pennsy," as she was called by her crew, was in drydock at Pearl Harbor on December 7, 1941, when she was hit with a 500-pound fragmentation bomb. After that, despite repeated attacks by kamikaze planes, four narrow torpedo misses, and five times announced as sunk by Radio Tokyo, she escaped enemy damage in thirteen consecutive operations, including seven in Micronesia. Her gunners shot down sixteen Japanese planes, and when she returned to drydock in March 1945 she was believed to have fired more ammunition at the enemy than any other battleship. Her luck ended the night before Japan surrendered, however, when a single torpedo from a Japanese ship opened a 32-foot-square hole in her stern, taking the lives of twenty men.[24]

The oldest heavy cruiser in Bikini's fleet was the *Salt Lake City,* which sank or helped to sink fifteen Japanese ships during the war. She first served in the Marshall Islands in February 1942, with the task force commanded by Admiral Halsey that struck at targets on Wotje and Jaluit atolls in the southern Marshalls. The raids did little damage, but they were America's first offensive strike of the war and they raised morale and gave carrier groups invaluable practice. After action in the battle of Cape Esperance, where she helped save the cruiser *Boise,* the *Salt Lake* joined a task force in the Aleutian Islands to intercept Japanese reinforcements heading for Attu Island. An hour before sunrise on the morning of March 26, 1943, the task force encountered a fleet of eleven Japanese ships in what became known as the Battle of the Komandorski Islands. It was the longest continuous long-range daylight gunnery duel in the history of the modern U.S. Navy, straight from the planning books of World War I. There were no airplanes or submarines, just ships trading gunfire at distances of eight to twelve miles.

The *Salt Lake* fought off two Japanese heavy cruisers for several hours, concentrating on the cruiser *Maya.* "Those who witnessed the action," wrote naval historian Samuel Eliot Morison, "compared these two big cruisers to a pair of graceful fencers, thrusting and parrying for three and a half hours over an ocean dueling ground."[25] After several hours of battle, the hydraulic unit on the *Salt Lake*'s steering engine was knocked out by the shock of her own gunfire. After her fourth hit, icy water poured into the engine room and she began to list. Seawater seeped into the ship's fuel tanks; one by one, her engines were flooded, and she lay dead in the water. "There was not a man aboard who did not expect to die within the next few minutes," wrote correspondent John Bishop.[26] But her gunfire never faltered. With a smokescreen concealing her plight from the Japanese, a daring torpedo attack by American destroyers saved her, and the Japanese broke off the action.[27] The *Salt Lake* went on to cruise 245,000 miles during the war, seeing action at Tarawa, Palau, Yap, Ulithi, Wake, Marcus, Iwo Jima, and Okinawa.

One of the newest capital ships at Bikini was the trim light aircraft carrier *Independence,* barely three years old. After being hit by a Japanese torpedo at Tarawa, the *Independence,* which had been converted from a cruiser, was outfitted at Pearl Harbor as the first aircraft carrier to function exclusively for night operations. Her airmen harassed the Japanese in the Philippines operations, while her gunners downed more than 100 planes.[28] Nicknamed the "Mighty I," the *Independence* was the first of many fast aircraft carriers that formed task forces and sported a new Navy plane, the F6F Hellcat, specially designed to outdive and outclimb the Japanese Zero.

In early October 1943, the *Independence* participated with five other carriers, seven cruisers, and twenty-four destroyers in a two-day bombardment of Wake Island. The task force was accompanied for the first time by submarines, whose crews would try to rescue downed aviators during the attack. The first successful submarine lifeguarding, as these missions were called, was made by the *Skate,* which now sat a mile away from the *Independence* in Bikini's lagoon. A Japanese plane strafed the *Skate* on the first day of the raid on Wake, critically wounding a crew member. As the submarine headed for Midway to seek medical care for the injured lieutenant, word came that six downed aviators were adrift on life rafts in the vicinity of Wake. The *Skate* immediately turned around and was able to rescue six airmen, although her crew member died of his wounds. From then until V-J Day, every major carrier attack was made with one or more submarines standing by as lifeguards.

Following her heroics at Wake, the *Skate* went on to earn a reputation as a "big game hunter" by damaging the superbattleship *Yamato,* flagship of Admiral Yamamoto after Pearl Harbor, on Christmas Day 1943. Less than two months later she became the second submarine to sink a light cruiser when she downed the new, fast light cruiser *Agano,* sister ship of the *Sakawa,* which was now anchored less than a mile away from the *Skate* in Bikini lagoon.[29]

The undisputed queen of Bikini's lagoon was the *Saratoga,* the oldest U.S. aircraft carrier afloat and once the most powerful ship of her time. Her crews gave her many affectionate nicknames—"Lucky Sara," "Saracobra," "Grand Old Lady," or just plain "Sara." She was originally planned as a battle cruiser when construction began in 1920, but the terms of the Washington Naval Conference of 1921 forced the Navy to scrap her or convert her to an aircraft carrier. She and her sister carrier, the *Lexington,* were the biggest aircraft carriers in the world, and it was on these twin giants that the U.S. Navy developed naval air tactics in the 1930s and the carrier task force operation that dominated fighting in the Pacific in World War II. She was commissioned on November 16, 1927, and two months later the first airplane landed on her deck, piloted by Marc A. Mitscher, who as commander of his own carrier task force during World War II would be recognized as the greatest master of the new carrier warfare.[30]

Luckily, the *Sara* was in San Diego when Pearl Harbor was attacked. Within 24 hours, she was under way in the Pacific. She was in the thick of seven Pacific invasions, from the early attacks on Guadalcanal to the final strikes at Japan's home islands, and she endured as much damage as any warship not actually sent to the bottom during the war. She steamed 1 million miles on combat patrol in Japanese waters. Her planes fought the Japanese at Bougainville and Rabaul, and her strikes at Nauru in the central Pacific made possible the Marine and Army landings in the Gilbert Islands. She supported the landings at Tarawa, and later returned to the Marshall Islands, where her planes flew 453 sorties against Wotje and other atolls. She then headed westward to support the landings on Enewetak.

The *Sara* was torpedoed twice, badly damaged at Guadalcanal, put out of action several times, and at Iwo Jima sustained the heaviest kamikaze attack on a single ship to that date. On the evening of February 21, 1945, fifty kamikazes headed for the invasion fleet. Two slammed into the *Saratoga* at the water line and hit fuel storage tanks and ammunition lockers. Flames engulfed the ship, but firefighters had the situation under control in 45 minutes. Suddenly, five more kamikazes broke out of the clouds, and one, all ablaze, hit the flight deck and left a gaping hole near the bow. Smoke billowed thousands of feet into the air as the crippled carrier, accompanied by destroyers, headed for Pearl Harbor, with 315 dead or wounded men. The carrier had seen her last action in the war.

The *Saratoga* held the record for the number of aircraft landed on a carrier, 89,195 in 17 years, and less than 28 hours after launching her last plane she went into Magic Carpet service, eventually transporting nearly 30,000 veterans home from the Pacific. More than 2,000 extra servicemen were crammed aboard the carrier, and they slept on the open flight deck, in the pilot room, even in the captain's flag cabin. The Japanese announced the sinking of the *Saratoga* seven times during the war, but that fate still awaited her when she arrived at Bikini.[31]

The scene in Bikini lagoon resembled Admiral Blandy's armada at Iwo Jima. The workhorses of his bombardment force there were its six battleships, and three of these "old ladies"—the *New York, Arkansas,* and *Nevada*—were at anchor in Bikini's lagoon, all within a few square miles. Barely a few hundred yards from the *Arkansas* and *Nevada* was the heavy cruiser *Pensacola,* sister ship of the *Salt Lake.* She, too, was under Blandy's command at Iwo Jima. On the second day of the bombardment, Blandy sent her in within a mile and a half of shore to cover his minesweepers, which had approached to within 750 yards of the coast. The *Pensacola* was right under Mount Suribachi's cliffs, firing her heavy guns at almost point-blank range, when the Japanese guns finally returned her fire. Their first round was 50 yards short, and the *Pensacola* began to turn. Then a heavy gun directed by a Japanese ensign found the range. The *Pensacola* took six hits within three minutes. Ammunition boxes were set off, and she was forced to draw off, with her crew fighting fires and trying to plug holes near the waterline. Seventeen men were dead and 120 wounded.

"Keep firing!" shouted the Japanese ensign. The *Pensacola* was a sitting duck now, retreating from the action with smoke pouring from her decks. But the Japanese gun fell silent, dismounted by the recoil from its last shots. Its barrel pointed uselessly to the sky. The ensign was in a rage, cursing, "We could have sunk her! We could have sunk her!"[32]

Now the guns were silent, the Japanese defenders gone. At Bikini, Admiral Blandy was in command again, with some of the same men who had served under him at Iwo Jima. The *Pensacola* had survived the Japanese guns. The *Salt Lake*, dead in the water, had withstood Japanese shells in the Aleutians. The *Nevada, Pennsy,* and *Sara* had all survived kamikaze attacks. But now they sat, leaders of the ghost fleet in Bikini's lagoon, no men aboard, no planes taking off, no guns in action. They were all sitting ducks now, not from Japanese torpedoes or kamikazes but from a lone B-29 about to take off from Kwajalein to drop the world's fourth atomic bomb.

19

"So We Strive to Save Civilization, and We Learn How to Wreck It, All on the Same Weekend"

As Able Day approached, the pace of activity at Bikini picked up rapidly. Admiral Blandy boarded a B-29 Superfortress at Kwajalein to observe an AAF practice drop on Erik Island at Bikini in early June. "It was a very respectable hit," Blandy told reporters, adding that the plane first flew over the *Nevada,* now painted bright red and orange to make a better target. "It showed up fine," he said. "It looked like a big, red lobster. The task force boys are now calling it the 'ship with scarlet fever.'"[1] Other pumpkins dropped in the lagoon fell within 200 feet of the *Nevada.* The hit, declared Crossroads's air chief Maj. Gen. William Kepner, was "well within our limits" of accuracy.[2]

The AAF held test runs every day for the four bombing crews still competing for the prize of dropping the Able Day bomb. "Bombing efficiency has improved steadily," reported Kepner from Bikini in mid-June to Gen. Carl A. Spaatz, AAF commander in Washington, D.C.[3] He said the drop would be safely within 600 feet of the target, and he was willing to bet that it would actually be less than 500 feet. Spaatz had every reason not to bet against Kepner, because the AAF had taken numerous steps to ensure accuracy. In addition to the visual aid supplied by the bright red target ship, a radar beacon was installed on the *Nevada,* specially stationed destroyers were lined up along the bombing approach as navigation aids, and other instruments supplied accurate wind data at all altitudes over the target. "We are doing all we can to help the Air Forces drop the bomb there," Blandy told a Washington press conference, leading some AAF partisans to question his self-professed objectivity.[4]

A full-scale dress rehearsal, dubbed "Queen Day," was scheduled for June 23, but it had to be postponed a day due to cloudy weather. The explosive but nonatomic bomb dropped right on target, as fragments gouged out holes in the *Nevada*'s wooden deck and caused minor damage to the *Independence*. The rehearsal was for the most part a technical success, but a series of mishaps dogged the operation, giving rise to talk of a jinx among many men of the task force. Certain timing signals controlled by the Los Alamos group for the purpose of starting up various cameras and instruments were sent out too early.[5] An AAF captain who was the maintenance supervisor for *Dave's Dream*, the B-29 Superfortress that would drop the bomb, was killed when he walked into the plane's propeller as it prepared to taxi down the Kwajalein runway. The plane's radar failed after takeoff, two Kwajalein-based photographic planes developed engine trouble and were forced to turn back, and miserable weather over the lagoon prevented the bombing crew from even seeing the *Nevada* until its last run.[6]

Within a few days, though, the intermittent rain showers that had plagued Bikini for several weeks at last moved off. The chief weather forecaster, Col. Benjamin G. Holzman, was a veteran of Trinity and the man who two years earlier had set the date for General Eisenhower's invasion of Normandy. Holzman's job now was even more difficult than on D-day due to the lack of data about Bikini. Early studies had raised serious questions about the atoll's swirling, unpredictable winds. Wind changes were so acute that at times an ellipse was formed above the lagoon, with easterly winds up to 25,000 feet, westerlies at 30,000, and easterlies again at 60,000 feet, just below the stratosphere. "It was foreseen that under serious circumstances the radioactive elements of the atomic cloud would 'fall-out' at different levels covering a large elliptical area," concluded a secret report on Operation Crossroads. "Also the possibility had to be considered of a scattered atomic cloud endangering nearby islands as well as ships of the Task Force."[7] In fact, suitable conditions for the bomb drop—with all winds up to 60,000 feet blowing toward the west—occurred only one day in four.

At 8:30 A.M. on June 30, Colonel Holzman climbed aboard the flagship *Mount McKinley* to brief Blandy and Navy Secretary Forrestal, who had arrived the day before. Winds would be favorable on July 1, Holzman reported, and there was only about a 25 percent chance of cloudiness over Bikini at 8:30 A.M. the next morning, the scheduled time for HOW hour, the moment of the drop. Blandy immediately radioed out his command. "One July is Able Day. HOW Hour is zero eight thirty."[8]

The lagoon immediately sprang to life, setting in motion last-minute preparations and evacuation plans. On Bikini Island, scientists made final adjustments on television, movie, and still cameras. Pontoon-supported docks and the roofs of some buildings were removed to prevent blast damage, and refrigerators, generators, and water distillation units were covered with tarpaulins. Sailors readied the experimental animals on twenty-two target ships. More than 100 pigs were released into special compartments on the decks of the target ships, thousands of caged rats and mice were placed into carefully prearranged positions, and 150 goats were tethered to cleats and stanchions on the decks of the target vessels.[9]

The 1,200 sailors aboard the battleship *Nevada* shut off valves, closed hatches, and checked the radar beacon and other equipment that would guide the B-29 to its target. A mile away, the *Saratoga*'s crew tightened lashings on the Navy Hellcats strapped to the carrier's flight deck. Men on other target ships propped up dummies dressed in all types of GI clothing, while technicians made final instrument checks and riveted empty five-gallon gasoline cans to exposed decks as simple but effective gauges of the strength of the blast. "If the bomb flattens the cans like a pancake," Deak Parsons told a press conference, "you will know it is effective."[10]

With preparations nearly complete, the first of more than 175 support ships headed out of the lagoon. Ten destroyers steamed south by the ghost fleet and out the Eneu channel, ready to track Able's radioactive cloud. Meanwhile, Rep. John J. Rooney paid a farewell visit to his state's battleship, the *New York*. Before leaving the ship, Capt. Lowe H. Bibby hauled down the Stars and Stripes from the fantail, slowly folded it, and handed it to Rooney. Bibby then took a piece of chalk and scrawled the words "Old sailors never die" on a gun turret. "That sign will still be there this time tomorrow," he told Rooney. With a farewell salute, Bibby stepped down the gangway, leaving to Rooney the honor of being the last man off the *New York*. "It was like a funeral," Rooney said. "A ship that had been so alive suddenly seemed dead, peopled by ghosts. I felt a little chill."[11]

By sunset, nearly all the support ships had moved to their preassigned positions at least 15 miles east and northeast of Bikini Atoll into grids code-named for automobiles, with such names as de Soto, Studebaker, Hudson, and Packard. Norris Bradbury of Los Alamos reported that Deak Parsons was being "continually pushed by various enthusiastic individuals to come closer and closer" than 15 miles, but Bradbury was comfortable with this distance. "There is no need to take a chance and if 15 miles is o.k. from a technical point of view, it is plenty close enough," he wrote his staff, adding, "Personally, I wish to be at least 15 miles away with plenty of room to turn around in."[12]

Back in the States, movie newsreels showed scenes of daily life on Rongerik—Bikini women combing their hair, men in their outrigger canoes, children swarming through the village, the community singing their Marshallese version of "You Are My Sunshine." "Here in the peaceful Pacific, where the natives sit in their courtesy and in their friendliness, with their smiles and with their happiness, they aren't sure exactly what the atom bomb means but at least they admit it," concluded the narrator.[13]

Just to be safe, the Navy evacuated as many people as possible from the area around Bikini. At Rongerik Atoll, 125 miles east of Bikini, an LST—the same type of ship that had moved the islanders in March—stood by in case the winds blew the wrong way. At one point after the shot, the ship actually loaded up the Bikinians and steamed away, but when the wind direction changed the islanders were permitted to return. Back in March, Stafford L. Warren, Blandy's radiological safety advisor, had prepared a plan for the evacuation of Rongerik, even though he believed that the likelihood of having to evacuate the atoll was remote. Warren recommended that the Navy tell the islanders prior to the tests that they would be "assembled and prepared to board evacuation ship to observe 'fireworks.'"[14] At Enewetak, 200 miles west of Bikini, 691 nonessential U.S. personnel were evacuated to Majuro in the southern Marshalls, and five C-54 air transports were in place to fly out the others on one hour's notice. Similar measures were taken at Kwajalein should the winds shift or the B-29 crash on takeoff, as nonessential personnel were moved over to Ebeye Island or to ships in the lagoon.[15]

At the recommendation of Stafford Warren, the Marshallese living on three other atolls close to Bikini—Rongelap, Wotho, and Enewetak—were also evacuated as a safety precaution for the duration of both tests.[16] The 128 Enewetakese were moved to Kwajalein, and the inhabitants of Rongelap and Wotho were moved to Lae Atoll, south of Kwajalein. Commodore Wyatt greeted the islanders at Lae with a speech similar to the one he had delivered at Bikini several months earlier, filled with references to the Bible and America's might. At Pearl Harbor, he said, Japan "slapped us on the left cheek and on the right cheek and in the face," and "all of that civilization which worships God, as do you people, was threatened." America came back, though, he continued, because "God looks after His people." He recounted the story of Moses and the flight from Egypt, telling how God, in the form of a pillar of smoke by day and a pillar of fire by night, guided and protected the people. America, he said, was developing something more powerful than the Army, Navy, and Air Force—"even as effective as the pillar of smoke by day and the pillar of fire by night. That something was in the hands of the great wise men of America. These men worked in their laboratories in America, quietly saying nothing, but working out the secrets of God. And under His guidance, out of that study came the atom bomb," which America could use "if in the future any nation attacked the peoples of God."

In thanking the islanders, he compared them to the Bikinians. "Where in the world," he asked, "could we find such a wonderful spirit of 'My God is your God; my house is your house; your people are my people,' a spirit which prevails amongst all of you people here! Those nations throughout the whole world that are looking here to you have a beacon light which shines through all Christianity."[17]

Wyatt did not have a monopoly on biblical references. At religious services around the United States the weekend before the test, several clergymen read out the scene of chaos and destruction in Revelation in which seven angels sound their trumpets before God:

> And the second angel sounded, and as it were a great mountain burning with fire was cast into the sea; and the third part of the sea became blood:
> And the third part of the creatures which were in the sea and had life, died; and the third part of the ships were destroyed.
> (Rev. 8:8–9)[18]

Nor was Wyatt the only Navy official to pontificate on the upcoming events at Bikini. "Crossroads is one of the greatest pageants of all time," declared the Navy's second-in-command, Vice Chief of Naval Operations DeWitt C. Ramsey, two days before the shot. "The immensity of spaces, the fantastic nature of the physical forces brought into play, the mighty array of ships and men moving across the Pacific, the imponderables of man and nature—these are the stuff of great drama." Ramsey's overblown rhetoric made Operation Crossroads sound like a cross between a ballet and a heavyweight bout. "It is like an hour glass," he continued. "Ships, men, brains, and material drawn from the ends of the earth and meeting for a brief moment in a tiny lagoon, brought into pinpoint fineness in the person of the bombardier and then, with the plummeting missile and the mushrooming explosion spreading out once again to encompass the future of mankind."[19]

Some reporters at Bikini were hopeful. "These may well be the last atomic bomb explosions the world will ever see," wrote one.[20] To a large extent, though, the media fostered an expectation of massive destruction, an expectation encouraged by some high-ranking officials. The chief Los Alamos scientist on Kwajalein, Dr. Roger S. Warner, hinted at a press conference that the Able blast might hurl one or more of the target ships clear out of the water. When a reporter then asked if the bomb might be a dud, an angry Warner jumped to his feet.

"Damn it, why'd you have to ask that?" he snapped. But Karl Compton, chairman of the Joint Chiefs of Staff evaluation board, interrupted Warner. "There is a certain possibility—though small—that this bomb might fizzle," he said. "I am anxious that this be realized so the public will not think we are alibiing if we get poor results."[21]

Overall, the quality of the reporting from Bikini led the public to expect something between Doomsday and the Fourth of July. One *Newsweek* correspondent wrote that the destruction was not likely to be spectacular, but another remarked in the same issue that "many could feel a secret tug of sympathy for the uneasy inhabitants of the low flat plain fronting the Pacific at the foot of the Sierra Nevadas." At the time of the blast, he added, many inhabitants of Los Angeles "will be picnicking up in the mountains—just in case," and the magazine reminded its readers that "all the worriers were not crackpots or alarmists." In Paris, according to another correspondent, the mood was "Eat, drink and be merry, for tomorrow we atomize," and newspaper headlines there trumpeted: "Tomorrow the world is going to blow up."[22]

Hanson Baldwin of the *New York Times* scorned "the 'crack-pot' assertions of pseudo-scientists, many with an axe to grind. They have been completely answered by the best scientific brains of the country." The *Times* itself saw no reason why its readers would not have a newspaper the following Sunday, "the chances being more than reasonably good that the world will still be there after the bomb drops on Bikini atoll."[23] Operation Crossroads "has been producing a psychology of fear," lamented Norman Myrick, a member of Fitzhugh Lee's press staff. "People are afraid just because they do not know the known facts about the atom bomb. That is a fundamental psychological fear."[24]

Others saw a more ominous side to Crossroads. On the eve of the tests, ABC radio commentator Gram Swing was struck by the juxtaposition of Crossroads and the UN negotiations. "At Bikini, the Navy is preparing itself for the failure of the UN Atomic Energy Commission," he told his listeners. "On the one hand, we're striving to rid the world of a weapon which may set back civilization for centuries . . . and, on the other hand, we're training ourselves in the use of this very weapon. So we strive to save civilization, and we learn how to wreck it, all on the same weekend."[25]

On Saturday night, June 29, ABC radio broadcast a one-hour prerecorded program on Operation Crossroads, as Forrestal, Nimitz, Eisenhower, Patterson, and Blandy all defended the tests. "Is Operation Crossroads a gesture of war?" asked Forrestal. "I can assert without reserve that these tests do not stem from aggressive plans. . . . It is precisely because we are not an aggressive nation, because we want nothing except the benefits of peace throughout the world, that we must not lag in our determination to have the means of enforcing peace."[26] To some critics, though, the speakers' sense of urgency seemed forced. "The phrases, 'save American lives' and 'national defense' ran through the program with the persistence of a Pepsi-Cola jingle," wrote one commentator.[27]

Across the international date line that night at Bikini, only eight support ships kept the ghost fleet company. Bikini Island, teeming with thousands of men for months, was virtually deserted. The only sounds other than the swaying coconut palms were the voices of forty-six men making last-minute instrument checks. Out in the lagoon, only three or four men were left on each target ship, checking for stragglers with their flashlights.

Holzman briefed Blandy and Forrestal at 10:00 P.M. and again at 4:00 A.M. on July 1. "The predictions still being upheld, the show was definitely on," noted Forrestal in his diary.[28]

As dawn broke on July 1, each target ship was scanned for a yellow and red flag, the sign that the last man had been taken off. The last support vessel had departed from the lagoon, leaving the ghost fleet to face the bomb. "These Pacific islands are tense with expectation," wrote one reporter. "No D-Day during the war produced the type of anticipation which is prevalent out here today."[29]

At Kwajalein, 250 miles to the south, 30-year-old Maj. Woodrow P. "Woody" Swancutt, of Wisconsin Rapids, Wisconsin, was awakened at 2:00 A.M. Swancutt, the national intercollegiate middleweight boxing champion in 1939–40 and veteran of forty-nine missions in the China-Burma Theater in World War II, was the pilot of *Dave's Dream*, the B-29 Superfortress that was about to drop the Able Day bomb on Bikini lagoon. The bombardier, Maj. Harold H. Wood, a former grocery clerk from Bordentown, New Jersey, had flown twenty-four bombing missions during the war, including the invasion bombing of Normandy, and had received two Purple Hearts. He sported the nickname "Lemon Bar" because of his luck at the slot machines in the officers' clubs.[30] Swancutt and his crew arrived for breakfast at the mess hall at 3:20 A.M., looking fit and confident. The men had had about five hours of sleep, much more than the many participants and reporters who had stayed up for the midnight weather briefing.

Despite the weather forecasters' predictions, heavy cumulus clouds hung over Bikini's lagoon at dawn. "It looked definitely bad," recalled Blandy, as he decided to hold up the test to see if the weather would clear.[31] It did. At 5:42 A.M., Blandy radioed the go-ahead to Brig. Gen. Roger M. Ramey of the AAF, who jumped into his jeep with Swancutt and sped across the tarmac at Kwajalein to *Dave's Dream*. Named after Capt. Dave Semple, the B-29 bombardier who died on a test flight in New Mexico while competing for the honor of dropping the Able Day bomb, the plane was easily identified by the large black letter *B* on its rudder.[32] A mobile crane had slowly hoisted the bomb into a trench beneath the B-29's open bomb bay at midnight, and from there it was drawn up into the bay. The bomb now had a name. It was called Gilda, after Rita Hayworth's latest movie, and a picture of the Hollywood star in a low-cut gown was painted on the bomb casing. "She kept us awake nights," explained one scientist. Crew members had asked for five pictures of the actress to ensure a good likeness.[33]

While Swancutt and his crew prepared to take off, the command plane, the first of eighty-five other planes that would fly over Bikini that day, was already in the air, carrying top-ranking officers and observers. Some passenger lists were still being finalized an hour before scheduled takeoff because of late changes and bumping. "Petty personal jealousies and feuds prompted a number of observers, chiefly congressmen, to demand changes," reported the Associated Press, while one group of scientists refused to fly in the same plane as a group of congressmen.[34] Meanwhile, Blandy moved the time of the drop back 30 minutes, to 9:00 A.M., to take advantage of decreased cloudiness over the lagoon.

In the United States and all around the world, Able Day was carried live over the radio. Operation Crossroads was an early media event, swamped in publicity and sensationalism, and the live radio broadcast of the Able Day shot drew huge audiences. "Around the world," reported *Time*, "ordinary men and women who would be the casualties in an atomic war bent their heads and cupped their ears to their radio sets to catch this preview."[35]

As the live coverage began, a correspondent interviewed Major Swancutt's mother, Caroline. "Do you feel a little bit anxious along with him?" the reporter asked.

"I certainly do," she replied, "but I have much faith and confidence in Woody and know that he will do the very best he can." She browsed through a letter she had received from him and read it out loud. "'Don't worry about me, mother. Believe me when I say we're in no danger at all in the test, no matter what you have heard. And have confidence in me. I'll be okay.'"[36]

The broadcast switched to the *Mount McKinley*, where Admiral Blandy assured the families of those participating in the tests. "No tidal wave," he proclaimed.[37]

Swancutt was confident that his crew would find the *Nevada*. "If we can see it, we'll hit it," he promised just before takeoff. His bombardier, Harold Wood, smiled in agreement. "My fingers feel good this morning," he said. "I think we'll do a job on the Navy."[38]

20

"Listen World, This Is Crossroads!"

At the western end of the Kwajalein runway, Woody Swancutt revved up the four motors on *Dave's Dream,* while the weaponeers, two 26-year-old ensigns, sat in the bomb bay, preparing to arm the atom bomb. Silverplated B-29s were nose heavy when loaded with an atom bomb, so 1,500 pounds of buckshot, stashed in aluminum cans, had been crammed into the farthest points aft in the fuselage compartment to make the takeoff easier.[1]

"Now the plane is swinging around," shouted Mutual radio correspondent Bill Chaplin into his microphone from a hangar roof overlooking the runway. "He's giving her the gun! The atom bomb plane, *Dave's Dream,* is starting down the runway. Fifty miles an hour, I should say, now sixty. He's on his way! Probably eighty miles now, one hundred, one-twenty. He's up! The plane is airborne. The atom bomb is in the air on its way to Bikini, for the greatest experiment, the most explosive experiment in history!"[2]

Dave's Dream was airborne at 5:53 A.M. on Monday, July 1. Three Navy planes and a B-17 followed at five-minute intervals for a possible air-sea rescue. Photographic planes took off next, each with a huge letter *P* painted on its tail against an orange field. Other B-29s followed, bearing black emblems of lightning bolts; they would measure the shock wave of the blast through the air. Then came the observers' planes, filled with reporters, congressmen, and military officials.

182

Over at Ebeye, several miles away, Navy seaplanes slid down the launching ramp and took off for the two-hour flight to Bikini, set to make low-altitude Geiger counter measurements over the lagoon immediately after the blast. Technicians set their instruments and passed out film badges, protective goggles, and even gas masks to the crew. No one, though, knew if the gas masks would prevent inhalation of the fission products from the test. A University of Wisconsin scientist told the technicians that the masks were not necessary. "You would all be dead from radiation before you could inhale enough to hurt you," he told them.

"And if you ran into a cloud of hot stuff, you would not bother to wear one?" they asked.

He hesitated. "Yes. Yes. I probably would, though I couldn't tell you why."[3]

Fifty miles southwest of Bikini, at 8:20 A.M., Swancutt spotted his guidepost, a destroyer, and began to level off for his trial run. Radio silence had been ordered throughout Bikini so that all planes could hear *Dave's Dream*, which had been given the code name Skylight One. Suddenly the silence was broken as Major Wood's slow, calm voice came over the radio. "This is Skylight One. Skylight One. Ten minutes before first simulated bomb release. Stand by. First practice run." Flying around the lagoon were sixty-four B-17s, B-29s, C-54s, Hellcats, and seaplanes, some of them pilotless, radio-controlled drones, ready to perform their radiological and photographic tests.

The dry run was a success. Swancutt clearly saw the *Nevada*, and his crew picked up the radar beacon at Bikini from 50 miles away and used it to approach and maintain the proper course. Visibility was excellent, and the ballistic wind data was encouraging. Surface winds were at eight knots, and wind speed was no greater than sixteen knots at any point between the water and *Dave's Dream*, five miles above the lagoon.[4]

At 8:32 Wood's voice came on again. "This is Skylight One, Skylight One. Predicted time of actual bomb release thirty minutes. Stand by. Mark." Ship captains called all personnel on deck and ordered them to ready their goggles. The sight of the reporters crowded on the starboard deck of the *Appalachian* made a fascinating contrast to the momentous occasion. All were sitting in deck chairs behind rows of typewriters on tables, goggles at the ready around their necks, many of them dressed in an assortment of pajamas, aloha shirts, boudoir slacks, and baseball hats.[5]

It was 5:32 P.M. on Sunday afternoon, June 30, on the East Coast, and NBC had returned to its normal program. The NBC Symphony

Orchestra was playing the last movement of Shostakovich's Fifth Symphony when an announcer came on the air.

> At this time NBC interrupts its regular program schedule to bring you a history making broadcast—the actual dropping of the atomic bomb at Bikini. In a matter of minutes now an Army Superfortress will drop that bomb on target ships in Bikini lagoon. There are those who predict it may be the last such test if nations now can agree to outlaw the bomb. The United Nations Atomic Energy Commission now is analyzing that problem, and the world waits to see whether there can be a compromise between our own plan for controlling atomic energy and that of Soviet Russia.[6]

A metronome placed aboard the *Pennsylvania,* electronically hooked up to a radio transmitter, started ticking away the last minutes before the blast. A radio correspondent aboard the *Appalachian* explained that the metronome was standing next to an open microphone on the *Pennsylvania,* which was now abandoned by all but goats, mice, and rats. "Listen to the ticking of the metronome," he said. "When the metronome stops, the atomic bomb has exploded." The steady beat was heard on radios around the world. It sounded "more and more like drums in the jungle," wrote William Laurence of the *New York Times.* "There came a time when the metronome drowned out the chopping of the ship's engines and the pulsings of the Pacific. It came to sound like a voice of doom tolling the world's last minutes."[7]

CBS correspondent Bill Downs was on an observation plane following *Dave's Dream* across the lagoon. "These few minutes we are talking are a sort of wake for the gallant ships in the lagoon below," he shouted over the engines' roar. "The Bikini target fleet, especially those proud old warriors, the *Nevada, Pennsylvania* and *Arkansas,* looked ominously lonely," wrote another reporter on the same plane. "At eight miles away they seemed like a small boy's toy fleet. As they awaited the atomic bomb over Bikini, you had a momentary feeling of pity for them. There was such an ominous peacefulness and quietness in Bikini before the atomic storm."[8]

A correspondent aboard the flagship *Mount McKinley* reported that Blandy was pacing the deck "like an expectant father."

"Of all the lousy metaphors!" muttered one listener back in New York. "This is a death watch, not a maternity ward!"[9]

A Navy seaplane made one last sweep across the ghost fleet and out over the nontarget ships. "You could see the people standing motionless at the rail," recalled David Bradley, a radiological monitor. "For all the roar of our twin engines, everything seemed to be holding a breathless silence."[10]

Finally, after 20 minutes, Major Wood's voice came over the ticking of the metronome. "Ten minutes to go, ten minutes to go."

"Five minutes to go, five minutes to go." Then three, then two. Each time he repeated himself like an echo.

"Two minutes to go, two minutes to go. Release minus two minutes."

Commanding officers on the support ships ordered all hands without goggles to look away from Bikini, to look down at the deck, to shut their eyes and cover them with one arm bent against the face.

"Adjust all goggles. Adjust all goggles. Stand by."

"Come in Bill Chaplin at Kwajalein," said the radio announcer. Chaplin started to explain the sense of relief at Kwajalein that Swancutt got Dave's Dream safely off the island, but he was cut off by bombardier Wood's voice.

"Coming up on actual bomb release. Stand by."

A few seconds passed. Dave's Dream was flying at 28,000 feet. Suddenly Wood came on again.

"Mark! Bomb away, bomb away, bomb away and falling!" It was 14 seconds before 9:00 A.M.[11]

Another voice came over the radio. "Listen world, this is Crossroads!"[12]

Aboard the Mount McKinley, Norris Bradbury grabbed Curtis Youngblood's arm. "Curtis, this has got to be good, this has got to be good," he said. "And I tell you," recalled Youngblood, "I thought during the countdown he was going to squeeze my arm off."[13]

Forty-eight seconds passed. There was nothing on the radio but the sound of the metronome.

The bomb, adorned with a picture of Rita Hayworth, never reached sea level. It was detonated 518 feet above the lagoon's surface, setting into motion the nuclear chain reaction.[14] A spectacular explosion thrust a huge ball of flame thousands of feet upward, like a meteor headed the wrong way. It was many times brighter than the sun, and its blinding light obliterated the morning sun. Suddenly the flame exploded, as if it were a balloon punctured by a pin. "Isn't that beautiful!" shouted Bradbury.[15]

Enormous swirling masses of flaming red, purple, and white clouds erupted from the lagoon. The clouds leapt upward, churning and coiling. Out of them emerged a column of white smoke that climbed to 20,000 feet, and from its top emerged the now-familiar mushroom-like cloud. The cloud initially surged upward at a speed of 100 miles per minute and eventually reached a height of more than 40,000 feet. Towering over the atoll like a genie escaped from its bottle, the cloud kept growing and changing colors. The mushroom head broadened as it rose, eventually widening to nearly two miles before it broke off into the upper atmosphere and floated off to the west.

The blast annihilated less than one gram of matter, converting it into energy. The energy released, though, was enormous. In an infinitesimal fraction of time, about one ten-millionth of a second, the bomb released the explosive energy of 23,000 tons of TNT, or 23 kilotons. The surface temperature of the fireball was over 100,000 degrees Fahrenheit, hotter than the surface of the sun, and interior temperatures were far higher. "It was like watching the birth and the death of a star, born and disintegrated in the instant of its birth," wrote Bill Laurence. "When the flash came it lighted up sky and ocean with the light of many suns, a light not of the earth."[16]

Assistant Secretary of War for Air W. Stuart Symington was in the observation plane closest to the blast, and his plane was immediately rocked by the shock wave. Symington looked down at the water. "I noticed a large ship turn over in the lagoon," he recalled, "as a child would turn over a toy boat in a bathtub." He saw the attack transport *Gilliam,* which was fewer than 50 yards from the blast; it sank within one minute.[17]

Almost all the other observers, though, were much farther away, and for them there was little drama. The ticking metronome had stopped, but for nearly 30 seconds there was no sound at all on the radio. The first reporter to speak on the global hookup was Bill Downs. "There was no tidal wave," he said in a disappointed voice. "The airplane did not receive any shock wave. I can't see any damage below." A reporter from the *Mount McKinley* followed. "I can see the palm trees. The island is still afloat. I can see the *Nevada,* too. She's still afloat."[18] Looking down from an observer plane, Gen. Joseph W. "Vinegar Joe" Stilwell looked down at the *Nevada* still floating majestically in the tropical sunlight, apparently unharmed. "The damned Air Corps has missed the target again," he mumbled. "Everyone had the feeling that something had gone wrong," wrote Groves's deputy, Kenneth Nichols.[19]

The next correspondent came on the air. It was just minutes after the explosion. "Scientists agree it's a big success," he said, apparently basing his opinion exclusively on the fact that the bomb actually went off. The broadcast then switched back to a San Francisco studio. "A tense and waiting world heard the broadcast of the explosion of the fourth atomic bomb," said the broadcaster, groping for something to say. "The sound of the explosion was not nearly what people had expected."[20] Flying over the target fleet, a team of radiation monitors was disappointed not to see more destruction. "There was much pooh-poohing of the Bomb over the interphone," wrote one, "and at last the co-pilot growled: 'Well, it looks to me like the atom bomb is just about like the Army Air Force—highly overrated.'"[21]

Some observers did not even see the blast through the dark goggles everyone was ordered to wear. "They're so black," reported one correspondent from an observation plane, "that I could see nothing at all through them." "The flash was so very dim through those black goggles that I felt for all the world as though I'd put my head in a rain barrel to avoid the glare of a flashlight bulb," said Senator Guy Cordon of Oregon.[22] The high humidity at Bikini absorbed a large amount of the brilliant light from the shot, and it turned out that the goggles were not needed. They were later determined to be 10 times too dark, cutting out over 99 percent of the light from the explosion. "If you turned your back at time zero and then turned around after the sensation of heat disappeared and the brilliance of the surroundings subsided, you were safe enough," recalled Stafford Warren, Operation Crossroads's radiological safety director.[23]

Representative Edouard Izac summed up the reaction of most of the observers. "It was one of keen disappointment, I'll say," he complained. "You could see very little, you could hear practically nothing and you could feel absolutely nothing."[24]

"Is that all?" reporters snorted incredulously. "This is a disaster," complained another. "This is Operation Chloroform, the logical sequel to Operations Build-up and Handout. Nothing could live up to the advance notices. Now the public will go back to sleep again."[25]

"Blast Force Seems Less Than Expected," ran the banner headline in the *New York Times,* while Bob Considine described the sound of the explosion as similar to a "discreet belch" from the far end of a bar.[26] Virtually all the reporters were disappointed. "As a spectacle," wrote one, Able "was, in Broadway parlance, a flop."[27] *Variety* expressed its views of the broadcast in a terse page-1 review: "ZZZ-ZZZ-Pffffz-Zzzz." One reporter compared the experience to small boys waiting for the circus to come to town. "There was the same high hope of a great thrill, and the same momentary disappointment when the bomb burst that one feels when a circus act proves less exciting than its billboard poster." A third observer was more blunt. "Blandy's inferno," he said, "has become Blandy's bust."[28] One congressman dismissed the blast as a "giant firecracker,"[29] while the Russian representative, Prof. Simon Alexandrov, shrugged his shoulders, pointed to the mushroom cloud and muttered, "Not so much."[30] Radio listeners were equally disappointed. "There were more explosions in that first [Red Sox] game at Fenway," complained one Bostonian, while another baseball fan referred to the "dud-by-dud" description of the test.[31]

Part of the disappointment was due to the fact that the observers were so far away from the blast. Reporters were prepared to be buffeted by a terrific shock wave. Observers at Alamogordo told of thunder reverberating like close-range artillery fire. The ground trembled under the observers' feet, they felt a wave of hot air followed by a mighty boom, and the light was so intense that some observers 20 miles away had blind spots for up to half an hour. One scientist had even been knocked off his feet by the blast, and another was blinded for a day and a half.[32] At Alamogordo, though, observers were as close as six miles away, while at Bikini the closest correspondents were about 15 miles away. Sound and light intensity fall off as the square of the distance increases, so these phenomena were nearly 10 times stronger at the Trinity test. Moreover, the high humidity at Bikini absorbed much of the heat and light. As a result, observers aboard the ships felt no shock wave and no heat, and the only sound of the explosion was a low-pitched rumbling blast, like a distant thunderclap, 90 seconds after the detonation.[33]

Several military observers were concerned. Adm. John H. Hoover, a member of the Joint Chiefs' evaluation board, thought the bomb had not gone off as planned. Deak Parsons thought the bomb was less powerful than either of the ones dropped on Japan, but Stafford Warren hastened to assure reporters that it was comparable in yield with the Nagasaki bomb, adding emphatically that it was not a "dud."[34]

Within eight minutes of the explosion, the first of eight drone planes launched from Enewetak and the aircraft carrier *Shangri-La* entered the mushroom cloud to take air samples. At the same time, four Navy torpedo bombers were launched from the aircraft carrier *Saidor* to photograph the target vessels and steer the drone boats, which took water samples in the lagoon to determine when the support ships could return. Small boats with radiological safety personnel reentered the lagoon two hours after the shot, threading their way through the target area with Geiger counters to detect radiation. As expected in an air drop, though, most of the deadly fission products were sucked up into the mushroom cloud and carried aloft into the stratosphere, where they were later dispersed.[35]

Admiral Blandy went on the air 90 minutes after the shot. "There have been no tidal waves, no earthquakes or any other unnatural phenomena," he declared. "The radioactive cloud . . . will not endanger personnel, ships or any Pacific island. . . . No one will be allowed in the lagoon until we make positive it will be safe."[36] At 2:30 P.M., he gave the all-clear signal, and the *Mount McKinley* led the support ships back into the lagoon.

The sight was staggering. The 446-foot attack transport *Gilliam*, which was located closest to the point where the force of the explosion hit the lagoon's surface, had sunk within one minute. "The forward part of the ship is mashed down as though the blast acted like the hammer and the water an anvil," reported a Navy diver. Fewer than 400 yards away was another attack transport, the *Carlisle*, loaded nearly to capacity with fuel and ammunition, including rocket heads and incendiary clusters. Thrown 150 yards by the force of the blast, the ship was smoking heavily within three minutes and sank within forty minutes. The *Gilliam* sits upright on the lagoon floor today, barely recognizable, with successive deck levels pancaked down into the hold and crumbled and torn wreckage all around. Close by sits her sister ship, the *Carlisle,* substantially more intact, but still showing evidence from the blast, with her port shell plating buckled, dented, and dished.[37]

The 338-foot destroyer *Anderson* was located 600 yards from under the Zeropoint. The blast destroyed most of the upper part of her superstructure, and she exploded violently within seconds when her magazines detonated. Within four minutes of the blast she was on her beam end, and four minutes later she was gone. Another destroyer, the *Lamson,* which had helped search for Amelia Earhart in 1937, sank in the late afternoon. As Blandy's flagship approached to within one mile of the target array, the Japanese cruiser *Sakawa* was burning fiercely, its superstructure flattened, but it was still afloat.[38]

From the flag bridge of the *Mount McKinley,* Forrestal sent out a message of congratulations to all Crossroads personnel. He then boarded the *Panamint* and asked the UN observers not to consider Operation Crossroads as a "gesture of war or aggression, or a threat."[39] Brig. Gen. Roger M. Ramey said that the bomb drop "was a complete and unqualified success," Admiral Blandy told reporters that it was made "with very good accuracy," and Major General Kepner sent a message commending all AAF personnel "for one of the most outstanding air operations in history."[40]

Nothing could have been further from the truth. Despite numerous practice runs, a brightly painted target, precise coordinates, and optimal visual aiming conditions, *Dave's Dream* badly missed its target. Instead of exploding over the *Nevada,* the bomb went off half a mile to the west, almost directly over the aircraft carrier *Independence.* The miss destroyed a large amount of data and equipment, made other instruments useless, and, in the words of a secret Air Force report, "invalidated much of what had been planned as a scientific test."[41] The blast was almost directly over a string of instruments designed to record shock wave velocity and other data. The bomb destroyed this equipment, sank the *Gilliam,* one of the most important instrument ships, and detonated so far from other instruments that it rendered them ineffective as well. "Unfortunately, the data secured from the . . . target ships were none too good," wrote Stafford Warren three days after the test.[42]

Scientists were aware that the bomb drop might be off-target, so they had placed backup equipment on several ships in case of a quarter-mile error in any direction, but, as the top-secret technical report on the tests noted, they "had not anticipated so large an error."[43] The explosion was missed by almost all the high-speed cameras, whose narrow lateral telephoto views were focused elsewhere. With so few instruments recording the actual blast, it became almost impossible to determine the precise location of the explosion because the lagoon's waters, unlike the surface shadows and burns at Hiroshima and Nagasaki, revealed no clues as to the exact point of detonation.

The *Nevada,* the ship that should have been sunk, suffered only superficial damage. The bridge was distorted and the orange-red deck was seared and blackened by the blast, but the hull and interior were not disturbed. There was virtually no damage below the decks; pictures of pin-up girls did not even fall from the bulkheads. The *Independence,* though, while still afloat, suffered spectacular damage. One observer described it as looking "battered and bent like a tin can."[44] Much of the superstructure was hopelessly torn and twisted, and the flight deck was destroyed. Part of it was blown off completely, while the rest was broken or buckled, and all twenty-five fighter planes on the deck were tossed overboard. The hangar deck was gutted and huge vertical steel beams were ripped loose and hung grotesquely. Six hours after the blast, internal explosions of torpedo warheads and gasoline touched off fires throughout the ship. Fireboats tried to save her, but she was wrapped in smoke, her hangar deck in flames.

The wooden deck of the despised *Nagato* was burning slowly. "We were terribly disappointed because she hadn't been sunk or at least badly damaged," wrote one observer in his journal. "Instead she stood there still in all her black and filthy ugliness—a little more battle scarred than before," and the mines strapped to her deck unexploded.[45] The *Arkansas* and heavy cruiser *Pensacola* were heavily damaged, all with blackened paint and topside structures twisted and distorted to the point of uselessness. Smokestacks had crumpled like paper, lubricants were burned out, and masts, radio antennae, and radar screens were snapped off or in complete tatters. The superstructure of the submarine *Skate* was a contorted mass of wreckage. Fires burned briefly on the *Pennsylvania, Arkansas, Saratoga,* and several other ships. Fourteen airplanes were either sunk with target vessels or were blown overboard from other ships that remained afloat, and twenty-nine other planes suffered major damage.[46]

The test animals were moved off the target ships seven hours after the shot. Only about 10 percent died instantly from the impact of the blast, and the first press reports, understandably, were about the survivors.

"Will we be as lucky as those goats on the battleship at Bikini?" asked one newspaper editorial writer, not knowing that most would be dead within a few months from radiation-related illnesses.[47] The goats were absolutely imperturbable. Close-up motion pictures showed one munching his hay without interruption as the shock wave struck and debris flew all around, and the goats aboard the smoldering *Pennsylvania* continued eating as fireboats pulled alongside to control the fires. And the heroine of the blast was a rat aboard the *Pennsylvania* who, apparently as the bomb burst, gave birth to three babies—appropriately named Alpha, Beta, and Gamma.[48]

Another survivor of the bomb and instant media star was "Pig 311," who was locked in an officers' toilet aboard the *Sakawa* before the test, but was found swimming in the lagoon the next day, and managed to survive with no sign of illness. She was sent to the Naval Medical Research Institute in Bethesda, Maryland, for observation, and her inability to produce offspring led scientists to speculate that she may have been sterilized by radiation at Bikini. She was eventually given to the Smithsonian Institution's National Zoological Park in Washington, D.C., where she died in 1950.[49]

The morning after the shot, Forrestal and Blandy "braved gamma radiation," according to a Task Force One press release, to inspect the damage. As Blandy's boat pulled up alongside the submarine *Skate*, James Nolan, a Los Alamos technician, reported that radiation readings on his Geiger counter were off the scale. Blandy laughed and shouted, "Let's get the hell out of here!" He then turned to Forrestal and laughingly explained that Nolan's counter was so delicate that "my luminous watch dial will make it go off the scale."

Blandy and Forrestal then motored over to inspect the *Independence*. Perhaps to emphasize the men's bravery, the Operation Crossroads press release noted that the two were "unmindful of radioactivity still lingering aboard ships in the target array's bull's eye circle." When someone shouted from a salvage tug that the *Sakawa* was going down a mile away, Blandy ordered his boat full speed ahead. Forrestal and Blandy watched for over 10 minutes from only 50 yards away, as the *Sakawa* slowly disappeared in greenish foam under the water.[50] The two men then boarded the *New York,* which had suffered less damage. Blandy told Forrestal that the battleship could sail back to port under her own power, but still had to undergo Test Baker. He also reminded Forrestal that the Navy had promised Governor Dewey that New York State would receive the battleship if she survived Crossroads. Not one to miss a political opportunity, Blandy said that he had promised Governor Dewey that the *New York* would not be exposed to as much radiation as other target ships.

Another group of correspondents and members of the two evaluation boards visited Bikini Island, four miles from the target center, and found it untouched. "Palm trees were not singed," wrote one reporter. The five high towers used to measure and photograph the test were intact, there was no evidence of high waves and no indication that vegetation had been affected by the heat or radiation.[51]

As scientists and technicians went ashore to recover their instruments, they discovered that an error that had occurred during the "Queen Day" rehearsal was repeated in the Able shot. The timing signal operator, tasked with starting numerous instruments at the moment of the bomb drop, sent out his signal 10 seconds late. As a result, dozens of cameras failed to record the blast, and numerous spectrographs, shock-wave instruments, and high-speed cameras recorded no data whatsoever. Reporters were never told of this multimillion-dollar mistake.[52]

After the huge buildup for Able, the disappointed media, which half-expected to see ships flying around in the air and most of the fleet sent to the bottom of the lagoon, began to downplay fears about the atomic bomb. "The A-bomb is a distinctly overrated weapon," concluded the *Christian Science Monitor,* and *Time* noted that "the Thing had grown a little less awful as a result of Bikini. Its apparently infinite power was finite after all."[53] ABC radio commentator Elmer Davis observed, "So far from disintegrating the ocean . . . , the explosion didn't even knock over the palm trees on the islands around the lagoon."[54] The *Nation,* echoing this sense of failure, lamented that "the meager results of . . . this giant Fourth of July explosion . . . may lull popular fears as to the potency of man's latest plaything." As one writer has noted, the Able shot "soothe[d] the fears of the American people almost as much as the bombs dropped on Japan had aroused them."[55]

21

"The Fleet Looked as Though It Had Returned from a Quick Trip to Hell"

Within two days of the Able test, Bikini's waters, ships, and shore were declared radiologically safe. A sense of relief pervaded the Crossroads personnel, and everyone was in a festive mood. The beaches and bars were packed, and poker games went late into the nights.

Eight of the fifteen congressmen returned to the United States, as did nearly two-thirds of the correspondents. No one missed the departing newsmen. Some were conscientious and workmanlike, but others were junketeers and phonies who viewed Operation Crossroads as an opportunity for an exciting vacation. Labeled "free riders" by their colleagues, these included a lawyer for a newspaper, a staff writer for a magazine that was never published, an assistant district attorney from Brooklyn, New York, and a freelance reporter who did not file a single story for the newspaper chain he purported to represent. Indeed, several newsmen wrote no stories at all because they were not reporters, but simply men who took advantage of their press connections to be accredited and come along for the ride.[1]

Other reporters wrote their Able test stories before the shot in order to file them early. The day before the test, a reporter handed Bob Considine ten typewritten pages and asked him to read them. It was a lurid, eyewitness account of the next day's events, borrowing heavily, and without credit, from Bill Laurence's descriptions of Alamogordo and Nagasaki. "Our hero," as Considine called him, wrote that he was knocked to the deck by the force of the concussion, after which "he shook off the terrible blow of the twenty-thousand tons of TNT, fought his way back to his post at the rail of the *Appalachian,* and beheld an enormous conflagration 'brighter, more dazzling, than 100 suns.'"[2] After reading the literary output from the *Appalachian,* an ensign in the ship's communication room said it would be hard for him ever again to believe anything he read in a newspaper.[3] "In retrospect," wrote Fitzhugh Lee nine months later, "it seems that a clearer overall coverage of factual information might have come from a group of twenty-five well-trained, hard-working, able newsmen. Having nearly two hundred resulted in their diffusing a lot of just plain verbiage, merely for the sake of sending in stories."[4] Much of the blame, though, lay with the Navy itself. With news coverage and interviews at Bikini strictly controlled by the Navy—and thus better suited to "pooled" coverage—it was not surprising that many reporters, in an effort to come up with good stories, concentrated so much of their efforts on the speculative nature of the tests rather than on the spoonfed "hard" news.

The press ship *Appalachian* brought reporters to Honolulu for a week, while observer ships toured Micronesia. Salvage teams worked to repair the surviving target ships from Able so that each one was able to steam under its own power and move to its position in the new target array for Test Baker. As soon as damage inspection from the Able test was completed, new instrumentation and experiments were set up on the target ships for the Baker test. Blandy met with his staff to set the date for the second test. "How long will it take you to get ready?" he asked Rear Adm. Thorvald A. Solberg, who was in charge of salvaging and repairing the target ships.

"Six weeks," replied Solberg.

Blandy asked the same question of Ralph Sawyer, his technical director. "I'll be ready in three weeks," Sawyer replied.

"We'll have it in three weeks," Blandy responded. The test was set for July 25. Solberg left the meeting muttering, recalled Sawyer. He had less work to do than Sawyer's team, "but my gang was willing to work day and night if they had to because they wanted to get done and get back."[5]

The media attention given the tests was phenomenal. Nearly 2.5 million words and 400 photographs were transmitted by radio from Bikini to newspapers and magazines, together with 615 radio broadcasts. "As for fanfare," the *New York Times* observed, "Operation Crossroads has been one of the most thoroughly press-agented shows in modern history, aside from war itself." The tests actually drew more press coverage than the McMahon bill or the Baruch Plan. In fact, in the days immediately following each test, more than 20 percent of front-page U.S. newspaper articles were devoted to Operation Crossroads.[6]

The foreign press reaction was largely jeering in tone. In Argentina, a radio reporter describing the tests worked up to a seemingly serious climax. "You will now hear the explosion of the bomb," he said, and then blew a small whistle.[7] Berlin newspapers reported on the spectators' disappointment, and a Paris newspaper cartoonist pictured a meeting of the Big Four Foreign Ministers after the test, with Secretary of State Byrnes looking sad and Soviet Foreign Minister Molotov turning to him with a contemptuous exclamation. Another cartoon showed the surviving Bikini pigs parading down Broadway in a rain of tickertape, with a caption reading "Broadway deliriously acclaims Bikini survivors."[8] London's *News Chronicle* criticized Joint Task Force One's own frivolous attitude toward the bomb, as expressed by "the vulgar high spirits that . . . painted on this instrument of fate the picture of a pinup star in a low-cut gown," while the *Economist* denounced the "circus-like atmosphere" and "nationalistic flavour" of the test. "For one nation, however peacefully disposed, to undertake on its own experiments in atomic warfare is hardly a good beginning to the process of taming the atom."[9]

Two days after the Able shot, Fitzhugh Lee accompanied a group of reporters on a tour of the damaged ships. Passing the wavy-decked and mangled *Independence,* Lee proclaimed that a good crew could have her underway in short order. It was not true, and no one there believed him. Parts of the carrier's 80-foot-high hull were ripped open and torn into shredded steel. "Three decks were a meaningless jumble of tangled iron and steel," wrote Norman Cousins of the *Saturday Review,* who described the carrier as a "floating graveyard of steel."[10] The Navy's technical report told the true story: The carrier suffered severe hull and superstructure damage; her flight deck "was put out of commission involving complete loss of military efficiency," and "she would have suffered progressive flooding in heavy seas."[11]

"Good as ever!" boomed Lee as the reporters slid by the submarine *Skate.* "For reasons comprehensible only to Annapolis graduates," wrote Bob Considine, "he was cheered by what short-sighted newsmen considered a pretty beat-up array of targets." Considine did not realize the accuracy of his statement. The sight of the *Skate* symbolized the dilemma the Navy faced by opening the tests to the media. The submarine was stationed less than a quarter of a mile from Zeropoint, and she looked it. Her entire superstructure was twisted and mangled, her antennae were lost, there was severe mast damage, and the outer hull was badly stripped and crumpled. What reporters could not see, however, was that her pressure hull suffered virtually no damage or impairment of military efficiency and did not experience flooding. Several ships more than 50 percent farther away from the blast than the *Skate* had

sunk from hull damage. The submarine looked like a wreck, but it survived the blast with its watertightness intact.[12]

Forrestal and Blandy were kept away from the *Skate,* which was dangerously radioactive until three days after the Able shot. "KEEP CLEAR
DANGER! VERY RADIO-ACTIVE!" read a makeshift sign on the *Skate*'s
superstructure, but within a day of the shot the mangled submarine was
cruising the lagoon under her own power with its full crew on board. As
she sailed by Admiral Blandy's flagship, the *Mount McKinley,* the entire
crew lined up on the *Skate*'s deck to salute. "That submarine was hotter
than all hell," recalled Robert Henderson, who worked with the Los
Alamos weapons assembly team, "but here was the Navy, all gung-ho,
lining up those sailors and showing that it was invincible."[13] The Navy
was not about to be deterred by radioactivity.

As preparations continued for Baker, debate raged over the significance of the Able test. Not surprisingly, Navy men downplayed the
damage, Army and AAF officials spoke of the bomb's destructive force,
and domestic newspapers continued to side with the service they had
favored all along. Crossroads critics felt vindicated, as speculation
mounted that the Navy had once again, as in 1921, rigged the tests in its
favor. The Navy "feels pretty smug," remarked one reporter, referring
to the air of self-congratulation and pious righteousness at Bikini; "you
almost expect to see meeting admirals tip their halos to one another."[14]
"Operation Crossroads is largely the Navy's show, and by the sheerest
coincidence only the Navy appears to be happy over the results so far,"
the *Nation* wryly observed. "The naval men are highly pleased with
themselves and their results."[15]

At a news conference the day after Able, Admiral Blandy refused to
draw any conclusions from the test and insisted that his job was simply
to put facts before the presidential and Joint Chiefs evaluation boards.
Having made that point, he announced that he saw no reason to declare
the Navy dead. "We had carriers and destroyers sunk in the war with
Japan, but we didn't stop building them," he said. "We continued to
build them because we needed them and that's what we will do in the
future." Blandy called the *Skate*'s shredded superstructure a "dimple"
and told reporters that "if you were inside you would never know there
had been an atomic blast." As to the crumpled and smoldering *Independence,* he said he had seen ships damaged more by kamikaze attacks.[16]
Forrestal, who said the test was "tremendous," echoed Blandy's comments. Photographed on the bulkhead of the battleship *New York* posed
under the legend "Old sailors never die" that her captain had chalked
the day before, he declared that "there will still be navies in the future,"
adding that the "American Navy will continue to be the most efficient,
the most modern and the most powerful in the world."[17]

True to form, the AAF saw things differently. "As I make this report," said Brig. Gen. Roger Ramey in a radio address four hours after the shot, "Bikini Harbor is still reacting from the effects of the blast and radiation of the world's mightiest bomb." Ramey painted a picture of massive destruction in the lagoon and triumph for the AAF. "But it is not destruction that we of the Air Forces are primarily concerned with," he added shrewdly. "Our primary task has been to demonstrate the flexibility of air power and atomic power. We have demonstrated that flexibility."[18] Four days later, Ramey told a press conference that the entire fleet would have been wiped out had the Able test been in real combat. While the Navy emphasized only the five ships sunk, Ramey pointed out that sixteen ships were completely eliminated from combat and twenty-five to thirty others were damaged. Eleven more suffered severely damaged boilers, caused by the force of the blast rushing down the stacks, and their power to maneuver was completely gone. "Unable to fight, they would be mere sitting ducks," Ramey declared.[19]

When Assistant Secretary of War for Air Stuart Symington arrived in Guam just after the test, Navy men were already boasting that the atomic bomb would not materially affect future war planning. "I had seen that one ship turn over," recalled Symington. "I knew also that feuding between the services had already started in Washington about the impact of this new nuclear force." Symington was on his way to represent President Truman at the independence celebration of the Philippines, but he was so disturbed by the downplaying of the test results that he immediately canceled his plans to fly to Manila and returned instead to Bikini to survey the damage firsthand. "The force shown us was unbelievable," he wrote.[20]

Groves's personal representative, Col. H. C. Gee, was amazed at Blandy's first report after the tests. "It painted a very optimistic picture from the Navy point of view," he wrote Groves. Gee and several members of the Manhattan Project team were left with a totally different impression following their on-site inspections. The stern of the *Sakawa*, wrote Gee, "had been pounded to a pulp," and a Navy official conceded that she barely resembled the ship that was anchored there the day before. After inspecting two more ships, Gee's group concluded that Blandy had greatly understated the condition of the ships. "The target fleet had indeed suffered a staggering blow," he wrote. The *Arkansas* sustained "spectacular damage," and the Army equipment on the deck "was for the most part a complete wreck." Nevertheless, their Navy escort "asked us to tell the folks at home 'that the oldest ship in the Navy had simply taken the Atomic Bomb in her stride.'" Gee tore into the Navy. "The attempts made by various Naval officers, including Admiral Blandy, to discount the effects of the bomb furnished a source of considerable amusement to our entire group," he wrote to Groves. "So much emphasis was placed on the fact that the various vessels remained afloat that all of us became convinced that the Navy was indeed grasping at straws in attempting to build up a case for the battleships."[21]

The press jumped on the blatantly pro-Navy comments by Blandy and Forrestal. "The Navy is running true to form in its propaganda on the effects and implications of Bikini," declared the *Chicago Sun*. A Detroit newspaper wrote that Forrestal "hardly waited for the smoke to blow away from Bikini before allowing himself a broad and general opinion on the outcome of the bomb test. . . . Mr. Forrestal has chosen to take his case to the jury before the evidence even is in. We hope to see in others concerned a graver sense of responsibility."[22] A *Washington Post* editorial derided Crossroads as a "three-ring circus," one-third completed. Able, it said, "was only the silliest of the three tests to be performed," because the results were along the lines of what the atomic scientists had predicted. "But the experiment . . . cost no more than a mere 70 million dollars, exclusive of the unknown cost of the bomb itself, and no doubt a good time was had by all . . . those who went along on the Navy's wondrous junket to the South Seas."[23]

Not even the official postmortems were free of interservice rivalry. In his classified summary of Operation Crossroads, Blandy reported that the tests were "successfully carried out . . . in exact accordance with the directives of the Joint Chiefs of Staff." The Joint Chiefs' plan, he wrote, "proved to be entirely adequate," and the cooperation he received from other government agencies "left nothing to be desired." He dealt with the Army-Navy sniping by denying its existence altogether. "An appreciable amount of interservice jealousy and discord might have been expected," he reported, but "throughout the Crossroads Operation, friction was notably absent."

In contrast, the formal report submitted by AAF Major General Kepner sounded defensive. The Able shot, he conceded, "produced a gross error which was four times the expected probable bombing error," and he still had no explanation. "Further study is being made on the subject," he reported tersely. On the subject of public relations, though, Kepner could not hide his annoyance with the Navy. He pointed out that all public relations officials were Navy officers, and he charged that the news releases "tended to create . . . the impression that the tests were primarily a naval activity rather than a joint effort in which all services were participating." This influenced reporting, he argued, and prevented the public from understanding the joint nature of the operation. He recommended that public relations in future joint service tests be controlled through a committee representing all participating services so

Karl Compton and Curtis LeMay said that the damage was far greater than they had suspected from aerial observation.[29] A few days later, a Manhattan Project scientist made headlines around the country by stating that under wartime conditions everyone within a one-mile radius of the target fleet would have been killed and the fleet immobilized.[30]

"Those who were expecting the atomic bomb dropped on Bikini to disintegrate all [the] combat vessels anchored in the lagoon will feel that the actual results are unimpressive," wrote the *New York Times* in its lead editorial the day after Able. However, many experts had predicted that the fleet would not be destroyed, and the *Times* urged the general public to withhold judgment as to whether the Able test was the "fizzle that so many seem to think that it was." In any case, the *Times* said, Able showed the atom bomb to be the "most monstrous weapon of destruction ever conceived," and its warning was blunt: "If there is any inclination to sell short the atom bomb, Don't!"[31]

The February debate over President Truman's independent evaluation board for the tests was all but forgotten as the president's evaluation commission and the Joint Chiefs of Staff's evaluation board issued nearly identical reports from the White House at precisely 4:00 P.M. on July 11. Probably as a result of the overlapping membership of the two groups, the structure, style, and conclusions of the two reports were remarkably similar. In fact, the presidential report, as one observer noted, "read like a layman's summary of the more detailed analysis by the experts for the Joint Chiefs."[32]

Both reports, in abstruse bureaucratese, reached the painfully inescapable conclusion that an atomic bomb dropped on a group of ships would kill almost everyone in the immediate area. As the presidential report put it, "Had the ships within the damage area been manned, casualties and psychological injuries would have required a large percentage of replacements." Both reports defended Crossroads and called for more testing. The military report found that the "importance of large-scale research has been dramatically demonstrated," and that the cost of the Able test was fully justified, and it concluded that the only way for the United States to maintain its position of scientific leadership was through "further large-scale research and development."[33]

Other observers contended that the test taught nothing that naval planners did not already know. In general, the superstructures of ships near the bomb suffered heavy damage, while most hulls and interiors remained intact. This lesson in ship design was identical to the lessons learned from kamikaze attacks, which were aimed at superstructures. In fact, ship designers during the war were already looking at ways to move as much equipment below deck as possible. As far as scientific measurements were concerned, the thousands of delicate instruments at

that the interests of all services would be properly fostered "and diffe
ences reconciled."[24]

Most observers did not begin to appreciate the true force of the Ab
blast until days and weeks afterwards. Reports of the colossal dama
were released in a piecemeal fashion, so the public never really got a fi
picture. "Greater Havoc at Bikini Revealed on Closer Inspection
Observers," ran a page 1 *New York Times* headline, but it was thr
days after the test. A diver reported that the destroyer *Lamson* had
"large wrinkle in the hull as if squashed down like a sandwich," a
wreckage from the transport *Gilliam* was "strewn about like all the st
from Pittsburgh was thrown on the bottom." The final tally of dama
was impressive. Five ships were sunk, including two destroyers and t
Japanese cruiser *Sakawa*. Six other ships, including two battleships a
two cruisers, were immobilized, and fires broke out on twenty-three t
get ships.[25]

Blandy announced that only 10 percent of the animals died in t
blast, but many of the survivors began to show sharply lower blo
counts within a few days. The *Chicago Tribune* charged that Bland
statement was a "definite misleading of an already confused publi
because many of the animals were near death after the blast. "T
admiral's clipped words imply that the majority of the beasts a
rodents pinch-hitting for men had escaped serious injuries," but t
simply was not true, reported the *Tribune*.[26] In mid-July an officer w
visited the *Burleson*, the Noah's Ark from which correspondents w
barred, reported that test animals were "dying like flies." Animals t
appeared healthy one day, he said, "drop off the next day." Asked
reporters whether any of the animals would be returned to the Uni
States for further study, the officer shot back, "What animals?"[27]
July 23, one-quarter of the animals were dead, including the three i
born on the *Pennsylvania* during the Able shot. In fact, more than
percent of the experimental animals died in the blast, and more th
half died five months after the Able test.[28]

The first impressions of anticlimax and disappointment quickly g
way to more somber appraisals. To *Newsweek*'s Samuel Shaffer,
Able test had been a disappointment. All but a few ships were afloat,
wrote in his July 1 dispatch. Bikini's palm trees still stood, and
watched the radioactive cloud "meekly" drift away. His July 15 p
mortem, though, sounded altogether different. "The sight of the stric
ships is one I'll never forget," he wrote. The ships near Zeropc
"looked as though an irresponsible, power-drunk giant had waded
with hammer and blowtorch, smashing the superstructures and scor
ing the paint into black blisters." Another observer remarked that
"fleet looked as though it had returned from a quick trip to hell," a

Bikini were placed on moving vessels to measure a bomb whose precise location was not known. The instruments were placed on the assumption that the bomb would explode over the *Nevada*, but it missed the mark by a wide margin. "From the standpoint of pure science," one critic noted, "no test was ever more haphazard."[34]

Crossroads's technical director, Ralph Sawyer, needed to know the TNT explosive equivalent of the bomb immediately, but most of the expensive instruments had been destroyed by the off-target drop. Luckily, William G. Penney, the British physicist, favored simple equipment. Just as Enrico Fermi had done at varying distances from the Trinity site, Penney had placed numerous five-gallon gasoline cans and beer cans on the target ships, tied them to the decks with life jackets in case they were blown overboard, and calibrated them. He collected the cans from the target ships hours after the test and made his calculations overnight, comparing pressure to distance from the epicenter. The next morning he had the bomb equivalent within 5 percent. "He always said beer cans made the best pressure gauges," recalled Horacio Rivero.[35]

The miss by *Dave's Dream* set off a series of charges and countercharges on two familiar Crossroads themes: interservice rivalry and public relations. Three hours after the shot, Walter Winchell said on his radio show that the error would set off "a terrific Army-Navy feud,"[36] and World War II hero James Doolittle saw "something fishy" in the matter.[37] An official investigation began on July 4, but speculation as to the cause of the miss intensified as Blandy refused for over a week to concede that any error had occurred.[38] Attention focused briefly on Los Alamos, but Norris Bradbury was quick to point his finger at the AAF. "Ignore newspaper reports," he cabled the laboratory. "All bomb behavior . . . completely normal in all respects. . . . Air Force having trouble explaining deviation from target point."[39]

Neither Los Alamos nor the AAF was willing to take the blame. The AAF suggested that the bomb may have scraped on something as it slid out of the B-29's bomb bay, knocking off part of the assembly and compromising its aerodynamics.[40] This charge, though, was contradicted by the air operations report issued after the tests. "The Bomb Commander watched the bomb clear the airplane," it reported, "and stated that it did not hit any part of the Bomb Carrier."[41] At a press conference, Major General Kepner expressed the AAF's "full satisfaction" with the bomb drop, but he conceded that the "fall of the bomb may be considered somewhat eccentric." AAF sources said the film of the bomb's fall showed that it was a "wobbler," and Kepner felt that there was something wrong with the bomb's fins and baffles.[42] Privately, Kepner remained bewildered. "We know that this bomb has poor ballistic qualities and everyone familiar with it admits that quite freely," he wrote on

July 5 to Carl Spaatz, "but even so that would not be enough, with our experience to date, to explain it." In fact, the Able Day miss was worse than any error made by Swancutt's crew during the training period.[43]

Public criticism of the AAF began to mount. *Newsweek* reported that the "bomber crew is in the doghouse," and the *New York Herald Tribune* wrote that the "Air Forces were guilty of gross exaggeration in their reports of precision bombing."[44] In late July, Senator Thomas C. Hart of Connecticut, a wartime admiral and fleet commander, tore into the AAF and its "flair for publicity." He charged on the Senate floor that the AAF's "overadvertised pinpoint accuracy was bound to be a delusion. It has always been a delusion." Operation Crossroads instruments and experiments, he said, had been adversely affected by the miss and there had been no need for Army participation in the tests. "The proper method, the way to insure that the explosion would be right where it was wanted," said Hart, "would have been to suspend the bomb from an anchored kite balloon. That method would have been sure, would have eliminated great difficulties in the timing of the entire operation and made it simpler and cheaper all around."

"Those facts are so evident," he continued, "that anyone would ask, Why did not the Navy use a kite balloon? The answer is just as evident, and is that the Army Air [Forces] insisted on being in the show. It could not be left out and thus miss the chance for publicity."[45]

Maj. Gen. William Kepner shot back a response from Bikini. He believed the bomb had merely lived up to its poor ballistics reputation, and he was certain that a kite balloon would have proved impossible. It was impracticable by the nature and design of the bomb, he cabled, and it would have been impossible in the time available to develop and produce the necessary equipment. Moreover, he believed that the accuracy of a balloon drop would not have been as good as from a B-29. Kepner was also suspicious of Senator Hart's motives. "Any statement indicating the AAF has dominated publicity is ridiculous," he wrote.[46]

Blandy told Senator Hart that technical difficulties had precluded suspending the atomic bomb from a balloon. All of his officers and scientists had recommended dropping the bomb from a B-29, and there was "no pressure from Army Air Forces." Blandy sympathized with the crew of *Dave's Dream,* whose pilot, copilot, and bombardier were later awarded Distinguished Flying Crosses for their service at Bikini. "You can't expect one bomb or one torpedo to go exactly where you want it to go," he wrote after the tests, and he praised the performance of AAF personnel as "outstanding."[47]

Returning to the United States, Kepner was still on the defensive, telling a news conference in late August that he had never promised "to drop the bomb down a rain barrel." At a press conference a month later, he cited three possible causes for the miss: crew capability, equipment malfunction, and trajectory. "I certainly eliminated in my mind the crew," he said, "and I have eliminated equipment such as bomb rack, bomb shackle and releasing mechanisms. . . . I think it gets down now to the trajectory of the bomb."[48]

Leslie Groves was furious at Kepner's remarks. "This is not conducive to the maintenance of security," he wrote to AAF Commanding General Carl Spaatz. "I had hoped . . . that public discussion as to the cause of the unexpectedly wide variation would be avoided by all responsible officers. Only harm could come from a newspaper debate on this subject between various scientists . . . and the Air Forces."[49] The AAF jumped at Groves's charge. Its deputy director of public information explained to Kepner that top AAF officials "are personally convinced of the accuracy of your statement, but . . . we have thus far failed to prove this point to General Groves to his entire satisfaction." Noting that the AAF was "not at all worried about our press and publicity, only our good relations with General Groves," the deputy director asked Kepner to refrain from any further public comments on the matter "until such time as final conclusions are more closely in accord with [Groves's] opinions."[50]

Kepner wrote an unctuous response to Groves. "I am very sorry that I did anything that might in any way embarrass you in the least," he apologized. "I didn't mean to do this and will govern myself to avoid such discussions in the future." Whether out of sycophancy or fear, Kepner went on to note that whenever he talked about Operation Crossroads, "I guard myself against saying anything more than I have heard you say in the press conferences which it has been my privilege to hear you conduct. Whenever questions arise, I find myself continually remembering the scope of your remarks and it surely is a big help. I wish I had heard you say more."[51]

Meanwhile, investigators questioned each member of *Dave's Dream* crew, reviewed all the calculations, and checked the bombsight, the bombardier's settings, shot photographs, bomb weight, and the altitude of the plane. No errors were uncovered. Swancutt and his crew flew the plane back to the United States and reenacted the bomb run at Sandia Bombing Range using the same bombsight and stabilizer as at Bikini and releasing from the same altitude. The pumpkin landed just 220 feet off target. Five more pumpkin drops were conducted later in the year. One investigator concluded that the photographs of the bomb fall showed "definite eccentricities," but another investigator saw none. A third concluded that movies showed something wrong with the bomb, but others disagreed with him, and the image in the film was too small to be regarded as conclusive anyway. In view of all the uncertainties, the investigators could only conclude that "some unusual force affected the bomb causing it to veer off in an unpredictable and erratic manner."[52]

Years later, Paul Tibbets, still bitter over losing out to Woody Swancutt and his crew, blamed incompetence on the part of *Dave's Dream*'s crew for what he called the "fiasco at Bikini." Tibbets wrote that he and two of his crew's bombardiers, Tom Ferebee and Kermit Beahan, went to the Kwajalein weather station on the morning of the Able test, obtained information on wind speed and direction, and then made their own calculations. "When we saw the figures that the other crew had arrived at, we were shocked," he wrote, and Ferebee and Beahan pointed out the "obvious miscalculation" to Swancutt's bombardier, Maj. Harold Wood. "Their advice went unheeded." Tibbets then spoke to Swancutt, but to no avail. He "listened a bit impatiently, thanked me for the advice, and then told me politely that they were satisfied with their own results." Ferebee and Beahan ran Wood's numbers and showed Tibbets where they thought the bomb would land—a point 1,600 feet short and to the left of the *Nevada*. Their predictions were off by less than 200 feet.[53]

In the end, the mystery was never completely solved. "We put more time and effort into solving that bombing error than any other problem at Operation Crossroads," recalled Frederick Ashworth. "And we simply don't know why it happened."[54] William Shurcliff, Operation Crossroads's official historian, was unable to explain the error in his November 1946 technical report. "Extensive studies have been made by several groups," wrote Shurcliff, "but neither separately nor collectively do the findings explain the miss . . . and it is likely that the cause will never be discovered."[55]

The AAF eventually pointed the finger at the bomb itself. After further studies and tests at the Aberdeen Proving Ground, which included dropping five bombs from 30,000 feet, the AAF reported that a large part of the error was attributable to the bomb's ballistics. "The Army Air Forces had virtually promised to drop the bomb within 500 feet of the target despite the fact that the poor ballistics of the Fat Man was common knowledge," noted a later Air Force study.[56] To Los Alamos, the investigation was a waste of time. "There was no such thing as pinpoint accuracy," recalled one of the technicians. "So we thought it was unrealistic to expect that one bomb could be dropped precisely where the Navy wanted it dropped. It couldn't be done."[57]

Bikini itself was unaffected by the controversies and debates raging over the Able test. "Bikini atoll was still there," wrote one reporter, "its waving palms confounding the punsters who had predicted that it would become 'Nothing Atoll.'"[58] The officers' club bar first reopened late on July 2, the day after the test, when Secretary Forrestal and Admiral Blandy went ashore for a drink. "I found that the island of Bikini had utterly ignored this world-shouted event," wrote a science reporter. "No frond of its coconut palms, no leaf of its pandanus trees, appeared out of place. There were no dead fish washed ashore on the lagoon beach. . . . Nature does not seem to know that anything important happened here."[59]

The lack of damage to Bikini led to speculation that the Bikinians could soon return to their homeland. "There seems to be an excellent chance that King Juda and his homesick Bikinians . . . may be able to return to their home eventually," wrote one correspondent, while another speculated that the Bikinians could have stayed on the island during the test.[60] "Some day King Juda may appear in Washington," mused one writer, "and ask the Army and Navy to please get going because HE has a little firecracker he'd like to explode. All in the interests of progress, of course."[61]

22

"The Water Near a Recent Surface Explosion Will Be a Witch's Brew"

With preparations for Test Baker well in hand, Admiral Blandy, Groves's deputy Kenneth Nichols, Commodore Wyatt, and Senator Carl Hatch of New Mexico, accompanied by several scientists, military officers, and reporters, paid a visit to the Bikinians at Rongerik on July 16. With all 167 Bikinians seated under coconut and pandanus trees on Rongerik Island, 125 miles from Bikini, Wyatt declared that the Bikinians had "set an example for the entire world" when they willingly gave up their homeland. Then Blandy spoke. "I wish to thank you for your kindness in giving up your homes so that we could conduct these experiments," he told the people. "I am glad to see that you have such a nice new home, and I hope that you are happy here."

They were not. "The Bikinians hid their sorrow with inbred dignity and courtesy," wrote one reporter. "From the silent semi-circle seated beneath waving palms at the edge of the beach, grave, sometimes tearful, faces were lifted to the great men who had arrived out of the sky to bring them greetings and word of their future." Although Nichols wrote that everything on Rongerik looked new and shiny, the Bikinians were already homesick, and they reported that the coconuts on Rongerik were smaller than Bikini's.[1]

The real purpose of the visit, though, was for Senator Hatch to give thanks to the islanders from President Truman. "The President knows the sacrifice you have made and he is deeply grateful to you for that," Hatch told Juda, who was dressed in Navy fatigues. "You have made a true contribution to the progress of mankind all over the world, and the President of the United States extends to you, King Juda, his thanks for all you have done."

As the message was translated, all the islanders applauded, and then, at the urging of Wyatt, sang one of their folk songs. After the Americans passed out chocolate bars, soft drinks, and salted nuts, the Bikinians presented Hatch with a large woven basket to give to the president, which Hatch did after his return to Washington.[2] Wyatt then presented to Bikini's schoolmaster a globe, the first the people had ever seen, and Blandy gave Juda a pipe, a carton of cigarettes, a cigarette holder, matches, and a set of aerial photographs showing the Able test over Bikini.

"Tell them this is Bikini," Blandy told the interpreter, "and tell them the palm trees are still there." He also invited Juda to come to Bikini to see the Baker shot, hoping that he would appreciate the tremendous size of the operations that necessitated the removal of the islanders.[3] After Blandy shook hands with all the Bikinians and the islanders took their visitors for a ride on an outrigger canoe to another island at Rongerik, the group left. "On the way back to Bikini," wrote Nichols, "someone asked Admiral Blandy where [Juda] would sleep when he came to visit. Admiral Blandy quickly responded, 'Out on the forward deck.'"[4]

Blandy was actually not sure Bikini's palm trees would be standing after the Baker shot. Stung by the unrealized expectations from the Able shot, though, he was already downplaying his estimate of the height of the waves Baker would create, lowering his prediction from 100 feet to 70. As he later recalled, "It was low tide at 7:20 and we wanted to blow the bomb as soon after that as we could, to minimize the waves reaching the islands."[5] The experts "do not intend to be caught out in any melodramatics such as gained currency before the first test," noted one reporter. The usual answers to questions were now "We will know more in a few days" and "Wait and see."[6]

Able and the two Japanese atomic bombs were exploded in the air, so most of their lethal fission products shot up into the earth's atmosphere. The Hiroshima bomb, for example, was detonated at an altitude of 1,800 feet, and its fireball did not actually touch the ground. Most of the vaporized and radioactive material rose up into the enormous updraft caused by the explosion, so ground contamination was minimized. Baker, though, would be an underwater shot, not a "self-cleansing" air burst, with the bomb detonated by remote control 90 feet below the surface of Bikini's lagoon. No one knew exactly what to expect from the test, but the head of Crossroads's radiological safety unit, Col. Stafford Warren, stated that the radiological hazard would not reach such a high altitude or extend over such a wide area as the Able test. Observation ships would therefore be stationed closer to the lagoon than they had been for the Able shot.[7]

In all matters involving radiological hazards or measurements, Blandy necessarily relied on Manhattan Project personnel. He and Groves agreed that the logical choice to head the Radiological Safety Section was Stafford Warren, chief of the Manhattan Project's medical section as well as Groves's personal medical advisor. Warren, who had just returned to his position as professor of radiology at the University of Rochester, took forty of his university colleagues to Bikini to assist him and to serve on the Operation Crossroads Medico-Legal Advisory Board, which was directed to review safety measures and, in its own words, "give what assurance was possible that no successful suits could be brought on account of the radiological hazards of Operation Crossroads."[8] Another safety team to deal with all nonradiological hazards was headed by Dr. George M. Lyon, who had trained at Johns Hopkins Medical School and practiced pediatrics until World War II. Blandy named Lyon as his safety advisor and Warren as his radiological safety advisor.

A tall, handsome man with a well-trimmed mustache, Stafford Warren was an energetic scientist, always amiable and polite. A dynamic speaker, he was also flamboyant and given to histrionics, as illustrated by his first day on the job at the Manhattan Project, when he arrived at work in combat boots with a .45 revolver strapped to his waist.[9] Warren graduated from medical school at the University of California in 1922 and had been affiliated with the University of Rochester for 17 years when he joined the Manhattan Project in early 1943. The Army surgeon general, aware of Warren's experiments with radiation to combat venereal disease, told Groves's aide that he could not understand why the Manhattan Project would want "that clap doctor."[10]

Warren, his deputy Hymer Friedell, and James Nolan, the chief safety planner for the Trinity test, drew up an evacuation plan for the area around the Alamogordo test site. At a meeting with Oppenheimer a week before the shot, Warren said he would not worry unless radiation readings reached a level that was nearly half the lethal dose for man. Safety monitors "took considerable risks knowingly," recalled Hymer Friedell, and he and Warren "set a pretty high level of radiation that was acceptable before we would evacuate for the reason that we didn't want to reveal the fact that there was an atomic explosion."[11]

Warren continued to work on radiological safety at Trinity, but he was also charged with supervising a team of psychiatrists that was ready to fly to the Trinity site in case panic broke out. In fact, he removed several people from the test site whom he deemed unable to withstand the pressures and uncertainties. He also sought to devise an eleventh-hour experiment to determine the effect of the atomic bomb on animals. He drove into the desert the day before the Trinity shot with a box of white mice and hung the animals by their tails from signal wire several miles from Alamogordo. His experiment, though, was a failure; all the mice died of thirst before the test.[12]

Weather conditions were unsettled the night before the Trinity test, and Warren and the head of radiological safety at Trinity, Dr. Louis Hempelmann, were concerned about the direction of the radioactive cloud. "If it went east," Warren later recalled, "I was sunk. If it went northeast, it was going to be all right."[13] As Hempelmann said, "We were just damn lucky. . . . All I could think of was, my God, all that radioactivity up there has got to come down somewhere."[14] As it turned out, though, no farmers or ranchers were evacuated from the area around the Trinity site, although several hundred cattle suffered superficial burns and hair loss.[15]

Radiological safety was not a top priority in the Manhattan Project. The Army had one goal: to develop a usable bomb. With a war on, it was deemed only fair for workers and scientists to take risks, risks that were far less than those being faced by U.S. troops. "Possible hazards were not too important in those days," recalled James Nolan. "The idea was to explode the damned thing," said Hymer Friedell. "We weren't terribly concerned with radiation."[16] Nevertheless, five days after the Trinity test, Warren told Groves that any future tests should not be held in the Alamogordo area, but rather at a site with no population for a 150-mile radius.[17]

Days after the Hiroshima bomb, Tokyo radio reported mysterious deaths among relief workers who had entered the city, but U.S. officials labeled this allegation a hoax. In mid-September, the *New York Times*'s William Laurence reported that "radiations on the surface have dwindled to a minute quantity, safe for continuous habitation." This evidence, he said, "gave the most effective answer today to Japanese propaganda that radiations were responsible for deaths even after the day of the explosion, August 6." Leslie Groves denied that there was any radiation danger at Hiroshima. "The Japanese claim the people died from radiation," he said. "If this is true, the number was very small."[18]

With American troops about to occupy Hiroshima and Nagasaki, Groves's deputy, Gen. Thomas Farrell, on direct orders from General Marshall, placed Stafford Warren in charge of a medical team to conduct a quick survey of the two cities to confirm that U.S. soldiers "shall not be subjected to any possible toxic effects, although [there is] no reason to believe that any such effects actually exist." The message was clear: Groves wanted assurance that radiation was not a problem. As

Farrell put it, according to one of the members of the U.S. team, "our mission was to prove that there was no radioactivity from the bomb."[19]

Warren and his team reached Hiroshima on September 8 and Nagasaki a few days later. On September 10, Warren sent a secret cable to Washington stating that only a small percentage of survivors suffered from radiation sickness. "Residual radiation alone," he wrote, "could not have been detrimental to the health of persons entering and living in the bombed areas after the explosion."[20] Back in Tokyo, Farrell told the press on September 12 that there would be no further deaths as a result of the bomb. He "denied categorically that it produced a dangerous, lingering radioactivity," although he did confirm Japanese reports that some people who suffered burns in the blast were now dying "from a marked decrease in the number of white corpuscles required to sustain human life."[21] In congressional testimony in early 1946, Warren claimed that radiation injuries at Hiroshima and Nagasaki resulted solely from the initial burst of gamma rays and accounted for only 5 to 7 percent of the casualties. His figures were immediately challenged by the U.S. Strategic Bombing Survey, which concluded that radiation caused as much as 20 percent of the deaths, and the figure could easily have been much higher.[22]

The battle over the lingering effects of radiation had begun. Warren, perhaps stung by the Strategic Bombing Survey's conclusions, was decidedly more wary of radiation hazards by the time of Operation Crossroads. The tests, of course, were going to occur in a time of peace, so radiological safety was a more important priority. At times, Warren even seemed to be overly cautious. When he first joined the staff of Joint Task Force One, for example, he urged Blandy to consider using a location other than Bikini for the underwater shot, reasoning that the Able test might produce so much lingering radioactivity that the second shot would have to be postponed. Blandy, though, decided that the danger of a delay from this possibility was not great enough to warrant preparing another test site.[23]

Warren's own handpicked Medico-Legal Advisory Board also minimized the possible adverse effects of radiation exposure at Bikini and expressed confidence in Warren's preparations—confidence that Warren would quickly lose. "There are some 40,000 persons engaged in these operations," wrote the committee in a largely self-serving memorandum on the eve of the Able shot, and "among them are sure to appear, soon or late, a number of . . . disease[s], some of which . . . will be attributed to the radiations from the Atomic Bomb." The board was confident, though, that such claims would be without merit, because these diseases "appear spontaneously in the human race without previous exposure to man-made radiations" and their occurrence would thus be statistically insignificant. "We expect that no such attribution will be well founded, and we expect that the records under the regulations of the Radiological Safety Section will in all such cases be adequate to show that the quantity of radiation received by that particular person was well below the threshold of perceptible biologic injury."[24]

Faced with the task of protecting Operation Crossroads personnel from radioactive hazards, Warren's group produced a safety plan by mid-April 1946, outlining the responsibilities of radiological (or "radsafe") monitors. A reconnaissance unit would track the spread of radioactive material in and above Bikini, a monitoring unit would take radiation measurements on personnel, and a technical service unit would repair and calibrate instruments, prepare and evaluate film badges measuring the radioactive dose to personnel entering hazardous areas, and conduct radiological analyses of water, soil, and fish samples.[25]

Warren's safety plan annoyed some of the Los Alamos scientists. Marshall Holloway complained to Norris Bradbury in late April that the operation plan for Operation Crossroads "has been seriously hampered by [Warren's] edict that no manned boats can enter the lagoon until pronounced safe by him." Calculating that "the radiation hazard for Baker Test *will be less* than for Able Test," he asked, "why Col. Warren's edict?" Bradbury sympathized with Holloway's concerns and explained that Warren "represents another extreme view."[26]

At first, Warren thought he would need between fifty and sixty radsafe monitors. He had already targeted half from the highly experienced personnel at Los Alamos who had worked on the Manhattan Project, and he hoped to recruit the other half from the armed services. This group would train for nearly three months at Los Alamos, Oak Ridge Laboratory, Berkeley, Chicago, and Rochester. As planning evolved, however, Warren realized that he had grossly underestimated his needs, and within weeks he was scrambling to recruit over three hundred monitors as well as to procure new equipment. "I need monitors badly," he wrote a friend in early March.[27]

"The test turned out to be literally a hundred times larger than the original conception," Warren later wrote.[28] As early as February, George Lyon, Blandy's safety advisor, told the Navy that Warren's inability to locate enough radiological safety monitors imposed a "*real and serious* threat to the essential safety requirements of the operation." Warren spoke to Blandy about the situation soon after the tests were announced, suggesting that a public statement by President Truman as to the importance of the tests would help his recruiting efforts. If adequately trained radsafe monitors could not be found, Lyon warned the Navy on February 6, "a serious delay may be occasioned, or the plans of the operation may have to be changed materially."[29]

Some of the monitors were scientists just back from wartime service. Few were eager for another stint with the government, and virtually all insisted on being back in the United States by the end of August to resume teaching positions. Warren's recruiting problems were thus dealt a major setback by President Truman's March 22 postponement of the tests. Two weeks later, George Lyon warned Deak Parsons that radsafe monitors were "increasingly reluctant to sign up" due to the possibility of more delays by the White House and the uncertainty of the dates of the tests.[30] Many recruits resigned, and Warren began what the government later described as a "frantic search for replacements," which "meant the loss of very valuable organizing, training and rehearsal time."[31]

By April 1, Warren had commitments from only thirty people. Eventually he was supplied with fifty-five officers from the Navy and fifteen from the Army, almost all of whom were reservists, but this was still not enough. Warren, hoping to attract more capable people, asked the Navy to delay as long as possible the sailing of the *Haven,* which was to carry all radsafe personnel to Bikini.[32] He wrote form letters to prospective monitors, telling them that their participation was urgently needed, especially for the Able test, and asking them, "Can I count on you for one or both tests?" Warren even arranged to have the sons of some of the scientists come along as monitors, and he "practically browbeat" his 18-year-old son, Dean, a freshman at Berkeley, to serve.[33]

The postponement of the tests, combined with Warren's recruiting problems, meant that only 33 of the more than 300 radsafe monitors received a thorough training course. Those who traveled aboard the *Haven* received their training on the ship's navigation deck in 12 days of lectures en route to Bikini, with one 50-minute discussion on protection against radiation hazards. Most were older men, and the majority had only a basic background in science. Warren recalled:

> We were so desperate in getting people that we took a lot of
> people we would not normally have considered. We could take
> people with a high school education. . . . From my standpoint
> anybody who could read and write and was mobile was useful.
> . . . They were to be trained to go to a certain place; measure it
> on the Geiger counter; record the reading, the location, and the
> time on a piece of paper, and maybe bring back a sample of that
> water. Well, this was not a highly skilled operation.[34]

Most of the radsafe monitors for the Able test did not arrive at Bikini until June 12, well behind other technicians and just weeks before the shot. Some did not arrive until after the Able or Baker rehearsals, which, as the government later admitted, "greatly decreased their value to the [radsafe] section and greatly increased the last minute mechanical and administrative load." Matters were made even worse by Warren's promise to release over one hundred monitors after the first test. "The loss between Able and Baker of so many people who had gained invaluable experience in Able was unfortunate," noted a government report. In fact, there were nearly fifty fewer monitors available for Baker than for Able, and Warren never got all the monitors he wanted.[35]

The radsafe monitors relied largely on Geiger-Muller counters to detect radioactivity. Unfortunately, the humid and salt-laden climate of the Marshall Islands played havoc with the monitors' instruments, as more than half of the 320 Geiger counters shorted out. "We had to admit we were having all kinds of calibrating trouble with our instruments," Warren recalled. "It would rain like mad, . . . and we had squalls, and you couldn't protect the equipment during those periods. . . . There was enough humidity so that the air was almost liquid. The humidity averaged about 85 percent all the time."[36]

Scientists knew that the atomic bomb produced different types of radiation. Alpha particles, which are difficult to detect, have a range of only one or two inches in the air and cannot even penetrate clothing or unbroken skin. However, when absorbed internally, even minute quantities of alpha-producing material can prove fatal over time. Beta particles can travel farther but are generally less damaging, although large doses on the skin can cause burns. Gamma rays, by contrast, can travel hundreds of feet in the air and are highly penetrating, although much less dangerous than alpha particles. In higher doses they can cause loss of hair, nausea, and aplastic anemia. As only dense materials such as lead and steel can shield humans against them, gamma rays posed the highest external exposure hazard from the bomb.

Stafford Warren set the maximum allowable exposure to gamma radiation at 0.1 roentgen per day, the same limit that had been set in 1934 by the National Bureau of Standards for manufacturing plants in the United States. A roentgen, named after the German physicist Wilhelm Konrad Roentgen, who discovered and studied x-rays, is a unit of radiation exposure that measures ionization in the air. (The term, first adopted in 1928, was eventually replaced in the late 1950s by the term *rem,* which is the amount of ionizing radiation required to produce approximately the same biological effect as one roentgen.)[37] Warren's Medico-Legal Advisory Board approved these guidelines, concluding that the tolerance dose was conservative and that the safety factor was correspondingly very large. The board did not share his concerns about the shortage of radsafe personnel or about their equipment. "We believe that the character, education and training and the number of the men of the Radiological Safety

Section are adequate to the management of the unexpected as well as the expected events," the board wrote on June 30. It concluded that the radiological monitoring instruments were "adequate in sensitivity" and that any possible breakdowns would not compromise safety.[38]

The radsafe team performed well after the Able shot. After the first team of monitors reported the Eneu channel free of contamination, ten other teams entered the lagoon and headed for the ships closest to the shot. The monitors boarded the target ships, surveyed the decks and the areas below, and then decided whether to declare each ship "Geiger sweet"—safe enough for salvage work to start—or "Geiger sour"—unsafe. The sight of the radsafe monitors was quite astonishing. "I've often wondered," one of them wrote in his journal, "what the Navy men thought when they came upon some mysterious figure, decked out in galoshes, gloves, coveralls, and mask, creeping along the passages of an able-bodied ship, waving a magic black box over the water pipes and listening intently through earphones as though tuned in on the supernatural. They must feel that the good old Navy is being taken over by screwballs."[39]

By the day after the Able test, no readings in the lagoon waters were higher than the tolerance standard of 0.1 roentgen per day, and all but a handful of target ships were declared Geiger sweet. The radiological readings held no surprises at all. The radioactive cloud had actually dissipated more quickly than anticipated, and radsafe teams soon settled into a routine of processing film badges and preparing for Baker. Warren's team was lucky, because there was tremendous pressure to board the target ships as soon as possible to minimize secondary damage caused by the bomb. Pumps were not running, firefighting and damage control crews were not on board, and it was not possible to flood the ships' magazines to prevent ammunition explosions or to compensate for a list due to flooded compartments. Warren, though, was more concerned about the Baker shot. As he later recalled, "The next question was: How will we get ready for the second bomb test?—because that was going to be the real mean one."[40]

In fact, an underwater shot originally seemed too reckless. As early as December 1945, Warren, Bradbury, and Parsons warned Blandy that an "underwater test against naval vessels would contain so many hazards that it should be ruled out at this time." They predicted that most of the radioactivity would not be dissipated into the atmosphere but instead would fall back into the lagoon. The contaminated water might well drift across shipping lanes or toward inhabited islands. "Fish life for a large area would be damaged," they wrote, and ships would pick up considerable contamination pumping saltwater out of the ocean. Warren predicted that there would be "terrific contamination" in the area for three weeks. Every ship in the target group, he said, would be "dangerously contaminated," and spray from the blast would make it difficult to observe the results of the shot. Parsons warned Blandy that the Manhattan District would oppose an underwater shot unless "the information which will be obtained therefrom can be demonstrated to be absolutely vital and obtainable in no other manner."[41]

Faced with these objections, Blandy at first ruled out an underwater shot and announced that the Baker shot would be a surface explosion, which was technically easier to accomplish, would produce the greatest wave effects, and would maximize the spread of radioactive contamination. However, Los Alamos scientists concluded in February that much more energy would be delivered to the water if the bomb were placed at a depth of between 20 and 60 feet in the lagoon. There were also political considerations to take into account. Bradbury complained to Groves at one point that planning for Baker had become "increasingly the province of political and civilian committees whose philosophy in these matters may be derived from several points of view." If plans continued for a surface shot, he warned, "we may be subject to the charge of 'rigging' the test in a favorable manner to the ships," as a surface shot would inflict less damage on the target ships than an underwater bomb.

Bradbury recommended that plans move ahead to design and construct a submersible tank to house a bomb at a depth of about 60 feet. Construction could be carried out under the auspices of Joint Task Force One at several remote locations, he said, while studies on the feasibility of an underwater shot would continue for two more months. "If the evidence is unambiguous," he told Groves, "then this tank will be ready for use without delaying the tests. If the argument goes the other way, . . . then this tank may be quietly junked."[42] These discussions continued until early May, when Joint Task Force One finally decided on an underwater detonation at a depth of between 75 and 100 feet.[43]

Warren was concerned that an underwater nuclear explosion would be muffled by the great mass of surrounding water. Los Alamos scientists predicted that the intense heat of the initial radiation would vaporize the water near the burst, forming a bubble that would expand as more and more energy was released. Depending upon the depth of the burst, detonation yield, and energy released, the bubble might break the surface of the water while still expanding or after all the released energy was expended. If the bubble was still expanding, some of the radioactive products would vent into the air, as in an air burst. But if the bubble did not rise high enough into the atmosphere, most of the fission products trapped in the rising water would collapse back into the lagoon.

An underwater detonation had never been attempted, and scientists could not predict exactly how the water would react to a nuclear explosion. An early Los Alamos report to Bradbury predicted that "the water near a recent surface explosion will be a witch's brew" and that "there will probably be enough plutonium near the surface to poison the combined armed forces of the United States at their highest wartime strength. The fission products will be worse."[44] Blandy did not pose the risk in such graphic terms to the Joint Chiefs, warning instead that "it will undoubtedly be some weeks before the lagoon and target ships are again habitable."[45]

Between March and May 1946, the University of California conducted several experiments for Joint Task Force One on the projected height of the water column and relative risks. "A rise of only 10,000 feet . . . would present the greatest hazard," one study concluded, "because most of the contamination would fall on the target ships or back into the lagoon."[46] Conversely, there would not be a serious risk if the bubble were either to rise much higher than 10,000 feet or barely break the surface of the lagoon. However, Operation Crossroads's own scientific team predicted a water column height that *almost exactly* matched the greatest hazard predicted by the University of California scientists. The Operation Crossroads Radiological Safety Plan, first circulated in February 1946, predicted that the dome of radioactive water and steam would rise to a height "estimated to be 5,000 to 8,000 feet." At least half the fission products formed by the nuclear reaction would then fall back and be "dispersed in the water of the lagoon." All ships in that area "thus will be heavily contaminated by radioactive materials falling from above," it warned.[47]

Moreover, on June 19, 1946, British explosives expert William Penney informed four of the top Operation Crossroads officials, including Warren, Parsons, and Sawyer, that "the true height of the column for a 20,000 ton explosion will be 8,000 feet." Penney noted that "the water column will be highly contaminated by fission products," and the last sentence of his two-page memorandum stated the obvious danger: "The collapse of the water column in the strong turbulence developed will certainly cover many ships with water and contaminate them."[48] Even Stafford Warren recognized that "the most serious concentration" of radioactivity in the lagoon would take place if the radioactive column did not rise above 10,000 feet. "Had [the cloud at Trinity] ascended to only 10,000 feet," he wrote, "the results might have been most disastrous."[49]

The warnings could not have been clearer. Blandy's own scientists predicted that the radioactive column would rise about 8,000 feet, and they also predicted that the men at Bikini faced the greatest hazard if the cloud only rose about 10,000 feet. Test Baker was a disaster waiting to happen. To make matters worse, although Blandy stated in January that the target ships would not be habitable for a matter of weeks after the Baker shot, Stafford Warren stated at a July 10 conference on board the *Mount McKinley* that access to the ships would be possible within five days of the shot.[50] The Baker test was about to become a great technical success—and a near-catastrophe.

23

"Why Doesn't the Captain Take This Ship Out of Here?"

Admiral Blandy may have forgotten his invitation to Juda to visit Bikini, but others did not. On July 23, two days before the Baker test, the Bikini leader flew to Bikini in Commodore Wyatt's personal seaplane. His arrival came as a complete surprise, and the result was a chaotic half hour in which Joint Task Force One officials were caught completely flatfooted.

Practically everything went wrong. As Juda approached Blandy's flagship in a small boat loaded with luggage, a gangway was cleared so that he could climb aboard in view of the newsreel cameras. Juda, though, insisted on unloading all the baggage himself until a reporter motioned him aboard. He showed that he had picked up some Navy customs as he saluted everybody in sight. With dozens of photographers and cameramen recording the scene, officers scrambled to receive him. His arrival alongside the *Mount McKinley* attracted more railside spectators than had the arrival of any military brass, including Navy Secretary Forrestal. Admiral Blandy, though, was elsewhere in the lagoon, so his chief of staff greeted the Bikini leader instead and led him to a stateroom where one of Stafford Warren's radsafe monitors was just settling in. "You're in the King of Bikini's room," the chief of staff barked, ordering the confused monitor to leave.[1]

The log book of the *Mount McKinley* duly noted Juda's arrival: "1535 His Majesty, King Juda of the people of Rongerik, formerly of Bikini,

218

boarded the ship to visit Vice Admiral Blandy."[2] The snaggle-toothed Juda, dark-skinned, with black hair, short, stocky, and muscular, wore Marine Corps utilities—khaki trousers and shirt—no tie, no socks, and black Navy issue shoes, one of which was tied with white twine. He carried a fountain pen and comb in his shirt pocket, which was closed with a huge safety pin. Grinning happily at the sight of Bikini Island, he told reporters through his interpreter that he was amazed to find the atoll unscorched. He added that he hoped to bring his people back that summer, but reporters told him that waves from the Baker shot would cover Bikini. "They say there be big waves," Juda responded. "But palm trees too tall to be hurt even if waves cover island."

Juda quickly found himself ensnarled in old-fashioned American red tape, and Blandy was in a bind. Despite his invitation to Juda to attend the Baker test, Blandy had told the Joint Chiefs that Juda would not be brought to Bikini unless they thought it proper. He scrambled to convene a top-level conference, and a few hours later he announced to surprised newsmen that Juda could visit Bikini Island, but only the Joint Chiefs could decide whether he would be permitted to watch the Baker shot. On a quick tour of Bikini, Juda inspected the tiny graveyard, stared in amazement at the huge towers rising above the coconut trees, and said he was surprised to find the foliage still green and fresh. He wanted to sleep on the island, so he was assigned to a bed in the small Seabees barrack, and the first sergeant on duty slept on the ground.[3]

Returning from Bikini to the *Mount McKinley* the next morning, Juda looked impassively at the target ships as a Navy officer explained the test. Making motions and pointing into the lagoon, the officer, perhaps unconsciously mimicking Juda's interpreter, explained that the next bomb would "blow much water up in air, way up, much water, high." Juda followed the hand motions and interpretation and then nodded his head understandingly without showing any amazement. "Onlookers got the impression that nothing the white men do now ever surprises these natives," commented one observer. Later that day Blandy finally received permission from the Joint Chiefs in Washington to allow Juda to witness the Baker shot from the *Mount McKinley*.[4]

Aboard the press ship *Appalachian* the mood was glum. It was pouring on the morning of July 24, and dark clouds filled the sky. A tropical low front lay almost directly over the atoll, but good weather was predicted for the test the next day. At 8:50 A.M., Blandy gave the go-ahead for Test Baker. Fitzhugh Lee, Blandy's press officer, grabbed the microphone in the *Appalachian*'s press room. "Flash—this is it!" he announced. "Baker Day will be held July 25. HOW hour will be 0835."

"There was an immediate burst of applause," wrote one reporter. "The faces lit up. The gloom ran out of the wardroom. All the press boys are homesick. We left San Francisco June 12, and all of us will be glad to get back home and leave the vast, empty, unneighborly stretches of the southwest Pacific to King Juda and the former occupants of Bikini."[5]

Evacuation procedures were similar to the Able test, as animals were put in place and instruments checked. Fewer animals were used this time. Two hundred white rats and twenty pigs were placed in the sick bays of four ships near the bomb, and all were well sheltered. By 4:00 P.M. all personnel were moved off the islands in the atoll. By sunset all but thirteen support ships had cleared the lagoon, although three sailors aboard one of the target ships, the attack transport *Gasconade*, were somehow overlooked. This very contingency had been anticipated, however, so, according to the operation plan, the men filled the ship's yardarms with the appropriate bunting and were picked up by a tug at 5:30 A.M. on July 25.[6]

At that moment, Deak Parsons and Los Alamos physicist Marshall Holloway were making final adjustments to the bomb. Less than a quarter of a mile to their south lay the *Saratoga,* and the *Arkansas* was just 225 yards to the north. The Baker Day targets included all the survivors of the Able burst, plus seven additional ships; forty were within one mile of the Zeropoint, and twenty of those were within a half mile.[7]

If this test were to prove a failure, no one would blame it on poor aiming. This time the bomb was suspended at a depth of 90 feet in a concrete caisson from a specially modified amphibious landing ship, *LSM-60,* which was anchored precisely where the Navy wanted it. The bomb was to be exploded by a radio impulse from the instrumentation ship *Cumberland Sound*. The Able test, as one observer noted, "had some sport about it." The weather had to be perfect, and the bomb had a chance of missing its target, which it did. The Baker shot, on the other hand, had "all the grim, cold, mechanical aspects of an electrocution"; the site of the detonation was set, as was the precise second.[8] Despite all the planning, though, on July 19, the day of the dress rehearsal, the bomb detonated prematurely, probably because of a stray radio signal from a newscast.[9]

Originally designed to make amphibious landings carrying twelve tanks, the 203-foot *LSM-60* was selected for its stability and peculiar construction. Working under strictest secrecy at Terminal Island, California, workmen cut through the opening in the tank deck and installed a bomb bay. The caisson holding the bomb was lowered into the water to the desired depth by means of specially designed winches. "No corners were cut" in modifying the ship, explained Deak Parsons. "It was over-designed to the last detail, and we carried three hundred percent spares for all equipment."[10] *LSM-60* was then brought to Bikini in another landing ship, towed to its position in the lagoon, and moored with two lines to prevent movement.

Parsons and Holloway spent the night of July 24 aboard *LSM-60*. After making a final check of the radio link for firing the charge, they left for the *Cumberland Sound,* which was waiting at the entrance to the lagoon. As the ship steamed out to sea 15 miles from the blast, Holloway moved to the transmitting room deep in the ship's hold and sat down before a walnut cabinet containing rows of buttons, each of which controlled one sequence in the firing mechanism. Following a precise schedule, he was ready to punch each button in rapid-fire succession until he came to the last one, which was set apart from all the others. At 30 seconds before the explosion his finger would push that button, which would start an automatic bomb-firing clock. The last button would send out a radio impulse setting off the bomb at precisely 8:35 A.M. Holloway was not particularly worried about his job. "This thing is just a glorified alarm clock," he told reporters before the test. "I just check the stuff, sit back and watch what will happen."[11]

Someone had anonymously scrawled the words "Helen of Bikini" on the side of the Baker bomb, and the name stuck. It was discovered when President Truman's evaluation commission, headed by Senator Hatch, made its final inspection of the bomb. Bradley Dewey, another member of the board, suggested the name Moby Dick, so that observers could shout "Thar she blows!" but he was voted down. Senator Hatch, not to be outdone by the anonymous Kilroy, got in a plug for Los Alamos and his home state by chalking the words "Made in New Mexico" on the outside of the watertight caisson holding the bomb.[12]

The countdown, again broadcast worldwide, was called the "Voice of Abraham," coming as it did from the control ship *Cumberland Sound,* which had the code name Abraham. The voice actually belonged to a British physicist, Ernest W. Titterton, whose British accent turned "One hour before How Hour" into "One owah befoah How Owah."[13] As they waited for the blast, many observers saw the Baker test as a harbinger of push-button warfare. Men pushed buttons, an atomic bomb was set off, and to add a Wellsian touch, crewless drone boats and robotic pilotless planes would move through the lagoon and over the ghost fleet of abandoned ships. No goggles were needed for Baker, because the lagoon's water would filter out the dangerous ultraviolet rays. Observers looked directly at the ships on the horizon as Titterton's solemn and calm voice counted down the last 30 seconds. This time, though, the world listened less in terror than in curiosity as to the damage the blast would cause.

The Baker shot more than made up for the Able blast. It was truly a spectacle beyond imagination. "The phenomenon in itself was one of the most spectacular and awe-inspiring sights ever seen by man on this planet," wrote William Laurence, "quite different from the spectacles seen in the earlier bombs."[14] So much happened at once that even a seasoned reporter such as Laurence admitted that the human eye could not follow all the phenomena at once. In fact, scientists had such a difficult time describing the explosion they saw that a conference had to be held two months later to develop a new vocabulary of thirty new phenomena, such as base surge, dome, and cauliflower cloud.[15]

"A gigantic dome of water, white, beautiful, terror-inspiring, at least a mile wide, rose nearly a mile in the air immediately," wrote Philip Porter of the *Cleveland Plain Dealer*. "It blanketed the entire target fleet. It left me staring open-mouthed. I was so moved I could hardly write intelligible notes." After the initial burst, Porter continued, "a strange thing happened. The dome of water which had surged into the air seemed to settle down into a doughnut-like circle. It hid everything. It seemed to wrap itself around the target fleet."[16]

The explosion "seemed to spring from all parts of the target fleet at once," wrote another observer. "A gigantic flash—then it was gone. And where it had been now stood a white chimney of water reaching up and up."[17] The flash was followed by what looked like a "giant mountain lighted up from within like a huge Christmas tree," Laurence wrote. "For a time it looked as though a giant continent had risen from the sea, as though we were watching the formation of a continent that had taken place at a time when the earth was young, and then it took the shape of a giant chain of mountains, covered with snow, glistening in the sun."[18]

New York Herald Tribune correspondent Stephen White described an "explosion so fantastic, so mighty and so beyond belief that men's emotions burst from their throats in wild shouts." He added a plaintive note to his editor at the end of his dispatch: "Don't take any superlatives out of my copy. This was SOMETHING."[19] The blast was "staggering," wrote *Newsweek*'s Samuel Shaffer. "A dome of water half a mile across was belched up by the lagoon," followed by the column of water. "The roar that came 40 seconds after the blast was frightening. One newsman shouted: 'Why doesn't the captain take this ship out of here?'" As the column began to collapse and disintegrate, "we saw the most terrifying sight of all. A bank of radioactive cloud and steam some two thousand feet high crept over the target fleet, swallowing the ships from view."[20] Even a seasoned veteran like Kenneth Nichols thought his observer ship, nine miles away, was too close. One of the drone planes flying over Zeropoint was suddenly lifted more than 300 feet, while the force of the blast blew in the bomb-bay doors on another, as well as another one of its doors, a window, and the tail gunner's hatch.[21]

"The entire target array with the exception of one, two, three, four, five vessels is completely obliterated by the spray and the mist!" shouted a radio reporter from the *Mount McKinley*. "Now everything has turned white. I can see nothing at all of the target vessels!" he continued breathlessly. "They are completely obliterated by the radioactive spray that is in the air, and all the time mushrooming along the very surface of the water. It has taken an entirely different shape from the classic mushroom design which we knew."[22]

The bomb's energy yield was about 23,000 tons of TNT, the same as the Nagasaki and Able bombs. The underwater shock wave, which dealt terrific blows to the target vessels, instantly spread throughout the lagoon as a rapidly expanding circle; aerial photographs clearly showed this phenomenon, now called a shock disk. The upward sweep of the shock wave and fireball bubble reached the surface of the lagoon within a few hundredths of a second. Coconut trees on Bikini and Eneu shook abruptly like giant dishmops as the shock wave reached the islands at a speed of 3,500 miles per hour.

As the steam and fission products hit the atmosphere, a huge condensation cloud formed, which looked like a gigantic bubble or dome. It shot upward at a rate of more than two miles per second. Within a few milliseconds, the bubble swelled up to a huge dome, lit from within by the explosion, and atop the dome rode the 203-foot *LSM-60*. In another hundredth of a second the dome burst. Five hundred thousand tons of water rushed into the cavity and were thrown upward into a water column. The radioactive contents of the bubble were vented through this hollow column and formed a cauliflower-shaped cloud. The cloud contained water and fission products, as well as mud, rocks, and other material sucked up from the floor of the lagoon. In fact, the blast carved out a hole in the lagoon floor as deep as 32 feet over a 2,000-foot area directly below the point of detonation, moving more than 2 million cubic yards of material on the lagoon floor.[23]

As the fireball and water column leapt upward from the lagoon, the landing ship *LSM-60* simply disintegrated. Cameras mounted on towers at Bikini were able to photograph a few of the flying fragments, and several pieces fell on the target ships, but no large fragments were ever found. The water column erupted to a height of over a mile in one second, carrying with it 2 million tons of water. It looked like Niagara Falls in reverse. The hollow column was nearly half a mile across, with a wall of water 300 feet thick. The column burst through the top of the bubble to form a cloud that resembled a cauliflower top, much wider than the familiar mushroom head. Then, a full 10 seconds after the detonation, the water column collapsed back into the lagoon, creating enormous rolling waves of spray, mist, and air. This extraordinary and unexpected phenomenon, later referred to as the base surge, looked like a great wave of water, much like the dense cloud of spray at the base of Niagara Falls. It was not predicted by any of the scientists, and it was about to become America's Chernobyl.[24]

"The base surge contained enormous quantities of radioactive material," Ralph Sawyer bluntly wrote in a secret report after the tests. It billowed outward at more than 60 miles an hour, engulfing all the target ships. Within four minutes it had spread more than three miles across and 1,800 feet high, towering over all the ships in the lagoon. As this huge wall of spray and mist spread outward, it left what Sawyer described as a "kiss of death" on the target ships, as total fallout amounted to more than an inch of rain on the surface of the lagoon and the target ships.[25] The lagoon, reported Bob Considine, had "regurgitated a monstrous fountain whose falling waters contaminated everything they touched." The base surge "did not merely pass by the ships," wrote the Navy; "its radioactive mist settled on the decks, moistened every bit of exposed metal, wood and canvas."[26] The cloud of radioactive spray, mist, and debris was carried downwind more than seven miles, and, according to the Navy's own report, "heavily contaminated" all but nine of the ninety-five target vessels.[27]

The Baker shot unleashed the greatest waves ever known to humanity, greater than any natural waves with the possible exception of those produced by the 1883 explosion of the island of Krakatoa. As the nuclear reaction carried millions of tons of water upward from the lagoon in those first few seconds, an enormous cavity resulted, which may have extended to the very bottom of the lagoon nearly 200 feet below the water's surface. The surrounding water rushed in to fill the cavity, thus creating a huge mound, which sank slowly. In the process of rising and falling over a few seconds, the mound set off a series of gigantic waves. "Momentarily, I thought, 'My God, we have miscalculated the height of the wave, the alarmists may be right,'" wrote Nichols.[28]

No one knows how high the waves were at the lagoon surface above the Zeropoint, because most of the measuring instruments located within one-third of a mile of the detonation were damaged by the explosion and provided little reliable data. However, photographs of the edge of the water column showed that the first wave was 94 feet high. About fifteen to twenty of these waves were created, each smaller than the previous one, moving outwards at 50 miles an hour. Their height and speed decreased gradually as they neared Bikini Island, three and a half miles away, but some were still 15 feet high as they came crashing over the beach onto the center of the narrow island. Thousands of tons of sand and coral were moved, beached landing craft were damaged and filled with sand, and a few structures on the island were affected. Meanwhile, the backrush of the huge waves carried more than 50,000 tons of the island's beach sand into the lagoon. Not surprisingly, thousands of fish were killed around Zeropoint.[29]

Damage to the target vessels was staggering. Water is a virtually incompressible liquid, so the explosion worked like a hammer on the water, which in turn hammered the hulls of the target vessels. The bomb sank nine ships and seriously damaged dozens of others. The huge battleship *Arkansas*, positioned 225 yards from the center of the burst, was lifted by the column of rising water and sank within seconds, as did a concrete barge, a 120-foot landing craft, and three submarines—the *Apogon*, *Pilotfish*, and *Skipjack*. The Japanese battleship *Nagato* took on a slight list after the blast and sank during the night four days later. Many observers reported that the *Arkansas* was heaved upward on one end like a toy boat and then disappeared in the rising water spout. Photographs clearly showed a darkened area perpendicular to the water at the exact location of the *Arkansas*, but Blandy later stated that this was created by a cloud of soot and debris from the ship's stacks and boiler tubes.[30]

The *Saratoga* was only 350 yards from the Zeropoint. The first big wave from the blast hit the carrier broadside, lifted her up 43 feet, and pushed her back 800 yards. This wave by itself did not cause much damage, and the ship's superstructure remained intact. But as the *Saratoga* fell into the trough created by this huge wave, she was hit hard by the second wave crest and the thousands of tons of water falling from the blast column, which caused her flight deck to collapse.[31]

Survey teams reentering the lagoon saw that the *Saratoga*'s stern was low in the water and that she had begun to list to starboard. The Navy desperately wanted to save her. Rear Admiral Thorvald Solberg, who was in charge of the salvage operations, headed directly for her in a fast tug just a few hours after the shot, hoping that a welder could cut her anchorage and that she could be towed toward Eneu Island's beach so she would not sink. "Through the glasses you could see this tug going like mad toward the [*Saratoga*]," recalled Stafford Warren, "and all of a sudden it looked as if it put heels in the water, slowed down, stopped, and then backed up furiously." Louis Hempelmann, head of the Los Alamos Health Group, was the radiological monitor aboard Solberg's tug, standing on the bow with a Geiger counter. The tug had suddenly run into heavily contaminated water, and Hempelmann ordered it to turn around immediately. "You couldn't get near these ships," said Warren.[32]

The *Arkansas* "died quickly and cleanly—as men and ships should die," wrote Hanson Baldwin. "But the carrier *Saratoga* fought sternly through the long tropical day for her life, and 40,000 pairs of eyes in the observing fleet watched her agonies."[33] "All day long we watched this Lady die with dignity," wrote another observer. "It seemed that just about everyone in the Navy had been aboard her at one time or another."[34] It was almost true. The *Saratoga* had participated with her sister ship, the *Lexington,* in dozens of fleet maneuvers just as naval aviation blossomed. She was the training ground for the most famous naval fliers of the war and home to as many as 100,000 Navy men. "There were scores who wanted to save her," wrote Baldwin, "and perhaps she might have been saved, had there been a crew aboard. But she died a lonely death, with no man upon the decks once teeming with life, with pumps idle and boilers dead."

As she started to sink fast in the late afternoon, the rest of the fleet kept a death watch. By 3:45 P.M., one corner of her flight deck was awash. All hands of the fleet were called on deck for the final moments. Fifteen minutes later, the bow reared high and the stern sank. "As if striving for immortality," wrote Baldwin, "the 'Sara' lifted her white numeral '3'—third carrier of our Navy—high into the sun before her bow slipped slowly under." The *Sara* slipped below the water's surface at 4:10 P.M. "Hail and farewell!" came across loudspeakers as thousands of sailors watched through binoculars, many weeping openly.[35] She rests at Bikini today, intact and upright, lying directly on the lagoon floor, the top of her mast readily visible just below the water's surface.

It was the end of an era, and the *Saratoga* was mourned and eulogized throughout the country. "She would have been nineteen years old on November 16," wrote the *New York Times* in an editorial headlined "Taps for the Saratoga." "Now she has gone down in her last battle, tethered to anchors, unable to fight back. . . . Perhaps there will be no more wars, and the mock Battle of Bikini will be looked back to as a final and determining event. . . . In admiration for men alive and dead, in hope that others will not have to endure what they endured, we look across the vast sea to the Saratoga's grave."[36]

24

"I Never Want to Go Through the Experience of the Last Three Weeks of August Again"

The amount of radioactive material that collapsed back into Bikini's lagoon moments after the Baker shot was simply staggering. Unlike the Able blast, the fission products at Baker did not dissipate in the atmosphere. The water surrounding the bomb trapped most of the radioactive material and rained it down over the target vessels. As much as half the bomb's fission products remained in the lagoon's water or in the mist remaining in the air after the surge of spray fell back into the lagoon.

Scientists knew from studies of radium-dial workers that only a few millionths of a gram of radium lodged within human bones could prove fatal. Plutonium, the main component of the Baker bomb, has the same effect and is even more toxic. Test Baker, though, did not involve millionths of grams of radium, or even hundredths of grams. It created the equivalent of *thousands of tons* of radium. Within one hour of the blast, radiation levels in Bikini's lagoon reached the approximate equivalent of 5,000 tons of radium, which is 1 billion times the radioactivity from just one gram of radium.[1] Initial dose rates on the decks of target vessels closest to the blast exceeded 8,000 roentgen per day, 80,000 times the daily tolerance standard and 20 times more than a fatal dose. During the first hour, wrote Ralph Sawyer, "the radiation was roughly equivalent to that from several thousand tons of radium." Even an hour after the shot the target ships a mile from Zeropoint showed a dose rate of

1,200 roentgen per day, more than three times the lethal dose, meaning that the daily tolerance dose would be reached in seven seconds.[2]

The difference between dose rate and dose is similar to the difference between what is measured by a speedometer and an odometer. Dose rate measures intensity of radiation at any given moment in time, just as a speedometer measures speed at any given moment. Dose measures cumulative radiation exposure resulting from various dose rates, just as an odometer measures cumulative miles traveled at different speeds. Thus, to say that a dose rate of 1,200 roentgen per day on a target ship was three times the lethal dose means that someone would receive a cumulative dose of 1,200 roentgen by staying in that place for 24 hours. Even staying in that location for one minute would result in a dose of 0.83 roentgen (1,200 divided by 24 divided by 60), or more than eight times the daily tolerance dose of 0.1 roentgen.

Stafford Warren's radsafe section had warned that Baker could cause severe contamination in the lagoon and that the target ships "may remain dangerous for an indeterminable time thereafter."[3] Virtually all of these warnings were ignored. Despite drone boat readings of 730 roentgen per day near the center of the target array (more than twice the lethal dose), the first patrol boats reentered the lagoon 41 minutes after the shot to measure radioactivity levels and to retrieve instruments. A salvage group reentered the lagoon less than two hours after the shot, and shortly after that radiological monitors and technicians temporarily boarded twelve target ships to retrieve data and instruments. Ten were declared radiologically safe, and by the end of the day forty-nine support ships returned to Bikini's lagoon with nearly 15,000 men on board.[4]

The warnings all came true. "About four o'clock," recalled Warren, "I began to notice that the deep-water Geiger counters were showing more circulation near and under the observation fleet. This was horrifying to all these commanders. They had to move the fleet."[5] Some ships moved over toward the Eneu channel, while others moved all the way out into open ocean. The blanket of radioactive mist had contaminated the target ships to a much greater extent than had been foreseen. Blandy was cautious in his first message back to the Joint Chiefs: "Detailed examination of target ships may be delayed several days by radioactivity persisting in water and on board."[6]

The day after the blast, Blandy tried to tour the ghost fleet with Stafford Warren, but the frantic ticks of the Geiger counter on their small boat confirmed that the ships were much too radioactive for anyone to venture aboard, and they were forced to retreat in less than 30 minutes. Everyone on deck, Blandy told reporters, would have been "goners—if not immediately, at least later on."[7] Three days after the shot, several support vessels again had to shift anchorage due to an increase in radioactivity near the target array. As the radioactivity decayed, though, all support vessels returned to their regular berths in the lagoon within a week after the blast, and many would remain there for the next five weeks.[8]

Radioactivity took a heavy toll on the experimental animals. High radiation levels prevented their removal for the first few days, but, as a Navy report conceded, there was "an urgent necessity to remove animals to obtain instrumentation records and to proceed with post-technical inspections."[9] However, many of the animals died from radioactivity before the ships were even reboarded; six of the twenty pigs were found dead, and all the rest died within two weeks.[10]

Nearly half the animals exposed to the Able test had already died or were critically ill, but a Navy medical spokesman assured the press that they had suffered "no real pain."[11] For decades, however, scientists and doctors had known that patients suffering from radiation-related illnesses experienced anguishing pain. As early as 1908, Dr. Charles Allen Porter delivered a paper to one of the first annual meetings of the American Roentgen Ray Society on the more than fifty cases of radiation poisoning he had treated. "The amount of pain which these patients suffer is variable, though usually extreme," wrote Porter. "From my experience and personal communications from patients, I believe that the agony of inflamed X-ray lesions is almost unequaled by any other disease."[12] Nevertheless, just as Leslie Groves had testified to Congress that radiation poisoning was "a very pleasant way to die," Joint Task Force One perpetuated this myth in its post–Operation Crossroads report on the status of the test animals. "Radiation sickness is painless in its effect on animals and humans alike," reported Blandy in late September, "and since the animal has no knowledge that it has the disease, there is none of the mental anguish that assails a human being. The animal merely languishes and either recovers or dies a painless death. Suffering among the animals as a whole was negligible."[13]

Radiation levels on some of the target ships remained dangerously high even a week after the Baker shot, and boarding these ships was unsafe except for brief visits. Some were so radioactive in the first few days after the blast that the daily tolerance dose of 0.1 roentgen per day was reached in less than a minute. Twenty days after the shot, a pile of sand on one ship gave off a reading of 200 roentgens per day, meaning that a person lingering over a "hot spot" like this would reach his daily tolerance limit in just 45 seconds. About half the radioactive material produced by the blast remained in the waters of Bikini lagoon, and the largest part of this was on the surface of the water.[14]

To make matters worse, radioactivity in the lagoon's contaminated waters quickly spread to the support ships. Ships use saltwater for many purposes, and planners were concerned that water lines might become contaminated with fission products from the lagoon. The radsafe plan therefore cautioned that no distilling plants, heat exchangers, or other apparatus on the support ships that used saltwater cooling should be operated after either test until the seawater in the lagoon was declared safe by the radiological safety section. Nevertheless, one day after the support ships entered the lagoon, Blandy authorized them to operate their evaporators, which distilled seawater for drinking. As a result, every nontarget vessel became contaminated just as the planners had feared, as fission products became concentrated on underwater hulls and in condensers, evaporators, and saltwater pipes.[15]

Despite all the warnings that the highly radioactive column of water would come crashing down on the ships, absolutely no one—not even Warren's radsafe section—had planned for the very disaster that had been predicted with amazing accuracy. As the Navy admitted a few months later, "Since the nature and extent of contamination of the targets was completely unexpected, no plans had been prepared for organized decontamination measures."[16] For all its thousands of pages of detailed plans, the U.S. Navy managed to expose tens of thousands of men and more than 200 ships to radioactive contamination more than 2,000 miles from decent port facilities without ever having attempted experimentally to irradiate a ship or parts of one to determine how—or whether—a ship could be decontaminated.

The examination of the target ships—the very reason for Operation Crossroads—could not proceed if the vessels were too radioactive for reboarding and examination. As a result, the science of ship decontamination was born at Bikini lagoon following Test Baker. The first experiment, on July 27, was to wash down the battleship New York with saltwater, using the huge fire hoses of the firefighting vessels. Then, beginning on July 28, the Navy began to try to decontaminate the ships using materials already at Bikini or obtainable from Pearl Harbor. It tried detergent action with foamite, soap powder, lye, and even naphtha and diesel oil, dissolving action with hydrochloric and sulfuric acid, and adsorption by flour, cornstarch, and charcoal. Using air compressors, other men blasted the contaminated ships with ground corn cobs, rice, barley, ground coffee, and two products readily obtainable from Bikini—sand and coconut shells. Crews even worked in two-hour shifts trying to decontaminate the ships with the tried and true Navy method—scrubbing.[17]

None of these measures worked very well. Prolonged washing with an acetic acid solution proved helpful but simply was not feasible for mass application, and the other reagents worked only to the extent that they actually removed contaminated surface paint or corrosion. "When you realize that even a small destroyer . . . had a superstructure that was about three acres," recalled Stafford Warren, "the job of cleaning the radioactivity off was just impossible."[18] There was some limited success during the early stages, as loose material from the ships could be washed off with seawater. Nevertheless, as the Navy later acknowledged, radioactive materials were "retained to a remarkable degree" by exposed organic materials such as rope, canvas, and wood decks. These materials were "heavily contaminated," as were painted and rusty surfaces.[19]

"The Navy considers this contamination business the toughest part of test Baker," wrote the Army Corps of Engineers' Col. Cy Betts to Kenneth Nichols, who had returned to the States. "They had no idea it would be such a problem and they are breaking their necks out here to find some solution." Betts toured the target area five days after the test, as several radsafe monitors boarded the *Pensacola* and *New York* to retrieve instruments. "Both these ships, although they had been fairly well washed down the day before, were still very hot," Betts wrote, "and the boarding parties had to work quickly to avoid receiving tolerance doses or higher."[20]

The radsafe monitors were ordered to be fully clothed at all times, including rubber gloves and boots. They knew the value of protective clothing, but teenage sailors did not. "No one told us about radiation or being exposed to anything," recalled John Smitherman many years later. "We saw these men coming aboard ship and they had these Geiger counters with them and they were walking all over the ship. They had regular shoes on but they had cloth pulled up over their shoes. . . . I still had on a pair of shorts and my tennis shoes and my . . . little t-shirt with a sailor hat. And that's all the clothing that I had on me."[21]

A Navy diver told a similar story. "We had scientists dressed for outer space, with instruments like I had never seen," recalled George McNish. "But when it came to diving or bringing up samples, all we had were skin and tanks." The Baker shot had pulverized the coral in the lagoon's floor into soft silt, and divers recovering samples sank in this highly radioactive silt up to their shoulders. Another group of sailors boarded the target destroyer *Hughes* just one day after Baker. "Out of the four hours we spent on her," recalled one of them, "two were spent vomiting and retching as we all became violently ill." After the Baker test, over 40 percent of the men at Bikini were assigned to tasks involving decontamination, inspection, or towing or salvaging the target ships, with the brunt of the boarding and decontamination effort being borne by the 8,463 crew members of those ships.[22]

Stafford Warren quickly realized that safety guidelines were not being followed. During hosing-down operations, all personnel on tugs were ordered to stay windward of the target ships to minimize contamination, but it was impossible not to get wet. "We'd have to take the clothes off these people," said Warren; "their clothes were all contaminated and so was the skin of their back. They would not wear their gloves, so they would get the palms of their hands contaminated. After a week of this, the deck of that tug got so bad we had to put it out of service because it was contaminated enough to be hazardous."[23] Some target ships remained so radioactive that salvage ships could not come closer than 50 feet. The situation was made worse because few of the 42,000 men were even aware of the hazards and the need to take radsafe precautions. For example, a group of experienced scientists motoring through highly radioactive water three days after the Baker shot to watch a firefighting ship hose down a target ship were caught in the spray. A radsafe monitor maneuvered over to ask if the scientists had a Geiger counter on board. "We said 'no' and asked 'why,'" wrote one of the scientists.[24]

Los Alamos scientists took a condescending view of the whole situation. "Believe that much of semi-hysteria at Bikini is due to ignorance of general facts of problem," read one cable in early August.[25] Stafford Warren, though, was worried, as radiation readings forced the nontarget fleet to move again on August 2, this time to the Eneu channel. Radsafe monitors were primarily concerned with the target vessels, but the support ships were beginning to show low levels of contamination. "The job here is very strenuous and we are pushed for time," wrote an exhausted and nervous Stafford Warren to his wife. "We moved the fleet today to cleaner water. . . . The radioactivity is a more serious thing than they tho[ugh]t."[26]

Another unexpected problem came from the marine life in the lagoon. One radsafe team cruised around right near the target ships after the Baker shot, recording the "hot" readings in the lagoon water. When they moved to "cooler" water, though, their Geiger counters showed that radiation levels below deck did not drop to their lower levels. "It looked as though we were somehow or other contaminated with radioactivity— as indeed we were," wrote one monitor.[27] It turned out that radioactive algae, barnacles, and other marine life that concentrated fission products clung to the ships' hulls below the water line and intensified the contamination problem. "Their hulls were just hotter than a firecracker," recalled Warren.[28]

Three days after the shot, outboard bunks on one support ship showed readings of 0.156 roentgen per day, and evaporator readings were at 0.104—both above the daily limit before men were even exposed to the target ships. "We had to move the bunks away from the hulls so that these boys wouldn't get exposed," said Warren. Later studies showed that some marine organisms can concentrate fission products by a factor of 100,000 times the background level in their environment.[29]

Extensive malfunctioning and breakdowns of the radsafe monitors' instruments only made matters worse. The X-263 Geiger counter, which was rushed into production and never field tested, performed poorly. It "too often failed to function entirely," wrote Dr. William Myers, a radsafe monitor and professor at Ohio State University Medical School, to Stafford Warren a month after the Baker shot. "Nearly everyone finally tried to get hold of three or four of them to assure himself that at least one would be working by the time he had reached his assigned post." When it did work, he continued, "it became very erratic and often misleading." Worst of all, the X-263 could only measure gamma radiation reliably (high energy rays such as X-rays), but it could not measure alpha radiation from extremely dangerous substances such as plutonium, and its measurements of beta radiation were often misleading. "I am not an alarmist, Colonel Warren," Myers wrote. "Probably no permanent radiation injury was sustained by any of the participants. I do believe, though, that many of us probably received much more penetrating, ionizing radiation than the instruments of very low beta-sensitivity were able to record."[30]

Warren agreed. Despite Blandy's assertion that no radiological safety risks would be taken in this peacetime operation, Warren replied to Myers that Operation Crossroads "was conducted as an emergency and a lot of compromises were made to meet this emergency." The X-263 "had a great many defects. . . . It never was designed to be used as a measuring instrument although we were forced, because of lack of other instruments, to use it as such." Nor did Warren disagree with Myers's conclusion that Crossroads personnel received greater doses of radiation than the instruments had indicated. "The air inhalation possibilities and all of the rest indicated conclusively that . . . we were certain to get into trouble if we did not close the operation shortly," he wrote. Warren knew all too well that Test Baker was a radsafe disaster. "I don't believe you are an alarmist," he told Myers, "but I never want to go through the experience of the last three weeks of August again."[31] A government report later confirmed that Warren's task force had several instruments for measuring alpha contamination. "None, however," it noted, "proved reliable for field surveys."[32] The extent of beta measurements was stated bluntly in another report: "Little effort was made to measure beta radioactivity."[33]

A large part of the problem was caused by the shortage of monitors. The peak strength of this group was 350 men, but only a maximum of about 150 was available on any one day to monitor decontamination efforts. The remaining personnel had to measure film badges, analyze water samples, maintain and repair the monitoring instruments, and carry out other technical and administrative duties. The 381 monitors available for the Able shot were just enough to meet the requirement, Blandy later wrote, but for Baker there was a "severe shortage."[34] "Those who have participated," Warren wrote Blandy, "have been worked hard for days and nights and they are approaching physical exhaustion."[35] There was virtually no monitoring of nontarget vessels, and hazardous conditions sometimes went unnoticed on the target fleet. Warren's staff, for example, reported that men were aboard the *New York* without film badges or monitors. "These men were in the super-structure where readings of 5R [roentgen] were common," wrote two monitors. "We obtained a dosage of 0.5R [per] day in thirty minutes in places where some of these men had been for a much longer time."[36]

David Bradley, a radsafe monitor, tried to see the situation from the Navy's perspective. "The whole business must seem like a very bad dream to the regular navy men," he wrote. "Decks you can't stay on for more than a few minutes but which seem like other decks; air you can't breathe without gas masks but which smells like all other air; water you can't swim in, and good tuna and jacks you can't eat. It's a fouled-up world." And into this world had come the radsafe monitors. One after-noon Bradley was assigned to survey the *New York,* whose decks had been sluiced with water, washed with soap, alkali compound, and lye, and then washed again. Radiation levels, though, remained dangerously high. The captain was "completely bewildered," wrote Bradley. "The deck was clean, anybody could see that, clean enough for the Admiral himself to eat his breakfast off of. So what was all this goddamn radioactivity?"[37]

25

"These Ships Must Not Be Considered as Casualties in the Sunken Ship Sense of the Word"

As the days passed after the Baker shot, the captains of the target ships became increasingly upset with Stafford Warren. "Everybody is sitting around . . . staring us in the face and saying 'when can we get aboard,'" he wrote his wife. "They wanted their ships back," he later recalled, despite the fact that they were highly contaminated and no one could go aboard for more than a few minutes at a time. "Well," remembered Warren, "time passed and ships sunk. The *Saratoga,* of course, was the most bitter one, because the Navy was convinced they could save her if they had only been able to get close to her."[1]

Admiral Blandy announced several days after the test that the carrier *Independence* would go to Pearl Harbor, adding that her crew wanted to take her all the way to the U.S. mainland under her own power, just to show how much punishment the ship could absorb and still function. Rear Admiral Thorvald Solberg, who was in charge of salvaging the target ships, shared this view; he expected that the decontamination measures would reduce radiation levels to the point where they could return to home ports under their own power. Warren, for his part, confiscated Solberg's radioactive shoes and all the personal belongings from the captain's cabin on the *Prinz Eugen*—even his clothes and family photographs. Navy pride was in conflict with the demands of radiological safety.[2]

One afternoon Blandy, who was caught in the middle between Warren's concerns and the Navy's increasingly angry sailors, ordered Warren to report to the *Wichita,* one of the support ships. "You could just feel a kind of a wall of hate when I walked in," Warren later related. "The tension was just terrific." In front of 1,400 officers and sailors, Blandy said, "Doctor, would you take the microphone and explain to the officers and men what you're trying to do."

Warren explained that his orders from Blandy and President Truman were to protect the men from radiation hazards, which were everywhere in the lagoon. His words fell on deaf ears. The captain of the *New York,* recalled Warren, "was just madder than he could be, because he had his 1,200 or 1,400 men sitting in a barracks ship . . . in that heat. There was his ship undamaged, but contaminated. I wouldn't allow him on board but twenty minutes, and I wouldn't clear his ship for occupancy. I was just a dirty stinker, you know. . . . It was all my fault."

The captain challenged Warren's radsafe measures. "He almost said, 'Any fool knows,' but he said, 'Most everybody knows that the radiation varies inversely as the square of the distance, but your men go around and some of them put the Geiger counters three or four inches from the deck, some hold it hip high and use any kind of way of doing it; there are no standards.'"

Warren did his best to field the criticisms. "I had it hot and heavy for an hour." Blandy closed the meeting, but the tension with the officers remained. "Here their whole careers were based on the use of a battleship as an instrument," said Warren. "They had lived heart and soul in it, giving up their families and everything else. This was their profession."[3] This episode was not an isolated incident. Warren's colleague George Lyon, who headed the nonradiological safety team, wrote about one captain "who insists on a 'hairy-chested' approach to the matter with a disdain for the unseen hazard, an attitude which is contagious to the younger officers and detrimental to the radiological safety program."[4] The Navy simply did not accept this talk about radiation, and it took Warren, a strong, vigorous, and honest man, to try to keep matters under control. "He was persuasive as hell," recalled one radsafe monitor. "He had to be. He was the only Army colonel who ever sank a Navy flotilla."[5]

A host of factors—lingering radiation on the target and nontarget ships, malfunctioning radsafe equipment, a shortage of monitors, failure to observe radsafe regulations, and the ignorance and indifference displayed toward the radiation hazard by officers and enlisted men alike— caused many Operation Crossroads participants regularly to receive radiation doses in excess of the daily tolerance dose. The anecdotal evidence is simply overwhelming. The radsafe section detected sixty-seven overdoses between August 6 and 9, with some men exposed to 20 times the daily tolerance dose. Less than a week later, Warren reported that 26 of 125 film badges showed overexposures, with 13 over twice the daily tolerance standard.[6] Four of the six monitors working on the *Salt Lake City* and numerous crew members were overexposed, leading the Medico-Legal Board to recommend that all work on the ship be suspended for 40 days to permit radioactivity levels to decline naturally. Despite strenuous efforts at decontamination, the topside of the ship showed daily readings 5 to 15 times above the tolerance level, with some areas over 100 times the permissible level.[7]

All decontamination work on two target vessels, the destroyer *Wainwright* and attack transport *Carteret,* was stopped due to the crew's overexposure from working and living on the ships; the crews were immediately evacuated to the United States. Similar examples abounded throughout the task force; not even the scientists and technicians were spared. "There were people, particularly the scientists, who thought they knew better," recalled Warren. "I had to send some home because they were already overexposed—not badly, but beginning to be questionable."[8]

To make matters worse, individual officers extended the crews' working hours on target ships without consulting radsafe monitors. "It appears that there is an attitude of indifference on the part of the ship's officer of the *Prinz Eugen* to the safety standard set by RadSafe," wrote two of Warren's men, who found readings of five roentgen per day on the superstructure, 50 times the maximum daily tolerance dose. Nevertheless, crew members stayed on board the ship for as much as 16 hours or more. Some were ordered to spend the night there, because the ship's officers believed that the daily tolerance dose "has such a large safety factor that it can be ignored."[9] Unfortunately, radioactivity from the ghost fleet followed the target vessel crews to transport ships, thanks to the Navy's improvisation. Recognizing that the transport ships were now overcrowded and uncomfortable, Joint Task Force One decided on August 6 to permit material from the target ships to be cannibalized and transferred to transport ships to "increase the . . . comfort of the crews."[10]

The radiological crisis developing at Bikini was made more acute with the daily departure of radsafe monitors. "Monitoring demands have been increasing steadily while our numbers are being depleted," Warren wrote to Blandy on August 7. "Attempts to delay these men have met with unanimous refusal." He was going to lose more than 90 percent of his men in the next week, leaving him with only a handful of monitors to protect the crews working on more than seventy target vessels. He also recognized the difficulty of enforcing radsafe regulations.

"It is almost impossible to enforce the wearing of gloves continuously on badly contaminated ships," he reported. "Nor is it feasible to expect [men] to take the proper care of their contaminated clothes."

Film badges, which were radiation-recording devices, were not designed to measure beta radiation. The Medico-Legal Board assumed a 5 to 1 ratio between beta and gamma radiation, but the actual ratios varied widely and were much higher, probably 10 to 1. "Contamination of hands and faces with beta emitters of intensities greater than tolerance . . . is exceedingly common," Warren warned two weeks after the Baker shot. "It is not infrequent to find personnel with amounts on the bare hands bordering on erythema dose levels"—a reddening of the skin caused by a dose of 300 roentgen or more.[11] Only about 6,300 of the 42,000 Operation Crossroads participants were issued film badges, and no one, except perhaps for a few radsafe monitors, wore a badge every day.[12] Moreover, the information obtained from them was only available after exposure had occurred and thus did little to warn or protect the men, a point not lost on the wearers. Told by a radsafe monitor that the film in his badge was exposed like X-ray film to determine "how much you've been getting," one sailor replied, "Sure, but that only tells you afterwards. A lot of good that is when you've been fried all day in X rays."[13]

Warren was most concerned about alpha emitters such as plutonium. The element was discovered only in 1941 and not studied seriously until 1944, because only two milligrams of it existed until the fall of 1943. Plutonium was new and unknown, and scientists still did not fully understand how it behaved in the body. Alpha particles pose little threat outside the body and can be blocked by even a sheet of paper, but once absorbed they can be lethal. Setting safety standards for plutonium at Los Alamos during World War II was pure guesswork. Like radium, the new element proved to be a bone seeker, but its alpha emission seemed to be smaller. Guessing that the body could bear up to one hundred micrograms of plutonium as opposed to two of radium, the Manhattan Project at first set five micrograms as the tolerance dose, 50 times the dose for radium. Further studies, however, showed that plutonium was eliminated from the body at a much slower rate than radium, and it seemed to be 5 or 10 times more toxic than radium despite its lower alpha activity. This led Manhattan Project scientists to lower the tolerance dose fivefold to one microgram, but the war ended with little knowledge about the behavior of plutonium in the lungs and elsewhere in the body. Moreover, although scientists had developed instruments to measure beta and gamma activity, they had no reliable field instruments to detect and measure alpha activity.[14]

Warren's Medico-Legal Board concluded three days before the Baker shot that the amount of plutonium would be "so small as to be un-hazardous," but this was not the case.[15] "In truth, we were grasping in a field that was new," recalled Robert Conard, a radsafe monitor who later worked on radiological conditions in the Marshall Islands. "We had no way of accurately assessing how much plutonium was present, so we relied almost exclusively on beta and gamma monitoring."[16]

Two weeks after the test Warren noted that many ships had beta and gamma intensities low enough in places to lead some monitors to think the ships were safe. "This is not the case," Warren warned bluntly, because of the "widespread presence" of alpha-emitting plutonium in the target area. "It accompanies the gamma and beta emitters everywhere in a definite proportion," he explained, "and the presence of beta emitters in even moderate intensities is an indication that it is present in dangerous if not lethal doses."

In another memorandum Warren told Blandy that "some of the most important ships have had many lethal doses deposited on them and retained in crevices and other places." He warned Blandy that "this alpha emitter is the most poisonous chemical known," and "it is insidiously toxic in very minute quantities." Moreover, he said, accurate detection and thorough decontamination were not possible. "It can only be measured with very precise equipment which is not available and cannot be made available," he wrote, adding that "decontamination requires meticulous care and an elaborate set-up of equipment and trained men, none of which are available."[17] And even though gamma readings were declining, they were still high even 10 days after the test. Thirty-five target ships still had average topside readings more than 10 times greater than the daily tolerance dose, and some, such as the *Pensacola,* had an average daily reading 70 times greater. Nevertheless, for weeks after the tests men routinely boarded target ships, swept them, scraped them, ate their meals on board, and even slept aboard them; they were constantly exposed to the danger of inhaling plutonium and fission products from the Baker test.[18]

On August 3, nine days after the Baker shot, Warren was convinced he had a disaster on his hands. Declining gamma readings resulted in more pressure from captains to return their men to the target ships, but this did not mean the plutonium situation was any better. Residual radiation on the target ships "presents an extremely difficult and dangerous problem," he wrote to Blandy. "In most cases, areas of dangerous intensities remain on deck surfaces in spite of strenuous efforts to remove them." He warned that decontamination efforts were largely useless. "No practical method of decontamination is known in the case of wooden surfaces and rough metal short of removal of the actual surface," he said, adding that there was "increasing evidence" of exposure well over the daily tolerance dose.

Warren was also worried about the daily tolerance dose of 0.1 roentgen as a limit for long-term exposure. He told Blandy that as little as *half* that level of daily exposure for three months "may cause progressively increasing sterility . . . which upon disappearing may still result in defective children," and that such daily exposure for even less than three months "may cause defects in children of the first and second generations." Warren realized that several more weeks of continuous exposure would be disastrous. "The majority of personnel exposed at Bikini are young," he wrote, "and their heredity is of prime importance to them and their families." Warren urged Blandy to end Operation Crossroads immediately, except for work on target ships with relatively little radioactivity. All the other ships, he recommended, "should be declared hopelessly contaminated and be towed to shallow water and beached and time allowed for radioactive decay to take place."[19]

The Medico-Legal Board met the next day and agreed with Warren's recommendations, but the salvage teams did not, as Admiral Solberg insisted that work was proceeding satisfactorily. At a staff meeting on August 6, he reported that decontamination methods developed since Baker "may result in the early cleanup" of target ships, adding that "it is entirely possible to decontaminate successfully all ships if given the necessary time and personnel."[20]

Blandy sided with Solberg. "Admiral Blandy would not go along with Warren's recommendation to close out altogether," wrote one participant. "He insists on continuing a program of decontamination no matter how long it takes."[21] Blandy was unwilling to admit that so many ships were contaminated, and he was concerned about the public relations aspect of what he called the "hot" ships. "These ships must not be considered as casualties in the sunken ship sense of the word," he said at the August 6 staff meeting, and he ordered that ships sunk or destroyed more than 30 days after the Baker shot "will not be considered as sunk by the bomb." Like Solberg, Blandy was convinced the ships could be decontaminated. "The idea must not be fostered," he told his staff on August 6, "that nothing can be done about the radioactive condition of the ships."[22]

Warren did not let matters rest there. "Control of the safety of the target ships' crew is rapidly getting out of hand," he asserted bluntly the next day, August 7. "The target vessels are in the main extensively contaminated with dangerous amounts of radioactivity. Quick decontamination without exposing personnel seriously to radiation is not possible under the present circumstances and with present knowledge." He was also alarmed about the state of his men and their equipment. "Relatively few instruments remain in trustworthy condition," he warned, and "adequate monitoring personnel and instruments are no longer available. . . . Those who have participated have been worked hard for days and nights and they are approaching physical exhaustion." He called for an end to Operation Crossroads by August 15. "No further gain can be obtained without great risk of harm to personnel engaged in decontamination and survey work."[23] Blandy reacted cautiously, taking no definitive action, but he was beginning to understand the magnitude of the problem. On August 8 he sent a cable to Washington asking Admiral Nimitz, the chief of naval operations, to allow him to decommission thirty-nine target ships. "They cannot all be made absolutely safe to board in the near future for sufficiently long periods to either prepare them for movement to Pearl [Harbor] or to assess fully the damage sustained," wrote Blandy.[24]

The turning point came on August 9. Lieutenant Commander William A. Wulfman, a physician in charge of the target ships' radsafe monitors, wrote Warren that "work on target ships has increased to the point that it is impossible to provide adequate protection for the personnel involved in this work." Wulfman, too, realized that many men had received doses well above the daily tolerance of 0.1 roentgen. "The large number of personnel to be protected when working in ships with radiation above tolerance has required that monitors and equipment be so widely scattered that proper protection and adequate control are not possible."[25]

On that same day when Solberg asked Warren to inspect and measure radiation levels on material obtained from the wardroom of the *Prinz Eugen,* Blandy finally realized that Geiger counters could not detect plutonium. Geiger counter readings showed radiation intensity sufficiently low to permit men to spend long periods of time on the ship without danger of injury, but other tests on more sophisticated instruments showed what the Navy later described as "widespread presence" of plutonium. The few instruments capable of detecting alpha radiation at Bikini could not operate outside the controlled laboratory conditions on board the *Haven,* the ship housing Warren's radiological safety section.[26]

Later on August 9, following a conference aboard the *Haven* with Parsons, Warren sent a teletype message to the Manhattan Project stating that an "urgent need exists for radiation measuring instruments." He ordered 300 X-263 Geiger counters, 100 dosimeters, 18 ionization chambers, 6 beta counters, and 50,000 film badges. By now, Warren was clearly worried that further overexposures would affect the health of the men at Bikini. "Strongly urge that . . . this [be] treated as an actual emergency involving safety to life," he teletyped.[27]

Blandy called a meeting for August 10 to discuss Warren's findings. Following a farewell luncheon for Blandy and Parsons, who were scheduled to sail for Hawaii at six o'clock that evening, the tables were cleared and Warren presented his case. His chief adversary remained Admiral Solberg, the head of salvage. "It was his group of ab[ou]t 2000 men whom I was fighting," Warren wrote his wife. "He felt he could clean up these ships & I'd been saying he was butting his head against a stonewall & was only fooling himself & risking a lot of men."

Parsons had seen the results of analyses flown in from Los Alamos just before the meeting. "This stops us cold," he told Warren, and supported him fully. Warren showed Blandy how alpha emitters in the scales of a fish created an x-ray picture when placed on photographic film. Blandy respected Parsons's judgment and said simply, "If that is it, then we call it all to a halt." Decontamination efforts were considered unsafe under the existing conditions, and Blandy ordered all further decontamination work discontinued. Warren was pleased. "A self x ray of a fish . . . did the trick," he wrote home.[28]

Blandy immediately proposed that Operation Crossroads be shifted from Bikini to Kwajalein. "Although all waters and land areas of Bikini Atoll are well within radiological tolerance," he cabled Washington just before leaving Bikini, "the tendency of radioactive matter to concentrate and accumulate in ships, especially in evaporators and in marine growth on the hulls, makes it mandatory to remove the ships of the Task Force from this atoll with its small and decreasing but nevertheless cumulative hazard." The Navy Department agreed. "This is a momentous decision, a momentous admission," wrote one radsafe monitor in his journal. "From a military point of view the Bomb which wreaked havoc in Hiroshima also knocked out Task Force One. We've just come to the count of ten."[29]

As a result of the August 10 conference, all decontamination work was halted. Undaunted, one ship commander proposed two days later that the external gamma readings were low enough for men to board the bigger target ships in order to start their engines for pumping. "This is not the case," replied Warren abruptly the next day in what a later government report described as a "didactic" memorandum. "The widespread presence of an alpha emitter has been demonstrated," he said, and the request was denied.

Warren's memorandum reflected his increasing frustration with the Navy's refusal to recognize the radiological hazard on its hands. Plutonium "is present in dangerous if not lethal amounts," he warned, adding that "every contaminated place as evidenced by the gamma or beta radiation or any surface of any vessel may be in fact the residence of many lethal doses of this alpha emitter." The ventilating systems, dust, and inner compartments of the target ships were heavily contaminated, he said, adding that the initial contamination from Baker was so great that reduction of radiation levels of "90% or more still leaves large and dangerous quantities of fission and alpha emitters scattered about." His assessment of the situation was chilling: "Contamination of personnel, clothing, hands, and even food can be demonstrated readily in every ship in the JTF-1 in increasing amounts day by day."

Warren also realized that some of the commanders of the target vessels were not complying with the radsafe guidelines, so he simply forbade further work on the ships. Stating that the continued use of crews for decontamination work without proper training and equipment "is exceedingly dangerous," he ordered that men could board the ships only to recover instruments, install pumping gear, and prepare the ships for towing to Kwajalein.[30] He warned Blandy on August 15 that "someone may become badly contaminated internally in the near future just upon the statistical basis of large numbers exposed to a wide area of low contamination," and his cable to the Manhattan Project was equally blunt: "Find inner compartments all target ships highly contaminated by alphas."[31] Warren's findings were later confirmed by Los Alamos based on analyses of target ships samples that had been flown back to the laboratory.[32]

For Stafford Warren, it was the end of what seemed to be a single-handed battle against the Navy. "[I] am still battling a rear engagement, but the battle [is] won in all details—namely to stop the program where it is now," he wrote his wife on August 11. "For over a week I have been trying to hold this task force within bounds. . . . I began to get proof that the boarding and 'clean up' parties were getting over the line and avoiding monitors, etc. . . . The officers and men began to take advantage of their numbers and my green men." With the tests definitely off, Warren had won his battle. "The navy is now beginning to believe me!" he wrote. He reported with near disbelief a few days later that the Navy had actually listened to him again. "Recommended today that the area be abandoned by 1 Sept. and they tow the ships they want to Kwaj[alein] & they will do so! If not sooner!" Thousands of Crossroads personnel began leaving Bikini within days, including Warren. "I'm getting the jitters," he wrote his wife just before sailing on August 13, and he sounded as if he had just avoided a close call: "We have pulled out of here the majority of the force . . . just in time."[33]

The reporters and observers had long since left Bikini. Operation Crossroads personnel were now flown out daily, target ships were towed to Kwajalein, and support vessels headed off to Hawaii. Most of the radsafe monitors left Bikini on August 16, leaving behind a skeleton force on the *Haven* to continue monitoring the ships. Warren, who was given a "Mark III" lead jockstrap by his staff to celebrate his fiftieth birthday at Bikini, was completely exhausted and slept off and on for four straight days. He also had time to reflect on the tests, and he hoped that the Navy may have finally developed a healthy fear of the bomb. "I think the Navy now has an idea, a very little idea of what a scourge it can be and what a boomerang," he wrote home. "Some very serious thinking is going on and many of the task force admit that war is unthinkable with atomic warfare."[34]

By early September the last ship had left Bikini, and the atoll was completely evacuated by September 26. For security reasons, some of the evidence was destroyed. In an attempt to erase all clues as to the size and weight of the bomb and the methods of loading and handling it, the AAF dropped its remaining pumpkins on Erik Island and even burned the boxes in which the pumpkins had been stored. At Kwajalein, meanwhile, the hoist that loaded the ramp and pit were dynamited and filled in with sand, so their location was obliterated.[35]

Most of the physical evidence, though, remained. More than a dozen ships now rested on the lagoon floor. The steel towers that had mounted high-speed cameras still stood, as did the concrete basketball courts, dispensary, and baseball fields. The story of Operation Crossroads was also evident on the lagoon side of the small islands in the western part of the atoll; beaches were strewn with oil drums, mattresses, bottles, tires, boxes, and rusting machinery, all smeared with tar and oil.

The invisible evidence—pervasive radiation—was still there, too. For reporters and the public, the story of Operation Crossroads was the heat, blast, and tally of sunken ships, but the real story was the powerful, uncontrollable—and invisible—radiation. At the edge of the cloud after the Baker shot, David Bradley's Geiger counter clicked wildly and the needle showing levels of radiation went off the scale. "It always seemed a little strange to me," he wrote, "that at such a time the pilot should be calmly looking down at the fleet, or glancing over his instrument panel. . . . Something was wrong. We should be able to feel the barrage of gamma rays tearing through our bodies. It was there. It was hot."[36]

That was the sad lesson of Operation Crossroads. Radiation has no direct impact on the senses. It cannot be seen, felt, tasted, heard, or smelled, and it was hard for all but a handful of Crossroads participants to react to and respect something they could not sense. "In the laboratory, radioactive material was handled by remote controls," said a Navy speaker at a 1947 conference on defensive atomic warfare. "At Bikini, it was scattered over the decks of the ships. Men walked through it, tracked it around, and got it on their clothing and hands and faces. There was some tendency on the part of the men to disregard a danger which they could not see, nor touch, nor smell." The greatest danger of atomic warfare lay not in the immediate blast and heat from the atomic bomb but from the deadly lingering radioactivity. However, as E. B. White put it, the Navy "is contemptuous of anything that isn't big and noisy and that refuses to come out in the open and fight."[37] The ghost fleet would not sail back under the Golden Gate Bridge, triumphant and invincible. The ships survived their familiar enemies of heat and blast, but the Navy had never fought an alpha particle.

26

"The Atomic Bomb Did Explode Something More Important than a Couple of Out-of-Date Warships"

In a battle between atomic power and naval power, Operation Crossroads could have had three outcomes. First, the entire target fleet might have been sunk, together with the Navy's future. Second, the fleet might have survived the bombs virtually intact. What did happen, though, was the third possibility, something in between: the ships were heavily but inconclusively damaged. "There is no doubt," wrote the *New Republic* after the Able test, "that prospects for world peace would be a lot pleasanter if every ship in the lagoon had been pulverized into steel filings." By sinking a few ships and damaging others, "the bomb accomplished enough havoc to salvage its reputation, yet not enough to maintain its 'absoluteness' in men's eyes. Most people now have the impression that, tremendous as it is, the bomb lacks the power to destroy mankind en masse."[1]

William Laurence of the *New York Times* summed up the popular mood in early August when he returned from the Baker test. "Before Bikini," he wrote, "the world stood in awe of this new cosmic force." Since the tests, though, "this feeling of awe has largely evaporated and has been supplanted by a sense of relief unrelated to the grim reality of the situation. Having lived with a nightmare for nearly a year, the average citizen is now only too glad to grasp at the flimsiest means that would enable him to regain his peace of mind." The bomb did not sink the whole fleet, make a hole in the bottom of the ocean, or create a

246

tidal wave, said Laurence, so the public was eager to conclude that the bomb was "just another weapon. As such, it is a problem concerning only the military and nothing for the average citizen to be worried about."[2]

Norman Cousins, editor of the *Saturday Review,* sounded a similar note. "After four bombs, the mystery dissolves into a pattern," he wrote. "By this time, there is almost a standardization of catastrophe." The tests had caused extraordinary damage, but these facts emerged only after the first impressions that the bomb was overrated. "The *Nevada* was afloat and some goats lived; what else mattered?" mused Cousins.[3]

In the summer of 1946, Bikini Atoll emerged as a symbolic ideological battleground. The first newsreels of Operation Crossroads were released by the War Department in early August, together with footage shot by Japanese cameramen immediately after the bombing of Hiroshima. The remarkably clear film of the Baker test, taken by automatic cameras mounted on Eneu Island, graphically showed the frightful explosion and grotesque beauty of the mushroom cloud and doughnut-like dome of water. Even more chilling were the pitiful scenes of the devastated city of Hiroshima. The victims looked as if they had been seared by an acetylene torch. The design of a dress was imprinted on a woman's body, and one man staggered along with half an ear.

President Truman saw a special advance screening of the newsreel at the White House movie room on August 7, and a few days later the film was shown to delegates at the Paris Peace Conference, leading one newspaper to recall Hitler showing films of his air force's power to impress satellite nations. Accusing Secretary of State Byrnes of using "atomic diplomacy" to intimidate smaller nations, a Yugoslavian journal deplored the showing of the movie during the peace conference as a modern version of Theodore Roosevelt's diplomacy: "Speak softly but keep an atom bomb in your hand."[4]

The military's reaction to the tests paralleled the political realities of the emerging Cold War. "These tests are one form of being prepared for war," proclaimed a Navy official just returning from Bikini, but Admiral Blandy was more diplomatic. Two days after his return to Washington in late August, he declared that he favored abolishing the atomic bomb, but that until it was outlawed he favored periodic testing. Thus, beginning in the summer of 1946, with U.S. diplomats hoping to sell the Baruch Plan at the United Nations and military experts analyzing the results of Operation Crossroads, America commenced its decades-long pursuit of two nuclear policies: a call for international control of atomic weapons matched by a buildup of its own nuclear stockpile. "You'd never convince a Russian factory worker that the Bikini experiment was made in the interest of world peace," asserted Senator Scott Lucas of Illinois in a radio interview. "He undoubtedly considers it a saber-rattling demonstration."[5]

President Truman's cantankerous and naive commerce secretary, Henry Wallace, the last New Dealer left in the Truman Cabinet, also saw the tests as contributing to a growing feeling in the United States that war with the Soviet Union was inevitable. Wallace had told Truman in mid-March that the Soviet Union's behavior was caused by its "dire economic needs and . . . disturbed sense of security." By the summer of 1946, convinced that the Baruch Plan was designed to be unacceptable to the Russians, Wallace decided to speak out against Truman's foreign policy in the hopes that the president would return to Roosevelt's stated policy of trust and cooperation toward the Soviet Union. In a twelve-page letter to Truman just before the Baker test, he asked, "How do American actions since V-J Day appear to other nations? I mean by actions the concrete things like . . . the Bikini tests of the atomic bomb. . . . I cannot but feel that these actions must make it look to the rest of the world as if we were only paying lip service to peace at the conference table."

Wallace made many of the same points in a September 12 rally at New York's Madison Square Garden, arguing that the United States should accept a Soviet sphere of influence in Eastern Europe. "The tougher we get, the tougher the Russians will get," he said, adding that "'getting tough' never brought anything real and lasting—whether for schoolyard bullies or businessmen or world powers." Wallace openly criticized Secretary of State Byrnes, who was attending the Paris Peace Conference, and declared, "The real peace treaty we now need is between the United States and Russia."

Five days later, Navy Secretary Forrestal, with Admiral Blandy at his side, discarded his prepared speech on Operation Crossroads and delivered an impassioned extemporaneous address to a New York audience, referring to "a certain atomic disturbance that happened in this town in recent days." He praised Secretary Byrnes as "a great American who has served this country well," and added that "if the world will permit it, he will serve it equally well." America, he said, was not planning for war against Russia, and he told reporters that he was "quite annoyed" with Wallace's comments.

Blandy, returning to Operation Crossroads, urged the audience of businessmen to help obtain congressional appropriations to support closer links between science and industry, and he chided those "deluded individuals" who thought the Navy was obsolete. "To think of abolishing the Navy while the sea is still needed for traffic in war would be as fatuous as abolishing the State Highway Patrol while passenger cars and trucks still used the roads." Three days later, with Byrnes threatening to resign, Truman dismissed Wallace from the Cabinet.[6]

Operation Crossroads was held at a critical moment in U.S.-Soviet relations. The bitter Paris Peace Conference was about to end. "We must make sure that others do not get the impression that they can impose their will on us," Secretary of State Byrnes had told the American people in a radio address in May during a recess in the conference. In reply, Molotov accused Byrnes of using "methods of pressure, threats and intimidation," and the new American ambassador in Moscow told Byrnes that Molotov "did not intend to withdraw or compromise." Nevertheless, Byrnes held his ground during the conference.[7]

By the summer of 1946, both America's public attitude and its policy toward the Soviet Union had changed radically from a year earlier. According to a *Fortune* poll in September 1945, 25 percent of the public believed the Kremlin wanted to spread communism to the rest of the world. More than half held that view in July 1946, and later polls showed this figure at two-thirds.[8] The Truman administration, meanwhile, had adopted a much tougher policy toward the Soviet Union, as Kennan had recommended in his "Long Telegram," and for the rest of 1946 it made no significant concessions to the Russians. By July, even the most liberal and optimistic members of the Truman administration were taking a hard line on dealings with the Soviet Union. One of the last converts, Dean Acheson, had hoped as late as March that the two countries could cooperate on atomic energy and economic matters. He had been working on a $3.75-billion loan package for Great Britain, which he hoped would be followed by a loan to Moscow, because he saw economic assistance as a means of improving relations and bringing the Soviets back into the world community. So, too, did he see the Acheson-Lilienthal Report as a bona fide effort to create global security in the new world of atomic weapons.

Although the Soviets had agreed in March to pull their troops out of Iran, the United States insisted on leaving the issue on the agenda of the UN Security Council, prompting the first of Soviet Representative Andrei Gromyko's many walkouts from the United Nations. Acheson was now convinced of the need to confront the Russians and show America's strength. As he later recalled, "The year 1946 was for the most part a year of learning that minds in the Kremlin worked very much as George F. Kennan had predicted they would."[9] By August, when the Soviet Union insisted on a joint Soviet-Turkish defense system—meaning Russian military bases in Turkey—Acheson had come around completely. Truman's military advisors feared that these Russian bases would ultimately make Turkey a Soviet satellite and might open the way to Russian control of Greece, the Persian Gulf area, and even the Suez Canal. "The only thing that will deter the Russians," Acheson told Truman at an August 15 White House meeting with military leaders, "will be the conviction that the U.S. is prepared, if necessary, to meet aggression with force of arms."[10]

Truman adopted this advice so rapidly that General Eisenhower asked if he understood that failure by the Russians to back down could lead to war. Without hesitating, Truman replied, "We might as well find out whether the Russians are bent on world conquest." Then he pulled a large map of the Mediterranean out of his desk drawer and proceeded to lecture Acheson and the generals on the strategic importance of the area. He was prepared to go to war. "When he finished," Acheson wrote, "none of us doubted he understood fully all the implications of our recommendations."[11] The policy of containment was born. The president dispatched an aircraft carrier task force, led by the *Franklin D. Roosevelt,* to join the *Missouri* in Istanbul and flatly declared the Turkish Straits to be an area of vital concern to U.S. strategic interests. The Russians shelved their plans. The lesson was clear: the Russians retreated when they were confronted with strength.

It is difficult to assess the influence of Harry Truman on Operation Crossroads and the early years of the nuclear age, because so many of his pronouncements seem contradictory. Upon hearing of the bombing of Hiroshima he exclaimed that the atomic bomb was "the greatest thing in history." Three days later, though, on the day of the Nagasaki strike, he said that he had "a human feeling for the women and children of Japan," and he told the American people that night that he understood "the tragic significance of the atomic bomb."[12] The same man who declared that America would hold the atomic bomb as a "sacred trust" for mankind also endorsed the Acheson-Lilienthal Report's call for a cooperative international venture to share the bomb. In 1945, believing that the successful test of the atomic bomb would strengthen his hand at the Potsdam Conference, he postponed the meeting until mid-July. Three years later he sounded a different note. "You have got to understand that this isn't a military weapon," he told a meeting of military leaders and AEC officials at the White House in July 1948. "It is used to wipe out women and children and unarmed people, and not for military uses."[13]

Truman probably saw Operation Crossroads as strengthening America's hand at a time of increasing tension with the Soviet Union. He had been impressed with Stimson's plea the previous September for direct talks with Moscow on the atomic bomb, but his interest in a policy of trust had disappeared by the summer of 1946 as he became increasingly frustrated at Soviet behavior. "The Russians are trying to chisel away a little here, a little there," he said at a July 12 staff meeting. "If the Paris conference busts up, I want to be ready to reveal to the whole world the full truth about the Russian failure to honor agreements." He then ordered his naval aide, Clark Clifford, to draw up a record of Soviet violations of international agreements.

Clifford's top-secret report, written with his assistant George Elsey, built on George Kennan's Long Telegram and formed the bases of the Marshall Plan, the Truman Doctrine, and the strategy of containment. They wrote that the Soviets had embarked on a massive program to develop guided missiles and atomic bombs, and they warned Truman that "the acquisition of a strategic air force, naval forces and atomic bombs in quantity would give the U.S.S.R. the capability of striking anywhere on the globe." In order to restrain Russia, Clifford and Elsey argued that "the United States must be prepared to wage atomic and biological warfare. . . . The mere fact of preparedness may be the only powerful deterrent to Soviet aggressive action and in this sense the only sure guaranty of peace." Truman was so shocked by the Clifford-Elsey report that he ordered all twenty copies to be delivered to him at the White House. "If it leaked it would blow the roof off the White House, it would blow the roof off the Kremlin," he told a startled Clifford.[14]

Lecturing at the National War College in Washington later in 1946, George Kennan clearly articulated the theory of containment. "There is no reason, in theory," he declared, "why it should not be possible for us to contain the Russians indefinitely by confronting them firmly and politely with superior strength at every turn." Averell Harriman sounded a similar note at an off-the-record talk to Kennan's class. To confront Soviet expansion, he called for a large air force capable of hitting Soviet industry and for the United States to have "guts enough to face the fact" that the atomic bomb had to be developed and maintained in readiness.[15]

American foreign policy had changed radically since September 11, 1945, when Henry Stimson had urged Truman "to meet Russian suspicion with American candor, to discuss the bomb directly with them and try to reach agreement on control." Exactly one year later, James Forrestal flew to New York to meet with the now-retired secretary of war. "He said," wrote Forrestal in his diary, "the way things had now developed he thought we should not delay in going forward with the manufacture of all the atomic missiles we could make."[16]

Nowhere was the deterioration of U.S.-Soviet relations more public than at the United Nations, where the United States actively played its nuclear card. The Baruch Plan was an extraordinarily shrewd American initiative. "As the first postwar plan on disarmament," two Cold War historians have written, "it is still a classic study in the art of political gamesmanship, in the technique of winning friends and embarrassing enemies."[17] The Baruch Plan ensured American safety and security. It called for an unrestricted survey of Russia's uranium and thorium reserves, with the mines and facilities needed to produce atomic fuel placed under international—meaning Western—control. A suspected violation of the plan by the Russians could result in "prompt and certain" penalties, including a military, even atomic, attack on the Soviet Union, and the Russians would have to give up their veto at the Security Council. Moreover, the United States would not even release technical information about atomic energy, much less destroy its arsenal of atomic weapons, until the end of the entire process, after an international system of controls and inspection was in place. The mere notion of inspections alone ran so contrary to everything the Soviet government stood for that it was out of the question that the Kremlin would agree. "We can't get into Rumania and Bulgaria much less Russia," said Byrnes at a meeting with Forrestal and Patterson. "It would be childish to think that the Russians would let us see what they are doing."[18]

A plan designed to perpetuate American security was, almost by definition, guaranteed to threaten Russian security. In this sense, the Baruch Plan was, pure and simple, a trap for the Russians. Acceptance meant placing themselves in a position militarily inferior to the United States. Rejection meant spurning America's altruistic offer to surrender its atomic monopoly, thus handing the United States a huge propaganda victory. There was also the question whether the fledgling United Nations was capable of taking on the job of international control. In a memorandum to President Truman from the Joint Chiefs, Admiral Leahy stated that the United States must recognize the "inability of the United Nations . . . to observe or control atomic research and development."[19] In a way, therefore, having the arms control issue before a UN commission without any hope of movement permitted the United States to move forward on nuclear testing without directly confronting the Soviet Union or losing the propaganda war.

The Soviet Union viewed Operation Crossroads as evidence that America was not interested in controlling atomic weapons, and it saw a direct link between the tests and the UN negotiations. Indeed, five of the foreign observers at Bikini, including the two Russians and the two Soviet sympathizers from Poland, returned to the UN negotiations immediately after the Baker test.[20] "Why are all other countries obliged to display blind confidence in the United States' intentions while the United States obviously distrusts not only its partners but also the international control organ?" asked *Pravda,* the official organ of the Communist party, a week before the Able test. "Can it be that it is considered in Washington that special confidence should be placed in the United States as a result of the noise raised about the forthcoming tests in the Pacific?" As one Russian told a reporter just before Crossroads, "What are the Bikini tests for? Don't the people in the United States know that the bomb is effective? Are the tests to reassure the Americans or frighten other people?"

"The test has political implications, of course," editorialized the *New York Times* in late June. "But there is certainly no validity in the charge that it is being made at this time in an effort to influence either the deliberations of the United Nations Atomic Energy Commission or the meeting of the Foreign Ministers in Paris." Just five days later, though, the *Times* noted that many people "think the events at the Pacific atoll and what they portend will have a more profound effect on the shape of the peace than the deliberations of the Foreign Ministers in Paris and the United Nations representatives in New York."[21]

Baruch played up America's monopoly of the bomb, insisting on verification and inspection before the United States would give up its "winning weapon." The Baruch Plan asked too much from the Russians. If implemented, it would have deprived the Soviet Union of the ability to develop the atomic bomb, guaranteeing America's monopoly over it, and modified the voting structure of the United Nations to the permanent disadvantage of the Soviet Union. "We wanted them to agree to international controls after we had already demonstrated our ability to make atomic weapons, but before they had the ability," recalled Dean Rusk. "Our hopes for the Baruch Plan and international controls went beyond what we Americans would probably have agreed to had our situations been reversed." Baruch's talk of atomic disarmament was just that—talk. It was good for propaganda, but it was a mere chimera, scorned in the minds of U.S. policymakers. Disarmament might come, but first there would have to be comprehensive and indefinite controls and inspections. Until that time, America would maintain its atomic monopoly.[22]

On June 19, five days after Baruch's speech, Gromyko and Soviet Foreign Minister Molotov finally responded. "The Baruch Plan is not in the interest of the United Nations," charged Molotov to the delegates. "There exists another plan for the atomic bomb proposed by the Soviet Union. . . . We, the people of the Soviet Union, do not have any future plans for an atomic bomb." Gromyko's comprehensive counterproposal differed in virtually every major respect from the U.S. initiative. The first order of business, he said, was to ban the bomb. The United States must destroy its stockpile of atomic weapons at the beginning of the process, and the manufacture or possession of atomic bombs would be prohibited. The Gromyko plan called for no immediate inspection and no sanctions, and any international agency would have to be subordinated to the UN Security Council, where the Soviets could continue to exercise the veto. The veto, he asserted, must be retained "under any circumstances." Here, for the first time, the two diplomats laid out opposing strategies that would form the bases of each country's negotiating platform for years to come. The American plan called for complete controls, with a future hope of disarmament, while the Soviet plan called for complete disarmament, with a future hope of controls.[23]

The gap between the two sides grew wider in late June and early July as negotiations between the two countries broke down on the veto issue. Baruch made little effort to negotiate, and Gromyko made none. Truman urged Baruch to stick to his hard line. "We should stand pat on our program," the president wrote Baruch. "We should not under any circumstances throw away our gun until we are sure the rest of the world can't arm against us."[24] The Soviets, though, may well have viewed American behavior with the same sense of foreboding that U.S. officials viewed Russian actions. Although the United States was rapidly demobilizing, it was also establishing a military presence in Germany, Korea, and Japan, asserting its power in Trieste, Iran, and Saudi Arabia, negotiating for overseas bases, developing jet fighters and a new intercontinental bomber, jockeying to impose the Baruch Plan—and planning to conduct a round of atomic tests at Bikini.

On July 5, just days after the Able test, Baruch rejected the Soviet counterproposal. *Pravda* saw an unmistakable connection between the two events, charging that the tests had been deliberately timed to coincide with and influence the UN debate on atomic controls. "Why carry out this costly test if the United States has made up its mind to denounce atomic weapons?" it asked. "The tests are not preparations to destroy this weapon but to work towards its perfection," *Pravda* charged. "The atomic bomb did explode something more important than a couple of out-of-date warships; it fundamentally undermined the belief in the seriousness of American talk of atomic disarmament."[25]

Some American commentators agreed with this assessment. Harold L. Ickes, secretary of the interior under Roosevelt and Truman, said in his syndicated column "Man to Man" that he was "perplexed" and "appalled" at the decision to hold the tests with the Baruch and Gromyko plans on the table and under negotiation. "Are [the tests] for scientific purposes?" he asked. Atomic scientists were not interested in them. He continued:

> Are they for military purposes? Perhaps. And yet it seems to me to be shocking that the United States . . . should at this time give any indication . . . that it is preparing for atomic warfare. Are they then diplomatic tests, designed to impress upon the peoples of the earth that some immediate international control is imper-

ative? Is the Bikini experiment diplomacy by intimidation? If so, it is in bad taste—and badly timed. Whatever its purpose, it is impossible to believe the United States will not be regarded as acting in bad faith.[26]

The Soviet line was simple: America was plotting an atomic war, and Operation Crossroads was the rehearsal. Other European Socialist and Communist parties took the same approach, denouncing the tests as a diabolical instrument of U.S. foreign policy. "The atomic bomb is on a level with the evil deeds of the Nazis, and places conquerors and vanquished on the same plane," proclaimed the Italian Socialist newspaper *Avanti*. *L'Unita*, the Italian Communist organ, described Crossroads as a "most startling, monstrous and at the same time tragically grotesque experiment."[27] Sweden's Socialist newspapers contrasted the blast to lectures in Moscow's parks on the peaceful uses of atomic energy. "The Statue of Liberty, which reminds one of the days the United States was a model democracy," wrote one paper, "ought to be supplanted by a statue of the Bikini goat, symbol of American imperialism's greatest propaganda fiasco."[28]

On the day of the Baker test, protesters marched down New York's Broadway leading a stuffed goat bearing a sign that read "Today Me, Tomorrow You." At the same time, up in the Bronx, the Russians rejected the entire Baruch Plan. "The United States proposals in their present form," Andrei Gromyko told the UN Atomic Energy Commission, "cannot be accepted in any way by the Soviet Union, either as a whole or in separate parts," and he warned that any attempt to "undermine" the great powers' veto would be "dangerous and maybe fatal." The *New York Times* headline the next morning demonstrated the proximity between Bikini and the Bronx:

ATOMIC BOMB SINKS BATTLESHIP AND CARRIER;
FOUR SUBMARINES ARE LOST IN MOUNTING TOLL;
SOVIET FLATLY REJECTS BARUCH CONTROL PLAN

The superpowers faced their first stalemate over nuclear weapons, three years before the Russians even had the bomb.[29]

27

"I Would Call Down the Wrath of God upon Such an Obscenity"

As debate raged over the Able and Baker tests, the Navy moved ahead with plans for the third test at Bikini, a deep underwater shot code-named Test Charlie. The bomb would be detonated up to one mile under the ocean, Admiral Blandy told Congress, and would require the construction of either a bathysphere or a specially designed bomb casing to withstand the tremendous pressure at these depths. His science advisors later determined that the optimum depth would be half a mile, although the bathysphere would have to be designed for pressure of nearly 1,000 pounds per square inch. Planning for Test Charlie continued at Bikini in the three weeks between tests Able and Baker, as Blandy tried to select between fifteen and thirty target ships and submarines and pick the best method of mooring them in the open ocean off Bikini. He eventually decided to bring several more target ships to Bikini for the Charlie test, including the battleships *Idaho* and *New Mexico*.[1]

At his last press conference before leaving Bikini, Blandy announced that the Charlie test would be held around April 1, 1947. Between fifteen and twenty target ships would be arranged over the bomb, which would be suspended several thousand feet below the ocean off the southwestern corner of Bikini Atoll, where the ocean floor forms a precipitous subterranean canyon that drops off more than one mile. By late August, engineers had anchored an enormous cable into the solid coral rock of Oruk Island, code-named Zebra, and huge chains stretched across the oceanside reef out into the deep water. The giant cable was to be anchored about one mile offshore, and smaller chains would be attached to it to provide moorings to hold the target ships in place.[2]

While the Navy continued to plan for the Charlie test, Leslie Groves, who had criticized Operation Crossroads all along, began a campaign to have the test canceled. "For your information no one has yet adequately explained to me Charlie's value to the United States," he sarcastically cabled Blandy on July 19. "I would welcome such explanation." In fact, all the top Los Alamos officials at Bikini—Norris Bradbury, Roger Warner, and Marshall Holloway—opposed the test. "Warner and Norris both want *no* part of Charlie," wrote Groves's deputy, Cy Betts, from Bikini on July 17. "The consensus of opinion is to the effect that Charlie is a sheer waste of time and effort. . . ." Betts said that it would take at least a year for a new team to work out the details of the test, but the Navy wanted the test sooner. "The toughest part of all will be to get a realistic Charlie date out of the Navy," he wrote. "I have no hopes at all that we could get them to cancel it altogether. Naturally that would be the easiest solution."[3]

On the same day he cabled Blandy, Groves also sent a lengthy message to Secretary of War Patterson urging the Joint Chiefs of Staff to cancel Charlie "before so much momentum is built up that the test cannot be stopped." After the Baker shot, Groves argued, Charlie would be of no scientific value. Baker would determine whether an atomic bomb could create the same amount of energy transfer from bomb to water as occurs in a bomb-to-air blast. Should it prove to be a poor mechanism of energy transfer, he argued, Test Charlie should be canceled, and if the energy transfer proved to be satisfactory, "this does not have to be reproved in another test." Like Baker, the Charlie test would determine how a ship would react to a strong shock over a large portion of its subsurface area. "Test Charlie, except for the engineering difficulties," said Groves, "could equally well be done with twenty thousand tons of TNT."

Groves also argued that the test was of no military value, because the target ships on the high seas could not be spaced as closely together as the ships for the Able and Baker shots. "The fact that one bomb will destroy one ship is now known," Groves told Patterson. Third, he was unwilling to commit Los Alamos to another test of a Nagasaki-type bomb when progress was being made on the lighter, smaller Mark IV bomb, "which appears to us to have a much higher national priority." Moreover, Congress was on the verge of passing the McMahon bill, which would transfer control of the test program from Groves's Manhattan District to a civilian-controlled Atomic Energy Commission. Groves had warned Blandy of the "complete loss of control" by the

War Department of personnel for the test, and he told Patterson that in the absence of legislation, it was "questionable" whether the Manhattan District could even provide the necessary radio instrumentation for the test.

Last, almost as an afterthought, he told Patterson that he was concerned about the use of another atomic bomb "when the stockpiling problem is particularly acute." Groves's concerns were well founded. Although an Army general told the *New York Times* in August that the United States possessed fifty atomic bombs and was manufacturing them at the rate of one a week, the fact was that the United States had only seven atomic bombs in its arsenal and was manufacturing four a year.[4]

Groves elaborated on some of these points three weeks later in an August 7 memorandum to the Joint Chiefs of Staff urging the cancellation of Test Charlie. The Charlie test would be less spectacular than the first two, he said, and "the important casualty producing radioactivity would be lost under water." Research and development work on new weapons at Los Alamos, he added, had been delayed considerably by Operation Crossroads, and he could not spare key personnel to carry out a third test at Bikini until 1949. This new weapons program, he said, "must be accelerated and nothing short of a national emergency should be permitted to interfere with it." His final point had the same ominous tone as his earlier cable to Patterson. "Even a single atomic bomb can be an extremely important factor in any military emergency," he wrote. "It is imperative that nothing interfere with our concentration of effort on the atomic weapons stockpile which constitutes such an important element in our present national defense."

Blandy was livid, and he wrote a scathing memorandum to Admiral Nimitz responding to Groves. For Blandy, the issue was not whether an atomic bomb could sink a ship. "Such an oversimplified question could have been answered in the affirmative a year ago without a test," he wrote. He also disagreed with Groves as to the probable effects of Charlie, asserting that it would inflict lethal damage over a greater area than Baker and would also produce a geyser of contaminated water that would rise hundreds of feet into the air. He took Groves's assertion that Los Alamos technicians could not be spared for more than two years and turned it on its head. He argued that it was unsound to have only a few civilian scientists and technicians capable of assembling the atomic bomb, and he suggested instead that Navy officers be trained by Los Alamos to take over the task of bomb assembly. Otherwise, he said, cancellation of the test "might relegate the assembly and delivery of the atomic bomb under combat conditions to the category of a lost art."

Blandy even attacked Groves personally. Now that President Truman had signed the McMahon bill Blandy argued that Groves's views should be given less weight. "Is it proper for him at this time to make a vital negative commitment probably binding the Commission and the nation throughout 1947 and 1948?" asked Blandy. Instead, he suggested that only the AEC itself could cancel the Charlie test. "The job we set out to do is unfinished technically and in the minds of the public," he told Nimitz. "If [Charlie] is canceled, it should be over the protest of the Navy. Otherwise the Navy will be essentially accused of dodging the 'most decisive Test.'" Other Navy leaders, though, disagreed with Blandy, including Nimitz and Adm. John H. Towers, commander-in-chief of the Pacific Fleet, who opposed Test Charlie because it would tax Pacific Fleet resources too much.[5]

Groves's memorandum persuaded Patterson to recommend to the Joint Chiefs of Staff that Test Charlie be canceled. "I am particularly impressed with [Groves's] final reason, the use of an atomic bomb for this purpose when our entire stockpile of this most potent weapon is so small," he wrote to the Joint Chiefs on August 21. "This factor of itself should dictate the utmost caution in the expenditure of funds for test purposes." Surprisingly enough, though, neither Truman, Byrnes, nor Forrestal had been formally briefed on the size of the nuclear stockpile. Only Groves and Eisenhower had routine access to such data, and Groves's severe restriction on the dissemination of this vital information was already posing a major obstacle to postwar planning and defense.

In preparation for a September 6 cabinet meeting, President Truman asked the chairman of his evaluation commission, Senator Carl Hatch, to poll the members on Test Charlie. With one exception, Hatch wrote on September 5, it was the view of the commission to postpone the test indefinitely, on the grounds that it would "seriously interfere with scientific and other personnel greatly needed for other more urgent projects." Nevertheless, he reported that all the members believed the test should be held in the future "and that it should not be too long delayed." Obviously unaware that Groves and Patterson were orchestrating the outright cancellation of Charlie, Hatch emphasized the commission's understanding that the postponement was not a cancellation of the test. "Had a cancellation been proposed, our recommendation might be different," he concluded. Truman met with General Eisenhower the next day, and it is likely that Eisenhower briefed him on the small number of nuclear weapons in America's arsenal.[6]

Separately, the Joint Chiefs' planning staff recommended that Test Charlie be canceled, both because of "the economy and personnel considerations involved" and the delaying effect it would have on atomic research and development. The Joint Chiefs concurred with this recommendation, and on September 6 the Cabinet, with no objections, voted to postpone Test Charlie. The information obtained from tests Able and Baker "will enable our scientific and military experts to make a proper evaluation of the effects of this weapon," Truman said in a statement released to the press on September 7. "The additional information of value expected to result from Test [Charlie] is such that the Joint Chiefs of Staff do not feel that completion of this test in the near future is justified."[7]

The press speculated on other reasons for the postponement. Some said the Navy was reluctant to tie up so many ships in the Pacific with tensions running high in Europe and the Middle East, while others saw the postponement as a cost-savings measure. "With both the Army and Navy scrambling to make a combined $1.6 billion budget cut," said *Time,* "Charlie looked like a $35-million baby who would not be missed." What the Navy did not say was that the fallout from the Baker test had left such high levels of radioactivity in the lagoon, in debris washed up on the beach, and in the atoll's water and fish that it would have been impossible to stage the Charlie test from Bikini.[8]

In Washington, Deak Parsons asked all sections of Joint Task Force One to send all documents relating to Test Charlie to central files to preserve the planning effort, but Blandy sensed that the test would never be held. "The President gave the whole story from Washington," he told reporters. "We'll cancel all preparations immediately."[9] Blandy, who was rumored to be Admiral Nimitz's likely successor as chief of naval operations, was said to be "boiling mad" at Truman's order, largely because he felt that the reporting on Able and Baker had left the public without a clear picture of the bomb's true destructive power. "We'll regret it if we don't stage the third test," said Blandy. "The deep-underwater explosion will give the bomb its full potential power." The deep-water shot would have been "even more horrible" than the other two, editorialized the *Washington Post.* "That is why men like Blandy, who have been doing everything possible to educate the public to the truth about atomic energy, are now pretty well disgusted."[10]

Unlike the previous March, when the White House was swamped with thousands of letters protesting the tests and many atomic scientists hailed the six-week postponement of Operation Crossroads, the postponement of Test Charlie brought little reaction. The public's attitude toward the Soviet Union had shifted dramatically in these six months, and only a dwindling band of liberals was still convinced that cooperation with the Kremlin offered the best hope for world peace.

In the meantime, the Navy was still grappling with problems on the target ships, all of which had left Bikini by September 5. Only twelve target vessels were reboarded and sailed back to the United States in August and September. The remaining ones, which were too contaminated to be boarded except for short visits, were towed to Kwajalein,

240 miles away. Virtually all the ships had some ammunition on board. Some was experimental ammunition, which could become unstable from the heat and pose a serious hazard. If removal were deferred, the radioactivity on the ships would be lower but the risk of an explosion would be greater.

The Navy decided to remove the ammunition at Kwajalein as soon as possible. As many as 1,500 officers and enlisted men worked for 45 days to remove more than 1,000 tons of ammunition from thirty-five target ships. The work was exhausting and, of course, potentially hazardous. Because of the high levels of radioactivity, men working below decks were required to work fully clothed and to wear special rescue breathing apparatus, which severely restricted their vision. Moreover, the heat and humidity at Kwajalein were such that the men could work below decks for only about 30 minutes before taking breaks.[11]

By mid-September there was an acute shortage of radsafe monitors and equipment at Kwajalein. Only ten X-263 Geiger counters were operable, no spare parts or replacements were on hand, and the ten instruments would be inoperable within three weeks.[12] With serious morale problems developing because of fatigue, the hazards of the ammunition, and unanswered fears about radiation, the Navy abruptly called a halt to the operation, with only about 40 percent of the ammunition removed.[13] Two of the ships at Kwajalein (the battleships *New York* and *Nevada*) were subsequently towed to Pearl Harbor and six (the aircraft carrier *Independence,* the cruisers *Pensacola* and *Salt Lake City,* the destroyer *Hughes,* and the attack transports *Crittenden* and *Gasconade*) to naval shipyards at San Francisco and Puget Sound for further decontamination work and examination. Another fourteen target ships were eventually sent to West Coast shipyards.[14]

The indefinite postponement of Test Charlie meant the end of Operation Crossroads, and Joint Army-Navy Task Force One was officially dissolved on November 1, 1946.[15] Even its dissolution, though, provoked public controversy. On November 7, several admirals and their wives held a reception for Admiral and Mrs. Blandy to commemorate the tests. The centerpiece, sent by several bakers from East St. Louis, Illinois, was a huge cake made of tiny angelfood puffs in the form of an atomic explosion, complete with a mushroom cloud. A photograph in the *Washington Post*'s society page showed the Blandys, looking like happy newlyweds, gaily cutting the cake, with Mrs. Blandy's hand gripping the admiral's as he holds the knife, and a delighted Adm. Frank J. Lowry looking on with a grin.[16]

The photograph infuriated the Reverend A. Powell Davies, Unitarian pastor of a fashionable Washington church. Waving the newspaper page aloft from his pulpit the following Sunday, he denounced the "utterly loathsome" photograph. "I hope to God the picture isn't reprinted in Russia—to confirm everything the Soviet government has been telling the Russian people," thundered Davies to an audience that included a U.S. Supreme Court justice. "How would it seem in Hiroshima or Nagasaki to know that Americans make cakes of angel-food puffs in the image of that terrible diabolical thing?"

"Try to imagine yourself for a moment a continental European, wondering, brooding, asking yourself a hundred times a day, will America lead us?" Davies asked. "Then imagine yourself being shown this picture. If I had the authority of a priest of the Middle Ages I would call down the wrath of God upon such an obscenity. I would damn to hell these people of callous conscience, these traitors to humanity."

Blandy dismissed the pastor's remarks as "too ridiculous to deserve comment," and the bakery supply salesman who helped design the cake termed the sermon "silly," adding, "We intended the cake as something to eat." The photograph, though, which was run by hundreds of newspapers and magazines around the country, made Blandy look like a fool. Reverend Davies's outburst was "a sign of the time, which I feel cannot be ignored," wrote the columnist Walter Lippmann to James Forrestal. "Public Relations officers of both the War and Navy Departments have been out of hand for some time, and I have detected for some months a growing undercurrent of feeling that will affect the whole military establishment if something isn't done about it." Forrestal responded that both he and Secretary of War Patterson were "in complete agreement" with Lippmann's views, and he ridiculed the incident as "adolescent competitive publicity."[17]

Operation Crossroads seized the public's attention for much of 1946. In fact, according to one poll the tests were the most important news event of the year.[18] Operation Crossroads was the source of countless editorials and news articles on the future of atomic energy, arms control, and the emerging Cold War with the Soviet Union, but the tests also permeated the popular culture as well. New phrases emerged, such as "fallout" and "countdown," and "Operation" became so overused that a New York Times editorial in early August expressed the hope that "we may soon see an originally vivid but now sadly overworked epithet pass out of the slang of the day." So many events, said the Times, "are now Operation something or another. People go down to the corner drugstore for Operation Chocolate Sundae, and at one o'clock sharp they ask the man at the next desk if he is ready for Operation Lunch." The Times hoped that the "epidemic" would soon burn itself out.[19]

Three weeks before the Able shot, the popular comic strip character Penny, having been slapped with a speeding ticket, cries out in despair,

"Gee, weepers, a ticket! Father will disintegrate me! I feel like Bikini Atoll the day before the big bang!"[20] In a "Grin and Bear It" cartoon, a woman at a fancy dinner party turns to a fat naval officer and asks, "Are you taking part in the atomic bomb trials, Admiral? Or is it only the ships they're using that are obsolete?" A Hollywood studio announced plans to use footage from the tests in a forthcoming movie, *Rendezvous 21,* described as an "atomic-bomb drama." Dozens of race-horses, sporting names like Atom Buster, Sir Atom, and Cosmic Bomb, were named in honor of the tests. A baby boy born in Louisville, Kentucky, was named Atomic Victory Trotter, and the Manhattan telephone book listed nineteen companies with the name "Atomic." "In New York one may buy atomic ties, in restaurants they serve atomic cocktails, and on variety stages there are atomic blondes," commented *Pravda* after the Able test, contrasting the social aspects of the bomb with its political force. "Against such a background . . . the results of the test were more modest than . . . expected."

The man in the street began to blame the bomb for everyday misfortunes. In Paris the day after the Able test a large, narrow mirror fastened to a wall suddenly fell to the ground for no apparent reason. As a crowd gathered about the broken glass, which boded seven years of bad luck, a disheveled woman muttered, "The atomic bomb," and the crowd, nodding gravely, agreed.[21] Meanwhile, with each new arrival of sailors from Bikini, Honolulu tattoo parlors were thronged with sailors seeking full-color reproductions—usually on their chests—of the atomic bomb cloud. "The aerial test is out in front so far," reported the Associated Press in mid-August, "but the underwater blast is catching up."[22]

Bikini Atoll also lent its name that summer to an alluring new bathing suit. While Bikini was dominating the news, a French couturier, Jacques Heim, was designing a new two-piece swimsuit. World War II had already seen pin-up girls photographed in two-piece outfits that, although hardly skimpy, were certainly daring for the times. Heim introduced a radically abbreviated two-piece suit at his store in Cannes on the French Riviera, called it the "atome," and hired a skywriter to bring his message to the Riviera bathers: "L'atome—the world's smallest bathing suit."[23]

On July 5, 1946, four days after the Able test, a new design was introduced by a competitor, 49-year-old Louis Reard, who made his navel-baring bathing suit even smaller, gave it a new name, and used the same advertising medium. Skywriters on the Riviera now touted the "Bikini," "smaller than the smallest bathing suit in the world." Reard at first had no way to launch his creation, though, because the professional models of Paris refused to wear his 129 square inches of bathing suit. As a result, he was forced to hire a striptease dancer, who gamely posed in the new bikini for the fashion press at the opening of a Paris swimming pool. Dozens of reporters showed up, including nine just from the *International Herald Tribune,* which reported on the "chain reaction" the bathing suit caused among the "stunned and incoherent" spectators. "Disrobement Race Seen," ran the story by the *Tribune*'s political correspondent, while the diplomatic correspondent, mimicking postwar Germany, wrote of the bikini's two zones, with the northern zone divided into two enclaves.[24]

America had dropped the bomb, but it was a Frenchman who dropped the bombshell. Even the French were scandalized. "That first suit was so daring that, to sell the idea, Reard had to add a bit more material all over," recalled Jacques Castle, who bought Reard's company in 1979. The bikini was immediately banned in the Roman Catholic countries of Italy, Spain, and Portugal, denounced in Australia and Belgium, and forbidden in Hollywood movies, but the name stuck, as "l'atome" faded away. For several years afterwards, in fact, the bikini was spelled with a capital "B" and identified with the atoll. It finally caught on in the 1950s in France, due in large part to Brigitte Bardot, who was frequently pictured in one on the Riviera. She first wore one at the 1953 Cannes Film Festival, a year before she appeared in a film, and she became a star before she ever made a movie.[25]

Reard never explained why he selected the name, leaving pundits to ponder whether he had in mind Bikini's small size, the exotic allure of the tropical Pacific, or the fact that the bathing suit was so tiny and yet caused such a big shock. *Sports Illustrated* has suggested the comparison to "the massive power of an atomic weapon, which, like a woman in a bikini, can devastate everything in its path," and *Webster's* agrees, stating that the name was derived "from the comparison of the effects wrought by a scantily clad woman to the effects of an atomic bomb."[26]

Several social historians have suggested that the Bikini tests and the bikini bathing suit were not a coincidence, but rather part of a psychological link between atomic destruction and sexuality that began with Hiroshima. Within days of Japan's surrender, "Atom Bomb Dancers" were featured at burlesque houses in Los Angeles. In the 1946 song "Atom and Evil," atomic energy was portrayed as an innocent, well-intentioned man led astray by a jaded "Miss Evil," and the bomb was equated with sexual arousal in a popular country music song in 1947, "Atom Bomb Baby." *Newsweek* compared the shape of the Baker Day explosion to a woman's hairdo, and *National Geographic,* reaching for a metaphor, wrote that the base surge from the Baker shot drenched the target ships with "a wet caress, a kiss of death."[27]

There was a decidedly feminine side to the bomb at Bikini. The Able bomb was named Gilda, and Baker's was Helen. Greece's Helen had launched a thousand ships, while Bikini's destroyed a dozen or so. And *Gilda* was Rita Hayworth's latest movie, a "film noir" in which Hayworth pretends to be a tramp to provoke her husband, played by Glenn Ford. "Didn't you hear about me?" she asks him at one point. "If I had been a ranch, they'd have named me the Bar-Nothing." Stripping in her husband's nightclub, Hayworth sings a song blaming women for San Francisco's earthquake and Chicago's fire. "Put the blame on Mame, boys, Put the blame on Mame," she sings in each refrain.

To some, the Gilda bomb symbolized America's postwar domestic dilemmas—a soaring divorce rate and millions of Rosie the Riveters wanting to maintain the hard-earned independence they had won during the war. The symbolism of the Gilda bomb, declared one movie critic, "is enough to frighten off any but the most intrepid Freudians," as the "phallic agent of destruction underwent a sex change."[28] In fact, though, the gender of the atomic bomb progressed from neuter to masculine to feminine and then back to neuter. The Trinity bomb was the "gadget," the two bombs dropped on Japan were Fat Man and Little Boy, and Bikini's were women. Since then, atomic and hydrogen bombs have been referred to simply as "the Bomb." Moreover, although the timing of Operation Crossroads in the summer of 1946 gave the bikini its name, fashion magazines had featured two-piece bathing suits as early as the 1930s. A 1940 issue of *Vogue* featuring Ronald Reagan and his wife, Jane Wyman, showed the actress wearing a two-piece suit, and *Life* in September 1945 featured a full-page photograph of a hitherto obscure MGM starlet, Linda Christian, now dubbed the "Anatomic Bomb."[29]

Was the two-piece bathing suit related to Bikini's erotic or exotic allure? Were the names of the Able and Baker bombs subconsciously related to men's love and fear of women or was the choice of these names simply the result of placing 42,000 men on an atoll for two months with no women? Perhaps Hugh Hefner, *Playboy*'s creator, deserves the last word. "Affairs of state will not be our province," he declared in the magazine's first editorial in 1953. "If we are able to give the American male a few extra laughs and a little diversion from the anxieties of the Atomic Age, we'll feel we've justified our existence."[30] Hugh Hefner, not Spike Blandy, was the real atomic playboy.

"General Groves Is Very Much Afraid of Claims Being Instituted by Men Who Participated in the Bikini Tests"

Despite the devastating impact of the Baker test, the Navy sought to minimize the results of Operation Crossroads. Deak Parsons told a New York audience in October 1946 that the tests had helped dispel "atomic neurosis" about the bomb. "Operation Crossroads has gone a long way toward substituting a healthy fear of the known for an unhealthy fear of the unknown," he asserted, adding that no one had died at Bikini as a result of the tests. Parsons told the audience that the bomb could be controlled so that it would not hurt people. "It is rather a question of controlling human beings," he declared.[1]

As press reports on the contaminated ships began to appear, though, a few cautionary notes were sounded. As one historian has noted, "It was Bikini, rather than Hiroshima and Nagasaki, that first brought the issue of radioactivity compellingly to the nation's consciousness."[2] The effects of the Baker test were so great that Admiral Blandy, more impressed by the lingering radioactivity than by the sunken ships, declared 10 days after the shot, "This is a form of poison warfare." One month later, back in Washington, Blandy reported that all but nine of the ninety-five target ships in Operation Crossroads were either sunk, damaged, or highly contaminated by radioactivity. "These reports," noted the *New York Times,* "serve to contradict further the early 'snap judgments' of some observers that the bombs were not successful because they did not sink the entire fleet."[3]

Stafford Warren, who left Joint Task Force One to become dean of the UCLA medical school in the fall of 1946, tried to explain to the public that the real menace of the Baker shot was its lingering radiation, which he described as "so insidious, so long drawn-out" as to be much more hazardous than the effects of the blast itself. "Two atomic bombs—dropped [in the water] on either side of the Statue of Liberty— and a nice upriver wind could turn the whole of Manhattan into a ghost town for 50 to 100 years," he said in one talk, and he later wrote that the health problems that would be created by the detonation of an atomic bomb in a large harbor were "beyond calculation or even imagining."[4] Blandy made the same point, calling atomic warfare "a scourge," whose effects would be felt not only by the immediate victims, but also by some of the survivors and their descendants.[5]

Operation Crossroads seemed to change Stafford Warren. He said that he "was totally unprepared" for the "great emotional impact" of the tests, and he wrote a chilling report in *Life* (later reprinted in *Reader's Digest*) on the Baker test in a special feature on the first anniversary of Operation Crossroads. "Radiation from fission products penetrated every crevice of the target ships," he wrote, and before the crews left Bikini, the radiological safety teams were monitoring "almost every bite of food, every drink of water, every piece of laundry, the handrails of ships, the beaches where the men went swimming." Warren, recalled his daughter, frequently said that he was "horrified" by the Navy's failure to appreciate the radiological hazards following the Baker test. "They just didn't believe there was any danger," he told her.[6]

"That second one at Bikini really ties this business up in a knot," he said in an interview six months after Operation Crossroads. "Literally astronomical quantities of radioactive material had become intimately mixed with the sea water, mist and spray which accompanied the formation of the giant mushroom of water which rose from the lagoon." If this cloud moved over a city, he warned, everyone would have to evacuate immediately or face death from gamma radiation. "You couldn't clean the area. The fissionable material would get into the water—into everything. It would get into next year's crop." He fully understood the sinister horror of Baker. "I'm not so worried about the killing of 50 to 75 million people as I am about the wiping out of resources."[7]

Nevertheless, despite his hair-raising descriptions of the effects of radiation from the Baker test on the target and nontarget ships, his dire warnings of overexposures and the shortage of monitors, and his plea to end Operation Crossroads early, Stafford Warren reassured the public one year after the tests that "not one of the 42,000 men who went to Bikini has been detectably injured by radiation." He never publicly entertained the thought that any of the men at Operation Crossroads—

men he was charged with protecting—had been adversely affected by radiation. Blandy echoed Warren and boasted of Operation Crossroads's perfect radiological safety record, assuring the Navy in a classified report that "no man was so exposed as to give rise to apprehension that he might become a casualty at a later date." Government civil defense manuals made this same point. Of the 42,000 participants in Operation Crossroads, noted the author of *How to Survive an Atomic Bomb,* "not a single one . . . was hurt by atomic rays."[8]

In May 1947, 10 months after the tests, Navy Secretary Forrestal ordered blood tests on all personnel still in service who were attached to Operation Crossroads or the Navy's radiological safety program. Wire services immediately picked up the story, but the Navy's press office quickly issued a statement describing the tests as "a routine followup of naval personnel for information only."[9] "I guess I made out okay," Admiral Blandy told reporter Bob Considine with a chuckle, and he questioned the value of the blood tests. "I understand that some of the men were proved to be anemic, but in view of the fact that no physical exam was taken just before the test . . . we can't be certain that the anemia came from the bomb." Blandy took the same view toward survivors of the atomic bombings in Japan. "As for the birth of a number of deformed children of residents of Hiroshima and Nagasaki, we can't be certain that it was the fault of the bomb," he told Considine. "There was considerable malnutrition in both cities when they were hit, which could have as much to do with the matter as the bomb."[10]

Did radiological hazards at the Baker test cause servicemen to contract radiation-related diseases? The evidence is not conclusive, although the issue has been raised in dozens of court suits and administrative claims brought by veterans who were at Bikini. Scores of expert witnesses have testified on both sides of the question, and the truth may never be known, largely due to so many unanswered questions. Few records were kept and some of those were lost. Only about 6,300 participants were issued radiation-dose film badges during one or more days of Operation Crossroads, and only a few radsafe monitors wore film badges every day. The results of the blood tests taken in May 1947 of all active Navy personnel involved in the tests have never been found.

It is impossible to recreate with any accuracy radiation levels on every part of the target ships over specific periods of time or how much time individuals spent at these specific locations, much less the actual energy spectrum for the radiation released by the two shots. It is equally impossible to determine who may have ingested or inhaled radioactive materials or received high doses from open cuts or wounds. Similarly, one sailor sleeping near an evaporator in close proximity to saltwater lines may have received much higher doses than someone sleeping three feet away. One man may have worn protective boots and gloves during a decontamination shift, while another just a t-shirt. Stafford Warren recognized the enormity of this problem shortly after the Baker test, telling Admiral Blandy that "the erratic location of high and low intensities on the target ships does not permit an accurate estimate of any one individual's exposure." A man "may hesitate longer near a high intensity location than was expected, thus accumulating more than a tolerance dose." One week later he cautioned that "no one can say any place is safe for any given length of time."[11]

Virtually all the available evidence points to the conclusion that radiation dangers following the Baker test were serious and that not enough steps were taken in time to prevent serious and widespread overexposures. First, the amount of contamination was overwhelming; as the Navy noted shortly after Operation Crossroads, "the nature and extent of the contamination of the targets was completely unexpected."[12] Second, there were not enough radsafe monitors to protect the men, and the vast majority of the monitors received inadequate training. Third, the tolerance level of 0.1 roentgen per day, deemed appropriate in 1946, has now been lowered for the general population by a factor of 365, so that today the current recommended maximum dose for *one year* is approximately the same dose that was recommended as the maximum exposure for *one day* at Operation Crossroads.[13] Fourth, the men at Bikini, starting at the top with the target ship commanders and their "hairy-chested" attitudes, simply did not appreciate the nature of the radiation hazard at Bikini.

Last, although crews were issued specific instructions and warnings about boarding target ships, the evidence suggests that these guidelines were largely ignored and, in some cases, not even distributed to the officers in charge. For example, despite new and more restrictive radsafe regulations issued for workers at Kwajalein in January 1947, a senior radiation safety monitor, Charles Coffin, was shocked at the violations he observed there. Crews regularly boarded target ships without radiation monitors, looted contaminated equipment from the ships, and ate and smoked aboard the ships. Monthly blood tests were not performed. Crews were not processed through the "change" ships, where men were issued protective clothing before entering contaminated areas and to which they later were supposed to return to shower and remove contaminated clothing. Contaminated clothing was not laundered, men wore clothing with readings in excess of 0.1 roentgen per day, and those showing positive contamination from urinalysis tests were not taken off work on target ships. Coffin and the officer in charge of the change ship found numerous high readings on the clothing, and it appeared that the officer was not even aware of the new regulations.

Coffin also had a great deal of trouble with his radiation-measuring instruments. "It was difficult to find any that were operable," he wrote to the Kwajalein Atoll commander. "No one seemed alarmed at this and I went out numerous times with instruments that were unreliable and inoperable altogether." Radiological safety guidelines were still evolving seven months after Operation Crossroads. "Inasmuch as there were very few standard precautions to refer to, the monitors were left more or less to their own discretion as to what was safe and what wasn't," reported Coffin. "Each invariably differed and as a result the working parties were confused as to the truth of the situation." No one, though, seemed to care, and by April the entire radsafe monitoring unit at Kwajalein consisted of one man.[14]

Dr. George Lyon, safety advisor to Admiral Blandy, was incensed at Coffin's report. In a May 5, 1947, memorandum to Deak Parsons, he described Coffin as "immature and inexperienced" and complained about the "lack of appreciation on the part of the younger officers as to the seriousness of their work." Accusing Coffin of "making a mountain out of a mole hill," Lyon warned that "having a little knowledge in this field is dangerous and can present more serious problems than the person with no knowledge." He admitted, though, that the incident showed that radsafe officers had to be trained to detect weaknesses in the technical and administrative aspects of the safety program. "Radiological safety officers must be instructed as to how to legally, but tactfully, get around such situations," wrote Lyon.[15]

The candor Stafford Warren displayed in his memoranda to Blandy after the Baker test was totally lacking in the period before Crossroads. While the documentary records do not suggest a conspiracy or intent to cover up the test results, they do show a deliberate attempt by the scientific and medical experts to cover their hindquarters by refusing even to consider the possibility that a serviceman's presence at Bikini might later result in a radiation-related disease. In fact, one of the main purposes of Stafford Warren's Medico-Legal Board was to provide a paper trail designed to lay the groundwork for future denial of legal claims that might be brought against the U.S. government arising from Operation Crossroads. Robert R. Newell, chairman of the Medico-Legal Board, readily admitted just weeks after the tests that the board "initially . . . served to reassure Col. Warren that the safety measures adopted by RadSafe were such as to attract no justifiable criticism, and to give what assurance was possible that no successful suits could be brought on account of the radiological hazards of Operation Crossroads."[16]

On the day before the Able test, all nine members of the Medico-Legal Board signed a five-page statement concluding that Warren's safety regulations were acceptable, even conservative. "We believe that in these operations radiation injury to personnel can be avoided," the board stated, adding that the anticipated radiation levels of the Able and Baker tests would be so low that they would not cause injuries. After the tests, the Medico-Legal Board expressed annoyance at the fears of overexposure. "What is needed is not emotional dismay at the discovery of radiation," admonished one of its draft reports, "but rather its careful measurement and the control of personnel adequate to prevent exposures above the permissible limit."[17]

Robert Newell expressed his disgust with all the talk of radiation. "It is not true that the boys returning from Bikini will glow in the dark— Walter Winchell to the contrary, notwithstanding," he wrote in a memorandum shortly after Operation Crossroads. The men at the tests, he declared, were limited to radiation exposure of 0.1 roentgen per day, and "through the whole operation, no person totalled more than this"—a blatantly false assertion that his own board conceded when it recommended that numerous men be taken off duty due to overexposure. Not a single man at Operation Crossroads, asserted Newell, received as much radiation as a radiologist is often exposed to on a daily basis. Indeed, he added, four of the doctors and scientists at Bikini (including Newell himself) took their sons along, and one had volunteered for the next atom bomb tests. The ships had picked up "some radioactivity and brought it home with them," he admitted, but "one doubts if there is any danger left."[18]

More cautionary notes, though, were sounded in a private conference of Operation Crossroads scientists and physicians at the San Francisco Naval Shipyard on October 1, 1946, which was called to discuss the results of two new acid treatment methods that had been developed at the shipyard to decontaminate saltwater piping on the target and support ships at Bikini. One of the conference participants, Dr. Kenneth G. Scott, was torn as to where to set the maximum permissible exposure levels for men working to decontaminate the ships and whether to decontaminate certain ships at all. "I think everyone realizes," he said, "that any radiation behind a pipe which gives you 1/10 [roentgen] a day over a long length may eventually turn into a lethal dose of radiation." The question, he asked, was "where can we set the limit?" Another option the group considered was simply to tear out the radioactive piping and dump it in the ocean. "It is difficult to get rid of radioactive matter," said one doctor. "It may be a lot cheaper to dispose of a valve than to try to get rid of the radiation hazard on the valve."[19]

Scott was no doubt aware of the paucity of data concerning tolerance to radiation doses over time. Most studies examined only the very low and lethal ranges (200–400 roentgen), so figures in between were merely extrapolations that had been made for Japan and the invasion of Normandy, when the United States feared Germany would unleash atomic weapons or some other form of radioactive material. As Stafford Warren told Deak Parsons shortly after the San Francisco meeting, scientists were learning that the time period over which the dosage was distributed was also important, because exposure of 0.1 roentgen per day over two years, or about 70 roentgen, caused serious diseases in dogs. The conflicting data led Warren to tell Parsons that "it is difficult, if not impossible, to say what is the lowest dose, on the average, which would cause mild or serious acute symptoms in humans." A figure of 60 roentgen for top exposure, he said, "is based on a pure guess and should be forgotten," and he recommended against any attempt to set a tolerance limit for military operations. "Once they are stated in writing or put in a manual, they are almost impossible to change," he wrote to Parsons. "They would hardly be worth the paper they were printed on and would be misleading in the light of subsequent findings."[20]

At a two-hour meeting three days later in Washington, Admiral Solberg briefed Admiral Blandy, Kenneth Nichols, and other top Operation Crossroads officials on the decontamination issues, "having in mind both medical and legal protection." Blandy and Solberg were also concerned about adverse publicity and possible legal problems resulting from Operation Crossroads. Blandy raised the question of classification of material relating to decontamination efforts, and according to the minutes of the meeting, all the participants agreed that such information should be restricted "and that the public relations angle should be considered carefully to remove confusion and the impression that the Navy is 'covering up.'"[21]

Meanwhile, on November 21, one of the top radiological monitors at Bikini informed George Lyon that plutonium contamination on the support ship *Rockbridge* was higher than would have been anticipated from extrapolating from the standard alpha-beta-gamma ratio used at Bikini. The monitor, Herbert Scoville, Jr., told Lyon that using the X-263 Geiger counter to measure plutonium contamination "is becoming increasingly difficult and open to question." In fact, he said that the conversion ratio could be off by a factor of 5 or even 10. Total plutonium readings on the ship were about 2,000 micrograms. "It would be difficult to visualize any mechanism by which an individual might obtain a lethal dose of plutonium from the *Rockbridge* since this material is spread over a considerable area," noted Scoville. "However," he went on, "there might nevertheless be considerable difficulty in demonstrating this fact from a legal point of view since the 2,000 micrograms represents a large number of lethal doses."[22]

Just six days later, on November 27, top Operation Crossroads officials met at the Navy Department in Washington to discuss security questions concerning the disposal of marine growth and sand-blasting sand from contaminated ships. Admiral Solberg told the group that Stafford Warren was concerned that dumping the sand in harbors might contaminate water supplies, but Dr. Joseph G. Hamilton of Berkeley saw no health or security risks. "The quantities of sand involved were so immense and the amounts of plutonium so small from any ship that the dilution of the radioactive material was sufficient to render it impossible for anyone to obtain any information from the sand," he said, according to the minutes of the meeting, so the group agreed that no special arrangements would be made for the disposal of sand from nontarget vessels. Dr. Hamilton recommended, though, that "if the sand should leave Navy property, the persons receiving it not be advised of the source because of their likely failure to understand that no hazard from radioactive materials existed."

Similarly, Hamilton recommended that the acid solutions used to decontaminate the ships be dumped right into the harbors where the ships were docked. "In most cases," he declared, "the material will settle into the mud where it will do no harm and the dilution factor in a large harbor such as at Puget Sound or San Francisco is so great that no concern need be experienced." He saw little danger in the plutonium on the ships and was "willing to state positively that there is absolutely no possibility of physical injury from radioactive materials in the amounts which are being worked with on the non-targets under present conditions." The other conferees agreed, concluding that "considerable effort and expense could be saved by dumping the acid solutions into harbors rather than at sea."[23]

Interestingly, though, each of Dr. Hamilton's recommendations was tempered with the equally strong admonition that none of the actions be made public, suggesting that he either viewed the public as stupid and the press as sensationalist or that he was not sure his recommendations really made sense. For example, he "advised that consideration be given to the public relations angle in not permitting the information to leak out regarding the local disposal of acid and sand containing some fission products, in spite of the fact that the quantities involved entail absolutely no health or security hazard." Given the fact that Hamilton's recommendations were completely at odds with what was known then about the lethal effects of even minute quantities of plutonium, his obsession about adverse public reaction suggests that he may well have been concerned about the wisdom of his own recommendations. Others at the meeting certainly did not share his confidence. Kenneth Nichols asked whether there was "any possibility of successful suits against the government by agencies receiving the non-target ships for scrap," and another participant added that "General Groves is very much afraid of claims being instituted by men who participated in the Bikini tests."

Dr. Hamilton responded that no such possibility existed because of the minute quantities of fission products in the scrap. There would probably be many suits by "cranks," he said, but "none of these would be valid, so it would be foolish to try to work towards avoiding them." Accordingly, contaminated sand and acid from as many as fourteen ships from Operation Crossroads, including at least five target vessels, were secretly dumped into San Francisco Bay over the next six months, with the Navy directing that "all procedures should be treated as routine in order to minimize any adverse publicity."[24] Records showing the quantities of materials dumped were lost, but the Navy assured the public in 1982 that the ships were decontaminated with "safe, technically advanced methods."[25]

Stafford Warren, by contrast, was much more concerned about radiation levels and possible lawsuits. "Most of the target ships have already undergone extensive decontamination," he wrote to Deak Parsons in January 1947, "and further efforts at decontamination with current information have not shown promise and are expensive and time-consuming." Warren told Parsons that it was hopeless to attempt any further large-scale decontamination work except on an experimental basis. Given the state of medical information, he foresaw possible lawsuits if decontamination efforts continued:

> The residual of even what are considered "safe" amounts of long life fission products will be the cause of uncertainty in the development of illness in so-called "susceptible individuals." Therefore, difficult and expensive medico legal problems will probably occur if previously contaminated target ships are "cleared" for constant occupancy or disposal as scrap.

He said that the target ships were so heavily contaminated that they would be a potential hazard and unfit for use for many years, so he recommended that they be sunk in deep water in the open ocean, except for ships to be used for radiological experiments or training,[26] and he cautioned against decontamination efforts at Pearl Harbor. "At Pearl, if much decontamination is attempted, contamination of harbor will result," he warned.[27]

Although the instantaneous bursts from Able and Baker sank only seventeen ships, radiological contamination eventually sank almost the entire target fleet. At first, though, Stafford Warren's recommendation to Parsons was ignored, as decontamination efforts continued on target ships that were towed to Kwajalein, Pearl Harbor, and the West Coast. However, most of the ships still had high levels of radioactivity one year after the tests. "They're still hot enough to make it inadvisable to have men on them more than 24 hours at a stretch," Blandy said in July 1947. Within the next year, the Navy ordered target ships not fully decontaminated to be sunk in deep water. Fifty were eventually sunk by bombardment and aerial attack, including thirty-six at Kwajalein. The *Prinz Eugen* sank in shallow water off Kwajalein in late 1946, while the *Nevada* and *New York* were sunk off Pearl Harbor in 1948 after undergoing extensive radiological study.[28]

As it turned out, radiation levels did not fall to the tolerance dose of 0.1 roentgen per day on some of the target ships for weeks, months, and, in one case, more than five years.[29] In the end, three-quarters of the ninety-five target vessels never left the Marshall Islands, and only twenty-two returned to the United States. All but six vessels were sunk by the atomic bombs or deliberately scuttled or sunk because of lingering radioactivity. (The appendix shows the disposition of all ninety-five target vessels used at Operation Crossroads.)

The Navy's Bureau of Medicine and Bureau of Ships issued a joint letter in late November 1946 seeking to put an end to speculation on the radiological condition of the ships at Bikini by setting new decontamination methods and standards to clear the ships. "All of the ships involved (target vessels not included) have low radiation intensities and small amounts of contaminating materials," said the Navy. "They present no danger from external radiation." As far as alpha emitters were concerned, the letter stated that "it is NOT LIKELY that personnel engaged in routine operations of maintenance of these vessels will suffer injury." The letter, though, raised as many questions as it answered because it referred only to the support ships, and many men spent considerable time on the target ships. Moreover, ongoing monitoring continued to show plutonium hazards on these ships.[30]

As the decades passed and participants in Operation Crossroads began to die, many veterans and their families became convinced that exposure to radiation at Bikini, whether deliberate or inadvertent, had caused or contributed to their sickness. "The common idea that huge numbers of people are dropping like flies is just wrong," declared Vice Adm. Robert R. Monroe, director of the Defense Nuclear Agency, in 1979. "The public has the perception that people were sloppy. The facts show the opposite. . . . A second idea is that there were massive overexposures. That's wrong. Wrong as hell. The average exposure was less than half a rem," a measure of radiation dose that is the approximate equivalent of 0.5 roentgen.[31]

Families, though, do not think in terms of averages. Joseph Quigley, a 25-year-old electrical engineer, boarded the *Saratoga* 24 hours after the Able shot to monitor electrical equipment. After the Baker shot, he wrote his family that his crew was "playing hide-and-seek with the radioactive water . . . anchoring and then reanchoring, moving ahead of the dangerously hot water." He died of cancer at the age of 45.

Richard Roehl spent nearly nine hours in the lagoon after the Baker shot, repairing the stern of a damaged ship. "My diving equipment was a face mask, swimsuit, and sneakers," he wrote. We even swam up close to the blast area to do some 'sight-seeing.'" In 1981 he was found to have a degenerative spine. Albert Tjeerdema, another Navy diver, examined sunken target ships and recovered specimens for testing after Operation Crossroads. He died in 1969 from a rare type of adenocarcinoma.

Jerome Martek worked in the engine room of one of the target ships to replace zinc plates in condensers, which converted radioactive seawater from the lagoon into drinking water. "A scientist walked by with a Geiger counter and asked me how I got so 'hot,'" he later wrote. "He told me to get out of my clothing and shower immediately." Martek became sterile shortly after Operation Crossroads, then suffered a brain abscess and internal bleeding and had part of his lung removed. With virtually his entire immune system destroyed, he died in 1983.

Frank Karasti's ship, the *Clamp,* returned to Bikini lagoon just hours after the Able shot to help put out fires on the deck of the *Nevada.* Karasti developed a lesion on his lung a month after the Baker shot and continued to suffer health problems in his bones and nervous system until his death in 1984.[32]

Ernest G. Erspamer and Thomas F. Kiley were members of a hydrographic survey team aboard the *Bowditch.* They traveled daily in small boats and rubber rafts throughout Bikini's lagoon, frequently passing over the Zeropoint of the Baker shot and almost always wading through the surf to carry their equipment ashore. Erspamer died at age 57 of chronic myelogenous leukemia, and Kiley had a malignant tumor removed from his thyroid in 1981.[33]

John Smitherman, the young Navy man who wore only tennis shoes, shorts, and a t-shirt on the contaminated ships, helped put out fires on the *Independence* after the Able test. A month after the Baker shot, he discovered five or six red burns on his feet and legs. The swelling was so bad that he could not wear shoes and the next year he received a medical discharge from the Navy. The swelling never did go away, and in 1977 he had both legs amputated. Before he left the hospital his entire left arm began to swell. "It was heavy, awful heavy," he told an interviewer. "And it was distorted, so ungodly looking." Suffering from cancer of the colon and liver, Smitherman died in 1983.[34]

Operation Crossroads was "carried through without irradiation injury to any persons," wrote Robert Newell after the tests. "I consider this conclusion well reasoned and founded on a sufficiently broad basis of measurements made by monitors sufficiently skilled and conscientious in their work." And in 1966, Warren himself wrote that "at the end of Operation Crossroads it could be said that no one had been injured by the 'peculiar hazards' inherent in it."[35]

This did not sound like the Stafford Warren of 20 years earlier. Were the alarms he sounded at Bikini merely a display of histrionics by someone more concerned about creating a paper record for posterity than managing the conflicting needs of radiation safety and nuclear testing? Did an exhausted and distraught Stafford Warren panic at Operation Crossroads in his first and only exercise of command authority?

A Los Alamos scientist complained to laboratory director Norris Bradbury one month after the Baker test that Warren's daily tolerance standard of 0.1 roentgen made no sense. "This is a preposterous limitation," the scientist argued, "in view of the fact that a man can without observable effect certainly take 0.1 R every day of his life, and can certainly take 1 R a day for a few days if he is not subsequently exposed to radiation for ten times that number of days."[36] A radsafe officer in later nuclear tests at Bikini deplored Warren's "over-cautious" safety standards with "large factors of safety built-in," and he criticized standards "carried to such extremes as to cause costly delays or extremely difficult and cumbersome methods for getting the job done."[37] One historian has argued that Warren was "unduly pessimistic" at Bikini, and it is true that some of his assertions were known to be wrong at the time.[38] For example, contrary to his statements to Blandy, there is no single ratio of alpha activity to gamma and beta emitters. Moreover, exposure to 0.05 roentgen per day for three months, resulting in a total dose of 4.5 roentgen, does not cause sterility or genetic defects in humans.

What exactly does "overexposure" mean, though? Was it "safe" to receive a tolerance dose of 0.1 roentgen per day over several weeks at Bikini but "unsafe" to receive a daily dose of 0.2 roentgen? How does radiation, once absorbed by the body, cause biological damage? How much radiation is harmful? Sudden massive exposure is obviously harmful, but is exposure to low levels of radiation also harmful? What exactly are "low" levels of radiation? One hundred years after Becquerel's discovery of radioactivity, science and medicine have not reached a final answer to these questions.

Some scientists plot the relationship between dose and injury on a straight line. Under this theory, the greater the dose received, the greater the injury. Thus, any exposure at all is deemed to result in injury. Others analogize radiation to biological agents such as certain poisons, which do not cause lasting harm below a certain threshold dose to the body. Under this analysis, there are virtually no long-term effects from exposure to low levels of radiation. Moreover, a Hiroshima victim who received a lethal dose of radiation might well have survived if he had received an identical dose gradually over months or years.

Hundreds of veterans who participated in Operation Crossroads and later atmospheric nuclear tests in the 1950s brought claims for service-connected radiation injuries before the Veterans Administration in the 1960s and 1970s, all with little success. In 1979, the Defense Nuclear Agency estimated that twelve additional fatal cancers would have occurred among the 250,000 veterans who participated in the entire U.S. nuclear testing program. "Of the 250,000 people, you would get 40,012 fatal cancers," said Admiral Monroe, "of which 40,000 are not related to radiation and 12 are."

"How do you find that 12?" asked the director of compensation and pension services at the Veterans Administration rhetorically.[39] From a legal and medical point of view, it is virtually impossible to state that an individual case of cancer was caused by earlier exposure to radiation, because cancers induced by radiation are impossible to differentiate from those that occur normally in a given population. It is possible to track acute exposures, but at lower doses the link to long-delayed injuries is weak, although there is no absolute proof one way or the other. As a result, the Veterans Administration ruled in favor of veterans in only 8 of 291 claims brought between 1967 and 1979 based on injuries arising from atmospheric nuclear tests. Almost all court suits met with similar results, based largely on legislation barring lawsuits against the government for injuries resulting from service in the armed forces.[40]

Faced with these legal, moral, and political concerns, Congress finally passed legislation in 1988 that removes the need to prove exposure, injury, or even the causal link between exposure and injury. If a veteran can show that he suffers from a form of cancer specified in the legislation and that he participated in a nuclear test or other activity likely to result in exposure to radiation, he receives compensation according to a set schedule.[41] The scientific questions remain unanswered, but the solution ultimately boiled down to politics, not medicine.

29

"The Best Defense against the Atomic Bomb Is Not to Be There When It Goes Off"

In the months following Operation Crossroads, military experts began to assess the impact of the tests on the ongoing controversy between the AAF and the Navy over the advent of the atomic bomb and its effect on military policy. The Navy had to demonstrate that its ships were not excessively vulnerable to atomic attack and that its carrier aircraft could deliver atomic weapons as well as AAF bombers could. For the most part, the Navy achieved its first goal at Bikini. Operation Crossroads was, at best, inconclusive on what the public saw as the key issue of whether a battleship could survive an atomic bomb, largely because the Navy focused on the small number of ships that were actually sunk, not on the fact that the surviving target ships would have been manned only by corpses had wartime conditions existed. "Bikini," wrote Hanson W. Baldwin, "showed to the public what more informed observers already had known—that one or two or four or five atom bombs of the present Nagasaki type cannot wipe out a fleet."[1]

The atomic bomb did not live up to its advance billing, so the Navy won a public relations victory. In response to the obvious devastation that had occurred to the guinea pig fleet, the Navy countered that the ships were obsolete, unmanned, undefended, and grouped in a much tighter formation than in battle conditions. The admirals argued that modern ships, properly designed, defended, and dispersed, would be far less vulnerable to atomic attack than other military targets, such as air bases. "Operation Crossroads demonstrated that the destructive power of the atomic bomb is much less at sea than it is over land," wrote a naval strategist after the tests.

> Naval vessels are engineered structures specifically designed to resist . . . enemy torpedoes and bombs. They are war machines. It is only too obvious that laymen and non-naval scientists prior to Bikini grossly underestimated the innate resistance of our naval vessels to damage. Operation Crossroads proved that ships . . . are immeasurably superior to any normal land structure in this respect.[2]

The Navy emerged from Operation Crossroads with an even bigger lead over the AAF in the field of atomic weapons. Naval officers were exposed to nuclear technology at Bikini, and by the summer of 1946 there were three significant scientific agencies within the Navy—the Naval Research Laboratory, the Office of Naval Research, and the Naval Bureau of Development—all of which worked closely with the Manhattan Project and academic scientists responsible for carrying out Operation Crossroads. By contrast, as the Air Force's own secret history conceded, the AAF after the tests "was still a Johnny-Come-Lately from the viewpoint of Manhattan's inner circle, and from the viewpoint of academic scientists as well."

After Operation Crossroads, the AAF still had very few officers versed in nuclear physics or nuclear weapons. Of the 130 military officers enrolled in the Navy's course in radiological defense in September 1946, 100 came from the Navy and only 5 from the AAF. "The Air Force must be particularly careful not to insist on action or responsibilities which might affect the general security policies," Gen. Curtis LeMay acknowledged in the spring of 1946. "Due to the general lack of information in the Air Forces concerning the technical problems of employment of this weapon, we are not in a very good position to submit specific recommendations at the present time." Needless to say, the Able Day "fiasco," as the Air Force history referred to *Dave's Dream*'s miss, did not enhance the AAF's standing. Nevertheless, it argued that the real lesson of Operation Crossroads was that the atomic bomb was an AAF weapon, as it alone possessed the means of delivery.[3]

In the weeks before Operation Crossroads, the very existence of the Navy was being questioned. After the tests, the talk turned to restructuring ship designs. Twenty of the Bikini target vessels were towed to the West Coast for what the Navy described as "an aggressive active program of radiological and atomic defense research to apply the lessons of Crossroads," and Admiral Blandy wrote of the "great mass of technical data" from the tests, "from which valuable lessons affecting ship design, training of personnel, naval and air tactics and strategy can be drawn." In fact, though, the few tactical lessons resulting from Operation Crossroads were obvious before the tests were conducted. Blandy wrote five months after the tests that wider spacing of ships was necessary as a protection against atomic attack. He added the equally obvious points that ships at anchor should be further separated and that large concentrations of ships in harbor should be avoided.

The tests clearly showed that the more modern ships, with newer construction techniques, were better able to withstand the shock of an atomic bomb. The Baker test, for example, caused extensive damage to the superstructure of the newer aircraft carrier *Independence,* but very little damage below decks, because her welded, as opposed to riveted, construction enabled her to absorb the underwater shock with relative ease. The older cruisers *Pensacola* and *Salt Lake City,* on the other hand, sustained much greater damage below decks due to their cast-iron fittings, which fractured easily under stress. Most of these construction design changes, however, had already been made during World War II in order to help ships better withstand the impact of shells and torpedoes.

In fact, few modifications were planned in the construction of new ships as a result of Operation Crossroads, and even fewer were actually implemented. As a passive defense against nuclear attack, planners recommended that ships' surfaces be made more rounded. Other studies from the Baker test showed that radioactive particles could be more readily removed from ships' surfaces if topside structures were wetted with seawater before an atomic attack. The Navy therefore outfitted some ships with remote-controlled "water curtains" for flushing weather surfaces at the time of an atomic attack and for automatically hosing down ships subject to fallout.[4] There was also speculation that superstructures would be streamlined in order to reduce the effect of the enormous pressure produced by an atomic explosion. Stacks would be made stronger and smaller, and radar and radio installations would be strengthened.[5] However, ship design has always involved balancing three factors: speed, armor, and firepower. Put simply, these three factors clash because a gain in one is usually obtained at the expense of another. For example, strengthening ships' hulls and stacks with more steel to withstand better the impact of an atomic bomb was theoretically possible, but only at the expense of speed.

The Navy consistently justified the tests as a way to learn about the structural strength of ships in relation to the atomic bomb. "A sound basis has been created for designing ships offering considerably increased resistance to the fury of the world's most powerful weapon," declared Operation Crossroads's official historian in summarizing the results of the tests.[6] "Alterations in naval design and hull structure are now clearly indicated," Blandy wrote two months after the tests, although he was vague about specifics. "It will take some time for all the data we have collected to be assimilated and put to practical use, but a start has already been made." Fourteen months later, though, at a speech in New York, he was forced to admit that no such changes had occurred or were planned: "I think that, at least initially, ship design will be affected little, at least so far as external appearance goes."[7]

In fact, the Navy realized that the lingering effects of radiation from an atomic attack on a ship would effectively accomplish the same result as sinking it, so very few design changes were made. Leslie Groves succinctly summed up the lesson of Operation Crossroads: "At present the best defense against the atomic bomb is not to be there when it goes off."[8] As a blast effects test, Operation Crossroads was a triumph for the Navy. Short of a direct hit, most ships did not sink, but the real blast effect was radiation. The Navy learned that its fleet would be literally dead in the water, floating but with no crews. This lesson, like others, showed that Operation Crossroads was not an end in itself but more a beginning. Having no detailed picture of the bomb's effects, America's military planners needed to gather as much data as possible in order to learn more about the new weapon's potential. Operation Crossroads helped strategists move from a position of virtual ignorance to a more informed understanding, so the armed forces were better able to pick those areas of research and development that would prove fruitful in developing a nuclear strategy. Los Alamos learned a lesson as well. Operation Crossroads kept the laboratory in business, but never again would it serve in a support role for the Navy in what it viewed as non-scientific weapons testing.

The Navy won a reprieve at Bikini—a reprieve both from possible extinction and from unification with the other services. In late September, President Truman put off action on the merger of the armed services. This stay of execution gave the Navy time to pursue its second goal, to demonstrate that the Navy could deliver an atomic attack as well as sustain one. At a press conference just one week after the Baker test, Admiral Blandy predicted the possibility of sea battles replete with "all the horror of atomic explosion" between ships driven by atomic engines, adding that the Navy intended to develop the latest atomic weapons and power plants "with all possible vigor." In fact, on the day of the Baker test, Acting Secretary of the Navy John Sullivan proposed to President Truman that several aircraft carriers be modified in order to carry atomic bombs.[9]

Six weeks later, the chief of the Navy's Bureau of Ships, Vice Adm. E. L. Cochrane, announced that two ships under construction—the 45,000-

ton battleship *Kentucky* and the 27,000-ton battle cruiser *Hawaii*—would be modified to become "guided missile warships," armed with "robot rockets" rather than guns. "Design studies now being made for the *Kentucky* and *Hawaii*," said Cochrane, "together with the development of missiles guided by carrier-based aircraft, will lead to a revolution in the striking power of naval warships." Several weeks later, the Navy announced that two other battle cruisers, the *Guam* and the *Alaska*, would be modified to fire guided missiles if the conversion of the *Hawaii* proved successful.

Operation Crossroads, far from proving the Navy obsolete, showed the need for "rebalancing the air forces," Cochrane argued, adding that other nations would soon develop sophisticated antiaircraft barrages and interceptor aircraft to stop atomic attacks. By contrast, he observed wryly, the AAF practiced for months at Bikini on hitting the *Nevada*, which put up no defense at all and was painted bright red with white turret tops—and still badly missed the target. Cochrane suggested that the AAF shift its emphasis to defensive aircraft, and he predicted that the Navy of the future would carry rockets and guided missiles armed with atomic bombs.[10]

In assessing the three factors in ship design—speed, armor, and firepower—the Navy realized virtually overnight that increasing armor to protect against the atomic bomb was useless. Instead, it saw atomic energy as a way to bolster speed and firepower while actually reducing weight. The concept of using a small nuclear reactor to propel a ship promised to increase speed and reduce the weight from huge fuel tanks, while replacing heavy guns with rocket-launched bombs would increase firepower and reduce the weight of gun installations. Indeed, during the very week of the Baker shot the Navy awarded a contract to St. Louis's Washington University to study the possibility of harnessing atomic power for ship propulsion. In announcing the contract, Chancellor Arthur H. Compton, brother of Karl Compton, envisioned a link between atomic energy and atomic weapons: "A battleship with an atomic power unit would use the unit to propel the ship," he said, "and at the same time might produce materials from which atomic bombs could be made."[11]

Operation Crossroads proved Oppenheimer's obvious point: If an atomic bomb came close enough to a ship, it sank it. As a result, the major strategic change in the Navy's thinking after Crossroads was not to adopt defensive measures, because none existed. Rather, the Navy shifted its emphasis from defensive measures to offensive ones, with the goal of taking the atomic bomb to sea as an offensive weapon. The AAF, just weeks after Hiroshima, had already articulated what would become the strategy of nuclear deterrence: devastating retaliation in response to aggression. "Real security against atomic weapons in the visible future will rest on our ability to take immediate offensive action with overwhelming force," wrote Gen. Hap Arnold in his final report on World War II. "It must be apparent to a potential aggressor that an attack on the United States would be immediately followed by an immensely devastating air-atomic attack on him."[12] Now the Navy, in the summer of 1946, began to embrace these same concepts of nuclear deterrence and massive retaliation through the use of nuclear weapons at sea, leading to the development of the nuclear-propelled and nuclear-armed submarine, aircraft carrier, and guided missile cruiser.

Operation Crossroads did, however, strengthen the case of one branch of the Navy that was seeking greater prominence as the war ended—the submariners. As early as December 1945, a Manhattan Project scientist, testifying before the Senate Special Committee on Atomic Energy, observed that the "navy of the future, if there is any such, will consist of submarines which will travel a thousand feet below the ocean."[13] Admiral Nimitz, an enthusiastic proponent of postwar submarine development, suggested that America's best defense against atomic bombardment was a strong Navy with the submarine as a means of carrying atomic weapons to within short distances of coastal targets.[14]

Postwar submarine research and development was also driven by the fact that the Russians had captured several advanced German U-boats at the end of the war, leading to concern that the Soviet Union might have as many as twenty of these fast submarines in operation by 1948, thus threatening U.S. control of the seas. By the summer of 1946, Nimitz and Forrestal had initiated a high-priority program of submarine development, which eventually led to the nuclear-propelled *Nautilus* submarine and the underwater-launched Polaris missile. The combination of Operation Crossroads and the Soviet threat gave this program an important psychological boost, as submarine technology and antisubmarine warfare quickly became the Navy's top postwar research and development priorities.[15]

The fact that AAF-Navy rivalry dominated Operation Crossroads does not mean that this rivalry dictated the postwar defense posture of the United States. In fact, the Army, which was responsible for the occupation of Japan, Germany, Austria, and Korea, played a much greater role than either the Navy or the AAF in shaping America's military strategy in the immediate postwar years. Even before Operation Crossroads, U.S. military planners assumed that the atomic bomb would form an important, if not exclusive, weapon in America's arsenal in case of future war—and that that war would be with the Soviet Union. As early as May 16, 1944, three weeks before D-day, the Joint Chiefs of Staff informed the secretary of state that Russia would emerge from the war as a leading world power and that war between Great Britain and the Soviet Union was possible as the two powers sought to enhance their strategic positions at the end of World War II. In October 1945, the Joint Chiefs' staff believed that the Soviet Union, although weakened economically, was seeking expansion by means short of war and intended to create a security zone around its borders. This would mean increased political, and perhaps military, pressure on Turkey and Iran.

Intelligence reports in early 1946 indicated that England alone could not halt a Soviet incursion into the Middle East. By April, the Joint Chiefs reported that the Soviets were capable of conquering the Middle East and Western Europe and that America would have no option but to assist the British in defending their homeland. In fact, on July 26, just after the Baker shot, the Joint Chiefs informed the White House that the Russians had forty-two divisions in Germany supported by 4,000 combat aircraft, capable of reaching the Rhine River in one day and overrunning the U.S. occupation zone in less than a week. The United States, by contrast, had eight divisions throughout Europe, less than half of which were combat ready. Asked that year whether the United States could stand up to Soviet ambitions in Eastern Europe, George Kennan replied, "Sorry, but the fact of the matter is that we do not have the power in Eastern Europe really to do anything but talk." By 1948 there would be exactly one combat-ready division in the entire U.S. Army. Its equipment was outdated, it had lost most of its elite troops, and in Omar Bradley's view it could not "fight its way out of a paper bag."[16]

The answer was simple. The atomic bomb would compensate for the lack of conventional forces. The Joint Chiefs of Staff issued its secret plan for war with the Soviet Union, code-named Pincher, on June 18, 1946, just four days after Bernard Baruch presented the United Nations with America's plan for the international control of atomic weapons. In light of the Baruch Plan, Admiral Nimitz had urged the Joint Chiefs "to avoid any specific affirmation at this time of any intention to use the atomic bomb," but the Pincher plan nevertheless called for the atomic bombing of thirty Soviet cities, including Moscow, Leningrad, and Gorki, which together produced nearly 90 percent of Russia's aircraft and tanks and 65 percent of its refined oil, and also housed its most important research centers.[17]

The results of Operation Crossroads led to an even greater emphasis on atomic warfare. At a top-level War Department meeting on August 1, 1946, Secretary Patterson mentioned a cable he had just received from the Joint Chiefs' evaluation board describing the results of the tests. "The conclusions as to the effect of the atomic bomb are clearly revolutionary and affect things up and down the line," Patterson told the group. What few military planners realized in the summer of 1946, though, was that it would have been virtually impossible for the United States to conduct atomic warfare. Although different versions of the Pincher plan called for the use of anywhere from 20 to 200 atomic bombs in a war with the Soviet Union, the Joint Chiefs' military planners were not told how many atomic bombs the United States possessed, and they were not given security clearance to receive this information until late 1947. In fact, there were only seven atomic weapons in the U.S. stockpile in July 1946, thirteen in July 1947, and fifty in July 1948. As late as August 1947, Leslie Groves refused to divulge this information to Maj. Gen. Curtis LeMay, one of the top Air Force military planners. "That information is quite complicated and is based on many factors," said Groves. "I cannot answer your question because I force myself to forget the numbers involved."[18]

The Navy had yet to develop a means of delivering the unwieldy atomic bombs from aircraft carriers. The Fat Man bomb weighed over 10,000 pounds, had a 5-foot diameter, and was nearly 11 feet long. Its dimensions and explosive power were limited by the size of the bomb bay of the B-29 Superfortress, the only American bomber that could carry such a large payload. Indeed, the atomic bomb was more than twice the weight and size of the largest conventional bombs carried by U.S. bombers during World War II. The only carrier plane that could carry the atomic bomb was the AJ-1 Savage heavy attack aircraft, but this plane was at least five years from delivery.[19]

With Operation Crossroads having come under constant attack from proponents of air power, it was perhaps only a matter of time before Admiral Blandy's Office of Special Weapons, known as OP-06, would fall victim to the same forces. In fact, this turned out to be the case but, in one of the final ironies of Operation Crossroads, OP-06 was brought down by aviators within the Navy itself, not by the AAF.

During World War II, the deputy chief of naval operations for air (OP-05) was responsible for overseeing the Navy's guided missile program, but Forrestal switched this function to Admiral Blandy's OP-06 Special Weapons office after the war. Blandy's gain represented a bureaucratic loss for Vice Adm. Arthur W. Radford, who became the new deputy chief of naval operations for air in January 1946. Politically astute and ambitious, Radford was determined to reverse this decision and at least return the guided missiles section of Blandy's office to the jurisdiction of his OP-05 organization, if not destroy OP-06 altogether.

Losing no time, Radford sent a scathing memorandum to Admiral Nimitz the day Operation Crossroads was announced. Using the same arguments as his AAF rivals, Radford invoked the Billy Mitchell tests of 1921, warned that AAF proponents would use Crossroads to their political advantage, and urged Nimitz to be wary of the Bikini tests. As soon as Blandy and his top assistants departed for Bikini in early June, Radford continued his bureaucratic war. Pointing out the technical similarities between the pilotless aircraft program under his control and Special Weapons' guided missile program, he argued that the reduction in postwar funding militated in favor of combining the two programs—under his Bureau of Aeronautics at OP-05.[20]

Vice Adm. George F. Hussey, Blandy's successor as chief of the Bureau of Ordnance, strongly opposed Radford's moves. His argument was simple: The guided missile was a weapon, and the development of naval weapons was the responsibility of his bureau, not the Bureau of Aeronautics. Virtually every other top officer under Nimitz sided with Hussey but Forrestal, himself a World War I reserve naval aviator, ruled in Radford's favor and ordered the guided missiles section transferred from OP-06 back to OP-05 on November 4, 1946, barely a year after he had created OP-06 and just three days after the dissolution of Joint Task Force One. The Office of Special Weapons was abandoned, as Blandy was named commander of the Atlantic Fleet and Deak Parsons took over a new organization within the Navy devoted exclusively to nuclear weapons. Blandy had successfully fought off the pro-AAF journalists, politicians, and military officers, but in the end his office was destroyed not by interservice rivalry but by the pro-air forces in his own backyard.[21]

30

"It Scared the Hell Out of Me"

Operation Crossroads ended as it began, shrouded in controversy, even within the meeting rooms of top U.S. military
planners. The Joint Chiefs of Staff Evaluation Board for Operation
Crossroads instantly recognized that the real power of the atomic bomb
lay not in sinking ships but in wiping out entire cities, but it was never
able to bring home to the American public the logical implications
imposed by this harsh reality.

"National security dictates the adoption of a policy of instant readiness to defend ourselves vigorously against any threat of atomic
weapon attack at any time," stated the board in the final paragraph of
its preliminary report on tests Able and Baker. "Therefore, so long as
atomic bombs could conceivably be used against this country, the
Board urges the continued production of atomic material and research
and development in all fields related to atomic warfare."[1]

The Joint Chiefs issued the preliminary report in the board's name in
early August, but it deleted several critical sections, including this last
paragraph, without telling the board. Karl T. Compton, chairman of
the evaluation board, was furious and resigned in mid-August. He told
the Joint Chiefs that he had received written assurances from Patterson
and Forrestal that the board would be free to make public comments on
any aspect of Operation Crossroads, except insofar as military secrets
were involved. "The result of these deletions," he wrote, "was to trans-

288

form a strong, straightforward statement into a weak, weasel-worded one." Accusing the Joint Chiefs of "unethical practice," Compton said that most of the deletions involved facts that had already been released to the public "or were already known to any almost 'kindergarten' nuclear scientist." The evaluation board, he said, did not expect its statements to be modified to conform to the views of the military, adding that "the civilian members of the Board have no desire to waste time in such a set-up." In submitting his resignation, he offered to stay on "only if there is a good guarantee that the board will not again be treated with similar lack of courtesy and respect." Bradley Dewey, the other civilian member, also wrote to protest, informing the Joint Chiefs that he intended to release the final paragraph to the press and to explain that it was omitted "due to a slip up somewhere along the line."

Admiral Leahy wrote back to Compton and Dewey explaining that the deleted paragraph, which called for increased production of atomic bombs, caused serious political problems for the military. As the board was an official agency of the Joint Chiefs, such a statement would imply that these views were those of the Joint Chiefs as well. This inference, he said, was unacceptable "in view of the fact that a national policy on the control of atomic energy has been announced and is now the subject of international negotiation." He admitted that the Joint Chiefs should have made clear that it was releasing only excerpts from the board's report, and he asked Compton to continue to serve as chairman, assuring him that "extra care will hereafter be exercised to avoid repetition of the type of incident that prompted your letter."

Compton and Dewey were not persuaded. "It was our expectation," wrote Compton on behalf of himself and Dewey, that "opinions or recommendations would clearly be the Board's and would not in any way be presented or understood as reflecting the judgment of the Joint Chiefs of Staff, which would remain wholly free to accept, reject, approve, disavow, or disregard them as they saw fit." The board's recommendation that the United States continue to produce atomic weapons, said Compton, was not contrary to announced U.S. policy or the current state of the UN negotiations. "It seems to us that some one ought to say these things," he added. "We can well understand some reasons why it might be unwise for the Joint Chiefs of Staff to say them, even if they agreed with the statements. So it seemed to us our duty to say them."[2]

Compton agreed to stay on, and the Joint Chiefs' evaluation board spent the next 10 months studying the dozens of volumes of technical findings and scientific data on the tests as it prepared a top-secret final report for the Joint Chiefs of Staff. Joint Task Force One had been disbanded, but a Joint Crossroads Committee, headed by Deak Parsons, continued to gather data and assist the evaluation board with its work.

Parsons also sought to involve his boss from the Manhattan Project, Robert Oppenheimer. He asked Oppenheimer, who had resigned from the evaluation board two months before the tests, to attend a February 1947 symposium on the effects of Operation Crossroads on planning for an atomic war. The key scientists who had been involved in Operation Crossroads had not met since the tests to compare notes on the data recorded there. The meeting was originally scheduled to take place at Bikini, but logistical problems and time pressures forced Parsons to switch the location to Washington. Karl Compton also called on Oppenheimer's expertise in preparing the evaluation board's report, asking him at one point to provide the board with "the number of air burst [atomic] bombs which would render the northern hemisphere ultimately uninhabitable—at least in general order of magnitude."[3]

Compton circulated a final draft of the report to other members of the board in early June. Rear Adm. Ralph A. Ofstie, a Navy member of the board, showed the draft to a colleague, whose response was, "It scared the hell out of me." Ofstie, clearly upset about this reaction, immediately wrote to Compton about the tone of the report. "If this should be the reaction of a highly experienced and keenly intelligent naval officer [it] suggests that somewhere or other we may have slipped a cog." The report, Ofstie noted, was largely directed at a possible atomic attack on the United States at a time when no other nation had developed an atomic bomb, and he wanted to avoid "criticism of extremism" against the board.[4]

The six members of the Joint Chiefs' evaluation board came to Washington on July 29, 1947, to present their top-secret report at the Pentagon at a meeting of virtually all the top U.S. military officials. The nearly sixty attendees in the heavily guarded conference room included Navy Secretary Forrestal, Secretary of War Kenneth C. Royall, Leslie Groves, the Joint Chiefs and their top planning staffs, the Atomic Energy Commission and its Military Liaison Committee, top Army, Navy, and Air Force officers, and all the top Operation Crossroads officials, including Admiral Blandy, Deak Parsons, Rear Admiral Solberg, Ralph Sawyer, and Stafford Warren.

After a brief introduction by Deak Parsons, Compton presented a 30-minute summary of the board's report and discussed in detail a diagram showing the effects of an atomic bomb attack on New York City. Speakers from the Army, Navy, and Air Force discussed the effects of Operation Crossroads on their services, and Blandy, who had been named commander-in-chief of the Atlantic Fleet following Marc Mitscher's sudden death in February, spoke on the strategic implications of the tests. The meeting began at 10:30 A.M. and was scheduled to be over by lunchtime, but it went on for nearly four hours. The discussion was considered so vital by Secretary of War Royall that he delayed for over an hour his scheduled departure for a trip to Germany, and Blandy's presence at the meeting led to press speculation that he might direct some new atomic bomb tests.[5]

Since the advent of the atomic bomb, countless volumes have been written on nuclear strategy, logic, and theory. Much of the writing is bureaucratic, sometimes inarticulate and dull, couched in terms of policy, planning, procurement, and other government terminology. The evaluation board's report contained none of this. The top military men in the United States heard nuclear reality, not nuclear theory. The report was frank, harsh, and sensational from beginning to end, raising many issues that planners still debate, from preemptive strikes to defenses against nuclear attack. The report, which remained classified for decades, is one of the most important documents in the history of the nuclear age, and it constituted the basic checklist for all atomic war planning until the advent of the hydrogen bomb in the 1950s.

"If used in numbers, atomic bombs not only can nullify any nation's military efforts, but can demolish its social and economic structure and prevent their reestablishment for long periods of time," began the board's report. "With such weapons, especially if employed in conjunction with other weapons of mass destruction, as, for example, pathogenic bacteria, it is quite possible to depopulate vast areas of the earth's surface, leaving only vestigial remnants of man's material works."

The Baker shot "threw large masses of highly radioactive water onto the decks and into the hulls of vessels," wrote the board, which recognized that the real weapon developed at Bikini was radioactivity. "These contaminated ships became radioactive stoves, and would have burned all living things aboard them with invisible and painless but deadly radiation." A Baker-type shot on a large city, it reasoned, "would have not only an immediate lethal effect, but would establish a long term hazard through the contamination of structures by the deposition of radioactive particles." This scenario, said the evaluation board, would result in horror beyond description:

> We can form no adequate mental picture of the multiple disaster which would befall a modern city, blasted by one or more bombs and enveloped by radioactive mists. Of the survivors in contaminated areas, some would be doomed to die of radiation sickness in hours, some in days, and others in years. But, these areas, irregular in size and shape, as wind and topography might form them, would have no visible boundaries. No sur-

vivor could be certain he was not among the doomed and so, added to every terror of the moment, thousands would be stricken with a fear of death and the uncertainty of the time of its arrival.

Rescue parties could enter the city only at the risk of death. The dead "would remain unburied and the wounded uncared for in the areas of heaviest contamination where certain death would lurk." Millions of refugees would flee the city in panic, causing a breakdown in transportation facilities and even more death, and "among these fugitives, for the moment unidentified from the rest, would be numbers whose contaminated clothing and any goods they carried could establish in others the fear of dangerous radioactivity." Indeed, the psychological impact of the bomb, now that the world knew its effects, could be even more powerful than the physical damage inflicted:

> In the face . . . of the bomb's demonstrated power to deliver death to tens of thousands, of primary military concern will be the bomb's potentiality to break the will of nations and of peoples by the stimulation of man's primordial fears, those of the unknown, the invisible, the mysterious. We may deduce from a wide variety of established facts that the effective exploitation of the bomb's psychological implications will take precedence over the application of its destructive and lethal effects in deciding the issue of war.[6]

Deak Parsons expressed these same views in a manual prepared at the same time by the Joint Crossroads Committee, in which he stressed that a Baker-type shot would produce many more casualties and over a far greater area than in Hiroshima and Nagasaki:

> While the atomic bomb was designed and used primarily for its direct destruction effects, no weapon has ever had such potentially widespread and serious psychological aspects, nor has any weapon even been used in war which has offered such rich opportunity for exploiting fear of the unseen and of the unknown. Indeed, the psychological effects of the atomic bomb may constitute its most significant feature from the military standpoint.[7]

The board's most controversial proposal was that the United States should maintain instant readiness in order to launch a preemptive nuclear strike against an enemy preparing to launch such an attack on the United States. The board recognized that U.S. policy, as evidenced by Pearl Harbor, was to declare war only after being attacked, but it called for a "revision of our traditional attitudes toward what constitute acts of aggression so that our armed forces may plan and operate in accordance with the realities of atomic warfare." Offense would be the only defense in an atomic war, it reasoned, and the United States should therefore wield a "superior striking power" to deter an enemy from attack or, if an enemy prepares an attack, to "overwhelm him and destroy his will and ability to make war before he can inflict significant damage upon us." It therefore recommended that Congress redefine what constitutes an "aggressive act" or an "imminent" attack to circumvent its own constitutional authority to declare war and provide authority for the president to order "prompt and effective atomic bomb retaliation should another nation ready an atomic attack against us."

Despite its graphic portrayal of the horrors of a nuclear holocaust, the report was also the U.S. military establishment's earliest call for an unlimited arms race. In the absence of acceptable guarantees of permanent peace, said the board, the United States should continue to manufacture and stockpile atomic bombs, conduct periodic weapons tests, and carry on continuous research and development in weapons development and delivery. It called for the initiation of a civil defense program in case of atomic attack on the United States, an intelligence system capable of monitoring a potential enemy's ability to develop nuclear weapons, and public recognition of the probability of surprise atomic attack on the United States.

As for targets, the board reached the same conclusion voiced by some of Operation Crossroads's critics before the tests: Because of the scarcity of fissionable material, the atomic bomb should be used as a strategic weapon and was much more effective against cities than against ships or soldiers. "The bomb is pre-eminently a weapon for use against human life and activities in large urban and industrial areas," it concluded, while "ships at sea and bodies of troops are, in general, unlikely to be regarded as primary atomic bomb targets." The board recommended against major ship design modifications. Recognizing the atomic bomb as the ultimate strategic weapon, it saw no reason to depart "from the principle that naval ship design should be based upon tactical function." Operation Crossroads, it concluded, did not indicate that the tactical design requirements of ships "should be compromised by emphasis upon additional protection from atomic weapons."[8] The evaluation board also recognized that no one branch of the armed services should have exclusive control of the atomic bomb. Choosing its words carefully, it called for the coordinated development of atomic weapons and weapons carriers, including airplanes, ships, and submarines, as well as rockets, guided missiles, and torpedoes launched from them.

Looking back at Operation Crossroads, the evaluation board con-cluded that the debate over the spacing of the target ships had been resolved in the Navy's favor. Only four ships instead of ten, as originally planned, were within relatively close range of the two bombs, and only eighteen, instead of the planned twenty-five, were within a "medium" range. The board also disagreed with the Navy's cost estimates for the tests, which had been placed as low as $10 million in the months after the tests were announced. The board found that Operation Crossroads cost the U.S. government $50 million beyond the fixed costs of salaries to the 42,000 military personnel and upkeep of the target and support ships. The board's conclusion was close to the Joint Crossroads Com-mittee's figure of $53,700,000, which was arrived at four months after the tests, although the official historian of Operation Crossroads referred to it as a "$100,000,000 experiment."[9]

As a final matter, the board recommended that the government reconsider several of the hard-fought civilian-versus-military issues that had been laid to rest less than a year earlier with the signing of the McMahon bill establishing the Atomic Energy Commission. These ques-tions included whether the military should have representation on the AEC, own and control atomic weapons, participate in the design and testing of weapons, and control all information relating exclusively to the military applications of atomic energy. When David Lilienthal, the chairman of the new AEC, expressed his concerns about these issues to the White House a week after the board presented its report at the Pen-tagon, he was astonished to learn that President Truman did not even know of the report's existence. Lilienthal rushed his copy of the top-secret paper to Clark Clifford, who called back three days later to say that Truman was "outraged" at the report.[10]

The Joint Chiefs and its Strategic Survey Committee were confronted with blunt recommendations and hard choices, the most immediate of which was whether to release the evaluation board's report. Dewey and Compton had hoped that portions of the report would be made public, but the White House intervened in October and declined to release any parts of it or even a summary. "Some of the findings about the effects of the atom bomb are so disturbing and frightening and the recommenda-tions are so sensational that the White House won't permit it to be made public at this time," a highly placed military source told reporters in mid-October.

Bradley Dewey demanded immediate public release. "I am fearful that the report has been suppressed because of political reasons, rather than for any top military secrets which could properly be deleted before the report is made public," he said on October 13.[11] Dewey was right.

Just one week later, Senator Bourke B. Hickenlooper of Iowa, chairman of the Joint Committee on Atomic Energy, perused Truman's copy of the report at the White House and concurred with the president's decision not to release it. "I find myself in agreement with you," Hickenlooper wrote Truman, "that making this report public at this time might create an area of misunderstanding outweighing in detriment such benefit as might result from publicity." Publication at a future date, he suggested, "will be necessary," but the public interest would be better served at that time by "proper secrecy."[12] Ironically, after informing his fellow senators that he had seen the report, Hickenlooper found himself in the somewhat embarrassing position of writing Truman in early December to report that the other members of his committee had voted unanimously to instruct him to ask the president to make the report available for them to review "in strict confidence."[13]

The *New York Times* reported on February 25, 1948, that the evaluation board's report would be released in about 10 days, following final White House approval. The release was held up, though, and when Secretary of Defense Forrestal eventually sent President Truman an extracted version of the board's report several months later, he included the Joint Chiefs' strong recommendation, based on "non-military considerations," that the report be kept secret. Forrestal also told Truman that both Secretary of State George Marshall and Undersecretary Robert A. Lovett strongly recommended against releasing the report. "They believe," wrote Forrestal, "that public disclosure of the report at this time might be misinterpreted both here and abroad, and considered as a preface to some brusque action which we do not, in fact, intend." In adding his own view that the report should be kept secret, Forrestal warned the president of Compton's repeated threats to make public statements on the report.[14]

The controversy over the report continued for years, and it followed Karl Compton to his grave. He wrote to his friend John H. Ohly, one of Forrestal's assistants, in early August 1948 to check on the status of the proposal to release the report. "The proposal is in abeyance," Ohly wrote back, "due to the very strong feeling of both the Secretary and Under Secretary of State that no release on this subject would be desirable at this time."

Meanwhile, Bradley Dewey wrote a "Dear Jim" letter to Forrestal, hoping to pry the report loose, without realizing that it was Forrestal himself who had recommended to Truman that it not be released. The report, Dewey told Forrestal, had gone from the Joint Chiefs to the AEC and then to the White House for final release. "There it remains, apparently entombed," wrote Dewey. Reminding Forrestal that in the "dark ages" he had told Dewey that the evaluation board's report would be made public after the necessary military censorship, he asked for the secretary's help.[15]

When Forrestal failed to act, Dewey wrote an article in the December 1948 *Atlantic Monthly* calling for the public release of the report except for deletions as required by military security. "Much of it was written for the American people and their Congress, and they should have it," argued Dewey. "We need a high policy governing our employment of atomic weapons in war. The American people must participate in this policy, must accept it and be willing to support it. To do this they must have facts which have been kept from them by the White House."[16]

At a press conference in early December, President Truman said that Dewey was mistaken in suggesting that the White House had suppressed the report, explaining that Forrestal had recommended months earlier that the report be withheld for reasons of national security. Forrestal, meanwhile, gave serious consideration to the release of the report following publication of Dewey's article, and he asked several friends for their views. Vannevar Bush suggested that disclosure by Truman at that time "would appear to be making a release under pressure, in the light of Dewey's article." On the other hand, he saw one good reason to release the report. "There is not the slightest question in my mind," he wrote Forrestal, "that if we were attacked, . . . we would use atomic bombs," and he believed that disclosure of this policy "would greatly aid to preserve the peace of the world."[17]

Forrestal again took no action, and one month later, in late January 1949, Compton again called for the release of the report. Senator Henry Cabot Lodge, Jr., could not understand why the report remained suppressed. In a February 1, 1949, letter to Brien McMahon, he praised Dewey's "provocative and disturbing" article and asked if McMahon could explain the situation. McMahon could not. "To the best of my knowledge," he replied on February 18, "no reason has been made public as to why this report was suppressed."[18]

That very day, columnist Drew Pearson, in his syndicated "Washington Merry-Go-Round" column, wrote that Forrestal had "bottled up" the report. "Secretary of Defense Forrestal and the Navy are moving frantically to hush it up," wrote Pearson, "but a full-fledged congressional investigation of the effects of the Bikini bomb tests is in the offing." Pearson reported that sixty-one of the target ships at Bikini had been sunk or destroyed due to radioactivity, but Forrestal, who was building $400 million worth of ships that year, "hasn't paid much attention to the problem." The "brass hats," he said, were "deliberately suppressing" the evaluation board's report, which was why Senator McMahon's Atomic Energy Committee "is now seriously planning a full-dress investigation of Bikini and its results." McMahon's committee did not investigate Operation Crossroads, as Pearson predicted, but neither did the Truman administration release the evaluation board's report. Despite pressure from other public figures, including prominent atomic scientists and businessmen, the administration reaffirmed its decision against releasing the Bikini report—or other atomic weapons information—based on the recommendations of an ad hoc committee that included James Conant, John Foster Dulles, and Dwight Eisenhower.[19]

As public debate raged over the release of the board's report, U.S. military leaders struggled for more than four years over its recommendations. Some naval officers, especially aviators, used the board's emphasis on the atomic bomb as an offensive weapon to argue that the Navy should develop an aircraft carrier capable of delivering an atomic attack. This argument would also solve the dilemma caused by the fact that the U.S. Navy's 4 million tons of combat vessels at the end of World War II made it larger than all the other navies of the world put together. With the AAF questioning the need of "a five-ocean navy to fight a no-ocean opponent," the Navy seized on airpower as the key to its future.[20]

Plans for the *United States,* a "flush deck" carrier with no island superstructure—to be the largest ship in the world—were unveiled in 1948, as the Navy sought to challenge the Air Force's mission of strategic bombing. "I think the time is right now for the Navy to start an aggressive campaign aimed at proving that the Navy can deliver the Atom Bomb more effectively than the Air Force can," wrote one Navy admiral in a memorandum leaked to Drew Pearson and published in February 1948.[21] The Navy's General Board, though, which provided policy guidelines to the secretary of the navy, questioned this view, and in early 1949, the new secretary of defense, Louis Johnson, canceled the project.[22]

The Navy had come full circle in less than three years. The advent of the atomic bomb seemed to make navies obsolete, but the Navy survived extinction at Operation Crossroads and went on to show that it could deliver the bomb, even proposing a leading role for naval aviation in strategic bombing. Three years after Operation Crossroads, the Navy no longer saw the bomb as the "winning weapon," and naval strategists, rejecting strategic nuclear warfare, reverted to the traditional view of the role of the Navy and naval aviation—control of the seas.

As U.S.-Soviet relations deteriorated, many of the evaluation board's conclusions became less controversial. By 1947, for example, the board's original call for the continued manufacturing and stockpiling of atomic weapons was no longer an issue. "The vital importance of this matter is recognized," noted the Joint Chiefs' Strategic Survey Committee, "and various programs designed to implement this recommendation are now being carried out to the extent that funds and materials permit."[23]

Most of the Joint Chiefs of Staff evaluation board's recommendations were eventually implemented, except for the two political initiatives: redefining the president's warmaking abilities to order a preemptive atomic strike and increasing the military's role in the AEC. By June 1950, the military's role in the atomic weapons program had greatly increased, so the Joint Chiefs finally dropped the evaluation board's proposals for changes in the AEC act. As to the board's proposal for legislation authorizing atomic bomb retaliation, the Joint Strategic Survey Committee noted that the Soviet Union had detonated its first atomic bomb, both countries were developing thermonuclear weapons, and there was an increased possibility of a surprise atomic attack by the U.S.S.R. against the United States. "These two nations are now, to all intents and purposes, engaged in war—except for armed conflict," declared the committee. The legislation would simplify the emergency use of atomic weapons, but the decision to push Congress to act was a political one. Two months later the proposal was finally dropped by the Joint Chiefs, largely at the recommendation of Adm. Forrest Sherman, the chief of naval operations, who wrote that such a law would be "highly questionable as to constitutionality."[24]

Meanwhile, the call for release of the evaluation board's report subsided until Karl Compton's death in 1954, when the Armed Forces Special Weapons Project, the successor organization to the Joint Crossroads Committee, sought unsuccessfully to recover his copy of the report. The Joint Chiefs ordered an investigation before dropping the matter, despite the recommendation that it ask the FBI to try to recover Compton's copy of the report or, failing that, to determine the probability that national security had been compromised.[25]

Dewey was also asked to return his copy, but he refused, despite the threat of possible criminal prosecution. The matter was raised with the Joint Chiefs of Staff, which declined to recommend further action. "In any decision concerning action to be taken in this case," wrote the Joint Chiefs' administrative secretary John B. Brady, "recognition must be given to the fact that this involves matters of policy at a very high level, including elements beyond JCS control." Dewey might have violated federal laws prohibiting the possible compromise of classified information, Brady suggested, but he found no conclusive evidence and the matter was dropped.[26] Dewey, like Compton, held onto his copy of the controversial report until his death, and the report remained classified for decades after Operation Crossroads.

31

"Leave 'Thermonuclear' Out of Press Releases and Speeches"

The Navy would never again test atomic weapons on its own after Operation Crossroads, but the military's connection with Bikini continued for many years after the tests. The surprising results of the Baker test, combined with the baseline data gathered by scientists before the tests, turned Bikini into a living laboratory, and it became a starting point for the science of radiobiology. In early 1947, Deak Parsons, head of the Joint Crossroads Committee, recommended to the Joint Chiefs of Staff that a scientific resurvey of Bikini be conducted under the direction of the Navy to retrieve test data from sunken ships, determine the exact cause of sinking, study the long-term effects of radiation from the Baker test on fish and coral, and "obtain data on which to base a decision relative to possible resettlement of the native population."

Parsons's plan was approved, and a group of more than fifty geologists, marine biologists, oceanographers, soil scientists, and other technicians and divers left Pearl Harbor on July 1, 1947, to rephotograph and reexamine Bikini Atoll. The group included officials from the Army, Navy, AEC, Smithsonian, U.S. Geological Survey, the Fish and Wildlife Department of the Interior Department, and scientists from the Scripps Institute of Oceanography, Stanford, Ohio State, Columbia, and the universities of California, Hawaii, Minnesota, Tennessee, and Washington. As the resurvey team entered Bikini lagoon on July 15, the sight was unmistakable. The tall camera towers, unused for a year and seeming so out of place, still stood out against the horizon, dwarfing the stands of coconut trees. The thatched roofs on Studs Saloon and the Up and Atom Club were sagging and rotting, and vines already grew over trucks and covered the basketball courts.

During their six weeks at Bikini, the resurvey team dredged soil samples from the lagoon floor for measurement and studied the atoll's flora, fauna, and fish. Thousands of specimens of fish and other marine life were caught, dissected, and analyzed at Bikini, while another 6,000 were brought back to the United States for further study at the University of Washington's Applied Fisheries Laboratory and other universities. The resurvey team also confirmed Charles Darwin's 1831 theory that coral atolls are formed by coral growing upward on reefs around a slowly sinking volcanic island. A series of holes drilled in the reef indicated that the atoll sits on a 2,000-foot-thick layer of coral, which in turn rests on volcanic rock and heavy rock of a buried mountain. In addition, more than 600 dives were made on the *Saratoga, Nagato,* and the submarines *Apogon* and *Pilotfish,* as divers photographed the vessels, tried unsuccessfully to recover pressure-measuring instruments from the *Nagato,* and sought to determine the exact causes of sinking. Much of the dive equipment, though, which had been used in Operation Crossroads, was still contaminated after one year.[1]

The resurvey team was cautioned to avoid unnecessary contact with barges and other objects in Bikini lagoon and with the debris found on the beaches, as well as to refrain from eating any fish from the lagoon or drinking water from any of Bikini's islands. Studies showed large amounts of radioactive material on the lagoon bottom, which made its way into the entire food chain, including many of the fish, invertebrates, algae, and plants. In fact, by the time the team left Bikini, the hull and evaporators on its flagship, the attack transport *Chilton,* showed radiation readings higher than normal background levels. With the exception of some dying coral on a reef north of Bikini Island, though, the resurvey team found no changes in the population or composition of the atoll's animal and plant life.[2]

Bikini would not be used again for nuclear testing until 1954. In late 1947 the AEC, after studying Amchitka in Alaska, the Azores in the Atlantic, and the northern islands of Kwajalein Atoll, announced that Enewetak Atoll in the Marshall Islands, about 200 miles west of Bikini, would be used for a series of nuclear tests. The AEC determined that Bikini was not suitable because it lacked sufficient land area for instrumentation and housing necessary for the tests. Operation Sandstone was held at Enewetak in April and May 1948, as three newly designed atomic bombs were detonated from towers to test improvements in weapons effectiveness and efficiency.[3]

At the same time, military and AEC officials began Project Nutmeg to study the feasibility of establishing a proving ground in the continental United States. Such an action, according to Deak Parsons, would have the "advantage of educating the public that the bomb was not such a horrible thing that it required proof-testing 5,000 miles from the United States."[4] The outbreak of the Korean War in 1950 gave new impetus to Project Nutmeg, as the National Security Council became concerned that the Russians or Chinese might invade Enewetak. After giving serious consideration to the Cape Hatteras–Cape Lookout area in North Carolina, the AEC finally decided on a 1,350-square-mile site northwest of Las Vegas, an area larger than Rhode Island. Operation Ranger, a set of five air-dropped atomic bomb tests, was held at the new Nevada site in January and February 1951.[5]

The AEC's return to the Pacific was occasioned by America's decision to develop the hydrogen bomb, a weapon triggered by an atomic bomb. With a force much greater than the atomic bomb, the new weapon could not be tested in the continental United States, so Enewetak was again prepared for a new round of tests. The world's first hydrogen bomb was tested at Enewetak on November 1, 1952, but it was not a usable weapon. The device, code-named Mike, was larger than a two-story house and weighed 65 tons. Robert Oppenheimer joked that in case of war it would have to be delivered by oxcart. Moreover, it required a massive refrigeration unit to keep the hydrogen fuel in a liquid state until detonation. A better bomb was needed.[6]

No plans had been made for more nuclear tests at Bikini. In fact, scientific teams returning to the atoll in the late 1940s and early 1950s detected such low levels of radioactivity that the AEC seriously considered repatriating the islanders. "The health hazard here is essentially negligible," said Dr. John C. Bugher of the AEC's Division of Biology and Medicine at a 1952 meeting, adding that his division saw "no reason why these people should not be returned as far as the hazards from persistent radioactivity may be concerned."[7] The AEC's only concern was whether Bikini should be held in reserve as a test site for thermonuclear hydrogen bombs. "It is possible that the tests planned for Eniwetok may result in the destruction of a part or all of the atoll," warned Bugher. "A severe shock may . . . cause the crumbling of the entire structure. In such case there would be no other test site feasible in the entire area other than Bikini." The AEC's fears were realized at the 1952 Mike shot at Enewetak. "The shot island Elugelab is missing," wrote AEC chairman Gordon Dean to President Truman.[8] Some of the next tests would have to be conducted at Bikini.

The Russians had tested their first atomic bomb in 1949. Then, in August 1953, U.S. scientists detected the first Soviet hydrogen explosion.

President Eisenhower told the American people that the Russians now possessed "the capability of atomic attack upon us, and such capability will increase with the passage of time."[9] Eisenhower did not want to reveal very much to the American public. "Keep them confused about 'fission' and 'fusion,'" he told the AEC, and "leave 'thermonuclear' out of press releases and speeches. Also 'fusion' and 'hydrogen.'"[10] He failed to tell the American public that the Russian hydrogen bomb did not require unwieldy refrigeration and could be placed in an airplane. The Soviets had not only caught up with American nuclear technology; they had actually moved ahead, and America had to develop and test a hydrogen bomb capable of delivery by aircraft.

The result was the first U.S. test of a deliverable hydrogen bomb, code-named Bravo, which was the first test in the Castle series of shots at Bikini and Enewetak in 1954. With a large share of America's hydrogen-bomb potential in its hold, the ship carrying the bombs to the Marshall Islands sailed under wartime conditions. Flanked by destroyers and protected by air cover, the convoy avoided normal shipping lanes and sailed at night with lights out and radios silent.

The AEC had taken extraordinary radsafe precautions at the Mike shot, but there had been very little local fallout. Accordingly, it placed little emphasis on emergency evacuations for Bravo. Scientists recommended that Rongelap and Ailinginae atolls, several hundred miles east of Bikini, be placed in the "danger" zone for the Castle series, but the U.S. Interior Department, reluctant to displace the islanders as had occurred during Operation Crossroads, disagreed, and suggested that the boundaries of the danger zone be drawn precisely to exclude these atolls. The AEC agreed, and the results were tragic.

As a last-minute precaution against a possible tidal wave, all personnel on Eneu Island except for the timing and firing technicians were temporarily moved offshore to a transport ship the day before the shot. Because everyone expected to be back the next day, the men took few belongings with them. Shaving kits, books, wallets, and clothing were left in the tent city erected on Eneu.

The experts were wrong, but they saved the men's lives. There was no tidal wave, but the March 1, 1954, Bravo shot was the most powerful nuclear weapon ever detonated by the United States and was, at the time, the largest manmade explosion in the history of the world, equal to the force of about 750 Hiroshima bombs. Bravo had an explosive force of about 15 megatons, or 15 million tons of TNT, nearly three times what its designer expected. A freight train carrying the bomb's equivalent in TNT would span the United States from Maine to California.

Bikini had not been used as a nuclear test site since the Baker shot, nearly eight years earlier. The atoll's ecosystem had almost fully recovered from the effects of Operation Crossroads, but the Bravo shot doomed Bikini. The bomb was detonated on the reef off Nam Island in the northwest corner of the atoll. It created a fireball nearly four miles wide that literally vaporized the entire test island and parts of two others, extirpating them from the lagoon and leaving a gaping hole in the ocean floor, one mile wide and 200 feet deep. It destroyed most of the buildings and scientific equipment on an island 14 miles across Bikini's lagoon, and its force actually moved the concrete timing and detonation bunker on Eneu Island, 24 miles away. Only a dramatic helicopter rescue of the men in the bunker saved them from certain death from the bomb's radioactive fallout.

The force of the explosion rattled buildings on Rongerik Atoll, 125 miles east of Bikini, and at Kwajalein, 250 miles away, there were high winds and barracks shook as if there had been an earthquake. A task force of ten U.S. Navy ships stationed 30 miles east of Bikini was hit with severe fallout, but the lessons learned from the Baker shot saved the sailors. After securing all hatches and portholes, all hands were ordered below decks in the stifling heat for more than four hours. Ventilators were covered to prevent the entry of radioactive dust, deck chairs were thrown overboard, and special hoses automatically sprayed the superstructure areas to wash off radioactive contamination. Radiation readings were as high as 5 roentgens per hour, with maximum readings of 25 per hour in deck drains.[11]

Moreover, what was described at the time as an "unpredicted" shift in wind direction sent the fallout eastward over Bikini Island and beyond, covering an area as large as 7,000 square miles. As the bomb cloud rose higher into the upper atmosphere than had been anticipated, high-altitude winds pulled it to the east rather than to the west. Pellet-sized particles fell to the earth quickly, but the smaller and less visible ones were carried east by the winds and drifted earthward more slowly. A soft rain of whitish ash began to fall 50 miles downwind one hour after the blast; several hours later the ashy rain began to fall 100 miles away. Those sprinkled with fallout included 28 American servicemen on Rongerik, the 236 inhabitants of Rongelap and Utrik atolls, other Marshallese who were camping at Ailinginae Atoll, and 23 crewmen of a Japanese fishing vessel, the *Lucky Dragon*.

The servicemen were evacuated to Kwajalein the day after the Bravo shot, but the Rongelapese were not moved for two days and the people of Utrík had to wait three. AEC chairman Lewis Strauss was determined to keep the evacuation secret, but when a Cincinnati newspaper broke the news on March 11, the AEC issued a statement the next day stating that "during the course of a routine atomic test," some Marshallese "were unexpectedly exposed to some radioactivity." They were moved to Kwajalein "according to plan as a precautionary measure," but "there were no burns" and "all are reported well."[12]

The press release was disingenuous at best. With poor wind forecasts, an explosive force equal to 750 Hiroshima bombs, and an unexpectedly large explosion at that, Bravo was hardly a "routine atomic test." The "plan" was an emergency evacuation, the "some radioactivity" equaled that received by Japanese located less than two miles from ground zero at Hiroshima and Nagasaki, and the statement that all were "reported well" belied the fact that virtually all the Rongelapese had already displayed the classic symptoms of radiation poisoning—hair loss, skin lesions, and lowered white blood cell counts. All but two of the nineteen Rongelapese who were under 10 years old at the time of Bravo developed abnormal thyroid nodules, and there has been one leukemia death. By 1982, the U.S. government had changed its views on Bravo. What the AEC had called a "routine atomic test" was now, in the words of the Defense Nuclear Agency, "the worst single incident of fallout exposures in all the U.S. atmospheric testing program," and the "no burns" had become "acute radiation effects."[13] If the wind had shifted just a bit farther to the south, everyone on Rongelap, Rongerik, and Ailinginae might have been killed. Persons just 15 miles north of Rongelap's main island would have absorbed a 400-roentgen dose, and people on the northern tip of the atoll would have received 1,000 roentgens, enough to cause certain death within a month.[14]

Several days after Bravo, scientists returned to Bikini and surrounding atolls to measure radiation levels. More than 100 miles away, on Ailinginae Atoll, birds too sick to fly staggered along in the sand. On Eneu, some poles had collapsed and a few cabinets were knocked over, but most of the tent city was intact. Except for a coating of highly radioactive gray dust, everything looked just as it had five days earlier. Clothes were draped over tent ropes, half-open books lay on tables next to watches and family photographs, and shoes were stored under bunks. The scene resembled a twentieth-century Pompeii.[15]

The tragedy of Bravo continues to haunt the Bikinians and its other victims. Bikini Island was hopelessly contaminated, and its radiation levels more than four decades later are still well in excess of acceptable international standards. The *Lucky Dragon* crewmen suffered severe radiation sickness, and the radio operator, Aikichi Kuboyama, died seven months later from the effects of the poisoning. More than 400,000 people attended his funeral, and by the following August over 30 million Japanese had signed a petition calling for a ban on nuclear testing.[16]

One of the lessons learned at Baker—that marine organisms greatly concentrate fission products—was brought home in a grotesque manner at the Osaka fish market, as Geiger counters held over tuna taken from the hold of the *Lucky Dragon* registered over 10,000 counts per minute. Panic swept through Japan, and overnight the bottom fell out of the fish market. Soon other fishing boats from the area around the Marshall Islands came to port with equally radioactive catches. A total of 683 tuna boats landed contaminated fish, and 457 tons of tuna were destroyed, roughly 1 for every 200 caught. Wary purchasers stopped buying fish altogether, and the Tokyo Central Wholesale Market was forced to close for the first time since a 1935 cholera epidemic had struck the city.[17]

Meanwhile, AEC chairman Strauss stated that "the facts do not confirm" stories about "the widespread contamination of tuna and other fish." He accused the *Lucky Dragon* of "inadvertent trespass," and stated, contrary to the evidence available to the AEC, that the ship was "well within the danger zone." He added that the crew's injuries "are thought to be due to the chemical activity of the converted material in the coral rather than to radioactivity."[18] Privately he declared that the boat, despite its 800 pounds of tuna, was really a "Red spy outfit" snooping on the American tests.[19]

Strauss's attitude was echoed by John M. Allison, the American ambassador in Tokyo, who cabled Secretary of State John Foster Dulles that the *Lucky Dragon* accident was followed by a "period of uncontrolled masochism, as the nation, aided by an unscrupulous press, seemed to revel in fancied martyrdom." Allison claimed that this breakdown was triggered by a small group of Japanese doctors, whom he described as "fuzzy-minded leftists" who had "vistas of nation-wide publicity at home and world-wide scientific prominence as exclusive proprietors of the world's first hydrogen bomb patients." Allison also recommended a quick lump-sum settlement with the crew in order to weaken "the position of neutralists, pacifists, feminists, and professional anti-Americans."[20] The tragedy revived the anguish from World War II and nearly caused Japan to sever diplomatic relations with the United States. "It has never been appreciated in the West," wrote British historian Richard Storry, that the "Bikini Incident," as it was called, "caused resentment in Japan at least equal to that occasioned by the atomic attacks on Hiroshima and Nagasaki."[21]

It also turned out that the AEC had received an alarming report about possible changes in the wind direction six hours before Bravo was detonated. According to a 1982 U.S. government report, the weather briefing at 11:00 A.M. the day before the shot predicted "no significant fallout . . . for the populated Marshalls." By 6:00 P.M., however, "the predicted winds were less favorable; nevertheless, the decision to shoot was reaffirmed, but with another review of the winds scheduled for [midnight]."[22] The midnight briefing "indicated less favorable winds at 10,000- to 25,000-foot levels." Winds at 20,000 feet "were headed for Rongelap to the east," and "it was recognized that both Bikini and Eneman Islands would probably be contaminated." With full knowledge that winds were not headed northward to the open sea but due east over Bikini's islands, the AEC proceeded to detonate the Bravo bomb.

Bravo set off an enormous public debate in the United States and abroad on nuclear testing and fallout. Americans did not understand the magnitude of this new bomb until President Eisenhower told a news conference in late March that U.S. scientists were "surprised and astonished" at the results of the Bravo test. Several days later Strauss casually mentioned that the hydrogen bomb could destroy a city the size of New York.[23] By April the White House was receiving more than one hundred letters and telegrams a day calling for a stop to all atomic testing. It was not until one year later, on February 15, 1955, that the AEC admitted that "about 7,000 square miles of territory downwind from the point of burst [of the Bravo bomb] was so contaminated that survival might have depended upon prompt evacuation of the area or upon taking shelter and other protective measures." Put another way, if Bravo were detonated at Washington, D.C., and the fallout pattern had headed in a northeast direction, the entire northeastern seaboard would be decimated. People in Philadelphia would receive a dose of 1,000 roentgens and in New York City a lethal dose of more than 500, while fallout in the 100-roentgen range, comparable to that received by the *Lucky Dragon,* would stretch through New England up to the Canadian border.

The Baker shot had revealed the true dimensions of fallout as a biological weapon of terror, but the media and the military had focused more on the instant effects of the bomb on the target ships. The Bravo shot, though, finally brought home to the American public and the world the realization that the killing power of radioactive fallout from a thermonuclear bomb greatly exceeds the fiery blast and heat of the direct explosion that causes it. Its impact and scope are mind-numbing. The fallout from Bravo covered an area as large as 50,000 square miles, with serious-to-lethal radioactivity falling over an area almost equal in size to the entire state of Massachusetts. The exclusion area prior to the Bravo shot covered more than 67,000 square miles, an area equal to the size of New England. After the fallout tragedy, the area was expanded to 570,000 square miles, an area almost equal to 20 percent of the continental United States and greater than the combined sizes of Arizona, Nevada, California, Oregon, and Washington. After learning that two or three hydrogen bombs could kill every person in Great Britain and Ireland, Winston Churchill ordered all work on air-raid shelters abandoned. Hiroshima paled in comparison to Bravo, which represented as revolutionary an advance in explosive power over the atomic bomb as the atomic bomb had over the conventional weapons of World War II.[24]

Although President Eisenhower privately ordered a test-ban study, another twenty nuclear tests would be held at Bikini over the next four years, despite the fact that Bravo had rendered the entire atoll uninhabitable, so that logistical and technical operations had to be staged from Enewetak or Navy ships off Bikini.[25] One of the tests, Romeo, three-quarters as big as Bravo, was so powerful that two messboys on a ship 40 miles from ground zero were thrown backward and down a flight of stairs by the impact of the air shock wave. Another, the 1956 Cherokee shot, was the first airdrop by the United States of a thermonuclear weapon. With all the shades of the 1946 Able test, the Air Force missed its target by four miles when the bombardier mistook a lighted island at Bikini for the ground zero site. All the cameras were pointed in the wrong direction, and nearly all the data was lost or useless. Meanwhile, the Zuni shot, detonated several weeks later, vaporized most of the western end of Bikini's Eneman Island.[26] Finally, in November 1958, following twenty-three atomic and hydrogen bomb tests at Bikini, President Eisenhower declared a moratorium on atmospheric nuclear testing, ending the twelve-year nuclear testing program at Bikini. Five years later, the United States and the Soviet Union signed an atmospheric test ban treaty. Meanwhile, the *Lucky Dragon* was rescued from the scrap heap in the early 1970s, restored, and placed in a Tokyo park. In May 1976 a stone monument was unveiled in the park with Aikichi Kuboyama's dying words: "Please make sure that I am the last victim of the bomb."[27]

32

"Bikini and Rongerik Look as Alike as Two Idaho Potatoes"

The Bikinians' odyssey is a sad one. They remained on Rongerik after Operation Crossroads, still homesick for Bikini and still dependent on the Navy. "Bikini was better," Juda told a group of reporters less than two months after the islanders were moved to Rongerik. "It was better because it was our home and our real place." As others nodded tearfully, Juda continued. "We want to go back. The coconuts were larger and the fish were not poisonous, as they are here."[1]

Navy Commodore Ben Wyatt, though, explained to the reporters that the Bikinians' claims were contradicted by a survey of Rongerik the Navy made before the islanders were moved. "Rongerik is in fact bigger and richer than Bikini," Wyatt said. "There are only two kinds of poisonous fish around here and there is plenty of tuna, bonito and other edible fish." The real problem, he said, was quite simple: "What this adds up to is that Rongerik isn't Bikini and they are homesick."[2]

Wyatt was wrong. In fact, the move to Rongerik was ill-conceived and poorly planned. Contrary to the Navy's assertions, Rongerik's land area is one-quarter the size of Bikini's, as is its lagoon. Its life-sustaining pandanus and coconut trees were considerably less productive than Bikini's, and many of the fish in the lagoon were poisonous. Moreover, because the Bikinians thought they would be living on Rongerik for only a short time, they had not bothered to tell the Navy that according to their mythology the atoll was inhabited by an evil spirit that contaminated the lagoon's fish.[3] The press, though, continued to follow the Navy line, and reporters were not permitted access to the Bikinians except in the presence of Navy officials, so the islanders' unhappiness on Rongerik was not taken seriously. The Bikinians, noted the *New York Times*, "will probably be repatriated if they insist on it, though the United States military authorities say they can't see why they should want to: Bikini and Rongerik look as alike as two Idaho potatoes."[4]

The Navy's decision to bring Juda to Bikini to witness the Baker test only increased the islanders' desire to return home. He reported that the coconut trees were still standing and the fish were plentiful. There was little visible damage, and the atoll looked especially fertile, as no food had been harvested in four months. The Bikinians became even more frustrated when they learned that the inhabitants of Enewetak, Wotho, and Rongelap, who had been evacuated for the tests, were repatriated in late July.

The Bikinians rapidly consumed Rongerik's entire supply of food, and its palm trees stopped bearing fruit in August 1946. In late September, five radsafe monitors on a one-week fishing trip stopped to visit the Bikinians on Rongerik. One islander, who identified himself as Pilip, could speak English. Dressed in a white shirt, castoff Navy dungarees, and a pair of surplus boots about six sizes too big, Pilip begged the group for help. "We . . . are very hungry," he said in his halting English. "We . . . have nothing to eat. This is . . . a very poor island. We . . . have not enough coconuts . . . no. For many days now we eat nothing but fish." Juda, speaking through Pilip, asked the same question that he had asked of every visitor: When could his people return home?

"It was no pleasant task to have to inform him that we thought it would be a long time yet," wrote one of the monitors. He and his colleagues tried to explain that the water and fish were still unsafe. The Bikinians did not understand the scientists' explanation of radioactivity (to this day, the word in Marshallese is "poison"), but they caught the gist. Pilip's short response was spoken with sorrow and resignation. "Oh. We very sorry to hear this."[5]

The situation on Rongerik worsened in the following months, and the Bikinians experienced severe food shortages during the winter of 1946–47. When a fire destroyed nearly one-third of the trees on Rongerik's main island in May 1947, the Bikinians were forced to sail by canoe the 18 miles to the neighboring atoll of Rongelap to place their children and elders with relatives and to ask for food. Following the fire, the Navy established a board of investigation to consider resettlement options for the islanders. Over the next two months Juda and several alabs surveyed three possible resettlement sites: Kili, an uninhabited island, and the populated atolls of Ujae and Wotho. In a July 25, 1947, letter to the Navy, the Bikinians announced their decision to move to Ujae, but then added, "Since these [sic] move will be the last move and the place we go to will be our home forever and ever therefore we wish to be removed to an atoll where there are no other people." The Bikinians' sense of helplessness and ambivalence was reflected in the letter's ending: "We will do whatever you'll say."[6] The Navy thereupon took the Bikini leaders to inspect Ujelang, an uninhabited atoll 300 miles southwest of Bikini. The islanders, though, decided to stay on Rongerik, where a doctor reported that they were "visibly suffering from malnutrition."[7]

The Navy board of investigation, at a complete impasse, came to Rongerik in early September. The transcript of its exchange with Juda revealed the islanders' frustration and desperate desire to return home:

> *Q:* They still want to stay [on Rongerik]?
> *A:* Yes.
>
> *Q:* They said they were going to starve here.
> *A:* If the government wants to move us it is okay.
>
> *Q:* It is better to move than stay here and starve.
> *A:* We still like Bikini.
>
> *Q:* Don't you want to move to a better island?
> *A:* Yes.
>
> *Q:* Why do you want to stay on Rongerik?
> *A:* Bikini is close.[8]

There seemed to be no adequate relocation site. Despite the resurvey team's optimistic reports, Bikini was ruled off-limits. Wotho was too small. It and Ujae were inhabited, and resettlement there would cause social problems. Ujelang and Kili, while uninhabited, were far from Bikini. Moreover, Ujelang lacked pandanus and Kili had no lagoon. In late September the Navy board reluctantly recommended resettlement on Ujelang.

Over the next three months the Bikinians became pawns in a series of developments involving the United Nations, the press, and the AEC. In July 1947, Bikini, together with the Marshall Islands and the former League of Nations Japanese Mandate, became part of the UN trusteeship system. The area had been under the U.S. military government since America's liberation of the islands from Japan in 1944. In fact,

Bikini was legally defined as occupied enemy territory during Operation Crossroads.[9]

Toward the end of World War II, there was little doubt that Micronesia would remain under U.S. control; the only debate was whether to annex the islands or place them under the trusteeship system of the new United Nations. United States military leaders urged outright annexation for strategic reasons. Secretary of War Stimson argued that the islands "are not colonies; they are outposts," and he claimed that annexation would be "merely the acquisition by the United States of the necessary bases for the defense of the Pacific for the future world."[10] The emotional appeal was equally strong. "These atolls, these island harbors," said Adm. Ernest King, "will have been paid for by the sacrifice of American blood." Secretary of State Cordell Hull, on the other hand, pointed to America's wartime principle of no territorial aggrandizement, and he urged that Micronesia be made a trusteeship, contending that Russia would use the military's annexation argument as a precedent for its own acquisitions.[11]

After the war, military leaders continued to push for annexation of Micronesia. "We wish to acquire . . . a few miserable islands of insignificant economic value, but won with the precious blood of America's finest sons, to use as future operating bases," declared Admiral Blandy shortly after the announcement of Operation Crossroads. "All that can be raised on most of these islands is a few coconuts, a little taro, and a strong desire to be somewhere else."[12] After lengthy negotiations within the U.S. government and between the United States and the United Nations, the islands became the Trust Territory of the Pacific Islands on July 18, 1947, the only one of eleven UN trusteeships to be designated a strategic trust. Under the Trusteeship Agreement with the United Nations, the United States, as the administering authority, was permitted to fortify the islands and close off parts of them for security purposes. Moreover, the United States reported to and acted under the jurisdiction of the Security Council, where it had veto power.[13]

The Bikinians were now citizens of the new Trust Territory of the Pacific Islands, and their welfare took on a worldwide dimension. Then, in late September, the Navy board's report was leaked to newspaper columnist Harold Ickes, former secretary of the interior, who had resigned from the Truman administration after charging that the president had urged him to commit perjury before a Senate Naval Affairs Committee hearing. Ickes now had the chance to get back at both Truman and the Navy. "The natives are actually and literally dying of starvation," he wrote in his September 29, 1947, syndicated column, "Man to Man." He charged that the Bikinians were "starving and forgotten," and he accused the Navy of "arrogant injustice to a native people." The Bikinians' plight was an "international question," wrote Ickes, and he compared "the assiduous care that the Navy has bestowed upon its experimental animals" with its treatment of the islanders.[14]

The public was outraged. "The Bikini people deserve a lot more than they have been given by the richest country in the world," editorialized the *New York Times.* "The debt can never be fully paid." It urged the Navy to "go out of its way to see that everything is done that can be done to make them comfortable," hoping that "the current publicity will make Navy officials more conscious of their responsibility."[15]

The Navy, concerned about public opinion and possible censure by the UN Trusteeship Council, acted quickly. One week after Ickes's column appeared, it announced that the Bikinians would be moved to Ujelang, and a team of ten Bikini men and twenty Seabees arrived at the atoll on November 22 to begin construction. Amazingly, the Navy had not consulted with the AEC, which announced barely a week later that it had selected Enewetak Atoll as a second site for nuclear testing in the Marshall Islands and that those islanders, not the Bikinians, would be moved to Ujelang! The Enewetakese were moved by Christmas, while the dejected Bikini workers returned to Rongerik.

An anthropologist from the University of Hawaii visited the Bikinians the next month on Rongerik. He found that the community store was stocked with only a 100-pound bag of flour, which was mixed with water into a thin gruel for meals twice a day. A fishing group caught 128 fish, of which 120 were slightly poisonous. Many people ate the fish and, not surprisingly, were afflicted with diarrhea and numbness. The people were starving. They were rationing themselves to one bucketful of water per household a day and were cutting down young palm trees in order to eat the heart of the palm because there was nothing else to eat.[16]

On March 14, 1948, two years and one week after their arrival on Rongerik, the Bikinians were moved off, this time to a temporary camp at Kwajalein. They explored relocation sites again that summer and selected Kili, an island 400 miles south of Bikini. The island was apparently inhabited until it was hit by a typhoon in 1875, after which the German trader Adolf Capelle purchased it for $300 and used it as a copra plantation, as did the Japanese. Kili is fertile, but it has a small land area (less than one-sixth the size of Bikini), no lagoon, and very difficult access.

The Bikinians chose Kili partly out of frustration and anger at their plight. Almost all land in the Marshall Islands is owned by paramount chiefs, or iroij lablabs, who had functioned in the past much like feudal lords, receiving tribute in the form of food and gifts from their subjects who worked their land and protecting them in times of danger. The deprivation and psychological stress the Bikinians experienced on Rong-erik led them to question their relationship with their iroij lablab, Jeimata Kabua, who had not even visited them on Rongerik. One of the strong attractions of Kili was that it was not controlled by any iroij lablab; the island had been public land under the Japanese and had passed to the United States that way. By moving to Kili, the Bikinians effectively rejected Kabua and adopted the United States as their surro-gate iroij lablab.

Even before leaving Kwajalein, though, many Bikinians were con-cerned about the move to Kili and the island's small size and lack of lagoon. Their one overwhelming and persistent desire was to return to Bikini, and they simply could not adjust emotionally to the fact that they could not go home. "The navy is running out of deserted islands on which to settle these unwitting, and perhaps unwilling, nomads of the atomic age," one Navy official told a Honolulu newspaper. "If they do not adjust to Kili," the newspaper commented, "the United States will have a new headache."[17]

Kili remains home to most Bikinians nearly a half-century after Oper-ation Crossroads, and life there has been difficult. Kili is an island, not an atoll. It has neither a lagoon nor sheltered fishing ground, so the skills the people developed for lagoon and ocean life at Bikini were use-less on Kili. Moreover, the island runs parallel to the northeast trade winds, so it has no leeward side and is thus virtually inaccessible by sea from November to May, when trade winds cause heavy surf to pound the shore. Visits by government ships were infrequent and irregular, and at times food supplies on the island ran critically low; in fact, in 1952 the U.S. government had to airdrop emergency rations onto the island.

The drastic change from an atoll existence, with its abundant fish and islands as far as the eye could see, to an isolated island with no lagoon and inaccessible marine resources, took a severe psychological toll on the people. Kili's soil is richer than Bikini's, but the Bikinians were fishermen, not farmers. They never accepted the move to Kili as anything but a tem-porary resettlement and were thus reluctant to adjust fully to life on the island. As one Kili resident lamented, "At Bikini, one could always go to another island, but here it's always the same. Sleep, wake up. Kili. Sleep, wake up. Kili. Again, sleep, wake up. Kili. Kili is a prison."[18]

As conditions on Kili worsened during the 1950s, the Trust Territory Government selected a site on nearby Jaluit Atoll to start a satellite com-munity. In 1956, the U.S. government gave the Bikinians $25,000 (in one-dollar bills) and a $3-million trust fund, which yielded annual pay-ments of about $15 per person. Typhoons in 1957 and 1958 caused extensive crop damage at Kili, sank the islanders' supply boat, and forced the Bikinians on Jaluit to return to Kili.

The Bikinians were completely self-sufficient before 1946, but after years of exile they virtually lost the will to provide for themselves. The Navy, meanwhile, was concerned that the islanders were becoming too dependent on the United States for help. "You must remain as independent as you were before we came," Commodore Wyatt told the Bikinians at Rongerik. "We will help you in every way we can, but you must not depend on us to do everything for you." These same concerns were voiced again during the Bikinians' brief sojourn at Kwajalein. "We don't want to dump the natives on an island where they will have any excuse for asking for more food contributions or another transfer," said one official. This was consistent with the Navy's overall view toward Micronesians, best summarized in a 1947 *Saturday Evening Post* article entitled "Let's Not Civilize These Happy People," written by Rear Adm. Carleton H. Wright, deputy high commissioner of the Trust Territory.[19]

The nuclear nomads of Bikini, though, saw matters differently. They gave up their islands in return for America's promise to care for them. Nearly 40 years after Commodore Wyatt's visit to Bikini, Lore Kessibuki remembered the bargain. "The promise that [Wyatt] made," said Lore under oath in a court deposition, was that "America would feed you and look after you, no matter where you are. Even if you were just out on a sand bar or on the water or on the reef. . . . We would take care of you. We would feed you."[20]

President Eisenhower's 1958 moratorium on atmospheric nuclear testing raised the Bikinians' hope for a return to their atoll, but it was not until 1967 that a blue-ribbon ad hoc AEC committee reviewed the results of a radiological survey of Bikini and declared that resettlement of Bikini would "not offer a significant threat to [the Bikinians'] health and safety."[21] Based on the recommendation of his advisors that "a White House announcement would give much greater visibility to this symbolic act of peace," President Lyndon B. Johnson announced in August 1968 that the Bikinians could return home, and he ordered the atoll rehabilitated and resettled. [22]

The Bikinians on Kili were jubilant at the news, and a group was taken to Bikini several weeks later. Their elation, though, soon turned to shock and sorrow. The idyllic homeland of their memories had disappeared. The coconut trees were gone, and only scrub vegetation remained. On seeing the site of the Bravo shot, where blue water and sand bars were all that remained of parts of several islands, the Bikinians declared that their islands had lost their bones. One leader was so overcome that he wept openly. "It's all changed, it's not the same," one man murmured, while the others nodded silently in agreement.[23]

The resettlement went forward, though, as the first Bikinians returned to their atoll in 1969. They lived there until 1978, when medical tests by U.S. doctors revealed that the people may have ingested the largest amounts of radioactive material of any known population, and they determined that the people had to be moved immediately. What went wrong? The AEC's blue-ribbon panel, in estimating the dose the returning islanders would receive, relied on an earlier 1957 AEC report that assumed a daily consumption of nine or ten grams of coconut, about one-third of a spoonful. "Obviously the people eat much more than that," admitted the AEC's Gordon Dunning, the author of the report. Both he and the AEC panel either ignored or overlooked the typographical error in his report, which put his numbers off by a factor of nearly 100. "We just plain goofed," he said. The AEC was dead wrong in 1967.[24]

History sadly repeated itself in late August 1978, as U.S. ships once again entered Bikini lagoon, and the 139 people on the island packed up their possessions and left. They remain scattered throughout the Marshall Islands, with the largest number of the nearly 2,000 Bikinians still on Kili. Following several lawsuits by the Bikinians against the U.S. government and congressional ratification of a new political relationship between the United States and the Marshall Islands, the Bikinians obtained a 15-year, $75-million settlement of claims against the United States for the taking and use of Bikini and a $110-million trust fund earmarked in part for the radiological cleanup and resettlement of Bikini Atoll.

A group of about thirty Bikini elders flew to Bikini in 1988 to attend a groundbreaking ceremony for the radiological cleanup of the atoll. The old men sang their haunting anthem, composed by Lore Kessibuki in 1946, about drifting on the waves until their return to Bikini. They raised their new flag, which closely resembles the American flag, except for the stars. Unlike America's fifty, Bikini's has only twenty-three, one for each of the atoll's islands, with symbolic gaps for those vaporized by the nuclear tests. "We've learned to dry our tears of sorrow with dollar bills," said Lore at the ceremony. "But money will never take the place of Bikini."[25]

A visit to Bikini today evokes many moods. Bikini Island has the beautiful charm of a remote tropical island, with its palm fronds, sprouting coconuts, and perfectly sloping beach that stretches for miles. From the air, as the eye moves from the necklace of islands toward the center of the lagoon, the color of the water turns from green to turquoise, then aquamarine and finally deep blue. On the northern islands, the silence is almost primeval, broken only by the pounding of the waves and the cries of noddy terns.

The atoll has the air of a house long unoccupied, but also the feel of an old battlefield, of great events that once were. Only a few remains of the test programs are evident on the land. The concrete communications bunker on Eneu, which once had a direct line to the White House, still stands, as do a few other vine-covered, crumbling concrete structures. The only remnant of the officers' club, though, is a stone retaining wall, and only the foundations remain of the bomb assembly building and the detonation and timing bunker, which was pushed off its foundation by the force of the Bravo shot. A close look at the reef shows hundreds of electrical and communications cables running into the lagoon, some of which transmitted the electrical impulses to detonate the bombs tested in the 1950s.

It is Bikini's waters that hide and preserve the atoll's legacy—the rusting hulls of target ships resting eerily on the lagoon's floor. Three miles off Bikini Island, in 180 feet of water, lies the *Saratoga,* victim of Bikini's second bomb. It sits upright on the lagoon floor, the top of its mast just below the water line. Four Navy planes sit ghostlike on her hangar deck—three Helldivers and an Avenger torpedo bomber—with 500-pound bombs stacked on nearby racks. Her antiaircraft guns are in place, facing skyward. Nearly a half century after Operation Crossroads, oil from the gigantic aircraft carrier still seeps slowly to the water's surface, marking the *Saratoga*'s grave.

Northwest of Bikini Island, on Aomen, a barren, windswept island with no trees and barely 200 yards wide, the low horizon is broken by a bulky, two-story bunker rising out of the sand, whose huge concrete slabs collapsed to shield camera equipment milliseconds after the nuclear explosions. This massive structure, miles from nowhere, slowly deteriorating in Bikini Atoll's harsh salt air, seems to call out like Ozymandias, King of Kings: "Look on my works, ye Mighty, and despair!" But nothing else remains. "Round the decay of that colossal wreck, boundless and bare, the lone and level sands stretch far away."

This is the legacy of Bikini.

Appendix

Disposition of Target Vessels at Operation Crossroads

CARRIERS

Independence (CVL-22): Towed to Pearl Harbor and then to Hunters Point (San Francisco) in October 1946. Sunk as target in special tests of new aerial and undersea weapons off San Francisco on January 27, 1951, in 1,000 fathoms.

Saratoga (CV-3): Sunk at Bikini by Baker shot on July 25, 1946.

BATTLESHIPS

Arkansas (BB-33): Sunk at Bikini by Baker shot on July 25, 1946.

Nagato (Japanese): Sunk at Bikini by Baker shot on night of July 29/30, 1946.

Nevada (BB-36): Towed to Kwajalein by USS *Preserver* (ARS-8), decommissioned on August 29, 1946, and then towed to Pearl Harbor. Sunk as target on July 31, 1948, 65 miles southwest of Pearl Harbor following four days of gunfire, bomb, rocket, and torpedo hits from Task Force 12. As of 1993, the USS *Preserver* was still on active duty as a salvage ship, assigned to the Naval Reserve Training Facility at Little Creek outside Norfolk.

New York (BB-34): Towed to Kwajalein by USS *Achomawi* (AFT-148), decommissioned on August 29, 1946, and then towed to Pearl Harbor. Sunk as target on July 8, 1948, 40 miles southwest of Pearl Harbor after an eight-hour pounding by ships and planes using bombs and gunfire in full-scale battle maneuvers with new torpedoes.

Pennsylvania (BB-38): Scuttled off Kwajalein on February 10, 1948.

CRUISERS

Pensacola (CA-23): Towed to Kwajalein and then to Bremerton, Washington, for radiological tests. Sunk as target off Washington coast on November 10, 1948, in 1,400 fathoms.

Prinz Eugen (German): Towed to Kwajalein and attempted to beach at Enubuj Island, but she capsized and sank in shallow water on December 22, 1946 (*New York Times* article indicates date was December 16).

Sakawa (Japanese): Sunk at Bikini by Able shot on July 2, 1946.

Salt Lake City (CA-25): Towed to Bremerton via Pearl Harbor for radiological tests. Sunk by torpedoes in 2,000 fathoms off San Diego on May 25, 1948, after a four-hour bombardment from planes and ships.

DESTROYERS

Anderson (DD-411): Sunk at Bikini by Able shot on July 1, 1946.

Conyngham (DD-371): Steamed from Kwajalein to Pearl Harbor in September 1946, and then to San Francisco area, arriving on October 22, 1946. Scuttled in July 1948 off California coast.

Hughes (DD-410): Beached at Eneu Island following Baker shot on July 26, 1946, and later towed to San Francisco for radiological tests. Sunk as target off Washington coast by air attack on October 16, 1948.

Lamson (DD-367): Sunk at Bikini by Able shot on July 1, 1946.

Mayrant (DD-402): Kept at Kwajalein for radiological tests until sunk there by guns and torpedoes on April 4, 1948.

Mugford (DD-389): Scuttled off Kwajalein on March 22, 1948.

Mustin (DD-413): Sunk by gunfire off Kwajalein on April 18, 1948.

Ralph Talbot (DD-390): Scuttled off Kwajalein on March 8, 1948.

Rhind (DD-404): Scuttled off Kwajalein on March 22, 1948.

Stack (DD-406): Sunk by gunfire from four destroyers off Kwajalein on April 24, 1948.

Trippe (DD-403): Sunk as target off Kwajalein on February 3, 1948.

Wainwright (DD-419): Sunk as target off Kwajalein on July 5, 1948, by Destroyer Division 172.

Wilson (DD-408): Scuttled off Kwajalein on March 8, 1948.

SUBMARINES

Apogon (SS-308): Sunk at Bikini by Baker shot on July 25, 1946.

Dentuda (SS-335): Steamed from Kwajalein to Pearl Harbor in September 1946, and the next month to San Francisco for radiological study. Decommissioned at Mare Island on December 11, 1946, and stationed in the 12th Naval District for training of naval reservists. Sold for scrap on January 20, 1969.

Parche (SS-384): Steamed to Pearl Harbor and then reported to Mare Islands Group 19th Fleet on October 14, 1946. Towed to the naval reserve docks in Oakland in February 1948 and accepted as a naval reserve training ship. Sold for scrap in July 1970.

Pilotfish (SS-386): Sunk at Bikini by Baker shot on July 25, 1946. Salvaged for examination and resunk as a target on October 16, 1948.

Searaven (SS-196): Raised from submerged position on July 29, 1946, after Baker shot. Steamed to Pearl Harbor from Kwajalein and then to San Francisco for radiological study, arriving there on October 22, 1946. Sunk as target off California coast on September 11, 1948.

Skate (SS-305): Towed to Kwajalein by *ATR-40*, then to Pearl Harbor by USS *Fulton* (AS-11), and then to San Francisco by USS *Clamp* (ARS-33). Decommissioned on December 11, 1946, and scuttled off California coast in 515 fathoms on October 4, 1948.

Skipjack (SS-184): Sunk at Bikini by Baker shot on July 25, 1946. Salvaged on September 2, towed to Pearl Harbor, and then to San Francisco. Sunk by aircraft rocket attack on August 11, 1948, off California coast in 700 fathoms.

Tuna (SS-203): Surfaced after Baker shot on July 27, 1946. Steamed to Kwajalein, Pearl Harbor, and then San Francisco. Scuttled off the West Coast on September 24, 1948, in 1,160 fathoms.

ATTACK TRANSPORTS

Banner (APA-60): Scuttled off Kwajalein on February 16, 1948.

Barrow (APA-61): Scuttled off Kwajalein on May 11, 1948.

Bladen (APA-63): Steamed to East Coast, decommissioned at Norfolk on December 26, 1946, and transferred to U.S. Maritime Commission on August 3, 1953.

Bracken (APA-64): Scuttled off Kwajalein on March 10, 1948.

Briscoe (APA-65): Scuttled somewhere in the Marshall Islands on May 6, 1948.

Brule (APA-66): Scuttled off Kwajalein on May 11, 1948.

Butte (APA-68): Scuttled off Kwajalein on May 12, 1948.

Carlisle (APA-69): Sunk at Bikini by Able shot on July 1, 1946.

Carteret (APA-70): Sunk in the Marshall Islands by gunfire of the USS *Toledo* (CA-133) on April 19, 1948.

Catron (APA-71): Sunk in the Marshall Islands by gunfire of the USS *Atlanta* (CL-104) on May 6, 1948.

Cortland (APA-75): Granted radiological clearance in December 1946, decommissioned at Norfolk on December 30, 1946, and transferred to the U.S. Maritime Commission on March 31, 1948. Later sold for scrap.

Crittenden (APA-77): Towed to San Francisco in January 1947. Towed to sea by USS *Tekesta* (ATF-93) and sunk off California coast by explosive tests on October 5, 1948, in 800 fathoms.

Dawson (APA-79): Scuttled off Kwajalein on April 19, 1948, in 2,290 fathoms.

Fallon (APA-81): Beached on Eneu Island on July 27, 1946, after Baker shot and then towed to Kwajalein. Scuttled off Kwajalein on March 10, 1948.

Fillmore (APA-83): Steamed to East Coast, decommissioned at Norfolk on January 24, 1947, and transferred to U.S. Maritime Commission on April 1, 1948.

Gasconade (APA-85): Towed to San Francisco and sunk as target by torpedoes off southern California coast on July 21, 1948, in 1,300 fathoms.

Geneva (APA-86): Steamed to East Coast, decommissioned at Norfolk on January 1, 1947, and received by the U.S. Maritime Commission at James River Reserve Fleet, Lee Hall, Virginia, on April 2, 1948. Transferred to Wilmington (North Carolina) Reserve Fleet in July 1955, and sold for scrap on November 2, 1966.

Gilliam (APA-57): Sunk at Bikini by Able shot on July 1, 1946.

Niagara (APA-87): Steamed to East Coast, arriving at Norfolk on November 23, 1946. After being used to test effects of special conventional explosives in the Chesapeake Bay in 1947–48, was sold for scrap on February 5, 1950, to Northern Metals Company of Philadelphia.

LSTs (LANDING SHIPS, TANK)

LST-52: Sunk off Kwajalein in April 1948 by gunfire of USS *Oakland* (CL-95) in 2,280 fathoms.

LST-125: Deliberately beached before Baker shot, then sunk by gunfire of USS *Fall River* (CA-131) off Bikini on August 14, 1946.

LST-133: Sunk off Kwajalein on May 11, 1948.

LST-220: Sunk off Kwajalein on May 12, 1948.

LST-545: Sunk off Kwajalein on May 12, 1948.
LST-661: Sunk off Kwajalein on July 25, 1948.

LSMs (LANDING SHIPS, MEDIUM)

LSM-60: Destroyed at Bikini as bomb carrier for Baker shot on July 25, 1946.

LCTs (LANDING CRAFT, TANK)

LCT-412: Scuttled off Kwajalein in September 1947.
LCT-414: Sunk by demolition charges at Bikini shortly after Baker shot.
LCT-705: Scuttled off Kwajalein in September 1947.
LCT-746: Scuttled off Kwajalein in March 1947.
LCT-812: Sunk by demolition charges at Bikini shortly after Baker shot.
LCT-816: Scuttled off Kwajalein in June 1947.
LCT-818: Scuttled off Kwajalein in September 1947.
LCT-874: Scuttled off Kwajalein in September 1947.
LCT-1013: Scuttled off Kwajalein in September 1947.
LCT-1078: Scuttled off Kwajalein in September 1947.
LCT-1112: Scuttled off Kwajalein in September 1947.
LCT-1113: Scuttled off Kwajalein in June 1947.
LCT-1114: Capsized by Baker shot and sunk by demolition charges at Bikini on July 30, 1946.
LCT-1175: Sunk at Bikini by Baker shot on July 25, 1946.
LCT-1187: Sunk by demolition charges at Bikini shortly after Baker shot.
LCT-1237: Sunk by demolition charges at Bikini shortly after Baker shot.

AUXILIARIES

ARDC-13: Sunk at Bikini by Baker shot on August 6, 1946.
YO-160: Sunk at Bikini by Baker shot on July 25, 1946.
YOG-83: Beached at Kwajalein on September 23, 1946, and scuttled off Kwajalein on September 16, 1948.

LCIs (LANDING CRAFT, INFANTRY)

LCI-327: Stranded at Bascombe (Mek) Island, Kwajalein, and destroyed there on October 30, 1947.
LCI-329: Scuttled off Kwajalein on March 16, 1948.
LCI-332: Scuttled off Kwajalein in September 1947.
LCI-549: Used at Kwajalein as patrol vessel until June 1948. Granted

final radiological clearance in August 1948 and towed to Port Chicago, California, in January 1949. Sold to the Learner Company in Alameda, California, on August 2, 1949, and delivered on August 19, 1949.

LCI-615: Sold to the Learner Company in Alameda, California, on August 2, 1949, and delivered on August 19, 1949.

LCI-620: Deliberately beached before Baker shot. Towed to sea and sunk off entrance to Bikini lagoon on August 10, 1946.

LCMs (LANDING CRAFT, MECHANIZED)

LCM-1: Fate unknown.
LCM-2: Fate unknown.
LCM-3: Fate unknown.
LCM-4: Sunk at Bikini by Baker shot on July 25, 1946.
LCM-5: Fate unknown.
LCM-6: Sold for scrap in Guam on unknown date.

LCVPs (LANDING CRAFT VEHICLES, PERSONNEL)

LCVP-7: Fate unknown.
LCVP-8: Fate unknown.
LCVP-9: Fate unknown.
LCVP-10: Sunk at Bikini by Baker shot on July 25, 1946.
LCVP-11: Fate unknown.
LCVP-12: Fate unknown.

SOURCES: Capt. A. G. Nelson, memorandum entitled "Crossroads Target Ships," May 25, 1978, DOE/CIC 48703; *Operational Report on Atomic Bomb Tests Able and Baker;* Mooney, ed., *Dictionary of American Naval Fighting Ships;* Delgado et al., *The Archeology of the Atomic Bomb,* 173–76; Berkhouse et al., *Operation Crossroads,* 173–77; Shurcliff, *Technical Report,* pp. 3.61–62; *New York Times.*

Notes

ABBREVIATIONS

AEC   Atomic Energy Commission
AFHRC   Air Force Historical Research Center, Maxwell Air Force Base, Mont-
            gomery, Ala.
CCS   Combined Chiefs of Staff
DASA   Defense Atomic Support Agency Records, National Archives, Washington, D.C.
DOE/CIC   Department of Energy Coordination and Information Center, Las Vegas
FRUS   U.S. Department of State, *Foreign Relations of the United States*
GRDN   General Records of the Department of the Navy, National Archives,
            Washington, D.C.
HSTL   Harry S. Truman Library, Independence, Mo.
JCS   Joint Chiefs of Staff
JPS   Joint Planning Staff
JTF-1   Joint Task Force One
LANL   Los Alamos National Laboratory Records Center/Archives, Los Alamos, N.M.
LC   Library of Congress, Washington, D.C.
MEDR   Manhattan Engineer District Records, National Archives, Washington, D.C.
NA   National Archives, Washington, D.C.
OAB   Operational Archives Branch, Naval Historical Center, Washington
            Navy Yard, Washington, D.C.
RG   Record Group
RJCC   Records of the Joint Committees of Congress, National Archives, Wash-
            ington, D.C.
RMCL   Robert Muldrow Cooper Library, Clemson University, Clemson, S.C.
RNOF   Records of the Naval Operating Forces, National Archives (Suitland
            Branch), Washington, D.C.
RUSS   Records of the U.S. Senate, National Archives, Washington, D.C.
SIA   Smithsonian Institution Archives, Washington, D.C.
TTPI   Trust Territory of the Pacific Islands
USDOE   U.S. Department of Energy Archives, Washington, D.C.
USJCS   U.S. Joint Chiefs of Staff Records, National Archives, Washington, D.C.

Notes appearing in abbreviated form at first reference appear in full in the bibliography.

PROLOGUE

1. *New York Times,* July 1, 1946, pp. 2, 5.
2. One writer has taken the allegory one step further, analogizing the sterility caused by atomic radiation to Moby Dick's destruction of Ahab's leg—"by some unknown, and seemingly inexplicable unimaginable casualty, his ivory limb having been so violently displaced . . . and all but pierced his groin." Melville, *Moby Dick,* chapter 106; Wilson, "Moby Dick and the Atom," 196; Saleh, *Science Fiction Gold,* 99–121.
3. Quoted in Lamont, *Day of Trinity,* 127; Groves, *Now It Can Be Told,* 298.
4. Groves, *Now It Can Be Told,* 296–97; Szasz, *The Day the Sun Rose Twice,* 122.
5. Quoted in Phillips, *The Truman Presidency,* 54.
6. Quoted in Lamont, *Day of Trinity,* 180.
7. Groves, *Now It Can Be Told,* 291–92; Szasz, *The Day the Sun Rose Twice,* 67–78.
8. Rhodes, *The Making of the Atomic Bomb,* 656, 677; Wyden, *Day One,* 208; Newhouse, *War and Peace in the Nuclear Age,* 40; *New York Times,* June 29, 1951, p. 4.
9. Laurence, *Men and Atoms,* 110–11.
10. *New York Times,* September 26, 1945, p. 16.
11. Quoted in Lamont, *Day of Trinity,* 12, 236–37; Groves, *Now It Can Be Told,* 294.
12. Groves to the Secretary of War, memorandum entitled "The Test," July 18, 1945, *FRUS: 1945,* 2:1363, 1374.
13. Quoted in Wyden, *Day One,* 16–17; Szilard, *Leo Szilard,* 185.
14. *New York Times,* August 25, 1946, p. 4.
15. Quoted in Wyden, *Day One,* 19; *New York Herald Tribune,* September 3, 1945, p. 3; *Washington Post,* August 25, 1945, p. 1.
16. Lamont, *Day of Trinity,* 270.
17. *New York Times,* February 16, 1946, p. 15; *New York Herald Tribune,* February 16, 1946, p. 5.
18. Wyden, *Day One,* 325–26.
19. Wallace, *The Price of Vision,* 530.
20. Rosenberg, "U.S. Nuclear Stockpile," 26; Zumwalt, *The Stars and Stripes,* 124.
21. Kauffman oral history transcript, 296.
22. *New York Times,* February 12, 1946, p. 9, and February 17, 1946, sec. 6, p. 8.

CHAPTER 1.

1. As Leslie Groves later noted, "This was the first time in history since the Trojan Horse that a new weapon was to be used without prior testing." Groves, "Some Recollections of July 16, 1945," 59.
2. Kurzman, *Day of the Bomb,* 455–58; Sherwin, *A World Destroyed,* 232.
3. Truman, *Year of Decisions,* 421.

4. *Public Papers of the Presidents, Harry S. Truman (1945)*, 197–98; Smith, *Thank You, Mr. President*, 258.

5. Quoted in Bernstein, "Roosevelt, Truman, and the Atomic Bomb," 61.

6. Donovan, *Conflict and Crisis*, 98.

7. Sherwin, *A World Destroyed*, 209, 234.

8. Truman, *Year of Decisions*, 419; Bernstein, "An Analysis of 'Two Cultures,'" 104.

9. Truman, *Harry S. Truman*, 5; Ferrell, *Off the Record*, 55–56. Secretary of War Henry L. Stimson had removed Kyoto, a shrine of Japanese art and culture, from the list of suggested targets, possibly fearing that its destruction would further alienate the Japanese and drive them into the Russian camp after the war. Stimson and Bundy, *On Active Service in Peace and War*, 625.

10. Diary of Harold Smith, October 5, 1945, HSTL.

11. Quoted in Herken, *The Winning Weapon*, 37.

12. JCS 1477, JCS 471.6 (8-15-45), Sec. 1, USJCS; Director of Ship Material, *Historical Report, Atomic Bomb Tests Able and Baker*, 1:ix.

13. *Hearings on Atomic Energy*, 395 (December 14, 1945); Davis, *Postwar Defense Policy*, 240.

14. Jones, *United States Army in World War II*, 505–8; "Manhattan Engineer District History," reprinted in Brown and MacDonald, eds., *The Secret History of the Atomic Bomb*, 273–76; Groueff, *Manhattan Project*, 346–49; Adm. George F. Hussey, Jr., to Secretary of the Navy, undated memorandum entitled "Chronology of Bureau of Ordnance Contributions to the Atomic Bomb," in *Selected Documents on the Navy's Role on the Development of Atomic Energy (1939–70)*, OAB. Vannevar Bush assigned the Army the task of developing the bomb both out of his "enormous respect" for Secretary of War Stimson and because of his antipathy toward the Navy's attitude on research and development. "When . . . work was first started in my own organization on anti-submarine warfare the Navy . . . stated to us that the Navy needed no help along these lines." Davis, *Postwar Defense Policy*, 338.

15. In fact, as the U.S. Strategic Bombing Survey concluded, strategic bombing had nowhere near the destructive impact on industry that the Army had predicted, and its demoralizing effect on the German population, if any, was never translated into political action. Against Germany, strategic bombings "came too late to have a clearly decisive effect; against Japan they were imposed on an enemy already prostrated by other forms of war." Brodie, *Strategy in the Missile Age*, 107; U.S. Strategic Bombing Survey, *The Effects of Strategic Bombing*; Caraley, *The Politics of Military Unification*, 76–77.

16. Millis, *The War Reports*, 462–64; Arnold, *Third Report of the Commanding General of the Army Air Forces*, excerpts reprinted as "The 36-Hour War," 27–35.

17. *Hearings Before the Senate Committee on Military Affairs on S. 84 and S. 1482*, 352.

18. Strauss, *Men and Decisions*, 208–9.

19. William S. "Deak" Parsons, ordnance division leader at Los Alamos, later served as the weaponeer aboard the *Enola Gay*. Frederick L. Ashworth armed the Nagasaki bomb in flight, and Horacio Rivero, a latecomer to the

Manhattan Project, was Parsons's assistant. Bruins, "U.S. Naval Bombardment Missiles," 126, 152; Hawkins et al., *Project Y*, 111; Rivero interview.

20. Streett to Arnold, letter, August 31, 1945, quoted in Bowen et al., *Air Force Atomic Energy Program*, 1:222–23. Arnold, like Forrestal, acted quickly; within three months he created an office for research and development headed by Curtis LeMay. Bowen et al., *Air Force Atomic Energy Program*, 2:126–27.

21. Quoted in Shurcliff, *Bombs at Bikini*, 10; *Washington Post*, August 26, 1946, p. 16. "Frankly, I never contemplated the widespread tests we had with some of our own ships," McMahon admitted a year later, but "I finally came to the conclusion that, personally, the tests should be held." Speech on September 11, 1946, in Joint Committee on Atomic Energy Files, Box 2 ("Atomic Energy Bill"), RG 128, RJCC. William Shurcliff, the official historian of Operation Crossroads, made no mention in his official history of the Strauss memorandum, which was written nine days before the McMahon speech and which obviously would have had more influence on Forrestal than a speech by a freshman senator.

22. Bowen et al., *Air Force Atomic Energy Program*, 1:161.

23. Arnold, memorandum entitled "Use of Combatant Vessels of the Japanese Navy as Targets," September 18, 1945, JCS 1490/3; King, memorandum entitled "Disposition of Combatant Vessels of the Japanese Navy," August 28, 1945, JCS 1490, RG 218, USJCS; *Operation Crossroads: The Role of the Army Air Forces*, 1:2–3.

24. Shurcliff, *Bombs at Bikini*, 9; Moll, "Operation Crossroads," 62–63; Herken, *The Winning Weapon*, 224; *New York Times*, July 25, 1946, p. 2.

25. JCS 1552/1 (Oct. 16, 1945), JCS 471.6 (10-16-45), Sec. 1, USJCS.

26. Rosenberg, "U.S. Nuclear Stockpile," 26.

27. Shurcliff, *Technical Report*, p. 3.5; *New York Times*, October 28, 1945, p. 35.

28. Howard Peterson to Gen. J. Lawton Collins, memorandum, February 12, 1946, Records of the Office of the Secretary of War, RG 107 (Atomic Energy Folder), NA.

CHAPTER 2.

1. Huntington, *The Common Defense*, 369.

2. Stimson and Bundy, *On Active Service in Peace and War*, 506–18.

3. Ibid., 506. Alfred Thayer Mahan, the father of modern naval warfare, maintained that the enemy of a navy is a navy and that concentrated fleets of battleships would win command of the sea in one decisive naval battle.

4. Quoted in Levine, *Mitchell*, 201.

5. Quoted in Morrison, *Wings over the Seven Seas*, 39.

6. *Hearings on Sundry Legislation Affecting the Naval Establishment 1920–21*, 422, 669; Shiner, *Foulois and the U.S. Army Air Corps*, 9–21.

7. Hurley, *Billy Mitchell*, 49; Sherry, *The Rise of American Air Power*, 29–38.

8. Mitchell, *Winged Defense*, 41.

9. Morrison, *Josephus Daniels*, 137.

10. Quoted in Melhorn, *Two-Block Fox,* 69.

11. Ibid., 70–71.

12. Mitchell, *Winged Defense,* 66–73; Morrison, *Wings over the Seven Seas,* 41–48; Roskill, *Naval Policy between the Wars,* 1:245–48.

13. *Congressional Record,* 67th Cong., 1st sess., 1921, 61, pt. 5: S 4708–9 (daily ed., August 5, 1921).

14. *New York Times,* July 23, 1921, p. 6.

15. Quoted in Ransom, "The Battleship Meets the Airplane," 22–23.

16. Quoted in Coffey, *Hap,* 102.

17. Quoted in Davis, *The Admirals Lobby,* 78.

18. Quoted in Ransom, "The Battleship Meets the Airplane," 24.

19. Melhorn, *Two-Block Fox,* 71.

20. Quoted in Moore, "A Bargain in Preparedness," 827.

21. Quoted in Levine, *Mitchell,* 318.

22. Davis, *The Billy Mitchell Affair,* 239–328.

23. Huie, *The Fight for Air Power,* 7.

24. Ibid., 155.

25. Spector, *Eagle against the Sun,* 12.

CHAPTER 3.

1. Brinkley, *Washington Goes to War,* 88; Prange, *At Dawn We Slept;* Lord, *Day of Infamy.*

2. Hezlet, *Aircraft and Sea Power,* 203–7; Middlebrook and Mahoney, *Battleship.*

3. Weigley, *The American Way of War,* 229–33; Stokesbury, *A Short History of Air Power,* 216, 243.

4. Davis, *Postwar Defense Policy,* 50–53; Yergin, *Shattered Peace,* 201–13.

5. Davis, *Postwar Defense Policy,* 54–63.

6. Stimson and Bundy, *On Active Service in Peace and War,* 519.

7. *New York Times,* May 12, 1944, p. 8.

8. Ibid., August 25, 1945, p. 1.

9. Quoted in Albion, *Makers of Naval Policy,* 601.

10. *New York Times,* November 10, 1945, p. 1.

11. Quoted in Huntington, *The Common Defense,* 369.

12. Ferrell, ed., *Dear Bess,* 462.

13. Quoted in Clifford, *Counsel to the President,* 146.

14. *First Report of the Secretary of Defense, 1948,* 141; *Second Report of the Secretary of Defense for the Fiscal Year 1949,* 218; Howarth, *To Shining Sea,* 476.

15. Quoted in Yergin, *Shattered Peace,* 215.

16. Quoted in Hagan, *This People's Navy,* 281, 308. "It is being assumed publicly that the President has become a partisan of the Army against the Navy," wrote George Elsey, the assistant naval aide in the White House, to Clark Clifford, Truman's new naval aide, in late 1945. Truman "developed prejudices against the Navy which cause him to disregard naval wishes," wrote Elsey, who believed that the president "will force the Navy into a sin-

gle Department of Defense which will be dominated by the Army and the Air Forces." Box 82 (Unification Folder), Papers of George M. Elsey, HSTL.

17. Quoted in Albion, *Makers of Naval Policy,* 603.

18. *Congressional Record,* 79th Cong., 1st sess., 1945, 91, pt. 8: H 10146 (daily ed., October 29, 1945).

19. *Composition of the Postwar Navy,* 1164.

20. Ibid., 1165–66; Herken, *The Winning Weapon,* 203.

21. *Composition of the Postwar Navy,* 1164, 1168–69.

22. *House Report No. 1107,* 79th Cong., 1st sess., p. 3; Hagan, *This People's Navy,* 335.

23. "For its time, the Truman administration was unusually leaky, partly because some of its senior figures feuded with a degree of hostility seen only occasionally since. . . . Bromley Smith, a State Department diplomat . . . recalled a time when he was Acheson's special assistant for leaks to the press. His only function, he said, was to leak stories to the newspapers." Newhouse, *War and Peace in the Nuclear Age,* 70.

24. *New York Times,* August 25, 1945, p. 1; *New York Herald Tribune,* October 24, 1945, p. 1.

25. *New York Times,* October 24, 1945, p. 4.

26. Ibid., November 16, 1945, p. 1, and December 11, 1945, p. 3.

27. Shurcliff, *Technical Report,* p. 3.23.

28. JPS 7705 (December 17, 1945), JCS 471.6 (10-16-45), Sec. 1, USJCS.

29. JCS 1552/5 (December 22, 1945), 1552/6 (December 29, 1945), CCS 471.6 (10-16-45), Sec. 1, USJCS.

30. Forrestal and Royall to Truman, memorandum, January 8, 1946, JCS 471.6 (8-15-45), Sec. 2, RG 218, USJCS, DOE/CIC 33020.

31. Shurcliff, *Bombs at Bikini,* 14–15.

32. Blandy, "Atomic Test Case," 39.

33. *Thirteenth Semiannual Report of the Atomic Energy Commission,* 80.

34. Transcript of telephone call from Capt. Richard Larkin to Commander Ashworth, December 19, 1945, p. 2, LANL; Rivero interview.

35. *New York Times,* January 14, 1946, p. 1.

36. Ibid., January 16, 1946, p. 1.

37. Shurcliff, *Bombs at Bikini,* 27; William S. Parsons to Shurcliff, memorandum entitled "Technical History of Operation Crossroads," January 7, 1947, Box 6, Rivero Folder, RG 38, OAB.

38. *New York Times,* January 25, 1946, p. 1.

39. *New Yorker,* July 27, 1946, 12.

40. Commodore William S. Parsons to Dr. Norris E. Bradbury, memorandum entitled "Possible Tests of Atomic Bombs against Naval Vessels," October 26, 1945, p. 2, LANL; Blandy, "Atomic Test Case," 39.

41. JCS 1552/1 (Oct. 16, 1945), JCS 471.6 (10-16-45), Sec. 1, USJCS; *Time,* January 28, 1946, 24; *Honolulu Star-Bulletin,* June 10, 1946, p. 3. Rivero recalled that the Interior Department's Fish and Wildlife Service ruled out the Galapagos because of its many rare species of birds and other animals. Rivero interview.

42. Smith, *A Peril and a Hope,* 566–67.

43. Ashworth interview.
44. Bowen et al., *Air Force Atomic Energy Program,* 1:164.
45. Shurcliff, *Bombs at Bikini,* 17. Bikini was selected as the site on December 21. G. K. Hartmann, memorandum entitled "Conference in Op-06 held on December 21, 1945, Concerning Atomic Bomb Tests—Notes On," December 27, 1945, p. 1, LANL. The formal recommendation to select Bikini was made by Blandy on January 21, but fishing industry spokesmen who were consulted expressed fear that the explosions would kill millions of fish, including whales and tuna, and thus cripple fishing activities throughout the Pacific. Two days later, however, the Fish and Wildlife Service of the U.S. Department of the Interior endorsed Blandy's choice of Bikini, reporting that it was not a spawning ground for West Coast tuna, that no danger to whales existed, and that the area was not of commercial importance for any kind of fish. Shurcliff, *Technical Report,* p. 4.3; Shurcliff, *Bombs at Bikini,* 20; *Hearings on Atomic Energy,* 459–60 (January 24, 1946).
46. Hope, "So This Is Peace," 119.

CHAPTER 4.

1. Perhaps to convey the sense of a calm and idyllic tropical setting, or simply because "south" seems warmer than "north," writers have consistently—and erroneously—placed Bikini and the U.S. nuclear tests in the South Pacific. James Michener's 1948 Pulitzer Prize–winning stories, *Tales of the South Pacific,* and the hit Broadway musical based on his book, *South Pacific,* only reinforced the stereotype. Even a popular Japanese song of the 1930s referred to a Marshallese sweetheart in the South Seas. Peattie, *Nanyo,* 216. No part of the Marshall Islands is located south of the equator.
2. Freeman, ed., *Geography of the Pacific,* 28–31. The word *atoll* is derived from *adal* or *atolu* (reef) in Malayalam, spoken along the southwestern coast of India, used to describe the Maldives Islands in the Indian Ocean. Gardiner, *Coral Reefs and Atolls,* 16–17; Bryan, "Life in the Marshall Islands," 30.
3. Quoted in Trumbull, *Paradise in Trust,* 38.
4. Streck, "Interim Report," p. D 31.
5. Parry, *The Age of Reconnaissance,* 41–42; Parry, *The Discovery of the Sea,* 71–75.
6. Morison, *The European Discovery of America,* 467.
7. Hezel, *The First Taint of Civilization,* 17.
8. Tobin, "The Resettlement of the Enewetak People," 15. At the instigation of the islanders, the spelling of the atoll was changed in the 1970s from Eniwetok to Enewetak. Another spelling change has seen Bikini's Enyu Island become Eneu.
9. von Chamisso, *A Voyage around the World,* xii–xiv.
10. Hines, *Proving Ground,* 29–30; von Chamisso, *A Voyage around the World,* 20.
11. Dodge, *New England and the South Seas,* 252.

12. The composer Nikolai Andreyevich Rimsky-Korsakov followed his uncle's path and joined the Russian navy before turning to music. Rimsky-Korsakov, *My Musical Life,* 25–47.

13. von Kotzebue, *A New Voyage Round the World,* 2:275–76.

14. *New York Times,* January 25, 1946, p. 4.

15. von Chamisso, *A Voyage around the World,* 79, 87.

16. Darwin, *The Structure and Distribution of Coral Reefs,* 85.

17. Anderson, *Melville in the South Seas,* 243–52.

18. Quoted in Mason, "Relocation of the Bikini Marshallese," 20.

19. Quoted in ibid., 21–22.

20. Ibid., 27–33; Richard, *United States Naval Administration,* 3:507.

21. Hezel, *The First Taint of Civilization,* 199.

22. Firth, "German Firms in the Pacific Islands, 1857–1914," 8–17; Brown, "Germany, Spain and the Caroline Islands," 165–69.

23. Grenville, ed., *The Major International Treaties,* 63.

24. Peattie, *Nanyo,* 230–56.

25. Morison, *Aleutians, Gilberts and Marshalls,* 225–81.

26. Spector, *Eagle against the Sun,* 267–73; Morison, *Aleutians, Gilberts and Marshalls,* 282–304, 315–32.

27. Heinl and Crown, *The Marshalls.*

28. Morison, *Aleutians, Gilberts and Marshalls,* 313; Atoll Commander to Commander Forward Area, Central Pacific, memorandum, April 14, 1944, p. 2; War Diary (T.U. 57.10.8) of Lt. J. B. Swann, Jr., Commanding Officer of USS LST #23; Marine Corps Maj. R. P. Felker to the Atoll Commander, Navy 3233, memorandum entitled "Report of Reconnaissance Conducted during Period 27 March–6 April," April 6, 1944; A. H. Colyer, Civil Affairs Officer, Roi Island (Kwajalein Atoll), memorandum entitled "Reconnaissance Trip—Bikini—Report on," April 10, 1944, Document No. 12453, Chief of Naval Operations, OAB.

The four contemporaneous reports on the occupation of Bikini are contradictory. Two indicate that the Americans killed the Japanese, while the other two say the Japanese committed suicide. Two Bikini elders confirmed the suicide reports in sworn depositions. Kilon Bauno, deposition, March 21, 1985, pp. 5–6; Lore Kessibuki, deposition, March 21, 1985, pp. 4–5.

CHAPTER 5.

1. Graybar, "The Buck Rogers of the Navy," 335–36; Graybar, "Bikini Revisited," 119; Blandy, "Possible Improvements in Our Gunnery Training," 1696–1702; Cope, *Command at Sea,* 159–74; *New Yorker,* July 17, 1946, 12.

2. Undated press release from Navy Department Incentive Division, "Admiral Blandy and the Development of Naval Ordnance," Blandy papers, OAB; *New York Times,* February 10, 1946, sec. 6, pp. 18, 45; Lenihan, *USS Arizona Memorial,* 40–46; Fahrney, "The History of Pilotless Aircraft and Guided Missiles," 241–44, 265–68.

3. Reynolds, *Famous American Admirals*, 37.

4. Furer, *Administration of the Navy Department in World War II*, 75–76, 987; Pfau, *No Sacrifice Too Great*, 66; *Washington Post*, December 7, 1942, p. 3; *New Yorker*, July 27, 1946, 12.

5. Furer, *Administration of the Navy Department in World War II*, 319–26; Christman, *Sailors, Scientists, and Rockets*, 1:179–95; Rowland and Boyd, *U.S. Navy Bureau of Ordnance in World War II*, 8–12, 469.

6. Forrestal, remarks before Navy Industrial Association, September 17, 1946, DOE/CIC 100964.

7. Albion and Connery, *Forrestal and the Navy*, 61; Steiner, *Bernard Brodie and the Foundations of American Nuclear Strategy*, 2; *Newsweek*, November 10, 1941, 40.

8. *Congressional Record*, 78th Cong., 1st sess., 1943, 89, pt. 10: A2552 (daily ed., May 24, 1943).

9. Friedman, *U.S. Battleships*, 353–56; *New York Times*, March 20, 1943, p. 1; Blandy to Secretary of the Navy, memorandum entitled "Final Report of Present Chief of Bureau of Ordnance," December 9, 1943, pp. 22, 24, Blandy papers, OAB.

10. Strauss oral history transcript.

11. Blair, *Silent Victory*, 1:275–77; Lockwood, *Sink 'Em All*, 85–86; Lockwood, *Down to the Sea in Subs*, 277–96.

12. *New York Times*, February 10, 1946, sec. 6, p. 18.

13. Quoted in Spector, *Eagle against the Sun*, 496–97.

14. Quoted in Costello, *The Pacific War*, 540.

15. LeMay and Yenne, *Superfortress*, 108.

16. Quoted in Buell, *The Quiet Warrior*, 319.

17. Spector, *Eagle against the Sun*, 496.

18. Quoted in Wheeler, *A Special Valor*, 348; Newcomb, *Iwo Jima*, 80–86.

19. Ross, *Iwo Jima*, 54.

20. Spector, *Eagle against the Sun*, 499; Wheeler, *A Special Valor*, 406.

21. Strauss, *Men and Decisions*, 135.

22. "Most Americans are profoundly ignorant of the military . . . history of their own country," Blandy told one audience during the war. "How many Americans, for example, know that in the War of 1812 we were decisively defeated on the seas or know why we were defeated? We read only of our glorious frigate victories and think those victories won the war for us, when as a matter of fact they counted scarcely at all in the total picture." Blandy, "Research for War," reprinted in *Congressional Record*, 78th Cong., 1st sess., 1943, 89, pt. 10: A2552 (daily ed., May 24, 1943); Blandy, "Command Relations in Amphibious Warfare," 569–72; M. Pierre Malaval, "Study of Transverse Resistance of Cylindrical Tubes," translated by W. H. P. Blandy (n.d.), Blandy papers, OAB; Cope, *Command at Sea*, 163–65.

23. *Honolulu Advertiser*, August 1, 1945, p. 3.

24. Strauss, *Men and Decisions*, 132, 135.

25. *Washington Star*, April 19, 1942, Magazine Section, p. 4; *New York Times*, January 14, 1946, p. 1, and February 10, 1946, sec. 6, p. 18.

26. *New York Times,* February 10, 1946, sec. 6, p. 45; Palmer, *Origins of the Maritime Strategy,* 7.

27. Commander, JTF-1, *Operational Report,* p. I-(B)-2; Daly, "Crossroads at Bikini," 66.

28. JTF-1, "Off the Record" Conference with the Press, April 26, 1946, pp. 1–2, Box 8 (Operation Crossroads), Callan papers, LC.

29. Gerrard-Gough and Christman, *The Grand Experiment at Inyokern,* 2:353; Blandy, "Final Report of Present Chief of Bureau of Ordnance," 19, Blandy papers, OAB.

30. *Honolulu Star-Bulletin,* May 19, 1946, p. 3. *New York Times,* February 10, 1946, sec. 6, p. 18; June 23, 1946, sec. 4, p. 10; and January 13, 1954, p. 31. *Newsweek,* July 1, 1946, 21.

31. Hoopes interview.

CHAPTER 6.

1. Quoted in McCullough, *Truman,* 372.

2. *FRUS: 1945,* 5:822.

3. Quoted in Gaddis, *The Long Peace,* 26.

4. Quoted in Harriman and Abel, *Special Envoy to Churchill and Stalin,* 444.

5. Morgan, *FDR,* 761–62.

6. *New York Times,* June 24, 1941, p. 7.

7. Wallace, *The Price of Vision,* 451, 502; Truman, *Year of Decisions,* 15.

8. Diary of Henry L. Stimson (hereafter Stimson diary), June 19, 1945, Yale University, New Haven; Isaacson and Thomas, *The Wise Men,* 342.

9. Stimson and Bundy, *On Active Service in Peace and War,* 639.

10. Ibid., 641, 644–45.

11. Quoted in Isaacson and Thomas, *The Wise Men,* 181.

12. Stimson diary, September 12, 1945.

13. Bundy, *Danger and Survival,* 136–37.

14. Forrestal, *The Forrestal Diaries,* 94–96; Maddox, *From War to Cold War,* 146–47.

15. Quoted in Yergin, *Shattered Peace,* 135.

16. *Public Papers of the Presidents, Harry S. Truman (1945),* 405–6.

17. Truman, *Year of Decisions,* 509; McCullough, *Truman,* 474; Leffler, *A Preponderance of Power,* 104–6.

18. Ward, "James F. Byrnes and the Paris Conference," 59.

19. Quoted in Leffler, *A Preponderance of Power,* 39.

20. "W. B.'s Book," September 24, 1945, Byrnes papers, RMCL.

21. Kennan, *Memoirs, 1925–1950,* 287; *FRUS: 1945,* 2:59–61; Gaddis, *The United States and the Origins of the Cold War,* 263–66.

22. *Public Papers of the Presidents, Harry S. Truman (1945),* 434, 437.

23. Stettinius, *The Diaries of Edward R. Stettinius, Jr.,* 439.

24. *New York Times,* December 31, 1945, p. 4; Gaddis, *The United States and the Origins of the Cold War,* 277–81.

25. Ferrell, ed., *Dear Bess,* 522; Wallace, *The Price of Vision,* 490.

26. Forrestal, *The Forrestal Diaries*, 124.

27. Truman, *Year of Decisions*, 551–52. When the letter was first published in 1952, Byrnes, who had by now broken politically with the president, denied that Truman had ever read it to him. Truman did have a habit of drafting speeches and writing letters that he would later file and never deliver. McCullough, *Truman*, 480; Ferrell, *Off the Record*, 100–102.

28. Quoted in Herken, *The Winning Weapon*, 39.

29. Isaacson and Thomas, *The Wise Men*, 326; *Congressional Record*, 79th Cong., 1st sess., 1945, 91, pt. 8: 11086 (daily ed., November 28, 1945).

30. Leffler, *A Preponderance of Power*, 101.

31. Yergin, *Shattered Peace*, 166–67; Isaacson and Thomas, *The Wise Men*, 349–50; Forrestal, *The Forrestal Diaries*, 134–35.

32. Quoted in Morris, *Iron Destinies, Lost Opportunities*, 26.

33. Kennan, *Memoirs, 1925–1950*, 294–95, 547–59.

34. *FRUS: 1946*, 7:413–15.

35. *New York Times*, March 6, 1946, p. 4.

36. Alperovitz, *Atomic Diplomacy*.

37. Blackett, *Fear, War and the Bomb*, 139.

38. McCullough, *Truman*, 444; Harriman and Abel, *Special Envoy to Churchill and Stalin*, 490.

39. Graybar, "The 1946 Atomic Bomb Tests," 888–907.

40. Quoted in Hershberg, *James B. Conant*, 267.

41. Joint Chiefs of Staff to Bernard M. Baruch, memorandum, June 5, 1946, "Atomic" Series (8-15-45), Sec. 3, USJCS.

CHAPTER 7.

1. *New York Times*, October 24, 1945, p. 4.

2. Ibid., February 17, 1946, sec. 6, p. 8. The article and drawing bore an eerie resemblance to illustrations in London newspapers in 1903 showing battleships in midair, which were based on the predictions of a British scientist who calculated that the energy in one gram of radium could toss the British Navy's entire fleet several thousand feet in the air. Weart, *Nuclear Fear*, 25.

3. *New York Times*, February 12, 1946, p. 9.

4. Ibid., April 7, 1946, p. 10.

5. *Boston Herald*, June 11, 1946, p. 7. Johns Hopkins authorities announced that the seismologist was a student, not a professor, and "of Soviet origin." In any case, they added, the university did not share his views. *Newsweek*, July 1, 1946, 20.

6. *New York Herald Tribune*, February 24, 1946, p. 6.

7. Moll, "Operation Crossroads," 64; Daly, "Crossroads at Bikini," 68.

8. Blandy, speech before the American Red Cross Chapter at the Bellevue-Stratford Hotel, Philadelphia, February 21, 1946, p. 4, Box 8 (Operation Crossroads), Callan papers, LC; Blandy, speech on *New York Herald Tribune* Youth Forum, April 13, 1946, DOE/CIC 100170; *New York Herald Tribune*, April 15, 1946, p. 36; "At the Crossroads," 8.

9. *Newsweek*, May 6, 1946, 58.

10. *Honolulu Star-Bulletin*, March 16, 1946, p. 1.

11. *New York Times*, April 19, 1946, p. 9.

12. *Atomic Energy, Hearings on H.R. 4280*, pp. 106–7 (October 9, 1945); Lawrence papers, Carton 22, Folder 31, University of California at Berkeley.

13. Quoted in Smith, *A Peril and a Hope*, 140.

14. *New York Herald Tribune*, October 24, 1945, p. 9; November 8, 1945, p. 8; and November 9, 1945, p. 11.

15. Hewlett and Anderson, *The New World*, 435–39; *New York Herald Tribune*, October 27, 1945, p. 6.

16. Truman to the Secretary of the Navy and the Secretary of War, letter, November 28, 1945, Records of the Secretary of the Navy, Double Zero File, Box 3, OAB; Truman, *Years of Trial and Hope*, 4–5; Herken, *The Winning Weapon*, 129–34.

17. *Bulletin of the Atomic Scientists* (March 1, 1946): 5.

18. Lawren, *The General and the Bomb*, 282–83.

19. Groves, *Now It Can Be Told*, 390, 392.

20. Hewlett and Anderson, *The New World*, 449–50.

21. *New York Times*, February 28, 1946, p. 12.

22. Herken, *The Winning Weapon*, 133.

23. For thorough accounts of the debate on the May-Johnson and McMahon bills, see Smith, *A Peril and a Hope*, 365–436; and Hewlett and Anderson, *The New World*, 428–55, 482–530.

24. *Bulletin of the Atomic Scientists* (February 15, 1946): 1.

25. *New York Herald Tribune*, February 8, 1946, p. 8.

26. *New York Times*, February 17, 1946, p. 32.

27. Wallace, *The Price of Vision*, 545; Wallace to Truman, memorandum entitled "Naval Atomic Bomb Tests," February 6, 1946, Matthew Connelly MSS, HSTL; *New York Times*, March 13, 1946, p. 6.

28. Patterson to Truman, letter, February 12, 1946; Truman to Secretary of Navy and Secretary of War, memorandum, February 8, 1946; Forrestal to Truman, memorandum, February 11, 1946, Matthew Connelly MSS, HSTL.

29. Dewey suggested at one point in their talk that another problem with the tests was the "fact that every little politician thinks that it's his duty to criticize the army and navy. . . . When you get fellows who are all disturbed because you're going to blow up the battleship that carries the name of my state you're getting down into human relations." Excerpts from telephone conversation between Forrestal and Dewey, February 4, 1946, File No. 39-1-37, RG 80, GRDN.

30. Ayers, *Truman in the White House*, 131.

31. Potter, *Nimitz*, 423; *Time*, February 25, 1946, 24; *New York Herald Tribune*, February 14, 1946, p. 18.

32. Memorandum re: "Atomic Bomb Tests," February 13, 1946, Forrestal papers, Princeton University, Princeton.

33. *New York Times*, February 20, 1946, p. 8; Wallace, *The Price of Vision*, 551. Another civilian advisor being considered was Robert M. Hutchins,

chancellor of the University of Chicago, but Truman was opposed and Hutchins's name was dropped. Notes on cabinet meeting of February 15, 1946, Box 19, Patterson papers, LC. In addition to Dewey and Compton, the Cabinet decided on February 15 to select William F. Gibbs, a ship architect, Dr. Robert G. Sproul of the University of California, and J. Robert Oppenheimer. Cabinet meeting, Friday, February 15, 1946, Matthew Connelly MSS, HSTL; Patterson to the President, memorandum, February 15, 1946, Official File, HSTL. Only Dewey and Compton accepted their appointments.

34. *New York Times,* April 11, 1946, p. 15.
35. Transcript of telephone conversation between Oppenheimer and "Will," May 27, 1946, Byrnes papers, RMCL. Although he directed the most top-secret program of the war, Oppenheimer was considered a security risk because of his past associations with Communists. His first wife, Kitty, was a member of the Communist party, as was his brother Frank and his wife. Oppenheimer's telephone and office had been bugged since his days at Los Alamos. Larsen, *Oppenheimer and the Atomic Bomb,* 62–63.
36. Goodchild, *J. Robert Oppenheimer,* 180. Ironically, Edward Condon suggested to McMahon in February 1946 that Baruch be considered as a possible chairman for a civilian review board for Operation Crossroads. E. U. Condon to McMahon, memorandum, February 14, 1946, Senate Special Committee on Atomic Energy, 79th Cong., Box 14, RG 46, RUSS.
37. Lilienthal, *The Atomic Energy Years,* 30; Acheson, *Present at the Creation,* 154.
38. Ferrell, *Off the Record,* 87; Ferrell, ed., *Dear Bess,* 526. On his appointment sheet for September 5, 1945, Truman listed Baruch's brother, Herman B. Baruch, as "Flatterer . . . Conniver like his Brother." Ferrell, *Off the Record,* 64. Truman, who referred to Baruch as "that old goat," told an aide that the only way ever to make Baruch happy was to consult him publicly. Clifford, *Counsel to the President,* 139.
39. Coit, *Mr. Baruch,* 564; Truman, *Years of Trial and Hope,* 7–8; Grant, *Bernard M. Baruch,* 306.
40. Lilienthal, *The Atomic Energy Years,* 43.
41. Herken, *The Winning Weapon,* 161; Lilienthal, *The Atomic Energy Years,* 32, 43.
42. Lilienthal, *The Atomic Energy Years,* 42–43. One of Oppenheimer's biographers theorizes that Oppenheimer hoped that his refusal to join Baruch's team would lead Truman to fire Baruch and replace him with someone like Vannevar Bush. Michelmore, *The Swift Years,* 129.
43. J. Edgar Hoover to Byrnes, May 23, 1946, "Atomic" folder, Byrnes papers, RMCL.
44. Herken, *The Winning Weapon,* 167–68. Baruch had already made this point publicly. *New York Times,* March 19, 1946, p. 1.
45. Blandy, speech, February 21, 1946, Box 8, Callan papers, LC; Blandy, "Sea Forces," 359.
46. J. Edgar Hoover to George E. Allen, letter, May 29, 1946, President's Secretary's File, HSTL.

CHAPTER 8.

1. Smith, *A Peril and a Hope,* 358; Schapsmeier and Schapsmeier, *Dirksen of Illinois,* 54–64; McCullough, *Truman,* 315.
2. McCullough, *Truman,* 470; Halberstam, *The Fifties,* 134.
3. *Congressional Record,* 79th Cong., 2d sess., 1946, 92, pt. 1: S 624 (daily ed., January 31, 1946).
4. *Hearings on House Joint Resolution 307,* 2422, 2430–31 (January 29 and 30, 1946); *Washington Evening Star,* January 29, 1946, p. 3; *New York Herald Tribune,* March 11, 1946, p. 5.
5. *Hearings on Atomic Energy,* 394–95 (December 14, 1945).
6. *New York Times,* January 30, 1946, p. 12; *Time,* June 3, 1946, 30.
7. Vandenberg, *Private Papers of Senator Vandenberg,* 167.
8. *New York Times,* January 24, 1946, p. 1; *Washington Evening News,* January 18, 1946, p. 3.
9. *Congressional Record,* 79th Cong., 2d sess., 1946, 92, pt. 1: H 2117–19 (daily ed., March 11, 1946); Hewlett and Duncan, *Nuclear Navy,* 23.
10. *Congressional Record,* 79th Cong., 2d sess., 1946, 92, pt. 1: H 2126, 2119 (daily ed., March 11, 1946).
11. Ibid., H 2119, 2125–26.
12. Ibid.; *New York Times,* March 12, 1946, p. 17.
13. *Congressional Record,* 79th Cong., 2d sess., 92, pt. 1: H 2120–22, 2126–27 (daily ed., March 11, 1946).
14. *New York Times,* April 17, 1946, p. 5; JTF-1, "Off the Record" Conference, Box 8, Callan papers, LC.
15. *Hearings on House Joint Resolution 307,* 2414 (January 29, 1946); Delgado et al., *The Archeology of the Atomic Bomb,* 21.
16. *Philadelphia Inquirer,* July 1, 1946, p. 3.
17. Blandy, speech before the Red Cross, February 21, 1946, p. 6, Box 8 (Operation Crossroads), Callan papers, LC.
18. *New York Times,* April 17, 1946, p. 5; *New York Herald Tribune,* April 15, 1946, p. 36.
19. *Congressional Record,* 79th Cong., 1st sess., 1945, 91, pt. 8: H 11085–86 (daily ed., November 28, 1945).
20. *Congressional Record,* 79th Cong., 2d sess., 1946, 92, pt. 1: H 2127–28 (daily ed., March 11, 1946); *New York Times,* March 12, 1946, p. 17.
21. *New York Times,* March 13, 1946, p. 6; *Congressional Record,* 79th Cong., 2d sess., 1946, 92, pt. 1: H 2130–31, 2118, 2125 (daily ed., March 11, 1946).
22. *New York Times,* March 20, 1946, p. 10.

CHAPTER 9.

1. *Bulletin of the Atomic Scientists* (March 1947): 70; Herken, *The Winning Weapon,* 111, 359.
2. Sherwin, *A World Destroyed,* 202; Smith, "Behind the Decision to Use the Atomic Bomb," 296.

3. Herken, *The Winning Weapon,* 359; Ermenc, *Atomic Bomb Scientists Memoirs,* 248.

4. *Newsweek,* December 3, 1945, 42; *Bulletin of the Atomic Scientists* (December 10, 1945): 1; Boyer, *By the Bomb's Early Light,* 51, 63. The atomic scientists' movement is described in detail in Smith, *A Peril and a Hope,* and Boyer, *By the Bomb's Early Light,* 49–106.

5. Lerner, *Actions and Passions,* 260; Swing broadcast of October 19, 1945, Swing papers, LC; Smith, *A Peril and a Hope,* 171.

6. Quoted in Kevles, *The Physicists,* 375–76.

7. *Philadelphia Record,* November 9, 1945, p. 32; *New York Times,* August 9, 1945, p. 8.

8. *Time,* November 19, 1945, 21; Michelmore, *The Swift Years,* 123.

9. Boyer, *By the Bomb's Early Light,* 62; Alsop and Alsop, *We Accuse!* 6.

10. Kurzman, *Day of the Bomb,* 107–9.

11. Goodchild, *J. Robert Oppenheimer,* 56–57.

12. Lilienthal, *The Atomic Energy Years,* 217–18.

13. Groves, *Now It Can Be Told,* 140; Herken, *The Winning Weapon,* 359.

14. Quoted in Royale, *The Story of J. Robert Oppenheimer,* 141; Lawren, *The General and the Bomb,* 260–62.

15. *New York Times,* December 11, 1945, p. 3.

16. *New York Herald Tribune,* February 3, 1946, sec. 2, p. 2, and February 28, 1946, p. 12.

17. *New York Times,* September 22, 1945, p. 3, and November 8, 1945, p. 4; *Hearings on Atomic Energy,* 61–62, 64 (November 29, 1945).

18. *Honolulu Star-Bulletin,* March 23, 1946, p. 4.

19. *FRUS: 1945,* 2:61–62.

20. Nitze interview; Boyer, "The Fences Are Gone," 452.

21. Goodchild, *J. Robert Oppenheimer,* 180; Donovan, *Conflict and Crisis,* 97; Warnke interview.

22. Bundy, *Danger and Survival,* 173.

23. *New York Times,* January 31, 1946, p. 8; *New York Herald Tribune,* January 31, 1946, p. 4.

24. *Life,* July 1, 1946, 41.

25. Ridenour, "Bikini: What Can It Prove?" 14.

26. *Honolulu Star-Bulletin,* March 4, 1946, p. 6.

27. *Bulletin of the Atomic Scientists* (May 15, 1946): 7.

28. *Time,* February 25, 1946, 24.

29. *Bulletin of the Atomic Scientists* (February 15, 1946): 1.

30. Shurcliff, *Bombs at Bikini,* 2.

31. *Bulletin of the Atomic Scientists* (February 15, 1946): 1, 11; (May 15, 1946): 7.

32. *Honolulu Advertiser,* June 19, 1946, p. 2.

33. *New York Herald Tribune,* February 20, 1946, p. 11.

CHAPTER 10.

1. Wallace, *The Price of Vision,* 565.

2. *Operation Crossroads: The Role of the Army Air Forces,* 99–101.

3. Wallace, *The Price of Vision*, 565.
4. Memorandum for the president re: "Atomic Bomb Tests," March 21, 1946, Forrestal papers, Princeton University.
5. Cabinet meeting, Friday, March 22, 1946, Matthew Connelly MSS, HSTL; Wallace, *The Price of Vision*, 565; Forrestal, *The Forrestal Diaries*, 150.
6. Notes for March 22, 1946, Papers of Eben A. Ayers, HSTL; diary of Charlie Ross, March 23, 1946 (hereafter Ross diary), Box 21, Ross papers, HSTL; *New York Herald Tribune*, March 23, 1946, p. 2; *Washington Post*, March 23, 1946, p. 2.
7. *New York Times*, March 23, 1946, pp. 1, 6; *Newsweek*, April 1, 1946, 21, 34.
8. *Newsweek*, April 1, 1946, 21, 34; *Washington Post*, March 23, 1946, p. 1; *New York Times*, March 23, 1946, p. 1.
9. *New York Herald Tribune*, March 23, 1946, pp. 1, 2; *New York Times*, March 23, 1946, pp. 1, 6, and March 25, 1946, p. 24; *Washington Post*, March 23, 1946, p. 1, and March 24, 1946, p. 1; Associated Press wire, March 23, 1946.
10. Howard C. Petersen to the Secretary of War, memorandum, March 22, 1946, Box 19, Patterson papers, LC; Herken, *The Winning Weapon*, 175–76.
11. *New York Times*, March 24, 1946, p. 1, and March 23, 1946, p. 1; *New York Herald Tribune*, March 23, 1946, p. 2; *Washington Post*, March 23, 1946, p. 1, and March 24, 1946, p. 1; JTF-1 Releases Nos. 25 and 26 (March 23, 1946), DOE/CIC 101018, 101019.
12. *New York Times*, March 24, 1946, p. 15.
13. Ross diary, March 23, 1946, Box 21, Ross papers, HSTL.
14. *New York Times*, March 26, 1946, p. 1, and March 29, 1946, p. 9.
15. Ibid., March 26, 1946, p. 1, and March 29, 1946, p. 9; minutes of Blandy press conference, March 28, 1946, p. 5, OAB.
16. *Public Papers of the Presidents, Harry S. Truman (1946)*, 172.
17. *Honolulu Star-Bulletin*, March 28, 1946, p. 4.1.
18. Memorandum for the Chief of Staff entitled "Reaffirmation of Necessity for Atomic Bomb Tests against Naval Vessels," April 2, 1946; Admiral Leahy to Patterson and Forrestal, memorandum entitled "Military Opinion as to the Importance of the Atomic Bomb Test," April 3, 1946: CCS 471.6, 10-16-45, RG 218, Sec. 5, USJCS; Patterson and Forrestal to Truman, letter, April 6, 1946, Official File, HSTL; JTF-1 radio message, April 15, 1946, DOE/CIC 0120860.
19. *Public Papers of the Presidents, Harry S. Truman (1946)*, 199–200.
20. *New York Times*, April 13, 1946, p. 12.

CHAPTER 11.

1. *Washington Post*, March 24, 1946, p. 2.
2. *Congressional Record*, 79th Cong., 2d sess., 1946, 92, pt. 3: S 2790 (daily ed., March 29, 1946).

3. Fulbright interview.
4. *Congressional Record,* 79th Cong., 2d sess., 1946, 92, pt. 3: S 2791–93 (daily ed., March 29, 1946).
5. Shurcliff, *Technical Report,* pp. 1.11, 6.7.
6. *Los Angeles Examiner,* May 15, 1946, p. 4.
7. *Congressional Record,* 79th Cong., 2d sess., 1946, 92, pt. 3: H 4023–24 (daily ed., April 18, 1946).
8. *New York Times,* May 26, 1946, p. 7.
9. *Newsweek,* April 1, 1946, 39.
10. Conant to Forrestal and Patterson, letter, February 4, 1946, File No. 39-1-37, RG 80, GRDN.
11. Kunetka, *Oppenheimer,* 110.
12. Col. H. M. Exton to General Handy, memorandum, February 15, 1946, RG 107, "Atomic Energy Safe File 2," Patterson Folder, MEDR. The draft of Truman's telegram is in Box 29, MEDR.
13. Quoted in Rhodes, *The Making of the Atomic Bomb,* 758.
14. Oppenheimer to Barnard, Lilienthal, Thomas, and Winne, memorandum, May 24, 1946, Box 191 ("Board of Consultants May-June 1946" folder), Oppenheimer papers, LC.
15. Oppenheimer to Truman, letter, May 3, 1946, Box 178 ("JCS Evaluation Board" folder), Oppenheimer papers, LC.
16. Kunetka, *Oppenheimer,* 111.
17. *New York Times,* June 26, 1946, p. 5.
18. Transcript of telephone conversation between Oppenheimer and "Will," May 27, 1946, Byrnes papers, RMCL.
19. Letter to Sen. Carl A. Hatch, June 21, 1946, Box 178 ("JCS Evaluation Board" folder), Oppenheimer papers, LC.
20. Lilienthal, *The Atomic Energy Years,* 49; Acheson, *Present at the Creation,* 135; *FRUS: 1946,* 1:790–95.
21. Nimitz to Baruch, letter, June 11, 1946, in *FRUS: 1946,* 1:853–54; Herken, *The Winning Weapon,* 167. Dean Rusk recalled "extensive opposition" to the Baruch Plan in Congress, the Pentagon, and the State Department. Rusk, *As I Saw It,* 139–40.
22. Baruch, *Baruch,* 366–67; Gerber, "The Baruch Plan and the Origins of the Cold War," 69–95; Hewlett and Anderson, *The New World,* 575–76; Lemmer, "The Air Force and the Concept of Deterrence," 11; Schnabel, "The History of the Joint Chiefs of Staff," 1:272–73.
23. Lilienthal, *The Atomic Energy Years,* 54–55, 59.
24. Truman, *Years of Trial and Hope,* 10.
25. *New York Times,* March 25, 1946, p. 24.
26. *Department of State Bulletin* 14, no. 364 (June 23, 1946): 1057–62.
27. *Toledo Blade,* June 15, 1946, quoted in Coit, *Mr. Baruch,* 585.
28. *Congressional Record,* 79th Cong., 2d sess., 1946, 92, pt. 6: S 6926–33 (daily ed., June 14, 1946); *New York Times,* June 15, 1946, p. 4; *New York Herald Tribune,* June 15, 1946, p. 7.

CHAPTER 12.

1. Richard, *United States Naval Administration,* 1:333–34; Mason, "Relocation of the Bikini Marshallese," 249–51, 260–61.

2. Advance Headquarters JTF-1, Press Release No. 33-46 (May 13, 1946), Box 6924, Folder 4, RG 313, RNOF.

3. *Hearings on House Joint Resolution 307,* 2425, 2429 (January 29, 1946).

4. CINCPAC to Navy Department, cable, January 13, 1946, CCS 471.6 (10-10-45), RG 218, Sec. 2, USJCS; JTF-1 to Navy Department, cable, January 17, 1946, Box 224, RG 374, DASA.

5. *Honolulu Star-Bulletin,* February 28, 1946, p. 13; *Time,* April 1, 1946, 28.

6. Richard, *United States Naval Administration,* 3:509–10.

7. Atoll Commander, Kwajalein, to ComMarianas, cable, February 18, 1946, Box 28 (Navy cables, January–February 1946), MEDR; Mason, "Relocation of the Bikini Marshallese," 261–62.

8. *Honolulu Star-Bulletin,* February 23, 1946, p. 11.

9. "Nuclear Exiles," National Geographic Explorer Series, Kessibuki interview, p. 9.

10. Kessibuki deposition, 10, 12.

11. *New Yorker,* June 15, 1946, 17.

12. Blandy press conference, January 24, 1946, 5, File No. 39-1-37, RG 80, GRDN.

13. Ibid., 8.

14. *Honolulu Star-Bulletin,* September 5, 1946, p. 13; Blandy, lecture at Constitution Hall, Washington, D.C., November 22, 1946, p. 2, DOE/CIC 100955; Associated Press wire, September 5, 1946.

15. *Time,* November 11, 1946, 31.

16. "The Atomic Bomb Test," 46.

17. Drucker, "The Ex-Bikini Occupants of Kili Island," 11.

18. Mason, "Relocation of the Bikini Marshallese," 266.

19. *Honolulu Star-Bulletin,* February 23, 1946, p. 11.

20. Richard, *United States Naval Administration,* 3:508–9.

21. Mason, "Relocation of the Bikini Marshallese," 264–65; *Washington Star,* February 24, 1946; Pratt, "How Bikini Became the Bomb-Testing Ground," 60.

22. "Nuclear Exiles," Kessibuki interview, p. 9.

23. Wyatt to ComMarianas, cable, February 18, 1946; CINCPAC to Chief of Naval Operations, cable, February 14, 1946, Box 28 (Navy cables, January–February 1946), MEDR.

24. Kessibuki deposition, 11.

25. Mason, "Relocation of the Bikini Marshallese," 248–51. "Jeimata is pretty unhappy about the whole thing," said Lt. Herbert Meade, a military government officer. "He wanted the Bikinians to go to another island in his jurisdiction rather than Rongerik." *Honolulu Star-Bulletin,* March 4, 1946, p. 4.

26. Wyatt to ComMarianas, memorandum entitled "War Diary—Submission of," April 13, 1946, RG 313, RNOF; CINCPAC to Navy Department, cable, February 14, 1946, Box 225 (JTF-1 Messages), RG 374, DASA.

27. Mason, "Relocation of the Bikini Marshallese," 270; Berkhouse et al., *Operation Crossroads,* 19.
28. Wyatt to ComMarianas, cable, February 18, 1946, RG 313, RNOF.
29. Markwith, "Farewell to Bikini," 108; *Time,* April 1, 1946, 28.
30. Notice from Lt. Herbert C. Meade, Military Government Officer and Officer-in-Charge, Bikini Resettlement Operation, March 6, 1946, Box 6924, Folder 4, RG 313, RNOF.
31. Quoted in Mason, "Relocation of the Bikini Marshallese," 273, 275.
32. Markwith, "Farewell to Bikini," 109.
33. "Radio Bikini" transcript, 3.
34. Markwith, "Farewell to Bikini," 112–13. Wyatt's meeting with the Bikinians was shown on newsreels in the United States and it, too, was the subject of a *New Yorker* cartoon. Islanders are shown sitting on the ground under a tree as a Navy official points to a drawing, nailed to a tree, of a chain of atoms. As he explains the chart, one Navy man says to another, "I don't see why he goes into all that detail. Why doesn't he simply tell them there's going to be one hell of a bang and let it go at that?" *New Yorker,* June 29, 1946, 27.
35. "Radio Bikini" transcript, 2–3.
36. Lt. Herbert C. Meade to Senior Military Government Officer, report entitled "Operation Crossroads—Resettlement of Bikini Population," April 5, 1946, p. 3 (hereafter Meade report), Enclosure C to Kwajalein Monthly Report for March 1946, Box 2246, RG 313, RNOF.
37. *Life,* March 25, 1946, 105; Mason, "Relocation of the Bikini Marshallese," 275–76; Mydans interview.
38. Meade report, 4.
39. Ramsey, address before the Jacksonville Chamber of Commerce, June 28, 1946, Navy Department Press Release, OAB.
40. Meade report, 5.
41. *Time,* April 1, 1946, 28; *New York Times,* March 31, 1946, sec. 6, p. 23.
42. *New York Times,* March 12, 1946, p. 17; *New York Herald Tribune,* April 15, 1946, p. 36.
43. *Honolulu Star-Bulletin,* April 1, 1946, p. 10; Weisgall, "The Nuclear Nomads of Bikini Atoll," 80.
44. *Honolulu Star-Bulletin,* May 4, 1946, p. 1.
45. *New York Times,* March 3, 1946, p. 31, and July 21, 1946, sec. 4, p. 8.

CHAPTER 13.

1. Berkhouse et al., *Operation Crossroads,* 32; Polmar, *Aircraft Carriers,* 479; Nichols, *The Road to Trinity,* 225.
2. Shurcliff, *Operation Crossroads,* 8–10. Director of Ship Material, *Historical Report, Atomic Bomb Tests Able and Baker,* 2:190–216.
3. Blandy, "Atomic Test Case," 13.
4. Blandy, memorandum entitled "Proposed Plan for Atomic Bomb Tests against Naval Vessels," December 1945, JCS 471.6 (8-15-45), RG 218, Sec. 2,

USJCS; Berkhouse et al., *Operation Crossroads*, 18; *New York Herald Tribune*, January 25, 1946, p. 12.

5. Kauffman oral history transcript, 298.

6. *New York Times*, April 24, 1946, p. 1; Shurcliff, *Bombs at Bikini*, 33; Blandy, statement before the Senate Special Committee on Atomic Energy, January 24, 1946, DOE/CIC 101073; Blandy press conference, January 24, 1946, File No. 39-1-37, RG 80, GRDN.

7. Quoted in Bowen et al., *Air Force Atomic Energy Program*, 1:193.

8. Shurcliff, *Bombs at Bikini*, 43; Berkhouse et al., *Operation Crossroads*, 32–42, 169; JTF-1, Press Release No. 23 (March 21, 1946), DOE/CIC 101021.

9. Shurcliff, *Bombs at Bikini*, 43–45, 100–102; *New York Times*, June 23, 1946, sec. 4, p. 10, and June 28, 1946, p. 15.

10. Berkhouse et al., *Operation Crossroads*, 515–17; Shurcliff, *Technical Report*, p. 4.4.

11. JTF-1, Press Release No. 33-46 (May 13, 1946), RG 313 (TTPI), RNOF; Berkhouse et al., *Operation Crossroads*, 84.

12. From Rear Adm. A. D. Struble, memorandum, February 19, 1946, Box 7706, Folder A-164, RG 313, RNOF; Blandy, speech, April 13, 1946, DOE/CIC 100170.

13. *Life*, July 1, 1946, 41.

14. Shurcliff, *Technical Report*, p. 8.6; Shurcliff, *Operation Crossroads*, 53; *New York Times*, May 14, 1946, p. 27; *Honolulu Star-Bulletin*, July 1, 1946, p. 41; Schultz papers, SIA; Commander, JTF-1, *Operational Report*, p. V-(D)-3.

15. Revelle, foreword to Emery et al., *Geology of Bikini and Nearby Atolls*, iii; Hines, *Proving Ground*, 32–35; Blandy, memorandum entitled "General Information on Atomic Bomb Tests," January 28, 1946, Box 7706, File A-1, RG 313, RNOF; *New York Times*, June 30, 1946, sec. 4, p. 9; Lyon oral history transcript, 11–14; Cumberledge, "Aerological Aspects of the Bikini Bomb Test," 140; *Popular Mechanics*, April 1946, 90.

16. Director of Ship Material, *Historical Report, Atomic Bomb Tests Able and Baker*, 2:186–87.

17. Berkhouse et al., *Operation Crossroads*, 81.

18. *Hearings on Joint Resolution 307*, 2417 (January 29, 1946); *Hearings on Atomic Energy*, 460 (January 24, 1946); *New York Herald Tribune*, January 25, 1946, p. 1; *Newsweek*, February 11, 1946, 13, and March 4, 1946, 33.

19. Blandy, "Atomic Test Case," 40; *Hearings on Joint Resolution 307*, 2417; JTF-1 Press Release No. 7 ("Scientific Data to Be Gained through Use of Animals in Crossroads Project"), OAB; Shurcliff, *Bombs at Bikini*, 84–85.

20. Goats were selected for the tests because their body mass is roughly equal a human's, and their respiratory systems are similar. Four goats were selected because of their psychoneurotic tendencies. Shurcliff, *Technical Report*, p. 8.4; Shurcliff, *Operation Crossroads*, 67; minutes of Blandy press conference, March 13, 1946, p. 56, OAB.

21. JTF-1 Press Release No. 48 (June 1, 1946), DOE/CIC 100995; *Time*, March 11, 1946, 56.

22. *Honolulu Star-Bulletin,* March 19, 1946, p. 9; Commander, JTF-1, *Operational Report* ("Special Reports—Photographic"), p. VII-(G)-19.
23. *New York Times,* June 23, 1946, sec. 6, p. 3.
24. *Honolulu Star-Bulletin,* March 19, 1946, p. 9; comments of Dr. Perregrine White, assistant historian of Operation Crossroads, in the radio broadcast "Atomic Preview," June 29, 1946, transcript p. 14, Box 29, MEDR.
25. *New York Times,* June 30, 1946, sec. 4, p. 9; June 23, 1946, sec. 6, p. 53; May 26, 1946, sec. 4, pp. 8–9; April 16, 1946, p. 33; and March 18, 1946, p. 3. *Newsweek,* July 1, 1946, 20; Shurcliff, *Bombs at Bikini,* 32; Shurcliff, *Operation Crossroads,* 9, 29, 72–73, 75, 81; Bradley, *No Place to Hide,* 16; de Ment, "Instruments of Operation Crossroads," 418.
26. Commander, JTF-1, *Operational Report,* pp. VII-(E)-107–9; Powell, "'Crossroads' Critique," 152, 155; *New York Times,* April 18, 1946, p. 9, and May 10, 1946, p. 8; Shurcliff, *Bombs at Bikini,* 98–99; Ramey, "Phantom Fortresses vs. the Atomic Bomb."
27. Quoted in Bowen et al., *Air Force Atomic Energy Program,* 1:188.
28. Berkhouse et al., *Operation Crossroads,* 160–63; de Ment, "Instruments of Operation Crossroads," 416–17.
29. Berkhouse et al., *Operation Crossroads,* 84–85; Shurcliff, *Bombs at Bikini,* 50–52.
30. Shurcliff, *Technical Report,* pp. 7.8, 10.8.
31. Berkhouse et al., *Operation Crossroads,* 208–14.
32. Blandy, "Atomic Test Case," 13.

CHAPTER 14.

1. Shurcliff, *Technical Report,* p. 6.9.
2. Bowen et al., *Air Force Atomic Energy Program,* 1:168–69.
3. Groves to Blandy, memorandum, February 7, 1946, DOE/CIC 33031.
4. Shurcliff, *Technical Report,* pp. 6.8–9.
5. Ashworth oral history transcript, 60.
6. Shurcliff, *Technical Report,* pp. 6.13–15.
7. Sawyer oral history transcript, 33–34; Coffey, *Iron Eagle,* 256; LeMay interview.
8. Shurcliff, *Technical Report,* pp. 5.4–5.
9. Ibid., p. 5.8; Parsons to Bradbury, memorandum, October 26, 1945, p. 2, LANL; Bowen et al., *Air Force Atomic Energy Program,* 1:168; *New York Herald Tribune,* February 27, 1946, p. 16.
10. Minutes of press conference held by Parsons and Sawyer, April 23, 1946, p. 3, File No. 39-1-37, RG 80, GRDN.
11. Shurcliff, *Technical Report,* pp. 5.5–6.
12. Minutes of meeting at Los Alamos, January 26, 1946, p. 11, LANL.
13. McCullough, *Truman,* 457.
14. *New York Times,* February 7, 1946, p. 8, and April 6, 1946, p. 2; Hopkins, *The Development of Strategic Air Command,* 1–5.
15. Bowen et al., *Air Force Atomic Energy Program,* 1:260–61.

16. Ibid., 1:263–64.

17. Commander, JTF-1, *Operational Report,* pp. VII-(E)-103–5; Krueger, "Operation Crossroads," 274; Bowen et al., *Air Force Atomic Energy Program,* 1:260.

18. Minutes of press conference held by Maj. Gen. W. E. Kepner, April 17, 1946, pp. 2–3, File No. 39-1-37, RG 80, GRDN.

19. Tibbets, *The Tibbets Story,* 248. Tibbets wrote that Col. William Blanchard was determined to keep him away from Operation Crossroads. Tibbets overheard Blanchard talking to another colonel in adjoining bathroom stalls, not aware of Tibbets's presence in a neighboring stall. "He's already had enough publicity," Tibbets heard Blanchard say, and he soon realized they were talking about him, "trying to figure out a way to keep me out of the spotlight" (246–47). Tibbets interview. Tibbets's account cannot be verified.

20. Groves to LeMay, undated memorandum, Box 24, MEDR. In Tibbets's view, the accident occurred because "many of the things we had worked out in painstaking practice for the Hiroshima bombings were not heeded by the less-experienced crews competing for 'Crossroads.'" The pilot, he wrote, lacked the precision needed to perform the diving turn after dropping the bomb to avoid the shock waves. Tibbets, *The Tibbets Story,* 248.

21. Groves to Col. H. P. Gibson, memorandum entitled "Atomic Bomb Information for Use by Joint Chiefs of Staff Committees," September 17, 1945, Records of the Office of the Chief of Engineers, Box 2, Entry 1, Folder No. 1, RG 77, MEDR.

22. Bowen et al., *Air Force Atomic Energy Program,* 2:175.

23. Groves to Blandy, draft memorandum, March 4, 1946, Box 26, MEDR; transcript of telephone conversation from Capt. R. R. Larkin to Captain Corrothers, February 19, 1946, LANL.

24. JTF-1, Release No. 46 (May 13, 1946), DOE/CIC 100997; draft of radio message from Groves to Blandy, May 15, 1946, Box 26, MEDR.

25. *New York Herald Tribune,* March 2, 1946, p. 5; *Time,* June 17, 1946, 48; minutes of Blandy press conference, March 1, 1946, p. 9, OAB.

26. *New York Times,* March 3, 1946, p. 12.

27. Ibid., March 9, 1946, p. 7.

28. *Time,* June 17, 1946, 48.

29. Groves to Chairman, Joint Crossroads Committee, undated memorandum entitled "Review of Crossroads Report," Box 26, Folder F-3-2, MEDR.

30. Radiological Safety Advisor, JTF-1, to Groves, telegram, August 19, 1946, Box 26, MEDR.

31. Gee, memorandum entitled "Report of Observations at Bikini, Test Able, 29 June–6 July 1946," July 6, 1946, p. 8 (hereafter Gee memorandum), Box 26, Folder F-2-7, MEDR.

32. Blandy, speech in New York, April 13, 1946, JTF-1 Release No. 36, DOE/CIC 100170; *New York Herald Tribune,* April 15, 1946, p. 33.

33. Blandy to Forrestal, undated memorandum entitled "Comment on Acheson Report," enclosure to memorandum from M. B. Gardner to the Chief of Naval Operations entitled "Discussion with Mr. Baruch," April 13, 1946, Records of the Secretary of the Navy, Box 3, Double Zero File, OAB.

34. Ferrell, ed., *The Eisenhower Diaries*, 156.
35. Forrestal, *The Forrestal Diaries*, 450.
36. Youngblood oral history transcript, 17.
37. Kauffman oral history transcript, 303.
38. Sawyer oral history transcript, 33; *New Yorker*, July 27, 1946, 11.

CHAPTER 15.

1. Bradbury interview.
2. Wyden, *Day One*, 289–90; Lamont, *Day of Trinity*, 265.
3. Rhodes, *The Making of the Atomic Bomb*, 755; Lawren, *The General and the Bomb*, 276; Groves, *Now It Can Be Told*, 378.
4. Quoted in Newhouse, *War and Peace in the Nuclear Age*, 54.
5. Shelton, *Reflection of a Nuclear Weaponeer*, p. 2-2.
6. Hawkins et al., *Project Y*, 268; Hewlett and Anderson, *The New World*, 625–26.
7. Hewlett and Anderson, *The New World*, 630; Bradbury to Blandy, letter, January 7, 1946, LANL.
8. Parsons to Oppenheimer, memorandum, November 22, 1943; Oppenheimer to Parsons, memorandum, December 27, 1943, LANL.
9. Parsons to Bradbury, memorandum, October 26, 1945; transcript of telephone call from Larkin to Ashworth, December 19, 1945, p. 2, LANL.
10. Hawkins et al., *Project Y*, 130–33; Hansen, *U.S. Nuclear Weapons*, 124–26; Bowen et al., *Air Force Atomic Energy Program*, 1:92–99, 2:394, 472–76; Rosenberg, "U.S. Nuclear Stockpile," 28–29.
11. Bowen et al., *Air Force Atomic Energy Program*, 4:61; Hewlett and Anderson, *The New World*, 626–27; Hawkins et al., *Project Y*, 274, 362.
12. *Time*, February 25, 1946, 24, and March 11, 1946, 54; *New York Times*, May 14, 1946, p. 1; Oppenheimer to Truman, letter, May 3, 1946, Box 178, Oppenheimer papers, LC; Lapp, *Atoms and People*, 97.
13. Hewlett and Anderson, *The New World*, 631; Blandy press conference of May 12, 1946, DOE/CIC 100997.
14. Schreiber interview; Bethe interview.
15. Weisskopf to Capt. L. W. McKeehan, letter, February 22, 1946, Navy Bureau of Ordnance, LANL; Wyden, *Day One*, 214.
16. Hawkins et al., *Project Y*, 282; Berkhouse et al., *Operation Crossroads*, 209.
17. Sam C. Adkins to *Louisville Courier-Journal*, dispatch, July 4, 1946, File Nos. 1109–1289, RG 374, DASA; Meade, "Crossroads Summary."
18. Transcript of telephone call from Larkin to Ashworth, December 19, 1945, p. 2, LANL; Hawkins et al., *Project Y*, 250.
19. Bradbury to Holloway and Warner, letter, May 7, 1946, DOE/CIC 0120521.
20. Bradbury interview.
21. Holloway to Bradbury, letter, April 23, 1946, p. 2, LANL.
22. Warner to Bradbury and Wilhoyt, letter, May 25, 1946, LANL.
23. Holloway to Bradbury, letter, May 26, 1946, pp. 7–8, LANL.

24. Frisch, *What Little I Remember,* 159–60; Rhodes, *The Making of the Atomic Bomb,* 610–12; Hacker, *The Dragon's Tail,* 72.

25. Frisch, *What Little I Remember,* 159.

26. Lawren, *The General and the Bomb,* 197; Lamont, *Day of Trinity,* 82, 199; Schreiber interview.

27. Quoted in Hacker, *The Dragon's Tail,* 73.

28. Quoted in Lapp, *Atoms and People,* 58.

29. Lamont, *Day of Trinity,* 271; Miller, *Under the Cloud,* 67–68; *New York Herald Tribune,* February 3, 1946, sec. 2, p. 1; Schubert and Lapp, *Radiation,* 138.

30. Warren oral history transcript, 2:846, 855–57.

31. Quoted in Lapp, *Atoms and People,* 61; Honicker, "The Hidden Files," 39–40; Lapp interview.

32. Hawkins et al., *Project Y,* 291; Honicker, "The Hidden Files," 40; Warren oral history transcript, 2:852–55; press release entitled "Statement of Manhattan Engineer Project Headquarters Regarding Death of Dr. Louis Slotin, Physicist at Los Alamos Laboratory," June 28, 1946, DOE/CIC 57619.

33. Lamont, *Day of Trinity,* 278; Schubert and Lapp, *Radiation,* 140–41; *Time,* June 10, 1946, 91–92; Hawkins et al., *Project Y,* 291; Schreiber interview.

34. *Hearings on Atomic Energy,* 36–37 (November 28, 1945).

CHAPTER 16.

1. Elizabeth May Craig (Gannett Publishing Co.) to President Truman, letter, June 26, 1946, Official File, HSTL; *New York Herald Tribune,* January 31, 1946, p. 4; *Newsweek,* March 11, 1946, 62–63; *Time,* June 17, 1946, 48; Littell, "The Voice of the Apple," 221; "Radio Bikini" transcript, 8, 10, 11, 14.

2. Considine, *It's All News to Me,* 199.

3. Littell, "The Voice of the Apple," 221.

4. Lee oral history transcript, 200–201.

5. Considine, *It's All News to Me,* 199.

6. Lee oral history transcript, 201; *Honolulu Star-Bulletin,* June 19, 1946, p. 2.

7. Littell, "The Voice of the Apple," 222–24.

8. Shurcliff, *Technical Report,* p. 3.13; *New York Herald Tribune,* January 25, 1946, p. 12, and January 26, 1946, p. 5; Australian Ambassador to Byrnes, letter, January 26, 1946; note from the Minister of New Zealand to Byrnes, February 13, 1946, Box 4617, File 811.2423, RG 59, General Records of the Department of State, Washington, D.C.; Byrnes to Truman, memorandum entitled "British Scientific Team," January 5, 1946, Official File, HSTL; notes of Byrnes's press and radio news conference, January 29, 1946, Byrnes papers, RMCL; report to Joint Chiefs entitled "Scientific Representation from British Admiralty and British Air Ministry at Atomic Bomb Trials," December 13, 1945, JCS 1552/4, USJCS.

9. Rhodes, *The Making of the Atomic Bomb,* 646.

10. *New York Times,* January 26, 1946, p. 12; *Washington Post,* January 30, 1946, p. 8.

11. Groves to the Joint Chiefs of Staff, memorandum, June 1, 1946, CCS 471.6 (10-16-45), RG 218, Sec. 7, USJCS; minutes of meeting of the secretaries of state, war, and navy, February 5, 1946; Byrnes to Kennan, cable, February 5, 1946, Box 4617, Folder 811.2423, State Department Archives, RG 59; *New York Times,* June 21, 1946, p. 5; *Washington Post,* January 30, 1946, p. 3.

12. Col. Horace B. Smith to C. L. Willard, memorandum, February 21, 1946, CCS 471.6 (8-15-45), RG 218, Sec. 3, USJCS; Press Kit, Operation Crossroads, p. 8, Vickery papers, Yale University, New Haven; waiver of Egyptian observers, May 30, 1946, DOE/CIC 100242.

13. Goldschmidt, *Atomic Rivals,* 303.

14. Ethan Pollock, letter to author, July 23, 1992, based on Pollock's June 30, 1992, interview with Igor Golovin.

15. "Panamint Passengers on Parade," Box 51 (Joint Committee on Atomic Energy folder), Hickenlooper papers, Hoover Library.

16. Goldschmidt, *Atomic Rivals,* 300, 303.

17. Telephone conversation between Forrestal and Anderson, March 19, 1946, File No. 39-1-37, RG 80, GRDN.

18. Byrnes, memorandum for the president entitled "Allocation of Observers and Press Representatives for Atomic Bomb Tests," March 8, 1946, Confidential File, HSTL; *New York Herald Tribune,* January 26, 1946, p. 5; *New York Times,* January 30, 1946, p. 4; February 18, 1946, p. 6; February 23, 1946, p. 14; April 9, 1946, p. 1; and April 10, 1946, p. 16.

19. *New York Times,* April 11, 1946, p. 15; *New York Herald Tribune,* June 13, 1946, p. 15; Shurcliff, *Bombs at Bikini,* 39.

20. Hoopes and Brinkley, *Driven Patriot,* 76; *New York Times,* June 18, 1946, p. 4; Clifford interview.

21. Forrestal, *The Forrestal Diaries,* 169–70, 463; Clifford, *Counsel to the President,* 148–51, 172–73; Rogow, *James Forrestal,* 295–97; Symington interview.

22. Nichols, *The Road to Trinity,* 233; Nichols interview.

23. Nichols, *The Road to Trinity,* 236–38.

24. Christman, "Deak Parsons, Officer-Scientist," 56–61; Rivero oral history transcript, 167; Rivero interview.

25. Groves, *Now It Can Be Told,* 160–61; Groueff, *Manhattan Project,* 347–48.

26. Sawyer oral history transcript, 29; Nichols interview.

27. Youngblood oral history transcript, 24–25.

28. Shelton, *Reflections of a Nuclear Weaponeer,* p. 2-10; Bethe interview.

29. Bradbury interview.

30. Williams, *Klaus Fuchs,* 87.

31. Secret memorandum from "T.O.J.," June 24, 1946, Records of the Office of the Chief of Engineers, F3-1 JCS 1552, Series Miscellaneous, No. 25, Entry 4 (Operation Crossroads), RG 77, MEDR; Commander, JTF-1, *Operational Report,* pp. VII-(D)-1–14; Kirkpatrick, "Panamint Parade," June 28, 1946.

32. Schultz logbook, April 23, 1946, SIA; Joseph Morrison to Alexander Wetmore, letter, May 17, 1946, Box 3, Folder 4, Morrison papers, SIA; Ladd oral history transcript; JTF-1, *Operation Crossroads: Fourth Cruise of the*

"Mighty Mac," 1; Krueger, "Operation Crossroads," 275; Berkhouse et al., *Operation Crossroads,* 66–67.

33. Shurcliff, *Bombs at Bikini,* 94–95; "United States Naval Construction Battalion 53"; Krueger, "Operation Crossroads," 273.

34. Bob Considine to International News Service, dispatch, July 5, 1946, Nos. 1289–1442, RG 374, DASA; Shurcliff, *Bombs at Bikini,* 89–96; JTF-1, Release No. 32 (April 1, 1946), DOE/CIC 101012.

35. Dr. Joseph G. Hamilton to "Don" [probably Cooksey], letter, June 29, 1946, Carton 8, Folder 14, Lawrence papers, University of California at Berkeley.

36. "Radio Bikini" transcript, 5; Quigley, "Swimming in the Atomic Lagoon," 34; Terkel, *The Good War,* 546; Lt. W. R. Prohs to Capt. R. R. Larkin, message, January 30, 1946, LANL; Guarisco interview.

37. Considine, *It's All News to Me,* 200. In its early years the United Nations was called the UNO (United Nations Organization). The *Panamint,* lead vessel of the three that transported observers to Bikini, had carried the famous World War II correspondent Ernie Pyle to the Pacific, where he was killed on Ie Shima. Nichols, ed., *Ernie's War,* 32.

38. *Crossroads,* nos. 1, 7, 8, Box 23, Folder 2, Record Unit 7222, Schultz papers, SIA.

39. Considine, *It's All News to Me,* 199.

40. Box 3, Parsons papers, LC.

41. *Washington News,* June 21, 1946.

42. Norman Cousins to *Saturday Review,* dispatch, June 18, 1946, Nos. 55–169, RG 374, DASA.

43. White, "Talk of the Town," 19; White, *The Wild Flag,* 161.

CHAPTER 17.

1. *Time,* January 28, 1946, 24, and February 25, 1946, 24; Toulmin, "Is Bikini a Fair Test?" 84; *Honolulu Star-Bulletin,* March 18, 1946, p. 4.

2. *New York Times,* February 21, 1946, p. 4; *Newsweek,* April 24, 1946, 11.

3. *Washington Post,* February 11, 1946, p. 7.

4. Toulmin, "Is Bikini a Fair Test?" 84.

5. "Analysis of Bikini's First Atom Bomb Test," 5.

6. Diary of James Forrestal, June 6, 1946, Forrestal papers, Princeton University; *Hearings on House Joint Resolution 307,* 2415 (January 29, 1946).

7. *New York Times,* January 30, 1946, p. 4.

8. Ibid., February 13, 1946, p. 13; *New York Herald Tribune,* June 18, 1946, p. 8.

9. *New York Times,* February 21, 1946, p. 4.

10. Ibid., February 13, 1946, p. 13; *Honolulu Star-Bulletin,* February 19, 1946, p. 1.

11. Peterson to Collins, memorandum, February 12, 1946, Records of the Office of the Secretary of War, RG 107 (Atomic Energy Folder), NA.

12. *Operation Crossroads: The Role of the Army Air Forces,* 1:90.

13. "Radio Bikini" transcript, 4.

14. *New York Times,* February 27, 1946, p. 17.

15. Protest letters and answers, Box Nos. 215, #4, #6, #8, and 216, #8 and #9, RG 374, DASA.
16. *Newsweek,* April 1, 1946, 26.
17. Blandy, remarks, September 5, 1946, p. 2, DOE/CIC 100967.
18. *Newsweek,* April 1, 1946, 26; Director of Ship Material, *Historical Report, Atomic Bomb Tests Able and Baker,* 2:185.
19. Box Nos. 216, #8, 217, #11, and 219, RG 374, DASA; *Newsweek,* April 1, 1946, 26.
20. Box Nos. 215, #3, and 219, RG 374, DASA; Senate Special Committee on Atomic Energy, 79th Cong., Box 14, RG 46, RUSS; *Washington Post,* March 8, 1946, p. 1.
21. *Los Angeles Examiner,* March 12, 1946, p. 7.
22. Box Nos. 216, #8, and 220, RG 374, DASA; Shurcliff, *Bombs at Bikini,* 85–86; Shurcliff, *Technical Report,* p. 8.3; *New York Times,* June 30, 1946, sec. 4, p. 5.
23. Commander, JTF-1, *Operational Report,* p. II-(A)-2.
24. Betts to Alexander Wilde, letter, April 2, 1946, RG 374, DASA; Shurcliff, *Technical Report,* p. 1.17.
25. Minutes of Blandy press conference, May 13, 1946, p. 9, OAB.
26. Box Nos. 216 and 219, RG 374, DASA.
27. Congressman Clifford Davis to Matthew Connelly, letter, March 29, 1946; JTF-1 to Clifford, memorandum, April 8, 1946; Clifford to Connelly, memorandum, April 10, 1946; Connelly to Davis, letter, April 12, 1946, Official File, HSTL; Clifford interview.
28. Shurcliff, *Bombs at Bikini,* 86; Box No. 218, #5, RG 374, DASA.
29. *Oregon Daily Journal,* May 3, 1946, p. 11; *Los Angeles Daily News,* May 10, 1946; *Seattle Post-Intelligencer,* March 7, 1946, p. 8; Box No. 215, RG 374, DASA.
30. White, "Talk of the Town," 18; White, *The Wild Flag,* 160–61.
31. Lee to Blandy, memorandum entitled "Public Information Estimate No. 1," March 7, 1946, Box 74, Folder 6, Warren papers, University of California, Los Angeles.
32. Transcript of telephone conversation between Forrestal and Dewey, June 10, 1946, Records of the Secretary of War, Safe File #2, RG 107, NA.
33. Box No. 104, Folder A13-7, RG 374, DASA.
34. Washington, D.C., *Times-Herald,* January 25, 1946.
35. Telegram to Maj. W. H. McAllister, JTF-1, Public Information Office, April 24, 1946, Box 28, MEDR.
36. Transcript of Navy newsreel excerpted in "Nuclear Exiles."

CHAPTER 18.

1. The major sources on Operation Crossroads disagree as to names, types, and numbers of target vessels at Bikini. In his *Technical Report of Operation Crossroads* (pp. 3.61–62), William A. Shurcliff, the official historian of JTF-1, listed ninety-three ships by name and/or hull number. He omitted

LCM-1, which was beached on Bikini Island, and *LSM-60,* a medium landing ship, which housed the Baker bomb. Inclusion of these two vessels would have raised the number of target vessels to ninety-five, which is the number used in this text.

The 1984 Defense Nuclear Agency report by Berkhouse et al., entitled *Operation Crossroads* (pp. 173–77), listed eighty-three ships, omitting twelve landing craft that were exposed on the beach at Bikini Island. Shurcliff, *Technical Report,* pp. 10.8, 10.10. The 1991 National Park Service study by Delgado et al. entitled *The Archeology of the Atomic Bomb* (pp. 173–76), listed ninety-four ships, inadvertently omitting the destroyer *Mugford.*

2. The size of Bikini's target fleet was surpassed only by the navies of the United States, Great Britain, the Soviet Union, and France. *New York Times,* July 1, 1946, p. 3.

3. Shurcliff, *Technical Report,* pp. 6.4–6.

4. Kurzman, *Fatal Voyage,* 1, 174–75.

5. Roscoe, *United States Submarine Operations in World War II,* 527–62.

6. Mooney, ed., *Dictionary of American Naval Fighting Ships,* 5:71; Navy Department press release entitled "USS New York," January 24, 1946, DOE/CIC 130097; *New York Herald Tribune,* January 26, 1946, p. 5.

7. *New York Times,* January 24, 1946, p. 1, and January 30, 1946, p. 12; *New York Herald Tribune,* January 30, 1946, p. 3; *Washington Evening News,* January 18, 1946.

8. Halsey and Bryan, *Admiral Halsey's Story,* 133.

9. *New York Times,* January 24, 1946, p. 7.

10. *New York Herald Tribune,* January 24, 1946, p. 3; dispatch to Scripps-Howard, July 2, 1946, Nos. 558–757, RG 374, DASA.

11. Whitley, *German Cruisers of World War II,* 118.

12. The *Prince of Wales* later hosted Roosevelt and Churchill at the Atlantic Conference in August 1941 and was then sunk by Japanese bombers at Singapore four months later.

13. Kennedy, *Pursuit;* Forester, *The Last Nine Days of the Bismarck;* Spengler, "Prinz Eugen," 1319.

14. Quoted in Ballard, *The Discovery of the Bismarck,* 142.

15. Bekker, *Hitler's Naval War,* 226–34.

16. *New York Times,* May 8, 1946, p. 12, and August 26, 1946, p. 2.

17. Howarth, *The Fighting Ships of the Rising Sun,* 134.

18. Prange, *At Dawn We Slept,* 382, 513–14.

19. Dull, *A Battle History of the Imperial Japanese Navy,* 309–16; Halsey and Bryan, *Admiral Halsey's Story,* 280–81.

20. *Crossroads,* no. 8 (May 4, 1946), Box 23, Folder 2, Record Unit 7222, Schultz papers, SIA; Kirkpatrick, "Panamint Parade," 15.

21. Navy Department press release entitled "USS Arkansas," January 24, 1946, DOE/CIC 128617; Mooney, ed., *Dictionary of American Naval Fighting Ships,* 1:62.

22. Shurcliff, *Technical History,* p. 6.10.

23. Prange, *At Dawn We Slept,* 514, 535–36; Mooney, ed., *Dictionary of American Naval Fighting Ships,* 5:52.

24. Mooney, ed., *Dictionary of American Naval Fighting Ships,* 5:250–54; Navy

Department press release entitled "USS Pennsylvania," January 24, 1946, DOE/CIC 130090.

25. Morison, *Aleutians, Gilberts and Marshalls,* 27.
26. Bishop, "Action Off Komandorski," 659–61, 665.
27. Spector, *Eagle against the Sun,* 179–80; Karig and Purdon, "The Komandorskis," 1411.
28. Polmar, *Aircraft Carriers,* 479; Navy Department press release entitled "USS Independence," January 24, 1946, DOE/CIC 130094.
29. Roscoe, *United States Submarine Operations in World War II,* 281–82, 289, 363–64; Blair, *Silent Victory,* 521–22.
30. Taylor, *The Magnificent Mitscher,* 82; Chesneau, *Aircraft Carriers of the World,* 201–4.
31. Ross, *Iwo Jima,* 116–17; Delgado, "What's Become of *Sara?*" 47; Eliot, "In Bikini Lagoon, Life Thrives in a Nuclear Graveyard," 76; *New York Times,* July 26, 1946, p. 20.
32. Newcomb, *Iwo Jima,* 75–76; Wheeler, *A Special Valor,* 345.

CHAPTER 19.

1. *New York Herald Tribune,* June 3, 1946, p. 11.
2. *New York Times,* May 31, 1946, p. 25, and June 3, 1946, p. 11.
3. Kepner to Spaatz, letter, June 15, 1946, Spaatz papers, LC.
4. JTF-1, Press Release No. 46, May 13, 1946; minutes of Blandy press conference, May 13, 1946, p. 2, OAB.
5. Shurcliff, *Technical Report,* p. 3.69.
6. *New York Times,* June 25, 1946, p. 4; Swancutt interview.
7. Commander, JTF-1, *Operational Report,* p. VII-(E)-14.
8. Ibid., p. VII-(E)-132; Forrestal diary, June 29 and July 1, 1946, Forrestal papers, Princeton University.
9. Berkhouse et al., *Operation Crossroads,* 86.
10. *Newsweek,* May 6, 1946, 56.
11. *Philadelphia Inquirer,* July 1, 1946, p. 3.
12. Bradbury to Marshall Holloway, letter, May 7, 1946, p. 2, DOE/CIC 0120521; *Newsweek,* May 6, 1946, 56.
13. "Bikini Preview: Report from Rongerik, June 18, 1946," "Radio Bikini" transcript file.
14. George M. Lyon and Stafford L. Warren to Blandy, memorandum entitled "Evacuation of Ronjerik [*sic*]," March 6, 1946, DOE/CIC 140583; Berkhouse et al., *Operation Crossroads,* 86, 265.
15. Berkhouse et al., *Operation Crossroads,* 86; Blandy, remarks, September 5, 1946, p. 4, DOE/CIC 100967.
16. *New York Times,* June 4, 1946, p. 17; Warren to JTF-1, memorandum entitled "Evacuation of Atolls Neighboring to Bikini," March 13, 1946, DOE/CIC 0140512. If it became necessary to jettison the atomic bomb on Able Day, Warren recommended that it be dropped in Taongi Atoll, an uninhabited atoll located some 225 miles northeast of Bikini and more than 200 miles from the nearest inhabited Marshallese atoll.

17. Document entitled "Commodore Wyatt's speech at Lae upon the arrival of the natives from Wotho and Rongelap," Box 6924, Folder 4, RG 313, RNOF; Shurcliff, *Technical Report,* p. 4.8; JTF-1 to Atoll Commander, Kwajalein, cable, March 14, 1946, Box 227, RG 374, DASA.

18. *Newsweek,* July 1, 1946, 22.

19. Ramsey, address before the Jacksonville, Florida, Chamber of Commerce, June 28, 1946, p. 4, OAB.

20. Nat Finney to *Des Moines Register-Tribune,* dispatch, June 15, 1946, Nos. 1–104, RG 374, DASA.

21. *New York Herald Tribune,* June 30, 1946, p. 17; *Time,* July 15, 1946, 28.

22. *Newsweek,* July 1, 1946, 20, 21; Boyer, *By the Bomb's Early Light,* 82; Hinds and Windt, *The Cold War as Rhetoric,* 113.

23. *New York Times,* June 30, 1946, sec. 4, p. 8.

24. John G. Harris to *Boston Globe,* dispatch, June 14, 1946, Nos. 1–104, RG 374, DASA.

25. ABC radio newscast of June 28, 1946, Box 30, Swing papers, LC.

26. "General Eisenhower and Other Military Leaders Speak on the A-Bomb Test," ABC radio, June 29, 1946.

27. Crosby, *Out of the Blue,* 3–4.

28. Forrestal diary, July 1, 1946, p. 2, Forrestal papers, Princeton University.

29. Tony S. Smith to Gannett Newspapers, dispatch, June 23, 1946, Nos. 368–481, RG 374, DASA.

30. Tibbets, *The Tibbets Story,* 248–49; *New York Times,* June 16, 1946, p. 8, and June 30, 1946, p. 4; *New York Herald Tribune,* June 16, 1946, p. 4; *Philadelphia Inquirer,* July 1, 1946, p. 2; Wood interview.

31. Blandy, remarks, September 5, 1946, p. 4, DOE/CIC 100967.

32. Semple served as the bombardier on the first "Silverplated" B-29 flown to accommodate the atomic bomb, and he played an active role in the Manhattan Project. He was also Swancutt's bombardier in practice runs in New Mexico, but his death on March 7, 1946, disqualified Swancutt's entire team. In late March, though, Harold Wood replaced Semple, and Swancutt's team performed well enough to qualify as the fourth competitor to go to Kwajalein for the final choice. Bowen et al., *Air Force Atomic Energy Program,* 1:98, 266.

33. *Philadelphia Inquirer,* July 1, 1946, p. 2. The actress's name still graces the Marshall Islands. To distinguish the two ends of Majuro Atoll, the Navy named the left side Lauren, for Lauren Bacall, and the right side Rita, for Rita Hayworth. The names stuck, in slightly modified form. The eastern, business end of the atoll is called Rita and the more rural area is called Laura.

34. Symington memoirs, 106; *New York Times,* July 1, 1946, p. 2.

35. *Time,* July 8, 1946, 20; Graybar and Graybar, "America Faces the Atomic Age," 68; Boyer, *By the Bomb's Early Light,* 83; "Analysis of Bikini's First Atom Bomb Test," 8; *New York Times,* July 1, 1946, p. 2.

36. "Radio Bikini" transcript, 10.

37. Crosby, *Out of the Blue,* 6.

38. *Philadelphia Inquirer,* July 1, 1946, p. 2.

CHAPTER 20.

1. Bowen et al., *Air Force Atomic Energy Program*, 1:287.
2. "Radio Bikini" transcript, 11.
3. Bradley, *No Place to Hide*, 22–23.
4. Shurcliff, *Technical Report*, pp. 10.4–6; Bowen et al., *Air Force Atomic Energy Program*, 1:284–86.
5. Littell, "The Voice of the Apple," 225.
6. "Radio Bikini" transcript, 11; Crosby, *Out of the Blue*, 7.
7. *New York Times*, July 1, 1946, p. 5.
8. Ibid., p. 4.
9. Crosby, *Out of the Blue*, 7.
10. Bradley, *No Place to Hide*, 53–54.
11. Shurcliff, *Technical Report*, p. 10.5; Berkhouse et al., *Operation Crossroads*, 87, 467; "Radio Bikini" transcript, 10–11.
12. *New York Times*, July 1, 1946, pp. 2, 4, 5; Crosby, *Out of the Blue*, 7–8; Bradley, *No Place to Hide*, 53–54.
13. Youngblood oral history transcript, 23.
14. Shurcliff, *Technical Report*, p. 10.5. Reporters were told that the bomb exploded at an altitude of several hundred feet, but the exact height remained a classified secret for more than 30 years.
15. Youngblood oral history transcript, 23.
16. *New York Times*, July 1, 1946, p. 1; Shurcliff, *Bombs at Bikini*, 106–7; Berkhouse et al., *Operation Crossroads*, 17.
17. Symington memoirs, 107; Shurcliff, *Technical Report*, pp. 10.10, 10.15.
18. Crosby, *Out of the Blue*, 8.
19. Nichols, *The Road to Trinity*, 236.
20. Ibid.
21. Bradley, *No Place to Hide*, 58.
22. *Atlanta Constitution*, July 1, 1946, p. 1; "Radio Bikini" transcript file, USAF 34282A, no. 31, NA.
23. Warren oral history transcript, 3:892; Shurcliff, *Technical Report*, p. 19.9; Moll, "Operation Crossroads," 66.
24. "Radio Bikini" transcript, 13. Interviewed just minutes after the blast, Rep. Albert J. Engel of Michigan was more cautious: "Until I have seen the destruction measured by the various instruments and seen the destruction itself, I want to reserve judgment as to whether or not I am ready to abolish the Army and Navy and go to throwing atomic baseballs from here on." Ibid.
25. Littell, "The Voice of the Apple," 226.
26. *New York Times*, July 1, 1946, p. 1; Considine, *It's All News to Me*, 202.
27. Jack Kofoed to *Chicago Daily News*, dispatch, July 1, 1946, Nos. 1–99, RG 374, DASA.
28. Volta Torrey to *Popular Science*, dispatch, July 1, 1946, Nos. 391–557, RG 374, DASA.
29. Boyer, *By the Bomb's Early Light*, 83.
30. *New York Times*, July 1, 1946, p. 3; *Newsweek*, July 15, 1946, 67; passen-

ger list, USS *Panamint*, Box 8 (Operation Crossroads), Callan papers, LC.

31. *Boston Globe,* July 1, 1946, p. 6.

32. Rhodes, *The Making of the Atomic Bomb,* 673–75; Laurence, *Dawn over Zero,* 11–12; transcript of lecture by Colonel Warren, October 7, 1946, pp. 3–4, DOE/CIC 140740; *Hearings on Atomic Energy,* 388 (December 13, 1945).

33. Shurcliff, *Technical Report,* pp. 12.3–4.

34. E. W. MacAlpine to *Australia Press,* dispatch, July 1, 1946, Nos. 391–557, RG 374, DASA; *New York Times,* August 3, 1946, p. 6; Graybar and Graybar, "America Faces the Atomic Age," 72; Groueff, *Manhattan Project,* 355–56.

35. Berkhouse et al., *Operation Crossroads,* 79–80; Shurcliff, *Bombs at Bikini,* 120–21, 127–28.

36. *New York Times,* July 1, 1946, p. 4; *Newsweek,* July 8, 1946, 20.

37. Director of Ship Material, *Technical Inspection Report, USS Gilliam,* p. 3; Delgado et al., *The Archeology of the Atomic Bomb,* 90–93.

38. Shurcliff, *Bombs at Bikini,* 110–12, 125–35; Shurcliff, *Technical Report,* pp. 10.9–10; Director of Ship Material, *Technical Inspection Report, USS Carlisle,* p. 9; Delgado et al., *The Archeology of the Atomic Bomb,* 90–93; Lovell, *The Sound of Wings,* 294.

39. *Philadelphia Inquirer,* July 1, 1946, p. 3; *New York Times,* July 2, 1946, p. 4.

40. *New York Times,* July 2, 1946, pp. 1, 4, 19; Bowen et al., *Air Force Atomic Energy Program,* 1:295.

41. Bowen et al., *Air Force Atomic Energy Program,* 4:53.

42. "Resume of Able Day Operations—Col. Warren 6 July 1946," p. 9, DOE/CIC 140588; Shurcliff, *Technical Report,* p. 11.6; Gerster, "The Special Weapons Center and Atomic Testing," 19.

43. Sawyer, *Report of the Technical Director,* 46.

44. James F. Chambers, Jr., to the *Dallas Times-Herald,* dispatch, July 2, 1946, Nos. 558–757, RG 374, DASA.

45. Kirkpatrick, "A-Bomb Tests as Viewed by the Editor," 96; Kirkpatrick, "Panamint Parade," 21–22.

46. *New York Times,* July 1, 1946, p. 1, and July 2, 1946, p. 1; *Time,* July 15, 1946, 26; Shurcliff, *Bombs at Bikini,* 125–34; Blandy to Joint Chiefs, memorandum entitled "Test 'A'—Preliminary Technical Report of Results," July 10, 1946, p. 3, Box 30, MEDR.

47. "Analysis of Bikini's First Atom Bomb Test," 9; *New York Times,* July 5, 1946, p. 3; Berkhouse et al., *Operation Crossroads,* 92; Commander, JTF-1, *Operational Report,* pp. VII-C-10–15.

48. Shurcliff, *Bombs at Bikini,* 140–41; *New York Times,* July 2, 1946, pp. 4, 19; C. J. Ryan to *St. Louis Post-Dispatch,* dispatch, July 4, 1946, Nos. 1109–1289, RG 374, DASA.

49. *New York Times,* July 11, 1946, p. 9, and April 3, 1949, p. 51; *Life,* August 11, 1947, 78; Tullis, "Pathologic Changes," 891; folder "P" in Animal Information Series and Animal Records Catalogue Entry 20.9.12, Records of the Office of the Registrar, National Zoological Park, SIA. There was some dispute as to whether Pig 311 was indeed the heroine she was made

out to be. Asked by a Texas town to attend a celebration after Operation Crossroads, she declined. "Regret to inform you that there was a slight error in the publicity I received relative to the long swim at Bikini Lagoon," wrote Pig 311 on Admiral Nimitz's stationery. "When you learn that I was actually on board a transport far from the big boom I fear you will want to retract your invitation." *New York Times,* August 8, 1946, p. 4.

50. JTF-1, "Able Day Plus One, Bikini," Box 104, Folder A13-8, RG 374, DASA; *New York Times,* July 3, 1946, p. 3.
51. *New York Times,* July 3, 1946, p. 3.
52. Berkhouse et al., *Operation Crossroads,* 93; Kemper interview; Peterkin interview; Shurcliff, *Technical Report,* p. 19.9.
53. *Time,* July 15, 1946, 29; Herbert B. Nichols to *Christian Science Monitor,* dispatch, July 2, 1946, Nos. 758–917, RG 374, DASA.
54. Quoted in Boyer, *By the Bomb's Early Light,* 84.
55. Jungk, *Brighter than a Thousand Suns,* 246; *The Nation,* July 6, 1946, 2.

CHAPTER 21.

1. *New York Times,* August 3, 1946, p. 6; *New York Herald Tribune,* July 11, 1946, p. 9; Littell, "The Voice of the Apple," 221–22; Shurcliff, *Bombs at Bikini,* 36; Lee, "The Press at Operation Crossroads," 27; Baldwin oral history transcript, 451.
2. Considine, *It's All News to Me,* 202.
3. Littell, "The Voice of the Apple," 226.
4. Lee, "The Press at Operation Crossroads," 28.
5. Sawyer oral history transcript, 37–38; Shurcliff, *Bombs at Bikini,* 145; Berkhouse et al., *Operation Crossroads,* 93.
6. "Final Report of the JCS Evaluation Board," 17; Graybar and Graybar, "America Faces the Atomic Age," 70; *New York Times,* June 23, 1946, sec. 4, p. 10.
7. *New York Times,* July 1, 1946, p. 19; Considine, *It's All News to Me,* 202.
8. *New York Times,* July 3, 1946, p. 3; *Life,* July 15, 1946, 28.
9. *Time,* July 15, 1946, 29; *The Economist,* July 6, 1946, 29–30.
10. *Saturday Review,* August 10, 1946, 18; Considine, *It's All News to Me,* 203.
11. Shurcliff, *Technical Report,* pp. 13.6, 13.12.
12. Ibid., pp. 13.6–12; Considine, *It's All News to Me,* 203.
13. Henderson interview; Berkhouse et al., *Operation Crossroads,* 119; JTF-1, *Operation Crossroads: Gross Damage Report—Test Able,* 14.
14. Keith Wheeler to the *Chicago Daily News,* dispatch, July 2, 1946, Nos. 1808–1948, RG 374, DASA.
15. *The Nation,* July 13, 1946, 29.
16. *New York Times,* July 2, 1946, p. 1, and July 9, 1946, p. 7.
17. Ibid., July 2, 1946, pp. 2, 18, and July 3, 1946, p. 3; *New York Herald Tribune,* July 2, 1946, p. 3; Harrington, "Bikini: War 1, Peace 0," 73.
18. *New York Times,* July 2, 1946, p. 18.

19. *New York Herald Tribune,* July 7, 1946, p. 5.

20. Symington memoirs, 107–8.

21. Gee memorandum, 4–8.

22. Quoted in "Analysis of Bikini's First Atom Bomb Test," 15–18.

23. *Washington Post,* July 2, 1946, p. 8.

24. Commander, JTF-1, *Operational Report,* pp. II-(A)-1–5, (B)-3–5.

25. "Final Report of the JCS Evaluation Board," 19–20; Associated Press wire, July 18, 1946; *New York Times,* July 3, 1946, p. 1.

26. Wayne Thomis to the *Chicago Tribune,* dispatch, July 21, 1946, Nos. 1649–1807, RG 374, DASA.

27. *New York Times,* July 15, 1946, p. 3.

28. Of the 3,619 experimental animals in the Able test, 656 died in the blast (619 rats, 23 goats, 11 pigs, 2 guinea pigs, and 1 mouse). By November 15, 1,953 of the animals, or 54 percent, had died. Shurcliff, *Technical Report,* p. 15.3; *Baltimore Sun,* July 23, 1946, p. 1; *Newsweek,* July 15, 1946, 35.

29. *Newsweek,* July 15, 1946, 35; *New York Times,* July 2, 1946, p. 19, and July 4, 1946, p. 1.

30. *New York Herald Tribune,* July 11, 1946, p. 8.

31. *New York Times,* July 2, 1946, p. 24.

32. Ibid., July 12, 1946, p. 1.

33. Preliminary Statement by the President's Evaluation Commission, July 11, 1946, *Department of State Bulletin* 15, no. 368 (June 21, 1946): 116–17; Preliminary Statement by the JCS Evaluation Board, July 11, 1946, *Department of State Bulletin* 15, no. 368 (June 21, 1946): 115–16; *New York Times,* July 12, 1946, pp. 1, 4. Both the chairman of the JCS board, Karl T. Compton, and his deputy, Bradley Dewey, served on the president's commission. Other members of the Joint Chiefs' board were Maj. Gen. Thomas F. Farrell (formerly with the Manhattan Project, then chief engineer of the New York State Department of Public Works), Gen. Joseph W. Stilwell (of the famous Burma campaign in World War II), Lt. Gen. Lewis H. Brereton (who had served under MacArthur in the Philippines), Vice Adm. John H. Hoover (a member of the Navy General Board), and Rear Adm. Ralph A. Ofstie (senior Navy member of the U.S. Strategic Bombing Survey). The members of the president's commission, in addition to Compton, Bradley, and Chairman Hatch, were Sen. Leverett Saltonstall (Massachusetts), representatives Chet Holifield (California) and Walter G. Andrews (New York), Edward Condon (director of the Bureau of Standards and unofficial aide to Senator McMahon), Fred Searls (one of Baruch's advisors at the United Nations), and William S. Newell, president of the Bath Iron Works Corporation in Bath, Maine, a major Navy contractor. Shurcliff, *Technical Report,* pp. 1.12, 1.15–16.

34. *New York Herald Tribune,* July 13, 1946, p. 5.

35. Sawyer oral history transcript, 36; Rivero interview; Lapp interview; Shelton, *Memoirs of a Nuclear Weaponeer,* p. 2-38.

36. Executive Office of the President, Bureau of the Budget, radio comments of June 30, Division of Press Intelligence, July 1, 1946, HSTL.

37. *New York Times,* July 24, 1946, p. 19; Moll, "Operation Crossroads," 69.

One historian, Greg Herken, wrote that the "error prompted some navy officers to suspect the AAF of sabotaging the test." Herken, *The Winning Weapon*, 225. Herken's cited sources do not point to this conclusion. If the AAF had any hidden motive, it would have been to cause as much destruction as possible to the target fleet. Moreover, a miss would only bring criticism of the AAF itself.

38. Hacker, *The Dragon's Tail*, 133; *Washington Post*, July 10, 1946, p. 13; Bowen et al., *Air Force Atomic Energy Program*, 1:300.

39. Bradbury to Los Alamos Laboratory, cable, July 10, 1946, Box 29, MEDR.

40. Considine, *It's All News to Me*, 203; *Newsweek*, July 22, 1946, 17.

41. Quoted in Shurcliff, *Technical Report*, p. 10.4. Frank Shelton, a former Defense Department official, wrote that a Los Alamos scientist, Bill Ogle, told him that Maj. Harold Wood, the bombardier, said over the radio immediately after the drop that he had "tossed that one," implying that he had made an error. Shelton also claimed that the inquiry into the bombing error revealed that the bomb "planed" as soon as it dropped, thus causing it to go off target. Shelton's statements are not supported by any contemporaneous documents, and have been denied by Wood and Frederick Ashworth. Shelton, *Memoirs of a Nuclear Weaponeer*, p. 2-44; Wood interview; Ashworth interview.

42. *New York Times*, July 22, 1946, p. 4; Bowen et al., *Air Force Atomic Energy Program*, 1:300.

43. Bowen et al., *Air Force Atomic Energy Program*, 1:302; Kepner to Spaatz, letter, July 5, 1946, Box 256, Spaatz papers, LC.

44. *New York Herald Tribune*, July 13, 1946, p. 5; *Newsweek*, July 22, 1946, 17.

45. *Congressional Record*, 79th Cong., 2d sess., 1946, 92, pt. 8: 9943–44 (July 25, 1946); *New York Times*, July 26, 1946, p. 3.

46. Kepner to General Eaker, memorandum, July 30, 1946, War Department, Box 26, miscellaneous USJCS papers, MEDR.

47. Blandy, "Statement on Participation of United States Army Air Forces in Operation Crossroads," July 31, 1946, DOE/CIC 100972; *New York Times*, August 3, 1947, p. 43.

48. *New York Times*, August 23, 1946, p. 9; *Washington Post*, September 27, 1946, p. 6.

49. Groves to the Commanding General, Army Air Forces, attention Col. Roscoe C. Wilson, memorandum, October 17, 1946, Kepner papers, AFHRC.

50. William Bownam to Kepner, letter, October 24, 1946, Kepner papers, AFHRC.

51. Kepner to Groves, letter, December 3, 1946, Kepner papers, AFHRC.

52. Bowen et al., *Air Force Atomic Energy Program*, 1:301–10; Swancutt interview.

53. Tibbets, *The Tibbets Story*, 250–51.

54. Ashworth interview; Shurcliff, *Technical Report*, p. 5.4.

55. Shurcliff, *Technical Report*, p. 19.8.

56. Gerster, "The Special Weapons Center and Atomic Testing," 19–20; Bowen

et al., *Air Force Atomic Energy Program,* 1:311.

57. Henderson interview.

58. *Time,* July 8, 1946, 21; Considine, *It's All News to Me,* 202; *New York Times,* July 1, 1946, p. 1.

59. Dr. Frank Thone to *Science Service,* dispatch, July 3, 1946; Keyes Beech to *Honolulu Star-Bulletin,* dispatch, July 3, 1946, Nos. 918–1108, RG 374, DASA.

60. Jack Kofoed to *Chicago Daily News,* dispatch, July 3, 1946, Nos. 1–99, RG 374, DASA; Robert K. Butcher to *Shreveport Times,* dispatch, July 3, 1946, Nos. 918–1108, RG 374, DASA.

61. Frank Conniff to *New York Journal-American,* dispatch, July 2, 1946, Nos. 558–757, RG 374, DASA.

CHAPTER 22.

1. Nichols, *The Road to Trinity,* 239; *Washington Evening Star,* July 17, 1946.

2. *New York Times,* September 5, 1946, p. 7.

3. Joseph L. Myler, dispatch, July 16, 1946, RG 374, DASA; *New York Times,* July 17, 1946, p. 7. Juda was impressed by the photographs and looked grateful. "We're inclined to believe, however," wrote E. B. White of the *New Yorker,* "that this was mere politeness on his part, noblesse oblige being as basic as uranium and sometimes just as handy." *New Yorker,* July 27, 1946, 11.

4. Quoted in Nichols, *The Road to Trinity,* 239.

5. Blandy, remarks, September 5, 1946, p. 7, DOE/CIC 100967; *New York Times,* July 6, 1946, p. 1, and May 22, 1946, p. 13.

6. McAlpine King to Press Newservice of New York, dispatch, July 23, 1946, Nos. 1949–2130, RG 374, DASA.

7. Notes on JTF-1 Conference on Test Baker on Board USS *Mount McKinley,* July 10, 1946, pp. 3–4, DOE/CIC 130043; JTF-1 Press Release No. 62, July 14, 1946, DOE/CIC 100975; "Transcript of Lecture by Colonel Warren," October 7, 1946, p. 9, DOE/CIC 140740.

8. Report of Medico-Legal Board, August 19, 1946, DOE/CIC 140683; *New York Times,* March 11, 1946, p. 8.

9. Hacker interview. Hacker was told this story by Hymer Friedell, Warren's assistant.

10. Quoted in Nichols, *The Road to Trinity,* 123; Jones, *United States Army in World War II,* 411–12, 421; Kemper interview; Ashworth interview.

11. Hacker, *The Dragon's Tail,* 93; Nichols, *The Road to Trinity,* 198.

12. Lamont, *Day of Trinity,* 189; Lawren, *The General and the Bomb,* 205; Goodchild, *J. Robert Oppenheimer,* 147; Warren oral history transcript, 2:786–87, 804.

13. Warren oral history transcript, 2:807.

14. Quoted in Szasz, *The Day the Sun Rose Twice,* 115, 144.

15. Lamont, *Day of Trinity,* 269–70.

16. Quoted in Hacker, *The Dragon's Tail,* 84–85.

17. Warren to Groves, memorandum, July 21, 1945, Folder 4 ("Trinity"), RG 77, MEDR.

18. *New York Times,* September 12, 1945, pp. 1, 4.

19. Quoted in Hacker, *The Dragon's Tail,* 110; Jones, *United States Army in World War II,* 543–45; Warren, "The Role of Radiology in the Development of the Atomic Bomb," 886–93.

20. Quoted in Hacker, *The Dragon's Tail,* 112.

21. *New York Times,* September 13, 1945, p. 4.

22. *Hearings on Atomic Energy,* 113, 510 (February 15, 1946); Hacker, *The Dragon's Tail,* 113.

23. Shurcliff, *Technical Report,* p. 3.57.

24. Report of the Committee for Review of Radiological Safety Measures, June 30, 1946, pp. 4–5, DOE/CIC 64028; Berkhouse et al., *Operation Crossroads,* 45. The committee was chaired by Robert R. Newell, and its members included John J. Morton, Frank Fremont-Smith, Joseph G. Hamilton, Louis H. Hempelmann, Alfred A. de Lorimier, L. D. Marinelli, James F. Nolan, and Eugene P. Pendergrass.

25. Berkhouse et al., *Operation Crossroads,* 451–84.

26. Bradbury to Holloway and Roger Warner, letter, May 20, 1946, p. 2, LANL; Holloway to Bradbury, letter, April 23, 1946, p. 3, LANL (emphasis in original).

27. Warren to Rear Adm. Ross T. McIntyre, memorandum, March 8, 1946, Box 2, Folder 3, Warren papers, UCLA.

28. Warren to William G. Myers, letter, December 31, 1946, DOE/CIC 140703.

29. Notes on JTF-1 Staff Conference of February 4, 1946, p. 2, LANL; Lyon to Ashworth, memorandum, February 6, 1946, DOE/CIC 460206.

30. Lyon to Parsons, memorandum, April 4, 1946, DOE/CIC 48586.

31. Commander, JTF-1, *Operational Report,* p. VII-(C)-5.

32. Berkhouse et al., *Operation Crossroads,* 54; Parsons to J1, J3, J5, entitled "Delay of HAVEN's Departure and Indoctrination of Radiological Safety Officers," Box 26, MEDR.

33. Warren, form letter, April 19, 1946, DOE/CIC 50615; Warren oral history transcript, 3:890; Warren interview.

34. Warren oral history transcript, 2:827, 859; 3:890; Commander, JTF-1, *Operational Report,* p. VII-(C)-6; Berkhouse et al., *Operation Crossroads,* 56–57.

35. There were 303 radsafe monitors at the Able test, but only about 225 were available at the time of the Baker shot. Berkhouse et al., *Operation Crossroads,* 54, 61; Shurcliff, *Bombs at Bikini,* 31–32.

36. Warren oral history transcript, 3:897–98; Bradley, *No Place to Hide,* 27; Berkhouse et al., *Operation Crossroads,* 49.

37. Warren, "Radiological Safety Section Activities at Bikini" (May 31, 1946), DOE/CIC 64029; Warren, "Radiation to Be Expected in Test Able," June 11, 1946, DOE/CIC 64030; Berkhouse et al., *Operation Crossroads,* 47; Hacker, *The Dragon's Tail,* 17–18, 41–42.

38. Report of the Committee for Review of Radiological Safety Measures, June 30, 1946, p. 4, DOE/CIC 64028.

39. Bradley, *No Place to Hide,* 104–5; Hacker, *The Dragon's Tail,* 131–36.
40. Warren oral history transcript, 3:898.
41. Thomas Farrell to Groves, memorandum, December 3, 1945; Parsons to Blandy, memorandum, December 3, 1945, Box 4, Entry 1, Folder 8, RG 77, MEDR.
42. Bradbury to Groves, undated memorandum entitled "Surface Shot for Naval Test"; memorandum entitled "Outline of Meeting 22 February 1946," Box 26, RG 77, MEDR; *Hearings on Atomic Energy,* 457 (January 24, 1946).
43. Shurcliff, *Technical Report,* p. 5.6.
44. Henry W. Newson to Bradbury, memorandum entitled "Possible Difficulties in Naval Tests," December 17, 1945, p. 4, LANL, DOE/CIC 120851.
45. Blandy to Chief of Naval Operations, memorandum, January 26, 1946, p. 7, LANL.
46. Quoted in Berkhouse et al., *Operation Crossroads,* 60.
47. Commander, JTF-1, *Operation Plan,* Annex E (Safety Plan), App., pp. 1286–89.
48. Penney to Parsons, Sawyer, Warren, and Revelle, memorandum entitled "Height of Water Column in Test BAKER," June 19, 1946, Box 74, Folder 1, Warren papers, UCLA.
49. Warren, "Safety Predictions—Test Baker," n.d., p. 5, DOE/CIC 140564.
50. Notes on JTF-1 Conference on Test Baker on Board USS *Mount McKinley,* July 10, 1946, pp. 3–4, DOE/CIC 130043.

CHAPTER 23.

1. Kemper interview.
2. Logbook of the USS *Mount McKinley,* July 23, 1946, OAB.
3. *Honolulu Star-Bulletin,* July 23, 1946, p. 3; dispatches from July 23–26, 1946, RG 374, DASA; *New York Times,* July 24, 1946, p. 8.
4. Frank B. Allen to International News Service, dispatch, July 23, 1946, RG 374, DASA.
5. John M. Carlisle to the *Detroit News,* dispatch, July 24, 1946, Nos. 2131–2336, RG 374, DASA; Shurcliff, *Bombs at Bikini,* 150.
6. Shurcliff, *Bombs at Bikini,* 149–50; *Time,* September 16, 1946, 100.
7. Berkhouse et al., *Operation Crossroads,* 97.
8. Philip W. Porter to *Cleveland Plain Dealer,* dispatch, July 19, 1946, Nos. 1649–1807, RG 374, DASA.
9. Memorandum entitled "Remarks on William and Baker Days—Col. S. L. Warren—22 July 1946," p. 1, Box 3, Folder 10, Warren papers, UCLA; Bowen et al., *Air Force Atomic Energy Program,* 1:319–20.
10. *Crossroads Pacific Breeze,* July 26, 1946, p. 2, Schultz papers, SIA.
11. *New York Times,* July 22, 1946, p. 4, and July 17, 1946, p. 1; Holloway interview.
12. William F. Tyree to United Press, dispatch, July 25, 1946, Nos. 2337–2534, RG 374, DASA; *Time,* August 5, 1946, 27.
13. Shurcliff, *Bombs at Bikini,* 151; *New York Times,* July 25, 1946, p. 1; Baker

Day detonation transcript, DOE/CIC 76360. In his book *No Place to Hide* (p. 91), David Bradley mistakenly referred to Titterton's voice as the "Harvard accent of the man who would detonate the bomb."

14. *New York Times,* July 25, 1946, p. 1.
15. Shurcliff, *Bombs at Bikini,* 151–52.
16. Porter to *Cleveland Plain Dealer,* dispatch, July 24, 1946, Nos. 2131–2336, RG 374, DASA.
17. Bradley, *No Place to Hide,* 92.
18. *New York Times,* July 25, 1946, p. 2.
19. *New York Herald Tribune,* July 25, 1946, p. 1; *Time,* August 5, 1946, 88.
20. *Newsweek,* August 5, 1946, 29.
21. Shurcliff, *Technical Report,* p. 24.3; Berkhouse et al., *Operation Crossroads,* 103; Nichols, *The Road to Trinity,* 241.
22. "Radio Bikini" transcript, 16.
23. Shurcliff, *Technical Report,* p. 21.6; Glasstone and Dolan, *The Effects of Nuclear Weapons,* 52, 251; Sawyer, *Report of the Technical Director,* 5–6.
24. Blandy, remarks, September 5, 1946, p. 7, DOE/CIC 100967; Nichols, *The Road to Trinity,* 242; Shurcliff, *Technical Report,* p. 28.3; Hacker, *The Dragon's Tail,* 138–39; Commander, JTF-1, *Operational Report,* p. VI-(D)-45.
25. Sawyer, *Report of the Technical Director,* 7; Glasstone and Dolan, *The Effects of Nuclear Weapons,* 53.
26. Shurcliff, *Bombs at Bikini,* 159; Considine, *It's All News to Me,* 203.
27. Fee, *Radiological Decontamination,* 1:14.
28. Nichols, *The Road to Trinity,* 242.
29. Berkhouse et al., *Operation Crossroads,* 107; Sawyer, *Report of the Technical Director,* 14; Shurcliff, *Technical Report,* pp. 9.14, 21.5, 28.5; Shurcliff, *Bombs at Bikini,* 160–62.
30. JTF-1 Release No. 65, August 26, 1946, DOE/CIC 100969; *New York Times,* August 3, 1946, p. 6; July 30, 1946, p. 8; and August 6, 1946, p. 1.
31. *Technical Inspection Report, USS Saratoga,* p. 14, RG 374, DASA; Shurcliff, *Technical Report,* p. 6.12; Glasstone and Dolan, *The Effects of Nuclear Weapons,* 249–50; Berkhouse et al., *Operation Crossroads,* 101.
32. Warren oral history transcript, 3:903–4; Berkhouse et al., *Operation Crossroads,* 104; Nichols, *The Road to Trinity,* 242; Hempelmann interview.
33. *New York Times,* July 26, 1946, p. 3.
34. Nichols, *The Road to Trinity,* 242.
35. *New York Times,* July 26, 1946, p. 3.
36. Ibid., 20.

CHAPTER 24.

1. Scoville, "The Atomic Bomb and the Resultant Phenomena," 19; Scoville, "Nuclear Radiation Effects in Tests A and B—Preliminary Report of" (September 25, 1946) (hereafter Scoville, "Nuclear Radiation Effects"), Enclosure J to Sawyer, *Report of the Technical Director,* p. J.7, LANL.
2. Sawyer, *Report of the Technical Director,* 25; Winant, "Command Prob-

lems of Atomic Defensive Warfare" (September 1947), DOE/CIC 0048678; Scoville, "Nuclear Radiation Effects," pp. J.1, J.9.

3. R. J. Buettner, "Safety Prediction—Test Baker," 14–16, n.d., DOE/CIC 140564.

4. Commander, JTF-1, *Operational Report,* pp. VII-(C)-53, VI-D-79. The bomb was detonated at 8:35 A.M. and the first manned patrols reentered the lagoon at 9:15 A.M. The salvage unit entered the lagoon at 10:15 A.M. and began checking and boarding target vessels. Berkhouse et al., *Operation Crossroads,* 97, 104; Shurcliff, *Technical Report,* p. 20.12.

5. Warren oral history transcript, 3:905.

6. Quoted in Hacker, *The Dragon's Tail,* 138–39.

7. *Newsweek,* August 5, 1946, 30.

8. Berkhouse et al., *Operation Crossroads,* 105; Blandy to Commanding General, AAF, cable, July 28, 1946, Box 26, Folder F-2-7, MEDR.

9. Fee, *Radiological Decontamination,* 1:8.

10. Berkhouse et al., *Operation Crossroads,* 68; *Time,* September 16, 1946, 100.

11. *New York Times,* July 23, 1946, p. 6.

12. Quoted in Caufield, *Multiple Exposures,* 13.

13. JTF-1 Press Release No. 78, September 24, 1946, OAB.

14. Radiological Safety Section to Technical Director, memorandum, September 25, 1946, App. 7, Sec. E, LANL; Fee, *Radiological Decontamination,* 1:14.

15. Herbert Scoville, Jr., to Warren, memorandum, April 27, 1946, Box 1, Folder 13, Warren papers, UCLA; Bureau of Ships Minutes of Conference of 3 May 1946 (May 7, 1946), Box 1, Folder 13, Warren papers, UCLA; Berkhouse et al., *Operation Crossroads,* 105.

16. Fee, *Radiological Decontamination,* 1:4.

17. Berkhouse et al., *Operation Crossroads,* 106–12; Fee, *Radiological Decontamination,* 1:5–7.

18. Warren oral history transcript, 3:908.

19. Fee, *Radiological Decontamination,* 1:7.

20. Betts to Nichols, undated memorandum, Box 26, Folder F-3-5, MEDR; Nichols interview.

21. "Radio Bikini" transcript, 17; Fee, *Radiological Decontamination,* 1:12.

22. Quoted in Wasserman and Solomon, *Killing Our Own,* 43–44; Shurcliff, *Operation Crossroads,* 219; Uhl and Ensign, *GI Guinea Pigs,* 38–41; Terkel, "The Good War," 72–75; *New York Times,* September 18, 1946, p. 1; Berkhouse et al., *Operation Crossroads,* 115.

23. Warren oral history transcript, 3:909; Fee, *Radiological Decontamination,* 3:84.

24. Kirkpatrick, "Panamint Parade," 49; Fee, *Radiological Decontamination,* 1:11; Blandy, naval message 292336Z, July 30, 1946, DOE/CIC 48641.

25. Los Alamos to Liaison Office, cable, August 2, 1946, Box 28, MEDR; draft cable message to Colonel Gee, LANL, DOE/CIC 128462.

26. Warren to Viola Warren, letter, August 2, 1946, DOE/CIC 140495.

27. Schubert and Lapp, *Radiation,* 223.

28. Warren oral history transcript, 2:875.

29. Schubert and Lapp, *Radiation,* 224; Warren oral history transcript, 2:875; Hacker, *The Dragon's Tail,* 141.
30. Myers to Warren, memorandum, August 27, 1946, DOE/CIC 140671; D. L. Collins, "Operation Crossroads Reports to Rad Safe Instrument Division," DOE/CIC 140718.
31. Warren to Myers, letter, December 31, 1946, DOE/CIC 140703.
32. Berkhouse et al., *Operation Crossroads,* 50.
33. Shurcliff, *Technical Report,* p. 9.11.
34. Commander, JTF-1, *Operational Report,* pp. VII-(C)-4, II-(A)-2; Shurcliff, *Technical Report,* pp. 3.42–43.
35. Warren to Blandy, memorandum, August 7, 1946, p. 3, DOE/CIC 140692.
36. Undated memorandum on radiological condition of *New York,* DOE/CIC 64036.
37. Bradley, *No Place to Hide,* 104, 109–10.

CHAPTER 25.

1. Warren oral history transcript, 3:907, 911; Warren to Viola Warren, letter, July 30, 1946, DOE/CIC 140484.
2. Warren oral history transcript, 3:914, 936; Berkhouse et al., *Operation Crossroads,* 112; *New York Times,* July 30, 1946, p. 8.
3. Warren oral history transcript, 3:909–11.
4. Lyon to Parsons, memorandum, May 5, 1947, DOE/CIC 140713.
5. Bradley interview.
6. Warren to Blandy, message, August 15, 1946, p. 2, Box 4, Folder 5, Warren papers, UCLA; list of overdoses evaluated on 9 August 1946, 8 August 1946, and 6/7 August 1946, Box 4, Folder 1, Warren papers, UCLA.
7. William A. Wulfman to Warren, memorandum, August 9, 1946, DOE/CIC 64034; R. R. Newell, August 10, 1946, meeting of the Medico-Legal Board, DOE/CIC 140672.
8. Warren oral history transcript, 3:937; F. G. Fahrion to Blandy, "Weekly Report for Week Ending 24 August 1946," p. 3, DOE/CIC 48648.
9. R. J. Rieckhoff and D. W. Jones to Wulfman, memorandum, August 10, 1946, DOE/CIC 140634.
10. D. R. Bergh, Flag Secretary, memorandum prepared on August 6, 1946, Conference on CJTF-1, August 8, 1946, p. 2, LANL (hereafter Bergh memorandum).
11. Warren to Blandy, memorandum, August 7, 1946, p. 3, DOE/CIC 140692; Bergh memorandum.
12. GAO, *Operation Crossroads,* 8; Lapp interview.
13. Bradley, *No Place to Hide,* 113–14.
14. Hacker, *The Dragon's Tail,* 3–5, 40–41, 52–53, 61–65, 77–79.
15. Report of the Medico-Legal Committee on Plutonium Hazard Associated with Test Baker, July 22, 1946, DOE/CIC 140586.
16. Conard interview.
17. Warren to Blandy, memorandum, August 7, 1946, p. 2, DOE/CIC 140692;

Warren to Commander Task Group 1.2, memorandum, August 13, 1946, DOE/CIC 140649.

18. Scoville, "Nuclear Radiation Effects," pp. J.11, J.46, LANL.

19. Warren to Blandy, memorandum, August 3, 1946, DOE/CIC 140630.

20. Bergh memorandum, 3; Fee, *Radiological Decontamination*, 1:13; minutes of Medico-Legal Board meeting, August 4, 1946, DOE/CIC 140613.

21. Betts to Nichols, undated memorandum, Box 26, Folder F-3-5, MEDR.

22. Bergh memorandum, 3.

23. Warren to Blandy, memorandum, August 7, 1946, DOE/CIC 140692.

24. Blandy to Navy Department, naval message 080303Z, August 11, 1946, DOE/CIC 48661.

25. Wulfman to Warren, memorandum entitled "Monitoring Problems," August 9, 1946, DOE/CIC 64034.

26. Berkhouse et al., *Operation Crossroads*, 27; Fee, *Radiological Decontamination*, 1:13.

27. Handwritten teletype message from the USS *Haven*, Box 4, Folder 5, Warren papers, UCLA.

28. Warren to Viola Warren, letter, August 11, 1946, DOE/CIC 140498; Warren to Admiral Fahrion, memorandum, August 13, 1946, DOE/CIC 140666; Fee, *Radiological Decontamination*, 1:13.

29. Bradley, *No Place to Hide*, 116–17; Blandy, naval message 100648Z, August 11, 1946, DOE/CIC 48663.

30. Warren to Commander Task Group 1.2, memorandum, August 13, 1946, DOE/CIC 140649.

31. Warren to Capt. S. P. Bednarczyk, naval message 130820Z, August 13, 1946, DOE/CIC 64045; Warren to Blandy, memorandum, August 7, 1946, DOE/CIC 140692.

32. Berkhouse et al., *Operation Crossroads*, 119.

33. Warren to Viola Warren, letter, August 11, 1946, DOE/CIC 140498; letters, August 13 and 15, 1946, DOE/CIC 140500.

34. Warren to Viola Warren, letter, August 20, 1946, DOE/CIC 140472; Warren oral history transcript, 2:844, 878.

35. Bowen et al., *Air Force Atomic Energy Program*, 1:325–26; Berkhouse et al., *Operation Crossroads*, 43, 58.

36. Bradley, *No Place to Hide*, 95–96.

37. White, "Journal of a Contaminated Man," 171; F. T. Winant, Jr., "Command Problems of Atomic Defense Warfare," September 1947, DOE/CIC 48678.

CHAPTER 26.

1. *The New Republic*, July 22, 1946, 73.

2. *New York Times*, August 4, 1946, p. 3.

3. Cousins, "The Standardization of Catastrophe," 18.

4. *New York Times*, August 12, 1946, p. 4, and August 8, 1946, p. 18; *Time*, August 26, 1946, 23.

5. *New York Times*, August 21, 1946, p. 18, and August 23, 1946, p. 9; Cof-

fin, "In the Light of Bikini," 370–71; *State Department Bulletin* 15, no. 370 (August 4, 1946): 210.

6. Wallace, *The Price of Vision*, 591, 661–69; Walker, *Henry A. Wallace and American Foreign Policy*, 149–58; Forrestal, *The Forrestal Diaries*, 206–10; Byrnes, *Speaking Frankly*, 239–42; Acheson, *Present at the Creation*, 190–92; *New York Times*, September 18, 1946, pp. 1, 18.

7. Ward, "James F. Byrnes and the Paris Conference," 66–68; Feis, *From Trust to Terror*, 121–25.

8. Gaddis, *The United States and the Origins of the Cold War*, 321.

9. Acheson, *Present at the Creation*, 196.

10. Quoted in Isaacson and Thomas, *The Wise Men*, 371.

11. Forrestal, *The Forrestal Diaries*, 192–97; Acheson, *Present at the Creation*, 196.

12. Truman to Sen. Richard B. Russell, Jr., letter, August 9, 1946, Official File, HSTL; *Public Papers of the Presidents of the United States, Harry S. Truman (1945)*, 212.

13. Lilienthal, *The Atomic Energy Years*, 391; Donovan, *Conflict and Crisis*, 172.

14. Quoted in Clifford, *Counsel to the President*, 110, 123–24; Krock, *Memoirs*, 470, 478.

15. Quoted in Isaacson and Thomas, *The Wise Men*, 374, 379.

16. Forrestal, *The Forrestal Diaries*, 200.

17. Spanier and Nogee, *The Politics of Disarmament*, 57.

18. *FRUS: 1945*, 2:69; Nogee, *Soviet Policy towards International Control of Atomic Energy*.

19. Leahy to Truman, memorandum, October 23, 1945, President's Personal File, HSTL.

20. The fifth, Frenchman Bertrand Goldschmidt, wrote, "I felt even more vividly the contrast between the two projects, the one inhuman and useless, the other unrealistic but indispensable." Goldschmidt, *Atomic Rivals*, 307.

21. *New York Times*, June 25, 1946, pp. 4, 20, and June 30, 1946, sec. 4, pp. 1, 5.

22. Rusk, *As I Saw It*, 139.

23. *New York Times*, June 20, 1946, p. 1; "Radio Bikini" transcript, 7; Kolko and Kolko, *The Limits of Power*, 99–109.

24. Truman, *Years of Trial and Hope*, 11.

25. Quoted in Nogee, *Soviet Policy towards International Control of Atomic Energy*, 62; *New York Times*, July 4, 1946, p. 4.

26. *Honolulu Star-Bulletin*, June 21, 1946, p. 9.

27. *New York Times*, July 1, 1946, p. 3, and July 2, 1946, p. 4.

28. Incoming State Department telegram from Stockholm, July 3, 1946, Box 4618, File 811.2423/7, General Records of the Department of State, RG 59.

29. *New York Times*, July 25, 1946, p. 1.

CHAPTER 27.

1. L. A. Kniskern to Blandy, memorandum, April 30, 1946; minutes of conference held aboard USS *Mount McKinley*, June 13, 1946; Director of Ship Material to Chief of Bureau of Ships, memorandum, June 21, 1946, JTF-1,

Box 2, "Test Charlie" folder, RG 374, DASA.

2. *Hearings on House Joint Resolution 307,* 2417 (January 29, 1946); Notes on Conference of Staff Division Heads, July 17, 1946, DOE/CIC 128475; *New York Times,* August 9, 1946, p. 35, and August 23, 1946, p. 9; minutes of March 14, 1946, conference entitled "Arrangement for Test 'C' (Deep Water Test)"; notes on conference on "Test Charlie" aboard USS *Mount McKinley,* July 15, 1946, LANL.

3. Letter to Groves enclosing July 17, 1946, letter from Cy Betts, July 26, 1946, DOE/CIC 78350; Groves to Blandy, cable, July 19, 1946, Box 26, Folder F-2-7, MEDR.

4. Groves to Patterson, cable, July 19, 1946, LANL; Rosenberg, "U.S. Nuclear Stockpile," 26; *New York Times,* August 16, 1946, p. 1.

5. Groves to the JCS, memorandum, August 7, 1946; Commander, JTF-1, to Chief of Naval Operations, August 17, 1946, JCS 1552/74, CCS 471.6 (10-16-45) (SCC 9), RG 218, USJCS; Reynolds, *Admiral John H. Towers,* 619 n. 25.

6. Rosenberg, "U.S. Nuclear Stockpile," 27; Hatch to Truman, letter, September 5, 1946, President's Secretary's Files, HSTL; Patterson to the Chairman of the Joint Chiefs of Staff, memorandum, August 21, 1946, Records of the Secretary of War, RG 107 (Atomic Energy Folder), NA. "The [AAF's] inability to get accurate information from the Manhattan Project . . . made it impossible to plan atomic operations on anything but sheer guesswork." Greenwood, "The Emergence of the Postwar Strategic Air Force," 230.

7. *New York Times,* September 8, 1946, p. 1; report by the Joint Staff Planners to the Joint Chiefs of Staff re "Test 'C' Operation 'Crossroads,'" JCS 1522/74, CCS 741.6 (10-16-45) (SCC9), RG 218, USJCS; Forrestal, *The Forrestal Diaries,* 203.

8. *Time,* September 16, 1946, 25; *Newsweek,* September 16, 1946, 24.

9. *New York Times,* September 8, 1946, pp. 1, 24; Parsons to JTF-1 Divisions, memorandum, September 13, 1946, DOE/CIC 0120892.

10. *Washington Post,* October 3, 1946, p. 5; *United States News,* September 20, 1946, p. 19; *Newsweek,* September 16, 1946, 21.

11. Berkhouse et al., *Operation Crossroads,* 67–68; Samuel W. McGovern to Commander Task Unit 1.2.12, memorandum, October 23, 1946, DOE/CIC 48679; F. G. Fahrion to Blandy, memorandum, September 1, 1946, DOE/CIC 48589; "Weekly Report for Week Ending 7 September 1946," p. 3, DOE/CIC 48649.

12. F. G. Fahrion to Blandy, memorandum, October 13, 1946, DOE/CIC 48652.

13. A total of 1,036 tons of ammunition were removed, out of a total of about 2,700 tons that was ordered for removal. Berkhouse et al., *Operation Crossroads,* 121–25.

14. These included eight to San Francisco (the destroyer *Conyngham,* attack transports *Bladen, Cortland, Fillmore, Geneva,* and *Niagara, LCI-549,* and *LCI-615*) and six to Mare Island, California (the submarines *Dentuda, Parche, Searaven, Skate, Skipjack,* and *Tuna*). Berkhouse et al., *Operation Crossroads,* 124, 139–40.

15. *New York Times,* November 2, 1946, p. 10.

16. Lowry was Commander of the Rear Echelon, placing him in charge of JTF-1 activities in the United States while Blandy was at Bikini. Shurcliff, *Technical Report,* p. 3.24.

17. *Washington Post,* November 8, 1946, p. C-1; *Washington Evening Star,* November 11, 1946, p. B1. *New York Times,* November 2, 1946, p. 10; November 11, 1946, p. 10; and November 18, 1946, p. 31. *Newsweek,* November 18, 1946, 68; Lippmann to Forrestal, letter, November 11, 1946; Forrestal to Lippmann, letter, November 12, 1946, Box 71, Section 3, Folder 794, Lippmann Manuscripts, Yale University, New Haven.

18. Weart, *Nuclear Fear,* 109. According to *Stars and Stripes,* the three biggest news stories of 1946 were Operation Crossroads, the Republican Party's takeover of Congress in the November elections, and Hermann Goering's suicide. Zumwalt, *The Stars and Stripes,* 124.

19. *New York Times,* August 4, 1946, sec. 4, p. 8.

20. Undated "Penny" cartoon strip, Blandy papers, OAB.

21. *Time,* July 15, 1946, 29; *New York Herald Tribune,* June 11, 1946, p. 41; *New York Times,* July 7, 1946, sec. 6, p. 15; Blandy papers, OAB; Graybar and Graybar, "America Faces the Atomic Age," 68.

22. *New York Times,* August 11, 1946, p. 30.

23. Ibid., March 1, 1970, sec. 6, p. 24. In fact, a mosaic from a third- or fourth-century Roman villa in Sicily shows women in a gymnasium dressed in rather skimpy two-piece bathing suits. *New York Times,* April 19, 1970, sec. 6, p. 12.

24. Martin and Koda, *Splash,* 139; Attwood, "The Birth of the Bikini," 78–82; *Newsweek,* July 7, 1986, 50; *New York Times,* March 1, 1970, sec. 6, pp. 24–25.

25. *Sports Illustrated,* February 1989 (25th Anniversary Swimsuit Issue), 34.

26. *Webster's Third New World Dictionary,* 215; *Sports Illustrated,* February 1989, 34; Bocca, *Bikini Beach,* 137–40.

27. *Newsweek,* August 5, 1946, 29; "Operation Crossroads: Color Photographs," 519; Boyer, *By the Bomb's Early Light,* 11–12; Wolfe, "Nuclear Country," 14; Farrell, "The Crossroads of Bikini," 57.

28. Wood, *America in the Movies,* 51.

29. Probert, *Swimwear in Vogue since 1910,* 38–48; *Life,* September 3, 1945, 53–54.

30. Quoted in McQuade and Atwan, *Popular Writing in America,* 235; *Newsweek,* August 4, 1986, 53.

CHAPTER 28.

1. *New York Times,* October 16, 1946, p. 33; Parsons, speech, October 9, 1946, DOE/CIC 100958.

2. Boyer, *By the Bomb's Early Light,* 90.

3. *New York Times,* September 5, 1946, p. 7, and August 5, 1946, p. 1.

4. Warren, "The Role of Radiology in the Development of the Atomic Bomb," 913; *Time,* February 17, 1947, 29.

5. *New York Herald Tribune,* November 3, 1946, sec. 10, p. 28.

6. Larson interview; Warren, "Conclusions," 88.

7. *Time,* February 17, 1947, 29.

8. Gerstell, *How to Survive an Atomic Bomb,* 6; Commander, JTF-1, *Operational Report,* pp. II-(A)-1–4; Blandy, "Operation Crossroads," 343; Warren, "Conclusions," 88.

9. Release by James Forrestal, May 19, 1947, DOE/CIC 48806; notes on "Information received over the telephone from the Press Section of Pubinfo," DOE/CIC 0048645.

10. *Washington Post,* July 6, 1947, sec. 2, p. 1, and May 23, 1947, p. 23.

11. Warren to Commander Task Group 1.2, memorandum, August 13, 1946, DOE/CIC 140649; Warren to Blandy, memorandum, August 7, 1946, DOE/CIC 140692; GAO, *Operation Crossroads,* 34, 109, 115.

12. Fee, *Radiological Decontamination,* 1:4.

13. Committee on the Biological Effects of Ionizing Radiations, *Health Effects of Exposure to Low Levels of Ionizing Radiation (BEIR V).*

14. R. T. Hadeer to Bureau of Medicine and Surgery, memorandum, April 7, 1947, DOE/CIC 48704; C. A. Swanson, memorandum, January 31, 1947, DOE/CIC 48653; Coffin to Kwajalein Atoll Commander, memorandum, April 9, 1947, DOE/CIC 48590; GAO, *Operation Crossroads,* 33–34.

15. Lyon to Parsons, memorandum re Ensign Coffin, May 5, 1947, DOE/CIC 140713.

16. Report of Medico-Legal Board, August 19, 1946, DOE/CIC 140683.

17. Reports of Medico-Legal Board meetings on August 12 and 13, 1946, DOE/CIC 140641, 140642, 140686; report of Medico-Legal Board, June 30, 1946, DOE/CIC 64028.

18. R. R. Newell, undated memorandum entitled "Technical Operation Ships Clearance," pp. 8, 9, Box 3, Folder 9, Warren papers, UCLA; Warren oral history transcript, 2:871, 890.

19. Fee, *Radiological Decontamination,* 3:61–62, 65–73.

20. Parsons to Warren, memorandum entitled "Wartime Radiation Tolerance," January 18, 1947, Box 5, Folder 4, Warren papers, UCLA; Warren, undated memorandum entitled "0930–1000 Radiation to Be Expected in Test Able," p. 2, DOE/CIC 64030.

21. Fee, *Radiological Decontamination,* 3:77–83.

22. Scoville to Lyon, memorandum, November 21, 1946, DOE/CIC 0048692.

23. Fee, *Radiological Decontamination,* 3:107–9; J. J. Fee, memorandum entitled "Conference on Radiological Safety; Report of," November 27, 1946, p. 3, DOE/CIC 0048697.

24. Fee, *Radiological Decontamination,* 3:53, 106–15.

25. Proposed Statement (Interim) for Release in San Francisco, January 22, 1982; Office of the Chief of Naval Operations to Mayor Diane Feinstein, undated letter, DOE/CIC 0048647.

26. Warren to Parsons, memorandum, January 6, 1947, DOE/CIC 140711.

27. Warren to all Naval Task Groups, JTF-1, teletype, August 29, 1946, DOE/CIC 126103.

28. Fee, *Radiological Decontamination,* 3:14; Berkhouse et al., *Operation Crossroads,* 126; Parsons, memorandum for OP-33 entitled "Crossroads

Target Vessels—Disposition of," February 20, 1948, Box 6, Rivero Folder, Records of the Atomic Energy and Guided Missile Division, RG 38, OAB; notes on Joint Crossroads Committee Conference of November 19, 1946, Box 104, Entry 47, RG 374, DASA. *New York Times,* January 9, 1947, p. 6; January 30, 1947, pp. 2, 10; May 11, 1947, p. 19; January 13, 1948, p. 8; March 25, 1948, p. 14; April 21, 1948, p. 54; and June 9, 1948, p. 9. *Washington Post,* July 6, 1947, sec. 2, p. 1; Delgado et al., *The Archeology of the Atomic Bomb,* 31–33, 173–76.

29. Table entitled "Tabulation of Decay Time from Various Intensities Down to 0.1r/day," in memorandum from Warren to Blandy, August 3, 1946, DOE/CIC 140630; Fee, *Radiological Decontamination,* 1:3–17, 67–123; Glasstone and Dolan, *The Effects of Nuclear Weapons,* chap. 10.

30. Fee, *Radiological Decontamination,* 3:31; Kenneth G. Scott to Capt. Philip Lemmler, memorandum entitled "Plutonium Hazard on the U.S.S. Crittenden," January 27, 1947, DOE/CIC 48673.

31. *New York Times,* June 20, 1979, pp. 1, 14.

32. Quigley, "Swimming in the Atomic Lagoon," 34–42; Uhl and Ensign, *GI Guinea Pigs,* 38–42.

33. *In re Veterans Administration Claim of Mrs. Jean A. Erspamer.*

34. Terkel, *The Good War,* 545–54.

35. Warren, "The Role of Radiology in the Development of the Atomic Bomb"; Report of Medico-Legal Board, August 19, 1946, DOE/CIC 140683.

36. William Rubinson to Bradbury, memorandum, August 26, 1946, DOE/CIC 120714.

37. Lt. Col. Richard A. House, memorandum for the record, April 29, 1953, DOE/CIC 126924.

38. Hacker, *The Dragon's Tail,* 151.

39. *New York Times,* June 20, 1979, p. 24.

40. *Feres v. United States,* 340 U.S. 135 (1950); *Inter-Agency Task Force,* vol. 4, Report of the Work Group on Care and Benefits, pp. 16–23.

41. Radiation-exposed Veterans Compensation Act of 1988, P.L. 100-321; *Federal Register,* October 18, 1989, pp. 42802–3.

CHAPTER 29.

1. *New York Times,* August 16, 1946, p. 6.

2. Strope, "The Navy and the Atomic Bomb," 1222.

3. Bowen et al., *Air Force Atomic Energy Program,* 1:340–41, 348, 2:379.

4. Fee, *Radiological Decontamination,* 2:165, 195.

5. Chief of Naval Operations to Commander-in-Chief, Pacific, memorandum entitled "Removal of Equipment and Supplies from Contaminated CROSSROADS Target Ships," February 18, 1947, OAB; Blandy, "Bikini: Guidepost to the Future," 8; *New York Times,* September 22, 1946, p. 34.

6. Shurcliff, *Technical Report,* p. 3.73.

7. Blandy, "The Future Value of Sea Power," 495–98; Blandy, "Report on Bikini," 2.

8. Quoted in Blandy, "Operation Crossroads," 343; *New York Times,* September 22, 1946, p. 34; Delgado et al., *The Archeology of the Atomic Bomb,* 39.

9. *New York Times,* August 3, 1946, p. 6, and September 25, 1946, p. 12; Davis, *Postwar Defense Policy,* 245–47; Sullivan to Truman, letter, July 24, 1946, Secretary of the Navy folder, President's Secretary's File, HSTL.

10. *New York Times,* September 8, 1946, p. 1, and October 1, 1946, p. 6.

11. *Time,* July 29, 1946, 68.

12. Arnold, "The 36-Hour War," 32–33.

13. Quoted in Davis, *Postwar Defense Policy,* 130.

14. *New York Times,* February 15, 1946, p. 1.

15. Davis, *Postwar Defense Policy,* 130–32; Hewlett and Duncan, *Nuclear Navy,* 11–15, 26–30; Rosenberg, "American Postwar Air Doctrine and Organization," 250.

16. Bradley, *A General's Life,* 474; Halberstam, *The Fifties,* 18.

17. Ross, *American War Plans,* 2–32; *First Report of the Secretary of Defense, 1948,* 143–45.

18. Rosenberg, "U.S. Nuclear Stockpile," 26–28; Box 23, General Correspondence, Patterson papers, LC.

19. Hansen, *U.S. Nuclear Weapons,* 124–29; Rosenberg, "American Postwar Air Doctrine and Organization," 255; Bruins, "U.S. Naval Bombardment Missiles," 153–57; Rosenberg, "U.S. Nuclear Stockpile," 27–28.

20. Radford to Admiral Ramsey, memorandum entitled "Public Relations in Connection with the Atomic Bomb Tests," January 24, 1946, Records of the DCNO (Air), OAB; Bruins, "U.S. Naval Bombardment Missiles," 136–39.

21. Bruins, "U.S. Naval Bombardment Missiles," 139–42; Graybar, "The Buck Rogers of the Navy," 339, 343; Rosenberg, "American Postwar Air Doctrine and Organization," 249; *New York Times,* November 13, 1946, p. 1; JTF-1 Press Release, November 1, 1946, OAB; Vice Adm. George F. Hussey to Vice Chief of Naval Operations, memorandum entitled "Coordination of New Developments," October 9, 1946, Atomic Energy Division Records, OAB.

CHAPTER 30.

1. Quoted in Dewey to the Joint Chiefs of Staff, letter, August 9, 1946, Box 32, Folder 740, Bush papers, LC.

2. Compton to JCS, letter, August 16, 1946, and Compton to Leahy, letter, September 5, 1946, CCS 471.6 (10-16-46) (SCC 10), RG 218, USJCS; Dewey to JCS, letter, August 9, 1946; Leahy to Dewey, letter, August 14, 1946; Leahy to Compton, letter, August 26, 1946, Box 32, Folder 740, Bush papers, LC.

3. Notes of Joint Crossroads Committee, November 5, 1946, Box 104, Folder A-19, RG 374, DASA; Parsons to Oppenheimer, letter, January 14, 1947, and Compton to Oppenheimer, letter, January 15, 1947, Box 178, Oppenheimer papers, LC; Parsons to Vannevar Bush, letter, January 20, 1947, Box 90, Folder 2034, Bush papers, LC.

4. Ofstie to Compton, memorandum, June 18, 1947, Box 3, folder marked "1947 letter filed outgoing," Ofstie papers, OAB.

5. "Persons Attending the Presentation of the JCS Evaluation Board Report to the Joint Chiefs of Staff," "Program for Presentation of JCS Evaluation Board Report to the Joint Chiefs of Staff and Discussion of Results of Crossroads," and Parsons to Buchanan, memorandum, July 30, 1947, CCS 471.6 (10-16-45), Sec. 15, Box 176, RG 218, USJCS. *New York Times,* February 4, 1947, p. 5; July 24, 1947, p. 1; and July 30, 1947, p. 10. *New York Herald Tribune,* July 30, 1947, p. 8; *Washington Times-Herald,* October 14, 1947, p. 3; *Washington Post,* July 6, 1947, p. B1.
6. "Final Report of the JCS Evaluation Board," 5, 29–31.
7. Fee, *Radiological Decontamination,* 1:1.
8. "Final Report of the JCS Evaluation Board," 10–13, 21, 25, 28, 32.
9. Shurcliff, *Technical Report,* p. 3.3; "Final Report of the JCS Evaluation Board," 16–17; notes on Joint Crossroads Committee Conference of November 26, 1946, Box 104, Entry 47, Folder A-19, RG 374, DASA. Yet another analysis placed the true costs of the tests at $25 million. According to Sen. David Walsh of Massachusetts, the fixed costs of maintaining the 240 target ships and support vessels at Bikini and paying the regular Navy crew was $75 million. The added costs of hiring extra scientific personnel, equipment, and other related expenses amounted to only $25 million. *Congressional Record,* 79th Cong., 2d sess., 1946, 92, pt. 6: S 6927 (daily ed., June 14, 1946).
10. Lilienthal, *The Atomic Energy Years,* 233–34.
11. *Washington Times-Herald,* October 14, 1947, p. 2.
12. Hickenlooper to Truman, letter, October 23, 1947, President's Secretary's Files, HSTL.
13. Hickenlooper to Truman, letter, December 4, 1947, Box 51, Hickenlooper papers, Hoover Library.
14. *New York Times,* February 25, 1948, p. 6, and November 27, 1948, p. 4; Forrestal to Truman, letter, April 6, 1948, DOE/CIC 33008.
15. Dewey to Forrestal, letter, September 16, 1948, CCS 471.6 (10-15-45) (SCC 9, part 2), RG 218, USJCS.
16. Dewey, "High Policy and the Atomic Bomb," 37–39; John H. Ohly to Compton, letter, August 3, 1948, Box 61, folders 44–45, Compton papers, MIT.
17. Bush to Forrestal, letter, December 20, 1948, Box 113, Presidential Papers, Eisenhower Library; *New York Times,* November 27, 1948, p. 4, and December 3, 1948, p. 28.
18. Lodge to McMahon, letter, February 1, 1949; McMahon to Lodge, letter, February 18, 1949, Box 105, RG 128, ("Bikini Tests"), RJCC.
19. Compton to Richardson, memorandum entitled "War Council Item on Bikini Report, BW, etc.," January 27, 1949, Box 113, War Council File, Eisenhower Library; *Washington Star,* February 18, 1949, p. 9; *Washington Post,* February 19, 1949, p. 13; Hershberg, *James B. Conant,* 377–90.
20. Knerr, "If We Should Fight Again," 24.
21. Quoted in Rosenberg, "American Postwar Air Doctrine and Organization," 254.
22. Steven Rearden has written that Navy designers concluded from Operation Crossroads that new aircraft carriers should be built without the traditional superstructure on the flight deck in order to withstand better the pressures

and winds from an atomic attack. Rearden, *History of the Office of the Secretary of Defense,* 1:389–90. There is no evidence for this statement, as plans for the flush deck carrier started as early as April 1945. Rosenberg, "American Postwar Air Doctrine and Organization," 254.

23. JCS 1805, September 23, 1947, CCS 471.6 (10-16-45), Sec. 9, Part 1, USJCS; Ross and Rosenberg, eds., *America's Plans for War,* vol. 9.

24. JCS 1805/19 (June 9, 1950, and August 8, 1950), p. 103, and JCS 1805/21 (June 26, 1950, and August 7, 1950), reprinted in Ross and Rosenberg, *America's Plans for War,* vol. 15: *Blueprint for Rearmament;* Rosenberg, "The Origins of Overkill," 17.

25. Report by the Joint Intelligence Committee to the Joint Chiefs of Staff on Final Report of the Joint Chiefs of Staff Evaluation Board for Operation "Crossroads," JCS 1805/32, CCS 471.6 (10-16-45) (SCC 9, part 4), RG 218, USJCS.

26. Maj. Howard D. Elliott, Armed Forces Special Weapons Project, to President, MIT, letter, May 24, 1955; Dewey to Elliott, letter, August 1, 1955; Maj. John B. Brady, Administrative Secretary, to Executive Secretary, Joint Chiefs of Staff, memorandum entitled "Final Report of the Joint Chiefs of Staff Evaluation Board for Operation "CROSSROADS," CCS 471.6 (10-16-45), Sec. 9, Part 3, RG 218, USJCS; *New York Times,* April 26, 1949, p. 4.

CHAPTER 31.

1. Joint Crossroads Committee to the Joint Chiefs of Staff, memorandum, April 18, 1947, JCS 1766, CCS 471.6 (10-16-45), Sec. 15, Box 176, RG 218, USJCS; Navy Department press release, June 27, 1947, DOE/CIC 100945; Joint Army-Navy press release, August 7, 1947, DOE/CIC 100933; Berkhouse et al., *Operation Crossroads,* 144–59; Hines, "Bikini Report," 106–7; Ladd et al., "Drilling on Bikini Atoll," 51–53; *Technical Report, Bikini Scientific Resurvey,* vol. 3. A newspaper entitled "Bikini Backtalk" distributed sixteen issues between July 10 and September 10 reporting on the day-to-day activities of the group. Box 26, Record Unit 7231, Schmitt papers, SIA.

2. Berkhouse et al., *Operation Crossroads,* 154–55, 158–59; Hines, *Proving Ground,* 74–75.

3. Russell oral history transcript, 269–71; Darol Froman to James R. Russell, memorandum, October 2, 1947, DOE/CIC 103592; Enclosure "D" to JCS SM 1908 (October 18, 1947), RG 326, USAEC, DMA Files, Box 3866, Folder "Sandstone—Basic Correspondence and References," USDOE.

4. Quoted in Col. Paul T. Preuss, USAF, to Capt. James S. Russell, memorandum entitled "Project 'Nutmeg'—Feasibility of Continental Proof-Test Site," February 10, 1949, RG 326, USAEC, DMA files, Box 3865, Folder MRA 7 Continental Test Site 1945–1956, USDOE.

5. Pringle and Spigelman, *The Nuclear Barons,* 180, 500–501.

6. Ferrell, ed., *The Diary of James G. Hagerty,* 6.

7. Bugher, memorandum to files entitled "Return of Natives to Bikini," April

10, 1952, AEC Division of Biology and Medicine, Box 326-78-3, Box 1, MRA Bikini and Eniwetok, Doc. No. 9458, USDOE.

8. Quoted in Hansen, *U.S. Nuclear Weapons*, 95.

9. Quoted in Strauss, *Men and Decisions*, 345–46; Divine, *Blowing on the Wind*, 16–17.

10. Quoted in *Health Effects of Low-Level Radiation*, 1:151; *New York Times*, April 20, 1979, p. 1; York, "The Debate over the Hydrogen Bomb."

11. Bascom, *The Crest of the Wave*, 150–56; Ellis, "Bikini: A Way of Life Lost," 821; O'Keefe, *Nuclear Hostages*, 178–96; Martin and Rowland, *Castle Series, 1954*, 205; Hewlett and Holl, *Atoms for Peace and War*, 171–75; Lapp, *The Voyage of the Lucky Dragon*, 159; *New York Times*, March 18, 1954, p. 1.

12. *New York Times*, March 12, 1954, p. 1; Voss, *Nuclear Ambush*, 37–39; Schubert and Lapp, *Radiation*, 220.

13. Martin and Rowland, *Castle Series, 1954*, 3, 235; Conard, *A Twenty-Year Review of Medical Findings*, 59–76, 81–86; *New York Times*, July 3, 1968, p. 12, and November 12, 1972, p. 26.

14. Voss, *Nuclear Ambush*, 39.

15. Bascom, *The Crest of the Wave*, 157–61.

16. *New York Times*, September 24, 1954, p. 10; January 4, 1955, p. 3; January 5, 1955, p. 6; and August 23, 1955, p. 7. Salaff, "The Lucky Dragon."

17. Schubert and Lapp, *Radiation*, 224–25; Lapp, *The Voyage of the Lucky Dragon*, 98–100, 117, 127–30, 178; *New York Times*, March 17, 1954, p. 1, and March 18, 1954, p. 3.

18. *New York Times*, April 1, 1954, p. 20; *Bulletin of the Atomic Scientists* (May 1954): 163–64; Pringle and Spigelman, *The Nuclear Barons*, 245; Hewlett and Holl, *Atoms for Peace and War*, 175–77.

19. Ferrell, *The Diary of James C. Hagerty*, 40.

20. Allison to Secretary of State, memorandum entitled "Fukuryu Maru," May 20, 1954, DOE/CIC 71978.

21. Storry, *A History of Modern Japan*, 261–62.

22. Martin and Rowland, *Castle Series, 1954*, 22.

23. *New York Times*, March 25, 1954, pp. 1, 18, and April 1, 1954, p. 1.

24. *New York Times*, February 16, 1955, p. 1; Schubert and Lapp, *Radiation*, 5; Lapp, *The Voyage of the Lucky Dragon*, 126; Smith interview.

25. U.S. Department of Energy, *Announced United States Nuclear Tests*, 4–11; Hewlett and Holl, *Atoms for Peace and War*, 178–82, 276–87.

26. Bascom, *The Crest of the Wave*, 165; Hansen, *U.S. Nuclear Weapons*, 72–73; *New York Times*, May 21, 1956, p. 1, and May 22, 1956, p. 1.

27. Salaff, "The Lucky Dragon," 23.

CHAPTER 32.

1. *New York Herald Tribune*, May 5, 1946, p. 6.

2. *Honolulu Star-Bulletin*, May 4, 1946, p. 1.

3. Mason, "Relocation of the Bikini Marshallese," 286–87. While Bikini's

twenty-six islands had a land area of 2.32 square miles, Rongerik's ten islands have a total land area of only 0.63 square miles and Rongerik's lagoon covers 55 square miles, while Bikini's covers 243 square miles. Kiste, *The Bikinians*, 29.

4. *New York Times*, March 31, 1946, sec. 6, p. 59.

5. Bradley, *No Place to Hide*, 157–63.

6. Quoted in Richard, *United States Naval Administration*, 3:519.

7. Quoted in Kiste, *The Bikinians*, 82.

8. Quoted in Richard, *United States Naval Administration*, 3:519–20.

9. The unconditional surrender of the Japanese in Tokyo Bay on September 2, 1945, did not officially end hostilities. The United States did not legally terminate hostilities until President Truman issued a proclamation on December 31, 1946 (Proclamation 2714, 12 Fed. Reg. 1), and the state of war continued until the United States and Japan signed the 1951 peace treaty.

10. Stimson and Bundy, *On Active Service in Peace and War*, 599–600.

11. Hull, *Memoirs of Cordell Hull*, 1466; *FRUS: The Conference at Malta and Yalta (1945)*, 78–81; *New York Times*, April 5, 1945, p. 4.

12. Blandy, speech, February 21, 1946, DOE/CIC 101039.

13. McHenry, *Micronesia*, 2–6, 32–35; *FRUS: 1946*, 1:544–711; McNeill, "The Strategic Trust Territory in International Law."

14. *Washington Star*, September 29, 1947, p. 9; *Honolulu Star-Bulletin*, September 29, 1947, p. 8; White and Maze, *Harold Ickes of the New Deal*, 230–35.

15. *New York Times*, October 3, 1947, p. 24.

16. Mason, "Relocation of the Bikini Marshallese," 339; Mason interview.

17. *Honolulu Star-Bulletin*, November 24, 1948, p. 3; affidavit of John P. W. Vest; Vest interview.

18. Weisgall, "The Nuclear Nomads of Bikini Atoll," 83.

19. Wright, "Let's Not Civilize These Happy People"; *New York Herald Tribune*, May 5, 1946, p. 6; *Honolulu Star-Bulletin*, May 23, 1948, p. 3.

20. Deposition of Lore Kessibuki in *Tomaki Juda et al. v. United States*, p. 10.

21. Shields Warren, "Report of the Ad Hoc Committee to Evaluate the Radiological Hazards of Resettlement of the Bikini Atoll," DOE/CIC 41847.

22. *New York Times*, August 13, 1968, p. 1; draft memorandum for the president from Bromley Smith re "Return of the Bikini People," August 2, 1968, National Security File, Lyndon B. Johnson Library.

23. *New York Times*, September 4, 1968, p. 13; Kessibuki interview.

24. *Washington Post*, April 13, 1978, p. 1, and May 22, 1978, p. 1; *Los Angeles Times*, July 23, 1978, p. 3; Dunning interview.

25. *New York Times*, April 10, 1988, p. 4.

Bibliography

INTERVIEWS

Frederick Ashworth, May 26, 1992
Hans Bethe, March 28, 1993
Norris Bradbury, April 9, 1991
David Bradley, October 29, 1992
Clark Clifford, March 4, 1992
Robert Conard, July 11, 1992
Gordon Dunning, June 8, 1986
J. William Fulbright, October 27, 1992
Anthony Guarisco, March 8, 1985
Barton Hacker, May 28, 1992
Louis Hempelmann, May 13, 1988
Robert Henderson, June 11, 1992
Marshall Holloway, April 17, 1989
Townsend Hoopes, March 5, 1992
William Kemper, April 22 and May 15, 1992
Lore Kessibuki, March 20, 1985
Ralph Lapp, November 10 and December 14, 1992
Jane Larson, July 4, 1992
Gen. Curtis LeMay, May 13, 1988
Leonard Mason, March 19, 1985
Carl Mydans, April 18, 1993
Kenneth Nichols, January 9, 1992
Paul Nitze, November 4, 1992
Ernest Peterkin, July 11, 1992
Horacio Rivero, May 5, 1992
Raemer E. Schreiber, June 29, 1991
Gerard E. Smith, June 1, 1993
Woodrow P. Swancutt, June 30, 1991
James Symington, February 20 and 24, 1992

Paul W. Tibbets, May 19, 1988
John P. W. Vest, October 18, 1989
Paul C. Warnke, January 28, 1992
Dean Warren, July 25, 1992
Harold Wood, May 8, 1987

UNPUBLISHED SOURCES

Libraries and Archives

Clemson University Robert Muldrow Cooper Library, Clemson, S.C.
   Papers of Walter Brown and James F. Byrnes
Defense Nuclear Agency (JAYCOR), Vienna, Va.
   Copies of all technical reports on Operation Crossroads and all ships' records
Dwight D. Eisenhower Library, Abilene, Kan.
   Papers of Dwight D. Eisenhower and James Hagerty
   War Council File
Herbert Hoover Library, West Branch, Iowa
   Papers of Bourke B. Hickenlooper and Lewis L. Strauss
Lyndon B. Johnson Library, Austin, Tex.
   National Security File
Library of Congress, Washington, D.C.
   Papers of Vannevar Bush, John L. Callan, Joseph E. Davies, William Leahy,
      J. Robert Oppenheimer, William S. Parsons, Robert Patterson, Carl Spaatz,
      and Raymond Gram Swing
Los Alamos National Laboratory Records Center/Archives, Los Alamos, N.M.
   RG A-84-019
Massachusetts Institute of Technology, Cambridge, Mass.
   Papers of Karl T. Compton
Maxwell Air Force Base, Montgomery, Ala.
   Research Studies Institute, Archives Branch
National Archives, Washington, D.C.
   Defense Atomic Support Agency, RG 374
   General Records of the Department of the Navy, RG 80
   General Records of the Department of State
   Manhattan Engineer District Records
   Office of the Secretary of War, RG 107
   Records of the Joint Committees of Congress
   Records of the U.S. Senate
   Trust Territory of the Pacific Islands
   U.S. Joint Chiefs of Staff Records
National Archives Branch, Suitland, Md.
   Records of Naval Operating Forces, RG 313
Princeton University, Princeton, N.J.
   Papers of James Forrestal

Smithsonian Institution, Washington, D.C.

Papers of Harry S. Ladd, Joseph Paul Eldred Morrison, George Sprague Myers, Leonard Peter Schultz, and Waldo LaSalle Schmitt

National Zoological Park, Records of the Office of the Registrar and Records of the Office of Public Affairs

Harry S. Truman Library Institute, Independence, Mo.

Papers of Eben A. Ayers, Clark M. Clifford, Matthew J. Connelly, George M. Elsey, Charles G. Ross, Harold Smith, and Harry S. Truman (including Confidential File, Official File, President's Personal File, and President's Secretary's File)

U.S. Department of Energy, Washington, D.C.

U.S. Department of Energy Coordination and Information Service, Las Vegas

U.S. Department of the Interior, Office of Territorial and International Affairs, Records Section, Washington, D.C.

Trust Territory National Defense—Military Defense

University of California at Berkeley

Papers of Ernest O. Lawrence

University of California at Los Angeles

Papers of Stafford L. Warren

Washington Navy Yard, Operational Archives Branch, Naval Historical Center, Washington, D.C.

Papers of William H. P. Blandy and Ralph Ofstie

Chief of Naval Operations

Operation Crossroads files, records, and reports

Records of the Secretary of the Navy (Double Zero file)

Yale University, New Haven

Papers of Hanson W. Baldwin, Max Lerner, Walter Lippmann, Henry L. Stimson, and Herbert B. Vickery

Oral History Transcripts

Ashworth, Vice Adm. Frederick L. Conducted by Albert B. Christman, Naval Weapons Center, China Lake, Calif. April 1969 (NWC-75201-S61).

Baldwin, Hanson Weightman. Conducted by Dr. John T. Mason, Jr., U.S. Naval Institute, Annapolis, Md. 1976.

Kauffman, Draper L. Conducted by Dr. John T. Mason, Jr., U.S. Naval Institute, Annapolis, Md. 1978.

Ladd, Harry S. Conducted by Pamela Henson, Smithsonian Institution Archives. October 1977.

Lee, Vice Adm. Fitzhugh. Conducted by Etta Belle Kitchen, U.S. Naval Institute. August 1970.

Lyon, Dr. Waldo K. Conducted by Etta Belle Kitchen, U.S. Naval Institute. 1972.

Rivero, Horacio. Conducted by Dr. John T. Mason, Jr., U.S. Naval Institute. 1978.

Russell, Adm. James S. Conducted by Dr. John T. Mason, Jr., U.S. Naval Institute. 1974.

Sawyer, Dr. Ralph A. Conducted by Albert B. Christman, Naval Ordnance Test Station, China Lake, Calif. May 1967 (NOTS-75201-S46).

Strauss, Lewis L. Conducted by Albert B. Christman, Naval Ordnance Test Station, China Lake, Calif. May 1967 (NOTS-75201-S47).

Warren, Stafford. "Stafford Warren: An Exceptional Man for Exceptional Challenges," 3 vols. Interviewed by Adelaide Tusler, University of California, Los Angeles. 1983.

Youngblood, Curtis. Conducted by Albert B. Christman, Naval Ordnance Test Station, China Lake, Calif. May 1967 (NOTS-75201-S51).

Dissertations

Brown, Richard G. "Germany, Spain and the Caroline Islands, 1885–1899." Ph.D. diss., University of Southern Mississippi, Hattiesburg, Miss., 1976.

Bruins, Berend D. "U.S. Naval Bombardment Missiles, 1940–1958: A Study of the Weapons Innovation Process." Ph.D. diss., Columbia University, New York, 1981.

Mason, Leonard E. "Relocation of the Bikini Marshallese: A Study in Group Migration." Ph.D. diss., Yale University, New Haven, Conn., 1954.

McNeill, John H. "The Strategic Trust Territory in International Law." Ph.D. diss., University of London, London, 1974.

Tobin, Jack A. "The Resettlement of the Enewetak People: A Study of a Displaced Community in the Marshall Islands." Ph.D. diss., University of California at Berkeley, 1967.

Manuscripts

"Analysis of Bikini's First Atom Bomb Test," prepared by Analysis Branch, IPR Headquarters, Army Air Forces. 1946. Document No. 7-7061. Maxwell Air Force Base.

Blandy, William H. P. "Research for War." Presented to the Maryland Historical Society, Baltimore, 1943; reprinted in *Congressional Record,* 78th Cong., 1st sess., 1943, 89, pt. 10: A2552 (daily ed., May 24, 1943).

Bryan, E. H., Jr. "Life in the Marshall Islands." 1972. Honolulu: Bernice P. Bishop Museum.

Drucker, Philip. "The Ex-Bikini Occupants of Kili Island." 1950. Honolulu: University of Hawaii Hamilton Library.

Fahrney, Delmer S. "The History of Pilotless Aircraft and Guided Missiles." n.d. Operational Archives Branch, Naval Historical Center, Washington Navy Yard.

Gerster, Max. "The Special Weapons Center and Atomic Testing." January 1957. Air Force Special Weapons Center Air Research and Development Command, Kirtland Air Force Base, New Mexico.

"History and Geography of the Northern Marshall Islands." 1991. Coordination and Information Center, Reynolds Electrical and Engineering Co., Inc., Las Vegas.

Kirkpatrick, Sidney D. "Panamint Parade of a Bikini Bum." Bourke Hickenlooper Papers, Box 51 (Joint Committee on Atomic Energy folder), Hoover Library.

Lemmer, George F. "The Air Force and the Concept of Deterrence, 1945–1950." 1963. Washington, D.C.: U.S. Air Force Historical Division Liaison Office.

Little, Robert D. "Organizing for Strategic Planning, 1945–1950: The National System and the Air Force." 1964. Washington, D.C.: U.S. Air Force Historical Division Liaison Office.

Meade, Roger A. "Crossroads Summary." 1991. LANL Records Center/Archives, Los Alamos, N.M.

"Nuclear Exiles." National Geographic Explorer Series, first aired October 14, 1987.

"Radio Bikini" (1987). The American Experience #102. Boston: WGBH Transcripts, 1988.

Schnabel, James F. "The History of the Joint Chiefs of Staff: The Joint Chiefs of Staff and National Policy," Vol. 1: "1945–1947." 1979. Washington, D.C.: Joint Chiefs of Staff Historical Division, Joint Secretariat.

Symington, W. Stuart. Memoirs (typewritten manuscript). n.d. James Symington, Washington, D.C.

"United States Naval Constructions Battalion 53." n.d. Item 95 in World War II Histories and Historical Report in the U.S. Naval History Division, Naval Historical Center, Washington Navy Yard.

Court Pleadings

Affidavit of John P. W. Vest in *Kabua Kabua v. Imada Kabua, et al.,* Nos. 1984-98 and 1984-102 (High Court, Republic of the Marshall Islands), November 15, 1989.

Depositions of Kilon Bauno and Lore Kessibuki in *Tomaki Juda, et al. v. United States,* No. 172-81L (U.S. Claims Court), 1985.

In re Veterans Administration Claim of Mrs. Jean A. Erspamer, Synopsis of Material Facts of Record Concerning Claimant's Motion for Reconsideration, Veterans Administration Board of Veterans Appeals (No. 82-04 889) (1984).

PUBLISHED SOURCES

Official Publications

Atomic Energy, Hearings on H.R. 4280 before the House Committee on Military Affairs, 79th Cong., 1st sess. Washington, D.C.: U.S. Government Printing Office, 1945.

Berkhouse, L., et al. *Operation Crossroads—1946.* DNA Report No. 6032F. Washington, D.C.: Defense Nuclear Agency, 1984.

Bowen, Lee, Robert D. Little, et al. *A History of the Air Force Atomic Energy Program, 1943–1953.* 5 vols. Washington, D.C.: U.S. Air Force Historical Division, 1959.

Christman, Albert B. *Sailors, Scientists, and Rockets: Origins of the Navy Rocket Program and of the Naval Ordnance Test Station, Inyokern.* 2 vols. Washington, D.C.: U.S. Government Printing Office, 1971.

Clarkson, P. W. *History of Operation Castle.* Washington, D.C.: Department of the Army, 1954. Extracted version prepared by Defense Nuclear Agency, Washington, D.C., 1983.

Commander, JTF-1. *Operation Plan, No. 1046, Annex E (Safety Plan).* Washington, D.C.: Department of the Navy, 1946.

——. *Operational Report on Atomic Bomb Tests Able and Baker (Operation Crossroads) Conducted at Bikini Atoll, Marshall Islands on 1 July 1946 and 25 July 1946.* XRD-206. NTIS Document No. AD473986. Washington, D.C.: Department of the Navy, 1946.

Composition of the Postwar Navy: Hearings on H.R. Con. Res. 80 before the House Committee on Naval Affairs, 79th Cong., 1st sess. Washington, D.C.: U.S. Government Printing Office, 1945.

Conard, Robert A., et al. *A Twenty-Year Review of Medical Findings in a Marshallese Population Accidentally Exposed to Radioactive Fallout.* BNL 50424. Upton, N.Y.: Brookhaven National Laboratory, 1974.

Delgado, James P., Daniel J. Lenihan, and Larry F. Murphy. *The Archeology of the Atomic Bomb: A Submerged Cultural Resources Assessment of the Sunken Fleet of Operation Crossroads at Bikini and Kwajalein Atoll Lagoons, Republic of the Marshall Islands.* Santa Fe, N.M.: U.S. Department of the Interior, National Park Service, Submerged Cultural Resources Unit, 1991.

Director of Ship Material, JTF-1, Bureau of Ships Group. *Historical Report, Atomic Bomb Tests Able and Baker (Operation Crossroads) Conducted at Bikini Atoll, Marshall Islands on 1 July and 25 July, 1946.* 3 vols. XRD-190. NTIS Document No. AD-A995213. Washington, D.C.: Department of the Navy, 1946.

——. *Technical Inspection Report, USS Carlisle (APA-69), Test Able, Operation Crossroads.* RG 374, DASA. Washington, D.C.: U.S. Navy, 1946.

——. *Technical Inspection Report, USS Gilliam (APA-57), Test Able, Operation Crossroads.* RG 374, DASA. Washington, D.C.: U.S. Navy, 1946.

——. *Technical Inspection Report, USS Saratoga, Test Able, Operation Crossroads.* RG 374, DASA. Washington, D.C.: U.S. Navy, 1946.

Emery, Kenneth O., Joshua I. Tracey, Jr., and Harry S. Ladd. *Geology of Bikini and Nearby Atolls: Part 1.* Washington, D.C.: U.S. Government Printing Office, 1954.

Fee, J. J. *Operation Crossroads: Radiological Decontamination Report of Target and Non-Target Vessels.* 3 vols. Technical Report XRD-185-87. NTIS Document Nos. AD 473 906. Washington, D.C.: U.S. Government Printing Office, 1946.

"The Final Report of the Joint Chiefs of Staff Evaluation Board for Operation Crossroads," June 30, 1947, JCS 1691/10, reprinted in Ross and Rosenberg, *America's Plans for War*. Vol. 9, *Concepts and Capabilities*, 101–39.

First Report of the Secretary of Defense, 1948. Washington, D.C.: U.S. Government Printing Office, 1948.

Furer, Julius A. *Administration of the Navy Department in World War II*. Washington, D.C.: Department of the Navy, 1959.

General Accounting Office. *Operation Crossroads: Personnel Radiation Exposure Estimates Should Be Improved*. GAO/RCED-86-15. Washington, D.C.: U.S. Government Accounting Office, 1985.

Gerrard-Gough, J. D., and Albert B. Christman. *The Grand Experiment at Inyokern: Narrative of the Naval Ordnance Test Station During the Second World War and the Immediate Postwar Years*, vol 2. Washington, D.C.: U.S. Government Printing Office, 1978.

Gerstell, Richard. *How to Survive an Atomic Bomb*. Washington, D.C.: U.S. Government Printing Office, 1950.

Glasstone, Samuel, and Philip J. Dolan. *The Effects of Nuclear Weapons*. 3d ed. Washington, D.C.: U.S. Departments of Defense and Energy, 1977.

Greenwood, John T. "The Emergence of the Postwar Strategic Air Force, 1945–1953." In *Air Power and Warfare: The Proceedings of the 8th Military History Symposium*, ed. Alfred F. Hurley and Robert C. Ehrhart. Washington, D.C.: Office of Air Force History, Headquarters USAF, 1979.

Health Effects of Low-Level Radiation. Joint Hearing before the House Interstate and Foreign Commerce Subcommittee on Oversight and Investigations and the Senate Labor and Human Resources Subcommittee on Health and Scientific Research, 96th Cong., 1st sess. 2 vols. Washington, D.C.: U.S. Government Printing Office, 1979.

Hearings before the House Committee on Naval Affairs on Sundry Legislation Affecting the Naval Establishment 1920–21, 66th Cong., 3d sess. Washington, D.C.: U.S. Government Printing Office, 1921.

Hearings before the Senate Committee on Military Affairs on S. 84 and S. 1482, Department of Armed Forces, Department of Military Security, 79th Cong., 1st sess. Washington, D.C.: U.S. Government Printing Office, 1945.

Hearings on Atomic Energy Pursuant to Senate Resolution 179 before the Senate Special Committee on Atomic Energy, 79th Cong., 1st sess. Washington, D.C.: U.S. Government Printing Office, 1945.

Hearings on House Joint Resolution 307, to Authorize the Use of Naval Vessels to Determine the Effect of Atomic Weapons upon Such Vessels, in Hearings on Sundry Legislation Affecting the Naval Establishment 1946, before the House Committee on Naval Affairs, 79th Cong., 1st sess. Washington, D.C.: U.S. Government Printing Office.

Heinl, Robert D., Jr., and John A. Crown. *The Marshalls: Increasing the Tempo*. Washington, D.C.: U.S. Marine Corps Historical Branch, G-3 Division Headquarters, 1954.

Hopkins, J. C. *The Development of Strategic Air Command 1946–1981 (A Chronological History)*. Washington, D.C.: Office of the Historian, Headquarters Strategic Air Command, 1982.

Joint Task Force One. *Operation Crossroads: Fourth Cruise of the "Mighty Mac."* Washington, D.C.: U.S. Government Printing Office, 1946.

——. *Operation Crossroads: Gross Damage Report—Test Able.* Washington, D.C.: U.S. Navy, 1946. Extracted version prepared by Defense Nuclear Agency, Washington, D.C., 1988, as XRD-213.

Jones, Vincent J. *United States Army in World War II, Special Studies, Manhattan: The Army and the Atomic Bomb.* Washington, D.C.: U.S. Army Center of Military History, 1985.

Lenihan, Daniel J. *USS Arizona Memorial and Pearl Harbor National Historic Landmark.* Santa Fe: U.S. Department of the Interior National Park Service Submerged Cultural Resources Unit, 1989.

Martin, Edwin J., and Richard H. Rowland. *Castle Series, 1954.* DNA Report No. 6035F. Washington, D.C.: Defense Nuclear Agency, 1982.

Mooney, James L., ed. *Dictionary of American Naval Fighting Ships.* 5 vols. Washington, D.C.: U.S. Navy Department, 1959–70.

Operation Crossroads: The Role of the Army Air Forces from the Project's Inception until May 7, 1946. 2 vols. Washington, D.C.: Strategic Air Command, 1947.

Palmer, Michael A. *Origins of the Maritime Strategy: American Naval Strategy in the First Postwar Decade.* Washington, D.C.: Naval Historical Center, 1988.

Public Papers of the Presidents of the United States, Harry S. Truman. Containing the Public Messages, Speeches and Statements of the President. 1945–1953. 8 vols. Washington, D.C.: U.S. Government Printing Office, 1961–66.

Rearden, Steven L. *History of the Office of the Secretary of Defense.* Vol. 1, *The Formative Years 1947–1950.* Washington, D.C.: Office of the Secretary of Defense, 1984.

Richard, Dorothy E. *United States Naval Administration of the Trust Territory of the Pacific Islands.* 3 vols. Washington, D.C.: U.S. Government Printing Office, 1957.

Rosenberg, David A. "American Postwar Air Doctrine and Organization: The Navy Experience." In *Air Power and Warfare: The Proceedings of the 8th Military History Symposium,* ed. Alfred F. Hurley and Robert C. Ehrhart. Washington, D.C.: Office of Air Force History, Headquarters USAF, 1979.

Rowland, Buford, and William B. Boyd. *U.S. Navy Bureau of Ordnance in World War II.* Washington, D.C.: Department of the Navy Bureau of Ordnance, 1953.

Sawyer, Ralph. *Report of Technical Director, Operation Crossroads.* Washington, D.C.: Department of the Navy, 1946. Extracted version prepared by Defense Nuclear Agency as XRD-210.

Scoville, Herbert, Jr. "The Atomic Bomb and the Resultant Phenomena." In *Radiological Defense.* Vol. 3, *A Series of Indoctrination Lectures on Atomic Explosion, with Medical Aspects.* Washington, D.C.: Armed Forces Special Weapons Project, n.d.

Second Report of the Secretary of Defense for the Fiscal Year 1949. Washington, D.C.: U.S. Government Printing Office, 1950.

Shiner, John F. *Foulois and the U.S. Army Air Corps, 1931–1935.* Washington,

D.C.: Office of Air Force History, 1983.

Shurcliff, William A. *Bombs at Bikini: The Official Report of Operation Cross-roads.* New York: William H. Wise and Co., 1947.

——. *Operation Crossroads: The Official Pictorial Record.* New York: William H. Wise and Co., 1946.

——. *Technical Report of Operation Crossroads.* XRD-208. NTIS Document No. AD 367 496. Washington, D.C.: Department of the Navy, 1946.

Streck, Charles F., Jr. "Interim Report: Archaeological Investigations on Eneu Island, Bikini Atoll, Republic of the Marshall Islands," in *Environmental Assessment for Initial Resettlement of Eneu Island, Bikini Atoll.* Supplementary Document No. 1, prepared by Environmental Resources Section, U.S. Army Corps of Engineers, Pacific Ocean Division. Berkeley: Bikini Atoll Rehabilitation Committee, 1987.

Technical Report, Bikini Scientific Resurvey. 3 vols. Washington, D.C.: Armed Forces Special Weapons Project, 1947.

U.S. Atomic Energy Commission. *Thirteenth Semiannual Report of the Atomic Energy Commission.* Washington, D.C.: U.S. Government Printing Office, 1953.

U.S. Department of Energy. *Announced United States Nuclear Tests, July 1945 through December 1990.* DOE/NV-209. Las Vegas: U.S. Department of Energy, Nevada Operations Office, Office of External Affairs, 1992.

U.S. Department of State. *Foreign Relations of the United States,* annual volumes, 1941–46. Washington, D.C.: U.S. Government Printing Office, 1958–70.

U.S. Strategic Bombing Survey. *The Effects of Strategic Bombing.* Washington, D.C.: U.S. Government Printing Office, 1946.

Warren, Stafford L. "The Role of Radiology in the Development of the Atomic Bomb." In *Radiology in World War II,* ed. Col. Arnold Lorentz Ahnfeldt, Kenneth D. A. Allen, Elizabeth M. McFetridge, and Mindell W. Stein, 831–921. Washington, D.C.: Office of the Surgeon General, Department of the Army, 1966.

Books

Acheson, Dean. *Present at the Creation: My Years in the State Department.* New York: Norton, 1969.

Albion, Robert Greenhalgh. *Makers of Naval Policy 1798–1947.* Annapolis, Md.: Naval Institute Press, 1980.

Albion, Robert Greenhalgh, and Robert H. Connery. *Forrestal and the Navy.* New York: Columbia University Press, 1962.

Alperowitz, Gar. *Atomic Diplomacy: Hiroshima and Potsdam: The Use of the Atomic Bomb and the Confrontation with Soviet Power.* New York: Simon and Schuster, 1965.

Alsop, Joseph, and Stewart Alsop. *We Accuse! The Story of the Miscarriage of American Justice in the Case of J. Robert Oppenheimer.* New York: Simon and Schuster, 1954.

Anderson, Charles Roberts. *Melville in the South Seas*. New York: Columbia University Press, 1939.

Ayers, Eben A. *Truman in the White House: The Diary of Eben A. Ayers*. Edited by Robert H. Ferrell. Columbia, Mo.: University of Missouri Press, 1991.

Ball, Howard. *Justice Downwind: America's Atomic Testing Program in the 1950s*. New York: Oxford University Press, 1986.

Ballard, Robert D. *The Discovery of the Bismarck*. New York: Warner, 1990.

Baruch, Bernard M. *Baruch: The Public Years*. New York: Holt, Rinehart and Winston, 1960.

Bascom, Willard. *The Crest of the Wave: Adventures in Oceanography*. New York: Harper and Row, 1988.

Bekker, Cajus. *Hitler's Naval War*. Translated and edited by Frank Ziegler. Garden City, N.Y.: Doubleday, 1974.

Bernstein, Barton J., and Allen J. Matusow, eds. *The Truman Administration: A Documentary History*. New York: Harper and Row, 1966.

Bishop, John. "Action Off Komandorski." In *The United States Navy in World War II*, ed. Stanley E. Smith. New York: William Morrow, 1966.

Blackett, Patrick M. S. *Fear, War and the Bomb: Military and Political Consequences of Atomic Energy*. New York: McGraw-Hill, 1948.

Blair, Clay, Jr. *Silent Victory: The U.S. Submarine War against Japan*. Philadelphia: Lippincott, 1975.

Bocca, Geoffrey. *Bikini Beach: The Wicked Riviera—As It Was and Is*. New York: McGraw-Hill, 1962.

Boyer, Paul. *By the Bomb's Early Light: American Thought and Culture at the Dawn of the Atomic Age*. New York: Pantheon, 1985.

Bradley, David. *No Place to Hide 1946/1984*. Hanover, N.H.: University Press of New England, 1984.

Bradley, Omar N., and Clay Blair. *A General's Life*. New York: Simon and Schuster, 1983.

Brinkley, David. *Washington Goes to War*. New York: Knopf, 1988.

Brodie, Bernard. *Strategy in the Missile Age*. Princeton: Princeton University Press, 1959.

Brown, Anthony C., and Charles B. MacDonald, eds. *The Secret History of the Atomic Bomb*. New York: Dial Press, 1977.

Buell, Thomas B. *The Quiet Warrior: A Biography of Admiral Raymond A. Spruance*. Boston: Little, Brown, 1974.

Bundy, McGeorge. *Danger and Survival: Choices about the Bomb in the First Fifty Years*. New York: Random House, 1988.

Byrnes, James J. *Speaking Frankly*. New York: Harper, 1947.

Caraley, Demetrios. *The Politics of Military Unification: A Study of Conflict and the Policy Process*. New York: Columbia University Press, 1966.

Caufield, Catherine. *Multiple Exposures: Chronicles of the Radiation Age*. Chicago: University of Chicago Press, 1990.

Chesneau, Roger. *Aircraft Carriers of the World, 1914 to the Present*. Annapolis, Md.: U.S. Naval Institute Press, 1984.

Clifford, Clark, with Richard Holbrooke. *Counsel to the President*. New York: Random House, 1991.

Coffey, Thomas M. *Hap: The Story of the U.S. Air Force and the Man Who Built It: General Henry H. "Hap" Arnold.* New York: Viking Press, 1982.

———. *Iron Eagle: The Turbulent Life of General Curtis LeMay.* New York: Crown, 1986.

Coit, Margaret L. *Mr. Baruch.* Boston: Houghton Mifflin, 1957.

Coletta, Paolo E., ed. *American Secretaries of the Navy,* vol. 2: *1913–1972.* Annapolis, Md.: U.S. Naval Institute Press, 1980.

Committee on the Biological Effects of Ionizing Radiations, National Research Council. *Health Effects of Exposure to Low Levels of Ionizing Radiation (BEIR V).* Washington, D.C.: National Academy Press, 1990.

Considine, Bob. *It's All News to Me: A Reporter's Deposition.* New York: Meredith Press, 1967.

Cope, Harley F. *Command at Sea: A Guide for the Naval Officer.* New York: Norton, 1943.

Costello, John. *The Pacific War.* New York: Rawson Wade, 1981.

Crosby, John. *Out of the Blue.* New York: Simon and Schuster, 1952.

Darwin, Charles. *The Structure and Distribution of Coral Reefs.* New York: D. Appleton, 1897.

Davis, Burke. *The Billy Mitchell Affair.* New York: Random House, 1967.

Davis, Vincent. *Postwar Defense Policy and the U.S. Navy, 1943–1946.* Chapel Hill: University of North Carolina Press, 1962.

———. *The Admirals Lobby.* Chapel Hill: University of North Carolina Press, 1967.

Divine, Robert A. *Blowing on the Wind: The Nuclear Test Ban Debate, 1954–1960.* New York: Oxford University Press, 1978.

Dodge, Ernest S. *New England and the South Seas.* Cambridge: Harvard University Press, 1965.

Donovan, Robert J. *Conflict and Crisis: The Presidency of Harry S. Truman, 1945–1948.* New York: Norton, 1977.

Dull, Paul S. *A Battle History of the Imperial Japanese Navy (1941–1945).* Annapolis, Md.: U.S. Naval Institute Press, 1978.

Ermenc, Joseph J., ed. *Atomic Bomb Scientists Memoirs, 1939–1945.* Westport, Conn.: Meckler, 1989.

Feis, Herbert. *From Trust to Terror: The Onset of the Cold War, 1945–1950.* New York: Norton, 1970.

Ferrell, Robert H., ed. *Dear Bess: The Letters from Harry to Bess Truman, 1910–1959.* New York: Norton, 1983.

———, ed. *The Diary of James C. Hagerty: Eisenhower in Mid-Course, 1954–1955.* Bloomington: Indiana University Press, 1983.

———, ed. *The Eisenhower Diaries.* New York: Norton, 1981.

———, ed. *Off the Record: The Private Papers of Harry S. Truman.* New York: Harper and Row, 1980.

Firth, Stewart. "German Firms in the Pacific Islands, 1857–1914." In *Germany in the Pacific and Far East, 1870–1914,* ed. John A. Moses and Paul M. Kennedy. St. Lucia, Australia: University of Queensland Press, 1977.

Forester, C. S. *The Last Nine Days of the Bismarck.* Boston: Little, Brown, 1958.

Forrestal, James. *The Forrestal Diaries.* Edited by Walter Millis. New York: Viking, 1951.

Freeman, Otis W., ed. *Geography of the Pacific.* New York: John Wiley and Sons, 1951.

Friedman, Norman. *U.S. Battleships: An Illustrated Design History.* Annapolis, Md.: Naval Institute Press, 1985.

———. *U.S. Cruisers: An Illustrated Design History.* Annapolis, Md.: Naval Institute Press, 1984.

Frisch, Otto. *What Little I Remember.* Cambridge, England: Cambridge University Press, 1979.

Gaddis, John Lewis. *The Long Peace: Inquiries into the History of the Cold War.* New York: Oxford University Press, 1987.

———. *The United States and the Origins of the Cold War, 1941–1947.* New York: Columbia University Press, 1972.

Gardiner, John Stanley. *Coral Reefs and Atolls.* London: Macmillan, 1931.

Goin, Peter. *Nuclear Landscapes.* Baltimore: Johns Hopkins University Press, 1991.

Goldschmidt, Bertrand. *Atomic Rivals.* Translated by Georges M. Temmer. New Brunswick, N.J.: Rutgers University Press, 1990.

Goodchild, Peter. *J. Robert Oppenheimer: Shatterer of Worlds.* Boston: Houghton Mifflin, 1981.

Grant, James. *Bernard M. Baruch: The Adventures of a Wall Street Legend.* New York: Simon and Schuster, 1983.

Graybar, Louis J. "The Buck Rogers of the Navy." In *New Interpretations in Naval History: Selected Papers from the Ninth Naval Symposium Held at the United States Naval Academy, 18–20 October 1989,* ed. William R. Roberts and Jack Sweetman. Annapolis, Md.: Naval Institute Press, 1991.

Grenville, J.A.S., ed. *The Major International Treaties 1914–1973: A History and Guide with Texts.* New York: Stein and Day, 1975.

Groueff, Stephane. *Manhattan Project: The Untold Story of the Making of the Atomic Bomb.* Boston: Little, Brown, 1967.

Groves, Leslie R. *Now It Can Be Told.* New York: Harper and Row, 1962.

———. "Some Recollections of July 16, 1945." In *Alamogordo Plus Twenty-five Years,* ed. Richard S. Lewis and Jane Wilson. New York: Viking Press, 1970.

Hacker, Barton C. *The Dragon's Tail: Radiation Safety in the Manhattan Project, 1942–1946.* Berkeley: University of California Press, 1987.

Hagan, Kenneth J., ed. *In Peace and War: Interpretations of American Naval History, 1775–1984,* 2d ed. Westport, Conn.: Greenwood Press, 1984.

———. *This People's Navy: The Making of American Sea Power.* New York: Free Press, 1981.

Halberstam, David. *The Fifties.* New York: Villard Books, 1993.

Halsey, William F., and J. Bryan III. *Admiral Halsey's Story.* New York: McGraw-Hill, 1947.

Hansen, Chuck. *U.S. Nuclear Weapons: The Secret History.* Arlington, Tex.: Aerofax, Inc., 1988.

Harriman, W. Averell, and Elie Abel. *Special Envoy to Churchill and Stalin, 1941–1946.* New York: Random House, 1975.

Hawkins, David, Edith C. Truslow, and Ralph Carlisle Smith. *Project Y: The Los Alamos Story*. Los Angeles: Tomash Publishers, 1983.

Herken, Gregg, *The Winning Weapon: The Atomic Bomb in the Cold War, 1945–1950*. New York: Knopf, 1980.

Hershberg, James G. *James B. Conant: Harvard to Hiroshima and the Making of the Nuclear Age*. New York: Knopf, 1993.

Hewlett, Richard G., and Oscar E. Anderson, Jr. *A History of the United States Atomic Energy Commission*. Vol. 1, *The New World, 1939/1946*. University Park: Pennsylvania State University Press, 1962.

Hewlett, Richard G., and Francis Duncan. *A History of the United States Atomic Energy Commission*. Vol. 2, *Atomic Shield, 1947/1952*. University Park: Pennsylvania State University Press, 1969.

——. *Nuclear Navy, 1946–1962*. Chicago: University of Chicago Press, 1974.

Hewlett, Richard G., and Jack M. Holl. *Atoms for Peace and War, 1953–1961: Eisenhower and the Atomic Energy Commission*. Berkeley: University of California Press, 1989.

Hezel, Francis X. *The First Taint of Civilization: A History of the Caroline and Marshall Islands in the Pre-Colonial Days, 1521–1885*. Honolulu: University of Hawaii Press, 1983.

Hezlet, Arthur. *Aircraft and Sea Power*. London: Peter Davies, 1970.

Hinds, Lynn Boyd, and Theodore Otto Windt, Jr. *The Cold War as Rhetoric: The Beginnings, 1945–1950*. New York: Praeger, 1991.

Hines, Neal O. *Proving Ground: An Account of the Radiobiological Studies in the Pacific, 1946–1961*. Seattle: University of Washington Press, 1962.

Hoopes, Townsend, and Douglas Brinkley. *Driven Patriot: The Life and Times of James Forrestal*. New York: Knopf, 1992.

Howarth, Stephen. *The Fighting Ships of the Rising Sun: The Drama of the Imperial Japanese Navy 1895–1945*. New York: Antheneum, 1983.

——. *To Shining Sea: A History of the United States Navy 1775–1991*. New York: Random House, 1991.

Huie, William Bradford. *The Fight for Air Power*. New York: L. B. Fischer, 1942.

Hull, Cordell. *Memoirs of Cordell Hull*. 2 vols. New York: Macmillan, 1948.

Huntington, Samuel P. *The Common Defense: Strategic Programs in National Politics*. New York: Columbia University Press, 1961.

——. "Interservice Competition and the Political Roles of the Armed Services." In *Total War and Cold War: Problems in Civilian Control of the Military*, ed. Harry L. Coles. Columbus: Ohio State University Press, 1962.

Hurley, Alfred F. *Billy Mitchell: Crusader for Air Power*. Bloomington: Indiana University Press, 1964.

International Physicians for the Prevention of Nuclear War and the Institute for Energy and Environmental Research. *Plutonium: Deadly Gold of the Nuclear Age*. Cambridge, Mass.: International Physicians Press, 1992.

Isaacson, Walter, and Evan Thomas. *The Wise Men: Six Friends and the World They Made*. New York: Simon and Schuster, 1986.

Jungk, Robert. *Brighter than a Thousand Suns: A Personal History of the Atomic Scientists*. Translated by James Cleugh. New York: Harcourt, Brace, 1958.

Kennan, George F. *Memoirs, 1925–1950*. Boston: Little, Brown, 1967.

Kennedy, Ludovic. *Pursuit: The Chase and Sinking of the Bismarck*. New York: Viking, 1974.

Kevles, Daniel J. *The Physicists: The History of a Scientific Community in Modern America*. New York: Knopf, 1978.

Kiste, Robert C. *The Bikinians: A Study in Forced Migration*. Menlo Park, Calif.: Cummings Publishing, 1974.

Kolko, Joyce, and Gabriel Kolko. *The Limits of Power: The World and United States Foreign Policy, 1945–1954*. New York: Harper and Row, 1972.

Krock, Arthur. *Memoirs: Sixty Years on the Firing Line*. New York: Funk and Wagnalls, 1968.

Kunetka, James W. *Oppenheimer: The Years of Risk*. Englewood Cliffs, N.J.: Prentice-Hall, 1982.

Kurzman, Dan. *Day of the Bomb: Countdown to Hiroshima*. New York: McGraw-Hill, 1986.

———. *Fatal Voyage: The Sinking of the USS Indianapolis*. New York: Atheneum, 1990.

Lamont, Lansing. *Day of Trinity*. New York: Atheneum, 1965.

Lapp, Ralph E. *Atoms and People*. New York: Harper and Bros., 1956.

———. *Must We Hide?* New York: Harper and Bros., 1949.

———. *The Voyage of the Lucky Dragon*. New York: Harper and Bros., 1957.

Larsen, Rebecca. *Oppenheimer and the Atomic Bomb*. New York: Franklin Watts, 1988.

Laurence, William L. *Dawn over Zero: The Story of the Atomic Bomb*. New York: Knopf, 1946.

———. *Men and Atoms: The Discovery, the Uses, and the Future of Atomic Energy*. New York: Simon and Schuster, 1946.

Lawren, William. *The General and the Bomb: A Biography of Leslie R. Groves, Director of the Manhattan Project*. New York: Dodd, Mead, 1988.

Leffler, Melvyn P. *A Preponderance of Power: National Security, the Truman Administration, and the Cold War*. Stanford: Stanford University Press, 1992.

LeMay, Curtis E., and Bill Yenne. *Superfortress: The B-29 and American Air Power*. New York: McGraw-Hill, 1988.

Lerner, Max. *Actions and Passions: Notes on the Multiple Revolution of Our Time*. New York: Simon and Schuster, 1949.

Levine, Isaac D. *Mitchell: Pioneer of Air Power*. New York: Duell, Sloane, and Pearce, 1943.

Lilienthal, David E. *The Journals of David E. Lilienthal*. Vol. 2, *The Atomic Energy Years, 1945–1950*. New York: Harper and Row, 1964.

Lockwood, Charles A. *Down to the Sea in Subs*. New York: Norton, 1967.

———. *Sink 'Em All: Submarine Warfare in the Pacific*. New York: Dutton, 1951.

Lord, Walter. *Day of Infamy*. New York: Henry Holt, 1975.

Lovell, Mary S. *The Sound of Wings: The Life of Amelia Earhart*. New York: St. Martin's Press, 1989.

McCullough, David. *Truman*. New York: Simon and Schuster, 1992.

McHenry, Donald F. *Micronesia: Trust Betrayed: Altruism versus Self-interest in American Foreign Policy.* Washington, D.C.: Carnegie Endowment for International Peace, 1975.

McQuade, Donald, and Robert Atwan. *Popular Writing in America: The Interaction of Style and Audience.* New York: Oxford University Press, 1974.

Maddox, Robert James. *From War to Cold War: The Education of Harry S. Truman.* Boulder, Colo.: Westview Press, 1988.

Martin, Richard, and Harold Koda. *Splash! A History of Swimwear.* New York: Rizzoli, 1990.

Melhorn, Charles M. *Two-Block Fox: The Rise of the Aircraft Carrier, 1921–1929.* Annapolis, Md.: Naval Institute Press, 1974.

Melville, Herman. *Moby Dick, or The Whale.* New York: Harper Bros., 1851.

Messer, Robert L. *The End of an Alliance: James F. Byrnes, Roosevelt, Truman, and the Origins of the Cold War.* Chapel Hill: University of North Carolina Press, 1982.

Michelmore, Peter. *The Swift Years: The Robert Oppenheimer Story.* New York: Dodd, Mead, 1969.

Middlebrook, Martin, and Patrick Mahoney. *Battleship: The Loss of the Prince of Wales and the Repulse.* London: Allen Lane, 1977.

Miller, Richard L. *Under the Cloud: The Decades of Nuclear Testing.* New York: Free Press, 1986.

Millis, Walter, ed. *The War Reports of General of the Army George C. Marshall, General of the Army H. H. Arnold, and Fleet Admiral Ernest J. King.* Philadelphia: Lippincott, 1947.

Mitchell, William. *Winged Defense.* New York: G. P. Putnam's Sons, 1925.

Morgan, Ted. *FDR: A Biography.* New York: Simon and Schuster, 1985.

Morison, Samuel Eliot. *The European Discovery of America: The Southern Voyages 1492–1616.* New York: Oxford University Press, 1974.

——. *History of United States Naval Operations in World War II.* Vol. 7, *Aleutians, Gilberts, and Marshalls.* Boston: Little, Brown, 1951.

Morris, Charles R. *Iron Destinies, Lost Opportunities: The Arms Race between the U.S.A. and the U.S.S.R., 1945–1987.* New York: Harper and Row, 1988.

Morrison, Joseph L. *Josephus Daniels: The Small -d Democrat.* Chapel Hill: University of North Carolina Press, 1966.

Morrison, Wilbur H. *Wings over the Seven Seas: The Story of Naval Aviation's Fight for Survival.* Cranbury, N.J.: A. S. Barnes, 1975.

Newcomb, Richard F. *Iwo Jima.* New York: Holt, Rinehart and Winston, 1965.

Newhouse, John. *War and Peace in the Nuclear Age.* New York: Knopf, 1989.

Nichols, David, ed. *Ernie's War: The Best of Ernie Pyle's World War II Dispatches.* New York: Random House, 1986.

Nichols, Kenneth D. *The Road to Trinity.* New York: William Morrow, 1987.

Nogee, Joseph L. *Soviet Policy toward International Control of Atomic Energy.* South Bend, Ind.: University of Notre Dame Press, 1961.

O'Keefe, Bernard J. *Nuclear Hostages.* Boston: Houghton Mifflin, 1983.

Parry, J. H. *The Age of Reconnaissance.* Berkeley: University of California Press, 1963.

———. *The Discovery of the Sea.* Berkeley: University of California Press, 1974.

Peattie, Mark R. *Nanyo: The Rise and Fall of the Japanese in Micronesia, 1885–1945.* Honolulu: University of Hawaii Press, 1988.

Pfau, Richard. *No Sacrifice Too Great: The Life of Lewis L. Strauss.* Charlottesville: University of Virginia Press, 1984.

Phillips, Cabell. *The Truman Presidency: The History of a Triumphant Succession.* New York: Macmillan, 1966.

Polmar, Norman. *Aircraft Carriers: A Graphic History of Carrier Aviation and Its Influence on World Events.* Garden City, N.Y.: Doubleday, 1969.

Potter, E. B. *Nimitz.* Annapolis, Md.: Naval Institute Press, 1976.

Prange, Gordon W. *At Dawn We Slept: The Untold Story of Pearl Harbor.* New York: McGraw-Hill, 1981.

———. *December 7, 1941: The Day the Japanese Attacked Pearl Harbor.* New York: McGraw-Hill, 1988.

Pringle, Peter, and James Spigelman. *The Nuclear Barons.* New York: Holt, Rinehart and Winston, 1981.

Probert, Christian. *Swimwear in Vogue since 1910.* New York: Abbeville, 1981.

Reynolds, Clark G. *Admiral John J. Towers: The Struggle for Naval Air Supremacy.* Annapolis, Md.: Naval Institute Press, 1991.

———. *Famous American Admirals.* New York: Van Nostrand Reinhold, 1978.

Rhodes, Richard. *The Making of the Atomic Bomb.* New York: Simon and Schuster, 1988.

Rimsky-Korsakov, Nikolai Andreyevich. *My Musical Life.* Translated by Judah A. Joffe. New York: Knopf, 1923.

Rogow, Arnold A. *James Forrestal: A Study of Personality, Politics, and Policy.* New York: Macmillan, 1963.

Roscoe, Theodore. *United States Submarine Operations in World War II.* Annapolis, Md.: U.S. Naval Institute, 1949.

Roskill, Stephen. *Naval Policy between the Wars.* Vol. 1, *The Period of Anglo-American Antagonism.* New York: Walker and Co., 1968.

Ross, Bill D. *Iwo Jima: Legacy of Valor.* New York: Vanguard Press, 1985.

Ross, Steven T. *American War Plans, 1945–1950.* New York: Garland Publishing, 1988.

Ross, Steven T., and David A. Rosenberg, eds. *America's Plans for War against the Soviet Union, 1945–1950.* 15 vols. New York: Garland Publishing, 1989.

Royale, Denise. *The Story of J. Robert Oppenheimer.* New York: St. Martin's Press, 1969.

Rusk, Dean. *As I Saw It.* New York: Norton, 1990.

Saleh, Dennis. *Science Fiction Gold: Film Classics of the 50s.* New York: McGraw-Hill, 1979.

Schapsmeier, Edward L., and Frederick H. Schapsmeier. *Dirksen of Illinois: Senatorial Statesman.* Urbana: University of Illinois Press, 1985.

Schubert, Jack, and Ralph E. Lapp. *Radiation: What It Is and How It Affects You.* New York: Viking Press, 1957.

Shelton, Frank H. *Reflections of a Nuclear Weaponeer.* Colorado Springs: Shelton Enterprises, 1988.

Sherry, Michael S. *Preparing for the Next War: American Plans for the Postwar*

Defense, 1941–1945. New Haven: Yale University Press, 1977.

———. *The Rise of American Air Power: The Creation of Armageddon.* New Haven: Yale University Press, 1987.

Sherwin, Martin J. *A World Destroyed: The Atomic Bomb and the Grand Alliance.* New York: Knopf, 1973.

Smith, Alice Kimball. *A Peril and a Hope: The Scientists' Movement in American, 1945–47.* Chicago: University of Chicago Press, 1965.

Smith, Merriman. *Thank You, Mr. President: A White House Notebook.* New York: Harper, 1946.

Spanier, John W., and Joseph L. Nogee. *The Politics of Disarmament: A Study in Soviet-American Gamesmanship.* New York: Praeger, 1962.

Spector, Ronald H. *Eagle against the Sun: The American War with Japan.* New York: Free Press, 1985.

Steiner, Barry H. *Bernard Brodie and the Foundations of American Nuclear Strategy.* Lawrence: University Press of Kansas, 1991.

Stettinius, Edward R., Jr. *The Diaries of Edward R. Stettinius, Jr., 1943–1946.* Edited by Thomas M. Campbell and George C. Herring. New York: New Viewpoints, 1975.

Stokesbury, James L. *A Short History of Air Power.* New York: William Morrow, 1986.

Stimson, Henry L., and McGeorge Bundy. *On Active Service in Peace and War.* New York: Harper, 1946.

Storry, Richard. *A History of Modern Japan.* Baltimore: Penguin Books, 1960.

Strauss, Lewis L. *Men and Decisions.* Garden City, N.Y.: Doubleday, 1962.

Szasz, Ferenc Morton. *The Day the Sun Rose Twice: The Story of the Trinity Site Nuclear Explosion, July 16, 1945.* Albuquerque: University of New Mexico Press, 1984.

Szilard, Leo. *Leo Szilard: His Version of the Facts: Selected Recollections and Correspondence.* Edited by Spencer Weart and Gertrude Weiss Szilard. Cambridge: MIT Press, 1978.

Taylor, Theodore. *The Magnificent Mitscher.* Annapolis, Md.: U.S. Naval Institute, 1954.

Terkel, Studs. *The Good War: An Oral History of World War II.* New York: Pantheon, 1984.

Tibbets, Paul W., with Clair Stebbins and Harry Franken. *The Tibbets Story.* New York: Stein and Day, 1975.

Truman, Harry S. *Memoirs.* Vol. 1, *Year of Decisions.* Vol. 2, *Years of Trial and Hope.* Garden City, N.Y.: Doubleday, 1956.

Truman, Margaret. *Harry S. Truman.* New York: William Morrow, 1972.

Trumbull, Robert. *Paradise in Trust: A Report on Americans in Micronesia, 1946–1958.* New York: William Sloane, 1959.

Uhl, Michael, and Tod Ensign. *GI Guinea Pigs: How the Pentagon Exposed Our Troops to Dangers More Deadly than War: Agent Orange and Atomic Radiation.* Chicago: Playboy Press, 1980.

Vandenberg, Arthur H. *Private Papers of Senator Vandenberg.* Edited by Arthur H. Vandenberg, Jr. Boston: Houghton Mifflin, 1952.

von Chamisso, Adelbert. *A Voyage around the World with the Romanzov*

Exploring Expedition in the Years 1815–1818 in the Brig Rurik, Captain Otto von Kotzebue. Translated and edited by Henry Kratz. Honolulu: University of Hawaii Press, 1986.

Von der Porten, Edward P. *The German Navy in World War II.* New York: Thomas Y. Crowell, 1969.

von Kotzebue, Otto. *A New Voyage Round the World.* 2 vols. London: Henry Colburn and Richard Bentley, 1930.

Voss, Earl H. *Nuclear Ambush: The Test-Ban Trap.* Chicago: Henry Regnery Co., 1963.

Walker, J. Samuel. *Henry A. Wallace and American Foreign Policy.* Westport, Conn.: Greenwood Press, 1976.

Wallace, Henry A. *The Price of Vision: The Diary of Henry A. Wallace, 1942–1946.* Edited by John Morton Blum. Boston: Houghton Mifflin, 1973.

Ward, Patricia. "James F. Byrnes and the Paris Conference." In *James F. Byrnes and the Origins of the Cold War,* ed. Kendrick A. Clements. Durham, N.C.: Carolina Academic Press, 1982.

Wasserman, Harvey, and Norman Solomon. *Killing Our Own: The Disaster of America's Experience with Atomic Radiation.* New York: Delacorte, 1982.

Weart, Spencer R. *Nuclear Fear: A History of Images.* Cambridge: Harvard University Press, 1988.

Weigley, Russell F. *The American Way of War: A History of United States Military Strategy and Policy.* New York: Macmillan, 1973.

Wheeler, Richard. *A Special Valor: The U.S. Marines and the Pacific War.* New York: Harper and Row, 1983.

White, E. B. *The Wild Flag: Editorials from the New York on Federal World Government and Other Matters.* Boston: Houghton Mifflin, 1946.

White, Graham, and John Maze. *Harold Ickes of the New Deal: His Private Life and Public Career.* Cambridge: Harvard University Press, 1985.

Whitley, M. J. *German Cruisers of World War II.* New York: Amrs and Armour Press, 1985.

Williams, Robert Chadwell. *Klaus Fuchs: Atom Spy.* Cambridge: Harvard University Press, 1987.

Wood, Michael. *America in the Movies: or, "Santa Maria, It Had Slipped My Mind."* New York: Basic Books, 1975.

Wyden, Peter. *Day One: Before Hiroshima and After.* New York: Simon and Schuster, 1984.

Yergin, Daniel. *Shattered Peace: The Origins of the Cold War and the National Security State.* Boston: Houghton Mifflin, 1977.

Zumwalt, Ken. *The Stars and Stripes: World War II and the Early Years.* Austin, Tex.: Eakin Press, 1979.

Articles

Arnold, H. H. "The 36-Hour War." *Life,* November 19, 1945.

"The Atomic Bomb Test." *Infantry Journal* (April 1946).

"At the Crossroads." *All Hands,* no. 352 (July 1, 1946).

Attwood, William. "The Birth of the Bikini." *Look,* May 19, 1970.

Bernstein, Barton J. "Roosevelt, Truman, and the Atomic Bomb, 1941–1945: A Reinterpretation." *Political Science Quarterly* 90 (Spring 1975).

——. "An Analysis of 'Two Cultures': Writing about the Making and Using of the Atomic Bomb." *The Public Historian* (Spring 1990).

Blandy, William H. P. "Atomic Test Case." *Collier's,* June 8, 1946.

——. "Bikini: Guidepost to the Future." *Sea Power* (December 1946).

——. "Command Relations in Amphibious Warfare." U.S. Naval Institute *Proceedings* (June 1951).

——. "The Future Value of Sea Power." *The Society of Naval Architects and Marine Engineers Transactions* 55 (November 14, 1947).

——. "The Navy's Tools of War." *Popular Mechanics,* April 1944.

——. "Operation Crossroads: The Story of the Air and Underwater Tests of the Atomic Bomb at Bikini." *Army Ordnance* (January–February 1947).

——. "Possible Improvements in Our Gunnery Training." U.S. Naval Institute *Proceedings* (September 1925).

——. "Report on Bikini." *All Hands* (September 1946).

——. "Sea Forces." *Air Affairs* (March 1947).

Boyer, Paul. "'The Fences Are Gone': American Policymaking in the Dawn of the Nuclear Era." *Reviews in American History* (September 1982).

Christman, Albert B. "Deak Parsons, Officer-Scientist." U.S. Naval Institute *Proceedings* (January 1992).

Coffin, Tris. "In the Light of Bikini." *The Nation,* October 5, 1946.

Cousins, Norman. "The Standardization of Catastrophe." *The Saturday Review of Literature,* August 10, 1946.

Cumberledge, A. A. "Aerological Aspects of the Bikini Bomb Test." *The Scientific Monthly* (September 1946).

Daly, Thomas M. "Crossroads at Bikini." U.S. Naval Institute *Proceedings* (July 1986).

Delgado, James P. "What's Become of *Sara?*" U.S. Naval Institute *Proceedings* (October 1990).

de Ment, Jack. "Instruments of Operation Crossroads." *The Military Engineer* (October 1947).

Dewey, Bradley. "High Policy and the Atomic Bomb." *Atlantic Monthly,* December 1948.

Dickey, Capt. George L., Jr. "The End of the *Prinz.*" U.S. Naval Institute *Proceedings* (August 1969).

Eliot, John. "In Bikini Lagoon, Life Thrives in a Nuclear Graveyard." *National Geographic,* June 1992.

Ellis, William S. "Bikini: A Way of Life Lost." *National Geographic,* June 1986.

Farrell, James J. "The Crossroads of Bikini." *Journal of American Culture* 10, no. 2 (Summer 1987).

Gerber, Lloyd G. "The Baruch Plan and the Origins of the Cold War." *Diplomatic History* 6 (Winter 1982).

Graybar, Lloyd J. "Bikini Revisited." *Military Affairs* (October 1980).

——. "The 1946 Atomic Bomb Tests: Atomic Diplomacy or Bureaucratic Infighting?" *Journal of American History* 72 (March 1986).

Graybar, Lloyd J., and Ruth Flint Graybar. "America Faces the Atomic Age." *Air Force Review* (January–February 1985).

Harrington, Alan. "Bikini: War 1, Peace 0." *New Republic,* July 22, 1946.

Hersey, John. "The Old Man, III: National Kibitzer." *New Yorker,* January 17, 1948.

Hines, Neal O. "Bikini Report." *Scientific Monthly* (February 1951).

Honicker, Clifford T. "The Hidden Files." *New York Times Magazine,* November 19, 1989.

Hope, Bob. "So This Is Peace." *Life,* October 21, 1946.

Karig, Walter, and Eric Purdon. "The Komandorskis—A Little Known Victory." U.S. Naval Institute *Proceedings* (November 1946).

Kirkpatrick, S. D. "A-Bomb Tests as Viewed by the Editor." *Chemical Engineering* (August 1946).

Knerr, Maj. Gen. H. "If We Should Fight Again." *Military Review* 27 (January 1947).

Krueger, Philip G. "Operation Crossroads." *Military Engineer* 38, no. 249 (July 1946).

Ladd, Harry S., Joshua L. Tracey, Jr., and G. G. Lill. "Drilling on Bikini Atoll, Marshall Islands." *Science* 107 (January 16, 1948).

Lapp, Ralph E., and Stuart Alsop. "The Strange Death of Louis Slotkin." *Saturday Evening Post,* March 6, 1954.

Lee, Capt. Fitzhugh. "The Press at Operation Crossroads." *Army Information Digest* 2, no. 3 (March 1947).

Littell, Robert. "The Voice of the Apple." *Harper's,* September 1946.

Markwith, Carl. "Farewell to Bikini." *National Geographic,* July 1946.

Moll, Kenneth L. "Operation Crossroads." *Air Force Magazine* 54, no. 7 (July 1971).

Moore, Samuel Taylor. "A Bargain in Preparedness." *Harper's,* May 1924.

"Operation Crossroads: Color Photographs." *National Geographic,* April 1947.

Potter, Robert D. "The Atom Bomb's Terrifying Test." *American Weekly,* May 12, 1946.

Powell, Herb. "'Crossroads' Critique." *Aviation* 45 (June 1946).

Pratt, Fletcher. "The Torpedoes That Failed." *Atlantic Monthly,* July 1950.

Pratt, William V. "How Bikini Became the Bomb-testing Ground." *Newsweek,* February 18, 1946.

Quigley, Eileen. "Swimming in the Atomic Lagoon." *Washington Monthly,* December 1984.

Ramey, Roger M. "Phantom Fortresses versus the Atomic Bomb." *Saturday Evening Post,* June 22, 1946.

Ransom, Harry H. "The Battleship Meets the Airplane." *Military Affairs* 23, no. 1 (Spring 1959).

Ridenour, Louis N. "Bikini: What Can It Prove?" *Science Illustrated,* May 1946.

Rosenberg, David A. "American Atomic Strategy and the Hydrogen Bomb Decision." *Journal of American History* 66 (June 1979).

——. "The Origins of Overkill: Nuclear Weapons and American Strategy, 1945–60." *International Security* 7 (Spring 1983).

——. "Reality and Responsibility: Power and Process in the Making of United States Nuclear Strategy, 1945–68." *Journal of Strategic Studies* 9 (March 1986).

——. "U.S. Nuclear Stockpile, 1945 to 1950." *Bulletin of the Atomic Scientists* (May 1982).

Salaff, Stephen. "The Lucky Dragon." *Bulletin of the Atomic Scientists* (May 1978).

Smith, Alice Kimball. "Behind the Decision to Use the Atomic Bomb: Chicago, 1944–45." *Bulletin of the Atomic Scientists* (October 1958).

Spengler, Wayne E. "*Prinz Eugen,* Little Brother of the *Bismarck.*" U.S. Naval Institute *Proceedings* (October 1946).

Strope, Walmer Elton. "The Navy and the Atomic Bomb." U.S. Naval Institute *Proceedings* (October 1947).

Terkel, Studs. "The Good War." *Atlantic Monthly,* June 1984.

Toulmin, Col. Harry A., Jr. "Is Bikini a Fair Test?" *Flying,* July 1946.

Truman, Harry S. "Our Armed Services *Must* Be United." *Collier's,* August 12, 1944.

Tullis, J. L. "The Pathologic Changes Induced by Ionizing Radiation in the Bikini Animals." *American Journal of Pathology* 23 (1947).

Warren, Stafford L. "Conclusions: Test Proved Irresistible Spread of Radioactivity." *Life,* August 11, 1947.

Weisgall, Jonathan M. "The Nuclear Nomads of Bikini Atoll." *Foreign Policy* 39 (Summer 1980).

White, E. B. "Journal of a Contaminated Man." *New Yorker,* December 4, 1948.

——. "Talk of the Town." *New Yorker,* March 9, 1946.

Wilson, Gilbert. "Moby Dick and the Atom." *Bulletin of the Atomic Scientists* (August 1952).

Wolfe, Charles. "Nuclear Country: The Atom Bomb in Country Music." *Journal of Country Music* 7 (January 1978).

Wright, Rear Adm. Carleton H. "Let's Not Civilize These Happy People." *Saturday Evening Post,* May 3, 1947.

York, Herbert F. "The Debate over the Hydrogen Bomb." *Scientific American,* October 1975.

Index

AAF. *See* Army Air Forces
ABC (network), 141, 178–79, 192
Aberdeen Proving Ground, 204
Able test, 1–2, 101, 117, 136, 159,
    182–92; aftermath of, 193–205;
    and animals in, 175, 190–91,
    195, 199; detonation of bomb,
    185–86, 189; disappointment
    concerning, 186–88, 190, 192,
    195, 200; effects of, 186,
    188–92, 195–97, 199–200; and
    evacuation of atolls, 176–77,
    302; height of bomb at, 126,
    185, 353n. 14; planning for,
    126–28, 173–81; and public
    response to, 187, 192; radsafe
    monitors at, 183, 186–87, 212,
    214; salvage operations after,
    194; weather conditions for,
    180, 183; yield of, 186. *See also*
    Atomic bomb; Operation Cross-
    roads; Target ships
Acheson, Dean, 328n. 23; and
    Acheson-Lilienthal Report,
    69–70, 99–100; and Baruch, 70,
    71, 99–100; and Crossroads,
    143; and Oppenheimer, 85; and
    Truman, 85; and views on Soviet
    Union, 55, 56, 72, 249, 250
Acheson-Lilienthal Report, 69–70,
    73, 85, 99–100, 131, 249, 250

Agano, 170
Ailinginae, 39
Ailinginae Atoll, 302, 303, 304
Aircraft carriers, 250; and atomic
    bomb, 86, 286; postwar debate
    over, 27, 29; and role in World
    War II, 25, 28, 169, 170–71,
    196; and role predicted by Billy
    Mitchell, 20
AJ-1 Savage airplane, 286
Alamogordo. *See* Trinity test
Alaska, 38, 39, 40, 300
Alaska (battle cruiser), 283
Albemarle, 122, 137
Alexander I (Czar), 39
Alexandrov, Simon, 187
Allen, George E., 72
Allison, John M., 305
Alpha particles, 213, 233, 238, 242,
    245, 277. *See also* Plutonium
Alsop, Joseph and Stewart, 83–84,
    85, 153–54
American Red Cross, 123
Anderson, 164, 189
Anderson, Herbert, 65
Anderson, Jack Z., 144
Andrews, William G., 88, 356n. 33
Apogon, 164, 225, 300
Appalachian, 122, 142, 151, 183,
    184, 194, 219
Arkansas: at Crossroads, 2, 168,

397

Arkansas (continued)
171, 184, 190, 197, 220, 225; in
World War I, 163; in World War
II, 3, 25, 167
Armed Forces Special Weapons Project, 298
Army, U.S.: biological-warfare division, 120; Corps of Engineers,
84, 122, 231; and postwar military strategy, 284–85; role of
in Crossroads, 122; Signal
Corps, 122; Strategic Air Command, 127; and unification of
services, 25–26. *See also* Interservice rivalry; Unification of the
services
Army Air Corps, 19, 23
Army Air Forces, U.S. (AAF): as
equal to Army and Navy in
World War II, 23; and competition to drop Able bomb, 127–28,
173–74, 180, 344n. 20, 352n.
32; and planning for Crossroads,
30, 67, 124–29, 137, 153; and
postwar atomic capability of,
13–14, 15, 62, 127, 197, 280,
283–84, 366n. 6; role of in
World War II, 13, 27, 134–35;
Strategic Air Command of, 127;
and unification of services,
25–26. *See also* Interservice
rivalry; Operation Crossroads;
Unification of the services
Army Air Service, 19–23
Arnold, Henry H. ("Hap"), 15, 23;
and criticism of Navy, 27; and
planning for Crossroads, 15–16;
and postwar atomic planning,
284, 326n. 20; role in World
War II atomic bombing, 14, 16
Ashworth, Frederick, 32–33, 125,
133, 134, 136, 204, 325n. 19,
357n. 41
Association of Los Alamos Scientists, 86
Atlantic Monthly, 296
Atolls, 34–35, 300, 329n. 2

Atomic bomb: ability of ships to
withstand, 14, 87, 163–64,
95–96, 371n. 22; assembly of,
134, 258; ballistics and trajectory of, 126–28, 134, 201–4;
biological warfare compared to,
4, 266, 291; delivery of, 13–14,
28–29, 280, 282–84, 286, 297;
as "destroyer of worlds," 86;
development of, 8, 147; as diplomatic tool, 57, 78, 80, 87–88,
97; doubts concerning, 5, 29,
135, 145, 178, 188; effect of on
ships, 126, 129, 154–55, 186,
188–91, 195–97, 225–26,
279–84; fear of and reliance on,
85; Germany's glide bomb compared to, 29; international control of, 59, 62, 69–71, 136, 143,
247–48, 251–55, 285; mobile
storage sites for, 123; Nagasaki-
type, 134–35, 257, 279; Navy's
attitude toward, 13–15, 27–29,
87, 120–21, 133–34, 136, 191,
195–96, 197–98, 229, 234, 240,
243, 244–45, 266, 279–80; and
Normandy invasion, 271–72; as
overrated weapons, 29, 187,
192, 246–47; possible demonstration of during World War II,
33; and postwar planning, 86,
244, 284–85; postwar production of, 133–35, 147, 258, 293,
297; psychological effect of, 292;
public attitude toward, 12–13,
87, 136, 160, 192, 246–47,
261–65; radiation injuries from,
4, 7–8, 138–40, 190–91, 199,
209–11, 213, 245, 268, 291–92;
Soviet Union's development of,
85, 301; stockpile of, 8, 9, 12,
16, 31, 247, 258, 259, 286; and
Truk lagoon, 16; as underwater
naval weapon, 133–34; used on
Japan, 1, 4, 7–8, 11–12, 27, 91,
146 (*see also* Hiroshima;
Nagasaki); use of on cities as

opposed to ships, 86–87, 98–99, 155, 288, 291–92, 293; U.S. monopoly over, 56, 61, 85; as "winning weapon," 86, 101, 297. *See also* Fallout, radioactive; individual tests by name; Operation Crossroads

Atomic Energy Commission (AEC), 31–32, 69, 78, 143, 250, 299, 310; and Bravo test, 9, 302–7; and Enewetak, 300, 301, 312; legislative proposals for, 65–67, 133, 257; and Nevada Test Site, 301; and Project Chariot, 40; proposed changes in, 294, 298; and safety of Bikini Atoll, 10, 301, 314–15; and search for test sites, 300–301; and weapons testing, 259, 300–307

Austin, Warren R., 14, 66

Australia, 143, 264

Avanti (Italy), 255

Avery Island, 122

Ayers, Eben A., 68, 91

Azores Island, as possible weapons test site, 300

B-29 bomber, 286; problems with, 48–49, 128; use of in Crossroads, 1, 33, 121, 127, 128, 134–35, 147, 172, 173, 176, 182, 201, 202; in World War II, 11, 27, 42, 48–49, 50, 352n. 32

Bacall, Lauren, 352n. 33

Bahrain, 61

Baker test, 2, 220–26; caisson for, 136, 215, 220; decontamination efforts following, 230–36; depth of bomb, 207, 215, 220; evaluation of, 291–92; overexposure of men following, 232–34, 236–41, 269–70, 275, 277–78; preparations for, after Able test, 194; prospective hazards of, 9, 63, 136, 214–17, 228; recovery operations after, 227–45, 362n. 4; rehearsal for, 220; safety

problems following, 227–43; as underwater shot, 207, 214–17; waves at, 117, 207, 224–25; weather conditions for, 219; yield of, 223. *See also* Atomic bomb; Operation Crossroads

Baldwin, Hanson W., 67, 141, 178, 225–26, 279

Baltimore News Post, 154

Bardot, Brigitte, 264

Baruch, Bernard M., 131; and Acheson, 70, 99–100; and Baruch Plan, 96, 99–102, 103, 143, 151, 253–54, 285; and Byrnes, 70, 100; and Crossroads, 335n. 36; and Groves, 71; and Lilienthal, 70, 99–100; named as U.S. delegate to UN AEC, 70; and Oppenheimer, 70, 71, 97, 98, 100; and Truman, 70, 253–54, 335n. 38; and views on atomic bomb, 71, 86, 101

Baruch Plan, 96, 99–101, 151, 194, 247, 248, 251–55

Base surge, 2, 222, 223–24

Battleships: and atomic bomb, 86, 279, 283; and Billy Mitchell tests, 20–23; and postwar planning, 51, 282–83; in World War II, 25

Bauno, Kilon, 112

Beahan, Kermit, 204

Becquerel, Henri, 5, 277

Bell Telephone, 123

Beta particles, 213, 233, 238–39, 277

Bethe, Hans, 65, 83, 147

Betts, Cy, 231, 257

Betts, Thomas J., 158, 159

Bibby, Lowe H., 175

"Big Apple," 142, 149

Bikar Atoll, 32

Bikini (bathing suit), 4, 263–65, 367n. 23

Bikinians: and Able test, 176; and Christian beliefs, 105, 106–7, 108, 112–13, 115; and compen-

Bikinians (continued)
　　sation from United States, 313,
　　315; exile of, 4; flag of, 315; iso-
　　lation of, 40; and Japanese, 43;
　　on Kili, 312–14; meeting with
　　Chramtschenko, 40; and mis-
　　sionaries, 41; and murder of
　　schooner crew in 1834, 41; and
　　possible return to Bikini, 205,
　　299, 301; prior to removal,
　　104–6; and promises of return to
　　Bikini, 9; and relationship with
　　United States, 104–6, 160–61;
　　removal of in 1946, 4, 106–14,
　　148; removal of in 1978,
　　314–15; returned to Bikini,
　　314–15; on Rongerik, 114–15,
　　176, 206–7, 308–12; and U.S.
　　forces in World War II, 43–44
Bikini Atoll, 3; agriculture of, 35,
　　230; archaeological discoveries
　　at, 36; climate of, 35; construc-
　　tion at, 148–49; discovery of,
　　37–39; effect of Bravo shot on,
　　302–3, 307; geology and geogra-
　　phy of, 34–36, 256, 329n. 1,
　　374n. 3; islands in, 118; as occu-
　　pied enemy territory during
　　Crossroads, 310; population of,
　　35; radioactivity at, 2, 207,
　　227–45, 260, 300, 301, 315;
　　rejected as weapons test site in
　　1947, 300; safety of in 1968, 10,
　　314–15; scientific resurvey of,
　　299–300, 372n. 1; selection of as
　　site for Crossroads, 31–33,
　　329n. 45; sunken ships in, 3,
　　188–89, 191, 225–26, 300, 316;
　　as symbol, 3, 247; weather con-
　　ditions at, 92–93, 128, 174; in
　　World War II, 43–44, 330n. 28
Bikini Island, 145–46, 147, 148,
　　175, 192, 205, 219, 223, 304,
　　306, 315
Bismarck, 4, 163, 165–66
Blackett, P. M. S., 61
Blanchard, William J., 151, 344n. 19

Blandy, Mrs. William H. P., 52, 261
Blandy, William H. P. ("Spike"),
　　24, 133, 143, 145; and AAF,
　　174; and Able test, 174–75, 179,
　　180, 181, 184, 188, 189, 201,
　　202; and Atlantic fleet, 287, 289;
　　and Baker test, 194, 210,
　　214–17, 225, 228, 230; as "bat-
　　tleship admiral," 51; and Bikini-
　　ans, 31, 106, 108, 109, 114,
　　176, 206–7, 218–19; at Bureau
　　of Ordnance, 45–48, 51–52; and
　　Charlie test, 256–60; and con-
　　gressional testimony, 13, 32,
　　74–75, 79, 81, 106, 120,
　　130–31, 164–65; criticism of by
　　media, 86, 198; and criticism of
　　Crossroads, 64, 78–79, 135,
　　156, 158, 159, 179; education
　　of, 45; and Leslie Groves, 127,
　　128–30, 257–59; and interna-
　　tional control of atomic bomb,
　　71, 131, 247; at Iwo Jima,
　　48–50, 171–72; on Micronesia,
　　311; on naming Crossroads, 32;
　　nominated to head Crossroads,
　　30–32; and Office of Special
　　Weapons, 15, 134, 286–87; and
　　placement of target vessels,
　　125–26; and postponement of
　　Crossroads, 90, 92–93; and pub-
　　lic relations, 52, 68, 272; and
　　radiological safety, 210, 211,
　　214–17, 229, 233, 236, 237,
　　239–43, 268, 270, 272; and
　　recreation at Bikini, 146, 204;
　　and reports to Joint Chiefs of
　　Staff, 198, 228; and review
　　boards for Crossroads, 67–69,
　　196, 290–91; on safety record of
　　Crossroads, 268; and scientific
　　value of Crossroads, 87, 117,
　　131; and Stafford Warren, 208,
　　210, 211, 235–36; and target
　　ships, 173, 191, 196, 197, 235,
　　266, 275; and termination of
　　Crossroads, 241–42, 261–62;

and views on atomic bomb, 191, 196, 197–98, 240, 266, 268; and views on postwar Navy, 51–52, 247, 258, 280–82; and views on postwar weapons testing, 51–52, 247; during World War I, 45; writings of, 31, 46, 50, 120, 123, 281, 282, 331n. 22

Bloom, Sol, 115

Boise, 169

Borah, William E., 21

Boston Herald, 64

Bowditch, 118, 119, 148, 150, 276

Bradbury, Norris E., 147; and Able test, 185, 201; and Charlie test, 257; on Crossroads, 132; as Los Alamos director, 132–33; and Navy, 133, 137; and planning for Crossroads, 125, 126, 134, 175–76, 214, 215; and radiological safety, 211, 277

Bradbury, Ray, 2

Bradley, David, 184–85, 234, 244, 361n. 13

Bradley, Michael, 106

Bradley, Omar, 285

Brady, John B., 298

Bravo test, 4, 9–10, 302–7, 314, 316

Brazil, 143

Brereton, Lewis H., 356n. 33

Brewster, Ralph O., 102

Brodie, Bernard, 47

Bugher, John C., 301

Bulletin of the Atomic Scientists, 83, 86–88

Bundy, McGeorge, 85

Burleson, 120, 122, 199

Bush, Vannevar, 12, 56, 99, 296, 325n. 14, 335n. 42

Butler, Thomas, 37

Byrd, Harry F., 66

Byrnes, James F., 15, 70, 82, 100, 247; and Crossroads, 68, 90, 91, 92, 143, 144; and Soviet Union, 57–58, 85, 195, 249, 252; and Truman, 56, 58–59, 331n. 27;

and U.S. nuclear stockpile, 8, 259; and Wallace, 248

Byron, John, 37

Cahn, Albert S., 86, 87

California Institute of Technology, 83, 86, 133

Canada, 59, 66, 143

Cannon, Clarence, 28

Capelle, Adolf, 41, 312

Carlisle, 164, 189

Caroline Islands, 32, 34, 42

Carteret, 237

Castle, Jacques, 263

Castle series, 302–7

CBS (network), 141, 184

Chamisso, Adelbert von, 3, 38–40

Chao, Chung-Yao, 144

Chaplin, Bill, 141, 182, 185

Charles I (king of Spain), 36

Charlie test, 90, 109, 256; cancellation of, 257–60, 261; prospective hazards of, 9, 63, 117

Charm (magazine), 141

Chernobyl, 224

Cherokee test, 307

Chicago Sun, 198

Chicago Tribune, 199

Chilton, 300

China, 143, 144

Chramtschenko, Ivan, 39, 40

Christian, Linda, 265

Christian Science Monitor, 192

Chukchi Sea, 40

Churchill, Winston, 54, 61, 166, 306–7, 350n. 12

Clamp, 276

Clay, Lucius, 54

Cleveland Plain Dealer, 222

Clifford, Clark, 159, 251, 294, 327n. 16

Cloves, 36–37

Cochrane, E. L., 282–83

Coffin, Charles, 269–70

Cole, Sterling, 74, 80–81

Collier's, 123

Compton, Arthur, 101

Compton, Karl T., 69, 93, 160, 178, 200, 283, 288–90, 294–96, 298, 356n. 33
Conant, James B., 97, 125, 297
Conard, Robert, 239
Condon, Edward U., 335n. 36, 356n. 33
Congress, U.S.: and atomic monopoly, 59, 74; and Billy Mitchell, 20, 21–22; and compensation to nuclear victims, 278, 315; and Crossroads, 65, 73–81, 89, 91, 95–97, 101–3, 143, 144–45, 180, 187, 353n. 24, 356n. 33; and postwar atomic planning, 83; and postwar budget, 29, 87; and preemptive atomic strike, 293; and unification of the services, 26; wartime criticism of Navy, 27–28. See also House of Representatives; Senate
Connally, Tom, 66, 76, 92
Considine, Bob, 141, 142, 149, 150, 187, 193–94, 195, 224, 268
Cook, James, 37
Copra, 41–42, 104, 105, 312
Cordon, Guy, 187
Cousins, Norman, 141, 151, 195, 247
Crittenden, 261
Cruikshank, George, 38
Cumberland Sound, 122, 137, 220, 221

Daghlian, Harry, 138–39, 140
Dahlgren Naval Proving Ground, 134, 146
Daily Worker, 80
Daniels, Josephus, 20, 21, 28
Darwin, Charles, 3, 39, 300
Dave's Dream, 147, 151, 174, 179, 180, 182–83, 184–85, 189, 201–4, 280
Davies, A. Powell, 261–62
Davis, Elmer, 192
D-Day (Normandy invasion), 26,

167, 168, 174, 271–72
Dean, Gordon, 301
De Lorimier, Alfred A., 359n. 24
Demobilization, 28, 29, 56, 116
Dentuda, 164, 366n. 14
Dewey, Bradley, 68, 69, 93, 160, 221, 289, 294–96, 298, 334n. 29, 356n. 33
Dewey, Thomas E., 164, 191
Dillinger, John, 66
Dirksen, Everett McKinley, 73
Doolittle, James H. ("Jimmy"), 27, 201
Dose, 213, 227–28, 238, 271–72, 275, 277, 303, 304. See also Tolerance dose
Douglas, William O., 60, 68
Downs, Bill, 141, 184, 186
Dr. Strangelove, 2
DuBridge, Lee A., 86–88, 151
Dulles, John Foster, 297, 305
Dunkirk, 73
Dunning, Gordon, 315
Du Pont, Henry A., 45

Earhart, Amelia, 189
Ebeye Island, 176, 183
Ebon Atoll, 41
Economist, 195
Einstein, Albert, 65, 82
Eisenhower, Dwight D., 131, 174; and Bravo, 396; and Groves, 84; and hydrogen bomb, 302; and Joint Chiefs Evaluation Board Report, 297; and planning for Crossroads, 68, 144; and test ban, 307, 314; and U.S. nuclear stockpile, 8, 259; and views on Soviet Union, 54, 250, 302
Elsey, George, 251, 327n. 16
Eneman Island, 306, 307
Eneu Island, 36, 147, 148, 223, 225, 247, 302, 303, 304, 316, 329n. 8
Enewetak Atoll, 309, 329n. 8; called Browne's Range, 37; and

Crossroads, 119, 122, 188; discovery, 37; invasion of, 42–43, 171; proximity to Bikini, 33; removal of islanders from, 176; as weapons test site, 300, 301, 302, 307, 312

Engel, Albert J., 353n. 24

Enola Gay, 11, 127, 128, 146, 147

Enterprise, 24, 76, 165

Erik Island, 173

Erspamer, Ernest G., 276

Eschscholtz, Ivan Ivanovich, 38–39, 41

Exposure standards. *See* Tolerance dose

Fairchild Camera, 123

Fallout, radioactive: at Able test, 188, 214; at Baker test, 214–17, 291, 306; after Bravo test, 4, 88, 303–7; at Crossroads, 88, 93, 262; at Trinity, 209; as weapon of terror, 4, 291–92

Farrell, Thomas F., 6, 209–10, 356n. 33

Fatalities: animals in Crossroads, 190–91, 199; in Crossroads rehearsal, 174; in Japan, 4, 8, 11–12; at Los Alamos, 138–40; of radium workers in World War II, 43, 50, 164, 165–66, 168, 170, 171

Fat Man, 12, 13, 127, 134, 135, 204, 265, 286

FBI, 70, 71, 298

Federation of American Scientists, 83, 86, 97

Federation of Atomic Scientists, 83

Ferebee, Tom, 204

Fermi, Enrico, 5, 65, 138, 201

Feynman, Richard, 138

Film badges, 234, 238, 241, 268

Flying (magazine), 154

Forrestal, James V., 14, 284; at Bikini, 144, 145, 174, 179, 189, 191, 196, 204–5, 218; and

Blandy, 47, 51, 131, 248; congressional testimony of, 28–29; criticism of, by media, 179, 198; and criticism of Crossroads, 94, 154, 160, 189, 262; and interservice rivalry, 27; and Joint Chiefs Evaluation Board, 288, 290, 295–96; and Office of Special Weapons, 14, 286–87; and planning for Crossroads, 14–15, 16, 31, 68–69, 89, 90–91, 96, 97, 143, 326n. 21; and radiological safety, 268; and Soviet Union, 54, 55–56, 58, 60, 248, 251, 252; and unification debate, 26, 28; and U.S. nuclear stockpile, 8, 259

Fortune, 249

France, 143, 178, 195, 263–64, 350n. 2

Franck, James, 82

Franklin D. Roosevelt, 250

Fremont-Smith, Frank, 359n. 24

Friedell, Hymer, 208, 209, 358n. 9

Frisch, Otto R., 137–38

Fuchs, Klaus, 140, 146–47

Fulbright, J. William, 96

"Gadget," 12, 265

Galapagos Islands, 32, 328n. 41

Gamma rays, 213, 238–39, 277

Gasconade, 164, 220, 261

Gee, H. C., 130, 197

Geiger counter, 138, 231, 272, 276; and Able test, 183, 188; and Baker test, 225, 228, 232, 241, 244; malfunctioning of, 213, 233, 261

"Geiger sour," 214

"Geiger sweet," 214

General Electric, 123

George V, 164

Germany, 41, 164, 165, 166, 195, 254, 264, 284, 285, 291, 325n. 15

Gibbs, William F., 335n. 33

Gilbert, Thomas, 37

Gilbert Islands, 37, 105

"Gilda," 180, 264–65
Giles, Barney, 15
Gilliam, 164, 186, 188–89, 199
Globe, 41
Godzilla, 2
Goering, Hermann, 106
Goldschmidt, Bertrand, 144, 365n. 20
Graves, Alvin, 139
Great Britain, 141, 142, 143, 144,
    147, 166, 221, 249, 285, 306,
    350n. 2
Gresham, Walter, 52
Grieve, Harold W., 111
Gromyko, Andrei, 92, 249, 253–55
Groves, Leslie R., 13, 71, 133; and
    Atomic Energy Commission, 65,
    66–67; and bombing of
    Hiroshima and Nagasaki, 7, 12,
    324n. 1; and concern about liti-
    gation, 273–74; and criticism of
    Crossroads, 125, 127, 128–30,
    197–98, 203, 257–59; and Man-
    hattan Project scientists, 82,
    84–85, 146; nominated to head
    Crossroads, 30; and planning for
    Crossroads, 94, 97, 118, 125,
    135, 143, 215; and possible
    attendance at Crossroads, 144,
    145; and postwar atomic plan-
    ning, 85, 131, 257–58, 282, 290;
    on radiation injuries in Japan, 7,
    140, 209, 229; and Stafford
    Warren, 208, 209; at Trinity test,
    5–7; and U.S. atomic monopoly,
    56, 85; and U.S. nuclear stock-
    pile, 8, 258, 259, 286
Guadalcanal, 117, 148, 170, 171
Guam, 36–37, 48, 148, 197
Guam (battle cruiser), 283
Guarisco, Anthony, 149

Hagemayer, Louis, 121
Halsey, William F. ("Bull"), 165,
    167, 169
Hamilton, Joseph G., 273–74,
    359n. 24
Harper's, 83

Harriman, Averell W., 53, 54, 55,
    60, 251
Hart, Thomas C., 66, 74, 202
Hatch, Carl A., 96–97, 99, 206–7,
    221, 259, 356n. 33
Haven, 122, 150, 212, 241, 243
Hawaii, 283
Hayworth, Rita, 180, 185, 265,
    352n. 33
Hearst, William Randolph, Jr., 141
Hefner, Hugh, 265
Heim, Jacques, 263
"Helen of Bikini," 221, 264–65
Hempelmann, Louis, 209, 225,
    359n. 24
Henderson, Robert, 196
Hickenlooper, Bourke B., 295
Higinbotham, William A., 86
Hirohito, Emperor, 111, 164
Hiroshima, 62, 132, 139, 147, 262,
    264, 268, 304, 307; as atomic
    bomb target, 1, 4, 7, 11, 127,
    146, 250, 305; casualties in, 7–8,
    247, 277–78; and Crossroads,
    77, 86, 87, 102, 124, 126, 129,
    164, 189, 207, 266, 292; Navy
    men imprisoned in, 11; radiolog-
    ical survey of, 209–10
Hiss, Alger, 72
Holifield, Chet, 356n. 33
Holloway, Marshall, 137, 211, 220,
    221, 257
Hollywood, 160–61, 263, 264
Holtzman, Benjamin G., 174, 179
Honolulu Star-Bulletin, 52
Hood, 4, 165–66
Hoopes, Townsend, 52
Hoover, Herbert, 55
Hoover, J. Edgar, 70, 72
Hoover, John H., 188, 356n. 33
Hope, Bob, 33
House of Representatives, U.S., 80;
    and hearings on postwar role of
    armed services, 26, 28–29; and
    Joint Resolution No. 307,
    76–78, 80–81, 96, 101–3; Mili-
    tary Affairs Committee, 77;

Naval Affairs Committee, 26, 28–29, 74, 75, 86, 106, 144. *See also* Congress, U.S.
Huffman, James W., 95–97, 102–3
Hughes, 231, 261
Hull, Cordell, 311
Huntington, Samuel P., 18
Hussey, George F., 287
Hutchins, Robert M., 334n. 33
Hydrogen bomb, 301–7

Ickes, Harold L., 254, 311–12
Idaho, 256
Independence, 169–70, 174, 189, 190, 191, 195, 196, 235, 261, 276, 281
Indianapolis, 164
Infantry Journal, 109
International Herald Tribune, 263
International News Service, 141
Interservice rivalry, 62, 297; over Billy Mitchell tests, 18, 19–23; over Crossroads, 8, 17, 29–30, 124–27, 130, 134, 153–55, 181, 186–87, 196, 197–99, 201, 283; during World War II, 18, 19, 25–26, 48–50
Iran, 59, 61, 249–50, 254, 285
"Iron Curtain" speech, 61
Iwo Jima, 3, 48–50, 164, 167, 168, 171–72
Izac, Edouard, 187

Jaluit, 41, 42, 169, 313
Japan: and Bikinians, 108; and Bravo test, 304–5, 307; and Mandate over Marshall Islands, 42, 310, 313; postwar occupation of, 209–10, 254, 284; and World War II, 42–44, 46, 49–50, 78, 166–67, 325nn. 9, 15, 374n. 9
Johns Hopkins University, 64, 208, 333n. 5
Johnson, Edwin C., 13, 59, 65, 74–75, 80
Johnson, Justin, 78
Johnson, Louis, 297

Johnson, Lyndon B., 10, 314
Joint Chiefs Evaluation Board, 68–69, 93, 160, 196, 200, 285, 288–98
Joint Chiefs of Staff, U.S.: and Evaluation Board report, 288–90, 294, 295, 298; and "King" Juda, 219; Military Advisory Board of, 125; and planning for Crossroads, 16–17, 30–31, 78, 94, 143, 216, 257–60; planning staffs, 30–31, 94, 259, 290; and postwar atomic planning, 13, 62, 100, 285–86; and Soviet Union, 60; Strategic Survey Committee of, 294, 297, 298
Joint Crossroads Committee, 289, 292, 298, 299
Juda ("King"), 149, 162, 220; at Baker test, 207, 218–19, 309; as hereditary chief, 40, 105; at Rongerik, 115, 205, 308, 309–10, 358n. 3; and Wyatt, 107, 112–13

Kabua, 41
Kabua, Jeimata, 110, 111, 313, 340n. 25
Kamikazes, 46, 168, 171, 172, 196, 200
Karasti, Frank, 276
Kauffman, Draper L., 9, 131
Kennan, George F., 57, 60–61, 62, 143, 249, 251, 285
Kennedy, John F., 24
Kenneth Whiting, 122
Kepner, William E., 128, 173, 189; and off-target bomb in Able test, 198, 201–3
Kessibuki, Lore, 108, 110, 113, 314, 315
KGB, 144
Kiley, Thomas F., 276
Kilgallen, James L., 141
Kili Island, 4, 309–10, 312–14
King, Ernest J., 15, 16, 49, 51, 311
"King" Juda. *See* Juda ("King")

Kistiakowsky, George B., 6
Knox, Frank, 26, 52
Kodak, 123
Kopplemann, Herman P., 95
Korean War, 301
Kotzebue, August von, 38
Kotzebue, Otto von, 3, 38–40, 41
Krakatoa, 224
Krock, Arthur, 30, 63, 69
Krohn, Robert, 5
Kuboyama, Aikichi, 304, 307
Kwajalein, 104, 111, 312, 313, 314;
    and Bravo, 303, 304; and Cross-
    roads, 118, 119, 122, 128, 147,
    172, 174, 176, 178, 179, 180,
    185, 242, 243, 244, 260–61,
    269–70, 274–75, 352n. 32; inva-
    sion of, 42–43, 48; as military
    base, 43, 105; as possible
    weapons test site, 300; proximity
    to Bikini, 33, 106

Lae Atoll, 110, 176
LaGuardia, Fiorello, 22
Lajore, 111
Lamson, 189, 199
Larkelon, 40, 105
Larkin, Ralph, 136
Laurence, William L.: on Baruch
    Plan, 151; and Crossroads, 1–2,
    141, 151, 184, 186, 221–22,
    246–47; and Hiroshima, 209;
    and Trinity test, 6, 193
Lawrence, Ernest O., 65
League of Nations, 42, 310
Leahy, William D., 5, 16, 22, 54,
    56, 58, 68, 94, 252, 289
Lee, Fitzhugh, 142, 150, 159–60,
    178, 194, 195, 219
Leffler, Melvyn, 59
LeMay Curtis E., 131, 200, 280,
    326n. 20; on B-29, 27, 49–50;
    and LeMay Subcommittee, 17,
    30; and Leslie Groves, 30, 286;
    and planning for Crossroads,
    125–26, 128

LeMay Subcommittee, 16–17, 30,
    124
Lenox Hill Hospital, 123
Lerner, Max, 83
Lewis, John L., 59
Lexington, 24, 164, 170, 226
Lie, Trygve, 143
Life, 14, 86, 113, 119, 265, 267
Lilienthal, David E., 69, 70, 71, 84,
    99, 100, 294
Lippmann, Walter, 154, 262
Little Boy, 11, 13, 133, 265
Lockwood, Charles A., 48
Lodge, Henry Cabot, 296
London Conference of Foreign Min-
    isters, 57
Los Alamos Laboratory, 5, 84, 191,
    196; and atomic bombing of
    Japan, 7, 98, 132, 146, 147; and
    attitude toward Navy, 136–37,
    282; Critical Assemblies Group
    at, 137–40; and mistakes at
    Crossroads, 174, 192, 201, 204;
    and planning for Crossroads, 88,
    90, 125–26, 129, 135–37, 139,
    149, 215, 216, 221; and postwar
    atomic bomb improvements,
    134–35, 257, 258; and postwar
    political dilemma of, 133; and
    radiological safety, 211, 225,
    232, 238, 242, 243
Los Angeles Daily News, 159
Lovett, Robert A., 295
Lowry, Frank J., 261, 367n. 16
LSM-60, 220–21, 223
Lucas, Scott, 73–74, 95–96, 101–3
Lucky Dragon, 303, 304–5, 306,
    307
Ludlow, Louis, 97
L'Unita (Italy), 255
Lyon, George M., 208, 211, 212,
    236, 270, 272

MacArthur, Douglas, 15, 19, 49
Magellan, Ferdinand, 36–37
Magnuson, Warren, 102

Mahan, Alfred Thayer, 18, 326n. 3
Majuro Atoll, 43, 176, 352n. 33
Maloelap, 42
Manhattan Project, 69, 133; and
    AAF, 13; and breakdown of sci-
    entific-military alliance, 82–83;
    creation of, 8; and Crossroads,
    88, 89, 127, 146, 197, 200, 208,
    214, 257–58; espionage during,
    146–47; and Navy, 13, 15, 280,
    284; and radiological safety,
    208–9, 211, 241, 243; role of
    Leslie Groves in, 5, 84; scientists'
    criticism of Crossroads, 78,
    87–88
Marcus Island, 119
Marianas, 34, 42, 49, 50
Marinelli, L. D., 359n. 24
Mark XIV torpedo, 48
Marks, Herbert, 72
Marshall, George C., 16, 54, 143,
    209; and postwar atomic plan-
    ning, 13, 295; on unification of
    the services, 26
Marshall, William, 37
Marshall Islands, 38, 136, 275,
    302, 315; discovery of, 37; geog-
    raphy of, 34–36, 329n. 1; and
    Germany, 41–42; and Japan, 42;
    and missionaries, 41; and para-
    mount chiefs, 41, 42, 110–11,
    312–13; as United Nations
    Trusteeship, 310; in World War
    II, 42–44, 48, 168, 169, 171
Martek, Jerome, 276
Massachusetts Institute of Technol-
    ogy, 69, 84
May, Andrew J., 65
Maya, 169
May-Johnson bill, 65–66, 71, 81
McCain, John S., 27
McCloy, John J., 72
McCormick, Anne O'Hare, 101
McCullough, David, 56
McKellar, Kenneth, 89
McMahon, Brien, 64, 66–67, 74,
    296–97; and Crossroads, 67–68,

91, 102–3, 143, 144; speech sug-
    gesting atomic tests on ships, 15,
    326n. 21
McMahon bill, 65–66, 70, 77, 81,
    90, 194, 257, 258, 294
McMahon Committee. See Senate,
    U.S., Special Committee on
    Atomic Energy
McNaughton, Frank, 66, 67
McNish, George, 231
McVay, Charles B., 20
Meade, Herbert, 340n. 25
Media: and Baruch, 70–71, 101;
    and Bikinians, 111–13; and Billy
    Mitchell, 20–22; and Cross-
    roads, 1, 122, 129, 130, 141–42,
    145, 149–54, 159–62, 178–79,
    180–92, 194–95, 196, 198–203,
    205, 207, 219–20, 243, 260,
    261, 273; leaks to, 29, 91, 273,
    328n. 23; and reaction to Cross-
    roads postponement, 91–94
Medico-Legal Advisory Board, 208,
    210–11, 213–14, 237, 238, 240,
    270–71
Melville, Herman, 39
Michener, James, 329n. 1
Micronesia, 32, 34, 42, 168, 194,
    311
Mike test, 301
Mili, 41, 42
Missouri, 61, 142, 250
Mitchell, William "Billy," 25, 47,
    121; and criticism of Navy,
    19–20; and Ostfriesland tests,
    21–22, 168; referred to in Cross-
    roads debates, 30, 68–69, 80,
    124, 154, 196, 286; in World
    War I, 19
Mitscher, Marc A., 27, 170, 290
Moby Dick (Melville), 221, 324n. 2
Moby Dick (movie), 2–3
Molotov, Vyacheslav, 54, 57, 58,
    143, 195, 249, 253
Monroe, Robert R., 275, 278
Monsanto, 123
Morton, John J., 359n. 24

Mount McKinley, 122, 148, 174, 180, 184, 185, 186, 188, 189, 196, 217, 218, 219, 223
Mount Wilson Observatory, 123
Myers, William, 233
Myrick, Norman, 178

Nagasaki, 62, 133, 147, 262, 268, 304; as atomic bomb target, 1, 4, 12, 127, 135, 250, 305; and Crossroads, 77, 86, 87, 102, 124, 126, 129, 164, 189, 266, 292; radiological survey of, 209–10
Nagato, 4, 166–67, 190, 225, 300
Nam Island, 303
Nation, 192
National Geographic, 112, 264
Nautilus, 284
Naval Ordnance Test Station, 47
Naval Weapons Center, 52
Navy, U.S.: and Bikinians, 4, 43–44, 104–15, 149, 160–62, 176, 177, 309–10, 311–12, 313, 314, 341n. 34; and Billy Mitchell tests, 20–22; Bureau of Aeronautics, 23, 287; Bureau of Medicine, 275; Bureau of Ordnance, 20, 45–48, 51–52; Bureau of Ships, 13, 275, 282–83; and Forrestal's plans for postwar period, 27–29; General Board, 20, 297; and lack of ordnance testing before World War II, 48, 52; and media coverage of Crossroads, 129–30, 142, 154–55, 159–62, 179, 194, 195–96; Office of Special Weapons, 14–15, 32, 51, 134, 286–87; possible litigation against, 111; and post-Crossroads evaluation, 279–84; postwar atomic capability of, 29, 258, 280, 282–84, 286, 293–94, 297; postwar plans to test weapons on captured enemy ships, 13, 51; postwar size, 28–29, 116, 297; public percep-

tion toward, 160, 279; role in bombing Hiroshima and Nagasaki, 13; Seabees, 111, 148–49, 150, 312; and sinking of target vessels, 275; and unification debate, 19–20, 26–27. *See also* Blandy, William H. P.; Interservice rivalry; Operation Crossroads; Unification of the services
NBC (network), 183–84
Nevada: at Crossroads, 3, 125, 128, 173–74, 175, 180, 183, 184, 186, 189, 190, 201, 204, 247, 261, 283; sinking of, 275; in World War I, 163; in World War II, 3–4, 25, 47, 168, 171, 172
Newell, Robert R., 270, 271, 276–77, 359n. 24
Newell, William S., 356n. 33
New Mexico, 256
New Republic, 246
News Chronicle (London), 195
Newsweek, 52, 83, 97, 110, 178, 199, 222, 264
New York: at Crossroads, 155, 164–65, 175, 191, 196, 230, 231, 234, 261; sinking of, 275; in World War I, 163; in World War II, 25, 50, 164, 171
New Yorker, 108, 131, 152, 159, 341n. 34, 358n. 3
New York Herald Tribune: on Baruch, 70; and Crossroads, 29, 88, 154, 202, 222
New York Times, 155; on alleged radiation injuries in Japan, 7, 209; and atomic bomb stockpile, 258; on Baruch Plan, 101, 253, 255; on Bikinians, 114, 115, 309, 312; on Billy Mitchell, 22, 30; on Blandy, 52; on Crossroads, 29–30, 63, 67–68, 69, 93, 94, 117, 141, 143, 153, 178, 184, 187, 194, 199, 200, 202, 226, 246, 253, 255, 262, 266, 295; on Eschscholtz Atoll, 39; on Groves, 85; on Truman, 81; on

unification of the services, 26–27
Nichols, Kenneth D., 272, 273; and Able test, 186; and Baker test, 222, 224, 231; at Bikini, 145–46; and Groves, 84, 145; at Rongerik, 206, 207
Nimitz, Chester W., 19, 32, 42, 43, 100, 284, 285; congressional testimony of, 27; and Crossroads, 68, 89, 94, 144, 154–55, 179, 241, 258–59, 286–87, 355n. 49; on destruction of captured Japanese ships, 15
Nolan, James, 191, 208, 209, 359n. 24

Oak Ridge Laboratory, 211
Office of Strategic Services, 53
Oftstie, Ralph A., 290, 356n. 33
Ohio State University, 233
Ohly, John H., 295
Okinawa, 48, 164, 167, 168
Omega site, 138
Operation Crossroads, 1–2; airplanes as targets at, 123, 175, 190; animals at, 120–21, 157–58, 175, 190–91, 195, 199, 220, 229, 247, 255, 342n. 20, 354n. 49; and Baruch Plan, 99, 101–2, 252–55; and blimp or balloon for delivery of bomb, 126, 202; cost of, 77, 78–79, 88, 91, 96, 98–99, 198, 200, 294, 371n. 9; creation of, 29–33; and creation of Joint Task Force One, 30; criticism of, 64, 73–74, 77–78, 86–88, 89–90, 95–99, 101–3, 132, 135, 151–61, 178–79, 195, 196, 198, 247–48, 254; drone planes at, 121–22, 188, 222; early proposals for, 14–17; evaluation of, 200, 246–47, 259–60, 288–98; and failure of Truman administration to control, 8; hazards of, 9, 63–65, 87–88, 93, 118, 143–44, 151, 178, 207–8, 210, 211,

214–17, 227–45, 269–70, 333n. 2; humor at, 149–51; instruments at, 175, 189–90, 200–201; and litigation, 111, 210–11, 270, 272, 273–74, 278; military value of, 257, 279–84; and missed target, 126–27, 186, 189–90, 201–4, 280, 283, 307, 357nn. 37, 41; as news event, 8, 141–42, 262–63, 367n. 18; newspapers published at, 150; as nonscientific experiment, 86, 132, 135–36, 201, 254, 257; observers at, 1, 69, 88, 89, 90, 92, 93, 98, 142–45, 180, 182, 186–88, 189, 193; official history of, 87, 281, 326n. 21; official reports on, 189, 190, 195, 198–99, 200, 201, 203–4, 213, 224, 229, 230, 231, 233, 288–98; photography at, 116, 117, 118, 121, 148, 182, 188, 190, 192, 194, 223, 224, 225, 247; and possible cancellation, 90–94 passim, 95–97; and possible radiation injuries, 268–78; postponement of, 89–91, 96, 97; and postwar atomic bomb development, 134–35, 293; preparations for, at Bikini, 105–6, 118–19, 137, 147–49, 175; and public relations, 68, 98, 99, 111–13, 137, 153, 158, 159–62, 198–99, 202, 272, 273; radiological safety planning for, 117, 176, 210–11, 213, 216–17, 228, 230 (see also Radsafe monitors); radiological safety problems at, 211–13, 228–43; recreation at, 148–50, 193; rehearsals for, 174, 192; reporters at, 1, 122, 129, 130, 141–42, 149, 150, 178, 179, 181–87, 192–96, 199, 205, 207, 219–20, 243; review boards for, 67–69, 80–81, 93, 136 (see also President's Evaluation Commission for the Atomic Bomb

Operation Crossroads *(continued)*
  Tests); as scientific experiment,
  87, 117, 189; scientific experiments at, 116, 119–21, 148; and
  scientific-military relationship,
  86, 131, 137; security at, 129,
  146–47, 203; selection of as code
  name, 32; sexual overtones concerning, 150, 180, 195, 264–65;
  and ship design modifications,
  117, 200, 280–83, 293, 303,
  371n. 22; and Soviet Union,
  61–62, 96, 135, 141, 143, 144,
  247–48, 252–55; and special
  stamp cancellation, 118; support
  ships at, 117, 145, 175, 188,
  228–30, 232; termination of,
  241–43, 261–62; weather for,
  92–93, 128, 174, 180; women
  at, 117. *See also* Atomic bomb;
  Bikini Atoll; Blandy; individual
  tests by name; Interservice
  rivalry; Medico-Legal Advisory
  Board; Navy, U.S.; Radsafe monitors; Target ships
Operation Magic Carpet, 167, 171
Operation Ranger, 301
Operation Sandstone, 300
Oppenheimer, Frank, 335n. 35
Oppenheimer, J. Robert, 132, 138,
  146; on atomic bombing of
  Hiroshima and Nagasaki, 7; and
  Baruch, 70, 71, 98, 100, 101,
  335n. 42; on Byrnes, 70; as
  celebrity, 83, 98; on legislation
  creating Atomic Energy Commission, 65; as observer at Crossroads, 88, 98, 334n. 33; opposition to Crossroads, 96, 97–99,
  160, 283; and planning for Crossroads, 118, 125, 135; and postwar atomic planning, 85, 290,
  301; as security risk, 335n. 35;
  and Trinity test, 5–6, 208; and
  Truman, 85, 98–99, 135; and
  underwater atomic bomb, 133–34
Oppenheimer, Katherine (Kitty),

  335n. 35
Oregon Daily Journal, 159
Ostfriesland, 21–22, 30, 69

Palau, 42, 48
Panamint, 144, 149, 189, 348n. 37
Paramount chief, 41, 42, 110–11,
  312–13
Paris Peace Conference, 76, 90, 195,
  248, 249, 250–51, 253
Parsons, William S. ("Deak"), 134,
  136, 270, 272, 274; and Baker
  test, 214, 215, 216, 220, 221; at
  Bikini, 151, 242; and Charlie
  test, 260; on Crossroads, 266;
  and Hiroshima, 133, 188, 325n.
  19; nomination of Blandy to
  head Crossroads, 30–31; and
  planning for Crossroads, 126,
  146, 175, 212; and post-Crossroads planning, 287, 289–90,
  292
Patterson, Robert P., 55, 145, 252;
  and Crossroads, 68, 94, 97, 143,
  144, 179, 257–59, 262, 285,
  288; and interservice rivalry, 27
Pearl Harbor, 27, 50, 94, 169, 171,
  299; attack on, 24, 167, 168,
  170, 293; and Crossroads, 79,
  176, 230, 235, 241, 261, 275;
  possible contamination of, 274
Pearson, Drew, 59, 296–97
Penney, William G., 125, 201, 216
Pennsylvania, 1, 163, 168, 172,
  184, 190, 191, 199, 231
Pensacola, 171–72, 190, 239, 261,
  281
Pentagon, 18, 84
Pescadores Islands, 37, 39
Petersen, Howard C., 17, 72, 92
Philippine Islands, 37, 49, 197
Pienkowski, Stefan, 144
Pilotfish, 164, 225, 300
Pincher war plan, 285–86
Playboy, 265
Plutonium, 138, 227, 233, 238–39,
  241, 242, 272, 273

Poland, 143, 144, 252
Polaroid, 123
Porter, Charles Allen, 229
Porter, Philip, 222
Potsdam Conference, 11, 54, 58, 61, 250
Prange, Gordon W., 168
Pravda, 252–53, 254, 263
Predpriatie (*Enterprise*), 39
Prendergrass, Eugene P., 359n. 24
President's Evaluation Commission for the Atomic Bomb Tests, 93, 97, 98, 99, 135, 145, 178, 188, 196, 200, 221, 259
Prince of Wales, 25, 165–66, 350n. 12
Pringle, Austin, 141
Prinz Eugen, 4, 165–66, 235, 237, 241, 275
Project Nutmeg, 301
Project Silverplate, 134–35, 182, 352n. 32
Puget Sound Navy Yard, 24, 261
Purnell, William Henry, 45
Pyle, Ernie, 348n. 37

"Queen Day," 174, 192
Quigley, Joseph, 275

Rabi, I. I., 6
Radford, Arthur W., 286–87
Radioactive contamination: of cities, 267; and Pearl Harbor, 274; of support fleet, 230, 232, 236, 237; of target vessels, 227–45, 268–69
"Radio Bikini," 149
Radium, 227, 238, 333n. 2
Radsafe monitors, 218, 268; at Able test, 183, 186–87, 212, 214; at Baker test, 231, 233–34, 236–41; and equipment malfunctions, 213, 233, 236, 261, 269–70; at Kwajalein, 261, 269–70; numbers of, 211–12, 233–34, 236, 237, 267, 359n. 35; and officers of target ships,

234, 235–36, 237; and overexposures, 233, 234, 236–37, 241; training of, 212
Ralph Talbot, 164
Ramey, Roger M., 151, 180, 189, 197
Ramsey, DeWitt C., 114, 177
Ramsey, Norman, 6, 7
Rankin, John, 80
Rayburn, Sam, 75, 89, 94
Raytheon, 123
RCA, 123
Reader's Digest, 267
Reagan, Ronald, 265
Reard, Louis, 263–64
Rem, 213
Repulse, 25
Revelle, Roger, 64
Reynolds, Quentin, 141
Ridenour, Louis N., 86
Rimsky-Korsakov, Nikolai (composer), 3, 330n. 12
Rimsky-Korsakov, Nikolai Petrovich, 39
Rimsky-Korsakov Islands, 39
Rivero, Horacio, 32–33, 134, 201, 325n. 19, 328n. 41
Roberts, Clete, 141
Roehl, Richard, 276
Roentgen, Wilhelm Konrad, 213
Romeo test, 307
Rongelap Atoll, 36, 37, 39, 119, 176, 302, 303, 304, 306, 309
Rongerik Atoll, 119, 218; and Bikinians, 110–15, 308–10, 312–13; and Bravo test, 303, 304; compared to Bikini, 308, 374n. 3; discovery of, 37, 39; evacuation of Bikinians from, 118, 176, 312; living conditions on, 308–10; visits to, by Americans, 115, 206–7, 314
Rooney, John J., 175
Roosevelt, Franklin D., 8, 14, 18, 22, 28, 53–54, 75, 82, 84, 350n. 12
Roosevelt, Theodore, 247
Rose, Tokyo, 7

Ross, Charlie, 91, 92, 93
Roswell Army Air Field, 118, 127
Royal Air Force, 19
Royall, Kenneth C., 31, 290, 291
Rurik, 38
Rusk, Dean, 253
Russell, Richard B., 66
Russia. *See* Soviet Union

Saidor, 122, 188
Saipan, 42, 48
Sakawa, 166, 170, 189, 191, 197, 199
Salt Lake City, 168–69, 237, 261, 281
Saltonstall, Leverett, 356n. 33
Sandia Bombing Range, 203
San Francisco Naval Shipyard, 261, 271–72
Saratoga, 3, 166, 316; at Crossroads, 76, 163, 175, 190, 220, 275; sinking of, 225–26, 235, 300; in World War II, 24, 25, 170–71, 172
Saturday Evening Post, 314
Saturday Review, 141, 151, 195, 247
Sawyer, Ralph A., 139, 216, 290; and Able test, 201; and Baker test, 194, 224, 227; on Blandy, 131; on hazards in Crossroads, 64, 65; and knowledge of atomic bomb, 88; and planning for Crossroads, 125–26, 146
Schreiber, Raemer E., 136
Schumann, Robert, 3, 38
Scientists, atomic: and academia, 90, 133; as celebrities, 83–84; and criticism of Crossroads, 78, 86–88, 89, 97, 136, 151, 178; and May-Johnson bill, 65–66; and military, 82–83; opposition to atomic secrecy, 84–85; opposition to Groves, 84; on U.S. atomic monopoly, 85
Scott, Kenneth G., 271
Scoville, Herbert, Jr., 272

Seabees, 111, 114
Sea Raven, 164, 366n. 14
Searls, Fred, 356n. 33
Seattle Post-Intelligencer, 159
Secrecy, 1, 8, 84–85, 127, 129, 130, 259, 366n. 6
Semple, Dave, 180, 352n. 32
Senate, U.S.: and Baruch, 70; and hearing on postwar role of armed services, 27; Joint Committee on Atomic Energy, 295, 296–97; Naval Affairs Committee, 81, 96, 311; reaction to Billy Mitchell tests, 21; Special Committee on Atomic Energy, 13, 15, 64, 66–67, 74–75, 76, 83, 84–85, 140, 284. *See also* Congress, U.S.
Shaffer, Samuel, 199, 222
Shangri-La, 122, 188
Shelton, Frank, 357n. 41
Sherman, Forrest, 298
Shurcliff, William, 204, 326n. 21, 349n. 1
"Silverplating." *See* Project Silverplate
Skate, 170, 190, 191, 195–96, 366n. 14
Skipjack, 225, 366n. 14
Slotin, Louis, 138–40
Smith, Bromley, 328n. 23
Smith, Harold D., 12
Smith, Holland M., 50
Smitherman, John, 149, 231, 276
Smithsonian Institution, 119, 148, 191, 299
Solberg, Thorvald A., 194, 225, 235, 240, 241, 242, 272, 273, 290
South Dakota, 47
Soviet Union, 311, 350n. 2; and atomic bomb development, 85, 301; and Crossroads, 91–92, 96, 135, 141, 143, 144, 156, 247–48, 252–55, 262; and hydrogen bomb development, 301–2; and Iran, 59, 61, 249–50;

as postwar enemy of America, 28, 53, 60, 248–51, 260, 284–86, 298, 301; spy rings of, 59, 66, 72, 146–47; use of nuclear weapons against, 251, 285–86; in World War II, 53
Spaatz, Carl A., 173, 202, 203
Spain, 36–37, 41, 264
Spector, Ronald, 23, 49
Spice Islands (Moluccas), 36–37
Sports Illustrated, 264
Sproul, Robert G., 335n. 33
Spruance, Raymond A., 49–50
Stalin, Joseph, 53–54, 58, 59–60, 92, 93
Stanford University, 133
Stettinius, Edward R., Jr., 54
Stilwell, Joseph W. ("Vinegar Joe"), 186, 356n. 33
Stimson, Henry L., 84, 311, 325nn. 9, 14; on interservice rivalry, 18; on postwar cooperation with Soviet Union, 54–55, 56, 57, 250, 251; on unification of the services, 26
Storry, Richard, 305
Strauss, Lewis L., 14, 48, 50–51, 303, 305, 306, 326n. 21
Streett, St. Clair, 15
Submarines: at Crossroads, 164, 195–96, 225; and postwar atomic capability, 284
Sullivan, John, 282
Sumner, 105, 106, 107, 111, 118
Swancutt, Woodrow P. ("Woody"), 179–83, 185, 202, 203, 204, 352n. 32
Swing, Gram, 141, 178
Symington, W. Stuart, 145, 186, 197
Szilard, Leo, 82–83, 84–85, 91

Taft, William Howard, 55
Taongi Atoll, 32, 351n. 16
Tarawa, 42, 43, 119, 164, 171
Target ships: in Able test, 1, 173–75, 183–84, 186, 188–90, 191, 195–98, 199, 214; age of, 73, 76, 77, 117, 163; ammunition and fuel on, 125–26, 167, 214, 261, 366n. 13; in Baker test, 2, 220, 225–45; captains of, 235–36, 243, 269; congressional approval for use of, 75–77, 96; decontamination of, 230–42, 274; histories of, 3–4, 163–72; instruments on, 116, 189; number of, 16, 96, 117, 163, 349n. 1, 350n. 2; placement of, 124–25, 129, 168, 171, 256, 257, 294; radioactivity on, 191, 196, 214, 227–45, 261, 266, 269–76, 291; reasons for selection of, 117, 163–64, 168; salvage and repair of, 117, 194, 228, 231, 242, 276; scrap value of, 77, 78–79, 273–74; sinking of, 136, 188–89, 191, 199, 225–26, 275; towed from Bikini, 260–61, 274–75; use of criticized, 73–74
Taylor, Geoffrey, 125
Teller, Edward, 6, 65, 147
Terminal Island (California), 220
Thomas, Charles A., 101
Thomason, Robert, 77–78
Tibbets, Paul W., 127, 128, 204, 344nn. 19, 20
Time, 83, 87, 135, 153, 180, 260
Tinian, 42, 48
Titterton, Ernest W., 221, 361n. 13
Tjeerdema, Albert, 276
Tolerance dose, 213, 229, 232, 237, 238, 241, 269, 271, 275, 277
Towers, John H., 259
Trinity test, 138, 143, 147; animal experiments at, 209; cattle burns from, 7, 209; compared to Crossroads, 126, 188, 201; contingency plans for, 5; doubts concerning, 5; effects of, 6–7, 135, 136, 188; fallout from, 209, 216; safety planning for, 208–9; weather conditions at, 5–6, 174, 209

Truk, 16, 42

Truman, Harry S., 5, 32, 58, 72,
97, 155, 156, 197, 247, 249,
301, 311; and approval of Crossroads, 31, 106–7; and atomic
bombing of Japan, 11–12, 85,
250; and Atomic Energy Commission, 65–66, 258; and
Baruch, 70–71, 253–54, 335nn.
38, 42; and Bikinians, 206–7; on
Billy Mitchell, 68–69; cabinet
meetings of, 29, 55–56, 69, 80,
90–91, 93; and Congress, 76,
295; and Crossroads, 9, 30,
68–69, 89–94, 143–45, 211–12,
236, 250, 259–60; on interservice rivalry, 27; and Joint Chiefs
Evaluation Board Report, 294,
295, 296; on Navy, 28, 327n.
16; and Oppenheimer, 85; and
possible attendance at Crossroads, 144; on Roosevelt, 70; on
Soviet Union, 54–59, 61–62, 93,
248, 250–51, 333n. 27; on unification of the services, 28, 31,
282; and U.S. nuclear stockpile,
8–9, 31, 259

Trust Territory of the Pacific
Islands, 311, 314

Tuna, 164, 366n. 14

Turkey, 59, 61, 249–50, 285

Turner, Kelly, 50

Tydings, Millard E., 66

Typee (Melville), 40

Ujae Atoll, 110, 310

Ujelang Atoll, 310, 312

Ulithi, 32

Unification of the services, 25; during World War II, 25–26; postwar debate on, 26–28, 145, 282

United Nations, 56, 61, 92, 115,
251–55; Atomic Energy Commission, 58, 100–101, 143,
178–79, 184, 253, 255; Security
Council, 92, 93, 100, 143, 249,
252, 253, 311; trusteeship of

captured Japanese islands, 32,
310, 311

United States, 297

University of California, 208, 216,
299

University of California at Berkeley,
211, 212, 273

University of Chicago, 73, 83, 86,
211

University of Hawaii, 299, 312

University of Michigan, 64, 146

University of Pennsylvania, 86

University of Rochester, 208, 211

University of Warsaw, 144

University of Washington, 84, 299,
300

University of Wisconsin, 183

Urey, Harold C., 83, 96, 101, 130

U.S. Defense Nuclear Agency, 275,
278, 304, 350n. 1

U.S. Department of Agriculture, 120

U.S. Geological Survey, 119, 148,
299

U.S. Interior Department, 302; Fish
and Wildlife Service, 119, 299,
328n. 41, 329n. 45

U.S. Strategic Bombing Survey, 210,
325n. 15

U.S. Veterans Administration, 278

Utah, 46, 47

Utrik Atoll, 303

Vandenberg, Arthur H., 66, 67, 76

Variety, 187

Versailles Peace Conference, 42,
100, 163

Veterans, 275–76, 278

Vinson, Carl, 75–78, 80–81, 144,
145; on postwar role of Navy,
28–29; on unification of the services, 26

Vogue, 265

Voorhis, Jerry, 80

Wainwright, 237

Wake Island, 119, 170

Wallace, Henry A., 54, 56; and

Crossroads, 68, 89, 90, 248; and Soviet Union, 55–56, 58, 72, 248–49; and U.S. nuclear stockpile, 8
Wallis, Samuel, 37, 39
Walsh, David I., 96, 371n. 9
Warner, Roger S., 127, 137, 178, 257
Warren, Dean, 212
Warren, Stafford L., 130, 290; and Able test, 176, 187, 188, 189; on Alamogordo as poor test site, 209; appointed head of radsafe section, 208; and Baker test, 214–17, 225, 228–44; and congressional testimony, 7, 210; and evacuation of atolls near Bikini, 176; on hazards at Crossroads, 207–8, 213, 228–44, 277; on manpower problems in Crossroads, 211–13; on Navy attitudes toward Crossroads, 235, 236, 237–38, 242, 243, 244, 267; on plutonium contamination in Crossroads, 238, 239; and post-Crossroads concerns about radiation, 267, 269, 270, 272, 273, 274; and safety planning for Crossroads, 210, 211–13, 216, 351n. 16; and safety planning for Trinity test, 208–9; and safety record of Crossroads, 267–68, 277; and survey of Hiroshima and Nagasaki, 209–10; and termination of Crossroads, 240–42
Washington Naval Conference, 170
Washington Post, 143, 198, 260, 261

Washington University, 283
Weisskopf, Victor F., 136
Western Electric, 123
Westinghouse, 123
Wharton, 122
White, E. B., 152, 159, 245, 358n. 3
White, Stephen, 222
Wichita, 236
Willkie, Wendell, 23
Wilson, Woodrow, 163
Winchell, Walter, 201, 271
Wood, Harold H., 179–80, 181, 183, 185, 204, 352n. 32, 357n. 41
Wood's Hole Oceanographic Institution, 119, 134
World War II, 11–12, 18, 24–26, 27, 42–44, 48–50, 53–55, 122, 146, 163–72, 350n. 12, 374n. 9
Wotho Atoll, 176, 309, 310
Wotje Atoll, 42, 169, 171
Wright, Carleton H., 314
Wulfman, William A., 241
Wyatt, Ben H., 106–15, 161, 162, 176–77, 206, 207, 218, 308, 314

Yale University, 63
Yalta Conference, 53–54, 74
Yamamoto, Isoroku, 4, 166–67, 170
Yamato, 170
Yorktown, 164
Youngblood, Curtis, 131, 146, 185

Zeropoint, 123, 164; at Able test, 124, 125, 189, 195; at Baker test, 222, 224, 225, 227, 276; defined, 7, 122; at Trinity test, 7
Zuni test, 307

About the Author

Jonathan M. Weisgall is an adjunct professor of law at Georgetown University Law Center. He graduated from Columbia College in 1970 and Stanford University Law School in 1973, where he served on the *Stanford Law Review*. After a judicial clerkship on the U.S. Court of Appeals for the Ninth Circuit he moved to Washington, D.C., where he has practiced law since 1974.

He has represented the people of Bikini since 1975, and he spent twelve years litigating three lawsuits against the U.S. government on behalf of the islanders. His articles have also appeared in *Foreign Policy*, the *Los Angeles Times*, and the *New York Times*. He was executive producer of *Radio Bikini*, a film about Operation Crossroads that was nominated for an Academy Award for best documentary in 1988. Weisgall now lives in Bethesda, Maryland, with his wife, Ruth, and their three children.

The **Naval Institute Press** is the book-publishing arm of the U.S. Naval Institute, a private, nonprofit society for sea service professionals and others who share an interest in naval and maritime affairs. Established in 1873 at the U.S. Naval Academy in Annapolis, Maryland, where its offices remain, today the Naval Institute has more than 100,000 members worldwide.

Members of the Naval Institute receive the influential monthly magazine *Proceedings* and discounts on fine nautical prints and on ship and aircraft photos. They also have access to the transcripts of the Institute's Oral History Program and get discounted admission to any of the Institute-sponsored seminars offered around the country.

The Naval Institute also publishes *Naval History* magazine. This colorful bimonthly is filled with entertaining and thought-provoking articles, first-person reminiscences, and dramatic art and photography. Members receive a discount on *Naval History* subscriptions.

The Naval Institute's book-publishing program, begun in 1898 with basic guides to naval practices, has broadened its scope in recent years to include books of more general interest. Now the Naval Institute Press publishes more than sixty titles each year, ranging from how-to books on boating and navigation to battle histories, biographies, ship and aircraft guides, and novels. Institute members receive discounts on the Press's nearly 400 books in print.

For a free catalog describing Naval Institute Press books currently available, and for further information about subscribing to *Naval History* magazine or about joining the U.S. Naval Institute, please write to:

Membership & Communications Department
U.S. Naval Institute
118 Maryland Avenue
Annapolis, Maryland 21402-5035

Or call, toll-free, (800) 233-USNI.